THE ROUTLEDGE HANDBOOK OF THE ETHICS OF DISCRIMINATION

While it has many connections to other topics in normative and applied ethics, discrimination is a central subject in philosophy in its own right. It plays a significant role in relation to many real-life complaints about unjust treatment or unjust inequalities, and it raises a number of questions in political and moral philosophy, and in legal theory. Some of these questions include: what distinguishes the concept of discrimination from the concept of differential treatment? What distinguishes direct from indirect discrimination? Is discrimination always morally wrong? What makes discrimination wrong? How should we eliminate the effects of discrimination? By covering a wide range of topics, and by doing so in a way that does not assume prior acquaintance, this handbook enables the reader to get to grips with the omnipresent issue.

The Routledge Handbook of the Ethics of Discrimination is an outstanding reference source to this exciting subject and the first collection of its kind. Comprising over thirty chapters by a team of international contributors, the handbook is divided into six main parts:

- conceptual issues
- the wrongness of discrimination
- groups of 'discriminatees'
- sites of discrimination
- causes and means
- history of discrimination.

Essential reading for students and researchers in applied ethics and political philosophy, the handbook will also be very useful for those in related fields, such as law, sociology and politics.

Kasper Lippert-Rasmussen is professor in political theory at University of Aarhus, Denmark, professor II in philosophy at University of Tromsø, Norway and Associate Editor of *Ethics*. His main work on discrimination is *Born Free and Equal?* (Oxford University Press, 2013).

Routledge Handbooks in Applied Ethics

Applied ethics is one of the largest and most diverse fields in philosophy and is closely related to many other disciplines across the humanities, sciences and social sciences. *Routledge Handbooks in Applied Ethics* are state-of-the-art surveys of important and emerging topics in applied ethics, providing accessible yet thorough assessments of key fields, themes, thinkers, and recent developments in research.

All chapters for each volume are specially commissioned, and written by leading scholars in the field. Carefully edited and organized, *Routledge Handbooks in Applied Ethics* provide indispensable reference tools for students and researchers seeking a comprehensive overview of new and exciting topics in applied ethics and related disciplines. They are also valuable teaching resources as accompaniments to textbooks, anthologies, and research-orientated publications.

Available:

The Routledge Handbook of Global Ethics
Edited by Darrel Moellendorf and Heather Widdows

The Routledge Handbook of Food Ethics
Edited by Mary Rawlinson

The Routledge Handbook of Neuroethics
Edited by Syd Johnson and Karen S. Rommelfanger

The Routledge Handbook of the Ethics of Discrimination
Edited by Kasper Lippert-Rasmussen

Forthcoming:

The Routledge Handbook of the Ethics of Consent
Edited by Peter Schaber

The Routledge Handbook of Ethics and Public Policy
Edited by Annabelle Lever and Andrei Poama

For more information on this series, please visit
www.routledge.com/Routledge-Handbooks-in-Applied-Ethics/book-series/RHAE

THE ROUTLEDGE HANDBOOK OF THE ETHICS OF DISCRIMINATION

Edited by
Kasper Lippert-Rasmussen

Routledge
Taylor & Francis Group
LONDON AND NEW YORK

First published 2018 by Routledge

2 Park Square, Milton Park, Abingdon, Oxon, OX14 4RN
605 Third Avenue, New York, NY 10017

Routledge is an imprint of the Taylor & Francis Group, an informa business

First issued in paperback 2020

British Library Cataloguing-in-Publication Data
A catalogue record for this book is available from the British Library

Library of Congress Cataloging-in-Publication Data
Names: Lippert-Rasmussen, Kasper, 1964- editor.
Title: The Routledge handbook of the ethics of discrimination / edited by Kasper Lippert-Rasmussen.
Description: New York : Routledge, 2017. | Series: Routledge handbooks in applied ethics | Includes bibliographical references and index.
Identifiers: LCCN 2017011639 (print) | LCCN 2017032950 (ebook) | ISBN 9781315681634 (E-book) | ISBN 9781138928749 (hardback : alk. paper)
Subjects: LCSH: Equality. | Discrimination. | Social stratification.
Classification: LCC HM821 (ebook) | LCC HM821 .R685 2017 (print) | DDC 305--dc23
LC record available at https://lccn.loc.gov/2017011639

ISBN: 978-1-138-92874-9 (hbk)
ISBN: 978-0-367-73588-3 (pbk)

Typeset in Bembo
by Saxon Graphics Ltd, Derby

CONTENTS

CONTRIBUTORS

Sean Aas is Assistant Professor of Philosophy and Senior Research Scholar at the Kennedy Institute of Ethics at Georgetown University. His work addresses the political philosophy of diverse embodiment, especially questions about disability, difference, and justice.

Richard Arneson holds the Valtz Family Chair in Philosophy at the University of California, San Diego where he has been a professor since 1973. He received the Ph.D. degree from the University of California, Berkeley, 1975. He has published extensively on a very wide range of topics in ethics and social and political philosophy.

Ronen Avraham is a Professor at Law at the University of Texas School of Law and Tel Aviv University Buchman Faculty of Law. He writes in the area of insurance and discrimination.

Erin Beeghly is an Assistant Professor at the University of Utah. She is currently at work on a book—*What's Wrong with Stereotyping?*—that examines the conditions under which stereotyping is wrong. She also writes and teaches about topics within legal theory, including discrimination law.

Juliana Bidadanure is an Assistant Professor in Political Philosophy at Stanford University. Her work is located at the intersection of Philosophy and Public Policy. Her research interests include egalitarianism, age group justice, unconditional basic income and youth quotas.

Paul Butterfield is a PhD student at CUNY.

Hugh Collins is the Vinerian Professor of English Law at All Souls College, University of Oxford, and is a Fellow of the British Academy.

Gideon Elford is a Departmental Lecturer in Political Theory at New College at the University of Oxford. His research interests are primarily concerned with questions of distributive justice, with particular emphasis on equality, agency and responsibility.

Carina Fourie is the Benjamin Rabinowitz Assistant Professor in Medical Ethics at the Program on Values in Society, Department of Philosophy, University of Washington.

Robert K. Fullinwider worked as a research specialist in the Institute for Philosophy and Public Policy at the University of Maryland for 27 years. He continues to write on public policy issues and maintains the websites http://newprostitutionwars.net and http://newprostitutionwarsblog.com.

J. L. A. Garcia is Professor in the Philosophy Department of Boston College in the USA, specializing in normative ethical theory, philosophy of race, and societal analysis. His article "The Heart of Racism" has been widely influential and often reprinted.

Sarah Goff is visiting assistant professor in the department of Politics & Public Administration at the University of Hong Kong. She works on topics in economic justice, including gender discrimination in the labor market and fairness in international trade.

Lena Halldenius is Professor of Human Rights Studies at Lund University. Her PhD is in Philosophy. She is the author of *Mary Wollstonecraft and Feminist Republicanism* (Pickering & Chatto, 2015) and numerous articles on political freedom, human rights, and early modern political thought.

Deborah Hellman is the D. Lurton Massee Professor of Law at the University of Virginia. Her work includes: *When Is Discrimination Wrong?* (Harvard Univ. Press, 2008) and *The Philosophical Foundations of Discrimination Law* (co-editor) (Oxford Univ. Press, 2013).

Jules Holroyd is a Vice-chancellor's Fellow in Philosophy at the University of Sheffield. She has published on the philosophy and psychology of implicit cognition, and is principle investigator on the Leverhulme Trust-funded research project on Bias and Blame.

George Hull is Senior Lecturer in Philosophy at the University of Cape Town, South Africa. He works on political and social philosophy, and he is the editor of *The Equal Society: Essays on Equality in Theory and Practice* (Lexington Books, 2015).

Tarunabh Khaitan is Associate Professor and Hackney Fellow in Law, Wadham College, Oxford. He is the author of *A Theory of Discrimination Law* (OUP 2015) and the co-editor of *Foundations of Indirect Discrimination Law* (with Hugh Collins, Hart 2017 forthcoming).

Frej Klem Thomsen is post-doctoral researcher at the department of Philosophy & Science Studies, Roskilde University, Denmark. He works on ethics and political philosophy, with particular interests in discrimination, criminal justice, neuroethics, and bioethics.

Carl Knight is Lecturer in Political Theory at the University of Glasgow, where he works primarily on distributive justice. He has published numerous articles on this topic as well as *Luck Egalitarianism* (Edinburgh University Press, 2009) and *Responsibility and Distributive Justice* (co-edited with Zofia Stemplowska, OUP, 2011).

Sune Lægaard, PhD, is Associate Professor in Philosophy at the Department of Communication and Arts, Roskilde University. He works within political philosophy on issues related to multiculturalism, including toleration, recognition, secularism, free speech and immigration. He edits *Res Publica*.

Hugh Lazenby is a Lecturer in Philosophy at the University of Glasgow.

Xiaofei Liu works on moral philosophy, philosophy of action, and the experimental approach to philosophy. He is currently an Associate Professor of Philosophy at Xiamen University, China.

José Jorge Mendoza is an Assistant Professor of Philosophy at the University of Massachusetts Lowell and is co-editor of *Radical Philosophy Review*. He is also the author of *The Moral and Political Philosophy of Immigration: Liberty, Security, and Equality* (2017).

Mari Mikkola is an Associate Professor of Philosophy and a Fellow at Somerville College at the University of Oxford (UK). She works mainly on feminist philosophy, social injustice and social ontology.

Andres Moles is an Assistant Professor at CEU in Budapest. He is interested in contemporary political and moral philosophy, with particular emphasis on discrimination, implicit biases, and free speech. His worked has appeared in Res Publica, and Social Theory and Practice among other venues.

Sophia Moreau is Associate Professor of Law and Philosophy at the University of Toronto, a Faculty Associate at the University's Centre for Ethics, and an Associate Editor of *Philosophy and Public Affairs*. She is writing a book defending a pluralist theory of discrimination, "The Many Faces of Inequality: Discrimination in Law and Morality."

Katherine Puddifoot is a Research Fellow at the University of Birmingham, United Kingdom, where she works on the ERC-funded 'Project PERFECT'. She was previously a Teaching Fellow at the University of Glasgow and the University of Bristol. She received her PhD in Philosophy from the University of Sheffield with a dissertation on epistemic naturalism. Her research fields are philosophy of psychology, epistemology, and philosophy of medicine.

Frederick Schauer is David and Mary Harrison Distinguished Professor of Law at the University of Virginia, and was formerly Frank Stanton Professor of the First Amendment at Harvard University. Among his six books are *Profiles, Probabilities, and Stereotypes* (Harvard 2003) and, most recently, *The Force of Law* (Harvard 2015).

Gina Schouten is Assistant Professor of Philosophy at Harvard University. Her research interests include gender justice, educational justice, and political legitimacy, including especially questions about whether political liberalism can constitute an adequate theory of legitimacy.

Re'em Segev is an Associate Professor at the Faculty of Law of the Hebrew University of Jerusalem. His research interests are moral philosophy (mainly normative ethics and especially distributive justice and uncertainty) and philosophy of law (especially criminal law and constitutional law).

Patrick Shin is Associate Dean and Professor of Law at Suffolk University Law School in Boston, Massachusetts. He received his JD and PhD in philosophy from Harvard University. His research interests include anti-discrimination law and the philosophy of equality.

Edward Stein is Professor of Law at Cardozo School of Law in New York City and the Director of the Gertrud Mainzer Program in Family Law, Policy, and Bioethics. He holds a B.A. from Williams College, a J.D. from Yale Law School, and a Ph.D. in Philosophy from M.I.T. He has been a visiting professor of law at Yale Law School and the UCLA School of Law and professor of philosophy at Yale University, NYU, Williams College, and Mount Holyoke College. He also clerked for Judge Dolores Sloviter on the U.S. Court of Appeals for the Third Circuit. Stein's research interests include legal and philosophical topics related to families, sexual orientation, reproduction, cognition and science. He has written extensively on these and other legal, philosophical, and scientific topics and is the author of two books, *The Mismeasure of Desire: The Science, Theory and Ethics of Sexual Orientation* and *Without Good Reason: The Rationality Debate in Philosophy and Cognitive Science*, both published by Oxford University Press, and the editor of an anthology, *The Forms of Desire: Sexual Orientation and the Social Constructionist Controversy*, published by Routledge.

Nenad Stojanović is a Senior Research Fellow and a Lecturer at the University of Lucerne. His main topic of research is democracy in multicultural societies. He currently works on the project "Racist voters and minority candidates" funded by the Swiss National Science Foundation.

Natalie Stoljar is Associate Professor in the Department of Philosophy and the Institute for Health and Social Policy at McGill University. She is co-editor of *Relational Autonomy: Feminist Perspectives on Autonomy, Agency and the Social Self* (OUP 2000) and has written articles on feminist philosophy, moral psychology and the philosophy of law.

Julie Suk is a Professor of Law at Cardozo School of Law, Yeshiva University in New York. She received a JD from Yale Law School and a DPhil in Politics from Oxford, where she was a Marshall Scholar. She was a visiting professor at Harvard, Columbia, University of Chicago, and UCLA, and a fellow at Princeton, European University Institute, and LUISS-Guido Carli. Her research develops theories of discrimination and equality in comparative legal perspective.

Peter Vallentyne is Florence G. Kline Professor of Philosophy at the University of Missouri, U.S.A. He writes on issues of liberty and equality in the theory of justice (and left-libertarianism in particular) and, more recently on enforcement rights (rights to protect primary rights).

David Wasserman is on the faculty of the Department of Bioethics, National Institutes of Health. He works on ethical issues in disability, reproduction, genetics, and neuroscience.

Garrath Williams is Senior Lecturer in Philosophy at Lancaster University. He has research interests in ethics, political theory and applied ethics. One major focus of his work is responsibility, while a second is collaborative research on children, health and public policy.

ACKNOWLEDGEMENTS

I thank the following persons for assistance in connection with this handbook:

Andreas Albertsen, Erin Beeghly, Kimberley Brownlee, Hugh Collins, John Corvino, Benjamin Eidelson, Gideon Elford, Carina Fourie, Robert Fullinwider, Joshua Glasgow, Sarah Goff, Lena Halldenius, Deborah Hellman, Nils Holtug, Klemens Kappel, Tarunabh Khaitan, Hugh Lazenby, Xiaofei Liu, Sune Lægaard, Tim Meijers, José Mendoza, Mari Mikkola, Sophia Moreau, Lasse Nielsen, Tom Parr, Frederick Schauer, Shlomi Segall, Re'em Segev, Adam Slavny, Nenad Stojanović, Frej Klem Thomsen, Peter Vallentyne, Kristin Voigt, David Wasserman, and Garrath Williams.

THE PHILOSOPHY OF DISCRIMINATION

An introduction

Kasper Lippert-Rasmussen

UNIVERSITY OF AARHUS AND UNIVERSITY OF TROMSØ

Introduction

Discrimination is an important topic. Many disadvantages and disrespectful forms of treatment endured by individuals result from or amount to discrimination. Not surprisingly, therefore, at least since the Civil Rights movement in the US, discrimination is often in the forefront when individuals complain about being unjustly worse off than others, or about being unjustly treated. Hence, understanding discrimination is important for understanding social inequalities as well as for understanding the politics and history of many societies. Indeed, because it is a tendency in many societies to see more and more disadvantages as reflecting discrimination, understanding discrimination could be an even more important task in the future.

Many different disciplines elucidate the nature of discrimination. Sociology, for instance, charts the social mechanisms whereby gender roles are reproduced. Psychology casts light on how implicit biases affect the way in which we respond to members of different groups and on the mechanisms whereby we perceive someone as being a member of a particular group. Political science explores how discrimination in the job market and in education affects social mobility. Law determines how Supreme Court rulings or human rights conventions weigh on the legal status of affirmative action schemes intended to counteract discrimination.

All of these disciplines are represented in the present handbook. However, the discipline of philosophy provides the main lens through which the handbook observes discrimination. This means that conceptual and normative issues, as opposed to causal and descriptive issues, play a central role in this handbook. This is not to say that the distinction between philosophical and other approaches to discrimination is sharp. Philosophical discussions of discrimination that are not informed about, say, what the main forms of actual gender discrimination are, empirically speaking, are bound to seem oddly irrelevant to real-life concerns. Similarly, sociologists who explore, say, racial discrimination by street-level police officers must rely on assumptions about what distinguishes racial discrimination from mere differential treatment on the basis of race. Moreover, legal theorists often engage in reflections on discrimination that go beyond determining what the law says about a certain case of differential treatment – for instance, in considering what it ought to say, morally or politically speaking.

While philosophical assumptions or claims about discrimination are omnipresent, there has been, surprisingly, relatively little philosophical discussion of discrimination until fairly recently. This is not to say that nothing has been written on the topic (cf. Alexander 1992; Cavanagh 2002; Edmonds 2006; Eidelson 2015; Gardner 1996; Hellman 2008; Hellman and Moreau 2013; Khaitan 2015; Lippert-Rasmussen 2013). However, much of this work was written in the context of legal theory and few philosophers gave it much attention. Despite being a central topic in philosophy in its own right, and through its many connections to other topics in normative and applied ethics, at present there simply is no comprehensive guide to the topic of discrimination. This is a considerable obstacle to students and faculties alike. This is so not only for philosophers, but for reasons indicated above, for students and scholars from other disciplines as well. This handbook aims to fill this gap in the literature.

Apart from this introductory chapter, this handbook has 36 chapters. These are grouped into six parts, which I describe below. Part I explores the concept and taxonomy of discrimination. Part II asks when discrimination is morally wrong and why it is, when it is. Parts III and IV say something about specific forms of discrimination, in terms of the individuals who are subjected to it, e.g., women (Part III), or in terms of the social sphere where discrimination takes place, for example in education (Part IV). Part V addresses the question of why and how we discriminate and the question of what we can and should do to eliminate discrimination or mitigate its effects. Part VI briefly casts a historical light on the use of the term "discrimination".

Conceptual issues

Perhaps the most basic question that any philosophical treatment of discrimination can ask is: "What is discrimination?" Initially, one might think that there is little need to answer this question, because we know discrimination when we see it. However, a moment's reflection tells us that this is not right. First, often people mean different things when they use the term "discrimination". For instance, some use the term in its most generic sense, where to discriminate simply is to treat individuals differently. There is no reason to think that to discriminate in this sense is in any way worse than not to discriminate, and accordingly there is every reason to think that when people complain about discrimination, this is not what they have in mind. Discrimination in the relevant and more specific sense is differential treatment plus something else.

There are different ways to go here. Some would say that the relevant "something else" is provided by some moral property such as injustice, moral impermissibility all things considered, or moral objectionableness. However, it is not clear that this captures central uses of "discrimination". There are lots of ways of treating people differently that are not normally thought to amount to discrimination. For example, nepotism involves differential treatment of family and non-family members, but few think of it as discrimination against non-family members. Others would favor a non-moralized concept of discrimination such that, unlike in the case of the moralized concept, one cannot infer from the fact that something falls under the concept of discrimination that it is unjust or morally impermissible. There are different descriptive, non-generic concepts of discrimination.

In a different context, I have defended the view that the "something else" refers to differential treatment on the basis of membership of a socially salient group. By this I mean a group, perceived membership of which structures social interactions across a wide range of different contexts (Lippert-Rasmussen 2013, 26-45). One advantage of this notion of discrimination is that it coheres well with standard anti-discrimination law that often lists a number of protected groups as groups which are protected by those laws, e.g., groups determined by sex, religion, race or sexuality. Invariably, such groups are socially salient in my sense.

Once we have distinguished between different concepts of discrimination, we can embark on the taxonomical task of distinguishing between different kinds of discrimination. One very important distinction, which is explored in Chapters 1 and 2 – by Frej Klem Thomsen and Tarunabh Khaitan respectively – is to distinguish between direct and indirect discrimination. Usually, this distinction is taken to be exhaustive, in that there is no form of discrimination which is neither direct nor indirect, and mutually exclusive in that an act of differential treatment cannot at one and the same time count as both direct and indirect discrimination. While Thomsen and Khaitan approach the distinction between direct and indirect discrimination from the perspective of different disciplines – philosophy and law, respectively – they agree that the distinction between direct and indirect discrimination is hard to draw and that one should be open to the idea that there might be different concepts of (in)direct discrimination employed by different agents in different contexts.

A standard view here is that, historically speaking, when people complained about discrimination they had in mind direct discrimination, i.e., differential treatment where the discriminator treated people – say, job applicants – differently, because he intended to exclude people on the basis of membership of a particular socially salient group, whose members he thought inferior in certain ways or to whom he was hostile. Direct discrimination was the kind of discrimination that was generally practiced. Currently, however, due to the dominance of anti-discrimination norms, direct discrimination has lost much of its former importance. Most discrimination that goes on now is indirect: it does not involve any intentions to exclude, but does in fact exclude because of how rules, practices, institutions etc. have been designed in a context where they serve the needs and match the capacities of particular groups.

Another distinction which cuts across the distinction between direct and indirect discrimination is that between statistical and non-statistical discrimination. Offhand, this distinction seems easy to draw: statistical discrimination is discrimination based on statistical beliefs about members of the group discriminated against, while non-statistical discrimination is not so based. However, as Frederick Schauer argues in Chapter 3, this simplistic dichotomy hides the truth that any evidence is statistical in nature and thus, as he puts it, pure individuation is impossible. If a female applicant informs the employer that she is likely to apply for maternity leave, refusing to hire her constitutes a clear example of sex discrimination, but, intuitively, it does not amount to statistical discrimination. Yet, ultimately the applicant's testimony about her intentions serves as evidence only given statistical background knowledge of the likelihood that, *inter alia*, the applicant will stick to her intentions. Schauer also points out that much statistical discrimination is morally benign, probably unavoidable, and that there are moral costs involved in not using statistically non-spurious indicators.

Much discrimination pertains to people's access to resources or opportunities. However, in recent years another site of discrimination has received increased attention, namely, where discrimination relates to people's status as knowers. As Kathy Puddifoot shows in Chapter 4, one can discriminate – often in ways of which one is unaware – by forming biased beliefs about whether or not other people are able to give or receive knowledge. Epistemic discrimination occurs when people are treated as if they are unable to give or receive knowledge due to their membership of a particular social group. While epistemic discrimination is distinct from the sort of non-epistemic discrimination that takes place when people sign documents, process job applications etc., obviously it is not unrelated to it. Underlying much discrimination in the sphere of action is discrimination pertaining to people's ability to give and receive knowledge.

The final conceptual problem which is covered in the first part of the handbook, pertains to intersectionality. As Natalie Stoljar shows in Chapter 5, the concept of intersectionality was introduced to describe the situation of black women (Crenshaw 1989). They experience racial as well as sexual discrimination. However, these two forms of discrimination interact in a complex way, such that the situation of black women is not just that of people who suffer the same sort of racial discrimination that black men do but in addition suffer the same sort of sex discrimination that white women do. Some theorists appeal to intersectionality to question an approach to discrimination that focuses on socially salient groups, and the corollary seems to be skepticism about group-focused anti-discrimination policies – and for that matter, group-focused definitions of discrimination such as the one I mentioned above. (A similar line of thought might motivate a concept of site-focused intersectionality in relation to sites of discrimination (see Part III). Being discriminated against in the job market and in housing might interact in complex ways.) However, as Stoljar argues, intersectionality does not mean that we have to dispense with the notion of social groups altogether.

The wrongness of discrimination

Once we are clear what defines discrimination, we can ask what makes it morally objectionable, when it is. In answering this question, we need to pay attention to several issues. First, as I mentioned in the previous section, there are different concepts of discrimination, all of which have legitimate uses. This plurality is unproblematic for analytical and moral purposes provided that we are clear about which concept we are employing. If we are not clear, what seems like a moral disagreement about discrimination might simply reflect that different interlocutors have different senses of "discrimination" in mind. In particular, we need to pay close attention to whether we use a moralized or a non-moralized notion of discrimination.

Second, the term "morally objectionable" is deliberately vague. It can mean morally impermissible. It can mean unjust, in which case some instances of discrimination might be unjust, but nevertheless morally permissible all things considered, e.g., in view of the bad consequences of not engaging in certain forms of discrimination. Or it might simply mean, loosely, that discrimination tends to have, but does not necessarily have, certain features, which render it morally problematic. For instance, some might think that discrimination tends to make badly-off people even worse off, and that it is wrong to do this. However, in such a view discrimination is not wrong non-instrumentally speaking, and many would say that discrimination is morally objectionable simply by way of being discrimination in the relevant sense.

The distinction between views according to which discrimination is non-instrumentally wrong and views according to which it is only instrumentally wrong is often conflated with the distinction between views according to which discrimination is very wrong, morally speaking, and views according to which discrimination is wrong, but not very wrong. However, this is a confusion and nothing prevents someone from holding that discrimination is non-instrumentally wrong, but not very wrong, or from holding that discrimination is instrumentally wrong, and seriously so whenever it has the relevant morally objectionable consequences.

Part II of the handbook presents the most influential accounts of what makes discrimination wrong. These accounts can be proposed as monistic accounts of the wrongness of discrimination, or they can be put forward in a pluralist spirit, where it is understood that discrimination can have different wrong-making features. Also, they can be proposed as broadly-scoped accounts that explain the wrongness of all forms of wrongful discrimination, or as narrowly-scoped accounts that explain the wrongness of some, but not all, forms of wrongful discrimination.

In Chapter 6 Erin Beeghly expounds the attractive view that at least some forms of discrimination are non-instrumentally wrong because of the disrespect they involve. Intuitively, some paradigm forms of discrimination – think of beaches reserved for white South Africans under Apartheid – involve disrespect against discriminatees. However, it is less clear what exactly disrespect amounts to, when it is not a matter of conventional disrespect or of not treating someone in the way that one is morally required to treat them, in which case disrespect seems epiphenomenal. Also, it is not clear whether all wrongful forms of discrimination need be disrespectful. Beeghly explores different answers to both questions on the basis of an account of which desiderata a theory of the wrongness of discrimination should meet.

In Chapter 7, Deborah Hellman sets out her influential meaning-based account of the wrongness of discrimination. Hellman argues that discrimination is wrongful when and because it is demeaning. To determine which acts are demeaning, she looks to their objective meaning, i.e., the sense which it is reasonable, given the social and historical context in which the discriminatory act took place, to ascribe to the action. Her account also focuses on the actual social power wielded by the alleged discriminator. Only denigrating actions taken by people or institutions with social power demean and thus wrongfully discriminate.

In Chapter 8, Lena Halldenius sets out another influential account of what makes discrimination wrong – namely, that to discriminate against someone is to treat that person disadvantageously relative to others on grounds that are irrelevant to how this person should be treated. To do so might be disrespectful, but on the present account this is not the core of the matter. Paradigm forms of discrimination involve treating discriminatees on irrelevant grounds. Think, for instance, of the employer who refuses to hire a female applicant despite her superior qualifications simply on the basis of her gender. Still, we would like to know what exactly it means for a feature to be irrelevant. In part this is so, because there are cases where gender in some sense *is* relevant but where it nevertheless might be wrongful discrimination to treat people differently on the basis of gender. For example, if customers have sexist biases against female economic advisors it might be relevant from a purely economic point of view what the gender of an applicant for a position as an economic advisor is. In this chapter, Halldenius provides an account of irrelevance, setting out some of the challenges that such an account must address.

Chapter 9 expounds the view that discrimination is wrong, because it involves treating people in ways that do not map onto their deserts. Such a view can be combined with the irrelevance-based view. One might think that all other factors than what people deserve are irrelevant to how they should be treated. If so, not treating people on the basis of their desert is to treat them on irrelevant grounds. Desert-based accounts need not be tied to an irrelevance account. As Andres Moles points out, a desert-focused account of the wrongness of discrimination is probably most at home in relation to accounts of why discrimination in the job market is wrong. Often, the idea is that in a free job market employers will select the best-qualified candidates and that these candidates deserve to be selected on the basis of their superior qualifications. Things, however, are much more complex and, according to Moles, there is little reason to believe that market outcomes track desert.

Considerations about desert sometimes connect with considerations about rights, in that the most deserving applicant is thought to have a right to the job for which he or she applied. There are, however, many other possible bases for rights and in Chapter 10 Peter Vallentyne looks at discrimination by private individuals from a left-libertarian, rights-based perspective. While many complaints about discrimination are often expressed in terms of rights violations, Vallentyne argues that there is no general right against discrimination in any non-moralized sense of the term. By this he means that provided the discriminator neither violates the discriminatee's self-ownership, nor brings about an unfair distribution of resources, even the most bigoted forms of discrimination do not violate the rights of the discriminatees. Some friends of respect-based accounts might find this view implausibly tolerant of discrimination (cf. Chapter 31). However, as Vallentyne emphasizes, acts that do not violate rights might be morally objectionable in other ways, e.g., they might be impersonally wrong.

Vallentyne's account presupposes an account of a fair distribution of resources and one of the most common objections to discrimination is that it results in unfair distributions, e.g., between men and women. Probably, the most common form this objection takes appeals to some ideal of equality of opportunity. Carl Knight scrutinizes this objection in Chapter 11. He points out that there are different notions of equality of opportunity. Formal equality of opportunity requires that positions be allocated on the basis of fair contest. Equality of opportunity in this sense is compatible with talented people having much better chances than untalented people. A different, luck egalitarian notion of equality of opportunity requires that opportunities be equalized by neutralizing all factors for which individuals are not responsible, natural talents included. However, Knight finds that luck egalitarian equality of opportunity is vulnerable to counterexamples, when understood as a broadly-scoped account. Hence, he proposes to explain the wrongness of discrimination by appealing to a conjunction of a particular prioritarian principle, which gives greater weight to benefiting people worse off and the more morally deserving they are, and formal equality of opportunity. The latter component is required to explain why it would be wrong to, say, exclude women from becoming army officers even if doing so maximizes value according to the desert prioritarian view.

In Chapter 12, Richard Arneson explores an account of wrongness of discrimination that can be seen as a genus for the previous account – the harm-based account. According to this account, what makes discrimination wrong is that it harms people – for example because it eliminates some of their opportunities. In this view, discrimination can be wrong even if it does not boost inequalities in opportunities. It can be wrong because it makes everyone worse off. One attractive feature of the harm-based account is that paradigm cases of wrongful discrimination clearly do harm discriminatees, and it is rare for people to complain about what they see as harmless discrimination against them. However, as Arneson shows, there are different notions of harm on offer, e.g., there is a difference between actual harm and probable harm. Accordingly, the view that discrimination is wrong only if harmful comes in many different versions. Arneson considers a number of putative counterexamples to this view – that is, cases of harmless, but wrongful, discrimination where the discriminator fails to respect the equal moral standing of the discriminatee in the knowledge that this will not actually harm the discriminatee. While he surveys a number of responses, proponents of the "no harm, no wrong" principle might offer in response such counterexamples (e.g., they might contend that the real source of our negative response to cases of harmless wrongdoing is not the deontic qualities of the action in question but the character of the deliberator), he does not take a stand on this principle, but simply clarifies the terms of the debate.

Chapter 13 offers a specific rights-based account of the wrongness of discrimination. As Sophia Moreau shows it is common for discrimination to reduce the freedom of discriminatees. It does so at a personal as well as a systemic level, and it does so in several ways on both levels. For instance, at a personal level if I know that many employers discriminate, directly or indirectly, against women, then I am deprived of my freedom to disregard my gender when I deliberate about my career. Intuitively, Moreau submits, we are entitled to the deliberative freedom to disregard our gender when making career choices. What makes discrimination wrong is precisely that it removes or reduces deliberative freedom along with other freedoms, e.g., the negative freedom to choose between an adequate range of options to which one is entitled. Perhaps, Moreau suggests in a pluralist spirit, discrimination is – sometimes at least – wrongful for other reasons as well, but any satisfactory account of the wrongness of discrimination must involve an appeal to its effects on our negative and positive freedoms. Interestingly, this freedom-based account implies that direct and indirect discrimination are morally equivalent, since both encroach on deliberative freedom. This distinguishes Moreau's freedom-focused account from, say, a disrespect-focused account, which seems best able to explain the wrongness of direct, as opposed to indirect, discrimination.

The final chapter in Part II – Chapter 14 – on the wrongness of discrimination explores a very different approach to the wrongness of discrimination. In normative theory it is common to distinguish between three main strands: consequentialism, deontology, and virtue ethics. Roughly, the accounts that we have touched upon so far fall under the first two headings. In his chapter, J. L. Garcia approaches the wrongness of discrimination from a virtue ethicist point of view. As he sees it, discrimination is basically a mental act. The relevant mental act could be an intention to exclude, but according to Garcia's account discrimination is much broader than that, and the relevant discriminatory mental act can also involve treating the discriminatee with callous indifference. Because Garcia's virtue-based account focuses on mental acts behind the relevant differential treatment, actual (as opposed to predicted) consequences in terms of harm, inequalities of opportunities, and so on are not relevant to the wrongness of discrimination.

As should be apparent from this brief survey of Chapters 6 to 14 the discussion of the wrongness of discrimination is likely to quickly lead us into the much more general discussion about what makes actions in general, i.e., whether discriminatory or not, wrong. Accordingly, it is inevitable that disagreements about the latter general question, e.g., between deontologists and consequentialists, reappear in a local form as a disagreement about what makes discrimination wrong. Hence, we should not expect any consensus to emerge soon on the wrongness of discrimination given the fact that normative theory is a contested issue. Still, some wrong-making features seem especially relevant to discrimination, or at any rate more relevant to discrimination than to other forms of wrongful action.

Groups of discriminatees

The first two parts of the book look at some general issues in relation to discrimination. Part III of the book distinguishes between different forms of discrimination on the basis of the relevant discriminatees. It explores three different types of discriminatees: those subject to classical, standard, and novel forms of discrimination.

Classical discriminatees include those groups of discriminatees that were the focus of the initial civil rights movements in the US and elsewhere in the 1960s: that is, discrimination on the basis of gender, race, or religion. Standard discriminatees include those groups that are now commonly recognized as such even if they were not initially at the center of discrimination discourse: that is, discrimination on the basis of disability, sexuality, age, and nationality. Novel forms of discrimination are forms of discrimination that are still not commonly recognized as such, for example, obesity discrimination, lookism, and discrimination against transgender people. This division between types of discrimination is rough and ready, and it is not intended to signal that classical forms of discrimination are somehow more important or more objectionable than novel forms of discrimination. Also, the selection of discriminatees in Part III should not be taken as exhaustive.

There are several reasons why it is interesting to compare different groups of discriminatees and the kinds of discrimination against them that the pertinent forms of discrimination involve. First, if not all forms of differential treatment qualify as discrimination, we could infer from an enumeration of those that do and those that do not which additional features differential treatment must have to qualify as discrimination. For example, does disadvantageous treatment of people with heavy facial piercings count as discrimination? Moreover, we can also learn about the contours of the concept of discrimination by noting which forms of discrimination are contested *qua* forms of discrimination. Hence, the present part of the handbook forms an important background to the conceptual questions addressed in Part II.

Second, discrimination against different groups takes different forms. While classical forms of discrimination on the basis of race might have involved beliefs about groups having a hierarchically ordered moral status, arguably no such thing is involved in discrimination on the basis of looks. Similarly, the case of discrimination against transgender people raises the possibility that discrimination might not be focused on socially salient groups (unless you think transgender people form its own socially salient group), or at least not exclusively so, because it might also target people precisely because they do not fit into a conventional sorting of people into recognized groups, that is, men and women.

Third, it is interesting to see whether discrimination against different groups is wrong for the same reason, as should be the case if "discrimination" refers to one particular kind of moral wrong rather than to a conjunction of diverse morally problematic acts. Also, an exploration of what makes particular forms of discrimination wrong can serve as a test for a more general account of the wrongness of discrimination, e.g., because it makes us attend to a wrong-making feature of discrimination that we might otherwise overlook.

In Chapter 15, Gina Schouten discusses probably the most widespread form of discrimination, discrimination against women. Focusing on contemporary discrimination against women, she notices the persistent gender inequalities in labor markets despite several decades of anti-discrimination legislation. She argues that part of the explanation of such unjust inequalities reflects something other than discrimination. Accordingly, even if we succeed in eliminating all forms of discrimination, direct as well as indirect, unjust gender inequalities would still persist. Schouten concludes that "the most promising policies for promoting gender justice are not policies aimed at ameliorating gender-based discrimination". The most promising policies are likely to benefit women, but they will also, Schouten contends, benefit men who in some ways are harmed by the present gendered division of labor, e.g., in relation to childcare.

In Chapter 16, Patrick Shin explores discrimination on the basis of race. Like with gender, race discrimination can be symmetrical, i.e., whatever race one belongs to, one can be subjected to race discrimination. However, if the wrong of racial discrimination is to be understood symmetrically, it becomes hard to understand why discrimination on the basis of race could serve as "an anchor for moral reflection", as Shin puts it, following Rawls. Indeed, as Shin sees it, race discrimination takes on its distinctive moral character only when it arises and coincides with pervasive systems of inequality and hierarchy. Specifically, Shin thinks that the wrongness of race discrimination so construed is best explained by a respect-based account of what makes discrimination wrong. He also notes that one particular form of disrespect is that involved in not seeing people as autonomous agents, but as more or less mere functions of their ascribed race. This form of disrespect, Shin contends, is what makes us object to statistical discrimination against racial groups even when based on valid generalizations.

Sune Lægaard takes a look at the third classical form of discrimination – religious discrimination – in Chapter 17. Part of his chapter is occupied with clarifying the very concept of religious discrimination, which, as he points out, can both refer to discrimination against people by virtue of their religion – here religion is the object of discrimination, as it were – and to religiously motivated discrimination, e.g., against people with different religious beliefs, where religion is the subject of discrimination. Lægaard also shows that it is tricky to define "religion" (is a practice a religious practice simply because it is endorsed by religious authorities, for example?), and tricky to tell what difference it makes to the moral qualities of discrimination if it is religious.

Moving from classical to standard forms of discrimination, in Chapter 18 Ed Stein takes a look at discrimination on the basis of sexual orientation. More specifically, he focuses on discrimination against gay men, lesbians, and bisexuals (LGB people for short). Stein's chapter starts with a discussion of what sexual orientation is, in the first place noting that sexual orientation – whether same- or different-sex orientation – is a result of a complex interaction of genetic and environmental factors. On that basis, he proceeds to demonstrate some problems with two standard arguments for discrimination against people who have or act on same-sex sexual orientation, that is, that such orientations are unnatural or non-procreative. He then proceeds to critically assess two arguments to the effect that discrimination on the basis of same-sex sexual orientation is unjustified: first, that sexual orientation is innate or immutable, and second, that the wrongness of sexual orientation discrimination can be accounted for in terms of sex discrimination. He concludes by outlining the kinds of arguments that better justify the wrongness of discrimination on the basis of sexual orientation.

In Chapter 19, David Wasserman and Sean Aas look at disability discrimination. Disability is interesting for several reasons. One reason why is that unlike most of the classical forms of discrimination, e.g., race discrimination, disability discrimination is something all of us face a non-negligible, though quite unequal, risk of being subjected to. Those who are not disabled now face a significant probability of becoming disabled later in life, e.g., as a result of an accident. Another reason is that it is at least controversial whether the disadvantages faced by disabled people are social through and through, or whether some of them, e.g., disadvantages that results from being paralyzed, would exist in a world in which there has never been any ableist discrimination against disabled people. In their chapter, Wasserman and Aas argue that the absence of discrimination against disabled people requires not just true equal opportunities for disabled people, but also a modification of the set of opportunities available in a way which accommodates disabled people.

Like disability discrimination, age discrimination is something that (almost) all of us can be subjected to. Indeed, the situation with respect to age discrimination – at least when it takes the form of discrimination against old people – is such that most of us are either presently subjected to it or will be so in the future, once we grow old. Interestingly, this means that from the point of view of equality of life-time opportunity, age discrimination need not be morally objectionable. Some infer from this that age discrimination is not morally objectionable, while others infer that this shows that causing inequality of opportunity cannot be all that is morally objectionable about discrimination. In Chapter 20, Juliana Bidadanure takes the latter view, suggesting that to understand the wrongness of age discrimination we must supplement the ideal of distributive equality with relational egalitarianism, i.e., the view that a just society is not simply one that realizes a certain distribution of money and resources, but is (also) one in which we relate to one another as equals. This ideal requires, for instance, that relations to the elderly not be based on pity or condescension. Similarly, it requires that young people not be stereotyped as lazy and irresponsible.

Chapter 21 concerns discrimination against immigrants. Throughout history newcomers have been treated disadvantageously. The topic is an especially pressing issue in the light of what is often described as the present refugee crisis. In this chapter, José Mendoza takes a slightly different perspective. His concern is not how immigrants are treated once they have entered a country, but the prior event of their entering their country of destination. More specifically, he looks at direct and, in particular, indirect racial discrimination in immigration policies, i.e., in policies that determine who is allowed to enter a state and eventually obtain citizenship. Some might think of immigration in analogy with personal relations. Just as I have a right to determine with whom I want to associate in my personal life, states have a right to determine who they allow in. However, Mendoza argues that such a view is not tenable when it comes to invidious discrimination against protected groups in immigration policies. In any case, even if one is within one's right to do something, it does not follow that one does not act wrongly in doing it.

Moving from standard forms of discrimination to new forms, Chapter 22 takes a look at discrimination against obese people. Interestingly, no one has suggested that, like race discrimination, obesity discrimination should serve as an anchor for our moral thinking (recall Shin's characterization above). Indeed, obesity discrimination is not frowned upon and jokes that would be socially unacceptable if they were about racial minorities are openly laughed at when about obese people. Indeed, obesity discrimination is institutionally sanctioned. As Garrath Williams contends, this is so despite the fact that obesity discrimination is a particularly widespread and harmful form of discrimination. Some might think that obesity discrimination is, if not permissible, then at least less wrong than other forms of discrimination. There are various rationalizations of this view, the most prominent being that obese people are responsible for their own predicament. Williams argues that such rationalizations are flawed in part because of the falsity of the empirical premises to which they appeal, e.g., that obesity is simply due to lack of self-control. Perhaps of more philosophical interest, however, is his further argument, that even if these factual claims were true, liberal principles require us to disregard such imputations of personal culpability when we relate to one another in civic, institutional, and public life.

In Chapter 23, Xiaofei Liu treats a related, though distinct, form of discrimination, lookist discrimination. Lookist discrimination overlaps partially with obesity discrimination, since being obese is generally taken to detract from the quality of one's looks. One can, however, be judged ugly without being obese and conversely, be judged beautiful yet obese. As with obesity discrimination, lookist discrimination is pervasive and has severe consequences for discriminatees. Moreover, it is generally seen as acceptable, especially in the private sphere, where we often respond to other people on the basis of their looks without compunction. Liu finds this permissive attitude problematic and notes some of the ways in which lookist discrimination can and cannot be seen as a "new form of racism". Drawing on the experience of fighting racist discrimination, Liu ends his chapter by listing a number of political actions which might help reduce lookist discrimination.

Chapter 24 takes a look at discrimination against transgender persons. This is a form of discrimination that has only recently attracted wider attention, e.g., in relation to bathroom access for transgender people. It is an interesting form of discrimination, because it seems different from standard discrimination on the basis of gender. Some trans people are treated disadvantageously not because they are perceived to be women or men, but precisely because they fit into neither category. In her chapter, Mari Mikkola details the unjust disadvantages faced by trans people. She argues that these can coexist with the enforcement of equal civil rights. Discrimination against trans people takes a very complex form and exploring it teaches us important lessons on how we should understand other forms of discrimination, e.g., discrimination against women. Moreover, discrimination against trans people is unlikely to end before trans identities are depathologized.

Having gone through the groups of discriminatees that are covered in this section, I should like to point to one particular group of discriminatees that is not covered. That group is working class people, or those at the bottom of the socio-economic ladder. It is a striking feature of contemporary discrimination discourse that class discrimination is rarely mentioned as a major form of discrimination – the word "classism" is hardly used and is all too liable to attract cries of "political correctness gone mad" – and, thus, that almost everyone believes that one can be against discrimination and yet not object to huge socio-economic inequalities, as long as they are not correlated with race, gender etc. However, it seems that many of the same mechanisms that are at stake in discrimination against the groups mentioned here are also at stake in class discrimination. Think, for instance, of how stereotyping of or implicit bias against working class people is a pervasive feature of everyday life. In the light of this, one might ask why discrimination against poor people should not be seen as a major form of new discrimination – not "new" in the sense that it is only recently that such discrimination has taken place, but "new" in the sense that it is only very recently that such differential treatment has been conceptualized as discrimination (cf. Lippert-Rasmussen 2013, 38–40). Perhaps tellingly, my efforts to find an author for a chapter on class discrimination was unsuccessful (but see Chapter 27).

Sites of discrimination

Part III looks at different groups of discriminatees. While in principle it could be true of a group of discriminatees that it faces discrimination in one site of discrimination only, generally, discrimination in one site correlates with discrimination in other sites. Take transgender people. It is not the case that trans people face discrimination in the job market, but face no discrimination in the housing market or in law enforcement. This fact of the multi-site nature of discrimination means that discrimination becomes a more serious problem than it otherwise would have been. Part IV of the book looks at seven different spheres of discrimination. No doubt one could have individuated sites of discrimination differently, e.g., in a more fine-grained way. Also, there is no implication that those sites that are covered exhaust the list of sites of discrimination, or even the list of important sites of discrimination.

Why is it interesting to look at different sites of discrimination? There are several reasons. First, a survey of different sites of discrimination serves as important background to our conceptual analysis of what discrimination *per se* is, e.g., we might need to reject a moralized, lexical definition of discrimination if it turns out that differentiation between the insurance premiums paid by men and women is generally labeled discrimination and yet is not wrong. Second, a survey of different sites of discrimination also serves as an important background to general accounts of the wrongness of discrimination. There are forms of discrimination that are thought by some to be wrong, yet discrimination in this site may not seem to involve what these people think makes discrimination wrong. For instance, there might be forms of discrimination in private life – e.g., racial discrimination in the choice of potential partners on dating sites – which might be wrong but yet do not involve, say, increasing inequality of opportunity. Moreover, even if we embrace a pluralistic account of the wrongness of discrimination it is interesting to see whether discrimination in different sites involves different wrongs.

Part III explores two classical sites of discrimination: the job market and education. Going back to the Civil Rights movement, discrimination in jobs and education were the main concerns in addition to undoing segregation in public spaces. In Chapter 25, Sarah Goff scrutinizes discrimination in jobs. She takes her point of departure in the different patterns of employment and income levels of socially salient groups, e.g., men and women. She then goes over various models that explain these differences. One model – the human capital theory – holds that employers hire on the basis of capacity to make productive contributions. According to this theory, different patterns of employment and earnings do not reflect discrimination in the job market. Rather, such differences reflect the fact that members of some socially salient groups have more human capital than others, due in part to their differential treatment within other major institutions of society. In the second part of her chapter Goff surveys different accounts of the wrongness of job discrimination and different normative standards for the allocation of jobs. Meritocratic hiring is plausibly the standard that adheres most closely to the predictions of human capital theory. However, she shows that meritocratic hiring may still require employers to bear significant burdens: in part because reaction qualifications – that is, qualifications one has in virtue of how others respond to one – imply that some applicants have more human capital than others. Yet this does not mean that they have greater merit in the relevant sense, in part because the meritocratic ideal might be problematic in itself.

In Chapter 26, Gideon Elford scrutinizes discrimination in education. There are many ways in which education can involve discrimination. Elford focuses on, first, the use of academic tests as a basis for the distribution of academic opportunities and, second, differential treatment on the basis of non-academic grounds, e.g., fees, gender, and faith. The use of academic tests is interesting, because how well students perform reflects in part the quality of the primary and secondary education that they have received, and that in turn is likely to be determined in large part by their membership of socially salient groups. Accordingly, the use of tests is likely to involve indirect class-based discrimination. With regard to differentiation on non-academic grounds Elford also submits that some such cases – e.g., single-sex schooling – might not involve discrimination against girls or boys, but simply discrimination between them. Elford notes that discrimination in education is likely to have repercussions for discrimination in other sites given that education is important for the distribution of other goods, e.g., jobs.

Part III also scrutinizes three sites of discrimination – politics, law enforcement, and insurance – which more recently have been the focus of anti-discrimination policies. In Chapter 27, Re'em Segev takes a close look at discrimination in law enforcement. His focus lies on rational, statistical discrimination, notably in cases of racial profiling, where law enforcement agencies use sound statistical information about crime rates across groups to set priorities about who, say, to stop and frisk. For obvious reasons, "racial profiling" is often taken to refer to a set of abusive or prejudiced practices. However, such practices are different from the ones Segev focuses on and, generally, there is little serious disagreement as to whether the former are wrong. Segev carefully lists *pro tanto* reasons that speak both in favor of statistical discrimination in law enforcement – e.g., that it may reduce the number of instances of criminal wrongdoing – and against it – e.g., the adverse effects of those who are subjected to profiling and may see themselves as victims of a racist society – and suggests that those which are most weighty will vary from context to context.

In Chapter 28, Ronen Avraham takes a close look at discrimination in insurance. One reason why this is interesting is that insurance discrimination seems immune to some of the standard objections to discrimination. Take, for instance, the practice whereby men are charged higher car insurance premiums than women based on the statistical fact that men have a higher probability of being involved in road traffic accidents than women. It seems to require a stretch of mind if one wants to argue that such differentiation of premiums is based on irrelevant factors, or is disrespectful to men (or women!) in a way that merits any attention from the point of view of justice. Another reason why insurance discrimination based on sound generalizations is interesting is that it raises some of the same issues as profiling. The problem here takes a particularly acute form, because differential treatment of risky and non-risky insurance takers is essential to insurance as a business. Unfortunately, and unlike what the case of gendered car insurance premiums suggests, this distinction tends to overlap with distinctions between advantaged and otherwise disadvantaged groups: unconstrained actuarial reasoning is likely to disadvantage already disadvantaged groups. Accordingly, Avraham explores what the contours of these constraints should be from the perspective of fairness and justice, and tentatively sketches a multifactorial approach to the ethics of insurance.

In Chapter 29, Nenad Stojanović provides an overview of discrimination in a pejorative sense in the political–electoral sphere of liberal democracies. As he observes, little attention has been devoted to this topic, and the electoral institutions of liberal democracies are often thought to be free of discrimination. Not so, according to Stojanović, who provides a rich account of the many forms of discrimination – direct as well as indirect – that take place in relation to citizens as voters. Examples include the racial dilution of districts, discrimination in relation to political parties (e.g. bans on parties representing ethnic minorities such as Kurds in Turkey – which, presently, probably is not the best example of a liberal democracy), and in relation to the selection and election of candidates for representative bodies, e.g., as when financial provisions disadvantage impoverished minorities. Stojanović notes that probably the most intriguing form of discrimination is that where citizens discriminate *qua* voters etc. against citizens *qua* candidates, e.g., men who are biased against female candidates for the presidency.

Finally, Part III also explores somewhere that traditionally has not been construed as an important site of discrimination, if a site of discrimination at all: private life. According to some views, unlike the state and unlike when people act in the public sphere and civic associations, people have a right to discriminate in their private lives. For instance, one has a right to choose to live in a neighborhood of town where one's ethnic group is in the majority, and one has a right to discriminate against potential partners on account of their religion. Note, however, that according to this view discrimination in private life might be morally impermissible, even if one acts within one's rights. The fact that one has a right to engage in discrimination in one's private life merely means that others do not have a right to prevent one from so doing. Moreover, many would agree that even in private life there are limits to the right to discriminate. For instance, while many find it unproblematic if a church – a private association – discriminates against applicants who do not share the relevant religious beliefs, fewer find it acceptable if the church discriminates against women (even if such discrimination is mandated by the relevant religion), and only very few find it acceptable if the church practices race discrimination (whether mandated by the relevant religion or not).

Part IV has two chapters that address discrimination in the private sphere. In Chapter 30, Hugh Collins notes the distinction between discrimination being immoral and discrimination being prohibited by discrimination laws. Arguably, much discrimination which takes place in the private sphere is immoral, but might nevertheless be something that the law should not interfere with. But how should one draw the distinction between discrimination within and beyond the boundaries of law? Collins notes that some standard ways of drawing this distinction, e.g., in terms of the distinction between state and non-state action or in terms of the harm principle, in one way or another have implausible implications. He then describes how the law in fact draws this distinction in order to ask the question of what, morally speaking, could justify doing so. Collins explores three suggestions. First, the purpose of anti-discrimination laws might be such that some forms of discrimination might be irrelevant, e.g., the purpose might be to prevent social exclusion. Second, the relevant form of discrimination might fall under the purpose of anti-discrimination laws but involve disproportionate interference with the liberty of duty-bearers. Finally, a proper balancing of the rights of the discriminatee and the rights of the discriminator to choose and express their values might in some cases fall out in favor of the latter.

Chapter 31 concerns discrimination on dating sites. Paul Butterfield and Hugh Lazenby start the chapter by presenting statistics showing racial disparities between ratings of attractiveness across different racial groups. Such disparities smack of racial discrimination. Yet this is discrimination in relation to something which is very personal and, thus, if it amounts to wrongful discrimination then at least some forms of personal discrimination can be wrong. Butterfield and Lazenby use the case to test various theories of the wrongness of discrimination. For example, they use my desert-prioritarian account as an instance of a harm-based theory and compare it with a rights-based theory, in the form of Sophia Moreau's deliberative freedom account. Against the former account, they argue that it is unable to account for how the wrongness of the relevant type of discrimination may depend on what explains these racial disparities, e.g., whether they reflect racist prejudice or not. In favor of the latter, they argue that Moreau's account suggests that the wrongness of discrimination is determined by a balancing of the freedom of the involved parties, and that different motivations for dating preferences involve reductions of freedoms that are not equally important, morally speaking. Accordingly, Moreau's account might possibly fit our intuitions about the differential wrongness of differently motivated dating discrimination. If so, this is *prima facie* support for her account and rights-based accounts more generally.

Eliminating and neutralizing discrimination

Suppose we know what discrimination is and what makes it wrong when it is. In that case, it is natural to ask what we should do to eliminate it, or at least to mitigate its effects. Note that these two aims are different, though clearly related. If one eliminates discrimination, one mitigates its effects in the trivial sense that one eliminates any effect of present or future discrimination. However, one can mitigate the effects of discrimination without eliminating it, e.g., one does nothing to prevent hiring committees from letting sexist biases influence their recommendations, but one adopts a quota system to counteract the effects of their recommendations being biased. To answer the question of what to do about discrimination one needs, *inter alia*, some knowledge about what causes discrimination. Part V of the handbook is devoted to these issues. In Chapter 32, Jules Holroyd surveys some of the literature on the psychology involved in and underpinning discrimination. More specifically, she addresses three psychological mechanisms: first, in-group favoritism; second, implicit biases in the form of automatic thoughts and feelings that the discriminator probably is unaware of and might even strongly disavow if he or she were made aware of them; third and finally, the mechanism whereby the threat of confirming a negative stereotype has deleterious effects on the discriminatee's performance. Attention to these mechanisms challenges how philosophers often think of discrimination. In particular, Holroyd argues that a definition of discrimination that I have proposed in a different context is better revised to accommodate the latter two mechanisms and, possibly, should be revised to accommodate in-group favoritism, which might be directed towards "arbitrary and artificial" groups that are otherwise not socially salient. Also, work in social psychology brings to our attention the fact that discrimination may take a form which is quite different from the paradigmatic case of racist or sexist discrimination informed by racist or sexist ideologies understood as a set of explicitly formulated and embraced ideas about racial or sex superiority.

Chapter 33 looks at what is probably the most discussed form of anti-discrimination policy: affirmative action. One reason for the attention paid to affirmative action is that it is often thought to resemble ordinary discrimination, which is why some refer to it as "reverse discrimination" (cf. Chapter 36). Affirmative action is, so this view has it, discrimination. The differences from standard discrimination are, first, who the object of discrimination is, e.g., men not women, and, second, its moral qualities: it is either not wrong at all or at least less wrong than paradigmatic discrimination. Julie Suk argues that this framework for thinking about affirmative action is misconceived. Affirmative action is not a form of discrimination because, unlike discrimination in the pejorative sense, it does not involve the loss of anything of moral value. More specifically, unlike discrimination in the pejorative sense, affirmative action does not reinforce or reproduce hierarchical social relations. Indeed, Suk defends the view that affirmative action is best seen as a necessary feature of the non-discrimination norm, where that norm condemns inegalitarian social relations.

Chapter 34 looks at another influential anti-discrimination policy, policies to promote diversity. As a matter of legal history, diversity and affirmative action are intimately connected because the famous *University of California v. Bakke* case in which the US Supreme Court left open that a public institution could have a compelling state interest in diversity, such that using means narrowly tailored to satisfy this interest might be constitutional. Over the years, it has become more common to justify affirmative action policies by an appeal to diversity. However, as George Hull notes, diversity is not always sought as a remedy to past or present discrimination, and in some cases diversity is valued independently thereof. In any case, appeals to diversity are open-ended in the sense that there is no such thing as diversity, as such. Something is always more or less diverse in relation to a particular set of factors. Accordingly, Hull devotes a good deal of his chapter to discuss what diversity is, e.g., which group identities are relevant to diversity and which numerical representations of differently-sized groups amount to more diversity. On that basis, he critically addresses a number of views about the social benefits of diversity, e.g., greater efficiency (in which case promoting diversity arguably should not be seen as a form of affirmative action), social justice (e.g., through the reduction of stereotyping through contact), and social harms (e.g., social divisiveness), that come from greater diversity.

Chapters 33 and 34 focus on what anti-discrimination policies the state and institutions such as companies and universities can adopt. However, some would argue that to effectively combat discrimination such initiatives are not enough. We also need to promote an egalitarian ethos, which informs people's conduct in their daily, private lives. Basically, such an ethos embodies a commitment to a social-relational egalitarian view. Obviously, an anti-discrimination norm regulating, say, how we select our dating mates, is one of the best candidates for being a constitutive norm of such an egalitarian ethos. In Chapter 35, Carina Fourie explores what such an ethos should look like and, more specifically, what anti-discrimination norms would partly constitute it. Generally, she holds that the ethos would be informed by the anti-discriminatory norm that underpins Deborah Hellman's account of the wrongness of discrimination. According to this account the wrongness of discrimination lies in a violation of equality *per se*. Part of the attraction of Hellman's account in the present context, Fourie argues, is that a suitably revised version of it provides us with a plausible account of the moral status of discrimination in the private sphere. As it is, Hellman's theory is able to account for why it is more wrong for white people to refuse to date black people – this is objectively demeaning – than for black people to refuse to date white people – this is not demeaning. It is, however, unable to explain why it is wrong for black men, say, to refuse to date black women. The latter fact, Fourie thinks, should leads us to revise Hellman's account of the efficacy conditions of demeaning someone – one can demean even if one is in a lower position in the social hierarchy relative to others, provided the discriminator is not in an inferior position relative to the discriminatee. Such a revised account initially seems more vulnerable to the objection that it would not be able to account for dating preferences that are intuitively acceptable, such as those based on gender. However, on further analysis, Fourie indicates that it is able to explain why it does not amount to wrongful discrimination when, say, straight men do not want to date gay men.

History of discrimination

The use of "discrimination" to articulate injustices is now ubiquitous in law and policy. This is a recent historical development. In Chapter 36, Robert Fullinwider takes his readers through a brief world history, noting that the term "discrimination" was seldom used in the past to describe unjust differential treatment. However, as he also notes, this does not mean that discrimination did not exist, or, for that matter, that people did not have the concept of discrimination. Quoting, for instance, passages from Dickens' *American Notes for General Circulation* from 1842, he shows how Dickens' depiction of the unjust situation of Afro-Americans was informed by the concept of discrimination, even if Dickens nowhere in the work uses the term "discrimination". As Fullinwider also points out, it has become more and more common to apply the concept of discrimination to differential treatment. In the early days of the Civil Rights movement few, if any, would speak of disability discrimination due to non-accommodation. Will this process not come to a halt? Not so, predicts Fullinwider. Nor should it. There are still groups out there, e.g., prostitutes, who are subjected to discrimination and receive no or inadequate legal protection.

Conclusion

As should be apparent from this introduction, discrimination raises a wide range of interesting and complex philosophical questions. However, I should like to end with a word of caution. As will be apparent to anyone who reads a handful or more of the chapters in this handbook, or, for that matter, to anyone who has read the present introduction, it does not reflect any uniform outlook on discrimination. Not only do authors approach its topic from different disciplinary angles, they also use "discrimination" to refer to different things. Some use the term in a moralized sense, others not. Some use the term to refer to the treatment of socially salient groups, others do not. Similarly, the authors have very different views on what makes discrimination morally wrong. This is as it should be, given the diversity of views held on the topic of this handbook. Still, it is worth keeping in mind as one reads through the handbook. I hope this confrontation with diverse points of view will help the reader make up his or her own mind about what is at stake, and what separates legitimate responses to the differences between people from invidious or unjust treatment.[1]

Note

1 I thank Garrath Williams and Robert Fullinwider for comments on an earlier version of this introduction.

Bibliography

Alexander, L. (1992) "What makes wrongful discrimination wrong?", *University of Pennsylvania Law Review* 141: 149–219.

Cavanagh, M. (2002) *Against Equality of Opportunity* (Oxford: Clarendon Press).

Edmonds, D. (2006) *Caste Wars: A Philosophy of Discrimination* (London: Routledge).

Eidelson, B. (2015) *Discrimination and Disrespect* (Oxford: Oxford University Press).

Gardner, S. (1996) "Discrimination as Injustice", *Oxford Journal of Legal Studies* 16: 353–368.

Hellman, D. (2008) *When Is Discrimination Wrong?* (Harvard University Press).

Hellman, D. and Moreau, S. (2013) *Philosophical Foundations of Discrimination Law* (Oxford: Oxford University Press).

Khaitan, T. (2015) *A Theory of Discrimination Law* (Oxford: Oxford University Press).

Lippert-Rasmussen, K. (2013) *Born Free and Equal?* (Oxford: Oxford University Press).

PART I

Conceptual issues

1
DIRECT DISCRIMINATION

Frej Klem Thomsen
ROSKILDE UNIVERSITY

Introduction

The concept of discrimination has been at the center of some of the most intense political and ethical debates of the late twentieth and early twenty-first centuries, from affirmative action and disability rights across police profiling and labor market inequality to multicultural accommodation and the limits of hate speech. The most paradigmatic and uncontroversial cases tend to be those of so-called direct discrimination. Few dispute that South Africa's 1948 to 1994 Apartheid regime constituted discrimination against Black South Africans, or that the disenfranchisement of female Swiss citizens before 1971 constituted discrimination against women. But even for direct discrimination there are unclear and controversial cases aplenty. Does a religious organization discriminate if it insists that its ministers and clerics must publicly profess belief in its religious creed, for example? Or does an underfunded hospital that chooses to prioritize scarce resources by preserving its maternity ward rather than its Alzheimer's clinic discriminate against the elderly, who are overwhelmingly more likely to require the second type of treatment than the first? What about a movie director who does not give consideration to a talented Black female actor when casting the lead role of a historical drama about Napoleon Bonaparte? Even though these examples are in many respects similar to paradigmatic cases of discrimination, most people will likely be unsure or skeptical that they themselves exemplify discrimination.

What makes matters worse is that it can be difficult to tell what the relevant difference is between cases that we intuitively want to label discrimination and those we do not. Consider the following trio of cases: first Abe, who has a strong preference for employees of his own gender, race, and ethnicity. As a result, he refuses to hire women and persons of other races and ethnicities. This, I take it, is an uncontroversial example of discrimination. Next consider Abe's sister Bea, who has strong sexual and romantic preferences for persons of her own race and ethnicity. As a result, she refuses to date persons of other races and ethnicities. I suspect that intuitions may differ and will in any case be less certain than above, but that some people might be willing to say, albeit probably with less confidence than in the case of Abe, that in so doing Bea discriminates against persons of those races and ethnicities (see Chapter 23). Finally, consider Bea's girlfriend Cynthia, who has a strong sexual and romantic preference for women:

that is, Cynthia is a cis-gender homosexual woman. Few of us would presumably want to say that Cynthia discriminates against men in her choice of romantic partners. At the very least, we do not ordinarily refer to the way that the vast majority of people employ gender preferences in their choice of romantic partners as discrimination.

What are we to say about these cases? The shift from the public context of labor market hiring practices to the personal and private choice of romantic partners may account for some of the shift in our intuitions between the first two cases. But as the contrast with the third case illustrates, at least some concern may remain. Nor can the difference between the second and third cases be explained by the shift in the target of the preferences. At least, the first case would appear to be equally discriminatory when it targets gender, and when it targets race and ethnicity.

Thinking about what discrimination really means will ideally help us settle such issues, by giving us principled and carefully thought through grounds for drawing the line between cases of discrimination and non-discrimination, where we eventually draw it, as well as enabling us to better understand what it is that the cases we label discrimination have in common with each other, and the ways in which they differ significantly from cases of non-discrimination.

In slightly more technical terms, there are benefits both to a lexical definition, which aims to clarify and spell out our inherent concept of discrimination as employed in linguistic practices by competent speakers, and to an explicative definition, which aims to produce a definition that will not merely reflect but enhance our understanding of what is at stake. The discussion in the following attempts to balance the considerations that speak in favor of each of these types of definition, that is, to retain enough of our inherent concept for it to be acceptable as more or less what we mean when we speak of discrimination, while noting where we have reason to revise, e.g. because the concept would otherwise blur an important distinction.

Given how complex and multi-faceted discrimination is, and the potential benefits of exploring the concept, it is surprising how recent most conceptual analysis on the issue is. Admittedly there were notable sporadic efforts throughout the second half of the twentieth century, but it is really only over roughly the past decade that the task of defining discrimination has attracted sustained scholarly attention. However, these efforts have produced an abundance of new insights, and it is probably no exaggeration to say that we are now in a much better position to understand and confidently define discrimination than we were just a few years ago.

This article first presents a definition of what we can call the generic or basic sense of direct discrimination, as an agent treating two groups differently because of the property that defines one of the groups as a group, in a way that is worse for that group. It does so by exploring each of the conditions in this definition in turn, showing why they are necessary for something to constitute direct discrimination, as well as clarifying how precisely they should be understood. Next, it considers two different arguments to the effect that the three conditions are not jointly sufficient for something to be direct discrimination, in that an act must target one among a particular set of groups to constitute discrimination, and that an act must be in some sense morally wrong to constitute discrimination. While these objections are forceful it may be the case that they illustrate that we employ multiple, partly overlapping concepts of discrimination. This review of direct discrimination thus concludes that it may be more important to recognize this heterogeneity and clarify individual debates about discrimination by making explicit which sense is at stake, than it is to attempt to establish a dominant or unitary definition.

Note finally that the focus of this chapter is on the specific form of discrimination conventionally labeled direct. Although I briefly note places where other forms of discrimination may differ below, generally speaking the chapter does not deal with the complications that emerge in the context of variations such as indirect or structural discrimination (for the many important different forms of discrimination see the subsequent chapters of this handbook). Hence, unless otherwise noted, when this chapter mentions 'discrimination', it means simply direct discrimination.

Defining generic direct discrimination

Discrimination is a surprisingly slippery concept, and much of the attention it has received in recent years has focused on constructing a precise definition of the term. At least in part this may be because the concept appears to cover such a wide variety of disparate cases crossing traditional boundaries in applied ethics and political theory, from distributive justice, medical ethics, and criminal justice to multiculturalism, liberal rights, and feminism. Consider again that charges of discrimination may appear in the contexts of social or economic programs designed to help deprived minorities, in both efforts to accommodate and in the failure to accommodate persons with disabilities in public spaces, in how police and courts treat minorities (including by profiling and through disparities in sentencing), and in employer policies of hiring and promotion. Such charges may also be made against parenting that assigns different gender roles to children, and in defining the limits of acceptable public speech and symbolic actions, including insulting or criticizing vulnerable groups and holding political rallies in the neighborhoods where they live. At first glance it can be difficult to see what the whole spectrum of such cases could have in common. We can get a somewhat firmer grip on the concept, then, by taking a closer look at certain features that appear to be essential to discrimination.

Different than...

Probably the most obvious essential feature of paradigmatic cases of direct discrimination is that they involve differential treatment, which is to say that in cases of direct discrimination, an agent treats a person or group of persons in a way in which she does not treat other persons (cf. Chapter 2). Classic examples, such as a racist being rude or hostile towards members of a different race, or a sexist being paternalistic or demeaning towards members of the opposite sex, illustrate this fundamental feature. Conversely, it would be counterintuitive to say of the misanthrope or the nihilist that they discriminate, when they treat everyone with rudeness, hostility, or disdain (Lippert-Rasmussen 2006).

Distinguishing equal from differential treatment may not be as easy as is often assumed, but we will set that complication aside here. It is worth noting two points, however. First, that we should probably allow the difference in treatment to be counterfactual, that is, include as discrimination cases where the discriminator treats the discriminatee differently than she *would* have treated someone else, even if she does not in fact treat or in any way interact with such persons. We should be willing to say, e.g., that Robinson Crusoe discriminated against Friday by treating him differently than he would have treated a European person (assuming that we can characterize Crusoe's treatment of Friday this way), had there been any European persons around to treat one way or the other. Second, that this may be a condition that distinguishes direct discrimination from indirect discrimination and structural discrimination. We might want to say, for example, that a university dean who made hiring decisions by subjecting both male and female applicants to an identical test of upper body strength was discriminating against women, even though men and women would in perhaps the most obvious sense be treated equally, by being subjected to the same test. If so, then arguably the discrimination is not direct precisely because it does not directly differentiate between men and women.

Worse for...

Secondly, in paradigmatic cases of discrimination, the treatment is disadvantageous to the members of the group treated differently. That is, the treatment is in some respect worse for the persons treated differently than the treatment is for persons in the non-discriminated group. The racist who treats Black persons with rudeness and hostility and White persons with civility, or the misogynist who belittles and patronizes female but not male colleagues, discriminates *against* these persons because they are treated in a way that others are not, and because the different treatment they are subjected to is worse (Lippert-Rasmussen 2007b).

A first clarification of this condition is that the badness of being discriminated against should probably be conceived of as tied to the specific respect in which the discriminatee is discriminated against. We would want to say, for instance, that a person who is fired for revealing her homosexuality at her workplace is discriminated against with respect to employment at that place, even if she is paradoxically made better off, all things considered, by being fired, because her being unemployed leads to her finding a superior position with a different employer. Note also that the evaluation here is value-based, not normative. To say that a person is discriminated against if she is treated *morally* worse, i.e., the treatment of her is less permissible or has stronger reasons against it than the treatment of others, would be to conflate the moral assessment of the action with its effect on the discriminatee. To emphasize these two points, we can say that discrimination against a person is worse for the discriminatee with respect to some particular good.

The next thing to note is that the way we have distinguished a form of discrimination as being against a group suggests that we should also recognize the possibility of discrimination *in favor of* a person or persons, which would involve treating them differently and *better* than the agent treats others, and discrimination *between* persons, which would involve the agent treating a person or persons differently than others, but neither better nor worse. A person who donates generously to charities working to help Christians in poor countries across the world but not to charities that aid atheists or persons of other religions might exemplify the former. Meanwhile, gender-separated changing facilities in a gym might exemplify the latter.

A potential objection at this point might note that some of the most reprehensible forms of historical discrimination against a group have labeled themselves as discrimination between groups rather than against one group. While this is undoubtedly true, we should bear in mind that cases of discrimination that appear superficially to be neither better nor worse for either party, and therefore to constitute discrimination between the parties, may on more careful consideration constitute discrimination against one group, as in the notorious case of "separate but equal" discrimination between US Blacks and Whites, which at once provided not equal but inferior conditions to US Blacks, and stigmatized them by suggesting that there were reasons to keep them separate from Whites. The existence of such cases of veiled discrimination against does not, therefore, rule out the possibility of actual cases of discrimination between groups that disadvantage neither. Similarly, even if it is true that gender-separated changing facilities discriminate between cis-gender men and women, this does not preclude that this way of organizing the facilities simultaneously discriminates against other groups, e.g., by disadvantaging transgender persons.

A second and important clarification is the baseline issue, which consists in determining what it means for treatment to be worse for the discriminatee. We fudged this issue in the above by saying merely that the treatment was worse than the treatment was for the non-discriminated group, but for a clear understanding of the concept of discrimination we require a more precise account. That is, what is the baseline against which we measure whether treatment is good/better or bad/worse? (Lippert-Rasmussen 2007a; Chapter 12).

A clear, simple, and mistaken baseline is the interpersonal comparison of outcomes, that is, how well off the different treatments leave discriminatees and non-discriminatees relative to one another with respect to the good in question. This view is mistaken because it entails that treatment is worse for a person if she ends up worse off than others, no matter what her position was prior to treatment, and whether and to what degree her position was improved by treatment. This would require us to say counterintuitively, e.g., that we treat cancer patients worse than others by giving them chemotherapy (unless, implausibly, the therapy can make the patient as well off with respect to health as people without cancer).

We can solve the problem above by looking not at where treatment leaves the discriminatee, but at how it affects her. However, a strictly intrapersonal baseline runs against the notion that discrimination is concerned with comparing discriminatees with non-discriminatees. That is, how a particular treatment has affected the discriminatee would not in isolation tell us whether the treatment is better or worse in the sense relevant to discrimination; for this evaluation, we need to know and compare with how treatment affects non-discriminatees.

A plausible suggestion therefore is to combine the two and evaluate first how treatment affects discriminatees and then compare with how the different treatment affects non-discriminatees. If the effect of the treatment on discriminatees is less beneficial or more detrimental than the effect of the treatment of non-discriminatees then discriminatees are treated worse, and vice versa for being treated better. A consequence of this approach is that cases of discrimination for and against become symmetrical, so that any case of discrimination against a group of persons defined by possession of a particular property is simultaneously discrimination in favor of persons who do not possess this property, and vice versa.[1]

A final complication awaits, for in order to make the intrapersonal assessment of how a treatment affects a person we require a counterfactual to compare with. That is, in order to evaluate what difference a treatment makes to an individual person, we must compare it with some situation in which that person does not receive that treatment: but which situation?

An obvious answer might be the counterfactual situation in which the discriminatee is treated as non-discriminatees are treated, that is, the situation in which treatment is equal, not different. This suggestion runs into difficulties, however, in those cases where differences between the groups means that equal treatment would be even worse for discriminatees. Consider a host who serves a seven-course meal of French haute cuisine to her omnivorous guests, but accommodates her vegan guests by offering them a plain salad. In this case, the vegans might well be worse off with respect to food if they had been offered the seven-course meal since even a plain salad is plausibly better than food one cannot eat (veganism is not ordinarily among the many culinary qualities of French haute cuisine). And yet, there seems to be an obvious sense in which the vegan guests have been treated worse than the other guests.

A better suggestion is the situation in which neither group is treated one way or the other. This allows us to say that the vegans receive a smaller benefit than the non-vegan guests in the example above, and are for that reason treated worse. In summary, a discriminatee is treated worse if the effect on her of the treatment, as compared with receiving no treatment, is less beneficial or more detrimental than the effect of treatment on non-discriminatees, as compared with their receiving no treatment.

Because of...

Third, and last, discrimination seems to require that there be a link between the property that defines the persons treated worse, which distinguishes them from those treated differently, and the fact that they are treated differently. Suppose for instance that the difference in treatment is accidental, because a lottery decides which persons are treated in one way and which persons in another, but that it just so happens that every member of a vulnerable minority is randomly assigned the worse of the two treatments, and every other person is randomly assigned the better treatment. While this might be in some respects unfortunate, and there is perhaps an argument to be made that choosing to use a lottery to assign treatments is wrong, because it allows these accidental disparities in treatment of groups to occur to the detriment of the already disadvantaged, it would be intuitively odd to say that it was a case of discrimination against minority persons (Lippert-Rasmussen 2007a).

The question, then, is how narrowly or broadly to construe the necessary connection between the treatment by the agent and the property that defines the group treated differently. A narrow answer is to require that the property be a decisive part of the agent's intentions, so that, e.g., differential treatment is only discrimination if the agent intends to treat persons with that property differently, and intends to do so *because* they possess that particular property. A different, broad answer is to require only that it be counterfactually true that had the discriminatee not possessed the property, then she would not have been treated differently; this leaves the specific way in which treatment and property is connected open. Finally, one can hold that the range of possibilities here concerns not whether something is or is not discrimination but rather what *kind* of discrimination it is, e.g., because although only intentional discrimination is direct, similar cases that fall within the broader category of being causally connected may constitute indirect discrimination.

A complication for either view is that we should probably allow for cases of mistaken identity, e.g., the misogynist who patronizes a young boy because he mistakenly thinks the child is a girl, or the racist employer who does not interview an applicant because she mistakenly believes her name to be associated with a particular racial or ethnic group.[2] Presumably, these cases should still be labeled discrimination, and arguably they ought to be labeled discrimination against the group defined by the property that caused the treatment to be different rather than the property actually possessed by the discriminatee, i.e. discrimination against women that mistakenly affects a boy, and discrimination against one racial or ethnic group P that mistakenly affects a person from a different group, in the examples above (Lippert-Rasmussen 2006).

An ecumenical answer that accommodates the above observation is to say that the difference in treatment must be explainable by the discriminatee(s) possessing the relevant property, or by the discriminator *believing* that the discriminatee(s) possesses or possess the relevant property.

A definition of generic direct discrimination

Together, the above considerations suggest that an agent engages in direct discrimination *against* a person or group of persons *iff*:

1 She treats persons with property P (P-persons) differently than she treats or would have treated others (non-P-persons);
2 The treatment of P-persons is worse for P-persons with respect to good G than the treatment of non-P-persons is or would be for non-P-persons; and
3 The difference in treatment is explainable by P-persons possessing or the agent believing that they possess P and non-P-persons not possessing P.

Two further conditions

While the above presents a relatively precise and plausible definition of a generic sense of discrimination (see the introduction to this book), there are at least two important respects in which one may question whether it adequately captures what we mean by discrimination. First, should discrimination be target-specific? That is, should it be part of the definition of discrimination that it targets particular groups, and if so, how should we determine the list of those groups that can be targets of discrimination? Second, is discrimination a purely descriptive or a moral concept? That is, should it be part of the definition of discrimination that discrimination is morally wrong – if perhaps not all things considered, then at least *pro tanto* or *prima facie*? In the following sections we will look at each of these questions in turn.

The targets of discrimination

The generic sense of discrimination we have defined above is neutral with respect to which property the discriminatees possess. Bluntly put, it labels differential treatment of, e.g., persons born on a Tuesday as discrimination just as readily as it does differential treatment of homosexuals, disabled people, women, Blacks, Muslims, or other minorities traditionally at the core of discrimination concerns. This will sound odd to many – is it really possible to discriminate against *any* group, no matter how strange or contrived? And even if it is, is there not something to be said for the idea that discrimination against those groups typically at the core of our concerns is somehow *more* discriminatory? If the generic concept is unsatisfactory in these respects, one solution is to introduce a restriction on the properties that can be targets of discrimination. This approach is common in both anti-discrimination law and philosophical definitions in the shape of a group criterion, which adds a condition to the definition that P is a member of a predefined set of properties.

While the group criterion can draw some support from its intuitive appeal, before adopting it we ought also to be able to specify which properties go on the list, and to explain why these properties can form the basis of discrimination while others cannot (Halldenius 2005; Heinrichs 2007). On one account the relevant groups are those identity-carrying groups that have been socially, economically or politically disadvantaged, e.g. because they have historically been denied equal status, subjugated and/or exploited. This has the benefit of fitting well with standard assumptions about the groups at the core of our concerns about discrimination, and of providing an immediately appealing explanation of how and why the groups are selected. As an account of the group criterion, however, the disadvantaged-group approach faces the obvious problem that it appears counterintuitively unable to label novel cases of disadvantageous differential treatment as discrimination until after such treatment has led to the target group becoming disadvantaged, so that we cannot say, e.g., of a country where a novel ideology takes hold, and leads the majority to treat a previously equal minority as inferiors, that in so doing they discriminate.[3]

On another influential account the relevant properties are those that are socially salient, which is to say that they are properties that are important in a broad range of social interactions (Lippert-Rasmussen 2006; Lippert-Rasmussen 2013). This has the advantage over the more common idea of making a stable list of the relevant properties – race, gender, religion, sexual orientation, political observation, etc. – of making the criterion contextual and flexible. Different social settings will make different properties socially salient, and thus allow for discrimination against different groups. The account also offers an explanation of why these are the properties that can form the basis of discrimination: such properties are important in virtue of being socially central, and thereby allowing differential treatment to be widespread in a way that will aggravate the badness of individual cases.

If we accept the suggestion of socially salient properties, then we should add a fourth condition to the definition above along the lines of:

4 P is a property that is socially salient in the circumstances of the differential treatment.

Critics can object that none of the above gives us a principled reason to delimit discrimination, and that supplying a principled reason by explaining the conceptual or moral relevance of the distinction the intuition tracks is difficult (Thomsen 2013). For example, to the extent that we want to condemn discriminatory practices, there is no obvious reason why idiosyncratic discrimination could not be wrong for the same reasons that paradigmatic discrimination is (at least sometimes) morally repugnant, even if as noted above it is likely in general to be less bad because it will be less common. Furthermore, critics can point out that while, e.g., an employer who refuses to hire persons born on a Tuesday is engaged in a much rarer and perhaps less grievous kind of differential treatment than one who refuses to hire women, it is itself counterintuitive to insist that the first is not idiosyncratic discrimination but something other than discrimination entirely (Arneson 2006; Heinrichs 2007; Hellman 2008; Thomsen 2013).

A persuasive compromise position is to hold that we employ discrimination meaningfully in both a broader and more generic sense, and in a narrower sense in which it is limited to certain groups. As long as we make sure to distinguish the two, recognizing both senses may in fact help us avoid confusion (Lippert-Rasmussen 2013).

Moralized and descriptive discrimination

The second way in which one may consider the generic definition inadequate concerns the fact that it is descriptive, and therefore allows for permissible or even laudable forms of discrimination. Surely, an objector might say, when we speak of discrimination we mean a policy or action that is in some respect morally problematic, or at the very least suspect? Is it not strongly counterintuitive, e.g., to label the way the criminal justice system treats convicted offenders worse than those exonerated (by imposing punishment on the former) as a form of discrimination? To accommodate this concern one can adopt a moralized definition of discrimination, which requires that the differential treatment be in some sense morally wrong, even if only *pro tanto* or *prima facie* (Horta 2010; Lippert-Rasmussen 2013).

As with the suggestion of restricting the potential targets of discrimination, a moralized definition adds a further condition to the definition of generic discrimination, along the lines of:

5 The differential treatment is at least *prima facie* morally wrong (cf. Chapter 7).[4]

The potential arguments for and plausibility of moralizing the definition will depend to a large extent on what particular account of the wrongness of discrimination one adopts, but a general worry is that a moralized definition robs the concept of a normative explanatory power that we take it to have in at least some contexts. It is not uncommon, e.g., for critics of a social practice to respond to a justificatory challenge – "Why do you think this practice is wrong?" – by claiming that the practice is wrong *because* it is discriminatory. But according to a moralized definition this move is dialectically vacuous because it is circular, since on this definition it is only if the practice can be independently demonstrated to be wrong that it can be labeled discrimination in the first place.

A comparison with a concept facing similar issues is suggestive: consider whether we ought to moralize the definition of lying. Certainly, just like discrimination, a charge of lying is ordinarily raised when the person raising the charge considers the act to be in some respect morally wrong. And yet we might hesitate to build into the definition the condition that something is an act of lying only if it is in some respect morally wrong. Any wrongness of lying is arguably better conceived as a consequence of (some of) the conditions that define something as an act of lying, along, perhaps, with certain conditions that are ordinarily but not necessarily fulfilled in cases of lying, than as a requirement of something being lying in the first place.[5] If so, could and should we not say the same about discrimination?

Irrespective of whether one prefers a descriptive or moralized definition, though, it is crucial to bear in mind that the question of what makes discrimination wrong (when it is wrong) is separate and must be answered independently. According to a descriptive definition this follows immediately, since labeling something discrimination does not in and of itself imply that it is wrong. Any claim that a discriminatory practice is wrongful will thus need to argue that it is one of the instances of wrongful discrimination. Obviously this is compatible with holding that all (or, more plausibly, many) practices that meet the descriptive definition are wrong by virtue of the features that make them descriptively cases of discrimination. According to a moralized definition one will need to present a similar argument before one can conclude that a practice constitutes a case of discrimination in the first place. As such, while there may in some contexts be practical reasons to prefer a moralized to a descriptive definition, or vice versa, little if anything of moral importance ultimately depends on which of the two definitions one adopts.

Conclusion

At the beginning of this chapter we considered a trio of cases, involving the employer Abe, who refused to hire certain people on gender, racial, and ethnic grounds; his sister Bea, who refused to date certain people on racial and ethnic grounds; and her girlfriend Cynthia, who refused to date certain people on gender grounds. I suggested that many would have strong intuitions that the first case constitutes discrimination, but less firm intuitions about the second, and that few would want to label the third case discrimination. I also noted that careful consideration of what discrimination means should ideally help us to settle such issues, by giving us principled and carefully thought-through reasons for drawing the line between cases of discrimination and non-discrimination where we draw it. Have we achieved this ambition?

On the generic definition of discrimination all three cases are clearly and equally discrimination. The different intuitions many will hold thus emphasize that the generic definition is unlikely to be all there is to discrimination. However, while the group criterion may help us delimit other cases it is of no use here: although strictly speaking we have not specified the social context, gender, race, and ethnicity are paradigmatic exemplars of socially salient properties, and all three cases thus remain discrimination even if we add this condition. A moralized definition will plausibly do better: although we require an account of what makes discrimination morally wrong to make a considered judgment, intuitively many are likely to judge the first case morally wrong, the second somewhat problematic, and the third morally permissible. If discrimination is at least *prima facie* morally wrong differential treatment, then the third case is therefore not discrimination, while the second may be on the fence, which fits the intuitions I attempted to elicit.

Does this mean that we should simply embrace the moralized definition? Not necessarily. Doing so might blind us to the way the generic concept plays its part in shaping our intuitions. It seems to me likely that at least part of our uncertainty about how to label many cases is based on a vague, and likely often unreflective, awareness that there are several different senses of discrimination, and that they can fall apart for cases like these. We hesitate or waver at least in part because it is unclear which of these senses we are being asked to apply in judging whether a case is discrimination or not. There *is*, after all, *some* sense in which Cynthia discriminates against men.

If so, the most important contribution of the clarifications we have attempted in the preceding text may be a heightened sensitivity to the different senses of discrimination, and an increased awareness of the importance of ensuring that we are employing the term 'discrimination' with reference to the same concept when we engage with others in discussions of whether or not some potentially contentious case is discrimination. In a field as fraught with controversy and confusion as the debates on discrimination, the resulting achievement of clarity and mutual understanding would be no meagre prize.[6]

Further reading

Larry Alexander's "What Makes Discrimination Wrong?" (Alexander 1992) is a seminal text on discrimination, which among other achievements neatly sets out a typology of the different forms of discrimination. A number of authors helped rekindle the discussion of discrimination over the past decade. Among these David Edmonds's "Caste Wars – A Philosophy of Discrimination" (Edmonds 2006) devotes more attention than most to the conceptual issues of defining discrimination. Similarly, Bert Heinrichs's "What is Discrimination and When is it Morally Wrong?" (Heinrichs 2007) and Lena Halldenius's "Dissecting Discrimination" (Halldenius 2005) are both important contributions that helped to move the current debate on the conceptualization of direct discrimination forward. Among recent contributions, Kasper Lippert-Rasmussen's "Born Free and Equal" (Lippert-Rasmussen 2013) is probably the most insightful, comprehensive, and precise analysis of discrimination as a whole currently available in the literature, while his earlier work in "The Badness of Discrimination" (Lippert-Rasmussen 2006) and "Private Discrimination" (Lippert-Rasmussen 2007b) set out detailed analyses of the concept and ethics of direct discrimination in particular. Another noteworthy recent and comprehensive analysis of discrimination is Ben Eidelson's "Discrimination and Disrespect" (Eidelson 2015). Finally, several legal scholars have approached the topic from a perspective informed by debates on discrimination law. Among these, Sophia Moreau's "What is Discrimination?" (Moreau 2010), Deborah Hellman's "When is Discrimination Wrong?" (Hellman 2008), and in particular Tarunabh Khaitan's "A Theory of Discrimination Law" (Khaitan 2015) offer valuable insights on the conceptualization of discrimination.

Notes

1 Does this symmetry constitute a problem for the approach? Not necessarily – if there is an intuition to that effect, I believe that it is based on a notion parallel to the idea that harming is worse than failing to benefit, that discrimination against a person must be morally worse than discrimination in favor of a person. If that were true, then it would count against conceptualizing discrimination in a way that made against and in favor symmetrical, but even if one accepts the moral distinction between harming and failing to benefit, one need not accept a moral distinction between discrimination against and in favor. In light of the conceptual problems alternative baselines encounter, it seems permissible to allow the symmetry at least until the question of why and when discrimination is morally wrong is settled in favor of an account that entails or defends the distinction.

2 Note that for ease of discussion I adopt examples of out-group discrimination throughout this text, which is not intended to deny the obvious fact that in-group discrimination (e.g. female misogynists

or Black persons who hold racist beliefs about Black inferiority) is both real and important. For this reason I refer to the misogynist discriminators here and elsewhere as male, while otherwise employing "she" to refer to non-descript exemplars.

3 The idea that disadvantaged groups are particularly relevant to discrimination may work better in the context of identifying what makes discrimination wrong. That is, it may be more plausible to hold that whether the target group is historically disadvantaged makes a difference to whether treatment is a case of *wrongful* discrimination (Hellman 2008).

4 Note that I list the condition here as number five, but if one adopts a moralized but not a target-specific definition then it will of course replace the group criterion as the fourth condition.

5 Although it bears mentioning that the view that we should accept a moralized definition of lying – so-called moral deceptionism – also has defenders.

6 I owe thanks to an anonymous Routledge referee for helpful comments and suggestions for this chapter. I should also thank Rune Klingenberg Hansen, Sune Lægaard, Thomas Søbirk Petersen, Jesper Ryberg, and Søren Sofus Wichmann, whose comments on a related article helped me refine my writing of this chapter too. Finally, and above all, I owe an enormous intellectual debt to Kasper Lippert-Rasmussen, whose contributions to the literature, personal encouragement, and kind and constructive critique over the years, on both this chapter and my other work on discrimination, have profoundly shaped and improved my understanding.

Bibliography

Alexander, L. 1992. "What Makes Wrongful Discrimination Wrong? Biases, Preferences, Stereotypes and Proxies." *University of Pennsylvania Law Review* 141: 149–219.

Arneson, R. J. 2006. "What is Wrongful Discrimination?" *San Diego Law Review* 43: 775–808.

Edmonds, D. 2006. *Caste Wars – A Philosophy of Discrimination*. Abingdon: Routledge.

Eidelson, B. 2015. *Discrimination and Disrespect*. Oxford: Oxford University Press.

Halldenius, L. 2005. "Dissecting Discrimination." *Cambridge Quarterly of Healthcare Ethics* 14: 455–463.

Heinrichs, B. 2007. "What is Discrimination and When is it Morally Wrong?" *Jahrbuch für Wissenschaft und Ethik* 12: 97–114.

Hellman, D. 2008. *When Is Discrimination Wrong?* Cambridge: Harvard University Press.

Horta, O. 2010. "Discrimination in Terms of Moral Exclusion." *Theoria* 76(4): 314–332.

Khaitan, T. 2015. *A Theory of Discrimination Law*. Oxford: Oxford University Press.

Lippert-Rasmussen, K. 2006. "The Badness of Discrimination." *Ethical Theory and Moral Practice* 9: 167–185.

Lippert-Rasmussen, K. 2007a. "Discrimination: What is it and What Makes it Morally Wrong?" *New Waves in Applied Ethics*, edited by Ryberg, J., Wolf, C., and Petersen, T. S. Chippenham and Eastbourne: Palgrave Macmillan: 51–72.

Lippert-Rasmussen, K. 2007b. "Private Discrimination: A Prioritarian Desert-Accommodating Account." *San Diego Law Review* 43: 817–856.

Lippert-Rasmussen, K. 2013. *Born Free and Equal?* Oxford: Oxford University Press.

Moreau, S. 2010. "What is Discrimination?" *Philosophy & Public Affairs* 38(2): 143–179.

Thomsen, F. K. 2013. "But Some Groups Are More Equal Than Others – A Critical Review of the Group Criterion in the Concept of Discrimination." *Social Theory and Practice* 39(1): 120–146.

2
INDIRECT DISCRIMINATION

Tarunabh Khaitan

UNIVERSITY OF OXFORD

Introduction

Discrimination is not a static phenomenon. It is changeable, and adapts to new circumstances; under attack it becomes subtle, even elusive. Its resilience rests on the self-perpetuating nature of power and on the hard-wired implicit biases carried even by those of us who cognitively abhor discrimination (Bagenstos 2007; Shin 2010). The prohibition on indirect discrimination (or 'disparate impact', as it is referred to in the United States) is, in some ways, the law playing catch up. As it responds to the various, and evolving, manifestations of discrimination in our society—highlighted as much through singular cases brought by pioneering litigants and innovative lawyers as through legislative change following organized political protects—the law has often led the popular understanding of what counts as discrimination, and our moral aversion to its evolving forms (Khaitan 2015, 1ff; cf. Eidelson 2015, 4–5). This is especially true of *indirect* discrimination, which continues to arouse the suspicions of non-lawyers; so much so that Eidelson doubts whether many cases of indirect discrimination involve any 'discrimination' at all (Eidelson 2015, chap. 2: Eidelson does not necessarily challenge the legitimacy of prohibiting indirect discrimination, only whether it is 'discrimination' properly so-called). Given the salience of law in developing the concept, this chapter will focus almost exclusively on the legal understanding of indirect discrimination. This is not meant to suggest that there is no viable conception of indirect discrimination outside of law, or that such conceptions are unimportant (Cook 2015; Thomsen 2015). Furthermore, there are good reasons why laws should not seek to enforce all our moral duties to their full extent. There will, therefore, necessarily be a gap between the legal understanding of indirect discrimination and a moral account of the same. The claims in this chapter do not therefore offer an exhaustive understanding of indirect discrimination as a general concept, but—given the centrality of law in its discovery and evolution—we can safely expect these claims to be more than merely relevant to a more general account as well. As Moreau explains:

> a focus on the law, far from muddying our moral thoughts, can help to clarify them... Whatever kind of injustice is involved in discrimination, it seems true that our understanding of it has been deeply shaped by our legal regimes for regulating it.
>
> *(Moreau 2016, 517)*

In law, indirect discrimination involves an apparently neutral practice or policy which puts members of a protected group (say, women) at a disproportionate disadvantage compared with members of a cognate group (say, men), and which fails to satisfy a means–end justification test (See *Griggs v. Duke Power Company* 401 US 424 (1971); s 703 of Title VII of the US Civil Rights Act of 1991; s 19(2) of the UK Equality Act 2010).

The concept was first developed in the landmark American case *Griggs v. Duke Power Company*. In that case, an employer required high school education or the passing of an IQ test as a precondition for employment. The rule had the effect of disproportionately excluding black applicants. The US Supreme Court held that the educational criterion which disproportionately disqualified blacks would violate Title VII of the Civil Rights Act of 1964 unless the requirement could be justified on the touchstone of business necessity. Since the employees hired before the new qualifications were introduced and did not satisfy them had continued to perform the job satisfactorily, the employer failed to justify the requirements. The Court explicitly held that the absence of a discriminatory intent was quite irrelevant to a finding of 'disparate impact'.

Soon after *Griggs* was decided in 1971, a visiting British Minister learnt about the judgment and incorporated disparate impact as 'indirect discrimination' in the British Sex Discrimination Act 1975 and the Race Relations Act 1976 (Hepple 2006, 608). The concept travelled to the European Union (and through it, to other member states), Australia, Hong Kong, Canada, South Africa and many other jurisdictions. Its focus on impact over treatment has been hailed as the institution, at least in part, of 'substantive equality' by courts as well as academics (*Law v. Canada* [1999] 1 SCR 497 [25]; Fredman 2011, 180–3).

The successful export of the concept to other jurisdictions is, however, only one side of the story. The backlash against it in its original home came swiftly. In 1976, the US Supreme Court refused to extend the logic of *Griggs* to the constitutional prohibition on discrimination under the 14th Amendment: this provision continues to prohibit only disparate treatment, not disparate impact (*Washington v. Davis* 426 US 229 [1976]). The next landmark is *Wards Cove v. Antonio* 490 US 642 (1989), where the Court tried to defang disparate impact law through a series of procedural and doctrinal innovations. Most of these changes were undone by Congressional statute. But the spark from *Washington v. Davis* was fanned by Justice Scalia's concurring judgment in *Ricci v. Destefano* 557 US 557 (2009). Given that voluntary compliance with disparate impact prohibition often requires race-conscious action, Scalia wondered whether such prohibition itself did not therefore violate the 14th Amendment's prohibition on the state undertaking or mandating disparate treatment. In her dissent, Justice Ginsburg argued that while disparate treatment law demanded race-neutrality in form, it did not prohibit race-consciousness of purpose (*Ricci*, 619–20; see also Siegel [2011]). In *Texas Department of Housing v. Inclusive Communities Project* 135 SCt 2507 (2015), the Supreme Court affirmed that although the Fair Housing Act, like the Civil Rights Act, prohibits disparate treatment *as well as* disparate impact, it did so with several caveats. Against the context of Scalia's threat in *Ricci*, Justice Kennedy held that 'serious constitutional questions' can be avoided only if the disparate impact prohibition is subjected to strict limitations. The extent to which these limitations bring the ghost of *Wards Cove* back to life remains to be seen. But some of the rhetoric suggests this could be a pyrrhic victory for the advocates of disparate impact law. Even in Britain, the Court of

Appeal sought to impose additional hurdles for a claimant seeking to establish indirect discrimination which, had they not been overturned by the Supreme Court, would have made successful litigation in this area very rare (*Essop v. Home Office* [2017] UKSC 27; Khaitan 2016).

These doctrinal developments have put a question mark over the legitimacy and the continued operation of the legal prohibition on indirect discrimination. In this chapter, I will highlight some of the theoretical controversies surrounding the legal conception of indirect discrimination as well as its prohibition, especially those which might have a bearing on its practical legitimacy. Section 2 explains the nature of the disproportionate impact requirement that qualifies as indirect discrimination and outlines some controversies that have arisen in determining the same. Section 3 explores two distinct ways, developed in the United States and the United Kingdom respectively, of categorizing discrimination into direct and indirect forms. Some of the conceptual difficulties associated with the US approach to the distinction are also canvassed in this section. Section 4 considers whether, as has been suggested by some academics, indirect discrimination constitutes a 'secondary paradigm' to direct discrimination in any way. It explores the possibility of a morally, temporally, or logically secondary character of indirect discrimination. Finally, section 5 briefly speculates upon the moral bases on which indirect discrimination may be thought to be wrongful or blameworthy.

Comparative disproportionate impact

Indirect discrimination occurs when an act impacts members of a protected group *disproportionately*, in comparison with its cognate groups. For example, to show that an act disproportionately affects women, one needs to establish that impact in relation to its impact on men. This notion of disproportionate impact on a protected group should not be confused with a subsequent—justification—inquiry which usually asks whether the discriminatory action was, all things considered, a proportionate means of achieving a legitimate end (cf. Lippert-Rasmussen 2014, 66). A criterion that requires fifteen years of teaching and research experience in physics for a professorship in physics may well affect women disproportionately, since they are less likely to have that experience for historical reasons. But, as a criterion, it may or may not be a disproportionate means of achieving the end in question: much will depend on how important the relevant fifteen years of experience is to satisfactorily perform as a professor in that discipline, and how this importance balances against the harm done by the discriminatory impact on women. Given this balancing requirement, the degree to which women are disproportionately affected is surely going to be relevant to the proportionality analysis at the justification stage, but the two inquiries are nonetheless distinct (Khaitan 2015, 180–92). Disproportionate impact of the relevant kind establishes *prima facie* indirect discrimination, the end-stage proportionality analysis tells us whether such discrimination is *justifiable* (and, therefore, permissible).

Indirect discrimination is structurally comparative, in the sense that it involves the disadvantaging of certain groups of persons *in relation to* others. The nature of the comparator analysis here is, however, very different from that used in direct discrimination cases. The comparative analysis for indirect discrimination involves groups rather than individuals. Section 19(2)(b) of the UK Equality Act 2010, for example, requires that the offending measure must put 'persons with whom [the claimant] shares the characteristic at a particular disadvantage when compared with persons with whom [the claimant] does not share it'. This usually avoids the need to find an *individual* 'appropriate comparator'—a search that has plagued direct discrimination jurisprudence (Réaume 2013). There are, of course, controversies surrounding comparison in indirect discrimination too—but they are of a different character.

Determining what counts as a disproportionate impact on a group is not straightforward. Two problems are involved. First, one needs to know the relevant pool in relation to which a judgment of disproportionality needs to be made (see *Wards Cove* 650–1). In the case of employment discrimination, for example, should the relevant pool be the entire population of the jurisdiction, or only the pool of persons qualified to perform the job in question, or simply the workforce of the employer? We will often arrive at different conclusions about whether a policy disproportionately excludes women in comparison to men depending on whether our relevant pool was the entire population (where women are likely to constitute half the pool) or only those who have the necessary qualifications to perform the job (say persons with graduate degrees, where women are likely to be less than half the pool).

In this regard, Lord Justice Mustill has suggested that the relevant pool against which disproportionality is to be judged should include everyone who satisfies all the other conditions of selection, except the one(s) that is/are being challenged (*Jones v. Chief Adjudication Officer* [1990] IRLR 533 [36]). This is easier to do in some cases than others. Consider an easy example first. Let us say that Company Inc. decides to give a one-off bonus payment to every employee who has worked for it for more than 15 continuous years. There are two criteria for eligibility for the bonus:

(i) The person must be an employee of Company Inc., and
(ii) He or she should have worked for Company Inc. for a continuous period of more than 15 years.

The rule that is under challenge as potentially indirectly discriminatory is (ii). Under the Mustill formula, the relevant pool consists of everyone who satisfies (i), i.e. all the employees of Company Inc. Say the total number of employees who work for Company Inc. are 150, and the total number of women in this group are 40. It is this pool against which those adversely affected need to be compared. Let us assume further that the adversely affected set (V)—employees who have not worked for 15 continuous years with this employer—contains 100 employees, of whom 35 are women. It turns out that the ratio of the number of women adversely affected to the number of women in the relevant pool is 35:40. Compare this to the ratio of men adversely affected to the total number of men in the relevant pool, which is 65:110. It turns out that 87.5 per cent of all women who could have been adversely affected were so affected, whereas the same percentage for men was 59.1 per cent. Even a rule of thumb analysis will suffice to conclude that women disproportionately constitute the adversely affected group V in this example.

Cases are harder when the relevant pool is more difficult to determine. Consider an employer who wants to hire 50 workers for a low-skilled factory job. In order to be eligible, every aspirant must:

(i) be between the ages of 18 and 55 on the date of appointment,
(ii) be living within, or willing to move to live within, a 30-mile radius from the factory, and
(iii) have an undergraduate university degree.

The group of 50 workers he eventually hires includes 4 black people and 35 white people, with the remaining 11 from other racial groups. An unsuccessful black aspirant challenges requirement (iii) as indirectly discriminatory against blacks (let us put age discrimination concerns in (i) to one side to focus the argument). In order to determine whether there is disproportionate impact, we need to know—under the Mustill formula—what the relevant pool of people who satisfied all conditions other than (iii) is, and what the racial composition of this pool is. The trouble is that in most cases it is almost impossible to determine this pool with any degree of certainty. Does one consider the entire population of the local area between the ages of 18 and 55 as the relevant pool? Even if one thinks this is appropriate, what counts as 'local' area, given that some people living elsewhere may be willing to move? Does one look only for those who might be considering a low-skilled factory job? Or, does the relevant pool only contain those who in fact want this particular job? It is hardly a trivial matter for a court trying to solve a real-world problem. Ultimately, the law must settle this issue by relying on its ability to deem certain facts as legally acceptable (as it does, for example, with a bright line age of majority). In doing so, it should consider what data is readily available, the relative position of the party which bears the evidentiary burden, and the broader objective that discrimination law seeks to achieve. In most cases, this will result in treating the entire population in the relevant age group living in the normal catchment area of that factory as the relevant pool for determining disproportionality. This rough determination will usually be more acceptable than rejecting the claim because of the epistemic difficulties involved.

A second, related, problem in determining whether there has been a comparative disproportionate impact is the type of evidence required to judge disproportionality. My example concerning bonus pay assumes that the relevant statistical data will always be available, even when the relevant pool is clearly defined. This will not always be the case. Again, if the epistemic constraint imposed by the absence of such data results in the wholesale rejection of indirect discrimination claims, the very purpose of discrimination law will be compromised. For example, section 1(1)(b)(i) of the UK Sex Discrimination Act 1975 required proof of the fact that 'the proportion of women who can comply with [the requirement or condition] is *considerably smaller* than the proportion of men who can comply with it' (emphasis added). Following developments in EU law, the UK Equality Act 2010 has now replaced this standard by only insisting on proof of 'particular disadvantage' (UK Equality Act 2010, s 19(2)(b); see also, Framework Directive 2000/78/EC, art 2(2)(b); *Homer v. Chief Constable of West Yorkshire Police* [2012] UKSC 15; *Wards Cove Packing Co v. Atonio* 490 US 642 [1989]; C-237/94 *O'Flynn v. Adjudication Officer* [1996] 2 CMLR 103). The move to the deliberately vague 'particular disadvantage' standard was designed to ensure that a rule of thumb assessment of disproportionate impact would suffice, and the claimant would not be required to satisfy demanding and expensive statistical standards.

Direct versus indirect discrimination

The line between direct and indirect discrimination is famously blurred. As discrimination law has evolved in different jurisdictions over the years, two distinct approaches to the divide have emerged. The approach in the US is to treat the difference as one of kind, whereas British courts tend to treat it as a difference in degree.

Before we examine the theoretical underpinnings of the distinction, some doctrinal differences between the implications of the characterization of an act as direct or indirect discrimination are worth noting. Both American and British courts treat indirect discrimination as almost always justifiable, i.e. they are open to the possibility that indirect discrimination in a given case might be justified. The discriminator is usually entitled to show that the discriminatory policy is a necessary and proportionate means to pursue a sufficiently important objective (or some variation of this means–end formula). Although the standard required to justify indirect discrimination is usually quite high, it tends to be less exacting than justifying direct discrimination, if that is permitted at all. Subject to strict affirmative action exceptions, American discrimination law treats any intentional use of a protected characteristic as cancelling out, or at least dramatically reducing, the possibility of justification. Canada, which adopts a unified approach to justifying all forms of discrimination, does not react so sharply to intention. It does, however, take *motives* more seriously: the absence of good faith on the part of the defendant would extinguish any justification defence (*British Columbia v. BCGEU* 3 SCR 3 [54]). Thus, the intentional use of race for a benign motive—for example, towards affirmative action—may be permissible (see Chapter 33). The second doctrinal distinction pertains to remedies. Jurisdictions often do not allow the award of damages if discrimination is not intentional, or make it easier to award damages, sometimes including special damages, when it is so (UK Equality Act 2010, s 124 [4] and [5]; 42 USC § 1981a; Canadian Human Rights Act 1985, s 53 [3]). In general, legal practice treats (intentional) direct discrimination as less readily justifiable (if justifiable at all) and liable to more onerous remedies.

These doctrinal distinctions, along with the fact that the two forms of discrimination are considered to be mutually exclusive, has led to expansionary pressures on the scope of direct discrimination. Ensuing difficulties in clarifying the boundary between direct and indirect discrimination in part motivated the Canadian Supreme Court to reject the bifurcated approach and adopt instead a common legal response to either form of discrimination (*British Columbia (Public Service Employee Relations Commission) v. BCGEU* [1999] 3 SCR 3). Let us now examine the basis on which a distinction between the two types of discrimination might be drawn.

The first—American—approach uses two different criteria to determine whether a discriminatory conduct is direct or indirect. There, discrimination is direct ('disparate treatment') if it is constituted by the intentional use of a protected characteristic—whatever the motive behind such use. This approach, hostile to any classification based on a protected characteristic, has been termed the anti-classification principle (Siegel 2004). On the other hand, the US treats discrimination as indirect ('disparate impact') if a facially neutral act nonetheless has a disproportionate impact on a protected group, when compared with a cognate group.

Normally when we classify a phenomenon into sub-categories, we can do so on a variety of different bases. People, for example, can be categorized based on their height (say, those under five feet, those between five and six feet, and those above six feet), or their citizenship (Bermudans, Australians, Ghanaians etc.), or their attractiveness (very attractive to not attractive at all). These examples demonstrate that different sub-categories can have different natures: height can generally be determined objectively; height-based sub-categories can be mutually exclusive so that a person who falls within one category is automatically excluded from all others; height admits to degrees so that a person can be taller or shorter. Citizenship, typically, can also be determined objectively, may not however be mutually exclusive for persons with more than one citizenship, and does not normally admit to degrees in that either one is a citizen of Ghana or not. Attractiveness, usually, cannot be determined objectively and admits to degrees, but on any one given approach to determination is likely to put every individual in a single sub-category rather than multiple ones (even though, given its subjective determination, different points of view may sub-categorize the same persons differently).

Similarly, discrimination may be intentional or unintentional. An act may also be sub-categorized based on its comparative impact on a protected group: it may adversely impact such a group in such a manner, or it may not. There are, of course, many other bases on which potentially discriminatory acts may be classified: based on the intensity of the impact, say, or the number of people impacted upon, and so on. However, a categorization of discrimination into intentional acts of discrimination (disparate treatment) on the one hand and unintentional acts that have a disproportionate comparative impact on protected groups (disparate impact) on the other is akin to categorizing persons based on their "cit-ractiveness": say, those who are Bermudans on the one hand and attractive non-Bermudans on the other. These are indeed sub-categories of the same phenomenon (persons), and they are mutually exclusive, yet there is something odd about the portmanteau classificatory basis of cit-ractiveness. It is all too reminiscent of Foucault's unease over a 'certain Chinese encyclopaedia' which divided animals into '(a) belonging to the Emperor, (b) embalmed, (c) tame, (d) sucking pigs, (e) sirens, (f) fabulous, (g) stray dogs, (h) included in the present classification, (i) *et cetera*, (m) having just broken the water pitcher, (n) that from a long way off look like flies' (Foucault 1970, xv).

Conceptual untidiness, on its own, may not be worrisome enough, especially for a practical discipline like law. But sometimes such untidiness matters. To see how, kindly permit a somewhat outlandish continuation of our example. For whatever eccentric reason, say a person has adopted a cit-ractiveness classification to determine who she will speak to. She resolves to speak only to people who are Bermudans or to attractive non-Bermudans. Let us say that she has a rather superficial approach to determining attractiveness, and judges it solely by looks. But citizenship cannot be so determined, and at least sometimes, determining whether a person is Bermudan or not will require her to speak to them. As such, the only way she can keep her resolve is by speaking to those unattractive persons who she already knows to be Bermudans, and to attractive persons. If the former category is small enough, in practice, she would have modified her rule and speak mainly to attractive people alone, Bermudans or not. She may or may not be comfortable with this new rule: what is clear is that her original rule has been effectively modified.

The analogy with the distinction we are concerned with is this: just as our eccentric heroine had to break one part of her rule in order to uphold the other, if one is to avoid inflicting disparate impact, one sometimes needs to intentionally use a protected characteristic, i.e., commit disparate treatment. This was exactly what happened in *Ricci v. DeStefano*, where a city discarded the results of a promotional test because no black firefighter passed it, and conducted a new test. This constituted disparate treatment because the city discarded the test owing to its racial impact: in other words, its action was based on race. The problem for the city was that it was worried that the original test may have been indirectly discriminatory. The city could not effectively abide by both parts of the prohibition on discrimination. The Supreme Court's solution to the dilemma was this: when in doubt, refrain from disparate treatment. The original two-pronged prohibition has been effectively modified, relegating disparate impact to a position subservient to disparate treatment. If the city cares about avoiding both disparate treatment and disparate impact, it will find the original rule debilitating. The hierarchy between the two types of discrimination matters in a world where we are increasingly more likely to encounter disparate impact than disparate treatment: as the Canadian Supreme Court acknowledged, 'a modern employer with a discriminatory intention would rarely frame the rule in directly discriminatory terms when the same effect—or an even broader effect—could be easily realized by couching it in neutral language' (*British Columbia v. BCGEU* 3 SCR 3 [29]).

In contrast to the United States, the United Kingdom has moved to an entirely different way of sub-categorizing discrimination. The understanding of direct discrimination in that jurisdiction has been overhauled. As Lady Hale, citing Advocate General Sharpston from the European Court of Justice, emphasized in *Bull v. Hall* ([2013] UKSC 73 [19]):

> I take there to be direct discrimination when the category of those receiving a certain advantage and the category of those suffering a correlative disadvantage coincide exactly with the respective categories of persons distinguished only by applying a prohibited classification.

In other words, if all those who are adversely affected by an act happen to be women, and all those who benefit from it (or are not adversely affected by it) are men, British law will hold such an act to be directly discriminatory. The coincidence must be total for *both* groups: if all members of the disadvantaged group fail, but so do some members of its comparator group, the discrimination is still *in*direct, albeit 'a form of indirect discrimination which comes as close as it can to direct discrimination' (*Rodriguez v. Minister of Housing* [2009] UKPC 52 [19]). The distinction between direct and indirect discrimination is then rendered one of degree: a total coincidence (or, a 'double-mirror' impact) amounts to direct discrimination, and less than total but disproportionate coincidence to indirect discrimination, on a graduated scale of seriousness depending on their proximity to the direct discrimination end of this scale.

What British law has effectively done is adopt the same basis for sub-categorizing the two forms of discrimination: it has opted for conceptual tidiness. Both types of discrimination now turn on the degree of comparative impact on protected groups. Since the law mandates a distinction, courts have fixed direct discrimination at one extreme end of the spectrum of comparative impact: if an act falls on this point, it is unjustifiable. This does make the law more certain: at least in these cases the parties know for sure where they stand, sans the muddying effect of a justification defence. It also mitigates the difficulties that an American-style portmanteau categorization leads to, where there is devaluation of indirect discrimination liability in practice because parties need to choose between refraining to commit direct discrimination on the one hand, and refraining from discriminating indirectly on the other.

This judicially developed conceptual neatness has not, however, mitigated the problem of false positives. The American hostility to all intentional uses of protected characteristics has been criticized for catching cases of benign affirmative action. Similarly, the British discounting of all intention and motives, even when benign, in the double-coincidence cases of comparative impact may also be over-inclusive (see *R (on the application of E) v. JFS* [2009] UKSC 15 [71]). It is little surprise, then, that there are calls for the adoption of the Canadian model of a unified justification approach in these jurisdictions too (Seiner, 2006).

Following legal developments in the United Kingdom and the United States, a key theoretical challenge for indirect discrimination law scholars is to see whether there remains a favoured coherent conceptual distinction between direct and indirect discrimination, and whether the distinction is one of kind or degree. This inquiry should remain sensitive to the practical nature of legal regulation, and not expect a perfect overlap between legal categories and conceptual ones. The question is, after making allowances for other pragmatic and principled constraints, can the distinction in the practice of a given jurisdiction be explained coherently? Theorists also need to figure out whether there would remain a point in distinguishing between the two forms of discrimination if the Canadian model of a unified approach to justification is adopted. What is the distinction, whatever its basis, supposed to track? Many assume that the distinction tracks a moral hierarchy, that direct discrimination is, in some sense, morally worse than indirect discrimination. To this question we will now turn our attention.

A secondary paradigm?

Gardner has suggested that 'the wrongfulness of discrimination is fundamentally linked to the fact that an improper ground of discrimination figures in the *operative* premisses of the discriminator's thinking'; this leads him to the controversial conclusion that direct discrimination (in the American sense) is the 'paradigm case' of wrongful discrimination, and that the legal prohibition on indirect discrimination constitutes a 'secondary paradigm' (Gardner 1998, 182).

In the previous section, we saw that drawing a bright line between direct and indirect discrimination is not straightforward, and that there are at least two different ways of approaching the distinction. For the purposes of this section, we will work with the distinction drawn in the United States, as that is the sort of distinction Gardner has in mind. So, assuming that the American distinction between them is coherent, this section will consider whether and in what sense indirect discrimination might be 'secondary' to direct discrimination. This theoretical question trades on doctrinal features such as the easier justifiability of and weaker remedies against indirect discrimination, which also suggest that it is a 'secondary' liability. There are at least three possible types of reasons—moral, temporal, and logical—behind any claim regarding its secondary character.

The first sense is a straightforward moral one, that indirect discrimination is morally less bad compared with direct discrimination. Now, an all-things-considered judgment about the moral badness of any action requires an account of one's moral worldview, and the place it has for concepts like harm and fault, and an understanding of whether and to what extent the two types of discrimination inflict harms or entail faults (see Chapters 6 to 14). Given the diverse ways in which discrimination, of either description, manifests itself, it would be surprising if any *general* claim that direct discrimination is morally worse than indirect discrimination turned out to be true. A *prima facie* claim is a bit more plausible, but even such an account will have to contend with the fact that indirect discrimination—because of its decidedly group orientation—often impacts very large numbers of persons, and sometimes quite gravely. Although Justices White and Stevens held in *Washington v. Davis* that dramatic impacts could sometimes 'evidence' disparate treatment, they do not, on their own, constitute it. Given the dramatic and morally compelling implications of some types of indirect discrimination and the morally trivial nature of certain acts of direct discrimination, a generally morally secondary status for indirect discrimination is difficult to sustain, unless one adopts the implausible view that intention alone is the full measure of the morality of all actions. What is more, the relevant 'intention' required to qualify for direct discrimination is simply an intentional—even if benign—use of a prohibited characteristic, rather than a prejudicial *motive* (cf. Chapter 32). We should be especially attentive to the contingent nature of the wrongfulness of discrimination given its dynamic and evolving nature.

The other two senses in which indirect discrimination might be 'secondary' are less obviously so, although worth interrogating at any rate. A second—temporal—explanation of the supposedly secondary nature of indirect discrimination is perhaps that it is parasitic on the prior existence of direct discrimination, even though it may be equally or possibly even more condemnable morally. In this version, direct discrimination is the original sin, one that creates the systemic patterns that differentially allocate social, economic, and political power between social groups (Lippert-Rasmussen 2014, 71). These patterns *then* manifest themselves in further acts of direct and indirect discrimination. Indirect discrimination is 'secondary', in this sense, because it comes about *because of*, and *after*, widespread acts of direct discrimination.

Although true in most cases, this explanation is not without problems. As Doyle points out, citing sexual orientation discrimination, the incidence of indirect discrimination can not only be more pernicious than, but sometimes even temporally prior to, direct discrimination (Doyle 2007, 549ff). Sexual choice has been criminalized for centuries without any reference to the orientation of the person concerned, or even before sexual 'orientation' emerged as a social phenomenon (Foucault 1978). Direct discrimination on the ground of sexual orientation is a much more recent phenomenon, and may itself be parasitic on the widespread indirect discrimination faced by sexual minorities. The same may be true of the discrimination historically faced by people living with certain types of disabilities.

A third—logical—basis of the claim might be that indirect discrimination generates 'secondary' protected grounds, alongside the primary grounds such as sex, race, religion, and sexual orientation on which discrimination is directly prohibited. The argument is that indirect discrimination is discrimination on secondary grounds such as educational qualifications, physical strength, and height, which are protected because of their contingent relationship with 'primary' grounds. This distinction may not, of course, be quite sharp in all cases: it is quite possible for the same case to entail direct religious discrimination (against, say, Muslims), which also amounts to indirect race discrimination (against persons of South Asian origin living in the UK). Even so, this seems to be the sense in which Gardner rests his claim. As an explanatory account, this might work, so long as it is made clear that these secondary *grounds* really are very different from the primary ones. It is easy for some theorists who endorse this view to go on to say that indirect discrimination simply 'expand[s] the relevant range of grounds. A ground which would not otherwise be a forbidden ground of discrimination (say, physical strength) becomes a forbidden ground of discrimination because it bears a certain relationship to the prohibited ground of distinction (sex)' (Holmes 2005, 184).

This *additional* claim, seeking to establish a conceptual continuity between primary and secondary *grounds* is problematic. Any theory of discrimination law needs to give an account of why certain characteristics (race, sex) are protected (Khaitan 2015, chap. 5). If all that indirect discrimination does is create new grounds of protection from direct discrimination, these new grounds (physical strength and educational qualification) need to jump through the same normative hoops that race and sex have crossed in order to be able to claim conceptual continuity. It should be obvious that discrimination law regimes do not treat these two categories of 'grounds' in the same way. The prohibition on race or sex discrimination is *comprehensive*. The prohibition on discrimination based on physical strength is *contingent*: only when such discrimination has an adverse effect on protected groups such as women does it qualify for protection. Physically weaker men who benefit from the voiding of a rule that indirectly discriminated against women decidedly piggyback on the coincidence that their lot was cast with women *in the particular context of that case*. A finding of indirect discrimination in such cases does not elevate physical strength to the same level of protection as sex, or even—on its own—to any level of protection at all. The point is that these secondary or apparent grounds do not matter for their own sake. They matter because—and only because—they are proxies for primary or protected grounds in certain circumstances (cf. Fishkin 2014, 246ff). Insofar as this third way of characterizing indirect discrimination as secondary to direct discrimination demotes its relationship with primary protected grounds, it is problematic.

It may well be, of course, that (at least the legal conception of) indirect discrimination is not secondary to direct discrimination in any sense. Any such claim will still have to make sense of some of the doctrinal features embedded in legal practice. Perhaps its easy justifiability and other such features are better explained on pragmatic rather than theoretical grounds. Indirect discrimination could, after all, be deeply disruptive of business as usual. Discrimination law is admittedly transformative in its objectives, and an in-built gradualism or incrementalism in its operation may well be a defensible policy choice.

Blameworthiness of indirect discrimination

Once it is established that a protected group has been disproportionately affected by the concerned act, *prima facie* indirect discrimination has been established. We already know that the defendant has done something which affects a protected group (usually a socially vulnerable group) disproportionately. Given that any plausible account of the purpose of discrimination law must contend with relative group disadvantage (Khaitan 2015, chap. 2), dealing with *prima facie* indirect discrimination lies at the heart of the entire edifice of this area of law. *Prima facie* indirect discrimination clearly harms protected groups. But is it also morally blameworthy on the part of the defendant?

The first thing to note is that like direct discrimination, indirect discrimination is an action-regarding norm. It is triggered by some provision, policy, practice, or criterion that the defendant applies (or seeks to apply) to the complainant (Holmes 2005, 184). A mere statistical disproportionality in, say, a workforce, will not amount to indirect discrimination unless it can be linked to some action, such as a provision or a policy (*Wards Cove Packing* 656). So, the liability attaches to something done (or purported to be done or to omissions in the course of something done) by the defendant. It is this complicity requirement that distinguishes indirect discrimination from affirmative action. But is it enough to suggest that the defendant has acted with blame?

Some theorists have argued that *prima facie* indirect discrimination is akin to the tort of negligence, inasmuch as it signals the absence of due care on the part of the defendant to avoid disproportionate impact on a vulnerable group, and is therefore blameworthy (Réaume 2001). Any such account will, however, need to explain the strict character of the legal liability, inasmuch as the law does not require proof of any culpable *mens rea* for establishing indirect discrimination. Another view might be that while the mere disproportionate impact on vulnerable social groups makes it wrongful and a legitimate object of legal regulation, such impact, on its own, does not indicate blameworthiness on the part of the defendant. This view is supported by doctrinal features such as the unlikelihood of securing damages for indirect discrimination. Others still could contend that *prima facie* indirect discrimination is blameworthy only if it fails the subsequent justification test, i.e. that in addition to having a disproportionate impact on a protected group, it is also a disproportionate means of achieving an aim (see generally, Collins and Khaitan 2017). On the outcome of this debate may well rest the perceived legitimacy of legal regulation of indirect discrimination.[1]

Note

1 I am grateful to Kasper Lippert-Rasmussen and an anonymous reviewer for helpful comments.

Bibliography

Bagenstos, S. 2007. "Implicit Bias, 'Science,' and Antidiscrimination Law". *Harvard Law and Policy Review* 477–493.

Collins, H. and Khaitan, T. 2017 (forthcoming). *Foundations of Indirect Discrimination Law*. Oxford: Hart Publishing.

Cook, R. 2015 "Discrimination Revised: Reviewing the Relationship between Social Groups, Disparate Treatment, and Disparate Impact". *Moral Philosophy and Politics* 2(2): 219–244.

Doyle, O. 2007. "Direct Discrimination, Indirect Discrimination and Autonomy". *Oxford Journal of Legal Studies* 27(3): 537–553.

Eidelson, B. 2015. *Discrimination and Disrespect*. Oxford: Oxford University Press.

Fishkin, J. 2014. *Bottlenecks: A New Theory of Equal Opportunity*. Oxford: Oxford University Press.

Foucault, M. 1970. *The Order of Things*. London: Routledge.

Foucault, M. 1978. *The History of Sexuality vol. 1*. New York: Pantheon Books.

Fredman, S. 2011. *Discrimination Law*. Oxford: Oxford University Press.

Gardner, J. 1998. "On the Ground of Her Sex(uality)". *Oxford Journal of Legal Studies* 18(1): 167–187.

Hepple, B. 2006. "The European Legacy of *Brown v. Board of Education*". *University of Illinois Law Review* 605–623.

Holmes, E. 2005. "Anti-Discrimination Rights Without Equality". *Modern Law Review* 68: 175–194.

Khaitan, T. 2015. *A Theory of Discrimination Law*. Oxford: Oxford University Press.

Khaitan, T. 2016. "Indirect Discrimination Law: Causation, Explanation and Coat-Tailers". *Law Quarterly Review* 135: 35–41.

Lippert-Rasmussen, K. 2014. *Born Free and Equal: A Philosophical Inquiry into the Nature of Discrimination*. Oxford: Oxford University Press.

Moreau, S. 2016. "Discrimination Law and the Freedom to Live a Good Life". *Law and Philosophy* 35(5): 511–527.

Réaume, D. 2001. "Harm and Fault in Discrimination Law". *Theoretical Inquiries in Law* 2(1): 349–385.

Réaume, D. 2013. "Dignity, Equality, and Comparison" in Hellman, D. and Moreau, S. eds, *Philosophical Foundations of Discrimination Law*. Oxford: Oxford University Press.

Seiner, J. 2006. "Disentangling Disparate Impact and Disparate Treatment: Adapting the Canadian Approach". *Yale Law and Policy Review* 25(1): 95–142.

Shin, P. 2010. "Liability for Unconscious Discrimination? A Thought Experiment in the Theory of Employment Discrimination Law". *Hastings Law Journal* 62: 67–101.

Siegel, R. 2004. "Equality Talk: Antisubordination and Anticlassification Values in Constitutional Struggles over *Brown*". *Harvard Law Review* 117: 1470–1547.

Siegel, R. 2011. "From Colorblindness to Antibalkanization: An Emerging Ground of Decision in Race Equality Cases". *Yale Law Journal* 120(6): 1278–1366.

Thomsen, F. 2015. "Stealing Bread and Sleeping beneath Bridges—Indirect Discrimination as Disadvantageous Equal Treatment". *Moral Philosophy and Politics* 2(2): 299–327.

3
STATISTICAL (AND NON-STATISTICAL) DISCRIMINATION

Frederick Schauer

UNIVERSITY OF VIRGINIA

Introduction

Discrimination is sometimes the product of what the discriminator takes to be a fundamental distinction between classes of people. For example, some religions treat men and women differently – in how they shall dress, in who can serve in the clergy, and in where they should sit during religious events – typically in the belief (whether sound or unsound is not the point, at least not yet) that the gender-based distinction is fundamental, foundational, natural, or constitutive. Those who distinguish between humans and animals for any of a number of reasons and in any of a number of contexts ordinarily understand the distinction between human beings and other creatures to be in some way ontologically or morally foundational. And placing a lesser value in war on the life of an enemy than on a country's own citizens is typically premised on a belief in a basic distinction between friend and foe, or between citizens and non-citizens.

By contrast, there are other forms of discrimination that appear even to the discriminator to be less fundamental. These forms of discrimination nevertheless exist, and that is because they are perceived to be instrumental to some other goal. For example, most countries discriminate against younger (than age eighteen, say) people for purposes of granting permission to drink or to drive, but such discrimination is not based on the belief that setting a minimum age to drink or drive tracks some sort of basic distinction. Rather, the discrimination against the young (at least in this context) is justified by the assumption that the distinction between the younger and the older is a reliable, even if imperfect, indicator of the more fundamental distinction between the responsible and the irresponsible. In much the same way, many universities discriminate in admission against those who achieve lower scores on standardized tests because the universities believe that scoring better on such tests is a plausible predictor of academic success. And employers often discriminate against those who have been convicted of crimes, typically in the belief that a past criminal conviction is predictive of future criminal conduct in the course of employment.

This chapter is focused on the latter form of discrimination, which is often labeled *statistical* discrimination. The discussion will deal with those forms of discrimination that are alleged by the discriminator to rest on a statistically valid empirical distinction – a correlation – between two (or more) people or categories. Statistical discrimination is thus defended by reference to the instrumental benefits of using a distinction that appears to have indicative or predictive value in pursuing a legitimate end existing independent of the discrimination itself.

Two types of discrimination

To discriminate is to draw a distinction between two or more people, places, things, categories, etc. And although the censorious use of the word "discrimination" is common, it need not always be so. When we non-pejoratively describe a person as having discriminating taste, for example, we mean that the person so described can distinguish the good from the bad, the true from the false, the fine from the crude, and so on. Here the identification of someone as discriminating is typically by way of praise and not condemnation. But although these days the language of discrimination is more often disparaging than commendatory, the basic point is that any form of discrimination, whether good or bad, presupposes drawing a distinction, and accordingly puts one or more items on one side of some line and one or more on the other side. To discriminate is to distinguish (cf. the Introduction to this book).

With this basic idea of discriminating as distinguishing in hand, and in order to focus on statistical discrimination, we can then draw a distinction between non-statistical and statistical discrimination (Hellman 1998). As noted in the Introduction, the former is that variety of discrimination purporting to rely on some non-instrumental distinction of importance between classes of, typically, people. Many forms of gender discrimination, for example, are based on some person's or group's belief that different genders have different roles to play, or simply that the sexes are fundamentally different. So too with many forms of racial discrimination, where those doing the discriminating often base their discriminatory acts on the belief that racial mixing is foundationally misguided because, they believe, the races are in some natural or foundational way different, or even that some races are superior to others. And many (most?) of the people who justify discriminating against non-heterosexuals do so on the belief that homosexuality and those who practice or prefer it are simply wrong.

What these forms of discrimination share is their non-instrumentality. The belief in the fundamental importance of gender or racial separation, for example, or in the foundational wrongness of homosexual practices and those inclined to engage in them, is most commonly justified in much the same way that people (especially non-consequentialists) might justify the wrongness of torture or the rightness of altruism. For the non-instrumental discriminator, the basis for the discrimination lies at or near bedrock, and is not justified by reference to further or deeper goals. Let us call this *foundational discrimination.*

To be contrasted with foundational discrimination is what we can label *instrumental discrimination.* Instrumental discrimination starts with some (presumably legitimate) goal that is itself independent of the discrimination at issue; but the discrimination is then based on the belief, assumption, or fact that drawing a distinction of a certain sort will, instrumentally, further the pursuit of that discrimination-independent goal. In other words, some discrimination is instrumental in the sense that possession of the trait that provides the basis for the discrimination is of significance to the discriminator only because of what it indicates about the likelihood that the person who is the subject of the discrimination possesses *another* trait. In a classic article, Joseph Tussman and Jacobus tenBroek (Tussman and tenBroek 1949) analyzed the same relationship under the rubric of an indicative instrumental connection between some "trait" and some "mischief" that the state sought to ameliorate, but, more broadly, the indicator need not be a natural human trait, and the goal need not be a mischief. Universities discriminating in favor of those with high test scores are an example, and there are many others. We might believe, say, that it is better to have airline pilots who have good rather than poor vision. This goal itself is of course a form of discrimination, because it distinguishes good pilots from bad ones, and distinguishes pilots who see well from pilots who do not. But in most contexts these forms of discrimination are not taken even to be worth worrying about, precisely because the goals underlying the discrimination are so plainly legitimate.

Given the existence of a legitimate goal, and given the desire efficiently or effectively to pursue that goal, instrumental discrimination consists of the use of some further distinction that is believed to be statistically indicative of (and thus supportive of) the legitimate goal. The distinction serves as an imperfect proxy for something else, and it is the something else that is the real concern (Alexander and Cole 1997). Thus a relevant form of instrumental (or proxy) discrimination would be discrimination on the basis of age. To continue with the example of commercial airline pilots, those who support imposing a maximum age for commercial airline pilots (traditionally 55 or 60, but now increasing) believe that age is a reliable even if imperfect indicator of poor vision (as well as impaired hearing and slower reflexes) (Schauer 2003, pp. 108–30). Consequently, if we exclude older people from serving as commercial airline pilots we will wind up, *ceteris paribus*, with a commercial airline pilot cohort that has better vision, better hearing, and faster reflexes than we would without the exclusion.

Instrumental discrimination, which we can now re-label as *statistical discrimination*, is ubiquitous (cf. Chapters 27 and 28). Using age again as an example, but in a different context, the widespread exclusion of those under a certain age (16, 17, 18, or 21, most commonly) from buying alcoholic beverages or from driving is based on the belief that safe driving is better than unsafe driving. Again, the goal itself is a form of discrimination, but few people are concerned about discriminating against bad drivers or dangerous drinkers. Rather, the relevant discrimination here – the statistical discrimination – is distinguishing older from younger drivers, or drinkers, in the belief that youth is a statistically sound predictor of irresponsible behavior. If that belief is sound, then if we restrict driving to those, say, over sixteen years of age we will wind up with a population of drivers that is, again *ceteris paribus*, more responsible than if we did not impose the age-based filter.

Many other forms of discrimination, some desirable and some deplorable, fit this model (Alexander 1992). If one believes that it is good to have aggressive lawyers, for example, and if one believes that women are on average less aggressive than men, then excluding women from the legal profession may represent this kind of statistical discrimination,[1] at least if we assume that the statistical discrimination is indeed an efficient way of pursuing the posited goal.[2] Or if one believes that women are less able at mathematics than men, and if one believes that it is better to have accountants (or mathematics teachers) who are better rather than worse at mathematics, then excluding women would involve the same kind of statistical discrimination. So too with excluding people of certain races from certain professions in the belief that those excluded are less intelligent, or preferring people of certain races for certain professions or activities in the belief that race is a statistically valid predictor of some talent or ability thought necessary or useful for successful pursuit of that activity.

The empirical foundations of statistical discrimination

That some people believe that a statistical (or probabilistic) relationship exists between some proxy and what it is a proxy for does not mean that they are correct in so believing. Indeed, much of the history of pernicious discrimination is a history of beliefs about the existence of some supposedly valid statistical instrumental relationship that turns out to have no sound empirical basis whatsoever. Historically, for example, the cultural (and sometime official) exclusion of women from serving as airline pilots was based on the belief that being female was a statistically reliable predictor of being worse at dealing with complex machinery, or being worse at reacting quickly and properly in case of emergency. We know now, however, that there is no basis for that belief, and that excluding women from the population of pilots would not produce a safer or more mechanically adept pilot population.

Such groundless correlations, which we can label as *spurious*,[3] are widespread. Consider the empirical basis for astrology. Those who believe in astrology believe that being born under a certain sign is an indicator of certain abilities or characteristics. Capricorns, for example, are thought to be ambitious, and thus the hiring practices of a business looking to hire ambitious people might prefer (discriminate in favor of) Capricorns to those born under the other signs of the Zodiac. But although many people believe that astrological sign is indicative in this way, there is no evidence to support this belief, and much evidence to refute it. Being a Capricorn actually tells us nothing about ambition, and thus the statistical claim is spurious. So too with the nineteenth century belief in phrenology, the pseudo-science based on the principle that certain cranial shapes were indicative of certain attributes of intelligence, personality, and other non-physical characteristics. In form, phrenological or astrological discrimination in favor of (or against) people with certain astrological signs or head shapes is the same as discrimination in favor of or against those of a certain age with respect to drinking, driving, and piloting. The difference is that in the latter cases the statistical discrimination has a sound empirical basis, but in the former we now know that the empirical basis is totally absent. And when that empirical basis is absent, as with the examples just used or with beliefs about, say, the intelligence of people of certain races or the courage of homosexual men, the basis for justifiable statistical discrimination disappears.

The statistical relationship between being a Capricorn and being ambitious is spurious and therefore unreliable, but just what is it that makes a statistical relationship non-spurious, and what is it for such a non-spurious relationship to be reliable? Or, what is it to say that a non-spurious relationship is accurate? The easiest cases, of course, are those in which all or virtually all members of some class (or having some trait) have the further trait in which we are interested. If we were to prohibit those under the age of three from having driving licenses, for example, we could be confident (at least in this world) that all members of the class of those under the age of three possessed the relevant characteristic of being unable to drive safely. More realistically, if we were seeking people for some task or job that required total linguistic fluency in Mongolian, limiting the applicant pool to those born and educated in Mongolia would produce an applicant pool of those almost all of whom possessed the necessary ability. The correlation would not be perfect. It is possible to be born and educated in Mongolia and not be proficient in Mongolian, and even more possible to be born outside of Mongolia and have developed native fluency in the language. Nevertheless, being born and educated in Mongolia is a very strong albeit non-universal indicator of the relevant ability, and is thus, in a statistical sense, reliable.

Much the same applies to those instances in which a majority of members of the class possess the relevant attribute. To continue with the same example, most people born in Latin America are fluent in Spanish, but there are large numbers of people fluent in Spanish who were not born in Latin America, and an appreciable number of people born in Latin America who are not fluent in Spanish. Still, even if being born in Latin America is a less reliable indicator of Spanish language fluency than being born in Mongolia is of Mongolian fluency, it is safe to say that the majority of people born in Latin America are fluent Spanish speakers, and thus being born in Latin America is a more-reliable-than-random indicator of Spanish fluency, even if, again, the reliable indicator is far from perfect.

Less obviously, but more importantly, some traits may be statistically *relevant* (the word is important) indicators of some other attribute even if the attribute is possessed by less than a majority of those who possess the trait. Most Jewish women of Ashkenazi background do not possess the genetic makeup that makes them disproportionately prone to breast cancer, but that genetic makeup is more prevalent among Jewish women of Ashkenazi background than among the class of women generally, and thus being a woman of Jewish Ashkenazi background is a non-spurious indicator of susceptibility to breast cancer, even though the relevant genetic marker is possessed by far less than a majority of those in the designated class. Similarly, most pit bull dogs are neither aggressive nor dangerous, but the percentage of dangerously aggressive pit bulls is higher than the percentage of dangerously aggressive dogs. As a result, a dog being a pit bull is a non-spurious indicator of dangerous aggressiveness, even though, again, most of the members of the designated class do not possess the worrisome trait.

For the sake of clarity, we can designate the trait at issue as the *indicator* – Latin American, Ashkenazi woman, pit bull, Capricorn, etc. – and the attribute or action or behavior that the indicator is thought to indicate as the *target* – Spanish speaker, breast cancer susceptibility, dangerous aggressiveness, ambition, etc. And so an indicator is statistically reliable insofar as it in fact probabilistically indicates (or *correlates* with) the existence of the target. As long as there is a positive correlation between the indicator and the target – if the relationship is better than random – then we can say that the indicator is reliable or accurate, although the degree of reliability or accuracy will vary with the closeness of the correlation.

It is worth emphasizing that the important relationship is an indicative or correlative one, and that the soundness of a statistical indicator is independent of the existence (or not) of a causal relationship between the indicator and the target, or vice versa. In some context we might well be interested in the existence or non-existence of a causal relationship, but indicators can be statistically sound even if there is no causal relationship. To take a shopworn example, air conditioner use does not cause people to eat ice cream, and eating ice cream does not cause people to use air conditioners. There is a common cause (heat) of both that produces the correlation, but there is no causation between the two effects of the common cause. Still, if we were interested in predicting the level of ice cream use, knowing the level of air conditioner use would be helpful – indicative – for this task, despite the absence of a causal relationship. And thus the statistical soundness of an indicator in predicting the existence or level of some target is independent of the existence of any causal connection between them.

In the language of conditional probability, an indicator is thus statistically sound, statistically reliable, or statistically accurate if the existence of the target is more likely given the indicator than it is without the indicator. In the law of evidence, such a relationship is described as logical relevance, and evidence is deemed logically relevant, to use the language of the American Federal Rules of Evidence, if "it has a tendency to make a fact more or less probable than it would be without the evidence" (Federal Rules of Evidence, Rule 401). So too with statistical discrimination, and an indicator is non-spurious if knowledge of it (or evidence of it) makes the existence of the target more or less probable than it would be without knowledge of the indicator.

Accuracy and reliability are of course matters of degree. There are strong and weak correlations, and thus strong and weak indicators, and thus indicators that are more or less reliable, or more or less accurate. Depending on the costs and consequences of using a particular non-universal indicator for some social or policy purpose, the degree of accuracy of the indicator will be important, and so although it is valuable to recognize the historical and contemporary significance of spurious indicators, the degree of non-spuriousness – the degree of accuracy of an indicator – remains a crucial consideration in the determination of which indicators should be used and in which contexts.

The conception of statistical relevance just sketched bears an affinity with modern work in the philosophy of language focusing on *generics* (Leslie 2008; Leslie 2015). As we know, a common feature of language is the use of descriptive statements about a class that are not universally true, even though the non-universality of the statement is not literally apparent from the statement itself. When we say that mosquitoes cause disease, that Volvos are reliable, that mathematicians are clever, or that Swiss cheese has holes, we do so knowing that many mosquitoes do not carry disease, that there are unreliable Volvos and dim mathematicians, and that some Swiss cheese does not have holes. Nevertheless, such generic statements are part of our language and our conceptual apparatus, and, to oversimplify, a generic statement is true if it bears the same non-spurious statistical relationship to facts about the world that we have just been discussing. Generic statements may not on the surface be explicitly comparative, but the truth of a generic statement presupposes some background or reference class with which the generic is being implicitly compared. "Volvos are reliable" is true if the class of Volvos is more reliable than the class of all cars, but false if being a Volvo is no more predictive of being reliable than simply being a car. Likewise, "pit bulls are dangerous" is true if a dog being a pit bull makes it more likely to be dangerous than just being a dog (or a dog of another breed), but if pit bulls are no more likely to be dangerous than any other type of dog then the statement that pit bulls are dangerous contains an implication that turns out to be false.

The virtues and vices of statistical discrimination

Within the broad category of statistical discrimination, the soundness of a statistical relationship between the indicator and the target will ordinarily be a necessary condition for its legitimate usability, but it is far from a sufficient condition (Hellman 2008, pp. 114–37). Of course we should not underestimate the importance of testing the empirical soundness of an alleged relationship between an indicator and a target, in large part because much of the history of unfortunate discrimination is a history of the erroneous belief in statistical relationships that turn out to have no basis in fact. It is simply untrue that homosexual men have less courage than heterosexual men, despite generations of belief to the contrary, and it is no more true that women inherently lack aggressiveness than that non-Capricorns lack ambition, again despite generations of belief to the contrary. So although the identification and rejection of spurious relationships between indicator and target may seem straightforward as a philosophical or conceptual matter, identifying such spurious relationships remains morally, politically, and practically important.

That said, however, the crucial question at the vortex of the conceptual, moral, and policy dimensions of statistical discrimination is the question of how and when, if at all, to employ non-spurious but non-universal indicators for the purpose of making decisions that have real consequences for individuals. Given the conception of statistical soundness (or reliability or accuracy) just explicated, the question remains as to how and when, if at all, such statistically accurate but non-universal indicators should be used as the basis for official or personal discrimination.

Initially, it is valuable to recognize that some statistically sound indicators exist as the residue of previous spurious ones. Within the class of non-spurious indicators there is a sub-class comprised of those indicators whose statistical soundness is itself a product of previous and non-statistically justified discrimination. Consider, for example, the case of gender. Suppose, as the American state of Idaho supposed until 1971 (*Reed v. Reed* 1971), that the government is interested in the qualifications of those who administer the estates of deceased persons. And suppose as well, as Idaho supposed, that financial and business training and experience were among the important qualifications for that task. Assuming, plausibly, that preferring those with financial and business expertise was a legitimate governmental goal, then how should we evaluate Idaho's decision to use gender as a proxy for financial and business expertise, and thus to prefer men to women to be administrators of estates?

Bearing in mind that this was 1971 (and earlier), it is difficult to deny that gender was then a statistically sound indicator of financial training and experience. Then (and still, but to a much lesser extent), few women possessed university training in business, economics, and finance, and even fewer benefited from such training at the graduate level. Few women were certified as accountants, and few held major positions in law or in the financial services industry. And so on for all of the other plausible markers of financial or business acumen. And thus at the time the policy was adopted, gender was in fact a non-spurious indicator of the skills reasonably thought desirable in the administrator of an estate.

Yet although gender was a correlated and thus (somewhat) reliable indicator of the legitimate target of financial and business expertise, it is almost certainly the case that this 1971 state of affairs was the product of earlier and persistent discrimination based on the erroneous belief that women were in some way genetically or naturally less able at financial tasks. Women were steered away from certain skills and profession (law and business, most relevantly here) and into others (grade school teaching and librarianship, for example) based on these beliefs. And it is thus highly likely that the 1971 non-spurious relationship between indicator and target was itself the product of an earlier and persistent belief in a relationship thought to be statistically accurate but which was in reality spurious, or was instead the product of a now properly-discredited belief in a foundational difference between men and women in the allocation of social and professional roles.

Whether a non-spurious relationship that is the byproduct of an earlier belief in a relationship that was in reality spurious (or was the product of a mistaken form of foundational discrimination) should now be employed presents difficult questions. It seems morally attractive to believe that we should not perpetuate the consequences of past wrongs, including past unwarranted discrimination, but the question remains one of allocating the costs of remedying past wrongs. If gender is now (or was in 1971) a non-spurious indicator of financial competence, as in the Idaho example, then refraining from its use entails the cost of excluding a factor that might now provide, *ceteris paribus*, useful information in pursuing a legitimate goal. And thus we can consider the question of just who it is that should bear this increased cost. In this instance the cost might turn out to be borne by the beneficiaries of less optimally managed estates, or, more plausibly and more desirably, by the society as a whole in paying for a more costly individualized system of assessment. Such allocations, especially the latter, seem appropriate in this and similar instances, but it is nevertheless important to recognize that the unwillingness to employ the most reliable (and efficient) indicator is not cost-free, and that the costs of that unwillingness must be borne somewhere and by someone.

Somewhat less conceptually or morally problematic, although again unfortunately frequent, are those reliable indicators that are employed as a pretext for some other form of discrimination. Gender, again, is a common example. Although it is true that men have, on average, greater upper body strength than women, and although it is hard to imagine (evolutionary explanations going back thousands of years aside) that such a state of affairs is a product of prior discrimination, employing this indicator in a hiring decision for a job in which upper body strength is not in fact valuable would be just such a pretext. The underlying basis for using such a pretext might be a belief in a relationship that is in fact spurious, as with using strength as a qualification for a job in the computer industry, where the real motivation was a belief that women were not mathematically adept enough to work in the industry. Or the real basis might be a form of non-statistical discrimination. When the Virginia Military Institute attempted before the Supreme Court of the United States to justify its male-only policy by claiming that women were less willing to endure and benefit from the particular form of "adversative" training common in the military (*United States v. Virginia* 1996), it is more than plausible to suppose that the underlying basis for the decision was a non-statistical belief that women simply do not belong in the military, rather than the claimed (and arguably true at the time it was claimed) lesser willingness of women to accept a particular form of education and training (Case 2000).

"Pure" statistical discrimination and the argument for individuation

Moving on from statistical discrimination based on spurious correlations, and moving on as well from statistical discrimination that is the product of previous spurious correlations or a pretext for something else, we then confront the "pure" case of statistical discrimination. How then should we evaluate statistical discrimination whose sole goal appears to be regulatory optimization, as with the age restrictions for driving, drinking, and piloting, or, far more controversially, highway or airport targeting (profiling) of those from certain countries, or with certain ethnic backgrounds, or of certain races, assuming, for the sake of argument, that there is a statistical basis for such actions, and that the motivation is nothing other than regulatory optimization? (Risse and Zeckhauser 2004).

When the question is framed in this way, it is apparent that it cannot be answered without presupposing a moral framework within which the analysis takes place. Under a broadly utilitarian or cost–benefit framework (Risse and Zeckhauser 2004; compare Lippert-Rasmussen 2006), the gains of engaging in statistical discrimination, gains that plainly vary with the degree of accuracy of the indicator and the frequency of mistaken indications, will be weighed against various costs, including the costs of mistaken indications. The analysis is a decision–theoretic one, where the expected costs of the errors (call them Type I errors) of mistaken indication are weighed against expected costs of the (Type II) errors of mistaken non-indication. Such a decision–theoretic analysis must, however, take into account the full range of consequences. For example, is the harm to a 66-year-old pilot discriminated against because she is, by virtue of her age, mistakenly believed to have poor vision the same as the harm to a Muslim pilot discriminated against for exactly the same job because he is mistakenly believed to be sympathetic to terrorists? Even assuming, counterfactually, that the degree of accuracy of both indicators is the same, the harms to the individual mistakenly excluded will be vastly different given the different social meanings of the two forms of discrimination. All of this, and more, must be incorporated into a complete utilitarian (or more broadly consequentialist) analysis (Lippert-Rasmussen 2014).

Indeed, the full utilitarian or cost–benefit analysis will also take into account the likelihood of error for different forms of discrimination, and the spillover effects of different forms of discrimination. For example, will even statistically justified discrimination against some group be overused because of background and non-statistically justified assumptions by those tasked with enforcement? Even if, say, there are relevant physical differences between men and women with respect to some task for which the physical attribute is relevant, will background beliefs lead those making decisions to exaggerate both the physical differences and their relevance? If so, mandatory underuse may be necessary to prevent mistaken overuse. Similarly, will the salience and literal visibility of race and gender lead decision-makers to exaggerate the importance of even relevant indicators compared to other indicators that may be more accurate and more relevant, even if less visible? None of these questions can be answered acontextually, but they show that even under a utilitarian framework the analysis will be complex, and must account for a wide range of positive and negative consequences in evaluating the use of even a statistically sound indicator.

Considering the question under various non-utilitarian frameworks is more complex yet, especially within frameworks that highlight the importance of equality as a pervasive good independent of consequences. Aristotle notwithstanding, equality is not about treating likes alike (Schauer 2003, pp. 199–207; Winston 1974). Rather, equality is an independent goal that requires treating unalikes alike. Just as the independent value of democracy will grant to all citizens the right to vote even in the face of knowing that some will vote more responsibly and knowledgeably than others, so too will the independent value of equality mandate treating people similarly even in the face of relevant differences. Equal access to the courts may require that those with weak claims for small amounts be treated, at least initially, the same as those with strong claims for larger amounts; equal access to public facilities typically requires that people be treated the same even if their qualifications to use the facility vary; and equal citizenship gives everyone a voice even if the quality of what is said is highly unequal. And thus when we evaluate statistical discrimination from a non-utilitarian or non-consequentialist framework in which values of equality, community, dignity, and respect, among others, have non-instrumental value, we find that treating everyone the same way in some contexts, or treating everyone with equivalent respect, dignity, and so on, are values that mandate ignoring even statistically relevant differences.

Some of the foregoing becomes more concrete in the context of contemporary debates about racial and ethnic profiling. Assuming that being a member of a certain group is at times a non-spurious indicator of a legitimate law enforcement or other governmental goal, and assuming as well that a pure cost–benefit analysis supports the discriminatory practice of focusing on members of those groups, it may be more important not to single out an already (or historically) discriminated-against group, for either consequentialist or non-consequentialist reasons, than to achieve some law enforcement or regulatory goal with maximum efficiency.

To repeat what was said above, however, refraining from statistically reliable discrimination entails a cost. Once we recognize that there is a cost to relinquishing the instrumental value of statistically non-spurious indicators, the question is how to allocate that cost. Will the cost of the comparative inefficiency of abstaining from using a reliable indicator be imposed on, and distributed among, everyone, as would be the case if we substituted targeted law enforcement screening with random searches and intensive examination of everyone? Will it be imposed on the best off or the worst off, as would be the case if government were to make available for a fee an exemption from intrusive screening? Obviously there are other possibilities, but the point remains that the avoidance of an instrumentally efficient and statistically justified discrimination comes at a cost that must be paid or borne by someone.

Typically, the chief alternatives to statistical discrimination have been understood to be individuation and randomization (Harcourt 2007). Individuation, or particularization, looks at each individual separately, attempting to determine whether *that* individual possesses the attributes that are the object of interest. An individuating approach would, for example, test every actual or aspiring pilot for vision, hearing, and reflexes, rather than relying on age as an indicator of decreased faculties on these dimensions. Such an approach would examine every dog for dangerous aggressiveness, instead of assuming that pit bulls were more dangerously aggressive than other breeds. And it would subject every airline passenger to the same scrutiny, rather than deploying more intensive scrutiny for those with certain ethnic, national, or physical characteristics.

In reality, individuation faces two obstacles. First, pure individuation is in the final analysis impossible. As the above discussion of generics in language shows, our language and our conceptual apparatus would be incomprehensible without generalizations, many of which are probabilistic and not universal. And even those attributes that appear particular are in some way generalizations. I observe a brown cow, and identify it as such, but that identification is based on the fact that the visual bombardments of sense data that I now interpret to indicate "brown cow" are arrays of sense data that in the past have reliably indicated "brown" and "cow" and so I rely on them now, even though those past indications might not be true on this occasion. More realistically, consider the idea of engaging in a particularized evaluation of pilot vision, without employing the proxy of age. We could test each pilot, but those tests would be based on the generalizations – proxies – that one's vision today is a reliable indicator of one's vision tomorrow or next week or next month, and that one's vision in the laboratory is a reliable indicator of one's vision in the cockpit. We could eliminate the use of standardized tests to predict academic performance, but we would still wind up predicting academic performance in the future based on academic performance in the past. And if we did not use race or ethnicity or national origin in airport screening, we would use something else that was in itself based on some generalization.

Even more serious than the virtual impossibility of complete or even maximum individuation is the reality of the necessity of using proxies in a world of limited resources of time, personnel, and money. We could eliminate the usual and suspect proxies in airport screening by scrutinizing everyone more carefully, at considerable cost and with imperfect success, and could accommodate for the possible mistakes by tripling the number of security personnel aboard each airplane, but the costs of such an approach are obvious. And the police, rather than focusing on the "usual suspects," itself a process of statistical discrimination, could investigate everyone whenever a crime was committed. More plausibly and more generally, every substitution of more rather than less individuation increases the costs of scrutiny, and also increases the possibility of error. Individuation requires individuators, and often the errors consequent on the use of imperfect proxies will, in some contexts, be less than the errors made by imperfect human beings attempting to take everything into account.

Recognizing the impossibility or the prohibitive cost of maximum individuation, some have suggested using randomization as a replacement for statistical discrimination (Harcourt 2007). Rather than using statistical indicators to select which taxpayers to subject to intensive audit, for example, the tax authorities could simply (as they do now, albeit not exclusively) conduct random audits, and the police could do much the same in deciding which drivers to stop for close inspection, and so on.

Although randomization would eliminate some of the problems associated with the non-universality of statistical generalizations, it would again hardly do so without cost. Some of these costs would stem from the perception that the application of state power should simply not be based on chance (Duxbury 1999, pp. 131–41). But other costs are more straightforward. If using a statistically reliable indicator allows us to train our attention and resources on those people, places, and things most relevant to some object of our concern, then relinquishing the use of the indicator, even if in the service of fairness or equality, is again not free. And at this point we can again no longer avoid the issues of just who statistical discrimination is discriminating against, and with what problems, and at what cost, and it is to this we now turn.

Conclusion: the inevitability of statistical discrimination

Statistical discrimination has been around for so long, and has so many benign applications, that until relatively recently it has rarely been a topic for discussion, academic or otherwise. Insurance companies, after all, are built around statistical discrimination – we call it actuarial decision-making – and in most contexts we have accepted that insurance companies will discriminate against smokers, drinkers, homeowners in floodplains, young drivers, and workers who are engaged in dangerous occupations (cf. Chapter 28). And although many forms of accepted statistical discrimination involve attributes voluntarily assumed – smoker, drinker, race-car driver – not all of them do. Statistical discrimination on account of advancing age, for example, is widely accepted, perhaps because the data on decreasing faculties is so strong, and perhaps because almost everyone is either elderly or hoping to get there. And statistical discrimination on account of youth is even less often questioned, again in part because youth is wisely understood to be a temporary status.

When the basis for the statistical discrimination is race, ethnicity, national origin, religion (sometimes), gender, or sexual orientation, however, the nature of the discussion changes, and the implicit presumption in favor of statistical discrimination in many domains shifts to a presumption in the opposite direction. There is nothing inherently problematic about this differential treatment. But what it reflects is an important aspect of the very idea of discrimination. Individuals, groups, associations, and governments discriminate constantly. And it could not be otherwise. When some people are hired and others not, when some are admitted to universities and others not, and when in countless other contexts distinctions are drawn, the entity doing the distinguishing is engaged in an act of discrimination. Sometimes these acts of discrimination are irrational, relying on spurious correlations between indicator and target. But often the relationship is non-spurious, and it is simply implausible to imagine that we could or should eliminate or even be skeptical about the use of non-universal instrumental relationships throughout our decisional or policy-making existence. Rather, it is essential to recognize that the aversion to statistical discrimination in domains such as race, ethnicity, citizenship, gender, sexual orientation, and the like is not an aversion to statistical discrimination *qua* statistical discrimination. Such aversions are specific to the grounds for the discrimination, and to the historical, moral, and psychological dimension of *some* forms of statistical discrimination. When the history, the morality, and the psychology suggest special concern about discrimination on certain grounds, it will be appropriate either to elevate the standard of statistical accuracy necessary to permit their use, or perhaps even to prohibit use entirely. But to suggest, as some of the popular discourse and some of the more academic literature (Harcourt 2007) suggests, that statistical discrimination can or should be eliminated entirely is neither possible nor desirable.

Notes

1 It is common to refer to statistical generalizations of this sort as *stereotypes*, but the word is misleadingly ambiguous (Bernstein 2013). For some, the word refers to all statistical generalizations, for others it refers to all statistical generalizations about classes of people, for others it refers only to those statistical generalizations that are inaccurate, and for others it refers only to those statistical generalizations that, whether because of their inaccuracy or because of their other consequences, are worthy of condemnation. Because of this radical divergence in meaning, it seems better to avoid using the term entirely.

2 If what appears to be statistical discrimination is not in fact less costly (in the broad sense of "cost") than examining the trait of primary interest, this may of course indicate that some more foundational discrimination is occurring.

3 "Spurious" as designating a claimed correlation for which there is no empirical support is consistent with ordinary usage, but is admittedly different from the technical use by statisticians to refer to a genuine relationship that nevertheless provides no basis for a causal inference.

Bibliography

Alexander, L. 1992. "What Makes Wrongful Discrimination Wrong? Biases, Preferences, Stereotypes, and Proxies." *University of Pennsylvania Law Review*. 141, 149–219.

Alexander, L. and Cole, K. 1997. "Discrimination by Proxy." *Constitutional Commentary*. 14: 453–463.

Bernstein, A. 2013. "What's Wrong with Stereotyping?" *Arizona Law Review*. 55: 655–721.

Case, M. 2000. "'The Very Stereotype the Law Condemns': Constitutional Sex Discrimination Law as a Quest for Perfect Proxies." *Cornell Law Review*. 85: 1447–1491.

Duxbury, N. 1999. *Random Justice: On Lotteries and Legal Decision-Making*. Oxford: Oxford University Press.

Federal Rules of Evidence 2011. Washington, DC: Government Printing Office.

Harcourt, B. 2007. *Against Prediction: Profiling, Policing, and Punishing in an Actuarial Age*. Chicago, IL: University of Chicago Press.

Hellman, D. 1998. "Two Types of Discrimination: The Familiar and the Forgotten." *California Law Review*. 86: 315–361.

Hellman, D. 2008. *When is Discrimination Wrong?* Cambridge, MA: Harvard University Press.

Leslie, S.-J. 2008. "Generics: Cognition and Acquisition." *Philosophical Review*. 117, 1–47.

Leslie, S.-J. 2015. "Generics Oversimplified." *Noûs*. 49: 28–54.

Lippert-Rasmussen, K. 2006. "Racial Profiling Versus Community." *Journal of Applied Philosophy*. 23: 191–205.

Lippert-Rasmussen, K. 2014. *Born Free and Equal: A Philosophical Inquiry into the Nature of Discrimination*. New York: Oxford University Press.

Reed v. Reed (1971). 404 U.S. 71.

Risse, M. and Zeckhauser, R. 2004. "Racial Profiling." *Philosophy & Public Affairs*. 32: 131–170.

Schauer, F. 2003. *Profiles, Probabilities, and Stereotypes*. Cambridge, MA: Harvard University Press.

Tussman, J. and tenBroek, J. 1949. "The Equal Protection of the Laws." *California Law Review*. 37: 341–381.

United States v. Virginia (1996). 518 U.S. 515.

Winston, K. 1974. "On Treating Like Cases Alike." *California Law Review*. 62: 1–39.

4
EPISTEMIC DISCRIMINATION

Katherine Puddifoot

UNIVERSITY OF BIRMINGHAM

Introduction

Epistemic discrimination is prejudice, bias and discriminatory action suffered by individuals in their position as epistemic agents, that is, as individuals who can acquire knowledge, justified belief or understanding. Epistemic discrimination can be intentional or unintentional. It can be the result of the actions of an individual or of deep structural inequalities in society, or a combination of the two. When epistemic discrimination occurs against someone, that person is unduly denied access to the resources and opportunities that they would need to be a successful giver and recipient of epistemic goods like knowledge. They are often denied these resources and opportunities as a result of their social group membership. Members of stigmatized and marginalized groups are especially vulnerable to epistemic discrimination because of the stereotypes that others apply to them and their exclusion from positions of power in which they could facilitate an improvement to their epistemic situation. Epistemic discrimination can be both an epistemic and an ethical harm because people suffer significantly from being denied the status of knower.

Fricker's epistemic injustice

To get a general handle on the phenomenon of epistemic discrimination, let us begin by considering a subset of cases of epistemic discrimination that have been widely discussed in the recent literature in philosophy and beyond: the cases of epistemic injustice identified in Miranda Fricker's *Epistemic Injustice: Power and the Ethics of Knowing*. Instances of epistemic injustice involve epistemic discrimination because when they happen people are treated unfairly "in their capacity as a subject of knowledge, and thus in a capacity essential to human value" (2007: 5). Fricker identifies two types of epistemic injustice: *testimonial injustice* and *hermeneutical injustice.*

Testimonial injustice

The first form of epistemic injustice, testimonial injustice, directly relates to the phenomenon of speakers providing testimony; aiming to bring hearers to understand something, by saying, telling or asserting something, via speech, writing or other means of communication. When a speaker provides testimony, an assessment is made about their credibility as a testifier. Things can go wrong in the process of assessing an individual's credibility: there can be *credibility excess*, where the speaker can be given more credibility than they deserve, or *credibility deficit*, where the speaker can be given less credibility than they deserve (Fricker 2007: 17). Fricker identifies cases of testimonial injustice with cases in which people suffer a credibility deficit. In her view, testimonial injustice occurs "if prejudice on the hearer's part causes him to give the speaker less credibility than he would otherwise have given" (ibid.: 4). What is the explanation for this credibility deficit? The application of a stereotype or stereotypes relating to the social identity of the speaker distorts the perception of the credibility of the speaker.

The example of Marge Greenleaf from Anthony Minghella's film *The Talented Mr Ripley* is used by Fricker to illustrate testimonial injustice. When her fiancé Dickie goes missing, Marge attempts to persuade his father that Tom Ripley is responsible for his disappearance. She has some strong evidence to support her claim but it is dismissed on the basis that her belief is mere women's intuition: "Marge, there's female intuition, and then there are facts" (Minghella cited by Fricker 2007: 9). Marge's testimony is dismissed on the basis of a stereotype about her gender: females are not driven by facts and are instead dependent on intuition. As a result of the application of the stereotype, Dickie's father has a distorted perception of the credibility of her testimony, failing to give her testimony the credibility that it deserves, so she suffers a credibility deficit.

The *Talented Mr Ripley* example can also be taken to support a point made by Jose Medina (2011, 2013): that credibility excesses can cause testimonial injustice. Medina claims that assessments of credibility are often comparative and contrastive by their nature. Where some people are given more credibility than they deserve, others are consequently given less. This can be seen happening in the *Talented Mr Ripley* case. Tom Ripley is trusted when he should not be. Marge's testimony is compared to his and unduly found to be unreliable. Because of the credibility excess given to Tom Ripley, Marge suffers from a credibility deficit.

Although instances of testimonial injustice are only a subset of the cases of epistemic discrimination, all instances of testimonial injustice are cases of epistemic discrimination. People who are subject to testimonial injustice are unduly treated as if they do not have the capacity for knowledge, understanding and insight. People who are treated in this way can consequently be excluded from discourses that would enable them to acquire more knowledge and understanding. They are therefore unduly denied the resources and opportunities that they would need to be successful givers and recipients of epistemic goods, like knowledge.

For Fricker, epistemic injustice is an epistemic vice that can be rectified by developing the epistemic virtue of *testimonial justice* (Fricker 2007: Chapter 4). The virtue of epistemic justice involves critical awareness of the distorting influence of identity prejudice on one's perceptions of the credibility of hearers. It involves recognizing that an imbalanced power relation between a speaker and a hearer, which is determined by their relative social identities, can lead to a distorted perception of who can be a possessor of knowledge, and of who can learn from whom. For example, it can involve recognizing that where a man has more power than a woman, the credibility of a woman can be perceived in a distorted way: she can become treated as someone who is unable to provide the man with knowledge. Simple critical awareness does not suffice for testimonial justice, however: the hearer must correct for the influence of identity, factoring in how their perceptions are likely to have been distorted by the application of identity stereotypes, and increasing the credibility given to the testimony of those whom they are likely to have judged too critically.

Fricker's discussion provides an important contribution to our understanding of how epistemic discrimination can occur as a result of stereotyping. It should not be assumed, however, that epistemic discrimination only occurs when someone has a *false belief* about the credibility of members of a particular social group.[1] Epistemic discrimination can occur as a result of a true belief about the credibility of members of a social group. For example, young children might be correctly viewed as statistically less likely to be reliable sources of information than adults. Nonetheless, a specific young child, Ben, might rightly claim to have been treated unfairly, and wronged in his role as an epistemic agent, if he gives testimony that contradicts that given by an adult and his testimony is not taken seriously. To see why this is a case of epistemic discrimination, compare it to a case in which Ben's testimony is not taken seriously because he is known to be a liar. In the latter case, Ben's testimony is not taken to be credible because of a true belief about his epistemic character, so the discrimination does not wrong him as an epistemic agent. The judgment that Ben is unreliable reflects that someone has made an effort to take him seriously enough as an epistemic agent to consider what sort of agent he is. In contrast, in a case in which Ben's testimony is not taken seriously simply because he is a child, he suffers discrimination because he is denied the status of knower without this being a reflection on his previous epistemic performance. Although the judgment that he is unreliable reflects the statistical reality that adults are generally more reliable testifiers than children, Ben could still claim to be a victim of epistemic discrimination (cf. Chapter 3).

Hermeneutical injustice

The second form of epistemic injustice identified by Fricker is *hermeneutical injustice* (2007: Chapter 7). Hermeneutical injustice occurs when the powerful within society have access to the hermeneutical resources required to understand their own experiences but the powerless lack these resources, owing to structural inequalities in society. As a result of the lack of hermeneutical resources, those who lack power are unable to gain self-understanding because they do not have access to the conceptual resources that would enable them to understand their own experiences, they are unable to articulate their situation to others, and can be rendered troubled, confused and isolated.[2] For example, women occupy a position of powerlessness relative to men. One consequence is that concepts like *post-natal depression* and *sexual harassment* did not enter common understanding until recently. Fricker claims that individuals suffering from post-natal depression or undergoing sexual harassment were consequently previously unable to develop a proper understanding of their negative experiences, or to articulate this understanding to others. The lack of conceptual resources was due to the way in which those in power constructed social understanding. Powerful men could, for instance, control how sexual harassment was interpreted by labeling it *flirting* and saying that those who complained lacked a sense of humor. Hermeneutical injustice is discriminatory because while a whole society might lack the hermeneutical resources to understand a phenomenon like *sexual harassment*, only the powerless victims suffer a systematic deficiency in their ability to understand their own experiences. This deficiency can lead to downstream disadvantages to the powerless, as they can lose confidence in their self-awareness and ability to articulate their experience. Others who lack the hermeneutical resources, such as a harasser in a sexual harassment case, do not suffer the same costs.

Fricker proposes that hermeneutical injustice can be corrected via the virtue of *hermeneutical justice*. Hermeneutical justice is structurally very similar to testimonial justice; they both involve reflexive awareness that leads to a correction of one's credibility judgments. When assessing the credibility of the testimony provided by members of social groups who may be marginalized due to their social identity, hermeneutical justice requires considering what an individual's testimony would be like if they possessed, rather than lacked, the hermeneutical resources to understand and articulate their experiences.

Limitations of Fricker on hermeneutical injustice

While Fricker's discussion of hermeneutical injustice provides important insights about how people can undergo epistemic discrimination, it can be criticized on the basis that it misrepresents both the epistemic harms caused to members of the non-dominant group and the epistemic damage done to members of the dominant group.

Rebecca Mason argues that non-dominant groups can develop non-dominant hermeneutical resources through which they can understand their own experiences, even while others, including those who are a part of the dominant group, cannot understand them (Mason 2011). She provides an alternative interpretation of the case of sexual harassment to illustrate her point. She claims that prior to the introduction of the term *sexual harassment* women understood their experiences of harassment and were able to discuss it among themselves. The lack of hermeneutical resources among the dominant group only prevented members of the non-dominant group from articulating their experiences to members of the dominant group. Misunderstanding of sexual harassment was not collective but instead restricted to those in the dominant group. The hermeneutical injustice suffered by the non-dominant group was therefore more circumscribed than Fricker suggests, although still serious and damaging.

Meanwhile, Medina argues that Fricker underplays the damage caused to the epistemic character of members of the dominant group (Medina 2013). He claims that hermeneutical injustice can lead members of the dominant group to develop poor epistemic character traits. They display *meta-ignorance*: ignorance about the insensitivity that they display to members of the non-dominant group due to their lack of hermeneutical resources. This meta-ignorance manifests epistemic vices such as arrogance, laziness and closed-mindedness. They therefore develop poor character traits in relation to their lack of hermeneutical resources.

These criticisms of the details of Fricker's account of hermeneutical injustice highlight a danger that can arise in discussions of epistemic discrimination. In cases of epistemic discrimination, the victims of the discrimination are harmed in their position as epistemic agents, but it would be wrong to assume that this always means that they lack understanding in contrast to others. As Mason (2011) argues, members of non-dominant groups can persevere and develop their own unique set of conceptual resources through which to understand their experiences. Meanwhile, as Medina argues, members of dominant groups can display systematic ignorance. There can be circumstances, then, when people who suffer epistemic discrimination can have an understanding that members of dominant groups lack, due to the epistemic discrimination perpetrated against them.

Other forms of epistemic injustice

While Fricker focuses solely on testimonial injustice and hermeneutical injustice, it is worth noting that there are other forms that epistemic injustice could take. For instance, Christopher Hookway emphasizes how a person can be wronged in her position as knower because she is taken to not be able to provide a contribution to a debate or discussion (Hookway 2010). She might be viewed as a credible recipient and source of information, but not as someone who can ask insightful questions that could progress debate and discussion. There are potentially numerous other forms that epistemic injustice can take.

In sum, then, the most prominent recent discussion of epistemic discrimination focuses on two forms that it can take, both of which are described as cases of *epistemic injustice*: testimonial injustice and hermeneutical injustice. Epistemic injustices count as instances of epistemic discrimination because they are cases in which people are unduly denied access to the resources and opportunities that they would need to be successful givers and recipients of epistemic goods like knowledge. It is important to note, however, that Fricker's discussion, in particular the discussion of hermeneutical injustice, can be viewed as over-estimating the lack of understanding of members of the non-dominant group while underplaying the epistemic deficiencies of the dominant group.

Epistemic discrimination and Black feminist thought

In contrast to Fricker's work on hermeneutical injustice, Patricia Hill Collins' work identifies ways in which people who suffer epistemic discrimination can gain understanding, particularly about injustice, as a result of being victims of the discrimination. Collins' work focuses on how a whole community of people—Black women—suffer epistemic discrimination by being excluded from political and social discourse. She describes how economic, political and legal forces have combined to lead to the burying of the ideas of Black female intellectuals, with the knowledge that they produce being ignored. Where Black females are employed as menial labor, denied educational opportunities and negatively stereotyped, it is possible for those in positions of power to ignore the knowledge that they produce. Meanwhile, the suppression of this knowledge is itself a social force, maintaining social inequalities by suggesting that Black women are willing collaborators in the processes that lead to their own oppression (Scott 1985, cited in Collins 2000). Their credibility is further undermined by this interpretation of their behavior, seeming to raise the question of why those who would willingly collaborate in their own oppression should be respected and listened to.

These harms are manifestations of epistemic discrimination. Black women suffer in their roles as epistemic agents, being denied the opportunities to give and receive knowledge through channels that are open to other people. However, Collins emphasizes that in spite of, and sometimes because of, suffering epistemic discrimination, many black women have gained a distinctive viewpoint opposing issues of social, political and economic injustice.

The economic, political and ideological dimensions of U.S. black women's oppression suppressed the intellectual production of individual black feminist thinkers. At the same time, these same social conditions simultaneously stimulated distinctive patterns of U.S. black women's activism that also influenced and were influenced by individual black women thinkers (Collins 2000: 12).

Racial segregation and the development of all-black communities have fostered the development of ideologies that resist the negative images of black women often used to control them. Meanwhile, the position of black women as *outsiders-within* (1986) in white households and academic communities has enabled them to develop a unique view of the inconsistencies, oppositions and contradictions found in the ideologies of the dominant group (Collins 2000: 11). The insights gleaned through these painful experiences have the potential to provide a unique contribution to understanding social oppression and inequality as it occurs more widely.

Collins therefore emphasizes how black women thinkers have made epistemic gains, developing unique insights, in part as a result of epistemic discrimination (as well as other forms of discrimination) that they have suffered. However, as a result of epistemic discrimination, black women thinkers and the black feminist thought that they produce remain buried on the periphery of intellectual thought. This means that members of other groups, including the dominant group, are unable to benefit from the insights that black women thinkers gain.

The discussion in *Black Feminist Thought* is thus in contrast to positions that focus predominantly on a lack of understanding on the part of victims of epistemic discrimination. Collins emphasizes how those who are subject to epistemic discrimination can consequently develop a unique understanding. Others, members of the dominant group who do not suffer directly from the discrimination, can lack the same understanding because the insights of the non-dominant group are marginalized.

Ignorance and epistemic discrimination

Charles Mills (2007) also emphasizes the relationship between epistemic discrimination and the ignorance of members of the dominant group. Mills focuses on what he describes as *white ignorance*. White ignorance occurs when people are ignorant about: (i) the privileged position of whites relative to non-whites, (ii) the adverse impact of the privilege on non-whites, and (iii) the need for action to reduce this impact. White ignorance prevents those who occupy a position of privilege from recognizing the need for action to reduce inequality, discrimination and their negative effects—action that would reduce their privilege. White ignorance is maintained through the concepts that people acquire from their social upbringing, and the way in which these concepts influence what they perceive and how they remember things. For example, the concept of "color-blindness" is acquired through social upbringing, and has obscured the need for action to repair the damage done by past inequalities. Those who aim for color-blindness might intend that people should be treated equally, but they fail to recognize the advantages afforded to whites over non-whites, and the need for differential treatment to rectify continued inequalities.

How does white ignorance relate to epistemic discrimination? Mills describes how white ignorance is maintained through testimonial injustice. Non-whites who might provide information to rectify misinformation and error about the privileged position of whites and the exploitation and discrimination of non-whites are prevented from having the opportunity to do so. For example, the work of black scholars is marginalized, predominantly being published in journals that are not read by the mainstream white academic community. Testimony about the systemic nature of oppression and white privilege and about efforts required to combat it that might be contained in this work is thereby marginalized, and given inadequate attention and credence.

Mills' discussion therefore shows how the ignorance of the dominant group can be maintained through epistemic discrimination. The dominant group makes material gain because they do not become aware of the need to change the social system to reduce their privilege. However, they gain as a result of an epistemic deficiency on their part: white ignorance.

White ignorance also relates to hermeneutical injustice, as non-whites who live in societies in which white ignorance prevails can lack understanding and the ability to articulate their experience of discrimination and marginalization. White ignorance is something that can be suffered by non-whites as well as by whites, if both are situated in a society in which the ignorance prevails (Mills 2013). Non-whites who are ignorant of white privilege can therefore lack the hermeneutical resources required to understand their experiences of discrimination and marginalization. However, it is also important to recognize that there can be an imbalance in the hermeneutical resources available to whites and non-whites. As Collins (2000) and Mason (2011) suggest, people who are a part of a non-dominant non-white group can develop a good understanding of their own experiences of discrimination and marginalization. They can develop non-dominant hermeneutical resources that remain unavailable to members of the dominant group. Where they can struggle is in articulating their experiences to others who lack the hermeneutical resources that they have gained through their experiences. In cases like this, epistemic discrimination will once again go hand-in-hand with ignorance on the part of the dominant group, to whom members of the non-dominant group will be unable to articulate their experiences.

In sum, then, Mills, like Collins, provides support for the conclusion that epistemic discrimination against members of a specific non-dominant group can lead them to suffer as they are denied opportunities in their roles as epistemic agents: to provide testimony and sometimes to understand their situation. But they both also emphasize how epistemic discrimination can contribute to an epistemic deficiency on the part of members of the dominant group: it can lead them to be ignorant.

Mechanisms of epistemic discrimination

The three sections above have described forms of epistemic discrimination and highlighted ways that discrimination can lead to epistemic harm to those who are victims of the discrimination and epistemic deficiencies in members of dominant groups who are not victims. This section focuses on providing details of two specific mechanisms through which epistemic discrimination can be perpetrated—silencing and implicit bias—highlighting how the two can interact.

Silencing

When silencing occurs, damage is done to the ability of individuals to speak and be heard. They are prevented from being fully fledged epistemic agents, engaging in the practice of giving and receiving reasons. Kristie Dotson (2011) identifies two types of silencing: *testimonial quieting* and *testimonial smothering*.

Testimonial quieting "occurs when an audience fails to identify a speaker as a knower" (Dotson 2011: 242). For Dotson, a person who commits testimonial quieting refuses to play their part in an exchange of testimony by failing to recognize the contribution that can be made by another person due to the person's membership of a certain social group. Dotson cites Collins' (2000) work as identifying an example of testimonial quieting: when black women are stereotyped and marginalized they are treated as if they are not knowers. Their testimony is silenced because they depend on the uptake of an audience which refuses to listen. There can be long term harms associated with testimonial silencing. It can damage the intellectual courage and epistemic agency of individuals who are systematically silenced and harm the intellectual traditions of whole communities.

It is important that any characterization of testimonial silencing is not too narrow. Collins' work, which is cited by Dotson, provides an example of testimonial silencing that occurs as a result of false stereotypes about black women: that they are not knowers. However, testimonial silencing can occur under other conditions. First of all, testimonial silencing can occur as a result of a true belief rather than a false stereotype about a social group. To see this point, re-consider the case of the young child Ben. Let us suppose once again that young children can be correctly viewed as statistically less likely to be reliable sources of information than adults. Ben's potential audience refuses to listen to a complaint that he makes against an adult because they truly believe that young children are not as reliable as adults. There would be a strong case for saying that Ben is discriminated against through the mechanism of testimonial silencing, although he is not listened to as a result of a true belief. Second, testimonial silencing might occur without the involvement of the specific stereotype that members of a certain group are not knowers. Suppose that a person correctly judges another person, Mary, to be very knowledgeable, perhaps more knowledgeable than she is. They are motivated to silence Mary to prevent her from exposing their lack of knowledge. They refuse uptake of her testimony, thereby damaging her intellectual courage and sense of agency. She is wronged as a result of actions that seem to be appropriately described as silencing without this being the result of the operation of a stereotype of members of a social group as lacking knowledge.

Whereas testimonial silencing involves one person acting directly to silence another, testimonial smothering occurs where a speaker self-silences. One remains silent because one "perceives one's immediate audience as unwilling or unable to gain the appropriate uptake of proffered testimony" (Dotson 2000: 244). The speaker remains quiet about certain matters, keeping her testimony to a minimum, to avoid being misinterpreted by hearers who have demonstrated an inability to comprehend her. To illustrate this phenomenon, Dotson provides the example of black domestic violence victims in the United States who remain quiet about their experiences in order to avoid appearing to corroborate the stereotype of black men as violent. They keep quiet because they believe that testimony about their experiences will be misinterpreted as supporting the general social stereotype. According to Dotson, epistemic violence is committed against people who are subject to testimonial smothering by hearers who display an inability to engage in appropriate uptake of testimony, thereby preventing the victims from providing fuller testimony.

Implicit bias

Increasingly, philosophers as well as psychologists are noticing that *implicit biases* can also provide a mechanism through which epistemic discrimination can be perpetrated. Implicit biases are "fast, automatic, and difficult to control processes that encode stereotypes and evaluative content, and influence how we think and behave" (Holroyd and Puddifoot, forthcoming; Chapter 32). They are mental states that associate members of a social group with some attribute or affective response (e.g. aversion or attraction) and can operate without the awareness of the agent. When implicit biases operate, they can influence the way that an epistemic agent perceives individual members of a social group. As implicit biases operate automatically and unintentionally, even those who are explicitly committed to egalitarian principles and hold egalitarian beliefs can be prone to making biased judgments when under the influence of implicit bias. An example of the operation of an implicit bias is the following: Ulmann and Cohen (2007) found that people ranked the characteristics *being streetwise* or *being well educated* as important to being a police chief when attributed to a man but the same characteristics were deemed unimportant when attributed to a woman. What seems to happen here is that people associate being a police chief with being male and view characteristics associated with males as more fitting with the role than characteristics associated with women. Where judgments of this sort are automatic and unintentional they are classified as implicit biases. Other widely studied implicit biases include those associating black men with violence and men, but not women, with careers.

How do implicit biases function as a mechanism through which epistemic discrimination can manifest? They can influence downstream evaluations of individuals' capacities as epistemic agents. Implicit biases can lead the testimony and evidence provided by members of low-status, stigmatized groups to be given less credibility and attention than it deserves while testimony and evidence provided by members of high-status groups is given more credibility and attention than it deserves (Saul 2013). Implicit biases can lead evidence that is consistent with a stereotype to be noticed, attended to and remembered while evidence inconsistent with a stereotype is ignored and/or forgotten (Levinson 2007; Puddifoot forthcoming). They can lead behavioral evidence about members of a social group to be viewed in a way that is consistent with the stereotype of their social group (Devine 1989; Puddifoot forthcoming). This means that if members of a social group are stereotyped as incompetent or unreliable sources of knowledge then evidence about their epistemic character will be attended and remembered in a distorted way that is consistent with the stereotype. Implicit biases can therefore lead to epistemic discrimination because they can lead members of stigmatized social groups to be treated as poor epistemic agents, and poor sources and potential recipients of knowledge, so they are denied the resources and opportunities to engage in the practice of giving and receiving epistemic goods like knowledge.

It is worth noting that implicit biases can have negative effects, leading to epistemic discrimination, whether or not the associations that they encode reflect some aspect of reality (Puddifoot: forthcoming). Let us return once again to the example of Ben. Suppose that you harbor an implicit bias associating adults more strongly than children with the provision of reliable testimony. This association might reflect the reality, which is that adults are generally more knowledgeable, and therefore more likely to provide accurate information, than young children. Nonetheless, if this implicit bias influences your judgment of Ben's testimony when he is trying to explain what an adult has done, then you are likely to view his testimony in a distorted way. For example, you will be likely to notice inconsistencies in, and implausible features of, his testimony rather than its strengths, such as the detailed descriptions he gives. You will be likely to judge his testimony unduly harshly, treating him as if he knows less than he does, and therefore harming him in his role as epistemic agent.

Silencing and implicit bias: where the two interact

While silencing and implicit bias can operate as separate mechanisms through which epistemic discrimination occurs, implicit bias can also lead to silencing and, more specifically, testimonial smothering. Recall that testimonial smothering occurs when people believe that their testimony will not receive appropriate uptake (Dotson 2011). When a potential hearer displays signs that they will not receive the testimony of a potential speaker in an appropriate manner, the potential speaker can self-silence, to avoid being misinterpreted. Subtle behavioral signs can indicate that there will be a lack of appropriate uptake, and levels of implicit bias have been found to predict signs of this sort. They have been found, for example, to predict the amount of eye contact and seating position choice (i.e. how closely people sit together) that occurs in inter-group interactions (see, e.g., McConnell and Leibold 2001; Dovidio, Kawakami and Gaertner 2002). If a person does not make eye contact or chooses to sit far from you, these behaviors can reasonably be taken as an indication that they do not want to speak with you, and that they will not willingly receive your testimony. Other subtle behaviors, as well as less subtle ones, caused by the influence of implicit bias could be taken to provide an indication that someone will not provide appropriate uptake. Under such conditions, testimonial smothering might occur.

Excessive discussion of implicit bias

While there has been increasing interest in implicit bias and the way that it results in epistemic discrimination, there is also growing recognition that the focus of attention on implicit bias has the potential to obscure other causes of epistemic discrimination. Sally Haslanger (2015), for example, argues that while implicit biases can explain some forms of discrimination, explanations that are too focused on the phenomenon are guilty of over-emphasis on the role of the individual and the individual's biases. By focusing too much on the individual's biases, the role of social structures—networks of social practices—is left underestimated and underexamined. Another thought that is commonly articulated is that discriminatory behavior is often attributed to implicit bias when a better explanation would focus on explicit, intentional bias.

In sum, then, silencing and implicit biases operate as mechanisms through which epistemic discrimination can occur. They can interact: implicit biases can lead to silencing. However, it is important to remember that implicit biases do not provide the only source of either silencing or of other forms of epistemic discrimination. Structural inequalities, unequal power relations and personal motivations to prevent other people from having a voice can lead people to engage in discriminatory practices, such as a lack of uptake of certain people's testimonies. Given that epistemic discrimination can occur through various mechanisms, successful actions to reduce epistemic discrimination are likely to need to take various forms. It is to this issue that we turn in the next and final section.

Correctional measures

Much of the most interesting discussion of epistemic discrimination has focused on the viability of various measures that might be adopted to reduce the discrimination. Fricker (2007) emphasizes the role of the individual, arguing that each person should engage in critical reflection with the aim of cultivating personal epistemic virtues, of testimonial and hermeneutical justice. However, doubts have been raised about whether attempts by individuals to develop epistemic virtues via critical reflection will suffice to combat the negative effects of epistemic discrimination. Motivated by these doubts, authors have proposed a number of alternative strategies to mitigate epistemic discrimination.

Problems with critical reflection

Benjamin Sherman (2016) highlights some practical problems with individual measures to mitigate testimonial injustice. Fricker (2007) claims that critical reflection can enable us to correct inappropriate credibility assessments, compensating for the negative impact of prejudicial social stereotypes. However, Sherman argues that critical reflection is unlikely to be useful in many cases in which people are prejudiced. Sherman thinks that most people are likely to judge their own beliefs to be correct, and are therefore unlikely to change them on critical reflection. With respect to testimonial injustice, they are likely to think that their current credibility judgments are appropriate. It might be expected that other people could persuade them of their errors, but their choice of advisers is likely to be influenced by their prejudice: they will choose to listen to people who agree with them. In addition, their critical reflection will be subject to confirmation bias, leading them to view evidence in support of their prejudice assessments to be of higher quality than evidence that challenges them.

Similar problems arise with respect to hermeneutical injustice. Attempts to mitigate hermeneutical injustice through critical reflection will only be successful if people are aware on reflection of any lack of hermeneutical resources. However, as noted by Medina (2013), people can display meta-ignorance, that is, ignorance about their available hermeneutical resources. If they are epistemically ignorant, they will be unlikely to notice their lack of hermeneutical resources even under the close scrutiny of critical reflection.

Where critical reflection does lead one to doubt one's existing credibility judgments, another problem can arise. According to Fricker, one must correct one's assignments of credibility, increasing them where they are found through critical reflection to be too low. But there is little reason to think that our processes of critical reflection will lead to an accurate assessment of precisely how much lower our credibility assessments are than they should be. Consequently, there is a danger that we can over- or under-correct our credibility judgments (Kelly and Roedder 2008).

Implicit biases can contribute to the problems associated with critical reflection. Because implicit biases can operate beyond the agent's conscious awareness, an agent can engage in critical reflection but fail to notice that they are biased, or the extent to which they are biased, and therefore fail to appropriately correct their judgments (ibid.).

Ameliorative strategies from social psychology

Social psychologists have developed a number of strategies to tackle epistemic discrimination that do not rely on individuals being able to identify the nature of their discriminatory practices or ways to rectify their judgments via critical reflection. This section introduces a small sample of illustrative strategies.

Many acts of epistemic discrimination occur as a result of social stereotyping, associating members of a social group more strongly than others with certain attributes.[3] The extensive literature within social psychology on social stereotyping outlines ways to reduce epistemic discrimination by reducing stereotyping and its negative effects. Irene Blair and colleagues (2001) present evidence that participants who consider counter-stereotypical examples, e.g. strong women, show reduced stereotyping (see Saul 2013 for philosophical discussion). Other evidence suggests that the formation of *implementation intentions*, specific "if–then" action plans such as "If I see a Muslim, I will think peace" can reduce the activation of negative stereotypes (e.g. Stewart and Payne 2008; see Saul 2013 and Madva 2016 for philosophical discussion). Meanwhile, reduced access to information that might activate a social stereotype—such as information about the social group membership of an individual—can prevent the activation of the stereotype (Steinpreis *et al.* 1999). While the former two strategies are measures that the individual should take if they want to prevent social stereotyping, institutions can implement the latter type of strategy. For example, employers can ensure that information about the social group membership of job candidates is removed from their application material so that those involved in recruitment do not engage in stereotyping (Steinpreis 1999; discussed in Saul 2013; Anthony 2016). Where stereotyping is reduced, a reduction to epistemic discrimination can follow.[4]

Structural changes

While social psychologists have tended to focus on measures that can be taken by individuals and institutions to reduce the negative impact of epistemic discrimination, some philosophers have emphasized the need for deeper structural changes to society. Elizabeth Anderson (2010) argues that integration is a prerequisite for the elimination of discrimination. Influenced by Anderson's work, Medina (2013) claims that reduction of epistemic discrimination will only be achieved if members of different groups confront each other's perspectives, so that the perspective of the dominant group and its unjust ideology are challenged. For Haslanger (2015), the social practices that prevent equality between groups need to be changed in order to produce the equality that would be required to reduce epistemic discrimination. Underlying many of these ideas is the thought that as the distribution of power—economic, social and political—determines the degree of epistemic discrimination encountered by individuals and groups. To remove or substantially reduce the threat of epistemic discrimination, changes are needed to existing power structures.

The implementation of strategies to change individuals or institutions is not inconsistent with deeper societal reform. Individualistic and structural explanations of epistemic discrimination do not have to be viewed as in opposition, providing competing accounts of how we should reduce discrimination. Instead, the take-home message is that we should avoid two forms of complacency. We should not think that if we have taken action to change our personal practices we are not complicit in more widespread epistemic discrimination. Nor should we get so focused on implementing changes to social structures that we forget to ask what we can do to change our institutions or ourselves as individuals.

Epistemic discrimination in discussions of epistemic discrimination

An interesting recent development in research on epistemic discrimination is the increased awareness that discussions of the phenomenon can lead to further epistemic discrimination. Dotson (2011) argues that it is possible to define epistemic injustice too narrowly, excluding many experiences of marginalized groups. Where new hermeneutical resources such as the concept of epistemic injustice do not capture some people's experiences, this can lead to further hermeneutical injustice and silencing. Rachel McKinnon (2016) describes how "there's a long history in black feminist thought, and other feminists of color, that should be seen as also working on issues of epistemic injustice" (438). The lack of uptake of these ideas, until a white academic philosopher, Miranda Fricker, raised them, can therefore be viewed as "an instance of epistemic injustice" (ibid.). Similarly, Jules Holroyd and I (forthcoming) highlight how members of stigmatized and marginalized groups have previously described their experiences of unintentional bias, yet wide-ranging interest in the phenomenon only arose in the wake of growth in scientific research on implicit biases. The lack of uptake of the testimony of marginalized groups can be viewed as an instance of epistemic discrimination. Circumstances like these can lead to silencing of members of marginalized groups if they recognize that their attempts to convince others of problems that they see within society fail while testimony to the same effect provided by scientists, or established white women, is widely discussed. These circumstances can lead, for example, to testimonial smothering (see section 5).

An important lesson about how to tackle epistemic discrimination can be learned from this self-reflection by philosophers, especially when it is combined with the insights discussed in section 3 from Collins (2000). The lesson is that it is counterproductive to ignore the testimony of those who are victims of epistemic discrimination. Reduction of epistemic discrimination might involve critical reflection on one's own practice and comprehension of psychological studies of prejudice and discrimination, personal efforts to tackle one's own bias, and structural changes to society (e.g. changes to laws and efforts to increase integration). However, solutions are likely to be most fruitful, and lead to minimum collateral damage in terms of the production of further epistemic discrimination, if they involve listening to the testimony of those who suffer due to the phenomenon. Those who have been subject to epistemic discrimination can contribute greatly to our understanding of the nature and scope of the problem. As Collins (2000) suggests, victims of injustice can gain a good understanding of it. And, as Medina (2013) suggests, the best way to reduce epistemic discrimination can be to confront other perspectives and experiences, especially those of marginalized groups.

Further reading

Miranda Fricker's *Epistemic Injustice: Power and the Ethics of Knowing* (New York: Oxford University Press) is the most-discussed work on epistemic discrimination. *Race and Epistemologies of Ignorance* (Albany, NY: SUNY Press), edited by Shannon Sullivan and Nancy Tuana, contains Charles Mills' "White Ignorance" and a series of other papers relating to ignorance. Patricia Hill Collins' *Black Feminist Thought* contains her ideas about the epistemic discrimination faced by black women. José Medina's *The Epistemology of Resistance: Gender and Racial Oppression, Epistemic Injustice, and Resistant Imaginations* (New York: Oxford University Press) is another important discussion of ignorance and epistemic discrimination. For an overview of research on epistemic issues arising from implicit bias see Brownstein, M. and Saul, J. (eds.). 2016. *Implicit Bias and Philosophy, Volume 1: Metaphysics and Epistemology* (Oxford: OUP). Sullivan, S. and Tuana, N. (eds.). 2007. *Race and Epistemologies of Ignorance* (Albany: SUNY Press).

Notes

1 There is some debate about whether stereotypes should be defined as inaccurate (see, e.g. Blum 2004; Beeghly 2015). Fricker is not committed to the idea that stereotypes must always be inaccurate but does focus on cases in which stereotypes lead to distorted judgments of the credibility of members of particular social groups.
2 A lack of hermeneutical resources, for example the resources to understand and articulate the experience of sexual harassment, can lead to an inability to understand other people as well as oneself. For instance, if I do not possess the concept of sexual harassment I might not be able to understand my friend's experiences in the workplace. However, Fricker focuses specifically on how a lack of hermeneutical resources can produce a lack of self-understanding. For more on why a broader conception of the negative consequences of hermeneutical injustice might be called for see the discussion below of the ways that people who are not victims of epistemic discrimination, and therefore do not lack self-understanding due to hermeneutical injustice, can nonetheless remain ignorant due to a lack of hermeneutical resources.
3 On some accounts of stereotypes, they are not all about members of social groups. For example, *birds have wings* might be a stereotype, but for the sake of the current discussion focus will be on what I call *social stereotypes*, which are about social groups.
4 Note that the claim here is not that all epistemic discrimination will be reduced if stereotyping is reduced. As has been highlighted elsewhere in this chapter, epistemic discrimination can occur in the absence of stereotyping, so even a full reduction of stereotyping would not guarantee a full reduction in epistemic discrimination.

Bibliography

Anderson, E. 2010. *The Imperative of Integration*. Princeton: Princeton University Press.

Antony, L. 2016. "Bias, friend or foe? Reflections on Saulish skepticism," in M. Brownstein & J. Saul (eds.) *Implicit Bias and Philosophy. Volume 1: Metaphysics and Epistemology*. Oxford: OUP.

Beeghly, E. 2015. "What is a stereotype? What is stereotyping?" *Hypatia*, 30 (4): 675–691.

Blair, I. V., Ma, J. E. and Lenton A. P. 2001. "Imagining stereotypes away: The moderation of implicit stereotypes through mental imagery." *Journal of Personality and Social Psychology*, 81(5): 828–841.

Blum, L. 2004. "Stereotypes and stereotyping: A moral analysis," *Philosophical Papers*, 33(3): 251–289.

Collins, P. H. 1986. "Learning from the outsider within: The sociological significance of black feminist thought." *Social Problems* 33(6): 14–32.

Collins, P. H. 2000. *Black Feminist Thought: Knowledge, Consciousness, and the Politics of Empowerment, 2nd edition*. New York: Routledge.

Devine, P. G. 1989. "Stereotypes and prejudice: Their automatic and controlled components." *Journal of Personality and Social Psychology*, 56(1): 5–18.

Dotson, K. 2011. "Tracking epistemic violence, tracking patterns of silencing." *Hypatia*, 26(2): 236–257.

Dovidio, J. F., Kawakami, K. and Gaertner, S. L. 2002. "Implicit and explicit prejudice and interracial interaction." *Journal of Personality and Social Psychology*, 82(1): 62–68.

Fricker, M. 2007. *Epistemic Injustice: Power and the Ethics of Knowing*. New York: Oxford University Press.

Haslanger, S. 2015. "Social structure, narrative and explanation." *Canadian Journal of Philosophy*. DOI: 10.1080/00455091.2015.1019176

Holroyd, J. and Puddifoot, K. Forthcoming. "Implicit bias and prejudice." *Routledge Handbook of Social Epistemology*.

Hookway, C. 2010. "Some varieties of epistemic injustice: Response to Fricker." *Episteme* 7(2): 151–163.

Kelly, D. and Roedder, E. 2008. "Racial cognition and the ethics of implicit bias." *Philosophy Compass*, 3(3): 522–540.

Levinson, J. D. 2007. "Forgotten racial equality: Implicit bias, decision-making, and misremembering." *Duke Law Journal*, 57: 345–424.

McConnell, A. R. and Leibold, J. M. 2001. "Relations among the implicit association test, discriminatory behavior, and explicit measure of racial attitudes." *Journal of Experimental Social Psychology*, 37: 435–442.
McKinnon, R. 2016. "Epistemic injustice." *Philosophy Compass*, 11(8): 437–446.
Madva, A. 2016. "Virtue, social knowledge and implicit bias." Brownstein & Saul (eds.) *Implicit Bias and Philosophy, volume 1: Metaphysics and Epistemology*. Oxford: Oxford University Press.
Mason, R. 2011. "Two kinds of unknowing." *Hypatia*, 26(2): 294–307.
Medina, J. 2011. "The relevance of credibility excess in a proportional view of epistemic injustice: Differential epistemic authority and the social imaginary." *Social Epistemology*. 25(1): 15–35.
Medina, J. 2013. *The Epistemology of Resistance: Gender and Racial Oppression, Epistemic Injustice, and Resistant Imaginations*. New York: Oxford University Press.
Mills, C. 2007. "White ignorance." *Race and epistemologies of ignorance*. S. Sullivan and N. Tuana (eds.). 11–38. Albany, NY: SUNY Press.
Mills, C. 2013. "White ignorance and hermeneutical injustice: A comment on Medina and Fricker." *Social Epistemology Review and Reply Collective*, 3(1): 38.
Puddifoot, K. Forthcoming. "Dissolving the ethical/epistemic dilemma over implicit bias." *Philosophical Explorations*.
Saul, J. 2013. "Scepticism and implicit bias." *Disputatio*, 5(37): 243–263.
Scott, J. C. 1985. *Weapons of the Weak: Everyday Forms of Peasant Resistance*. New Haven, CT: Yale University Press.
Sherman, B. R. 2016. "There's no (testimonial) justice: Why pursuit of a virtue is not the solution to epistemic injustice." *Social Epistemology*, 30(3): 229–250.
Steinpreis, R., Anders, K. and Ritzke, D. 1999. "The impact of gender on the review of the curricula vitae of job applicants and tenure candidates: A national empirical study." *Sex Roles*, 41(7/8): 509–528.
Stewart, B. D. and Payne, B. K. 2008. "Bringing automatic stereotyping under control: Implementation intentions as efficient means of thought control." *Personality and Social Psychology Bulletin*, 34: 1332–1345.
Uhlmann, E. L. and Cohen, G. L. 2007. "'I think it, therefore it's true': Effects of self-perceived objectivity on hiring discrimination." *Organizational Behavior and Human Decision Processes*, 104(2): 207–223.

5

DISCRIMINATION AND INTERSECTIONALITY

Natalie Stoljar

MCGILL UNIVERSITY

Introduction

According to one prominent analysis of discrimination, a necessary condition of discrimination is membership of a social group. Andrew Altman proposes that persons suffer discrimination as members of social groups and that the differential treatment that constitutes discrimination must be treatment 'relative to some appropriate comparison social group' (Altman 2015). Kasper Lippert-Rasmussen argues that differential treatment must be 'suitably explained' as making a distinction between members of 'different, socially salient groups' (Lippert-Rasmussen 2006: 168; Chapter 1).[1] The social group condition 'explains why we do not talk about discrimination against non-family-members, unqualified applicants or the undeserving' (Lippert-Rasmussen 2006: 169). 'Non-family members' and 'unqualified persons' do not correspond to salient social groups and therefore on this conception differential treatment with respect to these categories cannot constitute discrimination. On an alternative conception of discrimination, membership of a social group is not conceptually required for discrimination. Benjamin Eidelson argues that employment practices based on hair color or eye color (for instance) would be discriminatory even if there were no salient social groups constituted by people with a particular hair color or eye color (Eidelson 2015: 29). For Eidelson, wrongful discrimination is treatment that disrespects 'different attributes of personhood' such as intrinsic equal value or autonomy (Eidelson 2015: 8).

The intersectionality literature can be understood as presenting a challenge to the social group conception of discrimination and providing support for the alternative conception. Intersectionality questions several basic assumptions of the social group conception. First, it may be incompatible with the very idea of a social group. One way of characterizing social groups is as groups whose members share social identities, such as gender, race, religion or sexual orientation. The intersectionality framework offers an 'antiessentialist' critique of identity properties. It repudiates the idea that all members of social groups share *the same* identity properties and proposes that identity properties are *particular* to each individual. For instance, the gender 'woman' is not the same for everyone in the group 'women' because the qualitative features of gender are inflected by race and other intersecting dimensions of identity, such as religion or sexual orientation. If there is no identity property that effectively binds people into social groups, or if all dimensions of people's identities are particular to them rather than shared with other members of the group, it is difficult to maintain a notion of social group that is based on shared social identities. Second, even if the intersectionality framework is compatible with the existence of social groups, it seems to imply that people need not always suffer discrimination *as* members of social groups. Intersectionality emphasizes that disadvantage is relative to a person's particular location at the intersection of multiple dimensions of oppression. For example, the harm of sexual harassment often cannot be fully captured as sex discrimination or disadvantageous differential treatment that women suffer as members of the group 'women.' Sexual harassment can be reinforced by racist stereotypes – such as those about the sexual promiscuity of women of color – and other prejudice about victims' ethnic origin, age, sexual orientation or religion (cf. Ontario Human Rights Commission 2001: 9–10). Indigenous, transgender women might suffer a special form of sexual harassment in which multiple bases of discrimination intersect, yet it is debatable whether 'indigenous, transgender women' corresponds to an identifiable social group. Third, the intersectionality framework claims that disadvantage can be compounded by the fact that a person belongs to multiple subordinated social groups. If disadvantage can be compounded by the multiple group identifications of particular individuals, it seems that it could also be 'offset' when a person's group identifications allow them to occupy a position of privilege (Altman 2015). Consider a white, able-bodied, heterosexual woman who is privileged along the first three dimensions of her identity, yet disadvantaged by virtue of being a woman. Can this woman be said to suffer discrimination when her overall individual situation is one of privilege?

In this chapter, I explain the notion of intersectionality and evaluate whether the social group conception of discrimination survives a possible intersectionality critique. I also identify the consequences of the normative dimensions of intersectionality for the notion of discrimination. In section 2 (pp. 70–72) outlines the origins of the intersectionality framework, in particular Kimberlé Williams Crenshaw's argument that women of color are excluded by 'single-axis' approaches to discrimination. In section 3 (pp. 72–74), I introduce intersectionality critiques of the standard framing of antidiscrimination law, such as that found in section 15 of the *Canadian Charter of Rights and Freedoms* and Article 14 of the *European Convention on Human Rights*. These documents list 'grounds' of discrimination, for instance, sex, race, national or ethnic origin, religion or disability. Like the social group conception, the legal conception of discrimination seems to require that individuals base their claims of discrimination within social categories or 'pockets' (Iyer 1993). The intersectionality critique raises the possibility that certain forms of discrimination will not fit into the listed pockets or will not fit into pockets at all. In section 4 (pp. 74–75), I examine the antiessentialist implications of intersectionality and argue that antiessentialism need not undermine the very idea of a social group. Section 5 (pp. 75–77) turns to the normative significance of the intersectionality framework. Recent court decisions and scholarly writing have used intersectionality to analyze diverse forms of wrongful discrimination, including 'anti-queer' violence (Meyer 2012), discrimination against African migrant women sex workers (Yoshida 2013) and Muslim women who wear headscarves (Vakulenko 2007), and discrimination against members of Aboriginal groups excluded from voting rights because they live 'off-reserve' (*Corbière v. Canada*[2]). The intersectionality framework focuses attention on forms of disadvantage that are often marginalized and overlooked. I point out that a social group conception of discrimination, if it is to capture the wrongful discrimination identified by intersectionality, must analyze the relevant social groups as *normative* as well as socially salient. Wrongful discrimination is differential treatment of members of social groups that are historically or contextually disadvantaged.

What is intersectionality?

Writers on intersectionality have noted that the idea that black women are subject to multiple forms of subordination, which is a precursor to the notion of intersectionality, can be traced to black feminism in the United States of the late nineteenth century (e.g. Carastathis 2014: 305). The related idea that the oppression of women of color is distinct from that of white, middle class women became explicit through Latina and black feminist activism of the 1980s (hooks 1981; Moraga and Anzaldua 1991; Lugones and Spelman 1983; Spelman 1988). However, the articulation of intersectionality as a theoretical paradigm is usually thought to originate in two highly influential papers by the feminist legal scholar and critical race theorist, Kimberlé Williams Crenshaw (Crenshaw 1989; Crenshaw 1991). Although Crenshaw later commented that the notion of intersectionality in her early papers was supposed to function as a metaphor (Carastathis 2014: 305), intersectionality has now emerged as a standard theoretical paradigm in feminist theory (Cooper 2015; Carastathis 2014; Davis 2008; Nash 2008; McCall 2005). The basic idea is that disadvantage does not obtain exclusively along a single axis of social identity or group membership (sex/gender, race, class, sexuality, disability, religion etc.) but rather has multiple bases; further, disadvantage is often compounded due to individuals' multiple, intersecting group identifications. As I explain below, the paradigm has come to have both metaphysical (section 4) and normative (section 5) implications.

Crenshaw first articulated the notion of intersectionality through an analysis and critique of American antidiscrimination law (Crenshaw 1989). She argued that black women were denied the protection of antidiscrimination law in employment situations due to the intersecting nature of their disadvantage. Moreover,

> exclusion cannot be solved simply by including Black women within an already established analytical structure. Because the intersectional experience is greater than the sum of racism and sexism, any analysis that does not take intersectionality into account cannot sufficiently address the particular manner in which Black women are subordinated.
>
> *(Crenshaw 1989: 140)*

Crenshaw also provided a structural and ideological critique arguing that, without the recognition of intersectionality, legal categories such as those implicit in antidiscrimination law as well those pertaining to domestic violence and freedom of expression, will continue to replicate and reinforce sexist and racist hierarchies (Crenshaw 1989; Crenshaw 1991).

The critique starts with Crenshaw's discussion of *DeGraffenreid v. General Motors* (1977),[3] in which a group of black women brought a suit against their employer, General Motors, after having been laid off. They alleged that, since the company had not hired African-American women before 1964, *as black women* they faced disproportionate impact discrimination due to a 'last hired–first fired' policy (see Chapter 2). Neither (white) women employees nor African-American men suffered the same impact as the black women so the women could not establish either sex discrimination or discrimination on the basis of race. The Court however rejected the argument that a 'combination' of sex and race discrimination was a legitimate ground of discrimination. Crenshaw observes that 'Black women are protected only to the extent that their experiences coincide with those of either of the two groups… [but w]here the experiences of Black women are distinct, they can expect little protection' (Crenshaw 1989: 143); in other words, the 'single-axis framework erases Black women' (Crenshaw 1989: 140).

Crenshaw raises a different aspect of the problem of intersectionality through her discussion of *Moore v. Hughes Helicopters* (1983).[4] Moore, an African-American female employee of Hughes

Helicopters, alleged discrimination in promotion practices. Although in this case her strategy was intersectional – she alleged that she had been discriminated against *as a black woman* – the strategy backfired: 'The court would not allow Moore to represent white females because Moore had never claimed...that she was discriminated against as a female, but only as a black female. The court determined that this raised serious doubts as to Moore's ability to adequately represent white female employees... Mere membership in a sexual or racial group does not justify a finding that a plaintiff will adequately represent all members of a particular group.'[5] Because she was deemed not to be representative of all women, she was unable to avail herself of statistics 'reflecting the overall sex disparity in supervisory and upper-level labor jobs' (Crenshaw 1989: 148) and hence was unable to establish sex discrimination. Crenshaw argues that by denying an African-American woman the opportunity to represent all women, the Court privileged white women's experiences over that of women of color and in so doing rendered the latter invisible: '[d]iscrimination against a white female is thus the standard sex discrimination claim...because Black females' claims are seen as hybrid, they sometimes cannot represent those who may have "pure" claims of sex discrimination' (Crenshaw 1989: 145). In advancing the idea (contrary to intersectionality) that the standard for white women is the only or primary standard against which sex discrimination should be measured, the decision in *Moore* effectively reinforced existing racial hierarchies.

Crenshaw goes on to distinguish three different characterizations of intersectionality (Crenshaw 1991). First, *structural intersectionality* occurs when marginalized people occupy multiple burdened and subordinated social positions. In discussing minority women in a Los Angeles battered woman's shelter, Crenshaw notes that '[m]any women of color ... are burdened by poverty, child care responsibilities, and the lack of job skills. These burdens, largely the consequence of gender and class oppression, are then compounded by racially discriminatory employment and housing practices...' (Crenshaw 1991: 242). Structural intersectionality, which focuses on the complex material inequality of members of marginalized groups, is to be distinguished from both political and representational intersectionality.

Political intersectionality comes about when the political agendas of different social groups pull in competing directions. Crenshaw cites the example of domestic violence against women in marginalized and minority communities. The feminist political agenda of identifying and eradicating the domestic violence experienced by minority women is often thought to conflict with an antiracist political agenda promoting the interests of the minority community as a whole. For example, publicizing statistics about rates of domestic violence in a minority community might be taken to imply erroneously that domestic violence is an issue unique to that minority or reinforce racist stereotypes about the tendencies towards violence of minority men (cf. Crenshaw 1991: 1253). Women within minority communities or communities of color who are victims of domestic violence face a double bind: they can advance the feminist agenda only at the expense of the antiracist one or the antiracist agenda only at the expense of the feminist one. Without an acknowledgement of intersectionality, therefore, the political interests of women of color in such cases can be overlooked.

Representational intersectionality pertains to the ways in which 'production of images of women of color and the contestations over those images tend to ignore the intersectional interests of women of color' (Crenshaw 1991: 1282). For example, sexist and racist narratives that are part of public discourse often stereotype and homogenize the members of marginalized groups, camouflaging the individuality of people who are subject to intersecting oppression. In two recent cases, the European Court of Human Rights was asked to evaluate whether the forced sterilization (for no medical reason) of Roma women in public hospitals in Slovakia violated articles of the European Convention.[6] In both, the majority found that the forced sterilization violated a right under Article 8 to respect for private and family life but declined to consider whether it violated the Article 14 right to non-discrimination.[7] In a dissenting judgment in the earlier case, Judge Mijovic noted the historically entrenched racist narratives about the Roma:

> the sterilisations performed on Roma women were not of an accidental nature, but relics of a long-standing attitude towards the Roma minority in Slovakia…[T]he applicant was "marked out" and observed as a patient who had to be sterilised just because of her origin, since it was obvious that there were no medically relevant reasons for sterilising her. In my view, that represents the strongest form of discrimination.
>
> *(at 44–45; quoted in Yoshida 2013: 201–202)*

Keina Yoshida comments that an 'intersectional approach to Article 14 would have led the Court to look at the specific historical exclusion of Roma women and to conceive of the forced sterilisations as a form of gender violence in breach of the prohibition of non-discrimination' (Yoshida 2013: 202). One could add that in addition to the problem of structural intersectionality that Yoshida points to, this was an example of representational intersectionality because racist and sexist representations of the Roma rendered the intersecting interests of the Roma women invisible.

To sum up: Crenshaw's early articles described multiple-based, intersectional disadvantage that single-axis articulations of discrimination were unable to capture. She argued that women of color suffered a particular form of discrimination that was often not recognized by the standard categories of sex or race discrimination (cf. Chapters 15 and 16). More significantly, she offered the beginnings of an ambitious normative critique which 'aim[s] to expose and dismantle dominant systems of power…and to transform the epistemological grounds upon which [juridical and social] institutions conceive of and understand themselves' (Cooper 2015: 14). In other words, the intersectionality critique points out not only that particular excluded individuals need to be brought under the protection of antidiscrimination law, but that failing to acknowledge these hitherto hidden examples of discrimination serves to reinforce and further entrench existing structural inequalities. I turn now to applications of intersectionality in decisions by the Canadian Supreme Court in which both implications of the intersectionality critique are elaborated.

Intersectionality and 'grounds' of discrimination

The social group conception claims that people suffer discrimination as members of identifiable social groups. Antidiscrimination law often exemplifies this idea by listing 'grounds' of discrimination that can be understood as picking out salient social groups.[8] For instance, Article 14 of the *European Convention on Human Rights* reads:

> Prohibition of discrimination. The enjoyment of the rights and freedoms set forth in this Convention shall be secured without discrimination on any ground such as sex, race, colour, language, religion, political or other opinion, national or social origin, association with a national minority, property, birth or other status.

Similarly, Section 15 (1) of the *Canadian Charter of Rights and Freedoms* reads:

> Every individual is equal before and under the law and has the right to the equal protection and equal benefit of the law without discrimination and, in particular, without discrimination based on race, national or ethnic origin, colour, religion, sex, age or mental or physical disability.

Important questions arise in response to a definition of discrimination that uses 'grounds' corresponding to social groups. Should obesity constitute a ground of discrimination (Chapter 22)? Should having blue eyes? For instance, notice that neither s. 15 (1) of the Charter nor Article 14 of the Convention include groups defined by their sexual orientation. Does 'lesbian, gay, bisexual and transgender (LGBT)' count as a relevant social group (Chapters 18 and 24)? The intersectionality framework has been used both to expand the grounds analysis and to critique it.

The former approach of expanding the grounds analysis has been developed in the s. 15 jurisprudence of the Canadian Supreme Court, which allows both compound discrimination – discrimination that exists at the intersection of already existing grounds – and the introduction of new 'analogous grounds.' In *Egan v. Canada* (1995),[9] the Court addressed the issue of whether sexual orientation is an analogous ground. Egan was a same sex spouse who had been denied a spousal supplement under the *Old Age Security Act* that allocated spousal supplements only to legally recognized married or common law spouses. (The case arose before same-sex marriage was recognized under Canadian law.) He alleged that he had been subjected to discriminatory treatment on the basis of sexual orientation. The Court unanimously held that sexual orientation was analogous to the grounds enumerated in section 15. The majority adopted a test of an analogous ground, namely whether it corresponds to 'a deeply personal characteristic that is either unchangeable or changeable only at unacceptable personal costs' (*per* La Forest J. at 528). This apparently morally neutral test was subsequently revised to include normative and intersectional elements. For example, in *Law v. Canada*,[10] the Court argued that an analogous ground must have 'the potential to bring into play human dignity' (*per* Iacobucci J. at 555), (and thereby the identification of an analogous ground must promote the purpose of s. 15, namely, to protect equality conceived as protecting human dignity) and that 'there is no reason in principle ...why a discrimination claim positing an intersection of grounds cannot be understood as analogous' (*per* Iacobucci J. at 555).

In *Corbière v. Canada* (1999),[11] the Court recognized that Aboriginal people living 'off-reserve' were an analogous ground and that the members of an Aboriginal group who lived off-reserve had suffered discrimination due to a policy that allowed registered members to vote only if they lived on reserve. The majority held that 'Aboriginals living off-reserve' was, like the other enumerated grounds, 'a personal characteristic that is immutable or changeable only at unacceptable cost to personal identity' (*per* Lamer C.J. and Cory, McLachlin, Major and Bastarache JJ. at 206). However, the minority adopted a purposive, intersectional approach that adopted the social notion of personal identity implied by intersectionality as well as the important goal of rendering marginalized groups politically and legally visible. They proposed that the test 'must be flexible enough to adapt to stereotyping, prejudice, or denials of human dignity and worth that might occur in specific ways for specific groups of people, to recognize that personal characteristics may overlap or intersect, and to reflect changing social phenomena or new or different forms of stereotyping or prejudice' (*per* L'Heureux-Dubé J. at 253). Justice L'Heureux-Dubé in particular has been emphatic in developing an intersectional analysis of s. 15 (Ontario Human Rights Commission 2001: 18). For instance, in *Corbière*, she argued that 'Aboriginal women, who can be said to be doubly disadvantaged on the basis of both sex and race, are particularly affected by differential treatment of off-reserve band members' (at 259).

The jurisprudence of the Canadian Supreme Court exemplifies a normative and intersectional analysis of grounds and of the social groups relevant for identifying discrimination. A more radical response would be to reject the grounds framework altogether. For instance, Nitya Iyer argues that 'no matter how long or inclusive the list of protected grounds or characteristics, the mechanical, categorical, or category-based, approach...fails to comprehend complex social identities [and] therefore cannot accurately describe relationships of inequality, which is a precondition both for redressing particular rights violations, and for succeeding with the larger project of social reform' (Iyer 1993: 181). Although this criticism is aimed at s. 15 of the Canadian Charter, it also applies to the social group conception of discrimination. The idea that social identity is the complex product of intersecting group identifications that combine in individuals to form particular identities may imply that there is no shared social identity on which to base social groups. Even if there are social groups, disadvantage has multiple bases, and explaining disadvantage as relative to existing social groups may not capture the disadvantage experienced by individuals with these complex identities. The intersectional approach – and the purposive, contextual notion of discrimination offered in the dissenting judgments of the Canadian Supreme Court – perhaps imply an alternative conception of discrimination that does not require membership of a social group. I turn to these issues in the next two sections.

Intersectionality and the antiessentialist critique

The strand of the intersectionality literature that focuses on its implications for personal identity often articulates intersectionality as an 'antiessentialist' critique. For instance, Trina Grillo writes that 'the intersectionality critique has taught us, [that the experiences of a White woman and a Black woman] are different and not just additively…Race and class can never be just "subtracted" because they are in ways inextricable from gender' (Grillo 1995: 18). This is somewhat at odds with what Crenshaw herself says, namely that '[i]t is helpful to…distinguish intersectionality from the closely related perspective of antiessentialism' (Crenshaw 1991: 1296). Crenshaw is cautious about linking intersectionality with antiessentialism because she resists certain forms of the latter that conclude from the socially constructed nature and heterogeneity of social groups that 'there is no such thing as, say, Blacks or women' (Crenshaw 1991: 1296). In this section, I briefly assess the metaphysical, antiessentialist implications of intersectionality. Like Crenshaw, I do not think that intersectionality implies the disintegration of social groups. Indeed, intersectionality is compatible with relatively unified social groups, and hence does not directly undermine the social group conception of discrimination.

The antiessentialist strand of intersectionality is closely related to arguments that were developed by women of color in the 1980s pointing out that the interests, experiences, social standing and political goals of women of color are often different from those of white women. Feminism had developed norms that seemed inapplicable to women of color, women from poor families, and single women, because it had implicitly conceived of all women as white, middle class, and mothers in nuclear families (cf. discussion in Stoljar 1995: 264–267). One response to this exclusion of 'other' women was to develop an ideological critique that rejected the norms of white feminism and replaced them with norms applicable to the historical situation and political agenda of all women, especially women of color. Another response was to draw out the implications of intersectionality and diversity within social groups for the metaphysics of personal identity. For instance, Elizabeth Spelman argued that feminist writing had presupposed a false *metaphysics*, namely that all members of the group 'women' have the *same* gender property of being a woman: 'On this view of personal identity ... my being a woman means the same whether I am White or Black, rich or poor, French or Jamaican, Jewish or Muslim' (Spelman 1988: 136). Spelman denies that there is an essential 'womanness' or single, universal social identity in virtue of which women are members of the group 'woman' (Spelman 1988: 136).[12] Her argument also has the implication that the identity properties of each individual are *particular*. Crenshaw and other proponents of intersectionality argue that social identifications such as gender and race intersect in individuals in a way that is not just 'additive': hence, the intersection of race and sex discrimination is 'more than' the sum of race discrimination and sex discrimination conceived individually (Crenshaw 1989: 140; Grillo 1995: 18). If intersectionality were understood as 'additive', it would follow that group identifications – e.g. 'being a woman' or 'being black' – respectively correspond to universal properties that obtain in different combinations in different individuals and are simply added together to constitute individual identities. Rather, intersectionality is committed to a version of particularism in which a person's identity properties are each inflected by other intersecting identity properties and hence each has a particular quality that is different from that of the other members of the group.[13]

The denial that identity properties correspond to universals as well as the particularist account of identity properties suggest that there is a 'variety' of genders and other social identities (Spelman 1988: 175). If so, are social groups so heterogeneous that they fall apart and indeed do not exist? This question has been addressed in the feminist literature; it has been argued that, despite their internal heterogeneity, social groups track social reality. Crenshaw herself pointed out that 'to say that a category such as race or gender is socially constructed is not to say that that category has no significance in our world' (Crenshaw 1991: 1296). Indeed, there are different models for unifying people with particular identity properties into groups. For instance, feminist scholars have drawn on the notion of 'nominal essence' to explain the way in which women are unified into a group for political and other purposes (e.g. Fuss 1989). Nominal essences classify things into groups for certain purposes on the basis of their overt features without implying that members of these groups share the same underlying natures. An alternative approach has been to argue that there are resemblances among members of identity categories such as self-identifications, experiences, social roles and political solidarity. These resemblances provide a basis for relatively unified and stable social groups but do not imply that members of social groups share precisely the same social identities (Stoljar 2011). Hence, there are potentially fruitful strategies for characterizing social groups that are compatible with a particularist conception of individual identity. The antiessentialist critique implicit in intersectionality need not be taken to undermine the very notion of a social group.

Intersectionality and normative critique

The previous discussion suggests that although the intersectionality critique implies an antiessentialist account of identity categories, its primary significance is not to undermine the notion of a social group altogether. Rather, it provides important normative insights into the ways in which social groups should be understood for the purpose of identifying disadvantage and discrimination. In this section, I elaborate four aspects of the normative significance of the intersectionality framework. First, intersectionality makes the invisible visible. Crenshaw points out that the particular disadvantage of people subject to intersectional oppression is obscured by standard single-axis analyses. Although intersectionality originally focused on black women in the United States, there are now many additional examples: an intersectional approach renders visible the particular oppression of Muslim women who wear headscarves and are subject to simultaneous sex, religious and national origin discrimination (e.g. Vakulenko 2007; Chapter 17); the extension of the grounds of discrimination to include transgender identity illuminates the oppression of trans people whose disadvantage cannot be captured neatly by either sex or disability discrimination (Chapter 19);[14] and, as we saw above, the intersectionality framework counters stereotyping, homogenizing representations of groups that render invisible the rights to non-discrimination of individual members of those groups, as in the example of the forced sterilization of Roma women.

Second, the intersectionality framework seeks to undermine discrimination that is embedded in the status quo. Single-axis identity categories risk reinforcing sexist, racist and other power hierarchies. As Crenshaw notes, 'the process of categorization is itself an exercise of power' (Crenshaw 1991: 1297). In the *Moore* case, the marginal status of an African-American woman was taken to imply that she could not represent what was implicitly the standard for all women, namely the 'white woman standard.' One of the lessons of intersectionality is that identity categories are not fixed – they do not always correspond to immutable personal characteristics – but are often socially constructed in response to a history of disadvantage and subordination. There is nothing immutable about the personal characteristics of Aboriginal persons living 'off-reserve,' but as was pointed out in the dissenting judgement in *Corbière*, the legal identification of the social categories relevant for discrimination must 'reflect changing social phenomena or new or different forms of stereotyping or prejudice' (*per* L'Heureux-Dubé J. at 253). The intersectionality framework recommends that we focus on the histories and social contexts of the formation of group identifications to avoid replicating entrenched oppression (cf. Chapters 7 and 33).

The third normative implication of the intersectionality critique is to emphasize the compound nature of intersecting oppression. In section 4, I outlined the metaphysical implications of the idea that multiple basis disadvantage is not just 'additive.' This idea also has normative implications. For instance, the discrimination suffered by Aboriginal people who are disabled does not correspond to 'indigenous discrimination' plus 'disabled discrimination' because Aboriginal people who are disabled experience particular, contextualized disadvantage that is different from that experienced by disabled people who are not indigenous. Similarly, the experience of 'anti-queer' violence of people who are lesbian, gay, bisexual or transgender differs according to how sexual orientation or gender intersects with race and ethnicity (Meyer 2012); as well, the risks encountered by transgender people of color of hate crimes, sexual assault and other types of violence are significantly greater than for members of the transgender community who are considered non-racialized.[15] The phenomenon of compounded discrimination focuses our attention on the intractable situation of inequality of society's most marginalized individuals. However, it also introduces a number of puzzles. Compounded discrimination suggests that people experience particular disadvantage rather than disadvantage *qua* members of social groups, and hence Eidelson's conception of discrimination as disrespect for people's personal attributes might seem to be more congenial to compounded discrimination than the social group conception (Eidelson 2015). Further, if individuals can experience compounded disadvantage, can they also experience 'compounded privilege'? If a white, able-bodied, heterosexual woman is privileged overall, yet disadvantaged by virtue of being a woman, does she still suffer discrimination?

To answer these questions, I turn to the fourth normative implication of the intersectional framework. The social group conception requires comparisons between social groups. Intersectionality shows that, to capture disadvantage that would otherwise be invisible, selecting comparison groups must be a *normative* exercise. Consider again the *Egan* case, in which the Supreme Court of Canada was unanimous that sexual orientation is an analogous ground of discrimination. The legislation limited spousal benefits to legally recognized married and common law spouses, and hence excluded same sex spouses (who were not yet legally recognized in Canada). Despite the finding that sexual orientation was an analogous ground, the majority held that Egan had not in fact suffered comparative disadvantage on the basis of sexual orientation. They argued that the relevant comparison was between 'legally recognized couples who live together' and 'all other couples who live together,' such as siblings: 'the singling out of legally married and common law couples as the recipients of benefits necessarily excludes all sorts of other couples living together, whatever reasons these other couples may have for doing so and whatever their sexual orientation…' (*per* Lamer C.J. and La Forest, Gonthier and Major JJ at 515).

One way of explaining the majority's position in *Egan* would be to say that the differential treatment does not constitute discrimination because 'non-legally recognized couples who cohabit' are not a salient social group. However, this overlooks the normative implications of intersectionality and effectively renders Egan's disadvantage invisible. As the dissent pointed out, to identify the social groups that should be afforded protection under antidiscrimination law, it is necessary to ask questions such as: '"Is the adversely affected group already a victim of historical disadvantage?";… "Are group members currently socially vulnerable to stereotyping, social prejudice and/or marginalization?"; and "Does this distinction expose them to the reasonable possibility of future social vulnerability to stereotyping, social prejudice and/or marginalization?"' (*per* L'Heureux-Dubé J. at 554). On a normative and intersectional understanding, the differential treatment should be analyzed as directed towards a normatively salient group, namely 'same sex couples who cohabit.' The selection of this group is based on criteria that recognize the historical disadvantage of same sex spouses compared with opposite sex spouses.

The problem of 'compound privilege' can also be addressed by selecting comparison groups in a normatively informed way. When assessing whether a white, middle class same sex couple has suffered discrimination, the comparison group should be opposite sex couples of the same race and class. When evaluating whether a white woman has been subjected to discrimination, the comparison class should be that of white men who experience parallel privilege on the basis of other aspects of their identity, not men as a class. Although 'white, middle class, opposite sex couples' may not comprise a socially salient group, they are a group that is normatively salient in this context. Similarly, the group 'white men' is normatively salient for the purpose of comparison with similarly situated white women.

Conclusion

This chapter has argued that the social group conception of discrimination survives the intersectionality critique. Although intersectionality offers an antiessentialist account of social groups, it does not imply that social groups disintegrate altogether. Moreover, the particular disadvantage of people due to multiple and intersecting group identifications can be captured by articulating social groups using normative criteria. For example, although 'Aboriginal people living off-reserve' might not seem to comprise an identifiable social group, it is a normatively salient group given the history and social context of indigenous people in Canada. To explain the multiple-based discrimination identified by intersectionality, as well as to promote the goal of rendering visible hitherto invisible disadvantage, social groups need to be identified using normative not merely social or empirical criteria. Even on this normative understanding, however, the social group conception is incompatible with counting 'idiosyncratic' differential treatment as discrimination (cf. Lippert-Rasmussen 2006: 169). Differential treatment based on an arbitrary characteristic such as eye color when there is no corresponding normatively salient group would not count as wrongful discrimination. Thus, although the introduction of normative criteria can salvage the social group conception, the latter nevertheless may still be unsatisfactory to proponents of the alternative conception that focuses on disrespect for personal attributes.[16]

Notes

1 Lippert-Rasmussen's definition is as follows: 'X discriminates against (in favour of) Y in dimension W iff: (i) X treats Y differently from Z (or from how X would treat Z, were X to treat Z in some way) in dimension W; (ii) the differential treatment is (or is believed by X to be) disadvantageous (advantageous) to Y; and (iii) the differential treatment is suitably explained by Y's and Z's being (or believed by X to be) (members of) different, socially salient groups' (Lippert-Rasmussen 2006: 168).

2 *Corbière v. Canada (Minister of Indian and Northern Affairs)* [1999] 2 S.C.R. 203.

3 *DeGraffenreid v. General Motors* 413 F Supp 142 (E D Mo 1976).

4 *Moore v. Hughes Helicopters, Inc.* 708 F2d 475 (9th Cir 1983).

5 http://openjurist.org/708/f2d/475/moore-v-hughes-helicopters-inc-a-division-of-summa-corporation; accessed 16 September 2016.

6 *V.C. v. Slovakia* (2011) ECHR 1888; *N.B. v. Slovakia* (2012) ECHR 991.

7 The court also considered whether there had been a violation of Article 3 of the Convention, which provides that 'No one shall be subjected to torture or to inhuman or degrading treatment or punishment.'

8 It could be argued that in listing 'grounds,' legal documents do not imply a social group conception of discrimination. An anonymous reviewer pointed out that 'grounds' could refer to personal characteristics without implying that people with such characteristics form a social group. Although this is in principle possible, it does not appear to be how courts understand the function of grounds. For instance, the Canadian Supreme Court adopted the following test of wrongful discrimination: 'The first step looks to whether the law has drawn a distinction between the claimant and others. The second step then questions whether the distinction results in disadvantage, and examines whether the impugned law imposes a burden, obligation or disadvantage on a group of persons to which the claimant belongs which is not imposed on others, or does not provide them with a benefit which it grants others…The third step assesses whether the distinction is based on an irrelevant personal characteristic which is either enumerated…or one analogous thereto' (*Egan v. Canada*, [1995] 2 S.C.R. 513, *per* La Forest J. at 531). The differential treatment necessary for discrimination therefore is differential treatment of a person *qua* member of a group and this group is identified by whether its members have a characteristic that is either an enumerated or analogous ground.

9 *Egan v. Canada*, [1995] 2 S.C.R. 513.

10 *Law v. Canada (Minister of Employment and Immigration)* [1999] 1 S.C.R. 497.

11 See endnote 3.

12 Two conceptions of essentialism have often been run together by those employing antiessentialist critiques: (i) gender and other identity properties could be a *universals* or *kind essences*, namely the 'essences' that all members of a group instantiate in exactly the same way and in virtue of which they are members of the group; (ii) gender and other identity properties could be *individual essences*, namely properties that are necessary to an individual being the individual she is (Stoljar 1995). Once unpacked, antiessentialism usually corresponds to the rejection of (i). Many authors do not address (ii) explicitly, although sometimes both (i) and (ii) are implicitly rejected, such as in postmodernism feminist critiques.

13 In saying that identity properties are particular, or even in some cases unique to each individual, I am not implying that they are non-social. On the contrary, they are the product of the particular combination of multiple social group identifications of each person.

14 There is currently legislation before the Canadian Parliament that would address this problem. Bill C-16 seeks to: (i) amend the *Canadian Human Rights Act* to add 'gender identity' and 'gender expression' to the list of prohibited grounds of discrimination; and (ii) amend the *Criminal Code* to, e.g., 'extend the protection against hate propaganda' to people distinguished by gender identity or expression. www.parl.gc.ca/HousePublications/Publication.aspx?Language=E&Mode=1&DocId=8609176; accessed 2 December 2016.

15 http://thephoenix.com/boston/life/139051-trans-activist-gunner-scott-says-despite-increase/?page=2#TOPCONTENT; accessed 16 September 2016.

16 I am indebted to Kasper Lippert-Rasmussen and an anonymous reviewer for helpful comments on an earlier draft of this chapter.

Bibliography

Altman, Andrew. 2015. "Discrimination." *The Stanford Encyclopedia of Philosophy* (Fall 2015 Edition). Edward N. Zalta (ed.), Online at http://plato.stanford.edu/archives/fall2015/entries/discrimination/.

Carastathis, Anna. 2014. "The Concept of Intersectionality in Feminist Theory." *Philosophy Compass*. 9: 304–314.

Cooper, Brittney. 2015. 'Intersectionality,' in L. Disch and M. Hawkesworth (eds), *The Oxford Handbook of Feminist Theory*. Oxford: Oxford University Press.

Crenshaw, Kimberlé W. 1989. "Demarginalizing the Intersection of Sex and Race: A Black Feminist Critique of Antidiscrimination Doctrine, Feminist Theory and Antiracist Politics." *University of Chicago Legal Forum*. 1: 139–166.

Crenshaw, Kimberlé W. 1991. "Mapping the Margins: Intersectionality, Identity Politics, and Violence against Women of Color." *Stanford Law Review*. 43: 1241–1299.

Davis, Kathy. 2008. "Intersectionality as Buzzword : A Sociology of Science Perspective on What Makes a Feminist Theory Successful." *Feminist Theory*. 9: 67–85.

Eidelson, Benjamin. 2015. *Discrimination and Disrespect*. Oxford: Oxford University Press.

Fuss, Diana. 1989. *Essentially Speaking: Feminism, Nature and Difference*. New York: Routledge.

Grillo, Trina. 1995. "Anti-Essentialism and Intersectionality: Tools to Dismantle the Master's House." *Berkeley Women's Law Journal*. 10: 16–30.

hooks, bell. 1981. *Ain't I A Woman: Black Women and Feminism*. Boston: South End Press.

Iyer, Nitya. 1993. "Categorical Denials: Equality Rights and the Shaping of Social Identity." *Queen's Law Journal*. 19: 179–207.

Lippert-Rasmussen, Kasper. 2006. "The Badness of Discrimination." *Ethical Theory and Moral Practice*. 9: 167–185.

Lugones, Maria C. and Spelman, Elizabeth V. 1983. "Have We Got a Theory for You. Feminist Theory, Cultural Imperialism, and the Demand for 'The Woman's Voice'." *Women's Studies International Forum*. 6: 573–581.

McCall, Leslie. 2005. "The Complexity of Intersectionality." *Signs: Journal of Women in Culture and Society*. 30: 1771–1800.

Meyer, Doug. 2012. "An Intersectional Analysis of Lesbian, Gay, Bisexual, and Transgender (LGBT) People's Evaluations of Anti-Queer Violence." *Gender and Society*. 26: 849–887.

Moraga, Cherrie and Gloria Anzaldua (eds). 1981. *This Bridge Called My Back: Writings by Radical Women of Color*. Watertown, MA: Persephone Press.

Nash, Jennifer. 2008. "Rethinking Intersectionality." *Feminist Review*. 89: 1–15.

Ontario Human Rights Commission. 2001. "An Intersectional Approach to Discrimination: Addressing Multiple Grounds in Human Rights Claims." Discussion Paper, Policy and Education Branch: 1–30; Online at www.ohrc.on.ca/sites/default/files/attachments/An_intersectional_approach_to_discrimination%3Addressing_multiple_grounds_in_human_rights_claims.pdf

Spelman, Elizabeth. 1988. *Inessential Woman: Problems of Exclusion in Feminist Thought*. Boston, MA: Beacon Press Books.

Stoljar, Natalie. 1995. "Essence, Identity and the Concept of Woman." *Philosophical Topics*. 23: 261–293.

Stoljar, Natalie. 2011. "Different Women. Gender and the Realism-Nominalism Debate" in C. Witt (ed.) *Feminist Metaphysics. Explorations in the Ontology of Sex, Gender and the Self*. Dordrecht: Springer.

Vakulenko, Anastasia. 2007. "'Islamic Headscarves' and the European Convention on Human Rights: An Intersectional Perspective." *Social and Legal Studies*. 16: 183–199.

Yoshida, Keina. 2013. "Towards Intersectionality in the European Court of Human Rights: The Case of *B.S.* v *Spain*." *Feminist Legal Studies*. 21: 195–204.

PART II

The wrongness of discrimination

6
DISCRIMINATION AND DISRESPECT

Erin Beeghly

UNIVERSITY OF UTAH

Introduction

In her autobiography, Assata Shakur—a radical black activist who grew up in the United States during the 1950s and 1960s—describes her grandmother drilling her:

> "Who's better than you?"
> "Nobody."
> "Who?"
> "Nobody."
> "Get that head up."
> "Yes."
> "Yes, who?"
> "Yes, Grandmommy."
> "I want that head held up high, and I don't want you taking no mess from anybody, you understand?"
> "Yes, Grandmommy."
> "Don't you let me hear about anybody walking over my grandbaby."
> "No, Grandmommy."
> "I don't want nobody taking advantage of you, you hear me?"
> "Yes, I hear you."
> "Yes, who?"
>
> *(Shakur 1987, 19)*

"All of my family tried to instill in me a sense of personal dignity," she explains,

> but my grandmother and my grandfather were really fanatic about it. Over and over, they would tell me, "You're as good as anyone else. Don't let anybody tell you that they're better than you."
>
> *(Shakur 1987, 19)*

It is clear why Shakur's grandparents were fanatical. In the Jim Crow South, discriminatory treatment of black people was not just commonplace; it was the law.

Theorists of discrimination ask a great many questions about discrimination. One of the most basic ones is "when and why is discrimination wrong?" In the passage above, Shakur's grandmother suggests a compelling answer. Discrimination is wrong when—and because—it is disrespectful. "My grandparents were big on respect," Shakur says. "I hated when they would repeat everything so often. But the lessons that they taught me, more than anything else I learned in life, helped me to deal with the things I would face growing up in amerika" (Shakur 1987, 20).

Shakur's reflections are not merely anecdotal. Theorists of oppression and injustice have long argued that we ought to craft theories and concepts that facilitate resistance and, ultimately, liberation. By Shakur's own lights, "respect" is exactly the kind of concept to which historically marginalized persons can appeal in order to explain why discrimination against them is both wrong and ought to be resisted.[1]

This chapter is a philosophical exploration and test of Shakur and her grandparents' thought. In the next section, I articulate three conceptions of disrespect, each of which provides a special way to understand the way in which wrongful discrimination is disrespectful. After this, I ask what it would take for any of these conceptions to serve as the basis for a plausible theory of wrongful discrimination. I argue that any adequate theory of wrongful discrimination must be able to do two things well: *identify* cases of wrongful discrimination as such and, also, *explain* why they are wrong. Next, I examine the objection that respect-focused theories cannot reliably identify instances of morally wrongful discrimination. Were this objection correct, any and all respect-focused theories of wrongful discrimination would fail. On page 91, I contend that the objection does not apply to all respect-based theories; in particular, it does not apply to all versions of the deliberative theory of wrongful discrimination. In my conclusion, I argue that the most promising version of the deliberative theory, i.e., one with contractualist underpinnings evades what I call the misidentification objection only to face bigger challenges.

Three conceptions of disrespect

To explore different ways in which discrimination could be disrespectful, I will use a case of wrongful discrimination that personally mattered to Shakur and her grandparents. "In 1950," Shakur writes,

> The year we moved to Wilmington [North Carolina], the South was completely segregated. Black people were forbidden to go many places and that included the beach. Sometimes they would travel all the way to South Carolina just to see the ocean.
>
> *(Shakur 1987, 23)*

Laws that mandated segregated swimming spaces were clearly discriminatory. They treated white Americans and black Americans differently because of race. Black Americans were not permitted to swim at public beaches or pools, whereas white Americans were allowed to do so freely. These discriminatory laws were obviously wrong.

Shakur and her grandparents found a way to cope with the laws—and even to profit from them—because they were in a lucky position. Her grandmother had inherited a piece of beachfront property. "My grandparents," she writes, "decided to open a business on their land. It consisted of restaurant, lockers where people could change their clothes, and an area for hanging out and dancing" (23). Because of their business, they were able to provide a place for black folks to enjoy the ocean and to swim. "Cars and buses of people came," she explains, "from all over North Carolina, South Carolina, and Virginia. There were church groups, school groups, social clubs, women's clubs, boy scouts, girl scouts. All kinds of people would come to the beach…" (Shakur 1987, 24).

It is natural to say that laws prohibiting black Americans from using public beaches were wrong *because* they were disrespectful. But how, exactly, do we interpret this claim?

One possibility is that the laws were disrespectful because they were motivated by disrespectful beliefs about black people. This thought invokes *the mental-state conception of disrespect.* In "What Makes Wrongful Discrimination Wrong?" (1992) Larry Alexander proposes a theory of wrongful discrimination built on this conception. "When a person is incorrectly judged to be of lesser moral worth and is treated accordingly," he writes, "that treatment is morally wrong regardless of the gravity of its effects" (Alexander 1992, 159).[2]

On his view, discriminatory laws mandating white-only swimming spaces were disrespectful, hence wrong, because they were motivated by the false belief that black and white Americans were not moral equals. As one historian recounts,

> …the concern was that the black Americans, black men, would take advantage of the pool environment to brush up against white women, to touch them in the water, to visually consume them, as they were wearing, you know, relatively-revealing, relatively-tight fitting swimsuits.
>
> *(Wiltse 2016)*

Black women were also allegedly threatening. Donning bath suits, they would purportedly tempt white men with their unbridled sexuality and unruly bodies.[3] According to such views, black men and women were less capable of virtue—and more prone to vice—than white Americans and were thus not moral equals. Black Americans were also alleged to be dirtier than whites and, also, more susceptible to infectious disease. White patrons argued that swimming with black folks would result in being "polluted by their blackness" (Wiltse 2007, 151).

A second conception of disrespect—*the expressive conception*—conceptualizes disrespect in a more public way. According to this conception, disrespect is located in the *social meaning* of actions or policies. In his 2006 book *Moral Dimensions*, Thomas Scanlon argues that there is "something right about" the view that "decisions we call discriminatory are objectionable because they involve a kind of insult—an expression of the view that certain people are inferior or socially unacceptable" (Scanlon 2006, 72). "No one," he writes, "can be asked to accept a society that marks them out as inferior in this way and denies them its principal benefits" (Scanlon 2006, 73). In a similar vein, Deborah Hellman argues that discrimination is wrong when it is demeaning (Chapter 7). Demeaning treatment, she argues, is disrespectful "in an especially strong way as it is an expression of a lack of respect for the equal humanity of the other" (Hellman 2008, 36).[4] On both theorists' views, discriminatory treatment communicates disrespect because of its conventional meaning. Hellman puts the point like this:

> There are conventional methods of expressing respect—taking off one's hat when entering a room, writing a thank you note to one's dinner host, looking someone in the eye when speaking … In a similar way, albeit less formalized and defined, there are conventions for disrespect as well—giving someone the finger, spitting on someone, looking over someone's shoulder when she is speaking to one, and so on. Demeaning is, in part expressing disrespect (in an especially strong way as it is an expression of a lack of respect

> for the equal humanity of other) and as such depends on conventions regarding how disrespect is expressed in a particular culture.
>
> *(Hellman 2008, 36)*

We can now see a second reason why laws segregating swimming spaces were disrespectful. The laws publicly signified that black Americans did not have an equal right to inhabit public space. They also announced that black Americans were inferior to white Americans.

A third conception of disrespect—*the deliberative conception*—offers yet another way to understand disrespect. According to this conception, disrespect consists in a certain kind of deliberative failure—a failure to manifest what Stephen Darwall has called *recognition respect*. Recognition respect, says Darwall, is "a disposition to weigh appropriately in one's deliberation some feature of the thing in question and to act accordingly" (Darwall 1977, 38). In *Discrimination and Disrespect* (2015), Benjamin Eidelson invokes recognition respect to explain when and why discrimination is wrong. "According to my account," writes Eidelson, "an act [of wrongful discrimination] is disrespectful because of its roots in a certain kind of deliberative failing, and wrong because it is disrespectful" (Eidelson 2015, 80).

One of Eidelson's ambitions is to document the many ways in which deliberative failure can occur when people discriminate. He writes:

> You might discriminate against someone because you value her interests at a discounted rate relative to somebody else's. Or you might discriminate against her because the choice you make will affect you in some way, and (for example) you prefer contact with one kind of person rather than another. In yet other cases you might discriminate against a person on the basis of a judgment about what he is like that you form by appeal to your beliefs about a wider class of people. Despite their structural differences, we nevertheless perceive a common potential moral violation… Disrespect, I will argue, is the common thread.
>
> *(Eidelson 2015, 75)*

Invoking the deliberative conception of disrespect, we find a yet new way to explain what was wrong with Jim Crow laws regulating swimming spaces. These laws were justified by appeal to demeaning stereotypes of black Americans as dirty and dangerous and by the racist preferences of white swimmers. Black Americans' interests were, moreover, not respected or protected in the deliberative process that resulted in these laws. Elected officials did not, for example, take seriously black Americans' interest in having equal access to public goods like the ocean.

What makes a theory of discrimination plausible?

So far we have examined three ways to conceptualize disrespect. Each conception has been invoked in the literature on wrongful discrimination, and each offers a special way to understand how and why discrimination can be disrespectful. Each conception, I submit, sounds plausible when we use it to explain what's wrong with laws mandating white-only swimming spaces. But what if we wanted something more from the conceptions? Suppose, for instance, we wondered whether any of them constituted a promising foundation for a theory of when and why discrimination *in general* is morally wrong.

Given the conceptions, here would be the three theories on offer:

1. *Mental-state theory of wrongful discrimination*: discrimination is wrong when, and because, it is motivated by disrespectful mental states.

2 *Objective-meaning/expressive theory of wrongful discrimination*: discrimination is wrong when, and because, it expresses a disrespectful social meaning.
3 *Deliberative theory of wrongful discrimination*: discrimination is wrong when, and because, it manifests deliberative failure.

Each theory constitutes a branch in a family of related respect-focused theories, all of which orbit around a central idea.[5]

Are any of the above theories plausible? It's not immediately clear. A plausible theory of what's wrong with discrimination must satisfy two conditions:

1 *The identification condition*: the theory must be able to identify cases of wrongful discrimination as such.
2 *The explanatory condition*: the theory must be able to adequately explain why wrongful cases of discrimination are wrong.

To better understand (1), consider the following diagram:

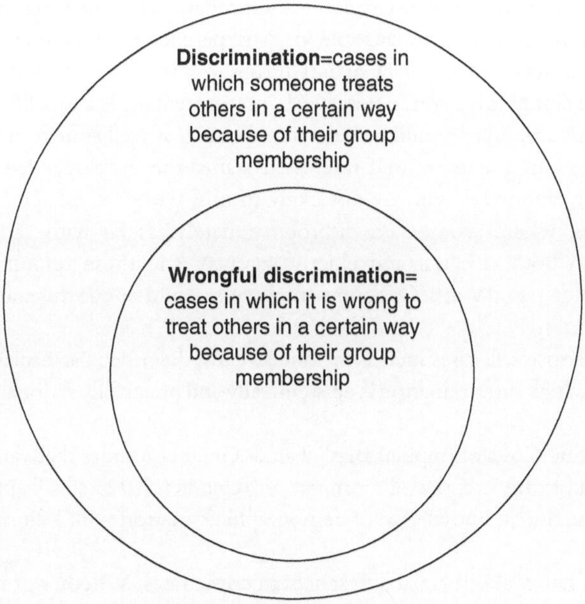

Right now, we know that each kind of respect-focused theory is capable of correctly identifying at least one central case of wrongful discrimination. That is, each classifies laws that prohibited black people from using public swimming spaces as wrongful. Each theory is thus off to an equally good start, as far as the identification condition is concerned.

On the other hand, it isn't good enough that a theory gets one—or even most—cases right. A theory that satisfies (1) must do something better. It must identify a feature that allows us to survey the whole range of cases in which people treat others in a certain way because of their group membership and, then, select from this group the subset of cases in which discrimination is wrong.

A plausible theory must do a second thing as well. It must be able to adequately *explain* why cases of wrongful discrimination are wrong. This second condition—the explanatory condition—is hotly contested and quite complex. People disagree about what the best explanation of a phenomenon like discrimination would look like.

In this chapter, I will mostly set aside the explanatory condition and the controversies associated with it. The reason is this: the most pervasive objection to respect-focused theories concerns *identification*. The objection—which I will call *the misidentification objection*—is that all respect-focused theories fail right out of the gate and in the most basic way by misidentifying paradigmatic cases of wrongful discrimination as cases in which discriminatory treatment is not wrong.

Were respect-focused theories to have this defect, they would be explanatorily inadequate too. You don't need fancy details about adequate explanations to understand why. The theories' explanatory failure would follow from failures of identification. If a theory would incorrectly classify Jim Crow laws as morally permissible, for instance, then it would have no way to explain why, in reality, these discriminatory laws were wrong.

The misidentification objection

Motivating the misidentification objection is easy. Think about the *mental-state theory of wrongful discrimination*. Were we to use this theory to identify cases of wrongful discrimination, we'd be hamstrung. There are many cases of wrongful discrimination in which the discriminator is not motivated, for example, by beliefs that some kinds of people are morally less than others.

Suppose an employer had a policy of not hiring women because women are statistically more likely to take family leave and to miss work intermittently because of family-related caring responsibilities. This employer would be behaving illegally, as well as unethically. Yet its motive would be "rational" in a narrow, self-interested sense: the employer has a strong business interest in selecting employees who are not likely to miss work (cf. Chapter 8). Moreover, we live in patriarchies, where women *are* disproportionately tasked with caring responsibilities (when it comes to both children and elderly parents), and these responsibilities can easily interfere with women's paid work. Of course employers would notice this and form expectations of individuals accordingly.

Lawyers and theorists call cases such as the one I've just described "statistical discrimination."[6] These are cases in which discrimination is epistemically and practically rational, but is nonetheless illegal and wrong.

In "The Epistemic Costs of Implicit Bias" Tamar Gendler implies that various kinds of racial profiling might constitute statistical discrimination (Gendler 2011; cf. Chapter 27). "A person who has accurate statistical knowledge of demographic variation will," she argues,

> by definition, know about racial differences in crime rates. Whether or not one is aware of the precise statistics, to know nothing of these data would require one to cultivate ignorance about a striking feature of contemporary American society. In the mid-1990s, for example, 23 of the 80 largest cities in the United States … had black homicide arrest rates that were more than 10 times higher than white rates (LaFree, Baumer and O'Brien 2010, 94) … This base-rate information has consequences for both reflective and non-reflective behavior, regardless of the degree to which one dislikes the correlation.
>
> *(Gendler 2011, 56)*

Echoing Gendler, Benjamin Eidelson writes:

> Disputing this empirical reality is a losing strategy for critics of racial profiling in immigration enforcement. More generally, it seems foolish to deny that there are often genuine

> correlations between certain perceptual features, such as race or sex, and other relevant traits, including some forms of criminality. Indeed, in light of the many correlations that traits like race and sex bear to other aspects of our lives, it would be surprising if there were not such relationship—if only because of the inequalities wrought by past and present discrimination on the basis of these same traits.
>
> (Eidelson 2015, 175)

For our immediate purposes, I will leave aside controversial assumptions within these passages and focus on the upshot in the present context. The upshot is this: so long as discriminatory profiling policies are not motivated by beliefs about the unequal moral worth of persons belonging to particular social groups, they are not wrong. Even if the epistemic basis of the policies turns out to be bogus—because, for example, there are more reliable heuristics available for policing—this conclusion follows if we accept a mental-state theory of wrongful discrimination, such as Alexander's.

Faced with the fact that mental-state theories systemically misdiagnose cases of wrongful statistical discrimination as cases in which discrimination is not wrong, theorists sympathetic to such theories have three options. The first option is to embrace the absurd conclusion that there is nothing wrong with, for example, an employer in the twenty-first century having a policy of refusing to hire women because of their disproportionate caretaking responsibilities (cf. Chapters 15 and 25). The second is to argue that statistical discriminators are, in fact, motivated by disrespectful—perhaps, more subtly prejudicial—mental states. The third option is to grant that statistical discriminators in cases like the ones above are not motivated by disrespectful mental states but, nonetheless, act wrongly.

Not surprisingly, Alexander picks option three. It is the only plausible option of the bunch. Option 1 flies in the face of discrimination law, not to mention common sense. Option 2 presents an uphill battle. As counterexamples multiply, there is little reason to believe that disrespectful mental states motivate every single case of wrongful discrimination.[7] Accordingly, Alexander argues that statistical discrimination—which he calls "rational proxy discrimination"—is not inherently disrespectful, though it does have "undesirable social consequences" (Alexander 1992, 170). Alexander cites these bad consequences when explaining why it is morally problematic (170–173).

Significantly, we see other theorists making this exact same move, even if they deploy quite different conceptions of disrespect. Consider Thomas Scanlon. In *Moral Dimensions* (2008), he invokes an expressive conception of disrespect to explain why discriminatory actions are sometimes wrong (cf. Chapter 16). But he *does not* argue that we should adopt a full-blown respect-focused theory of wrongful discrimination. On his view, discriminatory acts can be wrong for two reasons: "because of their consequences—the exclusion of some people from important opportunities—and because of their meaning—the judgment of inferiority that they express and thereby help to maintain" (Scanlon 2008, 73).

These wrong-making features can also come apart. For example, an act of discrimination might convey an insulting message, even though it does not harm anyone. The converse is also true: a discriminatory act or policy could be harmful, even if it is not insulting. Expounding on this last point, Scanlon writes,

> Once a practice of discrimination exists, decisions that deny important goods to members of the group discriminated against—and do so without sufficient justification—are wrong even if they express no judgment of inferiority …
>
> (Scanlon 2008, 73)

My hunch—because he never gives a concrete example to illustrate his claim here—is that Scanlon is talking about cases of *indirect discrimination.*

The concept of indirect discrimination was forged in legal contexts. In Title VII of the U.S. Civil Rights Act of 1964, indirect discrimination is discussed under the heading of "disparate impact." An employment practice or policy is indirectly discriminatory if it is facially neutral but unjustifiably causes "a substantially different rate of selection in hiring, promotion, or other employment decision that works to the disadvantage of a race, sex, or ethnic group."

Here is an example. Before 1977, the state of Alabama had minimum height and weight requirements for prison guards. The weight requirement was 120 pounds. The height requirement was 5 feet 2 inches. In *Dothard v. Rawlinson (1977),* the Supreme Court of the U.S. deemed the requirements discriminatory. Though the requirements were facially neutral—they applied to all persons equally regardless of race, ethnicity, gender, etc.—the court noted:

> When the height and weight restrictions are combined, Alabama's statutory standards would exclude 41.13% of the female population, while excluding less than 1% of the male population.
>
> *(Dothard v. Rawlinson 1977)*

The court also found that height and weight were imprecise proxies for strength—a qualification that was absolutely necessary for the job. A tall, heavy person could be flabby and weak. A petite person could be muscular and strong. Employers needed to test for strength directly, the court decided, rather than using height and weight in a way that unfairly diminished women's employment opportunities.

We can now better see what Scanlon had in mind—and how all this relates to the misidentification objection. Were we to adopt a full-blown expressive theory of wrongful discrimination, we could not explain why cases of indirect discrimination are wrong. Height and weight requirements do not communicate the message that anyone is of lesser moral worth or, more dramatically, less than human. Because they do not convey such a message, Hellman's theory would incorrectly classify such cases as not wrongful. While Scanlon's way of understanding insulting messages is somewhat broader—wrongful discrimination is understood as sending a message about *social* inferiority—the same point holds for a theory of wrongful discrimination built on his notion of disrespect. Alabama's policy does not communicate the message that petite people under 120 pounds are socially inferior to their taller, heavier counterparts. It says something about who is and who is not qualified to be a correctional officer. Scanlon understands this and that, I submit, is why he argues that discrimination can be wrong even in the absence of insulting social messages.

In *Discrimination and Disrespect,* we see Benjamin Eidelson making an argument analogous to Alexander's and Scanlon's, though he invokes the deliberative conception of disrespect. He writes,

> In part II of the book, I proposed an account of why discrimination is sometimes intrinsically objectionable … Roughly I suggested that paradigm cases of wrongful discrimination are objectionable in this way because they manifest a failure to appropriately recognize the standing of some people as persons [in deliberation] … One important consequence of this view is that much discrimination, and even much discrimination on the paradigm grounds of race and sex, may well not be intrinsically objectionable, because it does not manifest such disrespect.
>
> *(Eidelson 2015, 173)*

Like Scanlon and Alexander, Eidelson proceeds to argue that wrongful discrimination is wrong for one of two reasons: either it is disrespectful or it has bad consequences.

What kind of discrimination is only wrong because of its bad consequences, according to him? Statistical discrimination. Eidelson writes:

> The task facing critics of much *statistical discrimination*...is to explain why discrimination may be wrong *even if it manifests no disrespectful attitude* and constitutes an effective means to a legitimate goal.
>
> (Eidelson 2015, 175)

Racial profiling is his favorite example. Police who engage in profiling, he writes, are not necessarily treating persons disrespectfully. But they are nonetheless doing something wrong. He explains to readers:

> I will focus on the case of racial profiling here, both because it is of significant intrinsic interest and because it poses the broader question of the morality of respectful statistical discrimination in an especially clear form. Few deny the importance of the ends purporting to justify discrimination in this case: combating crime, preventing terrorist attacks, and so on. Moreover, racial profiling quickly brings to the surface the central challenge for developing a moral account of statistical discrimination that is not disrespectful: explaining what it is about the particular *grounds* of discrimination that might rule them out of bounds.
>
> (Eidelson 2015, 175–176)

Responding to the misidentification objection

As I have just shown, the misidentification objection is widely thought to show that we could not possibly adopt a full-fledged respect-focused theory of wrongful discrimination. But my hypothesis is this: the misidentification objection works against only two of the three respect-focused theories explored above; it *does not* work against the deliberative theory of wrongful discrimination, at least not in all its forms.

To test my hypothesis, let us return to the case of racial profiling. Eidelson assumes that statistical racial profiling may not be disrespectful and, hence, is not necessarily wrong, according to the deliberative theory of wrongful discrimination. But why does he think so?

As a starting point, consider the assumptions that underwrite Eidelson's support of the misidentification objection as it applies to the deliberative theory. Policies of racial profiling, if he is right, are *not* the result of deliberative failure. They are the result of deliberative success. In an earlier section of the book, Eidelson clarifies the notion of deliberative success as follows:

> On my view...discrimination is intrinsically wrong when and because it manifests a certain kind of failure of recognition. That failure to recognize someone as a person of equal value as others *may* be expressed in a belief or cognitive judgment that has a misestimate of her value as its content. Whatever you believe, however, the interest thesis implies that respecting someone as a being of equal value also entails *responding to* her status as a bearer of interests with presumptively equal normative weight. And to act consistently with what that presumption requires—to actually succeed in respecting it—it is not enough to reason in good faith. Your deliberation must track the actual facts.
>
> (Eidelson 2015, 103)

This quote is revealing. It tells us that people who deliberatively succeed aren't just trying—or hoping—to treat people as moral equals; they must *actually* be achieving this goal. On the other hand, the quote hides as much as it reveals. We know that deliberative success requires that we respond to persons as moral equals, where that means treating them as "bearers of interests with presumptively equal normative weight," but how exactly do we do that? Eidelson never says. This leads to the question: how should we understand what it means to treat persons as equals? And, is there a way to fill out the idea of deliberative success that vindicates his assertion that racial profiling is not necessarily disrespectful?

Consider, first, a classical utilitarian view of deliberative success. According to the classical utilitarian, one treats others as moral equals by giving every person's pain and pleasure equal moral weight. When deciding what to do, one aggregates the total pleasure and pain—or the likelihood of experiencing pain or pleasure—associated with particular courses of action. A good utilitarian picks the action with which the greatest hedonic total is associated.

Were Eidelson to adopt classical utilitarian assumptions about deliberative success, he could make the following argument. Racial profiling policies may hurt people of color. The policies are stigmatizing and humiliating, and they make people of color feel unsafe in public spaces.[8] But, as a matter of actual fact, the policies do a great deal of good, e.g., by "combating crime, preventing terrorist attacks, and so on" (Eidelson 2015, 176). Because they do so much good, he could then argue, all citizens have an interest in keeping the policies, despite their hedonic costs to vulnerable communities. Moreover, the policy would be respectful insofar as everyone's pain and pleasure would be valued equally in the decision-making process leading up to its selection.

Superficially, this imagined argument resonates with Eidelson's views on racial profiling. As demonstrated in the quotes in the last section, he contends that profiling policies are consistent with treating people as moral equals and, hence, are not disrespectful. He also argues that statistical profiling policies have something morally bad about them because they harm individuals of color. But the similarities end here. Eidelson never claims to adopt a maximizing view of morality. Moreover, he argues that racial profiling policies are morally wrong. This conclusion—a conclusion he very much wants to defend—is inconsistent with the claim that profiling is morally permissible, perhaps even morally required.

What does this show? We are looking for an account of deliberative success that vindicates Eidelson's endorsement of the misidentification objection. In order to vindicate that objection, we must attribute to Eidelson a view of deliberative success that makes it plausible for him to claim that racial profiling is respectful. Interestingly, we have found a classical utilitarian argument that could make his claim plausible. However, Eidelson cannot use this argument because it conflicts with what he ultimately wants to say about racial profiling, namely, that it is morally wrong to profile.

We have stumbled onto a second interesting result as well. Eidelson argues that statistical racial profiling is morally wrong when, and because, it is harmful. In order to defend this claim, he cites the "broad harms" associated with racial profiling. To explore these harms, he draws on Annabelle Lever's arguments against profiling. Lever writes:

> However scrupulous the police, racial profiling is likely to remind blacks, all too painfully, that odious claims about their innate immorality and criminality justified their subordination in the past, and still resurface from time to time in contemporary public debates. So, too, racial profiling will likely perpetuate, as well as reflect white tendencies to draw invidious and complacent racial distinctions, and exacerbate unmerited indifference and hostility to the legitimate interests of black people.
>
> *(Lever 2005, 97; cited in Eidelson 2015, 207)*

We should all agree that these are serious harms. But it is ironic that Eidelson should say so. He argues that paradigmatic cases of statistical racial profiling can be respectful. Yet someone interested in defending a respect-focused, deliberative account of wrongful discrimination can now say: "Ah ha! The misidentification objection clearly fails. Racial profiling policies *will* manifest deliberative failure. So they will absolutely be disrespectful."

Here is why. Suppose that racial profiling is more harmful than beneficial, according to the classical utilitarian calculus, once we appreciate the broad harms suffered by people of color due to profiling. If we pair a deliberative theory of wrongful discrimination with a classical utilitarian account of deliberative success, we will now find that people who racially profile deliberatively fail. After all, if Eidelson is correct, to count as deliberatively succeeding, a person must successfully track the moral facts. One is not tracking the actual moral facts if one ignores or discounts the broad harms associated with profiling. Doing so would constitute failing to value people of color's pain and pleasure—hence their interests—equally. Therefore the decision to engage in statistical racial profiling would be disrespectful and clearly wrong, according to the deliberative theory.

Maybe it was never very plausible that Eidelson held a utilitarian account of deliberative success. But investigating the matter has shown us something important. When we start thinking more carefully about deliberative success, it is not clear that Eidelson's central claim about racial profiling—specifically that it is ethically wrong but not disrespectful—is defensible, especially given what he says about its broad harms.

Consider a second view of deliberative success and failure inspired by Scanlonian contractualism, as articulated in *What We Owe to One Another.* On Scanlon's view, you count as successfully responding to the equal moral worth of persons only if you give each individual person affected by your action veto power over what you do. An action could be reasonably rejected, he writes, "*even if a small number of people* would be adversely affected" (Scanlon 1998, 205). Indeed, even if only *one* person were severely burdened by it, an action could be reasonably rejected.

Suppose we apply this way of thinking about deliberative success to racial profiling. Even if a policy serves a valuable aim, for example, the aim of promoting safety or stopping terrorism, it seriously harms individuals of color. Each one of them has viable grounds to reasonably reject the policy. Being constantly singled out causes stress and anxiety. It can lead to violent encounters with police and incarceration—even for minor, non-violent offenses such as traffic violations. Profiling policies also, as Eidelson notes, "legitimate pernicious stigmas and hostile attitudes [against people of color, especially black Americans] in social life writ large" (Eidelson 2015, 177). Accordingly, they send a humiliating public message. "No one," as Scanlon writes, "can be asked to accept a society that marks them out as inferior in this way and denies them their principle benefits" (Scanlon 2008, 73).

If this argument is right, a contractualist can say the exact same thing about racial profiling policies like stop-and-frisk as she said about Jim Crow laws regulating swimming spaces. Black Americans could reasonably reject all such laws. If legislators do not see this and enact such laws, they are guilty of deliberative failure. The same goes for police officers who enforce the policies and for civilians who informally profile.

The argument that I've just sketched needs to be filled out and supported. But it nonetheless renders my initial hunch very plausible. Only some versions of the deliberative theory of wrongful discrimination are susceptible to the misidentification objection. If the deliberative theory is paired with a contractualist account of deliberative failure and success, the misidentification objection goes away.

Not only does this version of the deliberative theory identify many cases of wrongful statistical discrimination in our actual world as disrespectful, it has the capacity to identify wrongful cases of indirect discrimination as well. Think about Alabama's height and weight requirements for prison guards. According to a contractualist account of deliberative success, women can reasonably reject being disqualified for employment on the basis of unjustified height and weight requirements. The basis of an individual's objection: the requirements arbitrarily favor the claims of men over the claims of women and are thus *unfair* (Scanlon 1998, 216). Because the state of Alabama did not respect women's objection to its exclusionary policy—and did not even believe that individual women had a legitimate objection—the state deliberatively failed.

Should we accept a deliberative respect-focused theory of wrongful discrimination?

Citing the misidentification objection, theorists often argue that respect-focused theories of wrongful discrimination are hopeless. However, if I am right, not all respect-focused theories are susceptible to this objection; in particular, the objection does not necessarily work against the deliberative theory of wrongful discrimination.

Many questions about the deliberative theory of wrongful discrimination remain, including questions about its relationship to more general ethical theories, including Scanlon's contractualism. Consider this question: does the deliberative theory of wrongful discrimination, when understood properly, converge with Scanlonian contractualism?

The answer is *no*! Eidelson's deliberative theory—if it successfully overcomes the misidentification objection by incorporating a contractualist account of deliberative success—says that wrongful discrimination is always wrong for a single reason: it manifests deliberative failure and is thus disrespectful. Scanlon, in contrast, endorses a hybrid view of wrongful discrimination: either wrongful discrimination expresses an insulting social message or it is harmful. Though he does not invoke his contractualist ethical framework explicitly, Scanlon's assumption seems to be that people may reasonably reject being discriminated against for these two basic reasons.

Which of these theories, if any, should we accept? This question pushes us back to our two desiderata for a theory of wrongful discrimination: *the identification condition* and *the explanatory condition*. If my argument in this chapter is correct, a respect-focused deliberative theory of wrongful discrimination and a hybrid theory of the kind described by Scanlon could be equally good at identifying cases of wrongful discrimination. But the explanations offered by the respective theories are different. In order to evaluate the theories, we will have to evaluate their respective explanations of why discrimination is wrong. Here, I suspect, the real weakness of the deliberative theory starts to show.

One problem is that the deliberative theory seems to render disrespect *explanatorily superfluous*. The theory says that disrespect is *the* wrong-making property of discriminatory acts. But that claim tells us very little. If discrimination is disrespectful, we know only that deliberative failure of some kind or other has occurred. One might ask: why not cut to the chase and explain what's wrong with discrimination by directly citing the reasons why deliberative failures occur? We know, for example, that Jim Crow laws mandating white-only swimming spaces unfairly excluded black citizens from public spaces, were stigmatizing, and entrenched racial prejudices and oppression. A theory of wrongful discrimination that appeals directly to such factors would be more informative and precise than the deliberative theory. Indeed, such a theory appears to make appeal to deliberative failure totally unnecessary.

A more direct theory would also locate the wrong of discrimination in a more plausible place. According to Eidelson's revised theory, when discrimination is wrong, it is wrong because of something defective in the minds of individuals or in collective decision-making processes. Disrespect is about deliberative failure, after all. But why not think that what makes discrimination wrong is external to deliberation?

My hunch is that a contractualist theory of wrongful discrimination—independent of the deliberative theory—gets us the better explanation of wrongful discrimination. Contractualist explanations permit us to appeal to people's actual reasons for vetoing discriminatory actions. For example, Scanlon argues that discrimination is wrong either because it is seriously harmful or because it conveys an insulting social message (and is therefore disrespectful). My own view is that he is on the right track, but does not go far enough. An even better hybrid theory would embrace a richer characterization of when and why discrimination is wrong. After all, there might not be only two reasons that explain why discrimination is wrong, but *many*. Such a theory would stay true not only to Shakur's and her grandparents' claims about the importance of respect and self-respect, but also to their observations about the ways in which discriminatory laws perpetuate, for example, the harms and prejudices associated with white supremacy.

Notes

1 The concept is not only powerful according to Shakur. In *Black Feminist Thought*, Patricia Hill Collins argues that respect is an essential concept for black feminists generally. "In a society in which no one is obligated to respect African–American women," she writes, "we have long admonished one another to have self-respect and to demand respect from others" (Collins 2000, 115).

2 You might worry, like I do, that the best version of the mental-state conception must be more expansive than the view advanced by Alexander. Alexander focuses on beliefs. Yet people who wrongfully discriminate might be motivated by a wider range of mental states, including implicit associations, dispositions, aliefs, or in-between beliefs. Relatedly, it is not clear what, precisely, Alexander has in mind when he says that wrongful discrimination is motivated by *incorrect* beliefs about unequal moral worth. See Lippert-Rasmussen for a discussion of different ways to interpret his thought here (Lippert Rasmussen 2014, 113–127).

3 For a discussion of this particular stereotype of black women, see Melissa V. Harris-Perry, *Sister Citizen: Shame, Stereotypes, and Black Women in American Politics* (New Haven, CT: Yale University Press, 2011), 53–69.

4 Hellman claims that her theory is equality-focused—not respect-focused—because she thinks that the most fundamental explanation of why discrimination is wrong will appeal to people's moral equality. Nonetheless I present hers as a respect-focused theory. Respect and equality are related notions on her account because to treat someone disrespectfully is to treat her in a way that signifies that she is less than equal to other people. As far as I am concerned, we could see either notion—respect or equality—as fundamental.

5 For the purposes of this chapter, I will interpret "wrong" in these formulations as "morally impermissible." But nothing in my argument hangs on this. You could equally interpret "wrong" as "prima facie wrong" and the same kind of objections work.

6 These are not the only cases the mental-state theory misidentifies. Suppose applicants are always asked about whether they will apply for parental leave and, because of this, that women have a harder time finding jobs. This is not statistical discrimination, but the same worry arises, namely, that the mental-state conception cannot identify the treatment as wrongful. The same worry applies to cases of indirect discrimination.

7 For a range of compelling counterexamples, see Lippert-Rasmussen, 2014, 115–127.

8 Some theorists argue that racial profiling could have the opposite effect. For a contrarian point of view, see Risse and Zeckhauser 2004. For an effective rejoinder, see Lever 2005.

Bibliography

Alexander, Larry. 1992. "What Makes Wrongful Discrimination Wrong? Biases, Preferences, Stereotypes, and Proxies." *University of Pennsylvania Law Review*. 141(1): 149–219.

Civil Rights Act of 1964 § 7, 42 U.S.C. § 2000e *et seq.* (1964).

Collins, Patricia Hill. 2000. *Black Feminist Thought: Knowledge, Consciousness, and the Politics of Empowerment*. New York, NY: Routledge.

Darwall, Stephen. 1977. "Two Kinds of Respect." *Ethics*. 88(1): 36–49.

Dothard v. Rawlinson. 1977. 433 U.S. 321.

Eidelson, Benjamin. 2015. *Discrimination and Disrespect*. Oxford: Oxford University Press.

Gendler, Tamar. 2011. "On the Epistemic Costs of Implicit Bias." *Philosophical Studies*. 156(1): 33–63.

Hellman, Deborah. 2008. *When is Discrimination Wrong?* Cambridge, MA: Harvard University Press.

Lever, Annabelle. 2005 "Why Racial Profiling is Hard to Justify: A Response to Risse and Zeckhauser." *Philosophy and Public Affairs*. 33(1): 94–110.

Lippert-Rasmussen, Kasper. 2014. *Born Free and Equal: A Philosophical Inquiry into the Nature of Racial Discrimination*. Oxford: Oxford University Press.

Risse, Matthias & Richard Zeckhauser. 2004. "Racial Profiling." *Philosophy and Public Affairs*. 32(2): 131–170.

Scanlon, Thomas. 1998. *What We Owe to Each Other*. Cambridge, MA: Harvard University Press.

Scanlon, Thomas. 2008. *Moral Dimensions: Permissibility, Meaning, Blame*. Cambridge, MA: Harvard University Press.

Shakur, Assata. 1987. *Assata: An Autobiography*. Chicago, IL: Lawrence Hill Books and Zed Books.

Wiltse, Jeff. 2007. *Contested Waters: A Social History of Swimming Pools in America*. Chapel Hill, NC: UNC Press.

Wiltse, Jeff. 2008. "Racial History of American Swimming Pools." *National Public Radio* Interview with Rachel Martin. May 6, 2008. For transcript of interview, see: www.npr.org/templates/story/story.php?storyId=90213675.

7
DISCRIMINATION AND SOCIAL MEANING

Deborah Hellman

UNIVERSITY OF VIRGINIA

Introduction

Laws that prohibit discrimination typically prohibit discrimination on the basis of particular, listed traits. For example, discrimination on the basis of race, sex, disability or religion is prohibited. This observation about discrimination laws gives rise to the question: is there a moral difference between "discriminating" on the basis of these sorts of traits and "discriminating" on the basis of other sorts of traits? For example, if an employer refuses to hire Adams because his last name begins with "A," is this wrongful discrimination (cf. Introduction and Chapter 1)? According to a meaning-based view of wrongful discrimination, acts and policies that differentiate between people on the basis of some traits have a social meaning in particular cultures and at particular times that differentiating between people on the basis of other traits do not, and this meaning is, in significant part, what makes the discrimination wrong (Hellman 2008).

Conceptual aside: what is discrimination?

In order to assess when discrimination is wrong, one must have some sense of what discrimination is (cf. Introduction and Chapter 1). Unfortunately, defining discrimination is itself a difficult task. First, the term "discrimination" is ambiguous between a moralized meaning and a non-moralized meaning. Sometimes we use the term "discrimination" in such a way that it is synonymous with "wrongful discrimination." To call something "discrimination," when we use the term in this way, is to assert that it is an action of a certain type and that it is wrong. For example, when the parents of a transgender teen assert that a school's policy requiring students to use the bathroom that comports with their biological sex is "discrimination," they mean that the policy treats their child in a particular sort of way and that it is unfair. Alternatively, sometimes the term "discrimination" means only that it is a certain type of action, but not that it is necessarily wrong. The common requirements that one must be 16 to drive and 18 to vote are examples of age discrimination in this non-moralized sense because they are policies of a certain type. If we use the term "discrimination" in this second way, we can go on to ask "when is discrimination wrong?" It isn't always wrong, only sometimes. If we use the term "discrimination" in the first, moralized sense, we don't ask "when?" it is wrong, only "why?"

Whether we mean the moralized or non-moralized concept of discrimination, the term "discrimination" picks out actions or policies of a certain type. What type? The requirement that one must be 16 to drive seems a plausible instance of discrimination (in the non-moralized sense) because the law distinguishes between people on the basis of age. What about a law that requires all people seeking a driver's license to pay a fee of $50? Is this law an instance of discrimination? At first blush, it seems that the answer here is no. Why? Because the law treats everyone the same. All would-be drivers must pay the fee. However, the law likely has a disparate impact on poor people, some of whom are unable to afford the fee. This impact strikes many people as also discriminatory. So potentially discriminatory laws and policies may include both laws that distinguish between people on the basis of particular traits (like the requirement that one must be 16 to drive) and laws that formally treat everyone the same but have a disparate impact on some people (like the fee for the driving license).

But now it seems that the term "discrimination" is too expansive. It could identify either policies of type X that are necessarily wrong *or* policies of type X that are possibly wrong and possibly not. Moreover, when we try to unpack X, we see that it includes policies that differentiate between people on the basis of a trait that they have or lack, or policies that treat everyone the same but have a disparate impact on a particular group of people. It is difficult to imagine a law, policy or practice that doesn't either treat people differently on the basis of some trait or have a disparate impact on some group (cf. Chapter 3).

It is true that many acts and almost all policies will either treat people differently on the basis of some trait, or differentially affect a group of people defined by a trait. Perhaps then, we ought not to focus on which acts or laws are potentially discriminatory (as almost anything might be) but rather on the sort of claim someone makes when she asserts that an action or policy constitutes discrimination. In claiming that some act or policy is *discrimination*, the claimant usually means that it is wrongful discrimination. Second, she claims that the fact that the act or policy distinguishes among people on the basis of having or lacking some trait is what makes the act morally troubling (direct discrimination), or she claims that the fact that the policy disadvantages a group of people defined by a particular trait as compared to others is what makes it problematic (indirect discrimination). In both of these claims, the key feature is a focus on traits, or what are also often termed "grounds."[1]

In what follows, I will assume the following definition of discrimination. An act or policy (directly) discriminates if the actor or the policy treats person A differently from B on the basis of A having or lacking some trait X. Alternatively, a policy (indirectly) discriminates if the policy has a disparate impact on persons with trait X as compared to persons with trait Y. In addition, I will use the term "discrimination" in the non-moralized sense, because it is by recognizing the pervasiveness of discrimination and comparing the benign cases with those that are morally problematic that we are able to see most clearly what makes wrongful discrimination wrong.

Which traits and why?

Sometimes actions and policies that treat person A differently than person B on the basis of A's having trait X wrongfully discriminate, even though treating A differently than B on the basis of A's having trait Y do not. For example, compare the case in which a law firm hires Adam rather than Bob, because Adam is white and Bob is black, with the case in which the employer hires Adam rather than Bob because Adam passed the bar exam and Bob did not. In each case, Adam gets the job and Bob does not. And in each case, the employer makes a hiring decision in response to some trait of Bob's (his race or his passing or not passing the bar). What explains the moral difference between these two instances of discrimination, making the first case wrongful discrimination and the second case permissible discrimination? The answer to this question may seem obvious. First, one might think the first case is impermissible because race isn't relevant to being a lawyer, while bar passage is (cf. Chapter 8). Second, one may think that in the racial discrimination case, the actor acts out of animus and this motive (to harm blacks) or belief (that blacks are inferior) makes the action impermissible. Third, one might think that because a person's race is outside of his control, while passing the bar exam is not, this lack of control makes the first case impermissible as compared to the second. These explanations do not exhaust the possibilities, but they constitute three prominent and familiar accounts of the wrongfulness of discrimination. Below, I briefly argue against each. I offer these arguments against alternative theories primarily to clear the ground and allow the reader to see that it is harder than one might suppose to explain why discrimination on the basis of certain traits in certain contexts is morally impermissible, while discrimination on the basis of other traits is not. With the mind of the reader open, the next section describes an alternative, less familiar, account that discrimination is wrong when and because it is demeaning.

Does the relevance of the trait used to discriminate matter? One might be tempted to say that an employer's discrimination on the basis of bar passage is permissible but his discrimination on the basis of race is not because bar passage is relevant to employment as a lawyer while race is not. But what does "relevance" mean here? Some suggest that relevance requires a reasonably close fit between the trait used to distinguish between people and some target trait that the discriminator seeks (Tussman and tenBroek 1949). If this is what relevance is, then discrimination on the basis of relevant traits will often be morally problematic. Consider the following example: an employer prefers to hire men rather than women because women are more likely to take leave when they have children than men are. If women *are* more likely than men to take extended leaves, then this policy may well be sensible from a business perspective. In that sense, the sex of the employee is a relevant trait. If relevance consists in a positive correlation between the trait used to select job candidates and a legitimate business purpose, then a relevance test for permissible discrimination leads to the result that the sex discrimination in this employment policy is permissible. This doesn't seem right. The wrongfulness of discrimination cannot be reduced to irrationality or overgeneralization (Schauer 2003; Chapter 3).

Alternatively, one might assert that the law firm employer who hires Adam rather than Bob because Bob is black acts from prejudice or dislike of blacks and that these beliefs or attitudes make his action impermissible (Alexander 1992). While racial animus is condemnable, such animus is also not what makes the employer's action wrongful discrimination. If it were, then an employer who lacked such animus, and still chose whites over blacks on the basis of race, would not act wrongly. Consider, for example, an employer who acts from unconscious bias (Lawrence 1989, Chapter 32). This employer may harbor no animus toward blacks or any conscious attitude toward them or beliefs about them, yet she may still repeatedly select white job applicants over black job applicants with comparable or even superior credentials. If animus is required for wrongful discrimination, then this conduct would not constitute wrongful discrimination. Again, that result seems mistaken.

A requirement that the actor be motivated by animus in order for his action to constitute wrongful discrimination also would permit race or sex discrimination in those cases where race or sex is a good proxy for a relevant characteristic. This is especially problematic if, as is likely, past injustice had led to a world in which race and sex are accurate proxies for traits employers and others legitimately seek. For example, return to the example of the employer who prefers to hire men rather than women because he believes, correctly, that women are more likely to take time out to care for children. In this case, the employer does not act from animus toward women. If the employer's preference for male employees is, nonetheless, wrongful sex discrimination, then an actor need not act from animus to act wrongfully.

Discrimination on the basis of race may seem different than discrimination on the basis of bar passage because a person has no control over her race while she has significant control over whether she passes the bar exam. Courts often focus on whether a trait is immutable and scholars emphasize that discrimination on the basis of traits within a person's control better respect a person's autonomy than does discrimination on the basis of traits a person cannot control (Eidelson 2015). But control, at least by itself, cannot sort permissible from impermissible discrimination either. First, discrimination on the basis of religion is often morally troubling, even when people can control their religious affiliation. Second, some traits that have seemed immutable in the past, like sex, are increasingly mutable, yet this fact does not appear to change the moral permissibility of discrimination on the basis of sex. But perhaps I am taking the idea of control too rigidly. Maybe traits that are difficult to control or that require some cost to control (as sex and religion certainly do) are different than those traits that are more easily chosen. Clearly more can be said here, but I am skeptical that such a modification will help to sort permissible from impermissible discrimination. Some would-be lawyers who exert great effort may still fail the bar exam and yet a law firm's discrimination against people who have not passed the bar would remain permissible.

If irrationality, animus, or immutability fail to sort permissible instances of discrimination from impermissible, the answer must lie elsewhere.[2]

Discrimination is wrong when it is demeaning

Discrimination, in the non-moralized sense, is ubiquitous. Many actions and policies distinguish between people on the basis of some trait (direct discrimination). And many policies have a disparate impact on a group of people defined by a particular trait (indirect discrimination). Which of these actions and policies are morally wrong, and why? In what follows, I focus on direct discrimination and at the end say something about indirect discrimination.

It is helpful to start with a paradigm case of wrongful discrimination: racial segregation of the Jim Crow South in the United States. When we consider what makes the racial segregation of schools, buses, water fountains (and more) wrongful, we note that one critical feature of these policies is that they each express that blacks are inferior. The U.S. Supreme Court appealed to just this sort of rationale in an early case to explain why the exclusion of blacks from jury service violated the Equal Protection Clause: this exclusion "is practically a brand upon them, affixed by the law, an assertion of their inferiority" (*Strauder v. West Virginia* 1879: 308). This law (excluding blacks from jury service) wrongfully discriminates according to a meaning-based account of wrongful discrimination *because* it expresses that African-Americans are inferior to whites.

Objective meaning

The claim that racial segregation of public facilities expresses denigration is a claim about the objective meaning of the policy. In other words, segregation has this meaning whether or not the people who enacted the policy or the people carrying out the policy intend to express this meaning and whether or not those affected by it interpret it in this way (compare *Plessy v. Ferguson* 1896, in which the Supreme Court denies that this is the objective meaning of segregation). The meaning the policy expresses is the objectively best interpretation of it in the particular culture, at the particular time. In the case of segregation in the American South, "the plain fact" that "the social meaning of segregation is the putting of the Negro in a position of walled-off inferiority" (Black 1960: 427) is, now, uncontroversial.

In other contexts, the meaning of distinguishing among people on the basis of particular traits in particular contexts is less clear. Consider laws that set a mandatory retirement age. Do these laws denigrate the elderly? Or do they instead convey a solicitude for the difficult employment situation of young people entering the workforce? The meaning-based account counsels that we cannot address this question in the abstract. Rather, we must look at the particular society, its general attitudes toward old people, whether it provides pensions for retired people, whether the young are having difficulty getting jobs, etc. (cf. Chapter 20). Yet still, even when we cast the question within a particular context, people may well disagree about the meaning expressed by mandatory retirement laws. If so, is there no objective meaning of this law? Perhaps.

As with interpreting the meaning of a statement, or perhaps more analogously, a story, sometimes there are clearly correct answers to what a particular statement or story means. The meaning of segregation in the Jim Crow South was clear. At other times, the meaning is ambiguous or contested. Whether mandatory retirement policies *really* do denigrate old people is up for debate. Sometimes there is a right answer to what the objective meaning of an action or policy is, and sometimes there is not. In addition, sometimes people disagree about which category a particular action or policy fits into. There may be no right answer to the question of the objective meaning of mandatory retirement laws. Alternatively, there may be a right answer, but people may simply disagree about what it is. Arguments for one position or the other must point to the plausible purposes that one could infer for the action or policy, its effects and the particular social context in which it occurs.[3] These are arguments that are internal to the interpretive project rather than arguments against the project itself (Dworkin 1986).

The meaning-based account of wrongful discrimination will not eliminate disagreement about controversial cases but it will channel it to particular questions and in doing so will make some arguments stronger than others. Consider, for example, affirmative action (see Chapter 33). When a city is hiring contractors or a university is admitting students, each might give preferential treatment to racial minorities in the competition for government contracts or places at school. If so, the city or university makes its selection, in part, on the basis of race. Is this wrongful race discrimination? According to a meaning-based account, the answer to this question depends on whether using race in selection in either of these cases expresses that either race – those benefited or burdened – are inferior. Let's consider the possibilities.

The claim that racial preferences denigrate whites seems weak. While whites may be harmed by a policy that provides a competitive advantage to non-whites, the fact that they are harmed does not convey that whites are of lower status. A preference by the university for students with high grades, or athletic ability, also harms those who lack the sought-after trait. Yet an admissions preference for high grades or sports prowess does not express that the person without these traits is the inferior of the person with them. Both the admissions policy in which minority applicants are preferred (to some degree) and those in which applicants with athletic ability are preferred (to some degree) disadvantage people who lack these traits as compared with a policy in which these traits play no roles. But the fact, standing alone, that a person would fare better under a different admissions policy doesn't denigrate the person comparatively disadvantaged. Thus, affirmative action doesn't demean the white student or business owner (Dworkin 1985).

The claim that blacks, rather than whites, are insulted by affirmative action policies is more plausible. Justice Thomas contends as much, arguing that minority preferences "teach many that because of chronic and apparently immutable handicaps, minorities cannot compete … without their patronizing indulgence" and that affirmative action programs thereby "stamp minorities with a badge of inferiority" (*Adarand v. Pena* 1995: 241). The claim that affirmative action sends a message of minority inferiority is more promising than the claim that such policies demean whites, because it tracks or picks up on the cultural meaning of blackness and on the stereotype of blacks as less intelligent than whites. Whether, in fact, affirmative action programs denigrate blacks is contestable, however. For example, Justice Stevens argued that the view that policies that afford preferences to racial minorities should be treated the same as policies that exclude blacks was to confuse "the difference between a 'No Trespassing' sign and a welcome mat" (*Adarand v. Pena* 1995: 245). The meaning-based account of discrimination focuses our attention on this question: does affirmative action, as practiced in the United States at a particular time, denigrate or insult blacks?

This example allows us also to see the role that context and culture play in determining the meaning of drawing distinctions between people on the basis of different traits. The social meaning of blackness connotes inferiority in the United States (Loury 2002) while the meaning of whiteness conveys the opposite. As a result, a policy of preferring blacks is different than a policy of preferring whites in the United States, because the exclusion of blacks conveys something quite different from the exclusion of whites due to that country's particular history and culture. In other countries, with different histories of exclusion, differentiation on the basis of other traits may have a similar social significance (Khaitan 2015).

But what meanings are morally problematic? A meaning-based account of wrongful discrimination must specify what meanings are morally troubling and why. In my view, an action or policy wrongfully discriminates when it is *demeaning* (Hellman 2008). "Demeaning," in the way I use this term, has two aspects: an expressive dimension and a power dimension. First, a demeaning action or policy expresses that a person or group is of lower status (the expressive dimension); and, second, the actor or institution expressing this meaning must have sufficient social power for this expression to have force (the power dimension).

Why is demeaning morally problematic?

In order to see why demeaning is morally problematic, return to the question discrimination gives rise to. Why might it matter, morally, that an action or policy treats people differently on the basis of some quality or trait? Differentiation among people matters because people are of equal moral worth. It is the underlying commitment to the equality of people that gives rise to worries about differentiation. Yet individuals and institutions cannot treat everyone the same. Sometimes doing so would be impractical (a state shouldn't license all drivers regardless of age and skill) and sometimes doing so would be impossible (an employer may have only one job opening available). So we might rephrase the inquiry by asking: when do actions and policies that treat people differently on the basis of having or lacking some trait fail to treat them as moral equals? Demeaning – the expression of denigration by an actor with power to lower their actual social status – fails to treat those affected as equals.

Lower status

The reason that differentiation among people is cause for moral concern is that people matter equally. Thus, the expressions that are morally troubling are those which deny this fact and express that a person or group is of lower status or rank than others (Waldron 2012). Again, racial segregation in the United States provides the clearest example. As Justice Harlan, dissenting in the 1896 case of *Plessy v. Ferguson*, explained: segregation of rail cars expressed that "colored citizens are so inferior and degraded that they cannot be allowed to sit in public coaches occupied by white citizens" (*Plessy v. Ferguson* 1896: 560). The more contemporary claim that laws restricting marriage to opposite-sex couples wrongfully discriminate rests on a similar contention that such laws express that same-sex couples lack a dignity equal to opposite-sex couples.

Perhaps more controversially, consider the objections of transgender people to policies requiring students to use the bathroom that matches their biological sex rather than their gender identity. A social meaning account of wrongful discrimination captures the heart of their complaint. Transgender students and their supporters object to these policies because the policies express that transgendered people are freaks (cf. Chapter 24). Defenders of these policies disagree with this interpretation in two distinct ways. First, they argue that the adoption of such a policy says nothing about transgendered people. Rather, they argue, because its purpose is to safeguard the privacy and safety of girls and women, it conveys no denigration of transgender people. Second, even if they concede that the law expresses something about transgendered people, supporters of the law contend that what it expresses need not be denigrating. Rather, they might argue, the policy merely reflects the fact that transgendered people are unusual – not freaks (with the insult that word connotes) but simply uncommon.

There are thus two different areas in which the meaning of an action or policy can be controversial. First, as we saw in the affirmative action example, people can disagree about what an action or policy in fact expresses. Second, as we saw in the debate about laws requiring people to use the bathroom that comports with their biological sex, people can also disagree about whether the expressive content of an action or policy conflicts with the equal status of some person or group.

Power

Not all actions or policies that denigrate also demean. To demean, the person or institution taking an action or adopting a policy must also have real power. To see the importance of actual power, we should first look to an example outside of the discrimination context. Suppose a referee at a sporting event shouts "foul." The referee *calls* a foul. If, instead, an enthusiastic fan shouts the same thing, the fan has not called a foul. Why not? The fan lacks the power or authority to call fouls (Austin 1962). In this example, the referee is able to call fouls because of the very explicit procedures or rules of sports events. However, the status of the speaker matters to what she can do with her words even in less formal environments as well. Suppose an employer says to her employee, "Bring me the report." This is an *order*. If the employee says the same thing to her employer, the employee may be impolitely *trying* to order the employer but nonetheless, she hasn't succeeded in doing so. To order requires a certain degree of authority or power.

Demeaning is like ordering, in this respect. To demean, the actor must have sufficient power such that her actions could lower the actual social standing of the people she affects. If she does not, then, like the rude employee, the would-be discriminator fails to demean and thereby fails to wrongly discriminate. Consider, for example, the contrast between an action by an employer who prefers white job applicants to black applicants with the action by an individual who prefers to make friends with whites rather than blacks. Because employers have more actual power in the world than most individuals, and denials of employment usually affect people in more consequential ways than denials of friendship, the actions of employers, in most cases, have more demeaning potential than do actions by individuals. This doesn't mean that actions by individuals cannot discriminate. But it does mean that individuals and institutions with more social power have more opportunity to wrongfully discriminate than do private individuals, particularly those without social power (cf. Chapters 30, 31 and 35).[4]

Moreover, the individual who chooses friends on the basis of race likely demonstrates a bad character, whether or not he demeans. He probably ought not to value the race of his friends. (I say "probably" because perhaps there are instances in which we might think this preference is appropriate.) But judging the character of the actor is not the same thing as judging the permissibility of the action (Scanlon 2008). Wrongfully discriminatory actions, on the account presented here, are denials of equal status by individuals and institutions with actual power. Isolated actions by persons without power are insulting, to be sure, but they aren't demeaning. By insisting on the importance of the discriminator's power to the wrongness of discrimination, this view identifies wrongful discrimination as the expression of denigration in a context in which that expression could actually lower the social standing of the person or group at whom it is directed.

This account may help explain and justify legal prohibitions on discrimination that provide carve-outs for small businesses and private clubs. While the exclusion of these small and/or private enterprises from antidiscrimination requirements can be explained on the grounds that the burdens of avoiding discrimination are especially difficult for small enterprises to bear, or particularly intrusive for private clubs, these legal exclusions can also be explained on the grounds that larger and more public institutions have more social power, and thus their denigrating actions are more likely to be demeaning.

A similar account provides an explanation for the fairly common intuition that it is morally permissible for individuals to select potential mates in part on the basis of race or religion. While alternative explanations for this view are surely possible, the account of wrongful discrimination as demeaning action provides a potentially attractive account. If wrongful discrimination is discrimination that demeans, a person's reliance on race or religion when choosing a spouse is less likely to be wrongful discrimination because the actions of individuals in making such choices usually lack the requisite social power to lower another's social status (cf. Chapters 30 and 31).

Demeaning depends on capacity not effect

Wrongful discrimination is the expression of denigration by an actor with power. This formulation leaves open two important questions. First, must the discriminator's reliance on a trait of the discriminatee be apparent and public? In other words, does an action express denigration if it is done in secret? Second, if the actor has power but nonetheless fails to lower the social standing of the person her actions affect, does she still wrongly discriminate? For example, are successful political protesters not actually wrongfully discriminated against because they succeed in resisting the actual lowering of social status?

Consider the second question first. Suppose an actor with power takes an action that is objectively denigrating. The police arrest Rosa Parks, an African–American woman, for sitting in the section of the bus reserved for whites, for example. The police certainly have the power necessary to lower the regard in which Parks is held by others, as does the state or city which enacted the ordinance. Moreover, segregation by race in the United States expresses that blacks are socially inferior in a particularly clear way. But still, Parks becomes an icon; her resistance to the police comes to symbolize black pride and the justice of the cause of civil rights. As a result, this action may fail to actually lower her standing in the community (Hellman 2014).[5]

Nevertheless, just as the boss orders the employee to bring him the report whether or not the employee obeys the order and brings the report, so too the police demean Parks, whether or not she feels demeaned and whether or not the situation plays out so that her social standing is affected in that way. The actor must have the requisite capacity to demean but demeaning, like ordering, does not depend on effect. For this reason, this action wrongfully discriminates against Parks even though she may be benefited by it, and indeed benefited in a way that relates particularly to her status in the community (cf. Lippert-Rasmussen 2014).

Now return to the first question: must an action be observable to constitute wrongful discrimination, according to the social meaning account? Consider, for example, an employer who prefers to hire men rather than women for a particular job but does not announce or otherwise make public his hiring policy. Thus, all that others see are the individual hiring decisions he makes. Suppose further that this employer only has the opportunity to hire one employee before he is laid off (for unrelated reasons). If no one knows that the sex of the potential employees affected the employer's decision-making process, can the meaning-based account of wrongful discrimination accommodate the intuition that this action is an instance of wrongful discrimination?

Here too, it is capacity that matters. So long as the action, if known, would have this meaning, then it expresses denigration even when no knows about it. While one can debate whether the tree that falls in the forest makes a sound when nobody is there to hear it, a person who sees a forest fire and shouts "fire" issues a warning, even if no one is there to hear it. The shout of "fire" is a warning because the utterance has the capacity to warn people. So too, a secret action (like the hypothetical employer's reliance on sex in the example under consideration) demeans the women who are passed over for this job.

Distinguishing intention from action

The focus on the capacity of actions and policies to demean sometimes makes the internal mental state of an actor morally relevant. From the outside, we may not know that the employer considers the sex of the employee in making a decision. For this reason, discrimination can be hard to prove. However, the fact that the mental state of the actor determines whether race, sex or some other trait played a role in his decision-making process does not entail (and should not be confused with) the claim that an actor's intentions are relevant to whether he has engaged in discrimination. What a person does and what a person aims to do often diverge. Sometimes intentions are unrealized. A writer intends to write a funny story, but this does not mean the story is, in fact, funny. Other times, we do things we do not intend to do. I may hurt you without intending to do so. If an actor distinguishes among people on the basis of having or lacking some trait, the actor discriminates on the basis of this trait – whether she does so intentionally or unconsciously. Discrimination is determined by action, not intention.

Yet, the relevant action may occur inside the head of the actor. A focus on the internal mental state of the actor and a focus on an actor's intentions are often confused, so it is important to be clear here. A meaning-based account of wrongful discrimination makes some mental states relevant because private, internal discrimination has the capacity to demean. But not all mental states are relevant. The meaning-based account I propose denies the significance of intentions.

Brief observations about indirect discrimination

If discrimination is wrong because it is demeaning, then this suggests that other demeaning actions – whether they are forms of discrimination or not – will also be wrong. As a result, we need not resolve the question whether indirect (disparate impact) discrimination *really* is a form of discrimination in order to conclude that some so-called "indirect discrimination" is also wrong and for a similar reason as is direct discrimination. However, not all instances of indirect discrimination will be demeaning. Of those that are not, forward-looking social policy reasons may support prohibitions on indirect discrimination (Eidelson 2015). In addition, non-demeaning, indirect discrimination may be wrong for others kinds of reasons.

On the view I describe in this chapter, discrimination is wrong when it is demeaning. To demean, a law, policy or action must express that the person affected is not of equal moral worth and the person or institution adopting the law or policy, or taking the action, must have a degree of power. This account leaves open many questions. How much power is needed? Must the action express that the person affected is inferior? Some seemingly wrongful discrimination expresses a limiting vision of others without expressing that these others are lesser. Perhaps we must broaden our understanding of the sort of expressive content that is morally troubling.

These are important questions. Some may call for refinement of the view and some might challenge its foundations. In addition, the view seems to announce itself as an account of why all instances of wrongful discrimination are wrong. In the years since I first articulated the view described here, I have become less confident that this is correct. Perhaps some discrimination is wrong because it is demeaning, and other discrimination is wrong for other reasons.

Notes

1 Scholars debate whether indirect discrimination (also known as disparate impact discrimination) is a genuine form of discrimination because they disagree about whether discrimination requires that a person is treated differently from others because she has a particular trait and they disagree about whether indirect discrimination amounts to treating a group differently on the basis of having or lacking some trait (compare Eidelson 2015 with Khaitan 2015).

2 Of course, it is also possible that no single criterion distinguishes permissible from impermissible discrimination. I do not consider a multi-factor approach here. Perhaps each factor is relevant but in order to show this, one needs to show how and why it is relevant as part of an account that explains why these factors matter and how they are to be weighed or included.

3 The reader may wonder why I suggest that the objective meaning of an action depends in part on plausible inferred purposes when I deny that the intentions of the actor matters. In my view, the meaning of the action is constituted in part by reasonable assumptions about its purpose, assumption that might well tract that actual purpose of the actor who adopted the policy or took the action at issue. However, the view I reject is that it is the *actual* intentions of the actor that matter.

4 Whether individual actions when aggregated have sufficient social power to discriminate raises an interesting question. I'm inclined to think that the more likely an individual's action is to be replicated by others, the more power the individual has.

5 By "social status," I mean to refer to her standing in the community. A wrongfully discriminatory action is an expression of denigration by an actor with the capacity to affect a person's standing in the community. While the actor must have actual social power for her action to be demeaning, she need not succeed in lowering the social standing of the person affected. The law at issue in this case demeans Parks even though her social standing is not lowered in fact.

Bibliography

Adarand Constructors v. Pena. 1995. 515 U.S. 200.

Alexander, L. 1992. "What Makes Wrongful Discrimination Wrong? Biases, Preferences, Stereotypes, and Proxies." *University of Pennsylvania Law Review*. 141: 149–219.

Austin, J. 1962. *How to Do Things With Words*. Cambridge, MA: Harvard University Press.

Black, C. 1960. "The Lawfulness of the Segregation Decisions." *Yale Law Journal*. 69: 421–430.

Dworkin, R. 1985. *A Matter of Principle*. Cambridge, MA: Harvard University Press.

Dworkin, R. 1986. *Law's Empire*. Cambridge, MA: Harvard University Press.

Eidelson, B. 2015. *Discrimination and Disrespect*. Oxford: Oxford University Press.

Hellman, D. 2008. *When is Discrimination Wrong?* Cambridge, MA: Harvard University Press.

Hellman, D. 2014. "Equal Protection in the Key of Respect." *Yale Law Journal*. 123(8): 3036–3062.

Khaitan, T. 2015. *A Theory of Discrimination Law*. Oxford: Oxford University Press.
Lawrence, C. 1989. "The Id, the Ego and Equal Protection: Reckoning with Unconscious Racism." *Stanford Law Review*. 39: 317–388.
Lippert-Rasmussen, K. 2014. *Born Free and Equal?: A Philosophical Inquiry into the Nature of Discrimination*. New York, NY: Oxford University Press.
Loury, G. 2002. *The Anatomy of Racial Inequality*. Cambridge, MA: Harvard University Press.
Plessy v. Ferguson, 163 U.S. 537 (U.S. 1896).
Scanlon, T. 2008. *Moral Dimensions*. Cambridge, MA: Harvard University Press.
Schauer, F. 2003. *Profiles, Probabilities and Stereotypes*. Cambridge, MA: Harvard University Press.
Strauder v. West Virginia, 100 U.S. 303 (U.S. 1879).
Tussman, J. and tenBroek, J. 1949. "The Equal Protection of the Laws." *California Law Review*. 37: 341–381.
Waldron, J. 2012. *Dignity, Rank, & Rights*. New York, NY: Oxford University Press.

8

DISCRIMINATION AND IRRELEVANCE

Lena Halldenius

LUND UNIVERSITY

Introduction

In this chapter, we will try to get a grip on the role, usefulness and challenges of invoking "irrelevance" as a deciding factor in an account of what discrimination is, and with what is wrong with it.

Let us tentatively agree that discrimination involves disadvantage through differential treatment. A person or a group is treated differently than others in such a way that the differential treatment represents or results in disadvantage for them. Not all differential treatment is discrimination, however. We need to add some constraining criteria. If high income groups are taxed differently than low income groups – say that they are required to pay a higher percentage of their income in taxes – the high income groups are subjected to differential treatment to their own disadvantage, but we would not count it as discrimination (cf. Introduction).

Some might say that since this example is about distributive justice it cannot have anything to do with discrimination because discrimination is not about such things at all, but we can change the example to see that issues of discrimination can arise also in relation to matters like tax policy.

Say that members of a racialized minority group is taxed to a higher percentage of their income than the majority population and that this has nothing to do with their level of income; if anything, the minority group is poorer than the majority population. This is a case of discrimination, surely. Why? An answer that we are considering in this chapter is that in order to say that a tax policy that differentiates on the basis of race is discriminatory, while a policy that differentiates on the basis of income levels is not, we do not need to delve into the history of racism, nor do we need to discuss contentious issues of fiscal fairness. All we need to show is that race is an irrelevant category where tax policy is concerned. Consequently, disadvantage through differential treatment counts as discrimination – and so gives rise to a legitimate complaint – when the differentiation is made on the basis of something that is irrelevant for the context or treatment at hand. "Irrelevance", then, is suggested as the criterion by which to distinguish between cases of disadvantage through differential treatment that count as discrimination, and cases that do not. The irrelevance criterion picks up on common-sense conceptions of discrimination, as well as of anti-discrimination law, as we shall see.

The tax example is on the level of law and policy. Now let's look at the irrelevance criterion as it applies to individual cases of decision making, such as hiring decisions.

Example 1. Hanna and Adam have the same employer and do a similar job, but Hanna earns considerably less. On a first scenario, Hanna's lower wage is correctly explained by the fact that she has worked for fewer years than Adam. She can expect to catch up as she gains more experience. On a second scenario, there is no difference between Hanna and Adam in terms of work experience and no other difference either that could reasonably account for why Adam's wage is higher. Hanna is paid less simply because she is a woman. The wage difference in the first scenario seems acceptable – Hanna has no legitimate ground for complaint – while the second scenario counts as a case of wage discrimination on the basis of sex.

Example 2. Helene and Rose apply for the same job. The employer chooses Rose over Helene (there are no other applicants). Helene has a physical impairment, which would not affect her performance on this particular job. On a first scenario, the employer's preference for Rose is correctly explained by the fact that she has worked for several years with similar tasks, while Helene is fresh out of college. In the second scenario, there is no such difference between them and no other difference either that could reasonably account for why Rose should be preferred. Helene is rejected because of her physical impairment. The first scenario looks unobjectionable – Helene has no legitimate ground for complaint – while the second scenario is a case of discrimination on the basis of disability.

Identifying the irrelevance criterion

Both examples illustrate the irrelevance criterion at work. One distinguishes between legitimate and illegitimate instances of disadvantage through differential treatment by asking whether the differentiation is made on grounds that are relevant in the context. If so, there is no discrimination. If not, there is discrimination. Getting to grips with the benefits and challenges of approaching discrimination in this way is important, not least because of how prevalent this approach is in political and moral discussions about discrimination, as well as in anti-discrimination law, even though it is not always explicitly framed in the language of relevance or irrelevance.

Grasping the moral intuition at play here is not difficult. Benefitting some while disadvantaging others on the basis of something that is irrelevant to whatever benefit is handed out or withheld is arbitrary. Peter Singer has referred to this as the "standard objection" to discrimination.[1] It harks back to the classic Aristotelian principle of justice through equal treatment, such that "equals be treated equally and unequals be treated unequally" (cf. Chapter 3). Settling whether justice requires that two agents be treated equally or not requires a non-arbitrary way of ascertaining whether they should be regarded as relevantly alike or not, in relation to the situation at hand. On this "standard objection", as Singer calls it, the key is what is reasonably regarded as relevant to the treatment in question. A moral principle of equality (which can be spelled out in various ways – "equal concern and respect",[2] "equal consideration of interests",[3] equal "entitlements to deliberative freedoms",[4] etc.) – may in certain instances require that people be treated unequally (or differently) for the sake of equality, as it were. Two schoolchildren, one of whom has dyslexia while the other does not, are differently situated in terms of gaining literacy skills. One has difficulties that the other does not have. A principle of equality therefore requires that these two children be treated differently. The fact that the child with dyslexia gets more resources and assistance does not give the child without dyslexia a legitimate complaint. The standard objection does not apply.

Pursuant to European Union (EU) directives, anti-discrimination law, at least in Europe, also follows this logic, even though the explicit language can be different. In EU Directive 2006/54/EC "on the implementation of the principle of equal opportunities and equal treatment of men and women in matters of employment and occupation"[5] *direct discrimination*[6] is defined thus:

> … where one person is treated less favourably on grounds of sex than another is, has been or would be treated in a comparable situation …
>
> *(EU Directive 2006/54/EC, Title I, Article 2.1[a])*

However, the directive allows states to make exceptions from this general rule:

> … a difference of treatment which is based on a characteristic related to sex shall not constitute discrimination where, by reason of the nature of the particular occupational activities concerned or of the context in which they are carried out, such a characteristic constitutes a genuine and determining occupational requirement, provided that its objective is legitimate and the requirement is proportionate.
>
> *(EU Directive 2006/54/EC,Title II, Chapter 3, Article 14.2)*

This definition of discrimination as well as the exception as it is formulated in the EU directive reappears almost verbatim in, for example, the Swedish Discrimination Act.[7]

What the exception in the EU directive says is that it is permissible and "shall not constitute discrimination" to treat someone less favorably than another on the grounds of (a characteristic related to) sex provided that this characteristic is required for legitimate reasons in the particular context, in this case for the occupation at hand. This exception introduces a version of the irrelevance criterion (only not in those words) such that sex counts as a relevant ground for differential treatment if the job requires it; in others words it is part of what makes a person qualified for the job in question. What kind of cases does this capture? In what kind of hiring decisions can it be legitimate to treat members of one sex less favorably than others? Say that a shelter for women who have suffered domestic abuse is hiring a therapist. It is not difficult to see that women who have just escaped and are hiding from male violence may find it difficult to trust a male therapist. In that circumstance, being a woman could be a legitimate occupational requirement. The character of the job makes sex a relevant consideration and so treating male applicants less favorably than female applicants because they are men would not count as discrimination. Other examples are not this clear cut, and I will get back to them in the sections beginning on pages 112 and 114 in order to highlight some of the challenges that come with the irrelevance criterion.

Our examples so far have all been from what we may crudely term the public sphere, and so apply to relations such as those between employers and job applicants, landlords and tenants, hotel managers and guests, school authorities and pupils, hospital staff and patients, and, of course, law and policy makers in relation to all of us as citizens. The irrelevance approach to discrimination makes sense of this limitation to relations of public concern, which are also what discrimination law regulates. Readily admitting that there will be hard cases and semi-public grey areas – such as subletting flats or hiring a babysitter for your children – a right to be treated non-arbitrarily, on relevant grounds, does not apply in relationships that are personal, where it is legitimate to distinguish between people on grounds such as loyalty and personal taste.

What discrimination is and what is wrong with it

We will now consider what the irrelevance criterion does in relation to how discrimination is defined. The definition of discrimination in the EU directive, together with how the exception is formulated, implies that irrelevance is part of the definition of what discrimination is, rather than a criterion for what makes discrimination wrongful: when there is differential treatment on the basis of sex in circumstances where sex is a relevant consideration (because it is a required job qualification) the differential treatment does not count as discrimination at all. A male applicant who is passed over for a job as a therapist in a women's shelter because of his sex has no legitimate complaint and has not been subjected to discrimination at all for that reason.

Neither our language nor legal provisions are consistent on this point. I have already said that the Swedish Discrimination Act repeats the definition and the exception in the EU directive *almost* verbatim. A difference is that in Swedish law, differential treatment on the basis of sex (or some other ground covered by the law, such as disability or sexual orientation) where sex is a relevant consideration, is framed as an exception from the *prohibition* against discrimination. It is consistent with the wording of the law to say that differential treatment on the basis of sex still counts as discrimination when sex is relevant; it is just not prohibited. If so, a male applicant in the shelter case, who was passed over because of his sex, has been subjected to discrimination but still has no legitimate complaint in the eyes of the law, since sex was a relevant consideration. Consequently, irrelevance can either figure as part of the definition of what discrimination is (making discrimination wrongful per definition) or as a criterion by which one assesses whether a case of discrimination is wrongful or not (discrimination itself being morally neutral).

There is no consensus among theorists over whether discrimination is best regarded as value laden or morally neutral.[8] I am on record in support of using discrimination as a value-laden term, as are Radcliffe Richards and Wasserman.[9] Peter Singer insists that it is best used as a value-neutral term, leaving it open as to whether a case of discrimination is wrongful until we know more about it. According to Singer, using discrimination as in itself value-laden is an "abuse of language" since to discriminate "is merely to distinguish, or differentiate".[10] But as Radcliffe Richards has pointed out, when we discuss discrimination as a political or moral term, it "comes trailing connotations of arbitrariness and injustice".[11] Using discrimination as a value-laden term tallies at least as well with our language as using it in a value-neutral sense, but, I think, explains our concerns better.

Importantly, using the term discrimination as value laden amounts, on the irrelevance approach, to counting the criterion of wrongness – being arbitrarily treated on irrelevant grounds – as part of what discrimination is. It does not mean that assessing a particular case as a potential case of discrimination involves making contentious normative judgments. The irrelevance criterion is invoked for normative reasons, but whether or not there has been differential treatment on irrelevant grounds can in principle be settled empirically, by looking at what has taken place and why. There is a complication here, however, which we will look at on page 114.

From what we have said so far, an account of discrimination that incorporates the irrelevance criterion might look something like this: discrimination is disadvantage through differential treatment, such that a person or group is treated worse than comparable others are, have been or would have been treated in similar situations, and where the differential treatment is correctly explained by – or grounded in – a distinguishing feature that is irrelevant in the context at hand. Think back to the examples where Hanna is paid less than Adam because she is a woman, even though sex is irrelevant to work performance, and where Helene is rejected because of a physical impairment which is irrelevant to the job she and Rose both applied for.

In the two sections that follow we will look at the benefits and challenges that come with the irrelevance approach, in terms of what distinguishing grounds count as possible grounds for discrimination, and why, and what applying the irrelevance criterion in individual cases requires us to consider.

Relevant and irrelevant grounds: on what ground?

On the irrelevance approach to discrimination our attention is turned to the grounds or reasons for differential treatment. If the ground or reason on the basis of which someone is disadvantaged is relevant in the context, there is no legitimate complaint, at least not one that can be cast in terms of discrimination (the differential treatment may, of course, be objectionable for some other reason). So far the irrelevance criterion looks like a negative criterion: any irrelevant distinguishing ground on which differential treatment is based makes the case a potential case of discrimination. But is that really right?

The examples that I have used so far all invoke familiar distinguishing grounds that typically feature in discussions about discrimination: sex, impairment and race. There are other grounds that I could have used instead to the same effect, and without confusing a reader. These can include sexual orientation, ethnicity, transgender identity, religion, age and minority status. The list will be open-ended, and some items on it will be more controversial and contested than others, but the point is that there is *a list*. If, in my initial examples, Hanna is paid less than Adam not because she is a woman but because she is curly-haired, while Rose is preferred over Helene not because of Helene's impairment but because Helene is left-handed, a reader might have objected: "The differential treatment in these cases does seem unfair, and the grounds are certainly irrelevant, but is discrimination really about things like that?" The objection makes sense. There should be something to explain, in a non-arbitrary way, why sex, impairment and race are readily accepted – by lawmakers and theorists alike – as grounds for discrimination, while being curly-haired or left-handed are not. It seems now that maybe irrelevance, although required, is not enough. Maybe we also need some kind of positive side-constraint such that not any distinguishing ground can make a case into a case of discrimination, however irrelevant it is. First, it needs to make it onto *the list*. How does it do that?

Before addressing that question, we should acknowledge that all of this might just be an unnecessary complication. An irrelevance account of discrimination with no restrictions on what distinguishing grounds qualify for the irrelevance test is perfectly viable, and would mean that *whatever* is irrelevant in the context is ground for discrimination. If being curly-haired is irrelevant, then being disadvantaged because of it is discrimination. The criterion is purely negative. Insisting on a list that screens features in or out simply deflects, one might want to say, from the general moral principle according to which it is unfair to be disadvantaged for arbitrary reasons. If Hanna is paid less than Adam then the disadvantage for her is the same, regardless of whether it is correctly explained by the irrelevance of her sex or by the irrelevance of the way her hair looks. Why should the irrelevance of one thing be more worthy of protection than another, if the disadvantage is the same?

So, what reason could there be for insisting on a positive requirement such that not all distinguishing grounds can, as it were, be irrelevant in the right way? How could we explain that?[12]

Let us first look at a couple of suggestions that are not dependent on the irrelevance condition but, arguably, compatible with it.

In her deliberations over things like career choices, Moreau maintains that distinguishing grounds that can in principle be ground for discrimination are such that they are "normatively extraneous",[13] by which she means that a person should not have to "factor [them] in *as costs*" (cf. Chapter 13). Moreau's examples are the familiar ones: religion, race, etc. So, maybe those grounds that are normatively extraneous can make a case into a case of discrimination provided that they are irrelevant in the context at hand? This suggestion does not seem to help us however, since something being "normatively extraneous" is purely negative too. Being left-handed or curly-haired are just as normatively extraneous as religion and race.

Lippert-Rasmussen suggests that those grounds that should make it onto the list are those that are "socially salient", meaning that they are "important to the structure of social interactions across a wide range of social contexts".[14] The idea is that people should be extra-protected from the effects of things that affect them wherever they go, from which social life offers no refuge. This criterion does do what we want it to do; it does screen grounds in or out. It also has the benefit of not essentializing what a ground of the right kind can be. If the fact that I am perceived as a woman affects how people interact with me in most social contexts, while the fact that I am left-handed does not, then that explains why sex is on *the list* while left- or right-handedness is not. In an androgynous but right-hand-biased society, where social status is tied to being right- or left-handed, while sex does not matter for how people interact with each other, the situation would be reversed. A good point to be made here is that any list of grounds of the right kind is conditioned by contingent social factors rather than preconceived moral notions.

There are similarities in that regard between Lippert-Rasmussen's "social salience" and Radcliffe Richards' position on social rules. They both insist that even though the disadvantage falls on an individual, we cannot understand what is going on in cases of discrimination without paying attention to the fact that individuals are treated as members of social groups, and ascribed characteristics and roles associated with that group and the position it has in relation to other groups. As Radcliffe Richards puts it, what "rules separating men and women" do is to "specify that the sexes should be kept in certain positions relative to each other".[15] Consequently, behind an individual case of discrimination against a woman on the basis of sex lies a social rule "putting one group [women] at a systematic disadvantage to another".[16] An instance of discrimination is an instance of acting on this discriminatory social rule. It need have nothing to do with a dislike of women or a wish to benefit men. Understood in this way, discrimination keeps up the systematic disadvantage of such social rules. Instances of differential treatment that cannot be explained in this way by a social rule might look like discrimination, but are something else entirely. A significant difference between Lippert-Rasmussen and Radcliffe Richards[17] is that social salience focuses on the structure of social interaction, while Radcliffe Richards' social rules concern systematic patterns of exclusion from opportunities.

A crucial implication of both analyses for an irrelevance account of discrimination is that before one considers whether a distinguishing ground that has decided the matter in an individual case is irrelevant or not in the particular context, one needs to assess the situation in relation to the larger social structure. In other words, a social analysis in terms of, say, Lippert-Rasmussen's "social salience" or Radcliffe Richards' "social rules that put one group at a systematic disadvantage to another" is logically prior to an assessment of irrelevance of distinguishing grounds in the specific decision-making context at hand.

So, any constraining criterion for selection of possible grounds for discrimination – be it social salience or rules that regulate relations between groups, or something else – has the implication for an irrelevance approach to discrimination that differential treatment on irrelevant grounds may still not be discrimination. If one is unhappy with that conclusion one has reason to drop the constraining criterion as a logically prior step, and go for context irrelevance directly.

Irrelevance in particular cases

We will now discuss the assessment of irrelevance in particular cases of differential treatment. We would do well to keep in mind that what is at stake is whether a distinguishing ground is irrelevant in the particular context in which the differential treatment took place; this involves considering what that context is like and how the distinguishing ground in question plays out in it. Do also remember what we just said about *the list*: an irrelevance approach may include a logically prior constraining condition, such that not all distinguishing grounds are of the kind that can make a case into a case of discrimination, however irrelevant it is.

Conversely, some cases that look deceptively similar to discrimination and often are labeled as such are not discrimination on the account we are discussing here. Article 7 of the *International Declaration on Human Genetic Data* says, under the heading "Non-discrimination and non-stigmatization" that

> a Every effort should be made to ensure that human genetic data and human proteomic data are not used for purposes that discriminate in a way that is intended to infringe, or has the effect of infringing human rights, fundamental freedoms or human dignity of an individual or for purposes that lead to the stigmatization of an individual, a family, a group or communities.[18]

Genetic information about a person can be used in all sorts of arbitrary, irrelevant ways, for instance in employment decisions, but a vexed matter is the use of genetic discrimination in decisions regarding health insurance policies. It might strike us as unfair that a person be denied health insurance because of known susceptibility to a genetic illness, but on the irrelevance account it is not discrimination provided that the information is relevant for the insurance company's calculation of risk (cf. Chapter 28).[19]

Requiring that differential treatment of persons or groups be made on relevant grounds is, one might say, an application of the moral principle that it is legitimate to expect of a person that they shoulder burdens and submit to disadvantages only if they have reason to accept them.[20] If you apply for a job that requires certain qualifications, you have reason to accept that another person is preferred if that person's qualifications are stronger than yours. Here lies a challenge to the irrelevance approach: what is a relevant qualification, and how can what it is be settled non-arbitrarily and without letting unfairness in through the back door?

A decision not to hire someone because of a physical impairment counts as discrimination on the irrelevance approach if the impairment would not affect how well the person could perform on the job, or if negative effects on performance could have been eliminated through reasonable accommodation of the workplace (Chapter 19). Not accepting persons with limited eyesight onto a pilot training program would – I think we could agree – not be discrimination since near perfect vision is a relevant requirement for flying an airplane (cf. Chapter 3). However, if a person with limited eyesight could operate a switchboard just as well as someone with full vision, as long as the workplace could be fixed with appropriate lighting, then not hiring a person solely because of her limited eyesight could be discrimination. Whether the distinguishing ground in question should count as irrelevant or not may, as this example shows, require considerations of what accommodations of the workplace – or whatever the setting is – can reasonably be required.[21] If an impairment would hamper work performance, given what the working environment is like now but would be insignificant if the workplace was amended in a way that would not be forbiddingly expensive, then it is reasonable to require that the assessment of irrelevance be made in relation to what the workplace could be like, not what it is like now. The irrelevance assessment could, then, be made in relation to what would be irrelevant or not given certain reasonable amendments to the context. This is important since it means that cases that would not count as discrimination judged in relation to the status quo, would count as discrimination if reasonable accommodation were taken into account. This does not apply only to questions of impairment.

In a gender equality project aimed at introducing women into the heavily male and masculine corps of firefighters in Sweden, the weight of the equipment was an issue. If women really did lack the physical strength to carry a hose, then not accepting them onto the training program would not be discrimination. The first thing to note is the matter of generalization: even if it were true for the average woman, or for women in general, that the equipment was too heavy to carry (which it probably was also for many men), this obviously does not work as an argument against accepting a woman who actually is strong enough. The project prompted a discussion about the equipment, and whether it needed to be as heavy as it was. Lighter equipment would not only make the job easier for women firefighters; it would make the job less taxing for all, regardless of sex. There was, however, another problem to contend with. Heavy equipment was part of a macho culture surrounding the profession, a culture cultivating the image of strong men – who could carry a heavy hose without flinching – as the saviors of women and children.[22] This introduces the question of attitudes.

On the irrelevance approach there is an important sense in which attitudes do not matter. Whether an alleged discriminator harbors hostile or demeaning attitudes towards persons who are differentially treated does not need to be investigated. It does not matter. Importantly, then, this approach does not say that discrimination is bad because it expresses demeaning or malevolent attitudes.[23] There are good reasons for this. Research into "implicit bias" shows that biased behavior may be prevalent even when the agent is committed to equality.[24] An employer who does not want to hire a person with limited eyesight to operate a switchboard might have no demeaning attitudes at all, only a desire to save money. It is still discrimination. But attitudes remain a complicating factor here. Consider these examples:

> Sara works as a sales representative for a hardware company. She abides by Muslim dress code and covers her hair. Her knowledge and her sales skills are strong, but due to prejudice against Muslims among the company's clients, her results are falling. No one doubts that had it not been for Islamophobic attitudes, her results would have been just as good as her colleagues, but because of her weaker results she is paid less than they are.
>
> Peter applies for a job as a primary school teacher. He has the appropriate training, long work experience and a raving letter of recommendation from his previous employer. However, after an upsetting incident at a neighboring school where a male teacher had been sexually molesting children, the principal concludes that parents would not trust a man to teach their children and so hires a woman instead, despite Peter's stronger résumé.

How should we think about these examples? On everything we have said so far one might conclude, with reason, that since religion has no bearing on selling hardware, and that neither is a person's sex relevant to teaching schoolchildren, the irrelevance criterion should say that the differential treatment of Sara and Peter counts as discrimination.

Wertheimer addresses cases like these using a distinction between "technical qualifications" and "reaction qualifications".[25] Technical qualifications are those that a person would put on their résumé, like training and prior experience, while reaction qualifications:

> refer to those abilities or characteristics which contribute to job effectiveness by causing or serving as the bases of the appropriate reaction in the recipients.[26]

More simply put, if people I interact with at work (in the examples just given: customers, pupils and parents) react well to me, I will function and perform better. Some reactions are such that I can control them. Any sales representative worth their salt knows that you do not go to a sales meeting chewing gum and wearing shabby clothes. How you present yourself may decide whether there will be a deal or not. But some reaction qualifications are beyond one's control and can only be explained by prejudice, and by social norms and attitudes – think of the social rules discussed by Radcliffe Richards – that may be completely irrational and unfounded, yet have a significant effect on how well a person can perform on the job. If we say, which we do on the approach to discrimination discussed here, that an employer may not differentiate on irrelevant grounds, we have to contend with the problem that something that should be irrelevant in actual fact may become relevant because of reactive attitudes in the environment.

The irrelevance criterion was supposed to be an empirical way of settling questions of discrimination – we said so on page 111 – but however deeply we resent the attitudes that affect the employers' decisions in the Sara and Peter examples, they do or would affect work performance, so how can we say that they are not relevant? This is a real problem. Saying that reaction qualifications are relevant and that these cases are not discrimination for that reason, is to let exactly such social and moral problems that give us reason to be concerned about discrimination in the first place, rule discrimination out. It would make the account self-defeating.

As Wertheimer points out, we can deal with this challenge only by differentiating between different reactive attitudes on grounds of justice. Some reactive attitudes are unobjectionable, even legitimate, such as the expectation we all have that shop assistants be polite, or that radio presenters have clear diction. (We might even say that such things challenge any easy distinction between technical and reaction qualifications.) Allowing some reactive attitudes while disallowing others to count as relevant considerations in decision making requires an analysis of how these attitudes sit within society, and it requires that we make judgments of social justice regarding what can be regarded as fair, and what cannot. [27]

The social analysis that we discussed in the previous section – the analysis that results in *the list* – which takes into account the structure of social relations and interactions or social rules that systematically distribute advantages and support hierarchies cannot be left behind when settling individual cases. It needs to be invoked in order to settle when reactive attitudes that *are* relevant as matters of empirical fact, *should* be counted as irrelevant for reasons of social justice, because they are racist, say, or sexist. That will inevitably be a contestable normative exercise.

Moreover, there are reasons of justice to look critically at features that are relevant in a decision-making context even when they are not a matter of reactive attitudes. In one of my first examples I let a difference in work experience between a man and a woman – Hanna and Adam – decide that a wage difference between them was not discrimination. But in a society where there are social rules about gender, rules and expectations that shape not only jobs but also family life and public benefits, a woman's lesser work experience can very well be due to an unequal distribution of child care responsibilities within families (cf. Chapter 15).

Sex, race, sexual orientation, religion, disability etc. – familiar items on *the list* – are social categories that make people who are associated with them comparatively vulnerable to differential treatment and disadvantage in contexts that are crucual for life opportunities: jobs, education, housing. The same categories shape the contexts in which decisions that affect individual people are taken, be they employment decisions or decisions about whether an employment decision is a case of discrimination.

Here lies a challenge for the irrelevance approach to discrimination: there is a risk that a distinguishing ground is relevant for reasons that are not only unfair in general, but unfair for exactly the same reasons that made us care about discrimination in the first place. The empirical, clinical tool that we maybe hoped the irrelevance criterion would be, turned out to be quite sticky. But that is as it should be. We are inescapably and already walking on contested political and moral terrain when questions of discrimination arise.

Notes

1 Singer 1978, p. 186. Singer's explicit focus is racial discrimination, but his discussion can be generalized to other forms of discrimination as well. On irrelevance and the equality principle, see also Schauer, 2003, pp. 216–223, who claims that "equality is at its core about treating unlike cases alike" (2003, p. 222).

2 Dworkin 1977, Wertheimer 1983.

3 Singer 1978.

4 Moreau 2010.

5 DIRECTIVE 2006/54/EC OF THE EUROPEAN PARLIAMENT AND OF THE COUNCIL of 5 July 2006, on the implementation of the principle of equal opportunities and equal treatment of men and women in matters of employment and occupation (recast).

6 On direct and indirect discrimination, see Chapter 1 and 2 in this volume.

7 Diskrimineringslag 2008: 567, Chapter 1, §4.1; Chapter 2, §2.1.

8 Lippert-Rasmussen 2014, p. 24. Lippert-Rasmussen defends a morally neutral concept, as does Cavanaugh 2002, p. 177. Neither of them subscribe to an irrelevance approach to discrimination.

9 Halldenius 2005; Radcliffe Richards 1985, p. 53; Wasserman 1998. I have suggested that a reasonable account of discrimination should specify where the badness lies, be context sensitive, not be conditioned on bad intention, offer a stable criterion for fairness, be resilient against unfair background factors, and contain a non-arbitrary and non-question begging principle for ground selection (Halldenius 2005).

10 Singer 1978, p. 202n.

11 Radcliffe Richards 1985, p. 53.

12 I will not dwell on the well-known suggestion that features that in principle can ground discrimination are such that they are immutable or that a person cannot help having them. If that which we try to explain is why things like sex and religion are on the list while left-handedness is not, these suggestions clearly will not work. A defence of immutability as a criterion in discrimination cases is in Hoffman 2011, and a critique is in Clarke 2015.

13 Moreau 2010, p. 149.

14 Lippert-Rasmussen 2014, p. 30.

15 Radcliffe Richards 1985, pp. 66 and 70.

16 Radcliffe Richards 1985, p. 75.

17 Remember also that Lippert-Rasmussen treats discrimination as morally neutral while Radcliffe Richards uses it as value laden.

18 The *International Declaration on Human Genetic Data*, UNESCO, 16 October 2003.

19 See also Halldenius 2007.

20 On the complexity of moral relevance for discrimination cases, see Nickel 1972. On the role of context for assessing relevance in moral terms, see Wasserstrom 1995.

21 See for example *UN Convention on the Rights of Persons with Disabilities*, 2006, article 27 (i).

22 A case raising similar questions is discussed by Schauer (2003). It concerns the Virginia Military Institute where only men were accepted onto the training program. It was claimed that certain skills were required and that women were less likely to have these skills, but evidence suggests that the Institute really wanted an all-male environment (Schauer 2003, 134–138). On the Swedish project for gender equality in the corps of firefighters, see Glans and Rother 2007.

23 Compare Hellman on discrimination conceived as inherently demeaning, 2008, pp. 35 and 172.

24 On the impact of implicit bias in discrimination cases, see Faigman et. al., 2008.
25 Wertheimer 1983.
26 Wertheimer 1983, p. 100.
27 See Bradley 1999, Chapter 5 for how background inequalities make differences relevant: "the assumption [is] that where such differences [in productivity enhancing characteristics] *do* exist and, howsoever derived (for example, as a consequence of unequal access to educational or training opportunities, or the gendered allocation of labour in the home) they *are* relevant to decision making, regardless of the gendered consequences which may flow from them".

Bibliography

Bradley, H. 1999. *Gender & Power in the Workplace. Analysing the Impact of Economic Change.* Basingstoke: MacMillan.

Cavanaugh, M. 2002. *Against Equality of Opportunity.* Oxford: Clarendon Press.

Clarke, J. A. 2015. "Against Immutability." *The Yale Law Journal.* 125(1): 2–102.

Dworkin, R. 1977. *Taking Rights Seriously.* London: Duckworth.

Faigman, D. L., Dasgupta, N., and Ridgeway, C. L. 2008. "A Matter of Fit: The Law of Discrimination and the Science of Implicit Bias." *University of California Hastings Law Journal.* 59(6): 1389–1434.

Glans, H. and Rother, B. 2007. *Bära slang som en man? En bok för aktivt jämställdhetsarbete i räddningstjänsten.* Karlstad: Räddningsverket.

Halldenius, L. 2005. "Dissecting Discrimination." *Cambridge Quarterly of Healthcare Ethics.* 14: 455–463.

Halldenius, L. 2007. "Genetic Discrimination". In Arnason, G., Arnason, V., Chadwick, R. and Häyry, M. (eds) *The Ethics and Governance of Human Genetic Databases: European Perspectives.* Cambridge: Cambridge University Press.

Hellman, D. 2008. *When is Discrimination Wrong?* Cambridge, MA: Harvard University Press.

Hoffman, S. 2011. "The Importance of Immutability in Employment Discrimination Law." *William & Mary Law Review.* 52(5): 1483–1546.

Lippert-Rasmussen, K. 2014. *Born Free and Equal?: A Philosophical Inquiry into the Nature of Discrimination.* Oxford: Oxford University Press.

Moreau, S. 2010. "What Is Discrimination?" *Philosophy & Public Affairs.* 38(2): 143–179.

Nickel, J. M. 1972. "Discrimination and Morally Relevant Characteristics." *Analysis.* 32(4): 113–114.

Radcliffe Richards, J. 1985. "Discrimination". *Proceedings of the Aristotelian Society, Supplementary Volumes.* 59: 53–83.

Schauer, F. 2003. *Profiles, Probabilities and Stereotypes.* Cambridge, MA: Harvard University Press.

Singer, P. 1978. "Is Racial Discrimination Arbitrary?" *Philosophia.* 8(1–2): 185–203.

Wasserman, D. 1998. "Concept of Discrimination". In Chadwick, R. (ed.) *Encyclopedia of Ethics.* San Diego: Academic Press.

Wasserstrom, R. 1995. "Preferential Treatment, Color-Blindness, and the Evils of Racism." In Cahn, S. (ed) *The Affirmative Action Debate.* New York: Routledge.

Wertheimer, A. 1983. "Jobs, Qualifications, and Preferences." *Ethics.* 94(1): 99–112.

Legal sources

Convention on the Rights of Persons with Disabilities, United Nations, 2006.

DIRECTIVE 2006/54/EC OF THE EUROPEAN PARLIAMENT AND OF THE COUNCIL of 5 July 2006, on the implementation of the principle of equal opportunities and equal treatment of men and women in matters of employment and occupation (recast). *Official Journal of the European Union,* 26.7.2006, L 204/23.

Diskrimineringslag. *Svensk Författningssamling* 2008: 567.

International Declaration on Human Genetic Data, UNESCO, 16 October 2003.

9

DISCRIMINATION AND DESERT

Andres Moles

CENTRAL EUROPEAN UNIVERSITY

Introduction

There are different views that purport to explain the wrongness of discrimination. An influential strategy appeals to some objectionable mental states of those who discriminate (Alexander 1992; Slavny and Parr 2015). Another popular view holds that discriminatory acts are wrong because of their objective meaning (Hellman 2008; Scanlon 2008; Chapter 7). Yet another view holds that discrimination is wrong when it has harmful effects (Lippert-Rasmussen 2014; Chapter 12). A fourth position points at the unfairness of discrimination that occurs when there is inequality of opportunity (Segall 2013; Chapter 11). The list, of course, is not exhaustive: there can be hybrid views that mix some of these elements or other factors that might be called upon.

In this chapter I will concentrate on arguments where desert plays an important role in explaining why discrimination is wrong. The first argument I will analyse concerns the distribution of economic benefits; in particular, access to jobs in competitive markets. According to this argument, desert explains why it is wrong, in principle, to refuse hiring the best-qualified candidate for a job.[1] The main idea is that a candidate who is best qualified for a job deserves it in virtue of the contribution that she makes to the satisfaction of other people's preferences. Well-functioning markets are closely linked to economic desert because they select the person who can best satisfy these preferences (cf. Chapter 25). Therefore, policies that permit offering jobs to less qualified candidates are, at least, presumptively wrong. Let's call it the 'economic desert' argument.

The main problem with this argument, I will argue, is that markets are unfit to track desert. I offer two reasons for why this is so. First, economic markets are insensitive to factors in virtue of which people become deserving. Although markets can track agents' contribution to supply others' demands, they are insensitive to purposeful effort, which also grounds desert. Second, markets are also insensitive to certain forms of luck that affect people's deserts.

The second part of the chapter analyses another discrimination argument where desert has a relevant role. Some people believe that "a world in which people are getting what they deserve is a better one than a world in which they are not" (Kagan 2012, 5). Clearly, things other than desert contribute to moral value. For instance, prioritarians argue that benefits (say, increased well-being) that accrue to the worse-off have more moral value than similar benefits to the better-off (cf. Chapter 11). By combining these two insights, desert prioritarians hold that a "given amount of well-being has greater moral value when it accrues to a badly-off, deserving person than it accrues to a well-off undeserving person" (Lippert-Rasmussen 2014, 166; see also Arneson 2007; Chapter 12). In this view, a discriminatory act can be bad when (and because) it brings about states of affairs that have less moral value than an alternative act.[2]

I will argue that desert prioritarianism has some counterintuitive implications and will suggest that we should abandon it. Instead, we should think about the wrongness of discrimination in terms of liability. The thought is that discriminators acquire certain duties in virtue of their discriminatory acts, and therefore they lack a legitimate complaint when they have to bear certain harms (for specific reasons).

I will proceed as follows. In the first section I clarify some issues that a plausible conception of desert must include. Then, I move on to analyse the economic desert claim. After laying out the argument for economic desert, I present, and dismiss, a conceptual objection to this view. After this I elaborate two objections to the idea that the best-qualified candidate has a claim to the job. One is that labor markets are unable to fully track economic desert: they are sensitive only to contribution, and not effort. The second objection is that forms of luck that affect people's desert are not captured by the best qualified principle. The last part of the chapter revises the desert prioritarian account of the wrongness of discrimination. In this section I argue that there are reasons to appeal to liability instead of desert. I sketch how these notions differ, and suggest that it will be costly for desert prioritarians to take up the liability view.

The idea of desert

The concept of desert usually consists in a relation among three elements: an agent, a treatment or good that is deserved, and the basis on which the agent is deserving (Feinberg 1970; Olsaretti 2004; Miller 1999; Feldman and Skow 2015). When we say that a person deserves a treatment X, we mean that it is fitting that she gets X (or that it is good that she gets X). One explanation of these kinds of judgments is that they square well with our basic moral phenomenology. Some authors make a connection between desert and 'appraisal attitudes' (Feinberg 1970, Miller 1999). In their view, both of these belong to a "complicated web of attitudes and feelings which form an essential part of the moral life as we know it" (Strawson 2008, 24).

The thought is that certain attitudes 'fit' some forms of conduct. It is fitting, for instance, to feel gratitude to a stranger who goes out of her way to help us when we are lost. At the fundamental level, these attitudes are not instrumental: we feel gratitude not because it has good consequences, such as making social relations easier (which it does), but because helpers deserve gratitude.

In order to make substantive judgments about when some treatment is justified by desert we need to elaborate (and defend) a conception of desert. A conception specifies the kinds of agents, treatments and basis that justify substantive desert-based judgments. In this section I sketch a conception of desert that includes three main features. Desert, in my view, has to be pre-institutional, distinctive and responsibility sensitive.

First, consider the distinction between institutional and pre-institutional desert. The former occurs when an institution sets up the criteria for desert. For instance, in competitive eating contests the person who swallows the largest amount of food in a given period of time deserves to win the contest.[3] If the institution ceases to exist or the rules are changed, then the criteria of desert will also disappear or change. Pre-institutional desert is, by contrast, more basic.[4] On the one hand, appealing to institutional rules is insufficient, and sometimes unnecessary, to understand desert claims. On the other hand, sometimes desert justifies the existence and rules of institutions. The admiration we feel for poetry justifies the existence of poetry contests and prizes.[5] Moreover, we can appeal to desert to criticize institutional rules that are not sufficiently sophisticated in tracking desert.

Consider, second, the idea that desert claims have to be distinctive. This feature is motivated because sometimes it is unclear whether desert judgments genuinely appeal to desert or are parasitic on other values (Olsaretti 2004). As an example, consider a sentence such as 'discrimination is wrong because everyone deserves an equal opportunity.' In this sentence desert does not play a distinctive role. The justification of the claim is not desert, but rather, a principle of equality of opportunity.[6] This consideration is important in the context of discrimination because we must be able to identify cases where discrimination is wrong because it fails to promote (or respect) desert. In the sentence above we can substitute 'deserves' with 'is entitled to' or 'should have' and nothing is lost. In cases of genuine desert, however, desert explains (or grounds) why the person should be treated as she deserves.

Third, desert claims have to be sensitive to responsibility. Miller argues that when genuine desert judgments are made, "some agent A is said to deserve some benefit B on the basis of an activity of performance P" (Miller 1999, 133). In his view, deserving agents must be responsible for the performance. Theories of responsibility differ in spelling out the necessary and sufficient conditions for responsibility. Thus, conceptions of desert will vary accordingly. Nevertheless, it seems clear that everyone assumes that some degree of control is necessary. One attractive feature of making desert conditional on responsibility is that it helps to explain why we tend to think that the mere possession of some properties (such as physical beauty) is insufficient to ground desert (even if it can ground admiration). Similarly, it explains Rawls' intuition that people do not become deserving because they are gifted (Rawls 1999, 89). Other circumstances where agents lack sufficient control over their performances include coerced actions (a cashier who hands over the money at gunpoint is fully excused and we do not think that she deserves criticism), and mere flukes (a footballer who scores a brilliant goal due to a sudden gust of wind does not deserve praise). Agents who lack the capacity for responsible agency also clearly fall outside of desert. We reprimand small children as a pedagogical strategy, but we do not think that they deserve to be reprimanded.

To sum up, I have argued that desert claims must be distinctive, pre-institutional and must track some form of responsibility. These features illuminate the 'fitness' relation between agents and their behavior. In making desert judgments, "we regard others as freely choosing agents like ourselves, and respond to their actions accordingly" (Miller 1999, 136).

One of the corollaries of subjecting desert to responsibility is that desert is always backward looking. For example, some theorists can justify higher wages to some workers in virtue of forward-looking considerations such as the effects of incentives. This justification is not open to desert theorists – at least not *qua* desert theorists. Higher wages must be justified by past performance. This feature will be further discussed in the following section.

Jobs and economic desert

This part of the chapter outlines the 'economic desert' argument and its relation to discrimination. Miller argues that desert can justify an anti-discrimination principle within labor markets (cf. Chapter 25). The principle holds that:

> candidate A deserves the job being offered when, on the basis of specific information about A's personal characteristics [...] he is the person likely to perform best in the job, once we discount illegitimate third-party reactions such as those stemming from racial or sexual prejudice.
>
> *(Miller 1999, 168–9)*

This view has some intuitive plausibility. In spite of its attractions, I will argue that the principle suffers from two main problems. On the one hand, the principle ignores effort as a plausible desert basis. On the other, it is unable to eliminate forms of luck that nullify desert.

Miller's principle is based on a restrictive view of desert that is grounded only in performances related to the job. It is implausible to think that judgments related to moral desert are relevant for hiring decisions. Consider the following:

> *Virtuocracy*. Adam and Ben apply for a job as a doctor. Both are equally well qualified, work equally hard, and will contribute to their patients' health to the same extent. Adam, however, is a great friend and a loving partner. Ben, on the other hand, is mischievous and has cheated on his partner on several occasions. The hiring committee decides to offer the job to Adam on those grounds.

Many will balk at the committee's decision. Since there is not a connection between being a good partner and being a good doctor, Ben's lack of desert as a partner should play no role in whether he deserves the job. The hiring committee's task is to assess Adam and Ben's deserts *qua* doctors, not *qua* partners. Perhaps it would be good if God arranged that Adam were happy and Ben unhappy.[7] Moral 'virtuocracy', however, gives no reason for action.[8] Even if it did give some reason it would not give a reason strong enough to generate a duty to hire Adam.

Economic desert is grounded in the contribution that agents make to the job requirements. Clearly, not everything that contributes to a person's job performance can ground desert. Contributions for which agents are not responsible must be excluded. No one deserves to play Queen Elizabeth II in a movie just because she looks like her (even if looks are relevant to the job). Nor does a person deserve a job because others will react favorably to one's ethnicity. The fact that Anna is a better waitress than José because the latter is Mexican, and customers prefer bars not waited by Mexicans, does not make Anna more deserving. More controversially, Rawls argues that since the mere possession of natural talents and the willingness to make effort are a matter of luck, benefits that flow from our talents are also not deserved (Rawls 1999, 89, 273–77).[9]

Miller suggests that job performance can be a basis for desert because jobs are socially valuable enterprises.[10] In societies where there is a labor market, jobs satisfy those activities for which there is social demand. The best-qualified candidate deserves a job because she is the person who can best contribute to social well-being by satisfying people's needs and preferences. It is controversial to think that there is value in the satisfaction of preferences independently from their content. We might plausibly think that the satisfaction of racist or sexist preferences has no value, so that jobs catering for these kinds of preferences would not generate desert claims. Imagine that a white supremacist magazine is hiring a new editor. The best-qualified candidate would not have a desert claim to the job, on the basis that he would increase sales better than others, because the desert basis would not be met: catering for white supremacist preferences is not valuable.

A well-functioning market is essential for this argument because it is the instrument by which the most deserving person is identified. Miller argues that "if we want to establish the relative value of *economic* contributions, then the market price of resulting good or service give us a nonarbitrary way of totaling up the value of a contribution to the many different people who may benefit from it" (Miller, 1999, 185, emphasis in original). By appealing to markets, Miller is able to rebut moralized accounts of value such as the one suggested in the previous paragraph.[11]

Desert and future performance

Since desert is backward looking, it is puzzling that someone can deserve a job when the performance has not yet occurred. Imagine that Leo has played wonderful football for years, but before signing a new contract suffers a crippling injury. Although he might deserve a prize for his past performance, he does not deserve a job: he is now unable to perform. Unlike deserving a prize, where the desert judgment is straightforward, deserving a job involves a secondary judgment of desert, linking backward-looking desert and forward-looking performance. The thought is that selectors use past performance as a proxy to predict future performance, and that this makes the candidate deserving (Miller 1999, 162). The best-qualified candidate has a claim to the job because it is more likely that she will deserve the intrinsic and extrinsic rewards that come with her position on the basis of her performance, than if a less qualified candidate is chosen (Clayton 2012, 422). It is in this sense that the best-qualified candidate deserves "the chance of becoming deserving" by putting in worthy performances (Miller 1999, 167). If this argument is sound, then it should be clear why discriminating against the best-qualified candidate is objectionable. Discrimination "predictably creates a state of affairs in which there is a discrepancy between deserts and income rewards [or jobs]" (Miller 1999, 166).

Notice, first, that the economic desert argument has a limited scope (cf. Introduction). It does not aim to give a general theory of discrimination: it does not claim that discrimination is wrong when and because it deprives persons of what they deserve. Needless to say, discrimination operates in many areas where desert is irrelevant: the disenfranchisement of women until the twentieth century did not depend on desert claims. This is because competent adults are entitled to vote for desert-independent reasons. Similarly, racial segregation by housing does not depend on desert. No one has a desert claim to live in a particular neighborhood. Second, the argument only states a sufficient condition: discrimination is wrong when it prevents people from getting their deserts, but it might be wrong even if people get their deserts.

A conceptual objection

A conceptual objection to Miller's claim that denying a job to the most deserving candidate wrongfully discriminates against her is that it uses an inadequately broad notion of discrimination. Some authors argue that discrimination necessarily focuses on socially salient groups. Group discrimination involves treating a person in some way because she is (or is thought to be) a member of a group that is socially salient (Lippert-Rasmussen 2014, 26–36). Social salience means that a "perceived membership of [a group] is important to the structure of social interactions across a wide range of social contexts" (Lippert-Rasmussen 2014, 30). Since the best-qualified candidates are not a socially salient group they cannot be objects of discrimination. Defenders of the group condition argue that normative worries about discrimination are focused on group membership. One reason for this is that we tend to think that discrimination is *prima facie* objectionable, whereas treating people differently is not: the fact that I spend more time with my children than with other children is not even presumptively objectionable (Lippert-Rasmussen 2014, 14–15). Now consider:

> *Horoscope*: Eva, a deserving university candidate, is refused a place because the admissions clerk thinks that candidates born under Sagittarius bring bad luck.

On the group-based view of discrimination, the clerk does not discriminate because being born under Sagittarius is not socially relevant across a wide range of social interactions. She only engages in idiosyncratic differential treatment. Of course, this does not mean that the clerk does not act wrongly by violating a principle of procedural fairness.

There are two possible replies to the objection that not offering the job to the deserving candidate does not constitute an act of discrimination. First, we could challenge the group-based condition of discrimination and insist that differential treatment is a form of discrimination.[12] Since many forms of differential treatment are acceptable, this move would imply that discrimination does not pick presumptively wrongful treatment. Some people might be willing to bite this bullet. Alternatively, one could appeal to a moralized definition of discrimination according to which discrimination involves wrongful differential treatment: whenever a person wrongfully treats people differently, she engages (by definition) in discrimination. The second variation suffers from a problem common to all moralized definitions. By introducing a normative component into the definition of discrimination, it eludes the important question of what makes differential treatment wrong. One risk with this type of objection is that we might think there is a substantive dispute, when we merely have a verbal disagreement (Chalmers 2011). We might agree that it is wrong to reject Eva, but disagree about whether this constitutes discrimination. I suspect that this kind of conceptual inquiry has limited interest. The question, 'What is discrimination?' is of little significance to those who aim to understand what the wrong properties of various forms of differential treatment are. Whether we call it 'discrimination' or not is of lesser importance.

Contribution, effort and desert

The economic desert argument holds that the best-qualified candidate deserves the job she applied for on the basis of her future performance. A second objection to this argument casts doubts on the idea that contribution, and contribution only, makes workers deserving. This seems too narrow. Intuitively, we are inclined to think that making an effort grounds desert too. For example, Rawls argues that "[t]he precept which seems intuitively to come closest to rewarding moral desert is that of distribution according to effort, or perhaps better, conscientious effort" (Rawls 1999, 274). Imagine this:

> *Tennis*. Robin is a talented, but not very hard-working, tennis player. Kevin, a second tennis player, is less talented but is hard-working. When they compete, Robin plays better and beats Kevin.

Intuitively, many of us think that because of his efforts, Kevin is to some extent deserving even if he plays worse than Robin. Clearly, pure effort is insufficient to create desert: a person who tries to write a poem with no aesthetic merit at all has no deserts. Similarly, effort towards a worthless activity is insufficient for desert. Someone who strives to count all the blades of grass in a field does not become deserving. Any effort they put into it is a waste (Rawls 1999, 379; Mason 2006, 46). So, this suggests that effort has a conditional relation to desert. When a person makes a contribution and puts effort into it, she deserves more than a person who makes a similar contribution with less effort. This hybrid view of desert (which includes both contribution and effort) raises difficulties for the principle that the best-qualified candidate has a claim to be appointed, because it is difficult to imagine that labor markets can track both elements of desert. Markets are sensitive to contribution by balancing demand and supply, but they seem incapable of tracking effort. Open competitions for jobs cannot establish how deserving Kevin is, either absolutely, or in relation to Robin. Now, Miller could insist that desert concerns only contribution and not effort. But, without further argument, this response is question begging.

Desert and luck

One reason to think that effort can be a basis for desert has to do with the effects of luck. It is often the case that people's performances are affected by luck. Miller distinguishes between two types of luck. First, 'integral luck' is the type of luck that affects the performance 'itself' of an activity (Miller 2004, 143). This kind of luck can frustrate the performance of an otherwise deserving agent. For example, the runner who stumbles upon a pebble on the verge of breaking the world record can still be deserving. Integral luck can also improve the performance of an otherwise undeserving agent; for example, a mediocre archer can get lucky by hitting the bull's-eye, and winning the competition. Despite being the winner, he does not deserve it. Miller acknowledges that integral luck nullifies desert (Miller 1999, 144–6). The real issue, then, is whether labor markets can factor out integral luck. A person can make a bad impression in a job interview by being too nervous, or some of her qualifications might have been affected by luck. Market mechanisms are not well-suited for detecting these facts.

Second, sometimes it is a matter of luck that a person has the opportunity to perform. Imagine that the deserving runner's plane is delayed and he does not show up on time. If he had run the race, he would have broken the world record. But he could not participate. Miller calls this 'circumstantial luck' (Miller 1999, 143). Miller argues that circumstantial luck does not affect desert. This is because desert has to be grounded on actual rather than hypothetical performance. Someone who would have performed well, but who did not perform at all, has no basis for desert. This claim is crucial for the best-qualified argument. It implies that selectors have to decide who deserves the job among the set of those who actually applied for the job. Someone who would be better qualified, but did not apply is not wronged by not being selected. This sounds plausible. Consider, however, cases where the person suffers bad circumstantial luck that prevents her from being better qualified for a job she would like to perform. Societies where people's qualifications are partly determined by their social circumstances strike us as especially unfair. So, when a person coming from a disadvantaged background cannot compete with those who got better education due to their social circumstances, we tend to think that the 'best qualified' principle loses force. Although circumstantial luck might not nullify desert, it might make desert-based principles unjustified. Consider cases of positive discrimination (cf. Chapters 33, 34):

> *Doctors*. There are two candidates for a job as a general practitioner. Elsa, a working class young doctor, is a good candidate but not as good as John who comes from a privileged background. Imagine also that there are weighty reasons to increase the overall number of female and working class doctors employed in the public health care system. It seems that discriminating against John violates the best-qualified principle.

Is offering the job to Elsa justified? One reply is to offer a conditional rendering of desert, according to which desert principles have force only when further constraints are satisfied. We might think, for example, that we should hire the best qualified only against a background of fair equality of opportunity (Clayton 2012). The plausibility of this response depends on how, exactly, fair equality of opportunity is spelt out. It might be a weaker principle requiring only the mitigation of social inequalities (Mason 2006), or a more ambitious principle requiring the neutralization of all sources of unchosen inequality (Segall 2013). Clearly, the broader the scope of equal opportunity, the harder it will be for desert principles to make a difference to our judgments.

A second response claims that desert is an unconditional, but defeasible principle. Discriminating against John is *pro tanto* wrong, but all things considered, permissible. So, from the point of view of desert, John should get the job. Desert, however, can be defeated by other considerations. This solution is attractive to value pluralists who think that normative judgments usually involve striking a balance between competing considerations or values. Now, those who endorse desert principles will insist that these principles must be sufficiently robust. That is, they might insist that even if desert considerations can sometimes be defeated, they should be weighty enough to determine, all things considered, judgments (such as the thought that the best-qualified candidate has a claim to get the job). Conceding too much to this objection amounts to a pyrrhic victory for desert.

A third strategy aims to accommodate positive discrimination within a desert theory. The claim that John is more deserving because he has better qualifications is not the only desert judgment we can make. Perhaps more complex desert judgments can justify offering the job to Elsa. For instance, let's assume that more resources have been spent on John's qualifications than on hers. Perhaps the state pours more money into public schools serving well-off neighborhoods, or perhaps John's parents bought him better qualifications through private schools and internships (cf. Chapter 26). So, we might think that relative to their potential, Elsa is more deserving than John. We might think that Elsa is more deserving of an opportunity to become deserving than John is, by virtue of how she has developed her potential (Miller 1999, 175–6). One problem with this reply is that it does not address cases where it is stipulated that the best-qualified candidate will also be the best doctor. We might think that we should still offer the job to Elsa even if John will always be a better doctor. A second problem is that the reply seems *ad hoc*. If it is legitimate to distribute jobs in relation to potential in the case of Elsa, why not generalize it? Instead of offering jobs to the best-qualified candidate, we might offer them to the candidate who is likely to achieve more in relation to their potential.

Friends of economic desert can still salvage the claim that it is wrong to deny the job to the best-qualified applicant on desert grounds, by conceding that markets are the wrong instrument to track desert. If this objection is correct, then I have not refuted the economic desert argument, but only Miller's claim that job markets identify deserving agents. There are two problems with this reply. First, it is difficult to imagine a non-market based institution that could track *economic* desert with sufficient reliability, or at least as reliably as markets do. Second, even if such an institution could de designed, there are weighty non-desert-based reasons in favor of markets. Some luck egalitarians plausibly believe that it is fair that the opportunity costs of people's choices and ambitions reflect the costs that these choices impose on other people (Dworkin 2000, Chapter 2). If this is correct, then markets are an essential component of fairness. This presents a dilemma for those who advocate the economic desert argument because they need to choose between fairness and desert. Choosing desert over fairness seems far too costly. So, perhaps they would choose fairness (and markets) and hold that there is a residual wrongness in not giving people what they deserve. This concession implies that the economic desert argument has no practical implications.

To sum up, societies where access to advantages such as jobs is distributed through market mechanisms (even if they are regulated) will fail to treat people as they deserve. This is because some grounds for desert, and some forms of luck, are beyond market mechanisms. From what I have argued, it does not follow that we should not appoint the best-qualified candidate. For instance, in *Doctors* patients might have a justified complaint if John is not hired, on the grounds that they will receive worse treatment. This complaint, however, has nothing to do with desert but with the effects of discrimination.

Desert or liability?

As we saw in the previous sections, the economic desert argument is unconvincing because contribution is too narrow for a desert basis, and because the argument cannot properly address issues of luck. In the face of these difficulties, perhaps we might try to formulate anti-discrimination principles in relation to the harmful outcomes they bring about (cf. Chapter 12). Lippert-Rasmussen, for instance, thinks that "an instance of discrimination is wrong, when it is, because it makes people worse off, i.e., they are worse off given the presence of discrimination than they would have been in some suitable alternative situation in which the relevant instance of discrimination had not taken place" (Lippert-Rasmussen 2014, 154–5). This account belongs to the family of harm-based accounts, because harm is understood as worsening people's situations against a baseline where this act token does not occur (Lippert-Rasmussen 2014, 157–60). Since Lippert-Rasmussen's is the most sophisticated version of this account, it will be the focus of this section. I will argue, however, that despite its initial attractiveness, Lippert-Rasmussen's view has some counter-intuitive implications that can be avoided by appealing to liability rather than desert.

Lippert-Rasmussen endorses a desert-catering prioritarianism according to which,

> [a]n act is morally right if, and only if, it maximizes moral value. The moral value involved in an action depends on three factors: (i) the greater the well-being for individuals affected by the act, the greater the moral value, (ii) the lower the level of well-being of those to whom additional units of well-being accrues, the greater the moral value, and (iii) the more deserving those to whom additional units of well-being accrues, the greater the moral value.
>
> *(Lippert-Rasmussen 2014, 166; see also Arneson 1999)*[13]

Desert-sensitive prioritarianism condemns discrimination because it fails to maximize value. It is easy to see how discrimination can be harmful. For instance, paying higher wages to men than to women who perform the same work harms women who are worse off (and *ex hypothesis*, no less deserving). This account also explains nicely why it is permissible to offer the job to Elsa in *Doctors*. Since women are worse off than men, there is more value in offering jobs to the former than to the latter.

Consider now a case similar to *Doctors*, but instead of Elsa, imagine that a clearly unqualified woman applies. In this case, prioritarianism recommends offering the job to John since having unqualified doctors is harmful for third parties. Prioritarianism can also be combined with a Miller type of desert principle. Since priority and desert are both independent values, we can combine them. We might hold that John is more deserving than Elsa by virtue of his better qualifications, but benefits to Elsa are more important than benefits to John because she is worse off.[14] Lippert-Rasmussen does not appeal to desert in Miller's sense. He introduces desert because prioritarianism can lead to counter-intuitive results. Consider:

> *Boris and Dalma*: Boris discriminates against Dalma. In a possible world, imagine that Boris ends up being badly off, and Dalma ends up better off. Let's say that the public finds out that Boris discriminates against females, shuns his shop, and he goes bust. Dalma successfully applies for a second job and thrives. In a second scenario, Dalma is unemployed, and Boris thrives (as much as Dalma thrived in the first scenario).

From the point of view of priority these two scenarios contain the same amount of moral value. If there was some benefit to be distributed, we should be indifferent between giving it to Boris in the first scenario, or to Dalma in the second. Intuitively, though, we think that we should benefit Dalma rather than Boris. Lippert-Rasmussen's explanation is that the second world is morally worse because Boris is less deserving than Dalma.

I believe that, in this case, Lippert-Rasmussen's account delivers the right verdict. However, there might be alternative explanations that generate this result and that have additional merits over desert prioritarianism (for an analogous strategy see Tadros 2017). Consider a case where a person faultlessly discriminates against another.

> *Aversive racism*: Lars wants to hire a junior professor. Two equally well-qualified candidates apply. Jasmine has great research potential and mediocre teaching prospects. Anna, on the other hand, shows mediocre research potential but great teaching prospects. Assume also that Jasmine is black, and Anna is white. Lars concludes that teaching weighs more than research and offers the job to Anna. *Ex hypothesis*, had Jasmine been white and Anna black, he would have considered research weightier. Lars has egalitarian convictions and has taken precautions against discrimination and has also evaluated the applications carefully.[15]

Let's say that Lars is an aversive racist, that is, a person who is explicitly egalitarian and non-prejudiced who nevertheless "possess[es] conflicting, often non-conscious negative feelings and beliefs about Blacks that are rooted in basic psychological processes that promote racial bias" (Pearson et. al. 2009, 3–4; Chapter 32). Lars neither endorses nor identifies with his prejudiced response. Moreover, he has taken precautions to neutralize his implicit biases, such as reading about biases or avoiding exposure to sources of bias. For these reasons his offering the job to Anna does not affect his level of desert: he is not at fault for discriminating against Jasmine. Imagine now, that we could benefit either Jasmine or Lars. Other things being equal, defenders of desert prioritarianism will argue that we should be indifferent between them. That is, since both are equally well-off and equally deserving, the moral value of benefits to either of them counts the same. In my judgment, however, we should still benefit Jasmine. The reason is that by harming Jasmine, Lars becomes liable to absorb some harm that would, otherwise, fall on her. The fact that he is not at fault (and therefore, no less deserving) is irrelevant. This is because, unlike desert, liability is not based on fault.[16]

Imagine a case where a group's range of occupational choices is restricted in ways which mean that moral value is maximized.

> *Governesses*: Middle-class women are discriminated against obtaining full-time jobs unless they spend time volunteering as governesses for disadvantaged children.[17]

Let's assume that the level of well-being of these women is higher than the level of well-being of these children, and will remain so during their lifetimes (or whatever period of comparison is correct). Let's also assume that these women are no less deserving than these children. In such situations desert prioritarianism seems to be compatible with upholding the occupational restrictions.

One reason why *Governesses* is wrong is that women are not liable to suffer harms for the sake of benefitting these children. Since I am assuming that the middle-class women have not disadvantaged these children, nor have they benefitted from any injustice done to them, it seems wrong to justify this form of discrimination on the fact that it maximizes moral value. Of course, this situation could be easier to justify if things were different. For instance, if they had a duty to benefit these children, then perhaps the case would be permissible. The explanation is, again, that under some circumstances, people become liable to suffer some harms for the sake of others.

Desert and liability can be confused for semantic reasons, but they are distinct notions. Typically, desert gives us a positive reason to treat people as they deserve. For instance, we might think the world is better when Boris is harmed just because he deserves it. Liability, on the other hand does not imply such as a positive reason. Rather, it means that a person is not wronged when she is harmed (for a specific reason) in particular circumstances (McMahan 2005). So, in *Boris and Dalma*, Boris is not wronged when he foregoes the benefit that goes to Dalma. He would, however, be wronged if the harm were avoidable.

Desert prioritarianism emphatically denies having this implication. Lippert-Rasmussen writes that, "saying that [it would be better if the harm follows on the less deserving] is not saying that it is in some way good if the harm falls on the discriminator – it is simply less bad that it falls on him" (Lippert-Rasmussen 2014, 166). Perhaps Lippert-Rasmussen, along with Richard Arneson, refers to 'liability' when they use 'desert'. If this is so, their usage is non-conventional. This is all very fine, as I mentioned earlier, little normative progress is achieved by analysing concepts. There is, however, a difference between the type of liability-based arguments I have offered and Lippert-Rasmussen's desert prioritarian account. Liability considerations are not consequentialist and are not concerned with promoting moral value. For those who are sympathetic to the liability account, we can remain agnostic about whether the world in which Boris is harmed has less value than the world in which Dalma is harmed. In order to understand what makes discrimination wrong, we need to focus on moral factors other than the badness of its consequences.

Conclusion

The findings of this chapter have been mostly negative. I have argued that neither the economic desert argument, nor the desert prioritarian harm account are fully convincing. I have given some reasons to think that liability and equal opportunity might provide accounts for understanding the wrongness of discrimination. Defending these views will have to wait for another occasion.[18]

Notes

1 Desert can also justify wage inequalities. But I will set this issue aside.

2 Although, for simplicity, I will focus on acts of discrimination, it is also possible to appeal to rules of discrimination instead. I don't think this affects the arguments I make in this chapter.

3 Institutional desert is different from institutional entitlement because a person can be entitled to some benefit without deserving it (in the institutional sense). A football team that wins a match because the referee wrongly awarded a goal in their favor is entitled to win, even if they do not deserve it.

4 Since I focus on pre-institutional desert, I will refer to it simply as 'desert.'

5 Controversially, I do not think there is any pre-institutional conception of desert that justifies the existence of competitive eating.

6 Miller calls these cases 'sham desert' (Miller, 1999, 137–8).

7 In this chapter I am agnostic about this claim.

8 The term 'virtuocracy' is taken from Lippert-Rasmussen 2014, 260.

9 Discussing Rawls's rejection of desert transcends the aims of this chapter. For instructive discussion see Miller 1999; Olsaretti 2004; Moriarty 2002.

10 A different view is that successful performance generates desert claims on its own by displaying mastery and skill. An implication of this view is that a criminal who masterminded a robbery deserves a bigger share of the loot than those who played a smaller role. I will set this question aside.

11 Relying on markets also enables him to reject the perfectionist objection according to which it is implausible to think that "a man who supplies matches to millions and thereby earns $200,000 a year

is worth more 'to society' than a man who supplies great wisdom or exquisite pleasures to a few thousand and thereby earns $20,000 a year" (Hayek, F. *Law, Legislation and Liberty* II, 76. Quoted by Miller 1999, 184).

12 Lippert-Rasmussen argues that differential treatment is 'generic discrimination,' (Lippert-Rasmussen 2014, 15-22).

13 Lippert-Rasmussen does not spell out what is the basis for desert. He (along with Arneson) seems to appeal to moral desert: the idea that it is the moral character of their actions that defines people's deserts. It is unfortunate that Lippert-Rasmussen does not develop further his account of desert.

14 This illustrates the second *pro tanto*, strategy described on page 25–26.

15 This case is inspired by Shin 2010.

16 To see this, consider cases where a person is liable to some harm if she has a duty to suffer this harm in order to spare someone else from suffering a bigger harm. It is permissible to bruise Miles in order to save Nick from losing a limb. This is true independently of whether Miles is guilty or responsible for the threat that Nick faces (Tadros 2012).

17 This case is inspired by Ferracioli 2015.

18 For valuable comments, I would like to thank members of the POLEMO research group at CEU, Kasper Lippert-Rasmussen, Tom Parr, János Kis and an anonymous referee.

Bibliography

Alexander, L. 1992. "What Makes Wrongful Discrimination Wrong? Biases, Preferences, Stereotypes, and Proxies." *University of Pennsylvania Law Review*. 141: 149–219.

Arneson, R. 1999. "Egalitarianism and Responsibility." *Journal of Ethics*. 3: 225–247.

Arneson, R. 2007. "Desert and Equality." In Holtug, N., and Lippert-Rasmussen, K. (eds.) *Egalitarianism*. Oxford: Oxford University Press.

Chalmers, D. 2011. "Verbal Disputes." *Philosophical Review*. 120: 515–566.

Clayton, M. 2012. "On Widening Participation in Higher Education Through Positive Discrimination." *Journal of Philosophy of Education*. 46: 414–431.

Dworkin, R. 2000. *Sovereign Virtue*. Cambridge: Harvard University Press.

Feinberg, J. 1970. "Justice and Personal Desert." In *Doing and Deserving*. Princeton: Princeton University Press.

Ferracioli, L. 2015. "Review of *Born Free and Equal?: A Philosophical Inquiry into the Nature of Discrimination*." *Economics and Philosophy*. 31: 486–492.

Hellman, D. 2008. *When Is Discrimination Wrong?* Cambridge: Harvard University Press.

Kagan, S. 2012. *The Geometry of Desert*. Oxford: Oxford University Press.

Lippert-Rasmussen, K. 2014. *Born Free and Equal? A Philosophical Inquiry into the Nature of Discrimination*. Oxford: Oxford University Press.

Mason, A. 2006. *Leveling the Playing Field*. Oxford: Oxford University Press.

McMahan, J. 2005. "Just Cause for War." *Ethics & International Affairs*. 19: 1–21.

Miller, D. 1999. *Principles of Social Justice*. Cambridge: Harvard University Press.

Moriarty, J. 2002. "Desert and Distributive Justice in *A Theory of Justice*." *Journal of Social Philosophy*. 33: 131–143.

Olsaretti, S. 2004. *Liberty, Desert and the Market*. Cambridge: Cambridge University Press.

Pearson, A., Dovidio, J., and Gaertner, S. 2009. "The Nature of Contemporary Prejudice: Insights from Aversive Racism." *Social and Personality Compass*. 3: 1–25.

Rawls, J. 1999. *A Theory of Justice*. Oxford: Oxford University Press.

Scanlon, T. 2008. *Moral Dimensions*. Cambridge: Harvard University Press.

Segall, S. 2013. *Equality and Opportunity*. Oxford: Oxford University Press.

Shin, P. 2010. "Liability for Unconscious Discrimination? A Thought Experiment in the Theory of Employment Discrimination Law." *Hastings Law Journal*. 62: 66–101.

Slavny, A. and Parr, T. 2015. "Harmless Discrimination." *Legal Theory*. 21: 100–114.

Strawson, P. 2008. "Freedom and Resentment." In *Freedom and Resentment and Other Essays*. London: Routledge.

Tadros, V. 2012. "Duty and Liability." *Utilitas*. 24: 259–277.

Tadros, V. 2017. "Moving Mountains: Variation on a Theme by Shelly Kagan." *Criminal Law and Philosophy*. 11: 393–405.

10

DISCRIMINATION AND RIGHTS

Peter Vallentyne

UNIVERSITY OF MISSOURI

Introduction

Discrimination can create serious injustices—ones for which there is often a moral duty to reduce or counteract the associated harms. Nonetheless, I claim that there is no kind of non-moralized discrimination for which there is a *general moral right* not to be discriminated against by private citizens. All that matters for justice is that people get their fair share of resources (including social resources, such as opportunities) and this is compatible with being subject to discrimination.

I will only be clarifying and motivating this claim, not defending it (except perhaps in a minor way). I will simply assume that individuals have a robust right to a fair share of resources, and I will give some examples where, I claim, there is no right against even despicable forms of discrimination. Dealing with discrimination via appeal to fair shares of resources is a well-known strategy, and it is subject to important objections. My goal here is extremely modest. It is simply to clarify and motivate the approach to discrimination issues based on a fair share of resources. I will not be resolving any of the difficult substantive issues.

My focus throughout is on whether there is a general moral right against discrimination. I will not be discussing any of the important issues concerning legal rights against discrimination.

Discrimination

I will argue that there is no kind of non-discrimination, in a non-moralized sense, for which individuals have a general moral right that others not discriminate against them in that way. I shall do this by focusing on the very worst kind of discrimination—having all the problematic features that are sometimes invoked. If there is no general right against such discrimination, there is, I claim, no general right (independent of contractual obligations, etc.) against any kind of discrimination.

I shall focus on despicable discrimination, where this is (1) harmful differential treatment of someone, (2) due to her membership in a significant and salient social group, (3) where the person is treated—subjectively (e.g., intentionally) and intersubjectively (e.g., in terms of social meanings)—with contempt (i.e., as though she had diminished moral status) and animosity on account of her group membership, and (4) the treatment makes the person more vulnerable to empirical domination (or subordination or oppression) by others. (Here I incorporate features discussed in Young 1990, Hellman 1998, and Lippert-Rasmussen 2014.) This should be understood as including the effects and expressive force of institutional discrimination, which need not involve any animosity, contempt, etc. on the part of the discriminator. I focus on cases where both the social meaning and the discriminator's meaning involve animosity and contempt so as to make the discrimination as morally problematic as possible.

Readers are free to add on additional conditions. The only stipulation I make is that discrimination is to be understood in the *non-moralized sense* that it is not a conceptual truth that discrimination in this sense *pro tanto* infringes someone's moral rights (instead, it depends on what the correct substantive moral principles are). Understanding discrimination as a kind of wrongful (rights-infringing) differential treatment would trivialize the question of whether discrimination infringes someone's rights, and shift the question to whether there is any discrimination so understood. It seems clearer to understand discrimination in a non-moralized sense.

Rights and wronging

Most people (e.g., Hellman 2008) think that despicable discrimination is morally wrong. The most natural thought is that it is wrong because it *wrongs the discriminatee*, that is, it infringes a right she has not to be so treated. I claim, however, that there is no general *moral right* against (non-moralized) despicable discrimination. In this section I clarify how I understand rights. Throughout, I am only concerned with moral rights (e.g., as opposed to legal rights). For simplicity, I focus on a choice-protecting (as opposed to an interest-protecting) conception of rights, but my core points apply to both.

In the broadest sense, a right is any of the four Hohfeldian normative advantages, or any combination thereof: *claim-rights* over the actions of others (e.g., a claim-right that others not discriminate in certain ways), *liberty-rights* over one's actions (e.g., a liberty-right to hire whom one wants), *powers to change* normative relations (e.g., making a contractual commitment not to discriminate), and *immunities* to such change (e.g., no non-contractual loss of one's claim-right against discrimination of a certain type). Our focus is on claim-rights that others not discriminate against one, and rights should be so understood in what follows. (See Kramer, Simmonds, and Steiner 1998 for a superb analysis of various aspects of rights.)

What, then, is a claim-right? One has a claim-right that an agent not do something just in case the agent *owes one a duty* not to do that something. The agent's doing that something *wrongs one* (and similarly for a right that the agent does something). That is to say that it is *pro tanto* (*prima facie*) wrong (impermissible) for the agent to do that something *without suitable authorization* from that person. For example, you have claim-right that I not slap your back. It is *pro tanto* wrong for me to slap your back without your authorization (i.e., valid consent), but it need not be *pro tanto* wrong for me to do so with your authorization. The *pro tanto* constraint protects *you* in the sense that it does not apply when the action (or failure of action) *is authorized by you*. For simplicity, we can here assume that authorization, for autonomous beings, is given by their valid consent (e.g., as opposed to advancing their interests), but nothing here depends on this.

Rights need only have *pro tanto* force in that it may be permissible to infringe them when there is an overriding justification (e.g., killing one person to save a million lives). Even when it is permissible to infringe a right, however, the rightholder is wronged. For example, the infringing agent may owe the rightholder a duty to rectify the situation (e.g., apologize and provide compensation), at least in those cases where he is suitably responsible for the harm from the infringement.

So, an action can wrong someone (infringe her rights) and still be permissible. It is also conceptually possible for an action to be wrong (impermissible) even though it wrongs no one. This can be so if there are *impersonal wrongs*, which are actions that are wrong even if they wrong no one (e.g., destroying an ancient religious relic, even if no one fully owns it and no one's interests, now or in the future, are adversely affected). I'm skeptical of such impersonal wrongs, but I do not address them here.

Compared with the claim that such discrimination is typically permissible, my claim that there is no right against discrimination is weaker in one sense and stronger in another. It is weaker, since it is compatible with discrimination typically being impersonally wrong. It is stronger in that it denies that discrimination as such even *pro tanto* wrongs the discriminatee (and thus overriding justifications are irrelevant).

I focus on *general* moral rights against discrimination, where these are rights that all right-bearers have, except as lost consensually (e.g., contractually) or in virtue of unrectified past wrongings. I do not question that some individuals have rights against discrimination against specific individuals, in virtue of a contract or owed rectification for a past wronging.

Finally, I do not assume that rights must be *enforceable*—that is, that the rightholder (or someone she has authorized) has a liberty-right to use force to prevent the infringement. Although I believe that rights are typically accompanied by such enforcement rights, I deny that this is a conceptual necessity. Nothing in my argument, however, depends on this.

Some problems with despicable discrimination

Consider an employer's refusal to hire the most qualified applicant because of her race, where (1) this disadvantages the applicant (e.g., because her other opportunities are not as good), (2) the employer intends this refusal to express his contempt and animosity toward the applicant because of her race, (3) this is also the social meaning attached to the act, and (4) the act is part of a racist system of domination. This despicable discrimination is morally problematic in several respects.

First, such discrimination is *morally undesirable*. It harms the discriminatee, expresses a mistaken view of her moral status, and creates or supports problems for social cooperation. That, however, leaves open whether it *wrongs* the discriminatee to perform such actions. Not everything that is morally undesirable need wrong someone. It may be morally undesirable for me to decline to help my neighbor shovel her snow, but it need not wrong her.

Second, such despicable discrimination may be impersonally wrong, even if it wrongs no one. As indicated above, I'm skeptical that there are any impersonal wrongs, but here I leave open this possibility.

Third, such despicable discrimination typically creates serious problems of injustice, for which the discriminator and others may have a moral duty to provide additional resources to offset the harms imposed. Even if (as I shall claim) despicable discrimination need not wrong the discriminatee, it harms her and often leaves her with less than her *fair share of resources* (where this includes social resources, such as opportunities). When this is so, she has a right against certain others that they provide her with additional resources. (One possibility is that she has this right against the discriminator, even if his discrimination does not wrong her. I shall suggest, however, that she has this right against those who have more than their fair share of resources.)

Our question is *not* whether despicable discrimination is (1) morally undesirable (it is), (2) impersonally wrong (I doubt it, but I leave this open), or (3) generates duties in others to provide additional resources to offset the harms imposed (it does). Our question is whether despicable discrimination wrongs (i.e., infringes a right of) the individuals discriminated against.

Here we need to distinguish between the actions of private citizens and those of government officials in their official capacities. There are many controversial issues concerning the proper role of government, but it seems quite plausible that the government owes a duty to its citizens not to engage in various forms of discrimination, including despicable discrimination. In addition, it seems plausible that governments are morally permitted (and perhaps owe a duty to their citizens) to require all *government contractors* not to engage in despicable and other kinds of discrimination. (Given that no one need be a government contractor, the government is permitted, within reason, to promote justice by imposing conditions on contractors.) Indeed, the government might also be morally permitted to require this of all *corporations*, as a condition of incorporation (which grants legal limited liability). In what follows, however, I shall focus on private discrimination, understood as excluding government officials, and employers who contract with the government, acting in these capacities.

So, our question is whether there is a right, against *private individuals* (either in their private lives, or in their public business lives), that they not engage in despicable discrimination. For brevity, let this be implicitly understood below.

Despicable discrimination sometimes *contingently* infringes the rights of others. This happens, for example, when the discrimination involves wrongful physical force, when the discriminator has a contractual duty not to discriminate, or when she has a duty of rectification (for a past wrong) not to do so. I therefore set aside such cases in what follows. Our question is whether despicable discrimination *as such* (always) infringes the rights of the person discriminated against, that is, whether there is a general right not to be despicably discriminated against.

There is no right against discrimination

Individuals, I assume, have some *negative (claim) rights* to their bodies and to certain things. These include the right not to be killed or assaulted and the right that others not use, damage, or destroy certain objects. What makes a right a negative right is a bit murky, but here I simply mean (roughly) that the rights are not infringed by a choice that initiates no new causal impacts on the world (beyond those of the mere presence of the agent's body in its current state). For example, your right that I (as an agent) not kill you is a *negative right*, since it is not infringed by my current choice, if it initiates no new causal impacts on you (e.g., I choose not to turn the trolley track to save your life). (Of course, some earlier choice of mine may infringe your negative right, as when I earlier turn the trolley switch so as to kill you, and then do nothing to change it back.) By contrast, *positive rights* can be infringed by a choice, even if it initiates no new causal impacts on you (e.g., your positive right to be saved is infringed, if I choose not to turn the trolley track to save your life).

The right against discrimination is a *positive right*, since it can be infringed by a choice that initiates no new causal impacts. Choosing not to initiate the hiring process, for example, can be a way of discriminating against someone. It can thus infringe a right of non-discrimination.

I claim (1) that there is a positive right to a fair share of resources, and (2) if there is such a positive right, then there is no (positive) right against despicable (or any other kind of) discrimination. I will explain, but not defend the first claim, and I will motivate, but not fully defend, the second claim.

Individuals, I assume, have a *right to a fair share of resources*. This right is sensitive to the adverse effects of discrimination, but it is compatible with despicable discrimination not wronging anyone, because its adverse effects can, in principle, be offset by other kinds of resource. Sometimes, of course, someone's right to a fair share of resources requires that agents not engage in despicable (or other kinds of) discrimination. Where it does not, I claim, there is no right against despicable discrimination.

It's crucial that resources are here understood broadly to include *opportunities*, and not merely things (land, machines, money, etc.). Two individuals with equally valuable property rights in things may have unequally valuable resources, if one has more valuable social opportunities (for cooperation or friendship, for self-respect and respect by others, for freedom from domination, etc.). Social resources are indeed extremely valuable, and any theory of fair shares of resources that ignores them is implausible.

I leave open here how shares of resources are evaluated: in terms of well-being, brute luck well-being, economic resource value, brute luck economic value, functionings, capabilities, etc.—except that I assume that they assign significant value to resources that are *significantly valuable to individuals*. I also leave open here the criteria for a fair share: a minimally decent share, an equal share, a prioritarian-maximizing share, etc.—except that I assume that the criteria for a fair share are *reasonably demanding*. For example, my own view (not invoked here) is that a fair share requires equality of initial opportunities for well-being to the extent compatible with certain other rights (e.g., bodily integrity). The demandingness is important, since it helps ensure that significant harms from discrimination tend to deprive a person of her fair share of resources.

I shall now identify four cases of despicable discrimination in which I claim that the discriminatee is not wronged (cf. Chapter 12).

> Case 1: Consider a society in which there are two equally-sized groups with mutual animosity and contempt, where each group has roughly equal overall power over the other group. Suppose further that each of the major institutions/industries of society (e.g., the shipping industry, which can be opposed to the trucking industry) is controlled entirely by one group or the other group, but in ways that give each group equal overall power over the other. Each group engages in despicable job discrimination (in hiring, promotion, etc.) against members of the other group (and thus individuals are subject to domination with respect to participation in the institutions controlled by the other group). Suppose further that each member of society has a well-protected right to bodily integrity (and certain other negative rights) and *has her fair share of resources*.

This is not an attractive society, and its practices are probably very inefficient, but, I claim, no one is wronged by despicable discrimination. Despicable discrimination definitely matters morally, given that it reduces the value of a person's share of resources, but an individual is not wronged by the treatment as long as it is compatible with her having a fair share of resources. Although there is, I would argue, a duty to try to reduce the amount of despicable discrimination in society (because it inefficiently increases the burdens on fair-share duties), this does not mean that the discrimination wrongs the discriminatee.

In this example, I stipulated that each individual has her fair share of resources. In the remaining three cases, I drop that stipulation, but I keep the other background assumptions. For concreteness, I will focus on despicable discrimination by an employer in hiring. We can suppose, for example, that an employer refuses to hire an applicant because of her race (membership of a significant and salient social group), where this disadvantages the applicant, expresses (subjective and intersubjectively) animosity and contempt, and subjects her to domination (with respect to employment in the company and industry). I will assume that in these cases non-discrimination imposes some costs on the employer (e.g., because of the prejudices of his customers). Discrimination when non-discrimination is costless may well wrong the discriminatee.

> Case 2: Like in Case 1, except for the fact that the employer has *less than his fair share* of resources even after the benefit (if any) to him of discriminating.

Here, I claim, the despicable discrimination need not wrong the discriminatee. One kind of case is where the applicant has *more* than her fair share of resources, even after the harm of despicable discrimination. Why would the employer, who has less than his fair share of resources, owe a duty to bear a cost (imposed by non-discrimination, in this case) for the benefit of an applicant who has more than her fair share of resources? Discrimination is typically a way of depriving individuals of their fair share of resources (and thus wrongs them), but it need not do so. When it does not so deprive them, it does not, I claim, wrong them. A second kind of case is where the applicant has *less* than her fair share of resources, but the employer is even more disadvantaged relative to his fair share of resources. Unlike the first kind of case, here non-discrimination does indeed move the applicant closer to her fair share of resources. Nonetheless, it seems implausible that the employer, who has a greater shortfall from his fair share, owes the applicant a duty to bear a cost for the benefits of the applicant (who is less disadvantaged with respect to fair shares).

> Case 3: Like in Case 1, except for the fact that the employer has *more than his fair share of resources, and so does the discriminatee.*

Again, I claim, the discrimination does not wrong the discriminatee. The employer does indeed have a positive duty to aid owed to those with less than their fair share, but the applicant is not such a person.

> Case 4: Like in Case 1, except for the fact that the employer has *more than his fair share of resources and the discriminatee has less than her fair share.*

Sometimes, in such cases, the employer may indeed owe the applicant a duty to hire her. My claim is only that this is not always (or even generally) so. First, the employer may not owe the applicant a duty of aid because he owes his aid (e.g., a job) to others who are even more disadvantaged with respect to fair shares than the discriminatee. (Note that the fact that the employer has a duty to hire someone else is fully compatible with this being a case of despicable discrimination.) Second, even if the employer owes the discriminatee a duty of aid, the aid need not take the form of hiring. A sufficiently large check might be better for the applicant (e.g., to go to college) and for the employer.

The core claim (Cases 1–3) is that despicable discrimination does not wrong the discriminatee when either the discriminator has less than his fair share of resources or the discriminatee has more. In addition (Case 4), despicable discrimination need not (although it can) wrong the discriminator when he has more than his fair share and the discriminatee has less. Obviously, the view just expressed is rejected from many moral perspectives. I shall not attempt a systematic defense. Instead, I will focus on two crucial assumptions implicit in the fair share view, and I will briefly comment on why they are rejected by social (relational) egalitarians (cf. Chapter 35).

The above view assumes that social resources (e.g., opportunities for self-respect and respect by others, non-domination, etc.) matter for rights only to the extent that they affect the value of people's shares of resources. Moreover, it assumes that, for this purpose, all social resources can be *traded off* for other resources (e.g., enough money can offset the harm of domination). Social egalitarians, however, reject one or both claims. They may claim, for example, that individuals have a right to be treated with respect (or as equals) and/or a right not to be dominated, independent of whether they have their fair share of resources. Moreover, they may claim, these basic social relationship goods (e.g., being treated with respect or not being dominated) are (morally) either lexically prior, or incommensurable with, other sources of individual well-being or advantage. (See, for example, Young 1990 (ch. 1), Anderson 1999, Hellman 2008, Allen 2014, Scheffler 2015, and Wolff 2015.)

These objections are indeed important and they deserve careful answers. The debate between social egalitarians and theorists of the fair share of resources is a fundamental debate in political philosophy, but it is beyond the scope of this chapter to address this issue carefully. I shall simply state how I would attempt to answer the objections.

I fully agree that having opportunities that are free of animosity, contempt, and domination is an extremely important factor in determining whether one's fair-share rights are respected. The more one is subject to such treatment, the less valuable one's opportunities are, and this can result in having less than one's fair share of resources. I merely insist that (1) such opportunities are not the only resources relevant to the fair-share rights that people have, and (2) trade-offs between such resources and other resources are often possible and relevant to people's fair-share rights. What matters for people's rights to resources is *the value to them* (e.g., on the correct theory of well-being, which need not be subjective, and need not be sensitive to prejudiced preferences) of the overall package of resources. Compared to one set of resources, a second set may involve more animosity, contempt, and domination, but it may be more valuable to the rightholder overall (e.g., more well-being), if it involves sufficiently more of other resources. (Of course, I do not claim that this is always so.) It seems like a fetish to require that each kind of resource be adequate when this involves a less valuable package for the rightholder. This is, however, merely to state my position. It does not adequately address the important concerns of social egalitarianism. For supporting discussion, see Fiocco (2012), Segall (2012, 2013), Arneson (2013), Lippert-Rasmussen (2012, 2014), Mason (2015), and Tomlin (2015). See also Vallentyne (2005, 2006).

Conclusion

I have suggested that there is no general right against despicable discrimination, and hence no general right against discrimination of any sort. Discrimination does often wrong the discriminatee, but when it does it is because the discriminator has more than his fair share of resources, the discriminatee has less, and the discrimination is incompatible with the discriminator's duty to the discriminatee to increase the value of her share of resources.

This does not mean that various sorts of discrimination are not seriously morally problematic. They are. They are often morally bad or undesirable. They may be impersonally wrong (even if they infringe no one's rights). They may be socially inefficient in that they impose costs on others to offset the harms imposed in order to give the discriminatee her fair share of resources.

The most fundamental challenge to this view is social egalitarianism, and I have only sketched why I think its focus on social relations to the exclusion of other resources is mistaken. So, I have only motivated and outlined a position, not defended it.

I have also only addressed discrimination by private individuals. Discrimination by government officials in their official capacities, by government contractors, and by corporations is quite another matter.[1]

Note

1 For helpful comments, I thank Joe Mazor, Kasper Lippert-Rasmussen, Eric Rowse, Shlomi Segall, and an anonymous referee for this chapter.

Further reading

Cavanagh, Matthew. 2002. *Against Equality of Opportunity*. Oxford: Oxford University Press. (A quasi-libertarian argument against any right to meritocratic treatment, equality of opportunity, or non-discrimination.)

Moreau, Sophia. 2010. "What is Discrimination?" *Philosophy and Public Affairs*. 38: 143–179. (An argument that the right to a roughly equal set of deliberative freedoms requires non-discrimination.)

Related topics: discrimination, justice, and morality; discrimination and equality of opportunity, discrimination and freedom, discrimination and personal life.

Bibliography

Allen, Amy. 2014. "Feminist Perspectives on Power." *The Stanford Encyclopedia of Philosophy (Summer 2014 Edition)*, Edward N. Zalta (ed.), online at http://plato.stanford.edu/archives/sum2014/entries/feminist-power/.

Anderson, Elizabeth. 1999. "What is the Point of Equality?" *Ethics*. 109: 287–337.

Arneson, Richard. 2013. "Discrimination, Disparate Impact, and Theories of Justice," in Hellman and Moreau, eds. (2013): 87–114.

Fiocco, M. Oreste. 2012. "Is There a Right to Respect?" *Utilitas*. 24: 502–524.

Fourie, Carina, Schuppert, Fabian, and Wallimann-Helmer, Ivo, eds. 2015. *Social Equality: On What It Means to Be Equals*. New York: Oxford University Press.

Hellman, Deborah. 2008. *When is Discrimination Wrong?* Cambridge, MA: Harvard University Press.

Hellman, Deborah and Moreau, Sophia, eds. 2013. *Philosophical Foundations of Discrimination Law*. Oxford, New York: Oxford University Press.

Kramer, Mathew H., Simmonds, N.E. and Steiner, Hillel. 1998. *A Debate over Rights*. Oxford: Oxford University Press.

Lippert-Rasmussen, Kasper. 2012. "Democratic Egalitarianism versus Luck Egalitarianism: What is at Stake?" *Philosophical Topics*. 40: 117–134.

Lippert-Rasmussen, Kasper. 2014. *Born Free and Equal? A Philosophical Inquiry into the Nature of Discrimination*. Oxford: Oxford University Press.

Mason, Andrew. 2015. "Justice, Respect, and Treating People as Equals," in Fourie, Schuppert, and Wallimann-Helmer, eds. (2015): 129–145.

Scheffler, Samuel. 2015. "The Practice of Equality." in Fourie, Schuppert, and Wallimann-Helmer (2015): 21–44.

Segall, Shlomi. 2012. "What's So Bad about Discrimination?" *Utilitas*. 24: 82–100.

Segall, Shlomi. 2013. *Equality and Opportunity*. Oxford: Oxford University Press.

Tomlin, Patrick. 2015. "What is the Point of Egalitarian Social Relationships?" in Alexander Kaufman (ed.) *Distributive Justice and Access to Advantage: G. A. Cohen's Egalitarianism*. Cambridge: Cambridge University Press: 151–179.

Vallentyne, Peter. 2005. "Capabilities vs. Opportunities for Well-being." *Journal of Political Philosophy* 13: 359–371. Reprinted in *Capabilities Equality: Basic Issues and Problems*, edited by Alexander Kaufman (New York: Routledge, 2006): 79–92.

Vallentyne, Peter. 2006. "Left-Libertarianism and Private Discrimination." *San Diego Law Review*. 43: 981–994.

Wolff, Jonathan. 2015. "Social Equality and Social Inequality," in Fourie, Schuppert, and Wallimann-Helmer eds. (2015): 209–225.

Young, Iris. 1990. *Justice and the Politics of Difference*. Princeton: Princeton University Press.

11

DISCRIMINATION AND EQUALITY OF OPPORTUNITY

Carl Knight

UNIVERSITY OF GLASGOW

Introduction

Discrimination, understood as differential treatment of individuals on the basis of their respective group memberships, is widely considered to be morally wrong.[1] This moral judgment is backed up in many jurisdictions with the passage of equality of opportunity legislation, which aims to ensure that racial, ethnic, religious, sexual, sexual orientation, disability and other groups are not subjected to discrimination. This chapter explores the conceptual underpinnings of discrimination and equality of opportunity using the tools of analytical moral and political philosophy.

Discrimination

Though discrimination is widely considered to be morally wrong, there are in fact forms of conduct that would meet the 'differential treatment of individuals on the basis of their respective group memberships' criterion, but not be considered wrong. The clearest case would be so-called 'affirmative action', which offers more favorable treatment for members of (historically) disadvantaged groups, and which is often referred to as 'reverse', 'positive', or 'compensatory' discrimination (Nagel 1973; Dworkin 1977: ch. 9; Chapter 33). Whatever one's attitude to particular real world cases of affirmative action, one is likely to accept that some possible cases of affirmative action would not be morally wrong: for instance, a policy that lowered a racial minority's university admission requirements by x% where high school examiners are known with certainty to systematically discriminate in their marking against members of this group by x%. This shows that discrimination is not, of itself, wrongful, and that identifying something as a case of discrimination does not, by itself, tell us whether to be positively or negatively disposed towards it.

The important question, then, is *what makes discrimination wrongful (where it's wrongful)*? Several answers to this question have been advanced.

A first account says that discrimination is wrongful where it shows *disrespect* towards the discriminatee (cf. Chapter 6). This account typically focuses on the *objective meaning* of the discriminatory act – a meaning that demeans or shows contempt for the discriminatee (Lippert-Rasmussen 2013: ch. 5). For instance, Deborah Hellman (2008: 6, 8; Chapter 7) writes that 'to demean is to treat another in a way that denies her equal moral worth', which is contrary to the 'bedrock moral principle' of the 'equal moral worth of all persons'. The disrespect account, in its various guises, is widely held in the literature (Cavanagh 2002; Hellman 2008; Scanlon 2008; Glasgow 2009; Clayton 2012).

A second account holds that discrimination is wrongful where it is based on *prejudice* towards the discriminatee. This account typically focuses on the objectionable *mental state* of the discriminator (Lippert-Rasmussen 2013: ch. 4). For example, Peter Vallentyne (2006: 982–983) says that 'invidious discrimination' involves 'the treatment of an individual less favorably because of some feature one believes the individual to possess, where (1) the person is not morally or prudentially responsible for having the feature in question; and (2) the treatment is based on (a) a mistaken belief in the moral inferiority of those having the feature, (b) a significantly mistaken empirical belief about people having the feature, or (c) hatred of those having the feature'. Other versions of the prejudice account identify wrongful discrimination with biases based on mistaken moral judgments, or flaws in how beliefs about the discriminatee were formed (Alexander 1992; Arneson 2006).

A third account maintains that discrimination is wrongful where it *harms* the discriminatee (cf. Chapters 11 and 12). This account typically focuses on the loss of advantage (e.g. welfare, resources, or capabilities) suffered by the discriminatee. However, it clearly cannot be the case that *any* discrimination that reduces an agent's advantage level is wrongful. Among other things, that would imply that all forms of affirmative action are wrongful, no matter how well they furthered justice and other moral goals. Thus, harm accounts must specify further conditions for reductions in advantage levels to amount to (wrongful) harm. Kasper Lippert-Rasmussen (2013) suggests a 'desert prioritarian' view according to which acts are morally right if and only if they maximize moral value, which depends on (1) the amount of well-being thereby realized, (2) how badly off well-being recipients are, and (3) the desert levels of well-being recipients (see also Arneson 1999a, 2000). On this view, discrimination is wrongful where it does not maximize moral value, and 'a given amount of well-being has greater moral value when it accrues to a badly off, deserving person than it does when it accrues to a well-off, undeserving person' (Lippert-Rasmussen 2013: 166). (Equality of opportunity views can be construed as a different kind of harm view – specifically, as a view about *comparative* harm. As I will treat these views at length in the next section, I will here focus on Lippert-Rasmussen's non-comparative version of the harm account.)

Finally, there are hybrid views, which include elements of more than one of the above accounts (cf. Introduction). For instance, Thomas Scanlon (2008: 73) seems to endorse a view according to which discrimination is wrongful on the grounds of both its disrespectful and harmful character, while Alexander's (1992) account of wrongful discrimination, while foregrounding prejudice, seems also to contain elements of the respect account.

In considering actual cases of wrongful discrimination, it is likely that disrespect, prejudice, and harm are all present. For instance, a sexist employer who refuses to promote female employees is, under usual circumstances, certainly disrespecting and harming them, and almost certainly on the basis of prejudice. This helps to explain the appeal of the disrespect account, prejudice account, and harm account: each captures a prominent feature of actual cases of wrongful discrimination. But it also means that, in order to find which of the features of disrespect, prejudice, and harm are actually responsible for the wrongfulness, we must consider unusual cases of apparently unjust discrimination in which one or more of these features is absent.

There is a kind of case that seems to defeat the disrespect view, by identifying cases of wrongful discrimination that would not be identified as such by the view. Lippert-Rasmussen describes two such cases:

> it seems that not all kinds of intentional discriminatory acts involve a judgment of inferiority, e.g., a patriarch who avoids hiring a certain applicant simply because she is a woman and thereby intends to avoid hiring women, not because he thinks, as most patriarchs do, women are inferior, but because he thinks that there is a clear division of labor between the sexes and women's place is in the home. A further complication derives from the fact that an employer may refrain from "giving a person a certain benefit," i.e., hiring him, because he thinks that the job is inferior and that it ought only to be performed by inferior persons. Should one say here that it is permissible not to hire the applicant—say, a Brahmin—considered superior by the employer, but not permissible not to hire the Brahmin with the intention to avoid hiring a superior person for an inferior job—say, a job the employer deems suitable only for Dalits?
>
> *(Lippert-Rasmussen 2013: 146–147)*

The first example is trickier, perhaps because a liberal will interpret the idea that 'there is a clear division of labor between the sexes and women's place is in the home' as a façade intended to disguise the true intention of subjugating women. But in the second case it seems clear that there is no disrespect to the discriminatee conveyed by the discriminator – the discriminator's reason for denying the applicant the job is precisely the high status the discriminator assigns to the discriminatee. Furthermore, we can extend the case so that this seems to be clearly wrongful. Suppose, for instance, that there are many Brahmins left unemployed by hiring decisions of this sort, and that this is not even of benefit to other groups, who are not interested in these jobs.

Such cases are also problematic for some versions of the prejudice view. An employer who refuses to hire Brahmins because she believes they are too good for the job is not acting out of hatred to Brahmins. Nor is she acting on an opinion that Brahmins are inferior – quite the contrary! It might be said, however, that she is acting on a faulty, or faultily formed, belief about Brahmins. Epistemic versions of the prejudice view, therefore, do not seem to be undermined by this case (cf. Chapter 4).

A different kind of case does challenge these views, however. Suppose Alexandra treats Barbara worse than Christina, because she falsely believes that Christina is more deserving than Barbara. This is, on the face of it, *less* wrongful than a second case in which Diana treats Barbara unjustifiably worse than Christina where she does not falsely believe that Christina is more deserving than Barbara (Lippert-Rasmussen 2013: 120). In the first case, it intuitively seems that Alexandra has at least something of an excuse for treating Barbara less favorably, namely, that she believes Barbara to be less deserving. The prejudice view says that holding that false belief makes the discrimination wrongful; but in fact it seems, if anything, to reduce the amount of wrongfulness. In the second case, there is no false belief, and the prejudice view under consideration takes that fact as implying that there is no wrongful discrimination. But in fact, the absence of a false belief that might explain why Diana treats Barbara unfavorably does not seem to remove any wrongfulness from her behavior (it may well make it worse). There are similar difficulties with epistemic versions of the prejudice view that say that wrongful discrimination is based on faultily *formed* beliefs. If Alexandra's views about Barbara's and Christina's desert levels were faultily formed, while Diana's were not, that hardly seems to justify the conclusion that Alexandra's harsh treatment of Barbara is wrongful, but that Diana's similarly harsh treatment of Barbara is not. If anything, Diana's epistemic advantage removes a possible excuse for her behavior, making it more blameworthy. Thus, it seems that there will be cases of wrongful discrimination in which none of the conditions for prejudice are satisfied. Just as wrongful discrimination is possible without disrespect, so too is it possible without prejudice. If we want an account of what it is that makes discrimination wrongful, we must look elsewhere.

This naturally takes us to the harm account. We should notice right away that this account, as set out by Lippert-Rasmussen, has little difficulty with the kind of case that sunk the disrespect and prejudice accounts. The employer that would not hire Brahmins would, typically, create disadvantages for Brahmins who are discriminated against. In some cases, such as that described above where the jobs are not taken by others, there would be no (or insufficient) offsetting advantages for other groups, in which case the discrimination is condemned by desert-accommodating prioritarianism. In others, there are sufficient advantages for other groups to offset the discrimination (e.g. they take the jobs), in which case the discrimination is not condemned by desert-accommodating prioritarianism and is instead considered a case of affirmative action. This seems like a plausible way of responding to the case.

There is, however, a further case that proves more problematic for desert-accommodating prioritarianism as an account of wrongful discrimination. Suppose that two applicants for a job are identical in all respects except one: their religious affiliation (cf. Chapter 17). Their expected job performance is identical. The employer discriminates against one of the applicants on religious grounds, and appoints the other applicant. Desert prioritarianism has no complaint with this outcome. The two applicants are, *ex hypothesi*, identical in well-being and desert levels, so assuming that there is only one job to be allocated and it cannot be divided, it makes no difference who the recipient is, nor – and here's the kicker – on what grounds the allocation is made. This seems to be a case where wrongful discrimination is overlooked by desert-accommodating prioritarianism.

Responding to a case that is in some respects similar to this, Lippert-Rasmussen comments that

> Friends of desert prioritarianism can concede that something may well be morally amiss in cases involving beneficial discriminatory acts, but insist that what is morally amiss is not that the act is wrong. To deny that a certain discriminatory act that maximizes moral value is bad is not to imply that the agent cannot be criticized for performing it; the agent might, for example, have had reason to believe that the act would on balance harm the discriminatee, and thus attract blame for performing the act.
>
> *(Lippert-Rasmussen 2013: 173)*

He adds that one may criticize the moral *character* of an agent, even where their *action* is morally right (see Lippert-Rasmussen 2013: 123–124, 160, 173). I agree that in many cases, an agent acts correctly, but for reasons that reflect badly on their character, perhaps leaving them open to blame. But I do not see that this could be a desert prioritarian's description of a case in which an employer deliberately satisfies desert prioritarianism, and with this done acts in a gratuitously discriminatory way. Such an agent is not even slightly criticizable from a desert prioritarian perspective. Moreover, we can criticize not just the agent's reasoning, but their action. Our intuitive response to the case is not that the employer acts correctly, for the wrong reason, as where a would-be wrongdoer inadvertently does right. It is that the employer acts wrongfully, for the wrong reason. She should not have discriminated against the applicant, just as she should not have been motivated by irrelevant religious reasons. I therefore conclude that, in spite of its strengths, the desert prioritarian harm account fails to identify some cases of wrongful discrimination.

Equality of opportunity

It is time to consider an alternative approach to discrimination – equality of opportunity (cf. Chapter 10). In this section I survey the three main accounts of equality of opportunity found in the normative political theory literature. It should be emphasized that these have not been developed primarily as accounts of wrongful discrimination, but rather as principles of justice. Nevertheless, on the assumption that a discriminatory act that breaches a principle of equality of opportunity amounts to wrongful discrimination, each principle yields a distinctive view of wrongful discrimination. I will argue that none of these three principles, by itself, offers a fruitful account of wrongful discrimination. In the next section I suggest that one of them can be combined with desert prioritarianism to make such an account.

A key section of John Rawls' famous *A Theory of Justice* considers two possible interpretations of the principle that 'social and economic equalities are to be arranged so that they are ... attached to positions and offices open to all' (Rawls 1999: 53). The first of these he refers to as 'careers open to talents'. This specifies 'a formal equality of opportunity in that all have at least the same legal rights of access to all advantaged social positions' (Rawls 1999: 62). Formal equality of opportunity requires that positions are allocated on the basis of a 'fair contest', in which 'one should be judged only on those characteristics relevant to one's future performance in the position for which one is applying' (Fishkin 2014: 25). This position rules out not just *de jure* but also *de facto* discrimination, such as racist or sexist hiring decisions.[2]

Rawls (1999: 63) himself rejects formal equality of opportunity, noting that it 'permits distributive shares to be improperly influenced by ... factors so arbitrary from a moral point of view'. For instance, according to formal equality of opportunity, a person who attended a private school that offers a high standard of education, and whose talents are therefore developed more effectively than equivalent state-educated people, will legitimately have a competitive advantage when it comes to applying for university places or jobs. Concerned to address such arbitrary factors, Rawls instead favors the second interpretation of 'attached to positions and office open to all', which he refers to as 'fair equality of opportunity':

> The thought here is that positions are to be open not merely in the formal sense, but that all should have a fair chance to attain them. Offhand it is not clear what is meant, but we might say that those with similar abilities and skills should have similar life chances. More specifically, assuming that there is a distribution of natural assets, those who are at the same level of ability and talent, and have the same willingness to use them, should have the same prospects of success regardless of their initial place in the social system.
>
> *(Rawls 1999: 63)*

Fair equality of opportunity is clearly a far more demanding principle than formal equality of opportunity. It requires not just that a contest is 'fair' at the moment of decision, but that certain background conditions are in place to ensure that people have a fair chance to develop their natural talents. As Rawls (1999: 63) observes, this requires that the 'school system, whether public or private, should be designed to even out class barriers' (cf. Chapter 26). It also justifies an inheritance tax in order to prevent inequalities growing so large that equal education is threatened (Rawls 1999: 245–246). In terms of discrimination specifically, fair equality of opportunity would seem to justify radical policies of affirmative action (cf. Chapter 33). As it requires those with similar natural abilities to have similar life prospects, it would appear to require that, where an individual's natural abilities have not been cultivated as well as others' (for instance, due to substandard state schools), they should be admitted to jobs and universities with lesser qualifications than persons who did not have this developmental disadvantage (see Arneson 1999b: 81). To see the radical implications here, note that the rationale for the affirmative action is not that the qualifications are thought to have failed to accurately estimate future performance.[3] Rather, the applicants are thought likely to underperform compared to non-disadvantaged people with better qualifications, but are admitted anyway in order to provide them with similar prospects to these people. A failure to provide affirmative action of this sort would amount to wrongful discrimination against those with a disadvantageous background.

Fair equality of opportunity faces some serious problems. Arneson draws attention to the fact that fair equality of opportunity only requires that people who are similarly talented *and motivated* have similar prospects. This implies that there is no injustice if men assume all positions of advantage in a society that socializes its women to believe that seeking positions of advantage is unladylike (Arneson 1999b: 78). In such a society, fair equality of opportunity simply considers men and women to have differential 'willingness' to use their natural talents, so differential outcomes are justified. A further objection is noted by Rawls himself. While fair equality of opportunity aims to neutralize the effects of social circumstance on people's life chances, it does not aim to neutralize the effects of natural circumstance, such as native talent. As Rawls (1999: 64) recognizes, '[t]here is no more reason to permit the distribution of income and wealth to be settled by the distribution of natural assets than by historical and social fortune'.

Rawls' response to this latter difficulty is to complement fair equality of opportunity with the difference principle, which ensures that inequality is to the benefit of the worse off and thereby mitigates the impact of lower natural talents. Some writers question whether it really achieves this objective (Kymlicka 2002: 70–74). In any case, the difference principle is of little interest for our purposes as it clearly cannot provide a more successful account of equality of opportunity.

A more promising response to the concerns about natural abilities is to develop a form of equality of opportunity that is even more radical than fair equality of opportunity. This third and final account of equality of opportunity is *luck egalitarianism*. As the name suggests, it aims to equalize (or neutralize) the effects of luck on distributions. In a famous formulation, luck egalitarianism is overtly presented as an account of equality of opportunity – specifically, as 'equality of opportunity for welfare' (Arneson 1989; see also Cohen 1989).

Shlomi Segall has recently presented an appealing luck egalitarian account of the badness of discrimination. According to Segall, '[d]iscrimination … is bad when, and only when, it upsets' equality of opportunity for welfare (Segall 2013: 109).[4] To see the appeal of this kind of view, note that an individual's natural talents are, just like her social circumstances, a matter of luck for her. Luck egalitarianism therefore aims to prevent natural talents from influencing distributions. This allows it to sidestep the objection to fair equality of opportunity that it arbitrarily distinguishes between social and natural contingencies. Affirmative action for those with social disadvantages *and* those with natural disadvantages would be justified. Luck egalitarianism would also not be satisfied, as fair equality of opportunity is, with a situation in which women are socialized to accept less advantaged positions: such a situation clearly disadvantages them as a matter of luck.

In spite of its attractions, luck egalitarianism faces significant difficulties. A variant of a familiar objection points out that luck egalitarianism, as a form of egalitarianism, will favor *leveling down* (Parfit 2000). Luck egalitarianism aims to reduce inequality of opportunity for welfare, and one way of doing that is to *reduce the opportunities for welfare of the better off.* Consider a case of discrimination with this feature. A council planning officer in a Western country is considering an application to build a Hindu temple. The town could easily accommodate the temple, and this would have beneficial welfare effects for local Hindus. However, it happens that the Hindus have greater opportunities for welfare than do other groups. If the planning officer denies planning permission for the temple, squandering the possibility of a welfare gain for local Hindus, luck egalitarianism will have no complaint with this decision. Nor, if we add that the planning officer's decision was a discriminatory one, will a luck egalitarian account of discrimination identify any badness with that discrimination, since it reduced inequality of opportunity for welfare.

Segall anticipates concerns about leveling down. He replies, first, that an unequal distribution makes the worst off 'potentially envious' of the better off, and second, that the inequality 'calls for a justification, whether or not there is a preferable alternative to it' (Segall 2013: 31). I am not quite sure what the relevance of the possible envy is intended to be, but in any case, it is easy to construct a case in which there is inequality but no envy – indeed, there is no reason to suppose that the non-Hindus in the above example are in any way envious. This leaves the fact that the inequality 'calls for a justification', but there seems absolutely no difficulty in providing such a justification. It could, for instance, be said that the inequality is justified because it benefits some members of the community and does no one any harm. Contra Segall (2013: 26–27), surely the defender of leveling down owes at least as much of a justification – his suggested defense for equality of 'why the hell not!' seems borderline offensive in a case where people are being forced to forego significant improvements to their lives, for the sake of a distribution that benefits no one at all. Of course, there is much more that could be said about leveling down,[5] but I doubt that it is compatible with a plausible account of the badness of discrimination.[6]

Discrimination and equality of opportunity

We have so far surveyed several accounts of wrongful discrimination and several accounts of equality of opportunity, but have found none of them truly satisfactory. In this section I argue that the desert prioritarian account of wrongful discrimination can be combined with an account of equality of opportunity to yield a successful overall account of wrongful discrimination.

To see the motivation for this combination, we should return to the case that seemed to defeat desert prioritarianism, in which a job application was rejected on religious grounds but in such a way that desert-prioritarian moral value was maximized. The discussion of equality of opportunity provides several different ways of branding this a case of wrongful discrimination. Formal equality of opportunity provides the most straightforward: it requires that there is a fair contest between applicants – that equally qualified candidates have equal chances – a condition that is clearly breached by the employer's actions. Careers are not open to talents if people of a certain religion are excluded.

We have seen the advantage of including a principle of equality of opportunity, but why include desert prioritarianism? The reason is that it answers the same challenges to formal equality of opportunity and, in turn, fair equality of opportunity, that luck egalitarianism does. On any plausible account of desert, individual desert levels do not decrease with poor social circumstance or natural talent. But advantage levels do decrease with these factors. Thus, the person with disadvantageous social circumstance or low natural talent will have a lower advantage level than their desert recommends. Desert prioritarianism treats such people as of high priority, as luck egalitarianism does.[7] And it does so without facing the difficulties of luck egalitarian accounts of wrongful discrimination, such as the implication that discrimination that levels down is not bad. This is because prioritarianism focuses on the absolute rather than relative position of the worse off, and their absolute position is not improved by leveling down. The disadvantaged's absolute position *will* be improved by (justified) policies of affirmative action, and other benign cases of discrimination.[8] Thus, desert prioritarianism seems to account for many cases of discrimination in a plausible way. Its one weak point can be reinforced by equality of opportunity.

Two questions lie before us. First, *which* form of equality of opportunity should be combined with desert prioritarianism? Second, *how* should equality of opportunity of the chosen kind be combined with desert prioritarianism? I will take these in turn.

It may seem that luck egalitarianism offers the most suitable form of equality of opportunity, given its accommodation of concerns about social and natural contingencies. However, it could be argued that this accommodation is otiose given the role of desert prioritarianism in the combined account. Indeed, it could even be counterproductive given the problems we found with leveling down – problems that are avoided by prioritarianism. Fair equality of opportunity also cannot work for our purposes: its requirements of background fairness are partial, favoring those with social disadvantages over those with natural disadvantages, and (like luck egalitarianism's similar but more demanding requirements) unnecessary given the role of desert prioritarianism.

What we need is an account of equality of opportunity that will filter out discriminatory acts. Adjustment of background conditions is already taken care of by desert prioritarianism. I believe, therefore, that formal equality of opportunity provides the appropriate supplement to desert prioritarianism.

To explain that claim, I need to explain the spheres in which the two principles are intended to operate. Desert prioritarianism provides an axiological account of the intrinsic goodness or badness of a distribution. If we were only interested in how good or bad a distribution was, we would need nothing in addition to desert prioritarianism. With some further assumptions, desert prioritarianism would also provide a full account of the justice or injustice of a distribution.

When we are asking about *wrongful* discrimination, however, we are asking about a certain kind of *action*. (This is why a naturally occurring distribution or event might be bad, but not wrong.) One way of identifying wrongful action is to check whether an individual's choices make a distribution as good or just as they can be in the circumstances. This explains the role of desert prioritarianism within my account. But this cannot be the whole account of wrongful action. A failure to promote desert prioritarian moral value is not a necessary condition for wrongful discrimination. As we have seen, someone may do everything they can to promote desert prioritarian moral value, but still wrongfully discriminate. In other words, *a good or just distribution may have been arrived at in a wrongful way*. This is where formal equality of opportunity comes in.

I now move on to our second question of *how* desert prioritarianism and formal equality of opportunity should be combined. I suggest the following 'hybrid account':

> First principle: maximize desert prioritarian moral value.
> Second principle: satisfy formal equality of opportunity.
> Wrongful discrimination is discrimination that fails to satisfy the first principle in any circumstance, or fails to satisfy both principles where both can be satisfied.

The hybrid view grants lexical priority to desert prioritarianism, as it says it must always be satisfied, whereas formal equality of opportunity must only be satisfied where this is compatible with desert prioritarianism. One motivation for this priority is to accommodate affirmative action. Some affirmative action, at least, is not wrongful. The hybrid view reflects this by allowing that violations of formal equality of opportunity are not wrongful provided they are necessary to satisfy desert prioritarianism, as I believe is true of some affirmative action.

To further illustrate the hybrid view, consider the case that created difficulties for desert prioritarianism, in which a discriminatory hire on the basis of religion, which was irrelevant to job performance, was perfectly consistent with desert prioritarianism. The first principle is satisfied, but the second principle is not satisfied, as a fair contest has not been provided – equally qualified candidates were not given equal chances of acquiring the job. As both principles could have been satisfied, but were not, this is a case of wrongful discrimination.[9] Had the employer flipped a coin, this would not have been a case of wrongful discrimination, as equally qualified candidates would then have been given an equal chance and a fair contest would have been provided.[10]

While a full defense of the hybrid account is not possible here, I hope to have said enough to offer some motivation for it. In short, it aims to capture considerations of both distribution, which explain why discrimination that disadvantages unfairly disadvantaged groups is wrongful, and procedure, which explain why some discrimination that is distributively fair is nevertheless wrongful.

Conclusion

The chapter first explored disrespect, prejudice, and harm-based accounts of wrongful discrimination, finding that each failed to identify some cases of wrongful discrimination. Three accounts of equality of opportunity – formal equality of opportunity, fair equality of opportunity, and luck egalitarian equality of opportunity – were then considered, and it was found that these too were subject to counterexamples. It was, finally, argued that an account combining desert prioritarianism and formal equality of opportunity provided a plausible account of wrongful discrimination.[11]

Notes

1 Discrimination in this sense is 'group discrimination'. For discussion see Lippert-Rasmussen 2013: ch. 1.

2 Here I follow conventional interpretation of Rawls – see, for instance, Freeman 2007: 88–90; Mandle 2009: 27–28. It is worth noting, however, that Rawls' definition quoted in the text does not explicitly say that formal equality of opportunity rules out de facto discrimination or requires a 'fair contest'. Everyone having 'at least the same legal rights of access to all advantaged social positions' could just mean that there are no legal restrictions on who can apply for which jobs, but that employers can review applications according to whichever criteria they choose. This shows that the 'fair contest' version of formal equality of opportunity is far from trivial; it rules out much actual discrimination that weaker versions of equality of opportunity would not.

3 Joseph Fishkin (2014: 33–34) mentions a 'formal-plus' equality of opportunity that would take this kind of strategy.

4 Segall discusses the badness of discrimination, rather than its wrongness, which is our focus. Though, as discussed below in a different context, there is an important difference here, it is not relevant for present purposes, as the failings of the luck egalitarian account as an account of the badness of discrimination are the same as its failings as an account of its wrongness.

5 Segall (2013: 138) gestures towards the different defense that leveling down is a problem for rules of regulation, rather than justice. But many would deny that leveling down is compatible with justice – it is plausible not just that the planning officer's discrimination was bad or wrongful, but also unjust. And Segall's response does not, in any case, look promising as a defense of a luck egalitarian account of the *badness* of discrimination, which is not on the face of it a matter of justice. For further relevant discussion that would take us too far afield see Segall 2016: ch. 6.

6 There are additional objections to the luck egalitarian account of the badness of discrimination. For instance, Sophia Moreau (2010: 172) considers a case in which there are many instances of *prima facie* discrimination but in such a way that they counterbalance one another, with an equal upshot. Segall denies that there is discrimination here, a position I find implausible. For discussion see Knight 2013a: 53–55.

7 A different route to a similar outcome would be to endorse *responsibility-sensitive prioritarianism*, which can be construed as a kind of luck egalitarianism (Arneson 2000). Indeed, I have done just this elsewhere (Knight 2009: ch. 6). In the text I focus on the very closely related view of desert prioritarianism for the sake of simplicity.

8 An example may be Arneson's (1999b: 88) communal workplace in which all employees are gay, which 'being small-scale and excluding members of a dominant majority that suffers no dearth of opportunities, does not impose significant costs on anyone'.

9 Kasper Lippert-Rasmussen and Hugh Lazenby suggested to me that friendships or romantic relationships may be more problematic for the hybrid view. Here equality of opportunity and/or desert prioritarianism seem to identify some ordinary and seemingly permissible conduct (e.g. choosing one person as a friend rather than another more disadvantaged person) as wrongful discrimination. There are at least three possible responses. First, I could distinguish public from private acts, and apply the hybrid account only to relevantly public acts. Second, I could bite the bullet, and accept that much *prima facie* permissible private conduct is in fact wrongful. Finally, I could argue that though the hybrid account applies to private acts, this does not generally have counterintuitive implications after all. The last of these responses is the most promising, I believe. It seems particularly important that the 'goods' of private acts, such as friendship, would often cease to be goods at all were they given only in order to satisfy moral requirements. A friendship or romantic relationship founded on, and sustained by, one party's begrudging sense of duty is likely to be harmful to both parties. Thus, desert prioritarianism, which has lexical priority on my view, would treat friendships or relationships that are primarily motivated by duty as usually self-defeating, creating space for more ordinary private conduct.

10 Some may feel that the coin toss is in a sense unfair. It may, for instance, fall foul of Segall's (2013: 86, 100) requirement that '*hiring must not be based on morally arbitrary considerations*', construed as '*hiring for relevant reasons alone*'. This suggestion is perhaps supported by Segall's (2013: 5) hostility to a lottery-based equality of opportunity. But I cannot see a fairer, less arbitrary, or more 'relevant reason'-based decision procedure in this case, given that both the candidates' qualifications and wider distributive considerations are conclusively tied. This is despite the fact that I share Segall's wariness of lotteries, and even go beyond him in identifying their outcomes as problematic from the perspective of equality where they only affect people that have chosen to take part. (That is, I endorse, all-luck egalitarianism, a view which aims to neutralize brute luck and option luck alike, and which Segall has powerfully criticized; see Knight 2013; Segall 2010: ch. 3.) Of course, in practice a coin toss would almost never be a sensible procedure to use, as a recruiter would rarely have our example's certainty that there is a tie. Something that initially looked like a dead heat would almost certainly change if further enquiries were taken (e.g. rereading CVs, considering additional opinions, further interviews, etc). But if a recruiter really were unable to split two candidates, a randomizing device seems a better last resort than the alternatives (such as discriminating on the irrelevant grounds of religion).

11 Earlier versions of this chapter were presented at Keele University in November 2016 and the University of Glasgow in December 2016. I thank the audiences on those occasions, and especially Kasper Lippert-Rasmussen, Hugh Lazenby and an anonymous reviewer for their written comments.

Bibliography

Alexander, L. 1992. "What Makes Wrongful Discrimination Wrong?" *University of Pennsylvania Law Review*. 141: 149–219.

Arneson, R. J. 1989. "Equality and Equal Opportunity for Welfare." *Philosophical Studies*. 56: 77–93.

Arneson, R. J. 1999a. "Equality of Opportunity for Welfare Defended and Recanted." *Journal of Political Philosophy*. 7: 488–497.

Arneson, R. J. 1999b. "Against Rawlsian Equality of Opportunity." *Philosophical Studies*. 93: 77–112.

Arneson, R. J. 2000. "Luck Egalitarianism and Prioritarianism." *Ethics*. 110: 339–349.

Arneson, R. J. 2006. "What is Wrongful Discrimination?" *San Diego Law Review*. 43: 775–808.

Cavanagh, M. 2002. *Against Equality of Opportunity*. Oxford: Oxford University Press.

Clayton, M. 2012. "Equality, Justice, and Legitimacy in Selection." *Journal of Moral Philosophy*. 9: 8–30.

Cohen, G. A. 1989. "On the Currency of Egalitarian Justice." *Ethics*. 99: 906–944.
Dworkin, R. 1977. *Taking Rights Seriously*. Cambridge, MA: Harvard University Press.
Fishkin, J. 2014. *Bottlenecks: A New Theory of Equal Opportunity*. Oxford: Oxford University Press.
Freeman, Samuel. 2007. *Rawls*. London: Routledge.
Glasgow, J. 2009. "Racism as Disrespect." *Ethics*. 120: 64–93.
Hellman, D. 2008. *When is Discrimination Wrong?* Cambridge, MA: Harvard University Press.
Knight, C. 2009. *Luck Egalitarianism: Equality, Responsibility, and Justice*. Edinburgh: Edinburgh University Press.
Knight, C. 2013a. "The Injustice of Discrimination." *South African Journal of Philosophy*. 32: 47–59.
Knight, C. 2013b. "Egalitarian Justice and Expected Value." *Ethical Theory and Moral Practice*. 16: 1061–1073.
Kymlicka, W. 2002. *Contemporary Political Philosophy: An Introduction*, second edition. Oxford: Oxford University Press.
Lippert-Rasmussen, K. 2013. *Born Free and Equal? A Philosophical Inquiry into the Nature of Discrimination*. Oxford: Oxford University Press.
Mandle, J. 2009. *Rawls's A Theory of Justice: An Introduction*. Cambridge: Cambridge University Press.
Moreau, S. 2010. "What is Discrimination?" *Philosophy and Public Affairs*. 38: 143–179.
Nagel, T. 1973. "Equal Treatment and Compensatory Discrimination." *Philosophy and Public Affairs*. 2: 348–363.
Parfit, D. 2000. "Equality or Priority." In Clayton, M. and Williams, A. (eds) *The Ideal of Equality*. Basingstoke: Macmillan: 81–125.
Rawls, J. 1999. *A Theory of Justice*, revised edition. Oxford: Oxford University Press.
Scanlon, T. 2008. *Moral Dimensions: Permissibility, Meaning, Blame*. Cambridge, MA: Harvard University Press.
Segall, S. 2010. *Health, Luck, and Justice*. Princeton: Princeton University Press.
Segall, S. 2013. *Equality and Opportunity*. Oxford: Oxford University Press.
Segall, S. 2016. *Why Inequality Matters: Luck Egalitarianism, its Meaning and Value*. Cambridge: Cambridge University Press.
Vallentyne, P. 2006. "Left Libertarianism and Wrongful Discrimination." *San Diego Law Review*. 43: 981–994.

12

DISCRIMINATION AND HARM

Richard Arneson

UNIVERSITY OF CALIFORNIA, SAN DIEGO

Introduction

Discrimination in a familiar, morally charged sense is making a selection that favors or disfavors a member of a group on a morally inappropriate or problematic basis. Selecting Jane over Janis as a friend on the ground that Jane is a white-skinned person and one prefers to befriend those who are white-skinned is arguably discriminating against Janis.

Discrimination might be thought to be a wrong uniquely perpetrated by governments or by public officials acting in an official capacity. Ronald Dworkin (2000) maintained that the state coerces its members and claims to act with authority in their name, and by virtue of these facts has a special moral obligation to treat all these members as equals, favoring none over others. In contrast, individuals executing their private affairs might be deemed to be under no such obligation (Chapters 31 and 35). Another related position is that norms against discrimination bind one when one is acting in a public sphere role, as when one chooses among candidates for promotion in a business enterprise, or engages in political activity, or acts in a capacity as state employee. I shall assume that norms against discrimination can bind individuals acting in a purely private capacity, but readers should be aware that the scope of these norms is contested.

Discrimination can be morally horrendous, with horrible consequences, as when a dominant racial group enforces systematic mistreatment of a disfavored group, gays suffer relentless persecution, or women are confined to inferior status and life prospects (cf. Chapters 15 and 18). Discrimination can be benign, or idiosyncratic, or harmless, as when members of an oppressed group club together in solidarity, or when someone tries to confine his friendship circle to those who attended a particular rock concert in 2005, or sports fans bestow their esteem disproportionately on home team favorites.

Arguably some but not all discrimination is morally wrongful. What makes acts of discrimination morally wrong when they are wrong? (For seminal discussion see Alexander, 1991 and Dworkin, 1978.) This chapter considers the relationship between discriminatory acts or policies being harmful and their being rightly deemed morally wrong. The discussion aims to clarify contending options; no conclusions are reached.

Must discriminatory wrongdoing be harmdoing?

An act might be *pro tanto* morally wrong or morally wrong all things considered (cf. Introduction). A *pro tanto* wrong act has a significant wrong-making feature, sufficient to render the act wrong unless there are significant countervailing considerations. An act is wrong all things considered just in case the overall balance of moral reasons bearing on the act determines that it is wrong to do. In argument about whether an act as specified is morally wrong, the reader needs to ask whether the disputants are attending to this distinction, and clear about what they mean.

The claim that an act is morally wrong, or permissible, or mandatory, might be interpreted in a belief-relative sense, or an evidence-relative sense, or a fact-relative sense, as Derek Parfit (2011) has observed. An act by an agent is wrong in the ordinary sense, says Parfit, when the act is rightly deemed wrong, on the assumption the agent knows all facts that might be material for choice. An act is wrong in the belief-relative sense just in case it would be wrong in the ordinary sense if the agent's beliefs about the morally relevant facts were all true; wrong in the fact-relative sense just in case it would be wrong in the ordinary sense if it were the case that the agent did in fact know all of the morally relevant facts; wrong in the evidence-relative sense just in case it would be wrong in the ordinary sense if the agent's beliefs about the morally relevant facts were in conformity with the available evidence. These are Parfit's formulations. He urges that we can and do speak about what is morally wrong in these different ways, which, when clearly distinguished, we can see not to be in conflict.

Certainly, many acts of discrimination that look to be plainly wrong will be acts that select among people in a way that proceeds from bigotry or prejudice or some other hostile attitude. Hating blacks, one refuses to serve black people who seek to be customers in one's restaurant. One possible view about discrimination and harm is that harmdoing is not necessary for acts to qualify as wrongful discrimination. Even if the blacks one turns away from one's restaurant invariably find better food at restaurants nearby that welcome their trade, and suffer no psychic harm, just bemusement at one's prejudiced behavior, and even if one's discriminatory acts cause no harm in more indirect ways, still, a prejudiced refusal to treat potential customers on equal footing, motivated by prejudice or similar hostile attitude, can be morally wrong. So some think (Arneson, 2006).

An opposing view holds that harmdoing is a necessary condition for wrongful discrimination (Lippert-Rasmussen, 2013). This view allows the possibility that harmless discrimination proceeding from bigotry, prejudice, or some similar hostile attitude can be blameworthy (cf. Chapter 14). Acting in this way is failing to show due consideration to others, and culpable. But, some might insist, wrongful discrimination involves some connection to harm (different accounts might spell out the idea of harmdoing in play here in different ways).

Although there are many possible views regarding the relation between discriminatory harming and discriminatory wrongdoing, this essay focuses on the following possible positions:

1 To be morally wrong, a discriminatory act must impose harm or excessive risk of harm.
2 To be morally wrong, a discriminatory act need not impose harm or excessive risk of harm.

Someone who affirms (1) might interpret "harm" in at least two different ways:

1a "Harming" an individual is doing what brings about that the person is worse off in well-being all things considered, by comparison with the alternative in which one refrains from doing that thing. Harming is distinct from failing to benefit.

Or:

1b "Harming" an individual is causing the person to be in a harmful condition, to be suffering any one of a list of bad situations, regardless of whether the person is rendered worse off overall. For example, if I break your leg, I harm you, whatever further consequences ensue.

Someone who affirms (2) might hold one or the other of two further views:

2a To be morally wrong, a discriminatory act need not impose harm or excessive risk of harm, but must be brought about by morally impermissible motivation or by morally defective deliberation on the part of the discriminating agent.
2b To be morally wrong, a discriminatory act need not impose harm or excessive risk of harm, but must frustrate some interest of the discriminatee that is protected by a moral right.

More needs to be said, to clarify 1a as intended. Consider the examples of a surgeon who slices into a patient as the first step of an operation that fixes her heart, and of a taxi cab driver whose faulty driving causes a crash that results in the passenger both suffering a broken leg, and missing a plane flight that crashed and so would have killed him. Of these examples, 1a says that neither the surgeon nor the cab driver harms the individual affected by his action. What about omissions? If I fail to invite you on a holiday, have I harmed you, given that you are worse off, not going on the holiday, than you would have been going on it? At a first pass, the response is No. Omitting to do what would make someone better off is not, generally speaking, harming the person. Omitting is not doing. But complications abound. When drawing bath water for an infant, omitting to shut off the tap may bring about a drowning. Also, omitting to provide someone a benefit one was duty-bound to provide should count as harming the person to whom one owed the benefit. Further discussion of these complications would be desirable.

Someone might hold specifically that harmdoing is a necessary feature of any act that qualifies as wrongful discrimination, or might hold the wider view that harmdoing is a necessary feature of any act that qualifies as wrongdoing.

The positions regarding wrong and harm canvassed here can be contrasted with act consequentialist views. Act consequentialism holds that one morally ought to do whatever would bring about the best outcome, so regarding discrimination, one morally ought to discriminate when and only when doing so would bring about the best outcome. On this view, harmdoing is neither necessary nor sufficient for its being the case that a candidate act one might do is morally wrong, all things considered (an act consequentialist account of discrimination is sketched in Arneson, 2013, following the lead of Wasserstrom, 1964). A nonconsequentialist might affirm any of 1a, 1b, 2a, or 2b (but no claim is made here that these specified options are exhaustive of the possibilities).

A nonconsequentialist who holds that all wrongdoing is wrongful harming may find discriminatory acts to be wrong that an act consequentialist will endorse as right, and may find discriminatory acts to be permissible that an act consequentialist will judge to be impermissible. Here are stylized, simple examples. Consider employment discrimination that favors members of formerly oppressed groups. The consequentialist will judge the compensatory discrimination permissible, and in fact required, just in case its overall consequences are better than anything else one might instead have done. The standard for assessing consequences might take into account various features of people who might possibly be affected by alternative policies. In contrast, a nonconsequentialist might find certain discriminatory policies to be wrong, regardless of their all things considered consequences, by virtue of the fact that they would impose harm or risk of harm on people who have moral rights against being harmed in that way. A nonconsequentialist might also judge a proposed compensatory discrimination program to be not morally required, even if permissible, on the ground that no one has any affirmative duty to be bringing about overall benefits to people in this way, in these circumstances.

Denying 2a and affirming 2b chimes in with the nonconsequentialist view that an act can be wrong by virtue of what is done, independent of the motivation or intention of the agent, but what makes an act morally wrong need not involve affecting the well-being or welfare of agents who might be affected. Judith Thomson (1991) states the irrelevance-of-intention-to-moral-permissibility idea in this way: "It is irrelevant to the question whether X may do alpha what intention X would do alpha with if he or she did it." (See also Kamm, 2007 and Scanlon, 2008.) One possibility is that moral permissibility turns in whole or in part on whether one's conduct would violate someone's moral rights. On such a view, if X's doing alpha now would violate someone's moral rights, then it would be impermissible for X to do alpha, independent of the intention with which he would do alpha if he were to do it. This position also affirms the possibility of harmless wrongdoing. For example, suppose the rights advocate holds that among the rights we have is a right that other people refrain from trespassing—venturing onto someone's property or using someone's property without the consent of its owner. Such trespassing can occur without bringing about any harm to the owner. You might trespass on my land when I am elsewhere, and you might trespass without damaging even a leaf or twig that belongs to me. The rights theorist will hold that your trespassing is morally wrong, a violation of my rights as property owner, even if it is, as in this case, entirely harmless (Ripstein, 2006).

Harm and Harmdoing

A person suffers a harm when her condition is made worse in some way. The unfolding of natural events can cause harm, as when lightning strikes. Human acts or omissions can cause harm. A person can be harmed either *in a respect* or *all things considered.* You are harmed, but not harmed all things considered, if a taxi in which you are riding crashes, breaking your leg but thereby preventing you from flying on your scheduled flight, which crashes in to the ocean killing everyone on board.

Ordinary usage might allow that one is harmed if one suffers loss in resources or opportunities, even if this loss triggers no loss in well-being, and no loss in how intrinsically well one's life goes for one. If someone steals an extra shirt from my bottom drawer, but I never notice the loss and never suffer any well-being loss from lacking the shirt, am I harmed?

From a nonconsequentialist moral perspective, the moral significance of harmdoing is generally thought to be modulated by two distinctions, one between doing and allowing, and another between harm and benefit. Doing harm might be thought worse, other things equal, than allowing harm. Causing someone to suffer harm might be thought worse, other things equal, than causing someone not to gain a benefit. Are there clear lines here? If we fail to put in place good schools for children are we harming them by causing them to be ignorant and lacking in reasoning skills, or are we rather failing to provide them the benefit of good education?

The idea of harming someone seems to include the idea of making the person's position worse by comparison with some baseline. Different ideas of harming might invoke different baselines.

One position is that an act that is rightly deemed morally wrong must be making a negative difference in the overall well-being of those affected by the act, by comparison with other acts that might instead have been chosen, including doing nothing. Whether one's choice of acts makes a difference in well-being depends on a counterfactual: if I do A or some other available act, what difference would it have made if I had chosen and acted differently, that is, done some other act instead? If the answer is "no difference at all," then on this view it cannot be morally wrong to do A rather than some alternative.

Making a difference is not exactly the same as the common-sense notion of causing effects. Suppose one is invited to join a firing squad that is going to execute an innocent man unjustly convicted of a crime at dawn tomorrow. The invitation specifies that if one accepts, one will shoot a fraction of a second sooner than other squad members and will (let us stipulate) be causing the death of the innocent person. But given that one's act only deprives the condemned person of a fraction of a second of anxious life, and we can suppose that this makes no difference at all to his well-being, one's act, on the making-a-difference view, cannot be morally wrong. At least, this is so if there is nothing else one could do instead of joining the squad that could make any difference to the person's lifetime well-being. The example illustrates the controversial character of the suggestion.

An alternate view is that one harms another by causing that person to be in a harmful condition, which might be true even if the person is not, all things considered, worse off. Elizabeth Harman (2009) suggests that "an action harms a person if the action causes pain, early death, bodily damage, or deformity to her." Another view relies on the distinction between a harm and a benefit, and holds that morality places greater weight on duties to refrain from harm than to duties to provide benefits (with intermediate status for duties to provide relief from threatened harm) (see Shiffrin, 1999).

If I operate a nuclear reactor in my basement for fun, my act imposes a large risk of causing an explosion that would harm my neighbors. Let us suppose, as is plausible, that this large risk imposition is unjustified. Suppose it turns out that no explosion occurs and no one is actually harmed. We might yet claim that my act is harmful by virtue of imposing risk of harm on my neighbors. This is stretching the idea of the harmful, because imposing a risk of harm on someone might not involve imposing any actual harm on anyone. But the stretch is arguably defensible. At least if we focus on excessive and unjustified imposition of risk in harm, it is plausible to allow that doing what imposes risk of such harm can be wrongful whether or not any actual harm materializes.

The idea that one's act is right or wrong, depending on the difference it makes, compared to alternative acts one might have done, is integral to an act consequentialist morality. If one faces a choice of doing A or B or C, the question is, what will come about if one does one or other of these options, and how good or bad is the outcome in each case. The act consequentialist holds that one ought always to do whatever would bring about the best outcome. (If one does not know what the outcomes of one's available acts would be, one will not know what one ought to do.) An alternative version of act consequentialism, also relying on the ideas of the difference one makes, holds that one ought always to do whatever would bring about the expectably best outcome (Pettit, 1997). On this view, for each act one might do, identify its possible outcomes and their value, multiply the value of each possible outcome by the probability that it will occur if one does this act, sum the results for each act one might do, and do the act associated with the highest expected value.

The expectably-best version of act consequentialism condemns as wrong the act of a physician who selects a treatment for her patient based on consulting the astrological signs, even if by a fluke the superstitiously selected treatment happens to deliver a cure. This version also condemns as wrong the act of a person who conducts nuclear experiments in her basement for fun, even if by good luck her conduct does not actually bring about a nuclear explosion destroying the neighborhood and harms no one.

The very same idea, that an act is right or wrong, depending on the difference it makes, can be deployed in a deontological morality of constraints and options. A morality of this type will hold that one is not always morally permitted to do whatever would bring about the best outcome, because the act that would produce the best outcome might violate a moral constraint, such as one against stealing, assaulting, or lying. A deontological morality will also hold that one is not always morally required to do whatever would bring about the best outcome, even if that would violate no moral constraints, because each person has moral options, up to a point, to act as she chooses, even if that brings about a less than best outcome. These formulations are fully compatible with the idea that moral constraints are constraints on making a difference in a way that harms someone (or fails to provide someone a benefit one owes that person; count that also as harming). On this type of deontological view, all wrongdoing is wrongful harming, with the exception of omitting to do what would bring about the greater good, when the greater good is of sufficient magnitude to override moral constraints, barring the acts that would bring it about. On this type of view, there are no acts of wrongful discrimination that harm no one. Or to be a bit more precise, since a deontological morality might take the *ex ante* (expectably harmful) rather than *ex post* approach, a deontological morality that relies on the notion of making a difference will hold that all acts of wrongful discrimination either harm someone or impose excessive risk of bringing about harm to someone. No harm, no foul, in a slogan.

In passing, I just note that one might also hold that whether one's discriminatory act involves opportunistic rather than merely eliminative agency can also affect the degree to which harming another by what one does is morally wrong. In opportunistic harmful agency, one benefits from the presence of the person whom one is harming, as when I grab a bystander and use his body to shield myself from a rockslide that is about to hit me (Quinn, 1989). Using someone in that way might be deemed especially wrong. Discrimination can involve harmful opportunistic agency. For example, suppose a committee examining applicants for a prestigious prize ignores all applicants except white-skinned males and chooses the best of these applicants for the prize, part of whose prestige value arises from the fact that it attracts so many apparently highly qualified applicants. The discriminator in this example is wrongfully using the ignored applicants.

For and against the claim that harmless discrimination can be wrong

Here is an example of a harmless discriminatory act, one involving racial discrimination.

> *Marta* is an Hispanic female who has just graduated from law school and is applying for entry-level positions in law firms. Her application is passed over by one firm acting on racial prejudice. The members of this firm's committee charged with assessing applications dislike the idea of having any coworkers except males of European ancestry, and on this basis decline to give her application a fair hearing. However, Marta's application is favorably reviewed at another law firm and she is offered a job on terms better than she would have received had the discriminating firm treated her application fairly. Given that her first-choice potential employer has offered her a job, it is a matter of indifference to Marta that the other firm has not followed suit. Moreover, given the current market pressures on law

> firms, the committee members of the discriminating firm know when they decline seriously to consider Marta's application that she will likely get very good job offers from other hiring firms. Finally, we add that the members of the hiring committee that is discriminating are aware that their discriminatory act will not cause harm to any other job applicants. Their discrimination against Marta will not cause any other applicant to fail to get a job for which he or she is best qualified.

Adam Slavny and Tom Parr (2016) introduce a similar example, which they regard as a counterexample to the claim that wrongful discrimination cannot be harmless. They suggest that certain defects in deliberation leading to choice can render the chosen action morally wrong, even if the action is harmless. The certain defects on their view involve failing to accord some person who might be affected by one's choice a proper consideration that respects the moral status of the individual. Brushing aside an application for employment on the basis of the race or ethnicity of the applicant fails to respect the equal moral status of the applicant—she is a person the same as any other person, and so entitled to equal consideration and fair hearing.

The contrary position would be to affirm that wrongful discrimination must, on the evidence available to the discriminating agent, impose harm or excessive risk of harm on the target—the person who will suffer the discrimination. If Marta is not harmed, the law firm committee cannot be guilty of wronging her.

Suppose in the grip of rancorous and hostile emotions, while standing on the sidewalk of a busy part of the city, I angrily stick pins in a Justin Bieber doll, expressing my unjustified hostility to him, but knowing this expressive act is harmless. This act might well be stupid, but it seems a long stretch to say it is morally wrong. Same goes if I stop eating pasta because I am angry at a victory by a team representing Italy in some international soccer competition. The intuition is, no harm, no wrong. Notice that in each of these examples, as in *Marta*, the act in question issues from morally faulty deliberation and morally bad attitudes. The claim would be that, contra Slavny and Parr, these features of acts are never sufficient to establish their wrongdoing.

One might still maintain that Marta is harmed, in a sense. She applies for a job at the discriminating firm and her application is not given fair treatment. This is in itself a setback to her interest in seeking a job. The discriminating firm harms her even though at the end of the day, given everything that happens, she is made no worse off overall. So one could accept that harmdoing is necessary for its being the case that a discriminatory act is wrong, but insist that in the *Marta* example—unlike the Justin Bieber and soccer resentment examples—the discrimination is harmful. This would be to affirm a 1b position.

Depending on the details of the account one gives of harming as not requiring bringing about reductions in anyone's well-being, one might end up with a position close to the 2b position. What 1b calls harming, 2b may identify as perpetration of harmless acts that are nonetheless violating someone's moral right.

But if we stand fast by 1a and stipulate that in the *Marta* scenario the discriminating hiring committee knows for sure that no loss will befall the discriminatee, doubt is cast on the judgment that the firm's behavior is wrong. The firm after all does not do what in the evidence-relative or belief-relative sense imposes any risk of harm (welfare loss), all things considered, on the target of discrimination. The behavior of the firm's agents nonetheless displays a nasty disposition and motivation, and may rightly be considered blameworthy on this basis. But regarding the committee members as culpable is compatible with holding that they do no wrong. Adopting that point of view is rejecting 2b. According to this way of looking at things, a morally bad deliberative process leading to action is one thing, the moral quality of the action chosen is another. You can never read off the second from the first.

The example of *Marta* resembles an example introduced by Derek Parfit (2011, at 216) to press the claim that having a culpable disposition and frame of mind toward a person one is treating in a certain way, might not force the judgment that what the agent does in this culpable spirit is morally wrong:

> *Mobster.* A hardened criminal wants to get hold of a pack of cigarettes, and to achieve this end enters a convenience store and gives the clerk the purchase price of the cigarettes and leaves the store with his purchase. The criminal has a thoroughly nasty disposition in this transaction. He would just as soon kill the convenience store clerk as look at him, if doing that would be advantageous. He is willing to run roughshod over other people's rights in order to satisfy his trivial, self-interested desire—here, a desire for having cigarettes. But the criminal knows before thinking of entering this particular store that shooting a convenience store clerk to get cigarettes would be a hassle, and the most effective way for him to get the pack of cigarettes is just to behave in the ordinary way—that is, ask for the cigarettes, and pay the requested price.

Parfit says the criminal displays bad character and a very bad disposition here, and is blameworthy on that account. But he does not do anything to the clerk that imposes harm or risk of harm on him, and so it is plausible to deny that the criminal is here guilty of wrongdoing. One might suppose that if the mobster is a loose cannon, his merely being near other persons renders it the case that he is imposing risk of harm on them. We have to understand the case as not involving risk imposition of that sort. The same is true in the *Marta* example, no harm or risk of harm is imposed on Marta, so on Parfit's view, as just construed, the hiring firm here does not commit wrongful discrimination.

One might suppose that we should see two acts here, one being the act of deliberating about a choice one faces, the other being choosing and pursuing one or other option from that set of choices. One might hold that the act of deliberating can be wrong, because it is done in a way that imposes excessive risk of harm on others, while the choosing and pursuing that results can be permissible, because it neither harms anyone nor imposes undue risk of harm on anyone. But this way of proceeding does not settle the questions, whether the deliberation leading to a further act can taint the further act as wrong, and whether one's being disposed in an evil way toward the person toward whom one is acting can make one's act wrong, even if the disposition does not here affect what is done.

We could heighten the disconnect between morally faulty deliberation and disposition leading to choice, and the act that as a result is chosen. Imagine that someone sees a stranger approaching, and deliberates in a thoroughly nasty way, thinking seriously about the ways he might dismember and kill this poor stranger just for the fun of it. In the end the person decides this rampaging would be too much hassle and just tips his cap politely to the stranger as he passes. The deliberation and choice-making are horrible in this example, but the actual act done is harmless and arguably not morally wrong. This example is now similar in relevant respects to the Slavny and Parr example. The judgment they make regarding it can be resisted, although whether this would be best advised is an exercise left to the reader. This essay just seeks to clarify some of the disagreements without settling them.

"Wrong in the evidence-relative sense" needs a qualification or at least a footnote. Consider an individual who intends to kill an innocent person for no morally respectable reason, and chooses the best means available for this purpose. Unfortunately for his plan, the best means available is terrible for the purpose at hand. The best he can do is shoot an arrow into the air, aiming at the distant figure of his intended victim. The distance is so great, and the winds so balky, that there is only a very small chance that the arrow will hit home. But it does, and the intended victim is killed. This is surely wrongful murder. But can the account that says harmdoing in the evidence-relative sense is a necessary condition for wrongdoing deliver this verdict? What the would-be murderer does has a tiny chance of imposing harm on the intended victim. But the risk of harm that is imposed is nonetheless excessive in the circumstances; there is no good reason to expose the arrow's target to any risk of harm at all, so any risk imposition is excessive. So there is excessive harm imposition in this sort of example. Moreover, the intention to kill for no good reason, and the choice of the best means at hand to achieve this bad end, surely contribute to the act's wrongfulness.

Beneficial discrimination?

In another type of example, the discriminatee is not only not harmed, but benefited by being treated in the discriminatory fashion. This sort of case might be thought to cast further doubt on the claim that harmdoing is a necessary condition or wrongdoing and *a fortiori* that discrimination must be harmful to qualify as morally wrong (Slavny and Parr, 2016; for critical discussion, see Lippert-Rasmussen, 2013). Here's a version:

> *Selection for dangerous duty*. The commanding officer of a military force is assigned the task of selecting soldiers who will then, under his leadership, carry out an extremely dangerous mission, one that is almost certain to result in death or grievous injury for those who do it. The commander is prejudiced against Jews and women, and is repelled by the thought of carrying out this heroic mission in such company. So he passes over eligible and qualified Jews and women under his command, and chooses English males for the mission. His deliberation leading to his selection is surely morally faulty, and faulty in a way that is wrongfully discriminatory. But his selection itself is clearly a benefit to those who suffer this discrimination, since any reasonable person prefers to stay able and alive and to be passed over for this assignment. So the view that wrongful discrimination must involve harmdoing seems incompatible with the judgment that in this example the discriminatory action of the commander is morally wrong. However, the example tugs us toward the judgment that the commander is indeed guilty of wrongful discrimination.

In response, it is not obvious that the example is one in which the discrimination is harmless, so this is not an example that tells against the view that says, no harm, no wrong. The discrimination brings about an unfair distribution of risk of serious harm among potential victims. If we accept the stipulation that being denied the opportunity to embark on a suicide mission is a benefit, then the discrimination in the example shifts risks that ought to be more equally shared. So interpreted, the example of beneficial discrimination pushes us to give up the idea that to be wrongful, discrimination must impose harm or excessive risk of harm on the target of the discrimination. In *Selection for dangerous duty* the discrimination might be claimed to be wrongful on the ground that it harms people other than those who are the targets of the discrimination.

In other cases of beneficial discrimination, the intuition that the target of the discrimination herself is wrongly treated, though not harmed, persists. Consider:

> *Nazi University*. The chancellor of a German university in the 1930s fires all Jewish professors without any good cause, as part of a campaign to rid prestigious institutions of non-Aryans. The professors cannot gain employment and flee the country, escaping the worst crimes of the Nazi era. They are better off for being fired.

As stated, the chancellor's act looks to be wrong in the belief-relative and evidence-relative senses even if it is, by historical fluke, fact-relative permissible. If one alters the case so that the evidence is that inducing the threatened Jewish professors to leave the country will benefit them, and their firing is necessary to the inducement, *and* the chancellor knows this, the advocate of the harm-is-necessary view will deny this revised case should be classified as wrongful discrimination.

Another possible move is to say that if the relevant baseline for deciding whether discrimination harms is a possible alternative scenario in which no one is treated unjustly at all, then the chancellor's act, even if necessary to benefit the professors in actual circumstances, is still wrong. But this just shows that the proposed baseline is inadequate for drawing lines of moral permissibility. Even if the chancellor is a secret anti-Nazi doing everything he can to save as many Jews as possible from death, his manipulation of the professors' circumstances, intended to benefit them and actually bringing about this result, still counts as morally wrong. This view we should definitely reject.

Discrimination as harmless violation of moral right

One who denies that the intention with which an agent does an act matters to whether his act is morally permissible might yet hold that there can be harmless wrongdoing, and in particular harmless discriminatory wrongdoing. This type of view might also hold that the quality of an agent's deliberation leading to a choice of action is morally independent of the moral assessment of the action that is chosen as permissible or impermissible. One view that has these implications affirms that violating someone's moral rights is always *pro tanto* morally wrong and that there are moral rights, the violation of which need not be harmful to the right-holder.

Assessing this view would require assessing all of the possible specifications of what moral rights people have that imply the possibility of harmless rights violations. Such an assessment is beyond the scope of this chapter.

To convey something of what is at issue, consider a non-discrimination example: harmless trespassing. Some hold that moral rights assign to each individual a morally protected sphere of liberty, and that acts that take away protected liberty are wrong even if harmless. One sort of liberty that might be protected in this way is the liberty of a property owner to determine what uses anyone will make of what she owns. If Smith is absent from her property and Jones crosses onto this property without her consent, Smith is wronged, even if no damage whatsoever is done and Smith never learns of the incursion, so suffers no displeasure or anguish arising from it. On the view under review, Smith is not harmed but is nonetheless wronged. Sophia Moreau (2010 and 2013; Chapter 13) develops an account of the wrong of discrimination that centrally involves the idea that norms against discrimination protect certain important freedoms of individuals, violations of which wrong the individuals even if they happen to be harmless.

The advocate of the idea that wrongdoing necessarily involves harmdoing can respond by appealing to a conception of moral rights as a set of important instruments for protecting people's welfare interests. Consider legal norms and allied public morality norms regarding discrimination. These are coarse-grained instruments. A good law might prohibit or otherwise disfavor a type of discrimination on the ground that it is generally harmful, and especially if it is generally harmful to members of the group that tends to suffer that type of discrimination. To be an appropriate law it is not necessary that each and every instance of the kind of discrimination that the law targets be an instance of harmdoing in some appropriate sense. If the law is justified in consideration of these general tendencies, then enforcement of the law will tend to reduce the morally disfavored harmdoing. Looking the other way and declining to enforce anomalous instances of harmless discrimination might not generate more fine-grained justice but rather decrease the degree to which there is deterrence of the legally prohibited conduct across the board. The law, and associated public morality norms introduced to support the law, can be defended in favorable circumstances as a more or less effective instrument for decreasing the discrimination that is genuinely wrongful, according to fundamental moral principles.

Regarding the harmless trespassing example, one who denies harmless wrongdoing will say that in the example, if the trespass is really harmless, it is really not morally wrong. But in reaching this judgment one needs to take into account the good consequences for the welfare of well-designed norms against trespass and the indirect harm that can result if acts are committed that erode these useful norms. A similar analysis will be available to defuse purported examples of harmless but genuinely wrongful rights-violating discriminatory acts.

Harmless discrimination motivated by prejudice

Another kind of case to ponder when considering whether discriminatory wrongdoing must involve harmdoing is discrimination directed against powerful, privileged, entrenched groups on the part of oppressed groups that propose separatist strategies aimed at reducing unfair distribution of opportunities that are hurting their group. For example, in the U.S. in the twentieth century, where black-skinned people of African lineage formed a racial underclass, some blacks turned their backs on integration in the larger society and proclaimed doctrines of racial self-help, independence, and separate black institutions. Some urged Back to Africa. Some sought political secession with the aim of establishing a separate black republic on land carved from part of the U.S. Although such movements often espoused doctrines of racial supremacy that denigrated possessors of white skin, their general aims and effects seemed benign to many observers.

We should accept that there can be separatist campaigns that involve no tincture of bias or hostile attitudes toward any social groups. The separatism is proposed as an effective strategy for improving the welfare prospects of group members, undoing oppression, and promoting social justice. If harmless, acts promoting separate institutions for different social groups are surely not morally wrong.

But suppose members of an oppressed group form an organization that promotes the separation of members of the group from the larger society and promulgates a doctrine that proclaims the inherent superiority of this group compared to others. Promulgation of such an ideology might have harmful effects. Today's oppressed can become tomorrow's oppressors. But suppose that in some situation no harm or risk of harm is being imposed; how should we assess the discriminatory practice and doctrine? Consider:

> *Harmless prejudice.* The Greens are an oppressed minority in a society dominated by Blues. A group of Greens urges that fellow group members should club together and favor each other, withdrawing from interaction with Blues. They urge that Greens should undertake this separation strategy because their blood is purer and better than the blood of the dominant Blues. Despite this pernicious and fanciful ideology, the acts of the Green separatists, though motivated by anti-Blue sentiment, have only beneficial consequences. The Greens form cooperatives and churches that increase the average labor force participation, income, years of schooling, and family stability of group members. We can sharpen the issue by stipulating that any similar reform movement by Greens that lacked the group superiority organizing doctrine would bring about less beneficial consequences.

A view that denies that harmdoing is necessary for discriminatory wrongdoing can find the Green separatist discriminatory acts morally wrong on the basis of their motivation, and the character of the deliberation that gives rise to them, even though the acts are entirely beneficial, not harmless. Such a view could allow the good consequences to weigh on the scales that determine moral wrongfulness status, and if the good consequences are sufficiently desirable, the all things considered judgment could be that these acts are permissible. But the harmlessness of the acts would not be a decisive bar to a judgment of wrongdoing.

Conclusion

The view that acts of discrimination are morally wrong only if harmful is supported less by a particular interpretation of the nature of discrimination than by the fact that this view is in harmony with a general moral position that wrongdoing is always harmdoing. This position allows that harmless discriminatory acts, even if harmless and therefore permissible, can proceed from bad motivation and qualify the doer as culpable. The advocate of this view probably should allow that someone who fails to provide morally required benefits to others counts as doing harm in a broad sense. Whether the view should be acceptable depends on the best account of what we owe to one another, whatever that turns out to be.

Bibliography

Alexander, L. 1992. "What Makes Wrongful Discrimination Wrong? Biases, Preferences, Stereotypes, and Proxies." *University of Pennsylvania Law Review*. 141: 149–219.

Arneson, R. 2006. "What Is Wrongful Discrimination?" *San Diego Law Review*. 43: 774–807.

Arneson, R. 2013. "Discrimination, Disparate Impact, and Theories of Justice," in Hellman, D. and Moreau, S. (eds), *Philosophical Foundations of Discrimination Law*. Oxford: Oxford University Press: 87–111.

Dworkin, R. 1978. *Taking Rights Seriously*, Chapter 9. Cambridge, MA: Harvard University Press.

Dworkin, R. 2000. *The Sovereign Virtue: Equality in Theory and Practice*. Cambridge, MA: Harvard University Press.

Harman, E. 2009. "Harming as Causing Harm," in Roberts, M., and Wasserman, D. (eds), *Harming Future Persons: Ethics, Genetics, and the Non-Identity Problem*. Dordrecht: Springer: 137–154.

Kamm, F. 2007. *Intricate Ethics: Rights, Responsibilities, and Permissible Harm*. Oxford: Oxford University Press.

Lippert-Rasmussen, K. 2013. *Born Free and Equal: A Philosophical Inquiry into the Nature of Discrimination*. Oxford: Oxford University Press.

Moreau, S. 2010. "What Is Discrimination?" *Philosophy and Public Affairs*. 38: 143–179.

Moreau, S. 2013. "In Defense of a Liberty-Based Account of Discrimination," in Hellman, D., and Moreau, S. (eds) *Philosophical Foundations of Discrimination Law*. Oxford: Oxford University Press: 71–86.

Parfit, D. 1984. "What Makes Someone's Life Go Best?" Appendix I in *Reasons and Persons*. Oxford: Oxford University Press.

Parfit, D. 2011. Chapters 7 and 9 of *On What Matters*, vol. 1. Oxford: Oxford University Press.

Parr, T. and Slavny, A. 2016. "Harmless Discrimination." *Legal Theory*. 21(2): 1–15.

Pettit, P. 1997. "The Consequentialist Perspective," in Baron, M., Pettit, P. and Slote, M. (eds), *Three Methods of Ethics: A Debate*. Oxford: Blackwell: 92–174.

Quinn, W. 1989. "Actions, Intentions, and Consequences: The Doctrine of Double Effect." *Philosophy and Public Affairs*. 18: 287–312.

Ripstein, A. 2006. "Beyond the Harm Principle." *Philosophy and Public Affairs*. 34: 215–245.

Scanlon, T. 2008. *Moral Dimensions: Permissibility, Meaning, Blame*. Cambridge, MA: Harvard University Press.

Shiffrin, S. 1999. "Wrongful Life, Procreative Responsibility, and the Significance of Harm." *Legal Theory*. 5: 117–148.

Thomson, J. 1991. "Self-defense." *Philosophy and Public Affairs*. 20: 283–310.

Wasserstrom, R. 1964. "Rights, Human Rights, and Racial Discrimination." *Journal of Philosophy*. 61(20): 628–641.

Further reading

For three recent, thorough, and contrasting accounts of the wrongness of discrimination, see Hellman, D. (2008) *When Is Discrimination Wrong?* Cambridge, MA: Harvard University Press; Moreau, S. (2010) "What Is Discrimination?" *Philosophy and Public Affairs* 38: 143–179; and Lippert-Rasmussen, K. (2013) *Born Free and Equal: A Philosophical Inquiry into the Nature of Discrimination*, Oxford: Oxford University Press.

13

DISCRIMINATION AND FREEDOM

Sophia Moreau

UNIVERSITY OF TORONTO

Introduction

There has been a longstanding debate in Anglo-American political philosophy about the relationship between freedom and equality. Isaiah Berlin argued that these two values are always potentially in conflict: full social and political equality can only be achieved by taking certain freedoms away from some people, and even though we may be justified in doing this, we must, according to Berlin, acknowledge the very real loss that this involves and not pretend that it can ever be fully compensated by a gain in equality (Berlin 1969). Many contemporary political philosophers have followed Berlin in assuming that freedom and equality are competing values, and they have offered us different accounts of the respective weight of these values in a theory of justice: libertarians emphasize the importance of protecting individuals' liberties, whereas egalitarians emphasize the need to promote social and political equality. Other philosophers, however, have denied that the two values stand in tension at all. Peter Westen and Joseph Raz have urged that equality is really an "empty" value: people are treated as equals when they are given what they are entitled to (Westen 1982; Raz 1982). On this account, freedom is the primary value, and people are treated as equals as long as each of them is given as much freedom as they are entitled to. By contrast, Ronald Dworkin argued that it is equality, and not freedom, that is the "sovereign virtue": far from being an empty value, the proper conception of equality will tell us which kinds of freedom we are entitled to, and why (Dworkin 2000).

But what about the relationship between freedom and *discrimination*? Legal and political philosophers are only beginning to think about this, since it is only over the past 15 to 20 years that philosophers have begun to think of discrimination as something worth theorizing about. Wrongful discrimination, broadly conceived, involves disadvantaging certain individuals because they possess, or are believed to possess, a certain kind of characteristic, in circumstances where this disadvantage is unfair. Sometimes this occurs intentionally or explicitly, and we call it "direct discrimination" or "disparate treatment"; sometimes it is a side-effect of a policy adopted for quite different and perhaps even beneficial reasons, and we call it "indirect discrimination" or "disparate impact." We can helpfully think of both kinds of wrongful discrimination as one way in which the state, and sometimes also ordinary people, can fail to treat people as equals. So if we were to draw a Venn diagram, we would map out unfair discrimination as a smaller circle within the broader circle that represents inequality. So understood, discrimination is not an "empty" value, or equivalent to failing to give someone their due – for it is only certain kinds of traits that we think of as the basis for unfair discrimination. But many questions similar to those that philosophers have asked about equality and freedom arise in the case of discrimination and its relationship to freedom.

It may seem, for instance, that the same tensions that Berlin noted between freedom and equality exist between freedom and discrimination. Certainly prohibitions on discrimination have effects on the freedom of contract of the *discriminator*: under such prohibitions, I am not free to exclude you or "people like you" from my bar because of your race; not free to deny you an apartment lease because of your religion; and not free to refuse to employ you because you are pregnant. One set of questions raised by discrimination and discrimination laws is whether these restrictions on freedom of contract are justified, and these questions have been explored by scholars such as Richard Epstein (Epstein 1995). However, it is a mistake to suppose that the only freedom at issue in such cases is the freedom of contract of the discriminator. For discrimination also has significant effects on the freedom of the *discriminatee*, and often also on the freedom of those who share the trait on the basis of which that person was disadvantaged. To take an easy example: Donald Trump's proposal to ban Muslims who are not U.S. citizens from entering the United States would clearly affect the freedom of movement of Muslims who are non-U.S. citizens, as well as their freedom to take up a variety of opportunities in the U.S. And such a ban would also have effects on Muslims who *are* U.S. citizens, and whose own freedom of movement is not at issue. Because the ban expresses and encourages prejudice against Muslims and stereotyping of "them" as a group – a group, moreover, that the ban conceives of as un-American and apparently homogeneous – there would be many ways in which it would lessen the social and political freedoms of all Muslims within the United States. So insofar as we are concerned with people's freedom in cases of discrimination, the real question is not how to balance the discriminator's freedom against the disadvantaged group's right to equal treatment, but how to balance different people's freedoms against each other.

One might think that this question of balancing is really more a question of normative ethics or of public policy than it is of political philosophy. At any rate, it is not the question that political and legal philosophers working on discrimination treat as most urgent. What primarily concerns these philosophers at the moment is whether the effects of discrimination on people's freedoms *are part of what makes discrimination unfair.*

It will help here to borrow a distinction drawn by the American political philosopher Judith Shklar. Shklar distinguished between "injustices" on the one hand, and "mere misfortunes" on the other (Shklar 1990). An injustice is a moral wrong that you have done to me, and it generates a strong claim on my part to have you put me back in the position I would have been in, but for your unjust action. By contrast, a misfortune is simply a disadvantageous effect of your action. It may harm me just as much as an injustice does, and it may generate a claim for some aid. But it does not leave me with a strong claim against others for full rectification. Using this distinction between injustice and misfortune, we can rephrase the central question for philosophers currently writing on discrimination and freedom: are the effects of discrimination on our freedom mere misfortunes, or are they a part of the injustice of discrimination? If they are mere misfortunes, then we can explain why discrimination is wrong without appealing to the value of freedom at all. By contrast, if these effects on people's freedoms are a part of the injustice of discrimination, then freedom will play a primary role in helping us understand the wrongfulness of discrimination.

I hope in the rest of this chapter to suggest that there are strong reasons for thinking that some of the effects of discrimination on our freedom *are* a part of the injustice of discrimination. But there are different conceptions of freedom – that is, different ways of understanding what it is to be free and why freedom is of value. Which of these is relevant to the unfairness of discrimination? And in what way? A subsidiary aim of this chapter is to explore these questions, and so to clarify exactly *which sorts* of freedom might be relevant, and *how*. I shall argue that although freedom cannot be the only value to which we appeal in explaining the injustice of discrimination, we do need to appeal to freedom in several different ways if we are to have a rich account of discrimination that captures all of our intuitive beliefs about why it is wrong, and that is faithful to the underlying purpose of anti-discrimination laws.

Wrongful discrimination, status, and disrespect

But why think that freedom is in any way relevant to the unfairness of discrimination? We can start to see why, I think, when we look at theories of discrimination that make no reference at all to freedom, and when we test these theories against certain core cases of discrimination. Take, for instance, theories of discrimination that locate its unfairness in some form of subordination or inappropriate valuation of others – such as Owen Fiss' idea that discrimination aggravates the subordinate social status of a specially disadvantaged group, or Deborah Hellman's suggestion that discrimination demeans people by implying they are less worthy than others and lowering their social standing (Fiss 1976; Hellman 2008; cf. Chapters 6 and 7). Many discriminatory acts do imply that the excluded group is less worthy, and many discriminatory acts do lower their social status or perpetuate their already low status. But do all of them – and is this the only reason why they are unfair? Consider the kinds of stereotyped workplace practices that are universally agreed to constitute discrimination. A grocery store channels new applicants in the following way: female job applicants get channeled into positions as cashiers, and male job applicants get channeled into positions in the re-stocking room. Suppose, as I think seems plausible, that neither of these positions is regarded as inherently superior to the other – they are both low-level jobs. When we challenge this arrangement as discriminatory, it can't be that our objection is that the women are being demeaned relative to the men, or the men relative to the women, or that the policy perpetuates a lower status for either men or women. The policy doesn't seem unfair because it demeans either group. Rather, it seems to stereotype them in ways that unfairly restrict their freedom: women have no chance of becoming or envisioning themselves as strong enough to work in a stocking room, and men have no chance of being seen as anything other than their muscles. Second, consider the many restrictive voting laws that are currently being challenged as discriminatory in the United States: for instance, restrictions on forms of I.D. recognized by voting stations, which have been used in order to lessen the number of ethnic minority voters who are able to cast a ballot, and roll-backs of early voting procedures that similarly result in far fewer members of ethnic minorities being able to go to the polls. When members of these minority groups challenge these policies as discriminatory, they are not doing so merely as a means to raise their social standing. They are doing so because they want these important freedoms that other Americans have: they want the freedom to cast a ballot in the election, and they want an equal chance of influencing American politics. It seems to be a misrepresentation of their aims, and their complaints, to suggest that their freedom matters only as a means to their achieving equal social standing, and it is this equal social standing that they really value in cases of discrimination. On the contrary, we might say, they care about their freedom as something that is of value in its own right. They believe they are done an injustice when they are denied it. And they think of this particular injustice as just as much a part of the wrongness of discrimination as they do the denial of equal standing.

The relevance of freedom and the inadequacy of a purely status-based account of the injustice of discrimination is even clearer in cases of indirect discrimination or disparate impact, in which a policy is not intentionally implemented so as to exclude a certain group, but rather has unforeseen but disproportionately negative effects upon them relative to other groups (cf. Chapter 2). Consider condominium rules that ban signs in hallways, and that therefore prevent Jewish families from placing mezuzahs over their doorways (and hence, prevent Jews that view this as a requirement of Jewish law from living in these condominiums). And consider height requirements for firefighters and police officers that result in disproportionately low numbers of women being admitted to these professions, and written tests for promotion that disproportionately large numbers of ethnic minority candidates fail. In cases of indirect discrimination such as these, it is more difficult to see the policy in question as a denial of someone's equal status, since the differential impact is usually not the purpose of the policy, but merely an unintended side-effect. It is true that such policies can still have the effect of perpetuating the lower status of certain groups. But it seems even less plausible here to suggest that this is the sole or the primary reason why they are unfair. Jewish families considering the condominium in my example would likely be far more concerned with the limitations that the policy places upon their freedom to live in and work in a certain place than they would be about its implications for their social standing; and both female applicants to the fire and police departments and minority employees seeking promotion want an equal chance at the job as much as, or even more than, they want recognition and equal social standing.

Wrongful discrimination and harms

I have argued that, both in certain cases of direct discrimination and in certain cases of indirect discrimination, theories of discrimination that appeal solely to a lowering of the victim's social standing fail to capture the victim's concern about discrimination. But why suppose that what is missing in the explanations yielded by these theories is an appeal to *freedom*? Why not appeal to the idea of a "harm," the way certain prioritarian theories of discrimination do? We could suggest, for instance, that discrimination is unjust because it harms people – most often, people who are worse off, the harms to whom generally are morally more problematic than are the harms accruing to people who are better off (Lippert-Rasmussen 2014; Chapter 12).

There are several reasons why an appeal to harms might seem inadequate here, and why we might prefer to think in terms of freedoms. First, what matters to each of the victims in the cases we have considered is not just voting or buying the condominium or being a firefighter – it is being able *to decide for themselves* whether to vote, or whether to take the condominium, or whether to apply to be a firefighter, not being prevented by others from accessing these opportunities or from making these decisions on their own. But this means that, at least from the claimant's standpoint, what matters is having the freedom to choose for themselves, and not just having achieved the particular outcome. Secondly, a focus on harms suggests that these freedoms matter from the standpoint of justice only insofar as they affect a person's *well-being*. And this seems false to our experience of such cases, and unnecessarily reductivist. We don't just care about having such freedoms insofar as they make us happier, or satisfy our preferences, or in some other way make our lives go well (such as in accordance with stipulations of an "objective list" theory of well-being). In many cases, we just think that it is fundamentally important that members of these social groups have these freedoms: they have a *right* or *entitlement* to them, irrespective of whether it helps or hinders their well-being. Suppose it could be proven that being given an equal chance at promotion in certain careers would actually lessen the well-being of women and ethnic minorities: they would be more stressed and their lives would be more uncertain, since they would no longer be forced to stay on the lower rungs of most employment ladders. Would we think that they had less of a claim on us to non-discrimination in employment?

Most of us would consider this fact about their well-being to be irrelevant to the justice or injustice of their employment situation. And that may be because questions of discrimination have more to do with questions of freedom than with well-being. Perhaps we have a right to certain freedoms, regardless of whether having them increases our well-being.

There is a further problem with thinking of harms as basic to claims of the injustice of discrimination, rather than freedoms. Most anti-discrimination laws do not protect against the worst forms of harm, and they do not help the groups that are least advantaged *simply because* they are least advantaged – on any metric or conception of "advantage". Significantly, poverty, or economic disadvantage, is not a prohibited ground of discrimination in most jurisdictions. So you cannot bring a claim of discrimination against a government simply because that government has failed to give you and others like you the most basic means of survival, such as food, clothing, and a rudimentary shelter. If discrimination were unjust because it continued to harm the groups that are worst off, surely poverty would be recognized as a prohibited ground of discrimination? To say this is not to suggest that our laws always do a perfect job of capturing the truth about discrimination, or that every legal doctrine is a good guide to what is truly just. But it seems most likely that the most basic features of our laws do capture our own basic understanding of the kinds of injustice that they are supposed to address; so from this standpoint, it does seem problematic that poverty is nowhere recognized as a prohibited ground of discrimination. Moreover, if discrimination were unjust largely because of the harm that it caused to underprivileged groups, it would seem mysterious why discrimination law only protects against disadvantage that arises from such a very limited set of traits, such as race, gender, and so on. Some of these traits, in some circumstances, do mark off the most underprivileged groups – but not in all circumstances. And in any case, if our real concern were to prevent harms to those who are most disadvantaged, surely it would be most efficient just to measure the impact of a policy on the well-being of the most socially disadvantaged groups, perhaps making certain allowances for such other relevant factors as ability or desert, but certainly not requiring that the groups have been disadvantaged on the basis of a certain kind of trait rather than others.

I have tried to suggest that at least part of what we object to, when we think of a given case of discrimination as unfair, is the fact that it denies certain groups certain freedoms. But what kinds of freedom, specifically? And how does unfair discrimination work to deny people freedom?

Wrongful discrimination and personal freedom

There are at least four kinds of freedom that philosophers have identified as relevant to the injustice of discrimination. Philosophers have suggested that unfair discrimination affects these four freedoms on two different "levels" – so I shall discuss each of these freedoms in the context of the level that is relevant to it. The first level is the personal level, at which the state and certain private actors, such as providers of goods and services and accommodation, owe particular people legal (and moral) duties of non-discrimination. When these duties are violated, this affects the victims' freedom. But discrimination also affects our freedom on a second level, a systemic level, which is concerned with the more indirect effects of discriminatory policies on the opportunities available to, and disadvantages faced by, the groups that share the trait on the basis of which a particular person has been discriminated against.

Let us look at each of these levels in turn. First, the personal level. We can identify at least three kinds of freedom that are affected at the personal level, when a person is excluded or disadvantaged because of some characteristic such as their race, or their gender, or their religion. First, what we call their "negative freedom" is lessened. Negative freedom is, broadly speaking, the absence of interference from others, whether in the form of removing options that used to be available to us, or in placing increased costs on remaining options (Berlin 1969; Miller 1983). Second, discrimination is also an indication of the potential of future interference by others: when it occurs, it indicates that these people are under the domination of others, subject to their potentially arbitrary control. So discrimination indicates a lack of a further kind of freedom, which Philip Pettit has called "freedom as non-domination" (Pettit 2001, 2014). We can think of this as freedom not just from *actual* interference but from the very *possibility* of arbitrary interference by others. Third, perhaps because victims of discrimination are in this way subject to others' domination, they are never allowed to forget their race, or their gender, or their sexuality: there is a very real sense in which, when deliberating about important (and even trivial) decisions in their lives, these traits, and other people's perceptions of them, must constantly be before their eyes (Moreau 2010). If I am African-Canadian, then wherever I go, I carry the burden of other people's assumptions about me and the burden of the increased costs associated with my skin color: if I am late for my job interview, the employer will assume I am scattered and lazy rather than assuming that my bus was late; when I pick up my biracial children, who look "white," the teachers will assume I am their nanny rather than their parent. This is, in my view, a serious and very real infringement of a person's freedom; and it seems to go beyond both sorts of freedom that I have mentioned, since it is primarily concerned, not with the options available to a person or their costs, but with the way her deliberation must proceed and with the burdens of always having to consider certain facts, and artfully side-step or try to avoid certain misperceptions about ourselves. In my earlier writings, I spoke of this kind of freedom and of the two other forms of freedom as together comprising our "deliberative freedom" (Moreau 2010, 2012). I now think this label is misleading: it invites us to focus too much on an individual's deliberative process and highlights the third understanding of freedom at the expense of the other two. But in the absence of a better umbrella term, I shall continue to use "deliberative freedom" to refer to all three of these forms of freedom.

Any theory of discrimination which implied that people were unjustly discriminated against whenever a policy lessened any person's deliberative freedoms would be hopelessly implausible. Most policies – even non-discriminatory ones! – infringe some people's freedom at least some of the time. But theories of discrimination that treat freedom as relevant to the unfairness of discrimination do not claim that any and all infringements of freedom are problematic. Rather, they claim that discrimination is unfair when a person is deprived of *those freedoms to which they are entitled.* How do we then determine whether, in a particular context, someone is entitled to a certain negative freedom, or to freedom from constant reminders of a certain trait of theirs and others' perceptions of it? We look, in part, to the prohibited grounds of discrimination, for we can see these as reflecting judgments about which traits it is whose costs we generally ought not to have to bear. Religion is a prohibited ground of discrimination in many jurisdictions, for instance: this, on a freedom-based account, signals that people should not have to think about their religion as a liability when deciding where to work or where to live, and that they should not have to choose between being able to practice their religion and being able to take up a certain job. Race is a prohibited ground of discrimination, for similar reasons. Notice, though, that when we ask *why* people generally should not have to bear these sorts of costs associated with being of one religion or one race rather than another, there is no single explanation we can give. In explaining cases of religion, we might appeal to how important a person's religion is to them; whereas in the case of race, we might appeal to the fact that a person can do nothing to alter it and should therefore not be penalized for it. So an account of why discrimination is unfair that appeals to our entitlement to different freedoms must rely, at bottom, on a number of diverse explanations of why we are entitled to these freedoms. I do not think this is a failing in such theories. We do not demand of theories of justice that they be reductive, appealing to some single ultimate underlying principle in all cases. Why should we demand this of theories of discrimination – particularly when the prohibited grounds of discrimination are so diverse? It is enough that the theory gives us a plausible explanation of why particular instances of discrimination are wrong or unjust, with an appeal to values, such as freedom, that we think are important.

I said that in determining which freedoms people are entitled to, in cases of discrimination, we can look in part to the prohibited grounds of discrimination. But there is also another set of factors we have to consider – namely, the competing interests of the discriminator and of others affected by his policy or action. In determining, for instance, whether as a visually impaired person travelling with a guide dog, I have a right to be given a lift by any cab that comes my way, we need to consider not just the impact on me and my freedom, but the impact on the cab driver. What if his religion requires him to clean his cab of all animal hair several times a day? Perhaps I do not then have an entitlement against *him*. Perhaps it is only against other cab drivers who are not of this religion. So which freedoms I am entitled to depends in part on the sorts of costs that we think I can reasonably be expected to bear – which are questions we ask when we think about prohibited grounds of discrimination; but it also depends on a weighing of my freedoms against the freedoms and other interests of other people affected. And indeed, we can see this weighing and balancing process at work in discrimination law itself, for there are many stages of legal reasoning in discrimination law complaints to which the freedoms and interests of other parties are considered relevant.

Systemic discrimination

I have now discussed the personal level, at which particular private actors and state actors have duties of non-discrimination toward particular people. But what about the systemic level, where we are concerned with a broader and often more indirect set of effects, and effects on *groups* of people marked out by the prohibited grounds? Certainly, all of the three kinds of freedom we have discussed could also be affected at the systemic level. But there is also a fourth kind of freedom that is affected at the systemic level. This fourth kind of freedom is what philosophers have called "positive freedom" or "autonomy." There are many ways of understanding positive freedom, but all of them involve some kind of appeal to the individual as self-governing and self-realizing. And all of them conceive of freedom not just as a set of opportunities that a person might have, but as a kind of personal achievement that requires a certain way of living: the person who is free in a positive sense has become self-governing and is living a life that fully reflects his choices or his values. Although it is possible that the most heinous cases of discrimination might directly limit a person's positive liberty, it is most natural to think of people's positive liberty as being affected over time, through many individual acts of discrimination both against themselves and against others, which then entrench social prejudices against and stereotypes about the groups to which they belong or are perceived to belong. Members of a Latino minority in part of the United States, for instance, do not have their autonomy lessened by being denied employment at one store. But discrimination in a number of places of employment and in a number of contexts over time – in employment, in accommodation, in education, in the availability of and quality of public facilities such as transportation and libraries and pools in their more run-down neighborhoods – all of these will together work to lessen the autonomy of members of this minority group. It is for this reason, I think, that this fourth kind of freedom is best understood as relevant to the systemic level. It may not explain why particular employers have duties of non-discrimination, but it could help to explain why discrimination is in general unjust and why we are justified in prohibiting it through our laws.

Discrimination and perfectionist conceptions of positive freedom

Tarunabh Khaitan has recently developed a theory of the unfairness of discrimination at the systemic level which appeals to a quite specific conception of positive freedom (Khaitan 2016). Khaitan argues that discrimination exacerbates and perpetuates significant disadvantages between social groups, and thereby makes it impossible for members of the least advantaged social groups to be free in the positive sense that they lead a life of flourishing through the pursuit of valuable activities. This is, in Khaitan's view, a large part of what makes discrimination unfair: quite apart from its direct impact on the person who is denied a job or denied accommodation, it works indirectly, at a systemic level, to prevent members of the most disadvantaged social groups from achieving positive freedom. Khaitan's positive conception of freedom is what we call "perfectionist," in that rather than allowing that each person can define for himself what a good life consists of, Khaitan maintains that there are certain objectively valuable activities, and it is only when a person's life involves the pursuit of these – as opposed to non-valuable activities or morally questionable ones – that he is truly free.

I have some doubts as to whether this perfectionist interpretation of positive freedom is the right one for Khaitan to use, in the context of understanding discrimination. In particular, it seems to me to sit uneasily with our common understanding of the aims of discrimination law. Whatever theory of discrimination we endorse, I think we cannot deny that part of the point of discrimination laws is to avoid placing some people in a position where they are making pronouncements about the moral value of belonging to a certain group or the moral value of having access to a certain opportunity. So a regime of discrimination law that required judges or tribunals to ask questions like "Is this proposed protected trait really objectively valuable?" or "Would eliminating this disadvantage between group X and group Y really increase the valuable options available to group Y?" would be problematic. It would require judges and tribunals to adopt a paternalistic stance towards the very groups who need to start speaking for themselves and helping us to understand their very different conceptions of value. Surely we want disadvantaged groups to have a chance to speak for themselves and to have their own conceptions of value taken seriously. Khaitan might reply that, for this reason, our laws should not inquire into the value of certain activities or certain traits: even though it is true that we can only live flourishing, worthwhile lives when we pursue activities that really are morally valuable, nevertheless because we would not want to adopt a paternalistic attitude towards disadvantaged groups, our laws themselves should not be constructed in such a way as to presuppose one moral truth rather than another. But this seems to leave us with a set of laws that responds very imperfectly to what is supposed to be, in Khaitan's view, a moral truth of the matter.

I think Khaitan's understanding of positive freedom could be modified so as to avoid these criticisms. There are conceptions of positive freedom that do not presuppose any objective conception of what is valuable but rather allow that this, too, is up to each person to decide. If we interpret Khaitan's theory of discrimination in light of this kind of conception of positive freedom, we can propose that discrimination is unjust in part because it exacerbates the disadvantages between social groups, and this leaves the least advantaged unable to be free in the sense that their lives are chosen by them and reflect what is important to them, whatever that may be. This modified theory, of course, gives rise to a different and difficult question: why should we think that autonomy in *this* sense is important to us? But it has the merit of remaining neutral as between different groups' ideals of the good life.

So modified, could Khaitan's account of the effects of discrimination on our positive freedom at the systemic level be conjoined with a freedom-based account of the personal level, such as the one I outlined earlier? Perhaps yes. Khaitan himself suggests such a conjunction of accounts, though he does not spend a lot of time discussing the personal level: he claims, somewhat briefly, that at the personal level, discrimination law aims to rectify personal wrongs that have been done by one individual to another, wrongs which consist in unfairly disadvantaging someone because of a trait whose costs she really should not have had to bear. One problem for such an account is that the different explanations given at the two levels risk crowding each other out. If, at the personal level, discrimination is wrongful because it infringes people's deliberative freedom in circumstances where they are entitled to it, isn't that enough to explain its unfairness? Why do we then *also* need to appeal to its systemic effects on our positive freedom? Conversely, if we begin with the systemic level and argue that this is the basis of the general injustice of discrimination, do we then need to argue that there is some personal duty owed by a discriminator to a discriminatee, which he violates when he infringes her deliberative freedom?

There is a genuine difficulty here. But it is not just a difficulty for freedom-based theories. It is a difficulty for *any* theory of discrimination: for much of discrimination law is structured in such a way as to suggest that we do owe personal duties to victims not to discriminate, and yet at the same time it is undeniable that discrimination has systemic effects on groups and the individuals that belong to these groups. Any theory of discrimination will have to find some way of acknowledging the effects of discrimination at both levels, and of drawing what it takes to be the relevant effects into a coherent whole.

Conclusion

In closing, I would like to mention a further difficulty that freedom-based theories must face. It seems implausible to think that discrimination is unfair *only* because it impacts on our freedom. Although, as I argued, victims of discrimination care about their freedom, they also care about other things: being given full recognition and equal social status, having the relevant opportunities, not being harmed. In other words, freedom might be a part of the story of why discrimination is unfair, but it may only be one part.

I think this is correct. I have tried to show in this chapter that freedom, as a value, has a strong claim to be a part of our theory of why discrimination is unfair. But I do not think it can be the whole of our theory. In fact, discrimination as a phenomenon is so diverse that it seems implausible to suggest that its unfairness could be reduced to any one value. We may need a pluralist account of discrimination if we are to capture all of what matters to us, in cases of discrimination. Of course, any pluralist account would owe us an explanation of how the different wrong-making features of discrimination cohere, and of how the different moral reasons that they give us interact. Must each wrong-making feature be present in each instance of discrimination, and does each of them yield a reason that is as weighty as the others? Or is it enough if one is present? Do some give us stronger reasons than others? These are all important questions that await further work.

Bibliography

Berlin, I. 1969. *Four Essays on Liberty*. Oxford: Oxford University Press.

Dworkin, R. 2000. *Sovereign Virtue: The Theory and Practice of Equality*. Cambridge, MA: Harvard University Press.

Epstein, R. 1995. *Forbidden Grounds: The Case Against Employment Discrimination Laws*. Cambridge, MA: Harvard University Press.

Fiss, O. 1976. "Groups and the Equal Protection Clause." *Philosophy & Public Affairs*. 5(2): 107–177.

Hellman, D. 2008. *When is Discrimination Wrong?* Cambridge, MA: Harvard University Press.

Hellman, D., and Moreau, S. eds. 2013. *Philosophical Foundations of Discrimination Law*. Oxford: Oxford University Press.

Khaitan, T. 2016. *A Theory of Discrimination Law*. Oxford: Oxford University Press.

Lippert-Rasmussen, K. 2014. *Born Free and Equal: A Philosophical Inquiry into the Nature of Discrimination*. Oxford: Oxford University Press.

Miller, D. 1983. "Constraints on Freedom." *Ethics*. 94: 66–86.

Moreau, S. 2010. "What is Discrimination?" *Philosophy & Public Affairs*. 38: 143.

Moreau, S. 2012. "In Defense of a Liberty-Based Theory of Discrimination," in Moreau, S. and Hellman, D. eds. *Philosophical Foundations of Discrimination Law*. Oxford: Oxford University Press.

Pettit, P. 2001. *A Theory of Freedom*. Cambridge: Polity Press.

Pettit, P. 2014. *Just Freedom. A Moral Compass for a Complex World*. Norton: New York.

Raz, J. 1982. *The Morality of Freedom*. Oxford: Clarendon Press.

Shklar, J. 1990. *The Faces of Injustice*. New Haven: Yale University Press.

Westen, P. 1982. "The Empty Idea of Equality." *Harvard Law Review*. 95(3): 537–596.

Suggestions for further reading

Khaitan, T. 2016. *A Theory of Discrimination Law*. Oxford: Oxford University Press.

Moreau, S. Forthcoming. "Equality and Discrimination," in Tasioulas, J. (ed.) *The Cambridge Companion to Philosophy of Law*. Cambridge: Cambridge University Press.

14
DISCRIMINATION AND VIRTUE

J. L. A. Garcia

BOSTON COLLEGE

Introduction

Here we explore ways in which virtues are relevant to discrimination's nature, morality, and forms, concentrating on racial discrimination as the most notorious, discussed, and illustrative type. Nowadays some draw on consequentialist accounts of moral justification such as utilitarianism to explain discrimination's moral status in terms of its deleterious effects, while others turn to the Kantian or contractualist stress on respect, rationality, reasonableness, and equality for the same purpose (cf. Chapters 6–13). In the last several decades, virtue ethics (or virtues-based moral theories) have been recognized as a third broad option beyond Kantian/contractualist and consequentialist approaches to moral theory. The literature on discrimination, however, has thus far neither caught up with nor reflected this alternative approach.

Our English term "virtue" derives from translating into Latin a Greek word for excellence. Aristotle influentially taught that a thing's virtues are what make it and its operation good instances of their type, and, among human virtues, he distinguished the intellectual from the moral, defining the latter specifically as states of character that concern choice and consist in a mean, or middle position, as determined by practical reason, and lying between extremes of vicious defect and vicious excess. Where classical Aristotelians saw in human nature an in-built purpose and teleology, medieval Christians added that this human purpose reflects God's creative will. Francis Hutcheson, a virtue theorist of the early modern epoch, identified benevolence as the central moral virtue, and David Hume saw virtue in any trait either agreeable or useful to the agent herself or to other people. Living before the mid-twentieth century concern with discrimination, these thinkers offered accounts of injustice, but none developed careful arguments against discriminating against people on the basis of groups to which those people belong. Most of these thinkers also left unclear the connection between someone's possessing vicious traits and her doing what is morally wrong, beyond their thinking that the former normally leads to the latter.

In Anscombe's (1958) radical view, at the twentieth century's rebirth of virtue ethics, no such connection could be explained, because she deemed the concepts of morally wrong action, the morally forbidden, what we morally ought not to do, and so on, to be incoherent without an understanding of moral law issued by a lawgiver, an understanding almost all modern philosophers reject. However, some recent versions of virtue ethics, such as Hursthouse's

(2002) and, especially, those variously called "agent-based" (Slote, 2001), "motivation-based" (Zagzebski, 1996), or "virtues-based," squarely face this gap between virtues and wrongdoing and attempt to close it. They hold that a person's acting wrongly, immorally, and doing what she mustn't consists in her acting viciously, that is, in ways opposed to or distant from relevant moral virtues. Since acting viciously is acting from certain (bad-making) motives, or contrary to certain considerations, e.g., acting neglectfully or inconsiderately, these approaches see such motivational input to an action, rather than its actual or probable effects, as what interacts with the agent's circumstances to determine its moral status. Taking this approach affects how we understand what is morally objectionable in invidious discrimination.

Discriminating against people

Discrimination, we need to remember, is originally and basically an act of the mind. Neither a lower animal, nor a baby, nor a severely retarded person, as we know, can discriminate, because none of them can perform the requisite mental operation. Rather, to discriminate among things is, first and fundamentally, to differentiate them (cf. Introduction). External actions, whether those of individuals or of collective agents, constitute discrimination when their agents act to treat things or people in different ways according to some perceived or assigned difference. We properly call such actions discriminatory in the sense important here when, as we say, in them an agent discriminates *against* someone by treating her with hostility, with callous indifference, with contempt, or with but meager or passive consideration. Thus, both discrimination and virtue are similar in that each is essentially mental. Moreover, discriminating against someone on account of her group (as in invidious racial, sexual, and religious discrimination) seems, as we have just described it, to involve morally vicious treatment, since acting hostilely or callously to someone, or acting in ways that manifest scant or merely passive consideration for her needs or rights is vicious, that is, unacceptably distant from the moral virtues of goodwill and justice (respect).

The kind of discrimination that concerns us here, discriminating against someone because she is in a certain group (or is thought to be in it), can be related to virtues and vices in diverse ways. First, both moral and intellectual vices have been imputed to groups so as to stigmatize them and to rationalize discriminating against them (cf. Chapter 32). Thus, in the West, Black people have been regarded as indolent, violence-prone, unambitious, and slow-witted, among other things, in ways that many took to justify keeping them out of influential positions and away from (or always subordinate to) White people. Similarly, women suffer stereotypes as irrational and overly emotional, Jews as greedy and conniving, Muslims as fanatical and violent, East Asians as crafty, and so on down the ugly and familiar list. Second, beneficiaries of past and current discrimination may face a challenge living moral lives, because it can be arduous for them to recognize as their equals those who have been degraded. That also makes it onerous for them to face up to the responsibilities they incur due to the undeserved benefits that discrimination continues to confer upon them. (Think of these as the burdens of so-called white privilege, for instance.) Third, those materially and socially disadvantaged by past or current discrimination may also find it difficult to live virtuous, admirable lives, since they may be sorely tempted to selfishness born of self-pity and a resentful inclination to treat others' needs and interests with as little consideration as their own have received. (The second point is stressed in Lebron [2013]; the third in Tessman [2005].) Fourth, and arguably most important, invidious discrimination often has roots in forms of bias and stigma that viciously dehumanize and degrade its victims. Again, contempt for and hostility to members of racial, religious, ethnic, and other groups has been a driving force behind the establishment and maintenance of discriminatory systems and practices.

This last idea has important explanatory breadth and power. Adams (2006) conceives of virtues as excellences in being for what is good. Focusing on what is good for people of a certain racial group, we can draw on this sort of account of virtue to generate at least four forms of vice (understood as grave departures from virtue): being against what is good for them, being neither for nor against their good, being for what is good for them but to such a paltry extent as to fall short of excellence, and being for their good but in some unsuitable way that keeps one's favoring the good from being excellent. If we now concentrate on racism from here on, and on discriminating against someone for her race, it follows that when we think of racism as vice, then there will likewise be at least four corresponding kinds of racism, understood as being less-than-excellent, for racial reasons, in favoring some people's having the goods of persons. These forms of racism comprise wishing Black people, for instance, harm (being against their good, in Adams's terminology), wishing them neither good nor ill (but instead being stonily apathetic about Black disadvantage and suffering), wanting them to do better (but doing so without fervor), and favoring their welfare but in the wrong way, for example, without any commitment or inclination to acting in order to improve their condition. Note that these comprise mental stances and dispositions, the traditional content of character, from which both actions and their moral status derive. This account can be adapted to accommodate other types of discrimination, for example, that derive from misogyny or disdainful indifference to women's needs.

Some kinds of virtue and some forms of discrimination

Such a taxonomy has significant implications for recent discussions of discrimination. Altman (2011), though he has now backed away from this claim, once proposed a "no-intent-to-harm" condition as what crucially distinguishes "indirect discrimination" from direct, where the latter is the more familiar type of (e.g. racial) discrimination that expresses (racial) disregard (cf. Chapters 1 and 2). However, we have just seen that there are forms of vicious racism that consist not in willing, say, Black people harm but in being callously indifferent to their welfare, or being only barely concerned for it, or caring about their welfare only in such inappropriate ways as a merely passive well-wishing that is largely disconnected from any real inclination to act. It stands to reason that there also can be forms of invidious anti-Black discrimination that are racist but lack anyone's intent to harm Black people. As there are vices of indifference, meagerness, and passivity, in addition to the vice of ill-will, so too there are multiple forms of racist vice. Similar moves are available to reconceive other types of discrimination, such as those based on sex or on one's status as an immigrant, but we do not pursue them here. When we combine the various types of racist viciousness with a variety of sites at which individuals' racism can infect an institution, we reveal a considerable breadth to institutional racism. We are now positioned, first, to illuminate the possibilities by understanding this last phenomenon as institutional*ized* racism (and, similarly, institutionalized anti-Semitism, anti-immigrant attitudes, and so on) and, second, to recognize a plurality of informal customs and practices as each of them tainted with one or another form of racist vice.

This positions us to expand and clarify our understanding of the connection between discrimination and the virtues of individuals. Adopting Aristotle's distinction between epistemic and moral virtues, and taking the former first, we should note that types of discrimination have sometimes been condemned for violating such epistemic virtues as rationality, open-mindedness, and responsiveness to evidence (cf. Chapter 4). Thus, a discriminating employer who hires a less competent applicant, even ignoring her competitor's test results, can be charged with failure both of practical rationality, since her hiring harms her company, and failure in theoretical rationality, for her obdurate belief in the face of the tests' counterevidence that the competing candidate is more competent. We have already observed ways in which wrongful discrimination can be wrong for offending against the moral virtue of benevolence/goodwill. We should also note that it has been regarded as viciously opposed to justice, which has itself been differently conceived in terms of equality, desert, rights and entitlement, respect for persons (recognition-respect, not evaluation-respect), and autonomy. We should not, however, assume a sharp distinction and significant distance between goodwill and justice. To be sure, Kant memorably saw justice as distancing us from one another, while love tends to bring us together. He meant that treating other persons justly, with respect, requires us to defer to many of their decisions, that is, to keep our distance; in love, to the contrary, we draw closer. Yet Kant's picture is rather simplistic. For we can think of virtuous love for persons as goodwill and of justice as a special disposition to respect them in their dignity by, among other things, willing each person the goods (such as rational self-direction) that are peculiar to persons as such. Seen in that way, the moral virtue of person-to-person love must include the deference that Kant's image visualizes as distancing. (We need not claim that the reverse implication, i.e., that justice includes the comprehensive goodwill that constitutes the virtue of benevolence, also holds.)

Not all virtues are in individuals. Rawls famously proclaimed justice the primary virtue of any society's political institutions. If we here apply Aristotle's general doctrine that anything's virtues are the features in it that make that thing and its work good according to its kind, then justice, as a virtue of society, must make a society a good one, and the operation of its institutions, similarly, to be good social action. Discrimination is sometimes seen as standing against such commonly acknowledged characteristics of a good society as fairness, equality, efficiency, democracy, reasonableness, and sensitivity to merit. It could be argued that some of these characteristics are virtues of society, making it a good one and its operations good social action. Thus, Anderson (2010; cf. Chapter 35) argues that democracy suffers, and is worse, when segregation renders its citizens unable to engage one another as equals. Further, there are grounds to worry that systematically unfair treatment undermines social comity. Lebron (2013) goes further, explicitly finding familiar kinds of bad moral character not only in individuals but also in their institutions.

We have spoken of racism, and we can add such similar attitudes as xenophobia, anti-Semitism, and misogyny, as being vicious in several ways and as broad enough thus to infect various forms of discrimination. We can explore this suggestion further. That invidious discrimination is vicious allows not only for different forms of racism to infect action, but also for it to occur at different levels. Levels of invidious discrimination may include the Personal, the Social (both customary and habitual), and the Formal, which is institutionalized. Moreover, racism can infect a course of action beyond its inception. Racist vice can contaminate a social institution, for instance, when racist response to persons is active when they first establish the institution or later operate it. Yet some (or all) of a society's institutions might instead be racist because its members' individual racism contaminates them much later, when they passively tolerate and permit its harmful operation or practice to continue. In this way, an institution not racist in its original design or set-up may nonetheless exist today because of racist indifference to the harm it does. Adapting the religious ethicists' distinction between sins of commission and sins of omission, we should acknowledge viciously discriminatory inaction, wrongful passivity, along with viciously discriminatory actions. When a society's members tolerate an institutional practice that harms Black people because they do not care about Black people's welfare, or because they regard harm to Black citizens as a "damn shame," but not as something about which they need to take action, they infect their social system with their racism. In this way, racism can explain more institutionalized discrimination than it is commonly thought to. If the police can be seen to be callously killing innocent and unarmed Black citizens with great frequency, for example, and the locality does nothing to fix this misconduct out of its members' minimal concern for Black people, then it is the citizens' racist neglect in demanding and implementing reforms that institutionalizes its police officers' behavior. Further, if a housing policy that disadvantages Black people is kept in place out of the community's lack of interest in the plight of Black people, that is racist discrimination, even if the policy's designers were not, and the officials currently implementing it are not, themselves racist. Rather, it is the community members who, by refusing to change it, infect the policy with their racism.

At the same time, understanding wrongful discrimination's essential connection to moral vice strongly suggests that, despite what is often said, mere social processes, structures, systems, and so on, cannot be viciously discriminatory because they are not themselves actions, and thus, by themselves, lack the mental inputs necessary for them to be tainted with racist, misogynist, anti-immigrant or other kinds of vicious ill-will, indifference, or passivity. Rather, they become wrongfully discriminatory, racially or otherwise, only insofar as persons' racism, etc., infects those processes and systems at some stage of their design, implementation, operation, or maintenance. For it is only therein that they become exercises of collective agency.

Current conceptions of wrongful discrimination

Lippert-Rasmussen (2013) influentially divides accounts of wrongful discrimination into those that ground its immorality in harms, those that ground its immorality in various mental states, and those that ground its immorality in the "objective meaning" of discriminatory actions. This division, however, is problematic, and due attention to virtues and vices can help us correct the problem. Suppose you think what makes relevant instances of discrimination immoral is that they make victims unhappy, insecure, or despairing. Lippert-Rasmussen would say that you have a harm-based view of the matter rather than one based in mental states (cf. Chapter 12). Notice, however, that the harms involved here are all mental states. So, you can as properly be said to base your criticism on those mental states as on harm. In contrast, if you think what makes such discriminatory behavior immoral is its being rooted in racist, misogynist, xenophobic, or anti-Semitic desire and intention to make its victims' lives worse, then he classifies your position as based on mental states. Again, though, notice that the mental states at issue are a desire and intention to cause harm. Thus, the objection to the discriminatory behavior derives from a prior objection to the mental state behind it, but what makes that mental state objectionable is that it is a desire precisely to harm. So, once more, we can validly describe your objection as harm-based as well as based on mental states. What this shows is that an adequate account needs to identify not only *what* factor grounds discrimination's immorality but also *how* it grounds it. Whether it is harm, a mental state, or both, we should ask whether the relevant factor makes the action wrong as part of its motivation or, instead, as part of its outcome. We can call these alternative approaches an input-driven account of immorality and an output-driven account, respectively. Moreover, what Lippert-Rasmussen proposes as a third option, objective meaning accounts, may pose no real alternative (cf. Chapter 7). For when we talk of an action's meaning we usually refer either to what it indicates about its agent's mentality ("What does her refusal to come tonight mean for her participation in this project?") or to its significance for those it impacts ("What does his withdrawal mean for our prospects?"). The former is input, the latter output. Of course, in principle, an account of immoral action might mix inputs with outputs or, perhaps, appeal to neither kind of factor.

Attending to virtues and vices, which are mental states and dispositions, helps illuminate this matter. What makes an action in any way vicious must be its connection to something vicious in its agent, and that can only be in her mind. Thus, all such familiar forms of discrimination as racism, misogyny, anti-Semitism, and so on, must be made wrong because of their connection to these vicious biases (that is, forms of bigotry). In contrast, when someone claims that what makes discrimination immoral lies only on the side of its output, that is, in its effects, results, or consequences (if those differ), she therein disconnects discrimination and its immorality from those biases. Unfortunately, that separation threatens to exclude all, or almost all, of the most familiar, common-sense, and outrageous instances of immoral discrimination. More generally, any theory that bases an action's immorality simply in its actual or probable effects, rather than its motivation, tends to dehumanize the agent, turning her into a mere mechanism that generates results, and it downplays her personhood, practical reason, and agency. Further, it allows mere luck to make an action immoral by shaping its effects, disconnecting an action's moral status both from what grounds its own status as virtuous or vicious conduct and from what grounds its agent's culpability or blamelessness. Finally, since no event is a human action except by being intended, and nothing is an act of cheating or murdering or degrading simply because of its results, such outcome-driven approaches to discrimination's immorality detach the question of whether the act is immoral from what makes it an action at all, as well as from what makes it the specific type of action it is. That is implausible, since discrimination is only morally significant as human conduct of a certain type.

A virtues-based approach to discrimination's immorality can accommodate the importance of both harms and mental states. Measures taken in order to harm, say, Black people, or out of heartless indifference to their being harmed, largely because they are Black, are plainly and therein wrong because of the mental states that they express. This exploits for explanatory purposes virtue ethics' traditional emphasis on what factors play a role in an agent's practical reasoning. Moreover, as we noted, the harm intended or thus accepted may itself be frustration, despair, a sense of being worthless, or some similar mental state.

Bearing this in mind, let us consider a few influential recent accounts of invidious discrimination's nature and immorality. To Shelby (2016), the function of classifying as "institutional racism" practices with racially disparate harmful impact is to protect unjustly disadvantaged racial minorities from further marginalization, by removing unnecessary barriers to equal opportunity (cf. Chapter 11). To his credit, Shelby doesn't himself use the term "discrimination" here. Nevertheless, in the political and legal literature, appeal to disparate impact is usually made in order to justify claims that operations without racist intent are "indirectly" racially discriminatory. Against this contention, note that "unnecessary," even unjust, obstacles need not therein be either racist or instances of discrimination *against* people because of their race. If the negative impacts occur without race being targeted or playing any role in the thinking of those designing, enforcing, or maintaining the causative institutional practice, it is implausible that racism has somehow infected that practice. The same holds *mutatis mutandis* for supposed indirect discrimination against women, immigrants, indigenous peoples, Jews, Muslims, and others.

Moreau (2010; Chapter 13) theorizes that what chiefly makes some discrimination so objectionable that it warrants criminalization is that it restricts victims' "deliberative freedom," meaning, roughly, their freedom to make decisions about how they shall live without needing to attend to others' view of their race, gender, and so on. She treats it as an advantage of her view that it shows how discrimination harms individual victims (as well as their groups). She thus highlights a negative aspect of discrimination that theorists often overlook or neglect. Still, Moreau seems to miss what is crucial. When we deem racism as vicious disregard, that explains not only that racist discrimination is wrong, but also that it wrongs individual victims (whether or not it otherwise harms them), and that it specifies the ways in which they are wronged: that is, they are treated unkindly, callously, inconsiderately, disrespectfully, cavalierly, and the like.

Lippert-Rasmussen (2013; cf. Chapters 11 and 12) himself argues for a harm-based consequentialist account of discrimination's wrongness that assigns priority to deserved harms and benefits to the worst off, and argues against any motivation-based account. He maintains that, "[T]he very idea behind [the concept of] indirect discrimination is that its injustice lies in the unequal outcome it generates, not in the indirectly discriminatory acts themselves...." His account may point out genuine flaws in understandings of racist, and therein unjust, discrimination that narrowly restrict racism to disrespect, and limit disrespect itself to a failure to discern victims' status. However, neither racism nor injustice is the same thing as unequal outcome, nor is inequality of outcome sufficient for either racism or injustice. Moreover, the concept of discriminating *against* someone is used chiefly to pick out conduct we find objectionable. Of course, not all vicious discrimination should be forbidden by law (cf. Chapter 31). But when the state itself discriminates against some people, or when it allows individuals or organizations to discriminate in ways that manifest the sort of disrespect against which it is the task of government to protect people, then the state conducts itself viciously, so as to warrant prohibition. Given that consideration, types of discrimination that need not be unjust, and types of racial discrimination that need be neither racist nor unjust, are of little political import. Lippert-Rasmussen rejects accounts of discrimination's immorality that focus on disrespect, because viewing wrongful racial discrimination as inherently disrespectful fails to allow for what he considers race-based discrimination that is purely systemic, involving negative beliefs without accompanying negative non-cognitive attitudes. He worries that such accounts also exclude wrongful racial discrimination that is rooted merely in personal favoritism. However, there is little reason to agree that such cases of racially differentiated negatively impactful treatment ought to be considered wrongful discrimination. Cases involving withholding benefits or imposing harm out of racial disregard are the clearest examples of invidious racial discrimination, and we can add behavior from a racialized paucity of goodwill or indifference, as well as situations where it is racism in a society's members that explains why they decline to end institutions that operate to the detriment of, for example, Black people. Lippert-Rasmussen, to the contrary, thinks wrongful racial discrimination is chiefly objectionable because of the harm it does. Yet harming someone is racist (or anti-Semitic, or xenophobic, or anti-immigrant) only when relevantly motivated, so this account slights what should be central, the targeting of someone's race, sex, and so on, or illicit attention to such personal features, in illicit discrimination.

Hellman (2008; Chapter 7) thinks that invidious discrimination wrongs victims by demeaning them, as Ely (1980) earlier identified its psychological origin in prejudice as the key to immoral discrimination. Both these views are close to basing their objection on vices insofar as demeaning someone, which is central for Hellman, is contemptuous and therein unjust, and prejudice, on which Ely focuses, is epistemically, and likely also morally, vicious. What is crucial to invidious discrimination is viciously biased treatment, not unequal outcome. Insofar as supposedly indirect discrimination is detached from such bias, it does not deserve classification as discrimination at all.

Finally, Garcia's (2004) volitional account of racism, according to which racism, at its heart, consists in some form of vicious departure from the moral virtue of respectful goodwill toward each person, can be interpreted to suggest an understanding of immoral racial discrimination based on virtues and vices. So conceived, really discriminating *against* someone, whether by an individual or by a social institution, is immoral chiefly when it is so infected by such racism as to be itself racist, an expression of racism. Perhaps this kind of account could be expanded from the racial to generate analogous accounts of sex-based, anti-immigrant, and other forms of invidious discrimination.

Explaining how discrimination goes, and is wrong, by appealing to moral virtues and vices has signal advantages. It offers a unified account of individual and institutional(ized) racist (and otherwise biased) forms of discrimination. It allows for the possibility of reverse racial discrimination (for instance, against Whites or the socially powerful), while denying that classification to many racial preferences within affirmative action programs (cf. Chapter 33). It grounds the important recent idea of invidious discrimination in familiar concepts and classical and recent traditions of virtue ethics. It contributes to the (still nascent) theoretical extension of virtue ethics to virtue politics, properly deriving political morality from individual morality. It captures the gravity of contemptuous (or otherwise hostile) discrimination's strong opposition to recognized moral virtues. Finally, it accommodates epistemic vice, while wisely subordinating its political significance as against moral virtue and vice.

Problems for virtues-based accounts of immoral discrimination

For all that, such a virtues- and vices-based account of wrongful discrimination faces its own serious objections. It remains to be shown that, even equipped with a broad conception of racist vicious attitudes that includes callous indifference, meager concern, and undue passivity, as sketched above, such an account can accommodate the varieties of institutional, structural, cultural, and systemic discrimination on which some insist; let alone offer a satisfying account of them. This type of approach is also criticized for misunderstanding the supposed centrality of racial beliefs and racial ideology in racism, and so too for discrimination against other social groups. Some complain that focusing in this way on racist and discriminatory agents and their mental states ignores or neglects what is most important in this realm, namely, the effects on victims. There are replies available to several of these objections. Prejudicial beliefs, ideological or not, can be seen largely as rationalizing viciously hostile, disrespectful, or indifferent attitudes toward groups. And, as we have seen, discrimination's bad effects may principally matter morally as indicators of vicious inputs. Still others object that a volitional view gets wrong what they see as the correct causal, explanatory, and evaluative ordering of structural racism and discrimination, as against individual forms of each. These critics, however, need arguments against the volitional conception's claim that it is vicious personal attitudes and dispositions that cause, explain, and make immoral the relevant discriminatory behavior of individuals, groups, and the operation of their social customs and institutions, rather than, as they claim, the other way around.

Conclusion

We can conclude by engaging a different kind of objection to the volitional account of racism's conception of racism itself and its derivative account of wrongful racial discrimination as racist: a political concern. The same objection also applies to virtues- and vices-based understandings of discriminating against women, immigrants, Jews, and others. Are both virtue ethics and virtue politics, to which Garcia links his account of racism and on which its adaptation to discrimination would also depend, just too "conservative" to serve as the basis for an adequate (and an anti-racist) account of racism? We think of conservatives as the political Right, after all, while it is the political Left who have spearheaded opposition to race-based, sex-based, and other kinds of discrimination. Before signing on to this critique, the reader should ponder Tessman's (2005) objection to racism and social oppression on the grounds that they "burden" victims, making it very difficult for them to live flourishing, virtuous lives. She should also think about Lebron's (2013) claims not only that the degraded victims of White supremacy suffer a consequent and unfair "ethical disadvantage" in living good lives, but also that its perpetrators' and their descendants are at a "moral disadvantage" in having now to acknowledge and compensate others for their own ill-gotten social and economic benefits. Finally, she does well to notice Paul Taylor's (2007) turn to virtue epistemology and virtue ethics as needed aids in successfully unlearning anti-Black social messages and biases. For all the references to Aristotle, Plato, and other Great Dead White Men that are common in the revived interest in virtue, approaches to ethics, politics, and epistemology that are grounded in moral virtues and vices may not be so old-fashioned or inherently conservative as some critics prematurely suppose.

Bibliography

Adams, R. M. 2006. *A Theory of Virtue: Excellence in Being for the Good.* New York: Oxford University Press.

Altman, A. 2011. "Discrimination." *Stanford Encyclopedia of Philosophy* (Feb. 2011 Edition). Edward N. Zalta (ed.). Current version available at http://plato.stanford.edu/archives/fall2015/entries/discrimination/.

Anderson, E. 2010. *The Imperative of Integration.* Princeton: Princeton University Press.

Anscombe, G. E. M. 1958. "Modern Moral Philosophy." In Anscombe, 1991, *Ethics, Religion, and Politics: Collected Philosophical Papers, vol. III.* 26–42. Oxford: Wiley-Blackwell.

Ely, J. H. 1980. *Democracy and Distrust: a Theory of Judicial Review.* Cambridge, MA: Harvard University Press.

Foot, P. 2003. *Natural Goodness.* New York: Oxford University Press.

Garcia, J. L. A. 2004. "The Sites for Racism: Social Structures, Valuing, and Vice." In M. Levine and T. Pataki (eds), *Racism in Mind.* 35–55. Ithaca: Cornell University Press.

Hellman, D. 2008. *When is Discrimination Wrong?* Cambridge, MA: Harvard University Press.

Hursthouse, R. 2002. *On Virtue Ethics.* New York: Oxford University Press.

Lebron, C. 2013. *The Color of Our Shame: Race and Injustice in Our Time.* New York: Oxford University Press.

Lippert-Rasmussen, K. 2013. *Born Free and Equal? A Philosophical Inquiry into the Nature of Discrimination.* New York: Oxford University Press.

Moreau, S. 2010. "What is Discrimination?" *Philosophy and Public Affairs.* 38(2): 143–179.

Shelby, T. 2016. *Dark Ghettos: Injustice, Dissent, and Reform.* Cambridge, MA: Harvard/Belknap.

Slote, M. 2001. *Morals from Motives.* New York: Oxford University Press.

Taylor, P. 2007. "Post-Black, Old Black." *African American Review.* 41(4): 621–640.

Tessman, L. 2005. *Burdened Virtues: Virtue Ethics for Liberatory Struggles.* New York: Oxford University Press.

Zagzebski, L. T. 1996. *Virtues of the Mind: An Inquiry into the Nature of Virtue and the Ethical Foundations of Knowledge.* Cambridge: Cambridge University Press.

PART III

Groups of discriminatees

15

DISCRIMINATION AND GENDER

Gina Schouten

HARVARD UNIVERSITY

Introduction

In modern liberal democracies, we no longer sanction open and explicit discrimination against women. And yet we have not achieved gender equality. Why not? At a first pass, anti-discrimination legislation seems to aim for equal treatment: For so-called "gender-blind" procedures for selecting among candidates for scarce jobs, college admissions spots, and other competitive positions. Critics find this aspiration problematic for many of the same reasons that so-called "race-blind" policy is problematic: Equal treatment against a background of inequality does not yield justice (Kymlicka 2002, MacKinnon 1987).

But anti-discrimination need not mean equal treatment. Against a background of gender injustice, gender-differentiated policy may be needed to secure equal access to social, economic, and political goods. If the structure *itself* is built in discriminatory ways, then we cannot secure justice by equalizing competition within it. Consider, for example, the ways in which the equipment used in certain jobs is built for male bodies (Kymlicka 2002). If machinery used by firefighters can be operated safely only by those who meet height and weight requirements that rule out significantly more women than men, then hiring based only on one's qualifications for the job—including one's ability to use the equipment in question—will not ensure equal access to the position regardless of gender. If, further, the machinery is built for male bodies *because its operators are presumed male*, then we can sensibly say that discrimination is built into the position itself, and something beyond equal treatment at the moment of hiring is necessary to overcome that discrimination: For example, supplementing or replacing the equipment with new versions that can be operated safely by women as well as men. Similar considerations might support affirmative hiring or admissions practices in some circumstances (Chapter 33).

The point is just this: Even if anti-discrimination requires that social positions not be awarded on the basis of characteristics that are irrelevant with respect to the position in question, we should not conclude that anti-discrimination supports a policy of ignoring such irrelevant differences in our *current* society. Accordingly, an adequate theory of discrimination must attend to different *kinds* of discrimination—including statistical discrimination (Chapter 3), private discrimination (Chapters 30, 31, and 35), and structural discrimination—in order to make visible different facets of injustice.

Particularly in the context of labor markets, we might think that a robust theory of discrimination can be a valuable theoretical lens. After all, labor markets seem to be a *paradigmatic* site of gender-based discrimination. Women are paid less than men on average; they are seriously underrepresented at high ranks in elite professions; and professions themselves remain highly segregated and unequally remunerated based on the coding of particular kinds of work as masculine or feminine (cf. Chapter 25). We might plausibly conclude that discriminatory practices persist in the face of policy aimed at eroding them, and that attending to different types of discrimination can improve our theorizing about gender injustice and our policy response to it.

This chapter explores some initially appealing ways of understanding persistent gender inequality in labor markets as a problem of discrimination. I think that attending to different types of discrimination *can* improve our theorizing about unjust gender inequality and our policy response to it. But a great deal of inequality seems not to result from discriminatory processes. Of course, not every inequality is *unjust*. My aim is to consider the concept of discrimination and ask how far it can take us in theorizing gender *injustice*; accordingly, I will suggest that a great deal of what we should regard as *unjust* inequality in labor markets is not best understood as a problem of discrimination. We have good reason to believe discriminatory practices persist, but eliminating wrongful discrimination will not suffice to secure gender justice in labor markets.

More conjecturally, I suggest that the most promising *policy response* to gender injustice is not one aimed primarily at ameliorating gender-based discrimination in the workplace. Rather, it is one aimed at incentivizing the performance of caregiving among men, somewhat counter-intuitively by offering family-friendly workplace benefits on different terms to men than to women. Whatever the success of anti-discrimination efforts in bringing about the gains so far achieved, such efforts constitute a highly limited approach moving forward.

Lessons from the classroom: a challenge for liberal feminism

In many ways, gender inequality in labor markets is a paradigmatic case of discrimination. We are confident that gender is an irrelevant consideration with respect to many of the positions and privileges to which women historically have been denied access. It was clearly wrongfully discriminatory for women to be denied access to college, for example. As a general class, cases of workplace discrimination against women seem easy to diagnose as such. These cases meet the most seemingly straightforward necessary conditions for wrongful discrimination: Differential treatment of two groups; in a way that is worse for one of the groups; based on the property that defines that group as a group (Thomsen, this volume, Chapter 1). They also meet a further condition that typifies paradigmatic cases of discrimination: The group whose members are differentially treated is a *socially salient* group. This means that perceived group membership is treated as socially relevant across a wide variety of contexts (Lippert-Rasmussen 2013).

Consider the gendered wage gap. It is widely recognized that women's average hourly earnings are significantly lower than men's. In the U.S. in 2015, for example, full-time working women made roughly eighty-eight cents for every dollar that men made (U.S. Bureau of Labor Statistics). At a glance, workplace discrimination seems a likely culprit. If women are less likely than their male counterparts to be hired into the highest ranks of job sectors due to discriminatory hiring, or if they are likely to be paid lower wages than men for performing the same work, then it should come as no surprise that women have lower earnings on average.

In political philosophy courses, I often give students a presentation assignment in which they identify a contemporary "problem" and think through it using some of the theoretical tools the course introduces. In nearly every class, at least one student has wanted to focus on the gender wage gap. Commonly, this is a student who presents the wage gap to his classmates as a problem of injustice against women: Wage inequality is *unjust because it is discriminatory*.

In every case so far, a sizeable number of students find this assessment apt. But just as reliably, some students think the data are misleading. The skeptics argue that the well-publicized raw data obscure a great deal that is essential to evaluating the case: The data show that women make less, on average, than men. But full-time working women also work shorter hours, take more leave, and generally have more career interruptions than men. They also disproportionally seek employment in less well-remunerated fields—fields in which they enjoy greater flexibility, but correspondingly less pay and shallower career trajectories. Surely, my students think, women should not be paid as much as men if they're working less, or working at lower levels, or working in less demanding positions. Most of these students grant that there's probably some "actual discrimination" lurking behind the raw data. But they want to insist that a great deal of the wage gap is *not* due to discrimination. Their objection is that, while some inequality in pay is discriminatory and thus unjust, some portion of it must be *not unjust because it is not discriminatory*.

And so we ask: What *is* being controlled for? Why measure the pay gap *that* way? Why not impose more controls, and in particular controls for more of the *choices* people are making? Are the raw data as morally and politically relevant as they first seemed? Surely women should not be paid equally for less work, and yet many still feel that *something* is wrong here.

We talk about the need for a more robust concept of discrimination—one sensitive to the reality that discrimination can be embedded in social mechanisms without being sustained by consciously discriminatory actions; that bias must actively be guarded against rather than merely not endorsed; that statistical discrimination can be objectionable even when the statistics reflect reality. The pay gap may still be due to objectionable discrimination, even if it isn't sustained by overt sexism. Still, some students wonder: Can these more subtle discriminatory processes really account for the full disparity? Or, coming at the question from the other direction: If women are, on average, working less than men, then we would not be surprised to find them making less. On its own, then, the pay gap can't be taken as evidence of discriminatory practices. And if no discrimination is occurring, how can we regard the pay gap as unjust?

My students are not alone here; nor are they unreasonable. It is tempting to think that discrimination exhausts the unjust or morally wrong sources of gender inequality in the workplace. And so we arrive at a perennial challenge for liberal feminists: How can unequal labor market outcomes between women and men be unjust if they result not from discriminatory practices but from women's own *choices* to prioritize caregiving and to *de*-prioritize paid labor?

The family and the gendered division of labor

It's a timely conversation to have. Women have made great gains in many domains of public life, but in the U.S., where I teach, the steady progress toward more gender egalitarian attitudes that characterized the three decades leading up to the twenty-first century began to slow in the mid-1990s.[1] Beginning around the same time, married mothers' labor force participation declined, as did women's entry into previously male-dominated fields. Recent years have witnessed an uptick of women seriously downshifting or exiting careers altogether in what's been termed the "opt-out revolution." Despite earning a majority of post-baccalaureate degrees, women remain underrepresented in high-skilled professions, both at entry levels and increasingly as they age. Only gains in women's educational attainment seem to have survived the slow-down of the gender revolution, and only to an extent; while women's rates of college entry and completion remain high, integration by field of study has stopped. Not only in the workplace but in politics and other domains, gender equality remains a long way off.

Of course, the U.S. is hardly alone in having failed to achieve gender equality, despite legislative efforts to end labor market discrimination. What accounts for the persistence of inequality? To some degree, no doubt, straightforward discrimination has survived efforts to eliminate it. Even if the pay gap alone doesn't prove this, we have plenty of other sources to draw on: Women's own accounts and the growing body of research on processes like implicit bias paint a compelling picture. Plausibly, many women who "opt out" of the paid labor market are motivated to do so by subtly inhospitable or overtly hostile work environments. Overt discrimination is no worse than it was before legislative attempts to end it, but what remains might be more discouraging for its resilience and seeming invisibility.

But a great deal of the inequality in labor market outcomes is due not to what goes on in the workplace, but rather to what goes on at home. To really understand gender inequality, we have to look to the institution that many contemporary feminists regard as the "core" or the "linchpin" of gender injustice: The family.[2] Unequal labor market outcomes are explained in large part by women's continued responsibility for the great bulk of the caregiving and domestic labor necessary to sustain the home and family. Household divisions of labor remain highly unequal, with women continuing to do the vast majority of housework and childcare.[3] This inequality persists in both urban and rural areas, in both developed and developing societies, and regardless of structural features about the family. On average, employed fathers in OECD countries spend less than half as much time caring for children as do their employed female partners, and mothers' time spent with children has not decreased despite the fact that mothers' working hours have gone up dramatically. Women have less time available for paid labor because they are still doing the bulk of the important work that was formerly done by full-time "housewives"—most notably, the work of caregiving.

Insofar as gender inequality in the workplace is attributable to women's disproportionally large burden of unpaid caregiving work, it seems difficult to understand as a problem of discrimination. The gendered division of labor is sustained by the choices individuals make about how to allocate paid and unpaid work within cooperative domestic relationships. And in many of these cases, women choose to prioritize caregiving and subordinate paid work because specializing in caregiving reflects their genuine preferences. Of course, choices and preferences might themselves be responsive to discrimination. But in a range of important cases, it is more difficult than we might think to diagnose unjust inequality as a problem of discrimination.

Is it *statistical* discrimination?

Statistical discrimination occurs when "there is statistical evidence which suggests that a certain group of people differs from other groups in a certain dimension, and its members are being treated disadvantageously on the basis of this information" (Lippert-Rasmussen 2013; cf. Chapter 3). In the case of statistical discrimination against women in labor markets, the process plausibly goes something like this: Employers (consciously or unconsciously) judge that mothers are likelier than fathers to take leaves or career breaks in order to take care of children or other dependent family members. Employers are often in a position to know little about prospective employees as individuals; thus, aggregate information can be highly salient in their deliberations. As a result, employers are less likely to hire or promote women into the most prestigious positions, and women continue to earn less than their male counterparts. Importantly, statistical discrimination imposes these costs whether or not the woman in question actually becomes a caregiver, and whether or not she takes leave even if she does (Gornick and Meyers 2009, Coltrane 2009).

Plausibly, some portion of existing inequality in labor market outcomes is due to mechanisms of statistical discrimination. And while some uses of aggregate data to make predictions about the behavior of individuals are morally unproblematic, it is safe to assume that statistical discrimination that perpetuates labor market inequality against women would be morally objectionable discrimination. But this explanation gets us only so far, because a great deal of labor market inequality does not fit this diagnosis. As evidence of this, notice how we would expect the pay gap to change over time if it were due entirely or primarily to statistical discrimination: We would expect to see the largest gap among workers at the *start* their careers, and then to see the disparity diminish as workers age—once caregiving responsibilities are statistically less likely to draw them out of the paid workforce. In fact, the pay gap *widens* over the life course (U.S. Bureau of Labor Statistics). The "motherhood penalty" that depresses women's labor market outcomes seems to result more from actual motherhood than from employers' anticipation of it (Correll et al. 2007). This observation casts doubt on the idea that the bulk of the disparity is due to statistical discrimination. It suggests that a larger factor is the difference between women and men in cumulative time spent out of work, or de-prioritizing work, to care for children—a difference that grows over the life course.

Statistical discrimination and implicit bias are real, and we should combat them. But the data suggest that something else plays a larger role in sustaining unequal labor market outcomes. Once more, we arrive at the difficult question: Insofar as unequal labor market outcomes result from women's choices to de-prioritize paid labor, does the concept of discrimination apply?

Is it *private* discrimination?

Perhaps we can get some traction by diagnosing persistent labor market inequality as a result of *intra-familial* discrimination: Men retain a larger share of bargaining power in most heterosexual partnerships, and so have been able to hold out for partners who are willing to shoulder the bulk of caregiving work. These men *discriminate* in partner selection against women who would insist on equal commitment to caregiving.

Plausibly, some men (and women) discriminate in partner selection in just this way. But is this unjust? We might find the very idea incoherent, on the grounds that legislative proscription against partner discrimination cannot legitimately be enforced. Consider a man who discriminates against possible mates based on body type (cf. Chapters 22–23, 30–31). We might judge him harshly, but we do not have recourse to the same legislative remedies as we would if an employer engaged in such discrimination in hiring. Still, private discrimination might be unjust even though we lack legitimate legislative means of eliminating or discouraging it. Similarly, when the guilty go free because of a legitimate but fallible system of trial by jury, we may say that their going unpunished is *unjust*, even though we must respect the jury's verdict. Concerns of legitimacy as well as practicality can limit our capacity to rectify injustices through political mechanisms.

This conceptual point aside, many will deny that partner discrimination is unjust. I think a response to these skeptics is available. Certainly, if widespread instances of partner discrimination systematically disadvantage women in labor markets, such discrimination is cause for moral concern. Whether such instances themselves constitute injustices depends in part on a longstanding debate in political philosophy about whether and how principles of justice judge the behavior of individuals in addition to the arrangements of social institutions (cf. Chapter 35). The point I want to make here does not depend on resolving these difficult questions. Instead, I challenge the plausibility of private discrimination as an explanation of persistent gender inequality.

Increasingly, women's aspirations for a gender equal domestic arrangement are well-aligned with men's aspirations. Many men now support their partners' careers and want, for themselves, a larger role in caregiving. Men's and women's preferences may diverge when they find equal sharing unattainable, but in most cases, the choice to maintain a gendered division of labor does not reflect the highest ideals and preferences of women *or* men (Gerson 2010). The private discrimination hypothesis might explain *some* of the choices women make to prioritize caregiving. But, whether or not partner discrimination is unjust, that hypothesis leaves a great deal of the gender inequality we observe unexplained.

Is it *structural* discrimination?

The choices women make to subordinate paid work are not made in a vacuum. Preferences surrounding paid and unpaid labor configurations are profoundly shaped by the social environment. Women *choose* to take time off, or work part-time, to accommodate caregiving demands. But they also develop and pursue their career aspirations in a social environment that presumes that women will specialize in caregiving (even if not to the exclusion of breadwinning), and that men will specialize in breadwinning (even if not to the exclusion of caregiving) (Okin 1989). Plausibly, our preferences in this domain are *malleable* preferences, and a great many of the choices we make are choices we are *socialized* to make.

Our choices are also heavily influenced by the contingent costs and benefits that attach to the options in question, and those costs and benefits—or our anticipation of them—plausibly play a role in shaping our preferences as well. For example, we might choose to share caregiving work more equally—and come to prefer equal sharing in the first place—when we anticipate that high-quality substitute childcare will be available and affordable. If the data are right that many women and men prefer, other-things-equal, to share equally in caregiving and wage-earning, then aligning contingent considerations to support that arrangement would facilitate actual choices that better align with families' highest aspirations. Under the status quo, choices may *not* align with other-things-equal best preferences, precisely because other things are not equal.

Indeed, gender unequal choices do seem largely attributable to socialization processes and to the arrangement of social institutions that makes gender-equal domestic arrangements contingently very costly. Social institutions have not evolved to accommodate our increasingly egalitarian ideals. Labor markets are still largely structured for the breadwinners of old: Breadwinners with "someone else at home" to see to life's other necessities. Jobs so structured do not suit those who *don't* have someone else at home; still less do they suit those who also *are* that someone else at home for another breadwinner. Against this backdrop, choosing for one partner to specialize in breadwinning and one in caregiving will often be—or at least appear to be—the least costly option. Even if they espouse egalitarian ideals, partners might choose to specialize—they may *prefer* to do so—when their first-choice option of equal sharing is so costly. Or they might choose to specialize because gender norms make specialization the least *socially* costly option. In either case, given gender socialization, it should come as no surprise that the terms of specialization as a second-best choice still largely favor women specializing in caregiving and men specializing in breadwinning.

Because the choices that sustain labor market inequality are subject to these external influences, we might think we can understand the resulting inequality as a product of discrimination built into the very social structure. But gendered choices are not unique in being subject to external influence. The social environment imposes contingent costs and benefits on *all* our choices, and these can motivate us to diverge from the path we would choose were we moved solely by intrinsic considerations. Nor are gendered choices unique in being influenced by socialization. I might choose to practice Catholicism because, having been raised catholic, I now find its doctrine and practice comfortable and congenial, and because, having come of age in a religious community, I judge the extrinsic costs of defection to be costs not worth bearing.

We may be inclined to regard this choice as unfree, but *no* choice is made in a vacuum, and few are made based purely on the intrinsic features of the options at hand. For the purposes of theorizing justice within a broadly liberal framework, we must regard citizens as capable of making genuine choices, even when those choices are responsive to extrinsic contingencies. It is in part because we regard citizens as capable of genuine choice that we have hope of building a workable system of social entitlement in which individuals can, under some circumstances, be accountable for what they do, and held to internalize the costs of their choices. We can meaningfully regard an employer as having *chosen* to discriminate, *even when not discriminating would have been contingently costly for him.* We can meaningfully regard religious affiliations as demanding respect, *even when they are influenced by social forces.* Thus, we cannot ground a claim of structural discrimination just by noting that extrinsic costs influence choice.

Can we argue that unequal labor market outcomes are a product of structural discrimination by invoking the *particular* extrinsic contingencies that influence the choices that sustain them? Are gender socialization or the contingent social costs of gendered specialization *themselves* products of discriminatory practices? Making that case is more difficult than it seems.

For one thing, the structure of social institutions, which causes the extrinsic costs to be what they are, is sustained by the very choices in question. Gender norms and the design of social and political institutions are mutually reinforcing, and there is a great deal of endogeneity in the mechanisms that account for gendered choices. On any plausible story, gendered behaviors themselves partly explain and sustain the institutional design that takes those behaviors for granted. For example, labor markets evolved to suit husband breadwinners supported by wife homemakers, and they remain predicated on the assumption that "ideal workers" will have relative immunity from caregiving work (Williams 2000). But that assumption and its persistence are due in part to the fact that breadwinners traditionally *have* enjoyed relative immunity from caregiving work. Workplaces are still able to take labor specialization for granted, even though the terms of specialization have changed, because workers comply with the expectations that presumed specialization imposes. Similarly, gendered behavior helps explain inadequacies in childcare support in countries like the U.S.: Traditionally, families have internalized the costs of the socially valuable work of caregiving by way of gendered work specialization, and this breadwinner/homemaker model of domestic cooperation relieved society of pressure to support high-quality substitute caregiving.

The *norms* that influence individuals' navigation of these gendered institutions also result from and are sustained by the aggregate behavior of individuals. Plausibly, the gendered division of labor persists—and has long persisted—because individuals choose, in sufficient numbers, to make gender a salient consideration in determining how to allocate labor within their domestic partnerships. Within the context of liberal theorizing about justice, we must regard the present-day compliance with gendered norms and institutions as genuine choice. Plausibly, so too must we regard as genuine the choices that have long sustained gendered norms and gendered institutional design. These mechanisms impose costs now on partners who prefer to share paid and caregiving work equally, because the cumulative choices of the many people who comply with the gendered division of labor make deviation from it costly for others. But here again, noticing that this is the case does not suffice to ground a claim of discrimination. Not every lifestyle choice can be made equally costly, and often extrinsic costs result from just these sorts of processes. For example, in a society where many choose Catholicism, path dependency and economies of scale may make catholic lifestyles less costly than other religious affiliations. But this should not be regarded as structural discrimination against those preferring other affiliations.

Can we sustain a charge of discrimination based on the *harm* of gender inequality, and the fact that it imposes unequally on women and men? Again, perhaps. But notice that in standard cases of discrimination, the goods being discriminatorily allocated are *competitive* goods like jobs and promotions (cf. Chapters 25 and 26). Because the goods are competitive, discrimination harms members of one group and unfairly privileges members of other groups. Initially, the same appears to be happening in the gendered division of labor: For the simple reason that caregiving responsibilities disproportionally interfere with women's sustained commitment to other pursuits, women are at a disadvantage in those domains. But it is far from obvious that men should be regarded as all-things-considered winners here. Labor markets are designed for breadwinning specialists who have the background support of a caregiving specialist to free the breadwinner up to prioritize paid labor. One consequence is that those with caregiving responsibilities are disadvantaged by having less time to devote to paid labor; another consequence is that *breadwinning* specialists have less time to invest in *caregiving*.

If caregiving is important and rewarding work—and surely it is—then this must be regarded as a genuine cost to men. If this is right, then women are not the *only* parties harmed by the gendered division of labor. Just as many women would be better off with more opportunities in the world of paid work, many *men* would be better off with more opportunities for the intimacy and fulfillment that caregiving enables. Some are harmed by their sub-optimal share of paid work; others by a sub-optimal share of caregiving work. The latter harms are due to the same kinds of extrinsic costs and benefits as are the former, and the configuration of extrinsic costs is due, plausibly, to the same historical processes. Perhaps we will ultimately want to say that there are two complementary discriminatory processes sustaining gender inequality, each with its own set of winners and losers. And even if there are harms befalling both women and men, it seems clear that women get it worse. Even so, since the system imposes costs across the population—since no social group is a *winner*, though losses befall groups to different degrees—that system does not fit comfortably with our understanding of structural discrimination.

I have acknowledged throughout this chapter that some of the gender inequality we continue to see in labor markets is due to discriminatory practices. But a great deal more of that inequality results from the accumulation of so many seemingly mundane choices: Those women make to be the family's caregiving specialist, and those men make to specialize in breadwinning. And discrimination seems not a particularly helpful concept for understanding those choices.

Nor does discrimination seem an especially useful concept when we turn to the task of formulating a policy response to the gendered division of labor. Because gender inequality is maintained largely by unequal performance of caregiving between women and men, there is good reason to think that caregiver support policies must be part of the solution. Such policies might involve socializing some of the costs of substitute caregiving through subsidized childcare provisions, or requiring employers to support caregiving through caregiving leave provisions. But given existing gender inequality, caregiving policies that are made available to men and women on equal terms will not serve gender egalitarian aims. Against a background of deeply entrenched gender inequality and deeply embedded social mechanisms reinforcing that inequality, gender neutral caregiving support even risks *reinforcing* gender inequality in caregiving (Gornick and Meyers 2009, Brighouse and Wright 2009). To be effective, caregiver support policy will need to incorporate components that are *gender non-neutral*.

To illustrate, consider family leave policies that require employers to provide paid time off for caregiving (Gornick and Meyers 2009). Due to gendered socialization in upbringing, women are likelier than men to feel competent to perform caregiving, and to have been encouraged and supported in caregiving pursuits and preparation (England 2010). And, while gender role attitudes have shifted in the direction of egalitarianism, prevailing attitudes still dictate that, when the demands of work conflict with caregiving, women should *prioritize* caregiving (Gerson 2010). For these reasons, leave policies offered on equal terms to women and men are likely to be taken up disproportionally by women. Other family support policy, if offered on equal terms to women and men, carries the same risk (Coltrane 2009). Against a backdrop of pervasive gender inequality, *take-up* of caregiver support policies will be highly gender non-neutral if the *provision* is gender neutral.

To overcome these problems, many have endorsed more radical, gender non-neutral alternatives that include mechanisms to induce take-up among men. For example, we might allocate leave to each member of a domestic partnership separately, on a "use-it-or-lose-it" basis, so that leave not taken by one partner would be forfeit rather than falling to the other partner (Gornick and Meyers 2009). Each parent might be allotted six months of leave individually, for example, so that if one parent opts out, the other parent gets only her six months; she cannot take the six allocated to her partner. Others propose, even more radically, that some portion of mothers' leave should be conditional on leave being taken by their partners. For example, mothers might be allotted six months off, but after three months, each subsequent month can be taken only if the father takes a month of leave as well (Brighouse and Wright 2009).

These policies have many critics, but the point to emphasize for now is this: Overriding deeply-entrenched gender norms requires near-term subsidies for non-compliance with those norms. Non-neutral policies can certainly constitute good strategies for confronting discrimination: We might endorse affirmative action as a corrective to pervasive discrimination against women in hiring, for example. As I pointed out at the beginning of this chapter, remedies for gender discrimination need not be gender-neutral any more than remedies for race discrimination need to be race-neutral. But gender non-neutral policies of the type described here are importantly different from policies like affirmative action (cf. Chapter 33): The policies described here explicitly aim to restrict the options of discrimination's putative *victims*. If leave time were transferrable among partners, a woman who preferred to be the family caregiving specialist would be able to take the full amount herself. The policies discussed here either remove that option or subsidize the alternative. Men's options are restricted by these policies as well, but given existing gender norms, the policies will constrain women far more than they constrain men. If progressive family support policies really are an essential component of any successful policy response to gender inequality in the workplace, then we have reason not only to question the adequacy of discrimination as a conceptual tool for theorizing that inequality; we have reason to question its adequacy as a practical tool for thinking through strategies to remedy it.

We should not mistake this as an argument that labor market inequality is morally unproblematic, or that policies for combatting it are morally optional. Not all social moral problems must be understood in terms of discrimination.[4] Women (and men) are worse off in many domains by virtue of making gender-norm-compliant labor allocation choices. In particular, women's vastly larger share of caregiving constitutes a disadvantage in professional, political, and social domains—whether women are discriminated against or not. These gender-norm-compliant choices are due in large part to extrinsic features of the social environment: Gender socialization and the design of workplaces. This state of affairs should strike us as morally problematic *whether or not* discrimination explains and sustains it. We tend to think of gender inequality in labor markets as principally a problem of discrimination, but questioning that diagnosis might yield improvements for both our theorizing about gender justice and our efforts to achieve it. In this spirit, many feminists have called for a reorientation of our theorizing about gender justice that incorporates concepts other than discrimination: Oppression (Frye 1983, Young 1990) or domination (MacKinnon 1987, Kymlicka 2002), for example.

This chapter has explored some of the challenges for thinking of gender inequality in labor market outcomes as principally a problem of discrimination. I have suggested that even a robust understanding of discrimination—one that includes statistical discrimination, private discrimination, and structural discrimination—cannot clearly account for gender inequality in that domain. Perhaps further work will show that gender injustice is ultimately understandable in terms of a single normative concept, like discrimination. In the meantime, we should consider the possibility that meaningful progress in theorizing gender injustice requires bringing a diversity of normative concepts to bear.

Notes

1 On the data canvassed in this paragraph, see Cotter et al. (2011), England (2010), Goldin (2006), and Buchmann and DiPrete (2006).
2 Okin (1989: 6); Gheaus (2012: 18). See Okin (1989) and Hochschild (1989) for foundational work on the gendered division of labor.
3 On the data canvassed in this paragraph, see Lachance-Grzela and Bouchard (2010), Davis (2010), Cotter et al. (2011), and Gornic and Meyers (2009).
4 Patterned principles of distributive justice are a case in point.

Bibliography

Brighouse, H. and Wright, E. O. 2009. "Strong Gender Egalitarianism." In E. O. Wright (ed.) *Real Utopias: Institutions for Gender Egalitarianism: Creating the Conditions for Egalitarian Dual Earner/Dual Caregiver Families*. Madison: University of Wisconsin Press.

Buchmann, T. and DiPrete, C. 2006. "Gender-Specific Trends in the Value of Education and the Emerging Gender Gap in College Completion." *Demography*. 43(1): 1–24.

Coltrane, S. 2009. "Fatherhood, Gender and Work-Family Policies." In E. O. Wright (ed.) *Real Utopias: Institutions for Gender Egalitarianism: Creating the Conditions for Egalitarian Dual Earner/Dual Caregiver Families*. Madison: University of Wisconsin Press.

Correll, S. J., Benard, S., and Paik, I. 2007. "Getting a Job: Is There a Motherhood Penalty?" *American Journal of Sociology*. 112: 1297–1338.

Cotter, D., Hermsen, J., and Vanneman, R. 2011. "The End of the Gender Revolution? Gender Role Attitudes from 1977 to 2008." *American Journal of Sociology*. 117(1): 259–289.

Davis, S. 2010. "The Answer Doesn't Seem to Change, so Maybe We Should Change the Question: A Commentary on Lachance-Grzela and Bouchard." *Sex Roles*. 63(11/12): 786–790.

England, P. 2010. "The Gender Revolution: Uneven and Stalled." *Gender & Society*. 24: 149–166.

Frye, M. 1983. *The Politics of Reality*. Berkeley: The Crossing Press.

Gerson, K. 2010. *The Unfinished Revolution: How a New Generation is Reshaping Family, Work, and Gender in America*. New York: Oxford University Press.

Gheaus, A. 2012. "Gender Justice." *Journal of Ethics and Social Philosophy*. 6(2): 1–24.

Goldin, C. 2006. "The 'Quiet Revolution' that Transformed Women's Employment, Education, and Family." *American Economic Review Papers and Proceedings*. 96: 1–21.

Gornick, J. and Meyers, M. 2009. "Institutions that Support Gender Equality in Parenthood and Employment." In Wright, E. O. (ed.) *Real Utopias: Institutions for Gender Egalitarianism: Creating the Conditions for Egalitarian Dual Earner/Dual Caregiver Families*. Madison: University of Wisconsin Press.

Hochschild, A. 1989. *The Second Shift*. New York: Penguin Books.

Kymlicka, W. 2002. *Contemporary Political Philosophy*. Oxford: Oxford University Press.

Lachance-Grzela, M. and Bouchard, G. 2010. "Why Do Women Do the Lion's Share of Housework? A Decade of Research." *Sex Roles*. 63: 767–780.

Lippert-Rasmussen, K. 2013 "Discrimination." In LaFollette, H. (ed.) *The International Encyclopedia of Ethics*. Oxford: Wiley-Blackwell.

MacKinnon, C. 1987. *Feminism Unmodified: Discourses on Life and Law*. Cambridge: Harvard University Press.

Okin, S. M. 1989. *Justice, Gender, and the Family*. New York: Perseus Books.

Thomsen, F. K. Forthcoming. This volume, Chapter 1.

U.S. Bureau of Labor Statistics, U.S. Department of Labor, *Current Population Survey*, Highlights on Women's Earnings in 2014. [www.bls.gov/opub/.../womens-earnings/.../highlights-of-womens-earnings-in-2014.pdf].

Williams, J. 2000. *Unbending Gender: Why Family and Work Conflict and What to Do about It*. Oxford: Oxford University Press.

Young, I. M. 1990. *Justice and the Politics of Difference*. Princeton: Princeton University Press.

16

DISCRIMINATION AND RACE

Patrick Shin

PROFESSOR OF LAW, SUFFOLK UNIVERSITY LAW SCHOOL

Introduction

Race Discrimination is the first named category of prohibited discrimination in the International Covenant on Civil and Political Rights, the Universal Declaration of Human Rights, and domestic legislation such as Title VII of the Civil Rights Act of 1964 in the United States. Invidious racial discrimination and subordination have been "enduring, if not classical, problems of democratic theory" (Shiffrin 2004: 1655), and most societies have found it necessary to enact legal measures to prohibit practices of race discrimination (Shelby 2004: 1707). The wrongness of race discrimination serves as an anchor for moral reflection (Rawls 1999: 17–18), a moral datum that must be accommodated by any theoretical account.

Because race discrimination is both widely familiar and universally condemned, its wrongness can serve as an axiom upon which a broader theory of discrimination might be built. Understanding the wrongness of race discrimination is often taken to inform an understanding of discrimination generally. But once a theory of discrimination is in place, one can also ask, looking in the other direction, whether there is theoretically anything special or distinctive about race discrimination. To put it another way, one can ask whether the reasons for the wrongness of race discrimination, or any particular forms of race discrimination, are identical with the reasons for the wrongness of discrimination generally; or whether there are reasons for the wrongness of race discrimination that are not shared in common with discrimination understood more generally. That question is the topic of this chapter.

In understanding race discrimination, we can distinguish among several different kinds of inquiries that one might undertake. One might ask, first, a conceptual question about what constitutes race discrimination and how it might be distinguished from neighboring concepts such as, for example, other non-racial modes of discrimination, non-discriminatory actions relating to race, and racism. One might ask, second, about the morality of race discrimination. What makes race discrimination wrong, and is the wrongness of race discrimination distinct from the wrongness of other forms of discrimination? Third, one might examine race discrimination as a social problem. Why does race discrimination persist? How does it contribute to social inequalities and injustices? How can the prevalence of race discrimination be reduced and its social effects ameliorated or remedied? Fourth, one might examine and critique legal conceptions of discrimination in relation to our best moral understandings and the aims of justice.

This chapter will focus mainly on the first two sets of questions. The third set raises empirical issues within the domains of social psychology, economics, and empirical legal studies. For a collection of essays on the fourth set of questions, which span the fields of moral and political philosophy and legal theory, see *Philosophical Foundations of Discrimination Law* (Hellman, D. and Moreau, S. (eds.) 2013).

The concept of race discrimination

I will not attempt to argue for any particular account of discrimination in this chapter. But under most plausible definitions, discrimination entails treating a person or group of persons worse than another because of some property attributed to that person or group (Lippert-Rasmussen 2014: 15; Eidelson 2015: 17). Roughly, then, discrimination generally involves a person being treated differently from members of some comparison class (actual or counterfactual) on the basis of some putative property of the person not shared by the comparison class. An act of discrimination, so defined, can be thought to constitute race discrimination when the property that distinguishes the comparison class is the person's race.

Like discrimination generally, race discrimination can be defined either as a moralized or neutral concept (cf. Introduction). When defined as a morally neutral notion, race discrimination merely describes a practice of differential treatment based on race, but the practice need not be morally wrong, even *prima facie* (Singer 1978: 186). Thus, for example, on a morally neutral definition, race-based affirmative action can constitute race discrimination even if it is morally permissible. In contrast, according to a moralized account, actions must have some wrongmaking feature (e.g., tendency to harm or demean) in order to count as race discrimination. Thus, on such a view, to claim that an action constitutes race discrimination entails a moral objection to it (Blum 2002: 95). On a moralized definition, if race-based affirmative action is not *prima facie* wrong, then it should not be called race discrimination at all.

Whether or not the general concept of discrimination is best understood in moralized or neutral terms, there are good reasons to favor a moralized definition of *race discrimination*. For one thing, the characterization of an action as race discrimination has a strongly pejorative connotation in ordinary public discourse. Insisting as a technical matter of definition that race discrimination is not inherently wrong could be confusing in such contexts. In particular, in the debate about race-based affirmative action, the adoption of a non-moralized definition of race discrimination might be regarded as a tendentious terminological move that favors those who oppose it, because such a definition implies that affirmative action, whether or not it is morally permissible, is conceptually kindred to invidious forms of racially differentiated treatment.

The remainder of this chapter will follow ordinary usage and assume a *moralized* notion of race discrimination. According to this understanding, race discrimination is not just a descriptive denotation of differences of treatment that track race, but a moral concept that embeds a judgment of wrongness, the content of which will be discussed below. Generally, according to a moralized view, the wrongmaking features of race discrimination are partly constitutive of it. On such a view, it makes sense to say that some but not all forms of racially differentiated treatment are wrong, and some but not all instances of such treatment are wrong *because* they constitute race discrimination.

Like other forms of discrimination, race discrimination can be intentional or unintentional; conscious or unconscious; direct or indirect. These variations in the possible modes of discrimination are not unique to race discrimination. Of course, the relative frequency of these modes of discrimination with respect to race might be different than for discrimination with respect to other characteristics, but that would seem to be a matter for empirical inquiry, not a function of the concept of race discrimination. Although the mention of race discrimination, without further specification, may call to mind an action based on intentional attitudes – such as desires, beliefs, animus, or other consideration of race as a reason-giving factor – it can also refer to action based on unconscious or implicit bias relating to race, as well as actions not motivated by racial bias that unintentionally create a significant disparity based on race. Race discrimination can thus encompass a variety of different scenarios, which may not all be reducible to a single structural form.

The concept of race

An account of race discrimination may not need to commit itself to any particular theory of race. But the concept of race is obviously embedded in that of race discrimination. Furthermore, holding certain kinds of beliefs about race (e.g., assumptions about racial essences) is sometimes associated with race discrimination; and, indeed, some acts might be considered racially discriminatory in virtue of being based on such beliefs. Thus, in seeking to understand race discrimination, one might also want to understand the concept of race.

Contemporary philosophical debates around the concept of race tend to center on ontological questions about whether and in what ways, if any, race can be thought to be "real" (McPherson 2015; Glasgow and Woodward 2015; Mallon 2006). The naïve view, which might be called "racialism" (Appiah and Gutmann 1996: 54) is that race denotes a robust natural (biological) kind; that different races of human beings have different geographic origins and genetic histories; and that each race is characterized by a distinctive set of essential biobehavioral properties, including particular somatic features, intellectual capabilities, and behavioral dispositions (Atkin 2012: 13; Blum 2002: 127).

Racialism has been widely discredited. There is general consensus that "[t]here are no biobehavioral racial essences" (Mallon 2006: 545) and that the ordinary concept of race cannot be derived from biology or other natural sciences (Atkin 2012: 46; Mallon 2006: 529; see also Zack 2002). Among other reasons, even basic putative somatic markers of race such as skin tone and facial morphology do not, on careful objective study, actually align with folk racial divisions. Thus, for example,

> [a]n east African will be classified as 'black' under our ordinary concept but this person shares a skin colour with people from India and a nose shape with people from northern Europe. This makes our ordinary concept of *race* look to be in bad shape as an object for scientific study – it fails to divide the world up as it suggests it should.
>
> *(Atkin 2012: 35)*

Furthermore, studies have established that "genetic variation within racially identified populations is as great as or greater than diversity between populations" (Mallon 2006: 529; see also Appiah 2006: 374), which is fatal for the supposition of genetic racial essences. The division of all humans into four or five races that roughly match up with continental origin is not justified by objective analysis of genetic clustering (Kitcher 2007: 113) or any biological taxonomy (Appiah and Gutmann 1996: 72), and racial groups in contemporary societies certainly do not satisfy scientific definitions of breeding populations (Zack 2002: 69). Finally, criteria for racial distinctions are not consistent from one culture to another. For example, "the Brazilian and US classification schemes for who counts as 'Black' differ" (Haslanger 2000: 43).

Thus, the traditional racial categories are, from a scientific viewpoint, arbitrary; and conversely, to the extent that human beings could be divided into subgroups of interest to biologists (e.g., Kitcher 2007: 114), those divisions would fail to capture the ordinary meaning of, and interest in, race (McPherson 2015: 682; Blum 2002: 144).

The general rejection of race as a scientifically defensible natural kind has led to disputes about the ontological status of race. The main alternatives to the naïve view that race is scientifically real seem to be that race is not real (Blum 2002; Zack 2002); that it is real in some deflated or minimal sense (Glasgow and Woodward 2015; McPherson 2015); that it is real as a social construct (Taylor 2004; Mallon 2006: 534; Haslanger 2000); or that its reality is rooted in a hybrid set of biological and social facts (Kitcher 2007; Andreasen 1998).

The conception of race as a social construct has become the dominant theoretical view (Andreasen 2000: S654) and perhaps also informs ordinary folk notions of race (Coates 2013). Constructivist theories of race branch out into their own sub-theories. Among the important insights that an account of race discrimination might pluck from such constructivist theories are that social ascriptions of race can cause people who are so categorized to have certain common experiences that then reinforce the ascription (James 2016); that racial classifications can identify a person's place within hierarchical social networks (Haslanger 2000) and racialized schemes of social interaction (Taylor 2004); and that social racial ascriptions can become important parts of personal identity (Mallon 2006; Taylor 2004).

It is not clear that the ontology of race has much significance for the concept of race discrimination. Granted, someone who clings to the idea of race as a set of biobehavioral essential properties might define race discrimination differently from a person who rejects the ontological reality of race. And someone who rejects the reality of race might hold the view that one of the reasons that race discrimination is wrong is that it entails treating people differently on the basis of a wholly delusory classification. But the reality of race does not determine the definition of race discrimination. A person can discriminate on the basis of race whether or not race is real; and discrimination can have differential consequences for socially "racialized" groups (see Blum 2002: 147), regardless of racial metaphysics. This is because intentional acts of race discrimination are characterized as such by virtue of being predicated upon ascriptions and imputations of race; but these ascriptions need not accord with any reality, biological or social. Consequence-based notions of race discrimination (such as indirect race discrimination) may depend on a construction of racialized groupings that arises out of historical and extant patterns of social inequality, but such functional understandings of race are orthogonal to any particular racial ontology.

The concept of race discrimination may presuppose the existence of folk understandings of race that form the basis of intentional and psychological attitudes, and perhaps social practices of racialization sufficient to support generally agreed upon schemes of classification; but an account of race discrimination can be agnostic about the metaphysics of race. The more relevant question about race for a theory of race discrimination is not metaphysical, but normative (Mallon 2006) and pragmatic (Haslanger 2000). For example, one might ask how race *should* be conceived, given the social fact of race discrimination and a shared commitment to its elimination.

Racism and race discrimination

Race discrimination may be distinguishable from *racism*. Racism is sometimes defined as a system of beliefs, judgments, or actions predicated upon the supposed superiority of one race over another, often coupled with attitudes of antipathy toward members of the supposedly inferior race (Blum 2002: 8; Atkin 2012: 115–16). In contemporary ordinary discourse, though, it is not clear that a belief of relative superiority is necessary for racism. An ideology that posited the (non-veridical) existence of significant cognitive differences between blacks and whites might well be characterized as racist, even if that ideology did not imply a judgment of moral superiority. Some might regard all pseudo-scientific claims that fall under the rubric of "racialism" as described above as racist. Perhaps this is because as a matter of fact, racialist views tend to be espoused in the service of tacit judgments of racial superiority or inferiority.

The class of acts that constitute race discrimination is not coextensive with the class of racist acts. For example, if a person goes out of his way to choose a queue at the supermarket that leads to a white cashier, and he does this because he believes minority cashiers are dishonest, we would likely characterize the person's act as racist. However, we probably would not say that the person has engaged in race discrimination, because according to most definitions, an action must cause or be aimed at causing some type of harmful or adverse consequence in order to constitute discrimination – although this depends on how broadly one understands the meaning of harm or adversity (see Slavny and Parr 2015; cf. Chapter 12). Similarly, if an employer without any racist motivation or belief institutes a hiring examination that unforeseeably turns out to disqualify job applicants of minority races at disproportionately high rates, this might constitute (indirect) race discrimination under some theories, even if the employer holds no racist beliefs.

Although the concepts of race discrimination and racism may pick out different sets of actions, I will argue below that the distinctive wrongness of race discrimination emerges when a discriminatory act expresses certain sorts of morally objectionable judgments, including judgments that could be characterized as racist.

The morality of race discrimination

Assuming a moralized definition of discrimination, to claim that an action constitutes race discrimination is to assert a moral objection against it. Insofar as race discrimination is a type of discrimination, the wrongness of race discrimination must overlap at least to some extent the wrongness of discrimination generally. Thus, the moral wrongness of race discrimination may be partly derivative of the wrongness of discrimination. On the other hand, because race discrimination is a central paradigm of discrimination, it may be that the wrongness of race discrimination informs the wrongness of discrimination generally. Perhaps the wrongness of discrimination generally can be extrapolated from the wrongness of race discrimination, and perhaps the wrongness of other modes of discrimination depends on the extent to which they can be analogized to race discrimination.

Whatever the order of explanation, one can ask how much space there is between the wrongness of race discrimination and the wrongness of discrimination generally. The well-known alternatives for explaining the wrongness of discrimination (e.g., Altman 2015; Arneson 2013; Alexander 1992; Blum 2002; Eidelson 2015; Hellman 2008; Lippert-Rasmussen 2014, 2006) all encompass the wrongness of race discrimination. For example, a harm-based account of discrimination would say that the wrongness of race discrimination lies in the particular harms caused by such conduct for members of particular racial groups. Similarly, an expressivist theory of discrimination might say that a racially discriminatory act is wrong insofar as it expresses a judgment that members of a particular racial group have lesser moral status or are somehow inferior to members of other racial groups (cf. Chapter 7).

There is, I think, some intuitive plausibility in the idea that treating a person worse than another on the basis of race is objectionable in a way that seems distinguishable from differential treatment on the basis of other discriminatory factors. As Richard Wasserstrom asserted in his

1987 address to the American Philosophical Association: "There is a special and distinctive kind of injustice when one's blackness or whiteness becomes the basis for fixing persons' unequal positions, opportunities, and status in a systematically pervasive fashion" (Wasserstrom 1987: 34). Wasserstrom's point is not that race discrimination is necessarily worse than other forms of injustice. It would not be difficult to name various kinds of wrongs that are equally unjust or detrimental, if not more so (Levin 1981). Wasserstrom's claim is that the wrongness of race discrimination is different from the wrongness of other forms of discrimination.

One plausible analysis of this difference has been suggested by T.M. Scanlon. He, like Wasserstrom, has observed that there seems to be "something particularly objectionable about discrimination on racial grounds" (2008: 72). After reflecting on the ways in which discrimination on racial grounds seems different from unequal treatment based on equally irrelevant but more idiosyncratic grounds, Scanlon argues that acts of discrimination on racial grounds are distinctively wrong because they arise out of, and help to maintain, a socially prevalent practice of depriving people of important benefits and opportunities on the basis of "prejudicial judgments" that mark certain groups as inferior (2008: 73). Thus, the particular wrongness of racially discriminatory acts, according to Scanlon, lies in their consequences and their social meaning, i.e., the socially resonant judgments of inferiority they express.

Kasper Lippert-Rasmussen criticizes Scanlon's view, arguing in part that a judgment expressing inferiority is neither a necessary or a sufficient component of an act of race discrimination (2014: 146–51). For example, employers might hold and express judgments that a particular racial group is inferior yet hire members at expected rates (2014: 146), perhaps because of legal compulsion or labor market conditions. Conversely, employers might limit the employment opportunities of members of a particular racial group by channeling them into one particular type of job, not based on any judgment of inferiority, but a genuine, albeit misguided, belief that members of that group are especially well suited to that kind of work (2014: 147). Lippert-Rasmussen argues that Scanlon's meaning-based account fails to properly account for such cases.

Lippert-Rasmussen's argument highlights the difficulty of casting expressive meaning in the role of a constitutive wrongmaking feature of race discrimination. But Scanlon's view is better understood as a claim that the distinctive wrongness of race-based adverse treatment is tied to its meaning within broader social contexts of systematic race discrimination. Scanlon does not assert that every individual act that constitutes wrongful race discrimination must express a judgment of inferiority. What he suggests, instead, is that we recognize acts as wrongful race discrimination when they can be seen as part of a social or institutional "practice" that imposes disadvantages on members of particular racial groups in a manner that expresses inferiority. This interpretation helps make sense of Scanlon's statement that "[o]nce a practice of discrimination exists, decisions that deny important goods to members of the group discriminated against – and do so without sufficient justification – are wrong even if they express no judgment of inferiority on the agent's part" (Scanlon 2008: 73).

More generally, one might concede (though this is not necessarily Scanlon's view) that acts of race discrimination can sometimes be wrong by virtue of features or consequences that do not involve expressions of inferiority and therefore are not wrong in any *special* way. It is possible, as Lippert-Rasmussen does, to posit or construct scenarios of racially differentiated treatment where the actor's known intentional attitudes or other contingent circumstances neutralize any judgment of inferiority that we might otherwise have reason to impute. But it is telling that such deliberate invention is necessary to deflect the inferences that would ordinarily (and reasonably) be drawn. In the main, our shared "history of mistreatment or current social disadvantage" of minority racial groups imbues racialized acts with a "demeaning" quality (Hellman 2008: 21–29).

We may agree, then, that "nonevaluational racial discrimination is *possible*" (Lippert-Rasmussen 2014: 149, italics added), but it would be difficult to deny that it is also possible, if not true in most cases, that race discrimination can be distinctively wrong by virtue of the special social meanings of race-based action. An understanding of the morality of racialized action in contemporary social settings cannot ignore the history of racial classification in the service of unjust exclusion, or the operative role of race in persistent patterns of social hierarchy and inequality. Absent specific context suggesting otherwise, treating someone unfavorably because of race can express an implicit endorsement of a social system of racial subordination.

Understanding the distinctive wrongness of race discrimination as tied to its resonance with historical oppression and persistent patterns of racial inequality helps answer an additional challenge posed by Lippert-Rasmussen to Scanlon. Lippert-Rasmussen states a worry (2014: 148) about Scanlon's argument that the wrongness of race discrimination is "unidirectional" in the sense that the charge of race discrimination "applies to actions or policies that disadvantage blacks, but not to all policies that employ race-based criteria" (Scanlon 2008: 74). Lippert-Rasmussen's challenge is that, though it might be rare as a matter of fact, an act of differential treatment disadvantaging a European American could express a judgment that whites are racially inferior to blacks. He argues that according to Scanlon's meaning-based account, such an act should be regarded as "morally wrong for exactly the same reason as acts of discrimination against African Americans" (Lippert-Rasmussen 2014: 148).

In an often-quoted passage, Alexander Bickel argued that race discrimination must be understood to be wrong regardless of the race of the persons who are advantaged or disadvantaged by the act, and that a rejection of symmetrical colorblindness would simply turn determinations of race discrimination into a "matter of whose ox is gored" (Bickel 1975: 133; for discussion see Appiah and Gutmann 1996: 119). In general, the question posed by proponents of "colorblindness" is that if it is wrong to subject members of minority races to disadvantageous treatment on the basis of their race, why is it not equally wrong to do so with respect to members of a majority race?

One possible answer is that race-conscious policies such as affirmative action are not wrong *qua* discrimination insofar as they can reasonably be expected to result in the overall reduction of the occurrence of invidious race discrimination (e.g., Appiah and Gutmann 1996: 133, cf. Chapter 33). This sort of answer works for conceptions of discrimination based on group harm or injustice (e.g., Young 1990), but it is unsatisfactory for any theory of discrimination that allows individual acts to constitute discrimination regardless of broader social consequences.

A more promising answer for such accounts is one that is partially suggested by Lippert-Rasmussen himself in a footnote (2014: 148 n.55). One can draw a distinction between acts of race discrimination that are wrong simply in virtue of having the features of wrongful discrimination, and acts of race discrimination that are *distinctively* wrong by virtue of the social meaning of race. According to the view I am proposing, the adverse differential treatment of members of a socially dominant group based on their race may very well constitute race discrimination. We can imagine a black employer, for example, who refuses to hire white employees due to feelings of racial resentment. But race discrimination in that sense becomes difficult to distinguish from discrimination on the basis of any other bad or arbitrary reason. Imagine, for example, an employer who passionately hates people who "went to Princeton, or … wear clothing in colors that clash" (Scanlon 2008: 71).

Even if a given act of discrimination against a member of a socially dominant racial group could reasonably be taken to express a judgment of inferiority about that group, such a judgment would seem eccentric or anomalous, giving the act the character of idiosyncratic discrimination rather than of paradigmatic race discrimination. The point is that discrimination against members of a socially dominant racial group can surely be morally wrong and impermissible, but such "reverse" discrimination does not seem open to the morally full-throated objection that applies to race discrimination against members of minority groups. The reason, according to a social expressivist view, is that in a white-dominated society, adverse treatment on the basis of being white simply does not have the same moral meaning as adverse treatment on the basis of being black, because being white is not reasonably associated with a "history of mistreatment or current social disadvantage" (Hellman 2008: 21–29). This is not to deny that anti-white action might also have a particular social meaning (cf. Khaitan 2015: 177–79), but the point is that the particular wrong of race discrimination is not just that it tends to express an arbitrary judgment of inferiority, but a judgment of inferiority that coincides with historic and prevailing patterns of racial injustice and subordination (Wasserstrom 1987).

I have tried to narrowly reframe Scanlon's view that race discrimination is wrong insofar as it expresses a judgment of racial inferiority to highlight the *distinctive* way in which race discrimination can be wrong. But this framing is arguably too narrow, because it may not capture other forms of race discrimination that might be regarded as distinctively wrong. First, my approach is informed largely by the history of anti-black discrimination in America. The social meaning of race discrimination might be significantly different in other societies. If so, then the distinctive wrong of race discrimination in those societies might have to be articulated differently. If there were a society in which race discrimination did not have any particular social meaning (e.g., if racial group membership was not "expressively salient," Khaitan 2015: 172), then it would have to be conceded that race discrimination would not be *distinctively* wrong in that society.

Second, there is an important category of wrongful race discrimination that seems objectionable not in virtue of expressing a judgment of inferiority, but in virtue of treating people as though their actions were a function of their race. We might think of an employer, for example, who clings to a racialist view that members of different races have differing levels of capabilities in various work-related areas. One race is better at detail-oriented work, another is better at management, another at sales, etc., or so the employer believes; but we can suppose that the employer does not believe that any one race is on the whole superior or inferior to any other (for each has its strengths). If the employer, based on these beliefs, relies upon racial classifications to separate workers into different job categories, the employer is surely engaging in wrongful race discrimination. Moreover, this type of discrimination – racial stereotyping (Appiah 2000; Shin 2013) – exhibits a wrongness that is quite characteristic of race discrimination, even though, by hypothesis, the act does not necessarily express a judgment of racial inferiority.

The wrongness of racial stereotyping is not necessarily that it expresses a judgment of racial inferiority, but that it is predicated on a rationale that fails to take persons seriously as individuals. We must be careful here not to fall into the trap of asserting that it is always wrong to treat individuals based on group classifications: that claim would be demonstrably false (Lippert-Rasmussen 2014: 275; Schauer 2003: 19; Chapter 3). Benjamin Eidelson analyzes the moral wrong of failing to treat someone as an individual as the expression of disrespect for a person's autonomy. He argues that we infringe a person's right to be treated as an individual when we fail to give reasonable consideration to that person's history of autonomous choices or "disparage" that person's agency, his capacity to make autonomous choices. Treating people as individuals for Eidelson means "respect[ing] the role they can play and have played in shaping themselves, rather than treating them as determined by demographic categories or other matters of statistical fate" (Eidelson 2015: 215–16). The employer who channels all employees of Race X into a particular type of work because of a belief that Xs, by virtue of their race, are generally suited for that work, can be criticized for a morally objectionable failure to treat Xs as individuals.

The employer treats Xs as fungible tokens of their racial group, as if the capabilities and talents of every X were predominantly a function of their race, not of the choices and efforts they might have made as autonomous individuals (see also Glasgow 2009: 85).

The moral objection of failing to treat persons as autonomous individuals is perhaps not distinctive of race discrimination – gender discrimination, for example, can also surely involve the same moral failing. But, in combination with the social meaning of racialized action, this objection helps answer a puzzle that is somewhat unique to race discrimination theory. The question is, why do we sometimes seem to have reason for moral concern over the use of statistically *valid* racialized generalizations? For example, if it is statistically true that crimes in a given local community are committed at a higher rate by members of minority races than whites, then why should it be morally problematic for law enforcement officers to engage in racial profiling – i.e., to expend more resources to monitor the activities of minorities than whites, especially if the expected benefit is a reduction of overall crime rates (Risse and Zeckhauser 2004; Bou-Habib 2011; Chapter 27)? Similarly, if it is statistically true for a given labor pool that minority workers are less likely to have a certain job-relevant skill than white workers, then why should it be objectionable for employers to use whiteness as a proxy for possessing that skill, especially if it is costly for the employer to directly test for that skill in the hiring process (Arrow 1998; cf. Chapter 25)?

The answer suggested by the autonomy and social meaning approaches is that depriving someone of a job, subjecting a person to police scrutiny or, less invidiously, channeling a person into a particular position based on the person's racial group membership constitutes a failure to respect the person's individual capacity for action and choice and instead treats the person simply as a function of his racial status. Furthermore, in the context of a society beset by racial inequality and a history of racial subordination, the practices of racial profiling, race-based statistical discrimination, and racial stereotyping bespeak acquiescence in the social injustices that likely explain the racial correlations in the first place. And such practices implicitly repudiate the capacity of disadvantaged individuals to do anything but sink to the level of their socially depressed expectations (Lippert-Rasmussen 2014: 300; Shin 2012: 176; Bou-Habib 2011).

Conclusion

Insofar as everyone is a member of some race, there is an important sense in which any person can potentially be subjected to wrongful discrimination on the basis of race. When understood in this broad way (for explanation, see especially Lippert-Rasmussen 2014: 49–53), race discrimination is not readily distinguishable from discrimination on the basis of a miscellany of arbitrary, idiosyncratic, or oddball considerations. Acts of race discrimination take on a more distinctive moral character, however, when they arise out of and coincide with pervasive social systems of inequality and hierarchy. We have special reason to object to discrimination on the basis of race, even when not facially non-invidious, when it expresses a judgment of racial inferiority or disrespect for individual autonomy that resonates with historical and persistent social schemes of subordination and racial stratification. In short, the distinctive wrongness of race discrimination derives from the complicated significance, significations, and etiology of racial status in contemporary society.

Bibliography

Alexander, L. 1992. "What Makes Wrongful Discrimination Wrong? Biases, Preferences, Stereotypes, and Proxies." *University of Pennsylvania Law Review*. 141: 149–219.

Altman, A. 2015. "Discrimination," in E. Zalta et al. (eds.) (Fall 2015 ed.), *Stanford Encyclopedia of Philosophy*, online at http://plato.stanford.edu/archives/fall2015/entries/discrimination

Andreasen, R. 2000. "Race: Biological Reality or Social Construct?" *Philosophy of Science*. 67: S653-S666.

Appiah, K. A. 2006. "How to Decide if Races Exist." *Proceedings of the Aristotelian Society*. 106: 365–382.

Appiah, K. A. and Gutmann, A. 1996. *Color Conscious: the Political Morality of Race*. Princeton: Princeton University Press.

Arneson, R. 2013. "Discrimination, Disparate Impact, and Theories of Justice," in Hellman, D. and Moreau, S. (eds.) *Philosophical Foundations of Discrimination Law*. Oxford: Oxford University Press.

Arrow, K. 1998. "What Has Economics to Say About Racial Discrimination?" *Journal of Economic Perspectives*. 12: 91–100.

Atkin, A. 2012. *The Philosophy of Race*. Durham: Acumen.

Bickel, A. 1975. *The Morality of Consent*. New Haven: Yale University Press.

Blum, L. 2002. *"I'm not a Racist but...": the Moral Quandary of Race*. Ithaca: Cornell University Press.

Bou-Habib, P. 2011. "Racial Profiling and Background Injustice." *Journal of Ethics*. 15: 33–46.

Coates, T. 2013. "What We Mean When We Say 'Race Is a Social Construct.'" *The Atlantic*: May 15, online at www.theatlantic.com/national/archive/2013/05/what-we-mean-when-we-say-race-is-a-social-construct/275872/

Eidelson, B. 2015. *Discrimination and Disrespect*. Oxford: Oxford University Press.

Glasgow, J. 2009. "Racism as Disrespect." *Ethics*. 120: 64–93.

Glasgow, J. and Woodward, J. 2015. "Basic Racial Realism." *Journal of the American Philosophical Association*. 1: 449–466.

Haslanger, S. 2000. "Gender and Race: (What) Are They? (What) Do We Want Them to Be?" *Noûs*. 34: 31–55.

Hellman, D. 2008. *When Is Discrimination Wrong?* Cambridge, MA: Harvard University Press.

Hellman, D. and Moreau, S. (eds.). 2013. *Philosophical Foundations of Discrimination Law*. Oxford: Oxford University Press.

James, M. (2016) "Race," in E. Zalta et al. (eds.) (Spring 2016 ed.), *Stanford Encylopedia of Philosophy*, online at http://plato.stanford.edu/archives/spr2016/entries/race

Khaitan, T. 2015. *A Theory of Discrimination Law*. Oxford: Oxford University Press.

Kitcher, P. 2007. "Does 'Race' Have a Future?" In Taylor, P. (ed.) (2012), *The Philosophy of Race*. New York: Routledge.

Levin, M. 1981. "Is Racial Discrimination Special?" *Journal of Value Inquiry*. 15: 225–234.

Lippert-Rasmussen, K. 2006. "The Badness of Discrimination." *Ethical Theory and Moral Practice*. 9: 167–185.

Lippert-Rasmussen, K. 2014. *Born Free and Equal? A Philosophical Inquiry into the Nature of Discrimination*. Oxford: Oxford University Press.

Mallon, R. 2006. "'Race': Normative, not Metaphysical or Semantic." *Ethics*. 116: 525–551.

McPherson, L. 2015. "Deflating 'Race'." *Journal of the American Philosophical Association*. 1: 674–693.

Rawls, J. 1999. *A Theory of Justice*, rev. ed., Cambridge, MA: Harvard University Press.

Risse, M. and Zeckhauser, R. 2004. "Racial Profiling." *Philosophy and Public Affairs*. 32: 131–170.

Scanlon, T. M. 2008. *Moral Dimensions: Permissibility, Meaning, Blame*. Cambridge, MA: Belknap Press of Harvard University Press.

Schauer, F. 2003. *Profiles, Probabilities and Stereotypes*. Cambridge, MA: Harvard University Press.

Shelby, T. 2004. "Race and Social Justice: Rawlsian Considerations." *Fordham Law Review*. 72: 1697–1714.

Shiffrin, S. 2004. "Race, Labor, and the Fair Equality of Opportunity Principle." *Fordham Law Review*. 72: 1643–1675.

Shin, P. 2013. "Is There a Unitary Concept of Discrimination?" in Hellman, D. and Moreau, S. (eds.), *Philosophical Foundations of Discrimination Law*. Oxford: Oxford University Press.

Singer, P. 1978. "Is Racial Discrimination Arbitrary?" *Philosophia*. 8: 185–203.

Slavny, A. and Parr, T. 2015 "Harmless Discrimination." *Legal Theory*. 21: 100–114.

Taylor, P. 2004. "Race: A Philosophical Introduction," in Taylor, P. (ed.) (2012), *The Philosophy of Race*. New York: Routledge.

Wasserstrom, R. 1987. "Preferential Treatment, Color-Blindness, and the Evils of Racism and Racial Discrimination." *Proceedings and Addresses of the American Philosophical Association*. 61: 27–42.
Young, I. M. 1990. *Justice and the Politics of Difference*. Princeton: Princeton University Press.
Zack, N. 2002. *Philosophy of Science and Race*. New York: Routledge.

17
DISCRIMINATION AND RELIGION

Sune Lægaard

ROSKILDE UNIVERSITY

Why religion and discrimination?

Religion is important in relation to discussions about discrimination. Discrimination in the generic sense is differential treatment on the basis of specific features. Religion (or at least, in a European context, certain newly arrived forms of religion, mainly Islam) is increasingly prominent in many social and political contexts, and as such it is also becoming increasingly common to distinguish between people on the basis of religious affiliation. A striking example of this is the fact that whereas immigration to Europe was earlier (i.e. during the 1980s and 1990s) framed in terms of the country of origin (e.g. Turks, Pakistanis, Iranians, Somalis), most immigrants are now framed as "Muslims". So, whereas differential treatment of these groups earlier would have been conceptualized as discrimination on grounds of nationality, language or race, it is now also necessary to consider it as discrimination on grounds of religion.

Apart from this empirical development, religion is picked out by many legal prohibitions against discrimination as a protected characteristic. According to European Council Directive 2000/78/EC, which has subsequently been implemented in national law in the EU member states, "any direct or indirect discrimination based on religion or belief, disability, age or sexual orientation as regards the areas covered by this Directive should be prohibited throughout the Community."[1] Because of such legal bans on religious discrimination, an increasing number of legal cases have appeared. This has in turn generated political controversies about whether there should be such bans at all and, if so, how they should be understood.

Discussion of such issues not merely as questions about what actual legal provisions *in fact* require as a matter of positive law, but as more principled philosophical issues about how we *should* understand religious discrimination and how it *should* be regulated, requires consideration of two very big sets of issues: one set of issues concerns what discrimination is and what makes discrimination wrong, when it is wrong. These are entirely *general* questions that can be and are being discussed without specific reference to religion (e.g. in Hellman 2014; Lippert-Rasmussen 2014; cf. Chapters 6–14). To consider religious discrimination in particular, we therefore also need to think about what (if anything) is special about religion. Religion is clearly a different category than, e.g. gender or race, since religion can be chosen and involves certain patterns of actions, both of which complicate the issue of when differential treatment on these grounds is discrimination and when it is wrong (cf. Chapters 15–16). But the question about what is special about religion also opens very big and general debates, e.g. about religion and politics, religious neutrality and freedom, etc. (e.g. Laborde 2017). The present chapter cannot possibly address the breadth of these two general debates. The aim therefore is more modest, namely to provide a sketch of *philosophical* questions *specifically* about religion *and* discrimination.

I will first distinguish between different philosophical issues about religion and discrimination (section 2). Then I will go through the distinguished issues in turn, which have to do with religion as object and subject of discrimination (section 3), the meaning of "religion" in religious discrimination (section 4), and religion as a justificatory category in relation to discrimination (section 5).

Different philosophical questions about discrimination

The most immediately obvious and discussed philosophical questions about religion and discrimination concern whether specific cases of religious discrimination should be permissible or not. Such questions are often prompted by concrete legal cases. A much-discussed case is the British case of *Noah v. Desrosiers*, which concerned the decision of a small hairdresser in London not to hire an applicant who insisted on wearing an Islamic headscarf, despite the stated policy of the salon requiring staff to make their own hair visible to customers to showcase the styling offered.[2] The Employment Tribunal found Desrosiers guilty of indirect discrimination. Cases like this generate lots of controversies over whether there should be bans on religious discrimination of this sort, whether the legal rules should be applied in the way they were in the given case, what counts as a legitimate requirement on employees, and whether people should bear the responsibility for their own beliefs (e.g. Jones 2015).

But underlying such first-order case-specific issues about religious discrimination there are a number of more general philosophical issues, which both inform the categorization of such cases *as* cases of religious discrimination and the normative assessment of them *as such*. These are the issues I will be discussing in the remainder of this chapter:

> **Structural:** Religion can relate to discrimination is several different ways. Roughly, one can say that religion can both be the *object* and the *subject* of discrimination.
>
> **Justificatory:** When it comes to the normative assessment of cases of religious discrimination, how does religion function as a *justificatory category* in relation to discrimination?

Religion as object and subject of discrimination

At the most general level, discrimination can be defined like this:

> *Generic discrimination*
> Agent A discriminates against (or for) patient P, if, and only if, A treats P worse (or better) than A would treat others because P has a certain feature F.
>
> *(For a more precise definition of generic discrimination, see Lippert-Rasmussen 2014: 15; cf. Introduction and Chapter 1)*

Given this generic understanding of discrimination, what, then, is *religious* discrimination? Although this might seem a straightforward question, this is actually not the case. The reason is that the definition includes several variables (A, P and F) all of which can be related to religion. So religious discrimination can mean several different things, depending on which of the variables in the definition are specified with reference to religion.

The most obvious illustration of this concerns the subject and object of discrimination. Religion can both enter in to the definition of discrimination in relation to the discriminator carrying out the discriminatory act (agent A) and in relation to the discriminatee, i.e. the person, group or organization at the receiving end of discrimination (patient P). The Desrosiers case mentioned above was a case of religious discrimination because the discriminatee was a Muslim, and did not get the job because of this. Cases involving the so-called "ministerial exception" under American First Amendment jurisprudence, which protects churches' right to select people who will preach and teach the church's values and doctrines free from interference from civil employment laws (Ahdar and Leigh 2013: 400), will be cases of religious discrimination because the agent selecting among candidates and preferring some over others on religious grounds is a religious organization.

Note that the difference between religious subjects and objects of discrimination is not the same as the difference between discrimination *for* and *against* religion. The definition offered above encompasses both (cf. "worse [or better]"). The difference between the subject (agent A) of discrimination and the object (patient P) is rather the difference between the agent carrying out the discriminatory act and the patient directly affected by the act – whether the latter is affected negatively (in which case it is discrimination against P) or positively (in which case it is discrimination for P).

When one speaks of religion as an object of discrimination, this means that the discriminatee (patient P) is *a religious entity*, e.g. as a religious person (a Christian or Muslim person), group (Christians or Muslims in general), organization (a religious school or charity) etc. To say that an act is an act of religious discrimination then is to say that the discriminatee is religious.

This implies that this particular religious patient (person, group or organization) is treated better or worse than some other patient (person, group or organization). This actually allows for several different relevant contrasts, so the contrast can either be to non-religious patients (e.g. if the state discriminates against all religious groups or in favor of secular organizations), or it can be to other religious patients (e.g. if the European Court of Human Rights treats Christians better than it treats Muslims, cf. Moyn 2016, Joppke 2016).

When one speaks of religion as a subject of discrimination, this can similarly mean that the discriminator (agent A) is a religious person (e.g. a priest refusing to marry homosexual couples), group (e.g. a sect whose members isolate themselves from non-members), or organization (e.g. a religious school dismissing a teacher who is not deemed to live up to the religion's requirements on personal conduct) (cf. Chapters 18 and 26).

But as is evident from the definition of generic discrimination above, there are not only two, but three variables. And once we consider that any act is only an act of discrimination in a certain respect, i.e. with respect to the feature F that is the basis of the differential treatment, things become even more complicated.

Then there suddenly is another way of understanding what it means to say that religion is the object of discrimination, in addition to the noted sense according to which it means that the patient is a religious entity. That religion is the object of discrimination can now also mean that the discrimination in question treats patient P differentially *on the basis of its religious aspects or traits* (feature F) – i.e. that a person, group or organization is discriminated against *because* and *insofar as* it is religious in some respect (because it possesses the feature of being religious). To say that an act is an act of religious discrimination, then, is to say that it takes place on the basis of a categorization of the patient as having feature F, which either is the agent's reason for discriminating (e.g. that I give the student the benefit of the doubt because I think the student is a Muslim, and that Muslims have generally been treated unfairly) or which properly explains the differential treatment (e.g. that a crash helmet requirement happens to burden Sikhs more than others, because their religion requires them to wear a turban). So if religious discrimination is specified in relation to the feature F, this is really a claim about the agent's reasons or motives or about what explains the differential impact of certain acts (cf. Chapter 2).

The difference between these two readings of the ways in which religion can be the object of discrimination is that the former (relating to patient P) focuses on the *outcome*, whereas the latter (relating to feature F) focuses on the *motivation* or *cause* of differential treatment. This is important for several reasons. These two different perspectives might in many cases provide different descriptions and conceptualizations of the same act, since the focus on feature F, for instance, picks out the categorization on the basis of which the agent acts, whereas the focus on patient P can deliver a description of an act that an agent does not necessarily share (this will often be important in relation to cases of indirect discrimination). But the difference, furthermore, is important because different theories about what makes discrimination wrong, when it is wrong, attach to different aspects – if discrimination is wrong because it is harmful, then the focus on the patient is the relevant one, whereas the focus on the reasons for discrimination is more relevant if what makes discrimination wrong is the mental state of the discriminator (for different theories of what makes discrimination wrong, see Lippert-Rasmussen 2014).

When one speaks of religion as a *subject* of discrimination, this can similarly mean that the *agent* doing the discrimination is a religious person, group or organization, or that the discriminator performs differential treatment *on religious grounds*.

The difference between these two readings is that the former focuses on *the type of agent* perpetrating differential treatment whereas the latter focuses on *the agent's motivation* for or the *effective causes* of differential treatment – so religion can be the subject of discrimination either in the sense that the discriminator is a religious agent, or that the reasons or causes for the discriminatory act are religious reasons or causes. This is one respect in which religious discrimination arguably differs from, e.g. racial discrimination – not only because racial discrimination is often about the *object* of discrimination being a racial group, but also because we usually do not speak of racial *reasons* in the same way as we speak of religious reasons.

This means that, when we speak of discrimination and religion, religion or religiously marked persons or groups can be either victims and perpetrators, or benefactors and beneficiaries, of discrimination. And "religious discrimination" can mean (at least) these four different things:[3]

Table 17.1 The meanings of religious discrimination

	Subject of discrimination	*Object of discrimination*
Nature of agent or patient of D	Agent of D is *a religious agent* E.g. the Catholic Church discriminates against women in hiring priests	Patient of D is *a religious patient* E.g. Muslims being discriminated against in uniform requirements prohibiting headscarves
Reasons or causes for discrimination	Agent of D acts *for religious reasons or causes* E.g. a registrar refusing to marry homosexuals because of a religious belief that marriage is only between man and woman	Patient of D is differentially treated *because it is religious* E.g. Arabic-speaking men being discriminated against because of fear of Muslims

This first of all means that we have to specify which meaning of "religious discrimination" we have in mind and take care not to confuse them. The different senses of religious discrimination are likely to behave differently in normative terms and, as noted, attach naturally to different theories about the wrongness of discrimination. Therefore, one cannot say anything general about religious discrimination across these different senses.

The distinction between the nature of the patient and the reason or cause for why the patient is being discriminated against is also relevant to highlight that it is often the very act of discrimination that constitutes or constructs a certain category. Sometimes it is only if a majority starts to treat a group of people in a certain way that this latter group becomes constituted as a minority group (e.g. the construction of the group of Hindus by British imperial colonists, who were not earlier thought of as either a unified group or categorized as "religious", in the Western sense, which is inspired by the monotheistic religions). Whereas the focus on the nature of the patient presupposes that people (if the patients are people) are already sorted into, in this case, religious and non-religious, or into different religious groups, religious discrimination is also possible when this is not the case – which is what the focus on the reasons or causes of discrimination picks out. In this case, religion comes in to the picture as a classificatory act on the part of the agent, which then either motivates or properly explains the differential treatment. One might then say that there is first an act of *cognitive* discrimination, in which the agent separates people in to different religious groups, and then a subsequent act of differential *treatment* based on this classification.

"Religion" in religious discrimination

This all presupposes that we know which agents and patients are religious, on the basis of possession of which features, and which grounds for discrimination count as religious grounds. In other words, we need a definition of "religion".

This same need arises in discussions of religious freedom, or in debates about secularism or religious neutrality, which all presuppose that we are able to specify what counts as religious (e.g. Audi 2000: 35). There are a lot of well-known problems about defining religion – all definitions pick out some features which tend to be more appropriate for some religions than others, and all risk either being overly general (in which case we get cases like the church of the flying spaghetti monster and the "Jedi" religion), or too restrictive (e.g. limiting religion to the already established theistic religions) (Ahdar and Leigh 2013: 141). Whichever criterion one points to, we get discussions about whether they are unique to religion or whether they are species of more general categories, in which case we should perhaps not focus on religion at all, and cannot make sense of claims that religion is uniquely special – e.g. discussion about whether we should focus on general freedom of conscience instead of freedom of religion, or on state neutrality towards conceptions of the good in general instead of religion in particular (cf. Leiter 2013; Laborde 2017).

I will not here try to offer any definition of religion, or to add to these well-known debates about the problems and theoretical issues to which this gives rise. One reason for this is that these are precisely *general* debates about religion and not specific to religious discrimination.

Another reason is that what I take to be the best solution to this general problem is to treat religion (incidentally, just as the concept of "discrimination") as what Ronald Dworkin called an "interpretive concept", i.e. a concept which does not have an independently settled semantic meaning. Instead, the meaning of interpretive concepts depends on what is (morally, politically) at stake, i.e. what is relevant from the point of view of applicable political values. For Dworkin, the politically relevant definition of religion is therefore not a conventional (functional or substantive) one. Rather, in the sense relevant for political philosophy (and in this case for discussion of issues of religious discrimination) Dworkin claims that religion denotes beliefs or practices that are central to personal ethics, or which are deeply controversial in the political community (Dworkin 2013: 108–9; see Laborde 2016 for discussion).

Such an interpretive understanding leads naturally to Cécile Laborde's "disaggregation approach", according to which religion has to be separated in to different components depending on which aspect of religion it is that is politically problematic or in need of protection. For some purposes, the relevant aspect of religion is that it is a comprehensive view about personal ethics, in other cases the relevant aspect is that religion is socially and politically divisive, and in yet other cases the relevant aspect is that religion is inaccessible for non-believers (Laborde 2017). None of these features are unique to religion – although religion might be special insofar as it often instantiates all of these aspects at once.

The four senses of religious discrimination sketched above further complicate the general problem about the meaning of religion. The four senses of religious discrimination make clear that a generic definition of religion would in any case be inadequate, since we need to define religion with respect to at least these four questions:

1 What counts as *a religious agent*?
2 What counts as *a religious patient*?
3 What counts as *a religious reason* (for which agents can engage in differential treatment)?
4 What counts as *a religious feature* (on the basis of which agents can single out patients for differential treatment)?

There is no reason to think that answers to these four questions will invoke identical conceptions of religion, since:

1 A group can be an object of discrimination without being an agent at all (e.g. the Danish People's Church, which is constituted without anyone being able to act on behalf of the church), so what counts as a religious agent is not necessarily the same as what counts as a religious patient.
2 A religious agent can evidently act for non-religious reasons (e.g. churches engaging in real estate investments for purely economic returns), and non-religious actors can arguably act for religious reasons (e.g. when juvenile delinquents with no history of religious observance or belief suddenly rationalize acts of violence in religious terms).
3 An agent may discriminate against a group (e.g. immigrants from the Middle East) because the agent understands the group in religious terms (e.g. as being Muslims) even if some or all of the group members do not possess this feature (e.g. are non-religious).
4 A religious patient can be discriminated against, but because the discriminating agent categorizes it (ascriptively) *as religious* on the basis of other features than those on the basis of which it self-identifies as religious (e.g. if Christian immigrants from the Middle East are discriminated against on the basis of hostility to Muslims).

This complexity further adds to the requirements for disaggregation of the notion of religion. In practice this means that one should not start a discussion of religion and discrimination by trying to settle on a definition of religion, since different definitions of religion are first of all likely to be appropriate in each of the respects noted, and because the relevant definition in each case – since religion is an interpretative concept – furthermore depends on what the normative issues raised by religious discrimination are.

Religion as a justificatory category

The interesting question about religious discrimination is when (if ever) it makes a difference for the wrongness or permissibility of discriminatory acts that they are religious. The question requires an investigation of the category of religion with a view to what normative difference it might make in relation to discrimination: When does the fact that the object of differential treatment is religious make this wrongful discrimination, and when does the fact that the subject of acts of differential treatment is religious make such acts permissible? How does religion function as a justificatory category for the purpose of such questions?

Given that there are several different senses of religious discrimination, where religion can both be the subject and object of discrimination, and where "religion" can have different meanings as well, there is no reason to expect a uniform and general answer to such normative questions. Especially if religion is considered as an interpretive category in the Dworkinian sense noted above, the question is not how a predefined category of religion functions normatively, but rather how we should understand religion for the purpose of discussions of religious discrimination in light of whichever values we think are relevant in this context. This means that we have to consider what the relevant values could be in relation to issues of religious discrimination.

There are two limiting-case views which mark the opposite boundaries of such a discussion. One possible view – probably held by some believers – is that religion or, for many believers perhaps more likely, a specific religion provides justification simply because it is *true*. This would be a *religion-internal* perspective which affirms dogmatic claims central to the religion, e.g. about how believers should conduct themselves, and advances these directly as justifications for acts, e.g. for why the Catholic Church should not ordain women as priests.

While religion-internal views might provide the right account of what believers' actual motivation for discriminating on religious grounds is, they are evidently problematic for justificatory purposes. The immediate problem is that people obviously disagree about religious claims, both across religions (is Islam or Christianity the true religion?), within religions (does Christianity actually allow for same-sex marriages?) and between believers and non-believers (are any religious claims actually true?). This means that religion-internal justifications will only be convincing and acceptable within religious groups that happen to agree on the truth of the dogmatic claims appealed to. Because cases of discrimination usually only arise when people disagree on exactly such questions, religion-internal justifications are simply unhelpful and unworkable for present purposes.

In addition to this practical problem, there are many other problems with religion-internal justifications. One is that religious justifications might be considered not only *practically* problematic but *in principle* inadmissible and illegitimate for the purpose of political argument. This is the view held by political liberals, public reason theorists and the like (Audi 2000; Rawls 1993). But there is also a different problem, which has to do with the fact that many religious acts are not based on dogmatic truth claims – much of what goes on under the heading of religion is not directly or mainly a matter of doing what believers think God requires of them, but rather a matter of taking part in a religious community, affirming a religious identity or continuing a religious tradition. So many religious acts are not justified, even in a religion-internal perspective, with direct appeal to religious truth claims. It would therefore be reductionist and artificially confining to limit possible justifications for religious acts to those that appeal to religious truth claims.

These and other problems mean that the justifications relating to religious discrimination cannot and should not appeal to the content of religion, but should rather focus on more general features of religious acts and practices.

When considering religion as a justificatory category, the opposite limiting-case view is that – despite common perceptions and actual formulations of positive law – religion is in fact *not* a justificatory category at all. Even if discrimination against religion is often wrong, and even if religious agents might sometimes be permitted to discriminate in ways that would otherwise be wrong, one might think that this can all be accounted for without reference to religion as a justificatory category. This is to say that what is doing the normative work in justifications for why religious discrimination is wrong or permitted is always something other than religion. The wrongness of discrimination against religion can always be explained with reference to something other than the fact that the object of discrimination is religious, e.g. that some act is required by a person's conscience, and that the permissibility of some forms of discrimination carried out by religious actors or on religious grounds can equally be explained without ultimate reference to the fact that the subject of discrimination is religious, e.g. that some group is a voluntary association. This would be a *deflationary* perspective on religion as a justificatory category (Nickel 2005).

One form of deflationary views is purely *justificatory*. Such views agree with normative claims that discrimination against religion is sometimes wrong and that discrimination by religion is sometimes permitted, but merely claims that the justification for why this is the case does not need to involve a reference to religion as a distinct justificatory category. Other forms of deflationary views are *normative*, in the sense that they reject claims that discrimination against religion is wrong or that discrimination by religion is permitted. In that case there is no need for religion as a justificatory category at all.

The question is whether something can be said about religion as a justificatory category, which on the one hand avoids the religion-internal perspective by abstracting from the actual content of religion, while at the same time still keeping the essential reference to religion as a justificatory category that might do some work in relation to claims about wrongness or permissibility of religious discrimination.

It is in this space between the two limiting-case views that different candidates for how we should understand religion interpretively can be considered. Let me briefly consider some of the central candidates for justifying answers to these questions (see also Ahdar and Leigh 2013: 69–83).

Justifications can be sorted into A) appeals to the consequences of discrimination and B) deontological justifications that appeal to features about the acts of discrimination in isolation from possible consequences. Given that the main questions concern C) whether discrimination against religion is wrong and D) whether discrimination by religious agents can be permissible, we get these main categories:

Table 17.2 Categories of religious discrimination

	A. Consequentialist justifications	*B. Deontological justifications*
C. Religion object of discrimination	1. Discrimination against religion wrong due to bad effects	3. Discrimination against religion is wrong in itself
D. Religion subject of discrimination	2. Discrimination by religious agents permissible due to good effects	4. Religious agents have a right to discriminate

The first set of justifications concern the bad effects of discrimination against religious patients. This is an instance of harm-based accounts of the wrongness of discrimination (Lippert-Rasmussen 2014, ch. 6), so the question is which reasons are there to think that discrimination *against religion* is especially harmful?

One reason is that religion is in many cases a socially salient division between people, which has either already been the basis for discrimination or which is, for other reasons, especially sensitive. Discrimination against religious persons or groups is therefore wrong because it will have especially bad effects. The worst kind of bad effect traditionally cited is the danger of *civil unrest* which could be harmful for all of society – sectarian civil war being the most radical version of this. Such claims need to be spelled out both in terms of what the causal mechanism linking discrimination and civil unrest is supposed to be, and in terms of the likelihood of the bad effects actually occurring. If the likelihood is low, then the justification might not be very convincing. If one adds considerations of responsibility to the consequentialist perspective, these types of justifications might also be problematic if the bad effects are mediated by acts which are themselves wrong, e.g. if it is not the acts of discrimination that directly cause the bad effects, but these only arise because some of those discriminated against respond in violent ways.

Another set of bad effects relates, not to society as a whole, but to the people discriminated against. One prominent concern here is that religious discrimination will lead to *alienation* of religious citizens, which is both assumed to be a bad thing in itself and to have further bad effects, e.g. in terms of reduced political participation (Ahdar and Leigh 2013: 71). Such arguments require a specification of what alienation is, and explanations for why religious discrimination is likely to have these bad effects (Lægaard 2017).

Consequentialist arguments for the wrongness of discrimination against religion hinge on bad effects actually obtaining. It is an empirical question whether discrimination against religion is actually wrong for these kinds of reasons. What is really doing the normative work in justifications like these is the badness of the noted effects, rather than the fact that the effects are linked to discrimination *of religion*. So religion only functions as a justificatory category here insofar as the causal links actually obtain between religious discrimination and the bad effects, which is an empirical matter.

The same goes for the second set of consequentialist arguments for why religious agents should sometimes be permitted to discriminate in ways that would otherwise be wrong, e.g. why churches need not comply with rules against gender discrimination. But in this case the kinds of consequences are different: the claim here must rather be that good consequences are likely to obtain if religious agents are allowed to discriminate in specific ways. Such arguments claim that there are good effects of allowing religious groups to organize themselves according to their religious beliefs, and that discrimination on religious grounds is sometimes necessary for obtaining these good effects.

Again, the good effects in question can both be for society as a whole and for the specific group in question. An example of the former is the classical claim that churches *strengthen civil society* and function as "schools of democracy" and civil engagement. In order for this to justify a right to discriminate, it has to be the case, furthermore, that these beneficial effects could not be obtained without churches having permission to discriminate. Both claims can of course turn out to be false: in some cases religious communities can be anti-social, and even when religious community life has beneficial effects, it is not always clear that these valuable effects could not be obtained without a right to discriminate.

Consequentialist justifications for permissions to discriminate can alternatively appeal to good effects for the members of the religious group rather than for society as a whole. This is on the one hand more promising, since it seems likely that members believing in a need for discrimination, e.g. in the hiring of ministers, will benefit if allowed to act according to this belief. At the least they will avoid the frustration attendant on being prohibited from acting according to their beliefs, and their religious community life will possibly also function more smoothly and contribute more to the members' sense of meaning and purpose. On the other hand, this is a more problematic justification insofar as the good for the members comes at the price of disadvantageous treatment of someone else, e.g. rejected applicants for ministerial positions. In a consequentialist justification the good and bad effects of a permission to discriminate will have to be weighed against each other, so in some cases good effects for members might not be sufficient to justify such a right.

Given the contingent and hence uncertain nature of consequentialist justifications, it is unsurprising that many justifications relating to religious discrimination are rather deontological. The first set of arguments aim at showing that discrimination against religious patients is wrong, not because of bad effects, but in itself. The most important argument in this category is a direct appeal to *civic equality* (e.g. Nussbaum 2012: 65). The claim is that discrimination against religious groups is simply wrong because it amounts to a differentiation into first- and second-class citizens, and an expression of lack of equal recognition (cf. Chapter 16). A state that allows discrimination against, e.g. Jews on the labor market, or which itself treats Christians better than others blatantly fails to respect the equal status of all citizens, a status which is a pretty uncontroversial component of a just society. This is a strong argument for the wrongness of discrimination against religion. The problem is that the argument is not at all specific to religion. It is the value of civic equality that is doing all of the normative work of explaining the wrongness of discrimination against religion, so on this account religion does not function as a justificatory category.

The fourth set of deontological justifications for why religious actors might have a right to discriminate on religious grounds appeals to the inherent value of acting according to religious beliefs (cf. Chapter 10). In order for such justifications not to be religion-internal in the problematic sense noted above, they cannot appeal to claims that something is actually a religious duty. The most promising accounts trying to justify such claims appeal to the general value of acting according to one's *conscience* or to live with *integrity*, i.e. to be able to live according to what one takes one's – in this case religious – duties to be (Leiter 2013; Maclure and Taylor 2011). Such justifications are quite strong, insofar as many people think it actually is important for a good life for people to be able to live according to their convictions. But they are problematic for the purpose of grounding a right to discriminate in the employment of ministers, since the discriminating agent here is not an individual with a conscience but an institutional actor. The right of churches to discriminate is therefore often instead justified with reference to a corporate right of "church autonomy" (Ahdar and Leigh 2013, ch. 11). The problem with church autonomy is that it cannot directly be derived from the more immediately plausible claims about the importance of individual conscience and integrity and that it involves controversial jurisdictional claims (Lægaard 2015).

Conclusion

Despite common discussion of religious discrimination, this term can mean very different things. I have sketched importantly different ways of understanding religious discrimination and the different philosophical issues these give rise to. The category of religion itself can furthermore have different meanings, and there are different ways of understanding what role it plays in relation to making religious discrimination wrong or permissible, when it is wrong or permissible.[4]

Notes

1 http://eur-lex.europa.eu/legal-content/en/TXT/?uri=CELEX:32000L0078
2 *Noah v. Desrosiers* [2008], (unreported) judgment of the Employment Tribunal, case number 2201867/2007, quoted and discussed in Jones (2015).
3 These categories are reminiscent of different senses of neutrality. This is interesting since issues of religion have often been discussed from the point of view of neutrality. Alan Patten's recent account of neutrality distinguishes between 1) "neutrality of intentions", which is reminiscent of my category focusing on agent's reasons for action, 2) "neutrality of effects", which is reminiscent of my category focusing on the outcome for the patient, and 3) "neutrality of treatment" (Patten 2014, ch. 4). An act is a form of neutral treatment in Patten's sense if it is not more accommodating of one conception of the good than another. This is distinct from neutrality of effect, because people are held responsible for their preferences as long as there are fair background conditions. So neutral treatment not only consists in absence of discrimination, but also in holding people responsible for their conceptions of the good, which might make a difference in relation to discussions of religion.
4 An early draft of this chapter was presented at the *Association for Social and Political Philosophy Annual Conference* at the London School of Economics, 29 June 2016. Thanks for comments from Monica Mookherjee, Jonathan Seglow, Kasper Lippert-Rasmussen and an anonymous reviewer.

Bibliography

Ahdar, R. and Leigh, I. 2013. *Religious Freedom in the Liberal State*, 2nd edition. Oxford: Oxford University Press.

Audi, R. 2000. *Religious Commitment and Secular Reason.* Cambridge: Cambridge University Press.

Dworkin, R. 2013. *Religion without God.* Cambridge, MA: Harvard University Press.

Hellman, D. 2008. *When is Discrimination Wrong?* Cambridge, MA: Harvard University Press.

Jones, P. 2015. "Toleration, Religion, and Accommodation." *European Journal of Philosophy.* 23(3): 542–563.

Joppke, C. 2016. "Pluralism vs. Pluralism: Islam and Christianity in the European Court of Human Rights." In Cohen, J.L. and Laborde, C. (eds) *Religion, Secularism, and Constitutional Democracy.* New York: Columbia University Press.

Laborde, C. 2016. "Liberal Neutrality, Religion, and the Good." In Cohen, J.L. and Laborde, C. (eds) *Religion, Secularism, and Constitutional Democracy.* New York: Columbia University Press.

Laborde, C. 2017. *Liberalism's Religion.* Cambridge, MA: Harvard University Press.

Lægaard, S. 2015. "Disaggregating Corporate Freedom of Religion." *Netherlands Journal of Legal Philosophy.* 44(3): 221–230.

Lægaard, S. 2017. "What's the Problem with Symbolic Religious Establishment? The Alienation and Symbolic Equality Accounts." In Bardon, A. and Laborde, C. (eds) *Religion in Liberal Political Philosophy.* Oxford: Oxford University Press.

Leiter, B. 2013. *Why Tolerate Religion?* Princeton: Princeton University Press.

Lippert-Rasmussen, K. 2014. *Born Free and Equal? A Philosophical Inquiry into the Nature of Discrimination.* Oxford: Oxford University Press.

Maclure, J. and Taylor, C. 2011. *Secularism and Freedom of Conscience.* Cambridge, MA: Harvard University Press.

Moyn, S. 2016. "Religious Freedom and the Fate of Secularism." In Cohen, J.L. and Laborde, C. (eds) *Religion, Secularism, and Constitutional Democracy.* New York: Columbia University Press.

Nickel, J. 2005. "Who Needs Freedom of Religion?" *University of Colorado Law Review.* 76: 941–964.

Nussbaum, M.C. 2012. *The New Religious Intolerance: Overcoming the Politics of Fear in an Anxious Age.* Cambridge, MA: Harvard University Press.

Patten, A. 2014. *Equal Recognition.* Princeton: Princeton University Press.

Rawls, J. 1993. *Political Liberalism.* New York: Columbia University Press.

18

DISCRIMINATION AND SEXUAL ORIENTATION

Edward Stein

CARDOZO SCHOOL OF LAW

Introduction[1]

For many years, in many countries, sexual activity between people of the same sex has been stigmatized, criminalized, and punishable by death. People who engage in such sexual activity, who identify as desiring to engage in it, or who are perceived as desiring it have been subject to discrimination. Although attitudes have changed in many countries, negative attitudes towards same-sex sexual activity and desire continue. This chapter considers ethical and jurisprudential issues concerning discrimination against people in virtue of their sexual orientations.[2] It begins by discussing the nature of sexual orientations. It then turns to two accounts meant to justify discrimination on the basis of sexual orientation—that same-sex sexual orientations are unnatural, and that they are non-procreative—and two accounts meant to show that sexual-orientation discrimination is wrong—that sexual orientations are innate and/ or immutable and that sexual-orientation discrimination is a form of sex discrimination. It concludes with a sketch of a better account of why sexual-orientation discrimination is wrong.

The nature of sexual orientations

Sexual orientations are clearly embodied. Humans can have sexual orientations but fruit flies—contrary to Burr (1996: 29–35)—cannot. This is because having a sexual orientation requires beliefs and desires, which in turn require a robust cognitive-psychological system. Sexual orientations are thus embodied in our brains, but the nature of this embodiment is not clear. Some clarification comes from looking at the distinctions between inborn traits and environmental traits, on the one hand, and between immutable traits and changeable traits, on the other.

The question whether sexual orientations are genetic or the result of environmental factors is based on a false dichotomy: no human trait is strictly the result of genetics or strictly the result of environmental factors; all human traits are the result of both. There are genetic factors that affect even the most seemingly environmental traits, like what a person's major will be in college. On the other hand, environmental factors contribute to the development of even the most seemingly genetic traits, like eye color—if I had not gotten enough of certain sorts of vitamins and minerals at crucial times, even though my genetic code would be the same, my eyes might have looked different. There is a range of the extent to which genes constrain a trait—one's blood type is more tightly constrained by genetic factors than is one's college major. Properly understood, the question of whether sexual orientations are innate concerns where they fit on the continuum between blood type and college major.

Turning to immutability, the evidence is strong that people's conscious choices do not play a significant role in the development of sexual orientations (Shidlo et al. 2002; American Philosophical Association 2009). The evidence is almost as strong that for most adults it is very difficult, if not impossible, to change sexual orientations, although "reparative therapists" think otherwise. Conceptually, sexual orientations do not need to be innate in order to be immutable: something can be shaped by early childhood experience and, thereafter, not changeable. Also, even if sexual orientations are innate, choices can play a significant role in the development of sexual orientations. Even if a person is gay, lesbian or bisexual (LGB) in virtue of genetic or other strongly biological factors, one still has to *choose* to be open about same-sex desire, to show affection towards people of the same sex, and/or to have sex with and to build families with people of the same sex.

Same-sex sexual orientations are unnatural

I turn now to arguments to justify discrimination on the basis of sexual orientation. In *The Laws*, Plato (1934: 840d-e) says that people should not "behave worse than birds and many other creatures" who "live in continence and unspotted virginity" until "the age of procreation" whereupon "they pair together, the male with the female ... and they live thereafter in piety and justice, steadfastly true to their contract of first love." According to Plato, humans ought to follow the example of birds and avoid same-sex sexual activity, because such behavior is *unnatural*. This argument is not exclusive to Plato. At the opposite end of the intellectual spectrum, Anita Bryant, former Mouseketteer and opponent of LGB rights, made roughly this argument in a 1970s interview with *Playboy* magazine: "Homosexuality is a perversion of a very natural thing ... it is a sin and very unnatural ... [and] even barnyard animals don't do what homosexuals do" (Kelley 1978: 82). This is an empirical argument to justify discrimination on the basis of sexual orientation: such discrimination is warranted because same-sex sexual orientations are unnatural.

This argument can be turned on its head by showing that animals of many species engage in same-sex sexual activity (Bagemihl 1999). Does this, following the logical structure of Plato's argument, show that same-sex sexual activity is natural and not immoral? This empirical argument did not persuade Anita Bryant when her *Playboy* interlocutor informed her that many non-human species do engage in same-sex sexual activities. She responded—without apparently realizing she was rejecting an argument isomorphic to one she herself had just made—that the existence of same-sex sexual activities in animals "doesn't make it right" (Kelley 1978: 82).

Stories of animal sexual activity, although perhaps interesting in their own right, have little to tell us about what sexual activity is moral for humans. Animals engage in many behaviors that are morally wrong for humans to engage in, and there are many behaviors that animals do not engage in that are central to human existence. Some non-human animals eat members of their own species and many non-human species kill other animals in especially gruesome ways. Non-humans animals do many things that seem unnatural or morally problematic when done by humans. On the other hand, non-human animals do not communicate in complex languages, and yet it is natural for humans to do so. Non-human animals do not prevent diseases that affect them through the use of vaccines, and yet it doesn't seem unnatural for humans to use vaccines.

Research on the sexual desires and behaviors of animals may be relevant to understanding some aspects of human sexual orientations, but such research is not relevant to legal and ethical issues concerning human sexual orientations and behaviors.

Others scholars have claimed that same-sex sexual desires and same-sex sexual acts are unnatural without referencing other species (Levin 1984; Finnis 1995; George 2006), while others have refuted such claims (Murphy 1987; Macedo 1995; Perry 1995; Koppelman 2002: 79–93). One significant problem with such arguments is that the word "natural" gets used in various and contradictory ways, and which acts and desires are seen as unnatural change over time and in various cultures. Consider for a moment what you think makes a trait, a behavior, or a desire (sexual or not) unnatural? In general, it is not clear whether the claim that a (sexual) behavior is unnatural amounts to anything more than that certain people think the behavior is unappealing. When people say same-sex sexual activities and desires are unnatural, it is unclear what they mean.

That said, there are several general problems with arguments that try to show that homosexuality is unnatural (Mohr 1990: 21–45; Murphy 1997: 165–192; Ruse 1988: 176–202). One problem is that such arguments prove too much, that is, such arguments, if successful, entail that a whole range of behaviors—for example, celibacy, masturbation, contraception, vaccines against diseases, and even air travel and skiing—are unnatural when, in fact, most are natural in any morally relevant sense. This suggests one of two responses to the "unnaturalness" argument justifying sexual-orientation discrimination: reject the claim that same-sex sexual orientations are unnatural, or reject the claim that their unnaturalness—like the unnaturalness of celibacy, vaccines, and air travel—is relevant to the moral assessment of same-sex orientations. Taking the second response, even if there is a sense in which sexual desires for, and sexual activities with, people of the same sex are unnatural, it is not clear what ethical conclusions follow from this; it is not at all clear why unnaturalness entails immorality. Air travel for humans might be "unnatural" in some sense of the term, but it does not follow from air travel being unnatural in *that* sense that air travel is immoral or unethical.

More generally, empirical facts alone cannot entail moral and ethical conclusions. Arguments of this form commit the *naturalistic fallacy* (Moore 1903), that is, the mistake of trying to derive an "ought" claim (that is, a claim about how humans ought to act) from an "is" claim (a claim about how things are). Just because, for example, humans have teeth that resulted from evolution and that are capable of ripping flesh does not entail that we *should* use our teeth to rip flesh. Moral arguments for vegetarianism might entail that we should not eat meat despite empirical facts about our teeth and their evolutionary function. Similarly, ethical questions concerning sexual orientations will not be settled solely by appeal to empirical facts about the naturalness of certain sexual orientations.

Same-sex sexual orientations are non-procreative

Another argument for justifying sexual-orientation discrimination focuses on the extent to which same-sex sexual activities are linked to *procreation*: sexual activities desired by people of some sexual orientations—but not others—are, on this account, morally wrong because they do not lead to procreation.[3] This argument has been made in the United States legal context in relation to whether people of the same sex should be allowed to marry, but the argument can be made about sexual-orientation discrimination generally as well. The idea is that sexual-orientation discrimination is justified because sexual activity—and the desire for it—is morally permissible only when such activity leads to procreation.

In the 1970s in the United States, in response to an early litigation attempt to allow marriage between two people of the same sex, an appellate court in Washington state offered the following justification for allowing only couples consisting of a man and a woman to get married:

> [T]he state's refusal to grant a license allowing [two men] to marry one another is... based upon the state's recognition that our society... views marriage as the appropriate and desirable forum for procreation... This is true even though married couples are not required to become parents and even though some couples are incapable of becoming parents and even though not all couples who produce children are married. These, however, are exceptional situations.... Further,... no same-sex couple offers the possibility of the birth of children by their union.
>
> *(Singer v. Hara 1974: 1195)*

This argument from procreation can be made into a more general argument for sexual-orientation discrimination by distinguishing between sexual orientations that involve desire for sex that can be procreative and those that do not. Those that make this argument realize that some heterosexuals cannot or will not procreate, but they deny this is a serious threat to the procreation argument to justify sexual-orientation discrimination. They focus on the fact that procreation can result from sexual activity between a man and a woman, while no such possibility exists from sexual activity between two people of the same sex (Bennett 2001: 133–134).

A strong rejection of this argument came from the Supreme Judicial Court of Massachusetts in 2003. Massachusetts's Attorney General, in defending the state's ban on same-sex marriage, argued that the purpose of marriage is to provide a favorable setting for procreation. The Massachusetts court responded:

> Our laws of civil marriage do not privilege procreative heterosexual intercourse between married people above every other form of adult intimacy and every other means of creating a family. [They] contain... no requirement that the applicants for a marriage license attest to their ability or intention to conceive children by coitus. Fertility is not a condition of marriage... People who have never consummated their marriage, and never plan to, may be and stay married. People who cannot stir from their deathbed may marry. While it is certainly true that many, perhaps most, married couples have children together (assisted or unassisted), it is the exclusive and permanent commitment of the marriage partners to one another, not the begetting of children, that is the sine qua non of civil marriage. Moreover, the Commonwealth affirmatively facilitates bringing children into a family regardless of whether the intended parent is married or unmarried, whether the child is adopted or born into a family, whether assistive technology was used to conceive the child, and whether the parent or her partner is heterosexual, homosexual, or bisexual. If procreation were a necessary component of civil marriage, our statutes would draw a tighter circle around the permissible bounds of nonmarital child bearing and the creation of families by noncoital means. The attempt to isolate procreation as "the source of a fundamental right to marry" overlooks the integrated way in which courts have examined the complex and overlapping realms of personal autonomy, marriage, family life, and child rearing.
>
> *(Goodridge v. Department of Public Health 2003: 961–962)*

Some commentators have responded to the comparison between LGB people, on the one hand, and infertile heterosexual couples, on the other, by pointing to what they see as the crucial difference between infertile heterosexual couples and same-sex couples. They say that even though procreation is not possible for the sexual behaviors in which either type of couple typically engages, infertile heterosexuals, but not LGB people, can engage in "reproductive-type" acts. Infertile heterosexuals—but not LGB people—participate in what John Finnis calls "the marital form of life":

> because they can make every commitment and can form and carry out every intention that any other married [male–female] couple need make, form, and carry out in order to be validly married and to fulfill all their marital responsibilities. By their model of fidelity within a relationship involving *acts of the reproductive kind* (and no other sex acts), these infertile marriages are, moreover, strongly supportive of marriage as a valuable social institution.
>
> *(Finnis 1997: 128 [emphasis added])*

On this view, the crucial difference between infertile heterosexual couples and same-sex couples that explains why the former, but not the latter, should be able to marry is that some of the sex acts in which infertile heterosexual couples engage are of the "reproductive sort" even though, since they are infertile, their sex acts are not reproductive.

A married *same-sex* couple, however, has the same potential to "participate in the marital form of life" as does the infertile different-sex couple *except* with respect to engaging in "penis-in-vagina" sex. "Potential" procreative capacity aside, what is special about penis-in-vagina sex as compared to " penis-in-anus," "penis-in-mouth," or "tongue-in-vagina" sex? Finnis's focus on "penis-in-vagina" sex seems arbitrary when the procreative capacity of this sex act is not at issue, as it is not when focusing on *infertile* heterosexual couples. Further, some infertile heterosexual couples who cannot even engage in penis-in-vagina sex are still allowed to marry. Such couples include those involving men who have been castrated or women who suffer from vaginismus, a condition involving the involuntary tightening of the vagina during sexual intercourse or attempts at it. In *T. v. M.* (1968), an annulment was granted to a husband whose wife suffered from vaginismus despite there being nothing preventing him from staying married to his wife and seeking sexual pleasure through other marital sex acts or simply not having sex with her. The point is that women with vaginismus—like men without penises—can still legally marry, even though penis-in-vagina sex is difficult, painful, or impossible for them. This attempt to justify sexual-orientation discrimination because same-sex sexual activity lacks procreative potential fails because it also justifies discrimination against infertile people (and couples), which is—to say the least—a quite counterintuitive result.

Sexual orientations are innate or immutable

Having considered two arguments justifying sexual-orientation discrimination, I now turn to two arguments *against* such discrimination. I begin with the *etiological argument* against sexual-orientation discrimination. This argument draws support from theories of how sexual orientations develop, in particular, that sexual orientations are innate, that sexual orientations are immutable, and/or that sexual orientations are not chosen. Although I have strong views about these accounts of sexual orientations (Stein 1999, 119–257), I here set aside my concerns about the veracity of these empirical claims. Granting these claims, the etiological argument against sexual-orientation discrimination faces a serious problem: even if sexual orientations are innate, immutable, and are not changeable, much of what is ethically relevant about being an LGB person is *neither* innate *nor* immutable. Actually *engaging* in sexual acts with a person of the same sex, publicly or privately *identifying* as an LGB person, deciding to *establish* a household with a person of the same sex, and raising children as an openly LGB person are *choices*, choices one might not make. On any reasonable view of human nature, these decisions go beyond innate and immutable characteristics. Even assuming that sexual orientations are inborn and/or immutable, LGB people need protection against discrimination for their *actions* and *decisions* rather than simply for their orientations, especially when they engage in same-sex sexual acts, openly identify as LGB people, or are in spousal, spouse-like or co-parenting relationships with people of the same sex. The etiological argument is unable to deliver these basic and important legal and ethical needs.

Martha Nussbaum has offered a defense of etiological arguments for LGB rights:

> [W]e need only supply one further premise [to save the etiological argument]:... people should not be doomed to a life of sexual misery and frustration.... [M]ost Americans think of sexual fulfillment as one of the greatest goods of life, and are inclined to think that it is unreasonable to demand that people utterly forgo sexual fulfillment. If they can be persuaded that sexual orientations lie very deep in the personality, then they think that same-sex conduct is not at all like adultery or gambling or nude dancing[,]...conduct [that] could, they think, be omitted without crippling the personality.... [But] asking people not to engage in same-sex conduct is a cruel and unreasonable demand.... [because doing so] den[ies] people a form of sexual fulfillment that cannot be substituted for because of deep factors about the organization of their personalities...
>
> *(Nussbaum 2002: 332)*

I unfortunately disagree with Nussbaum's optimistic assessment of most Americans' attitudes about sex (and even if she is right about their attitudes, her defense would not work in other contexts where attitudes are different). Many people think some sexual behaviors involving consensual sex are immoral and that people should be discouraged from acting on desires to engage in these behaviors. Such people accept that some people should forgo sexual fulfillment that comes through activities that are unappealing or shameful. For example, there are some people who get sexual fulfillment through adultery, masturbation, "sadomasochistic" sex, or group sex. Many Americans (and many others) still find these sexual practices immoral and the people who engage in them deserving of discriminatory treatment. Regardless of how widely accepted it is, I agree that Nussbaum's "further premise"—people should not be forced to forgo a life of sexual fulfillment (if the activities in question are consensual)—is plausible, but it is unrelated to the innateness or immutability of the desire to engage in the sexual activities in question. The core of Nussbaum's revision to etiological arguments, then, is not really about etiology. Empirical evidence about how sexual orientations develop is not relevant to the morality of sexual-orientation discrimination.

There are other problems for etiological arguments. The etiological argument is impotent when sexual orientations are neither innate nor immutable. Some scientists claim that women's sexual orientations are more fluid than men's (Diamond 2008). If some women's sexual orientations are neither innate nor immutable, then the etiological argument against sexual-orientation discrimination fails with respect to such women. A similar problem exists related to bisexuals, who, simplifying matters somewhat, are sexually attracted to both men and women and can be sexually and emotionally fulfilled by relationships with either. Even if being bisexual is innate, immutable, and not a choice, a bisexual could choose to have sex with and build a relationship with someone of a different sex. The etiological argument is thus problematic applied to bisexuals. Something is seriously wrong with a purported argument against sexual-orientation discrimination that does not reach lesbians and bisexuals.

In sum, the etiological argument against sexual-orientation discrimination faces serious ethical problems. Neither this nor my previous discussion of the naturalistic fallacy entails that empirical considerations are never relevant to ethical and political issues. Science has some bearing on certain legal, ethical, political and philosophical questions. For example, if you have the view that it is wrong to cause wanton pain and suffering to animals that can feel pain and be conscious of it, then the empirical discovery that pigs are conscious of their pain would be relevant to the morality of the "factory farming" of pigs. Empirical facts do not, however, establish that it is wrong to cause unnecessary pain and suffering. Similarly, scientific facts about sexual orientation might be relevant to convincing people that there is no risk that an openly LGB school teacher could make her students LGB. Scientific facts about sexual orientation are not, however, able to establish the general wrongness of sexual-orientation discrimination.

Sexual-orientation discrimination is sex discrimination

I turn now to the *sex-discrimination argument* against sexual-orientation discrimination, which sees laws that discriminate on the basis of sexual orientation as necessarily discriminating on the basis of sex (cf. Chapter 15). Sexual orientation concerns the sex of people to whom one is sexually attracted; to determine a person's sexual orientation, we need to know the person's sex and the sex of the people to whom he or she is primarily sexually attracted. In virtue of what a sexual orientation is, any law that discriminates on the basis of sexual orientation seems to necessarily discriminate on the basis of sex. To see the sex-discrimination argument in action, consider a legal regime that allows sexual-orientation discrimination. Under this regime, a woman may be fired because she has sex with women, is married to a woman, or is sexually attracted to women, but a man who has sex with women, who is married to a woman, or who is sexually attracted to women will not be fired. In this regime, women can be fired for doing the precise thing that men can do without fear of being fired. As this treats similarly situated people differently because of sex, this constitutes sex discrimination.

The sex-discrimination argument, as stated, faces a straightforward response: simply deny that sexual-orientation discrimination in fact constitutes discrimination because of sex. A European Court of Justice (ECJ) decision did this in rejecting the sex-discrimination argument about sexual-orientation discrimination (*Grant v. Southwest Trains* 1998). Lisa Grant took a job working for Southwest Trains, Ltd. (SWT), replacing a man who had received a travel pass for his non-marital female partner as a benefit of his employment. Grant applied to SWT for the same travel pass for her non-marital female partner. SWT refused to provide Grant's partner with a travel pass because Grant and her partner were of the same sex. Grant sued, arguing that SWT violated Article 119 of the treaty establishing the European Community, that says "men and women should receive equal pay for equal work." In particular, Grant argued that SWT failed to give her equal pay by denying her the benefits it gave to the man who had held the same job that she held. SWT responded saying (1) the treaty does not prohibit discrimination on the basis of sexual orientation and (2) it was not discriminating on the basis of sex because its policy was *sex-neutral*—neither men nor women were eligible for travel benefits for a same-sex partner. The case eventually reached the ECJ which held that SWT's policy did not constitute sex discrimination because it applied the same to both men and women—both receive the same benefits for their partners under precisely the same circumstances, namely, only if they have a different-sex partner. This effectively denies that sexual-orientation discrimination constitutes sex discrimination.

The first problem facing the sex-discrimination argument is that statutes that use sex classifications to discriminate on the basis of sexual orientation can be seen as treating men and women equally. Advocates of the sex-discrimination argument can reply to this objection by noting that the mere equal application of a law with respect to two different classes does not entail that the law does not discriminate on the basis of a classification that includes these classes. In *Loving v. Virginia*, the United States Supreme Court considered a Virginia law prohibiting interracial marriage. Virginia defended this law by claiming it treated individuals equally regardless of their race: both whites and non-whites were prohibited from marrying outside of their race.[4] The Supreme Court rejected this reasoning, holding that, even if the law prohibiting interracial marriage applied equally to whites and non-whites, it was unconstitutional because it made use of racial classifications that lack an exceedingly compelling justification (*Loving v. Virginia* 1967: 11). In reaching this conclusion, the Court "reject[ed] the notion that the mere equal application of a statute containing racial classifications is enough to remove the classifications from the Fourteenth Amendment's proscription of all invidious racial discriminations" (*Loving v. Virginia* 1967: 8). Even granting the Virginia marriage law applied equally to all races, the Court found that, because the law makes use of racial classifications, the state must provide an exceedingly strong justification for the law.

Comparing the sex-discrimination argument to the Court's argument in *Loving*, a potential disanalogy appears. In *Loving*, there is a fit between the class disadvantaged by the law and the suspect classification the law employs. The class disadvantaged by the law at issue in *Loving* is "miscegenosexuals:" people, regardless of race, who want to marry outside of their race (Marcosson 1992: 6). The Virginia anti-miscegenation law employed racial classifications and disadvantaged blacks and other non-whites. In contrast, laws that discriminate on the basis of sexual orientation, as characterized by the sex-discrimination argument, seem to lack this fit: such laws make use of sex classifications, but they disadvantage LGB people.

Advocates of the sex-discrimination argument have addressed this potential disanalogy, arguing that to understand the discrimination involved in laws that discriminate on the basis of sexual orientation, we must look to the conceptual underpinnings of discriminatory laws. The thought is that doing so will reveal that the underlying justification for sexual-orientation discrimination is sexism and the associated idea that men and women should play different roles in our society. Andrew Koppelman, in his articulation of the sex-discrimination argument, offered multi-disciplinary evidence on the role of sexism in laws that discriminate on the basis of sexual orientation.

> Much of the connection between sexism and [homophobia] lies in social meanings… accessible to everyone.… [O]rdinary experience [shows] that the stigmatization of the homosexual has something to do with the homosexual's supposed deviation from traditional sex roles.… Most Americans learn no later than high school that one of the nastier sanctions that one will suffer if one deviates from the behavior traditionally deemed appropriate for one's sex is the imputation of homosexuality.… [T]he homosexuality taboo enforces traditional sex roles.
>
> *(Koppelman 1994: 234–235)*

He concluded that sexual-orientation discrimination is "the product of … sexism.… [and] implicitly stigmatize[s] women, and … reinforce[s] the hierarchy of men over women" (Koppelman 1994: 256–257).

This sophisticated version of the sex-discrimination argument distinguishes between three features of a law: the group whose behavior the law regulates, the class the law disadvantages, and the belief system that justifies it. Anti-miscegenation laws regulated (heterosexual) miscegenosexuals by preventing them from marrying the people they wanted to, they disadvantaged people of color and miscegenosexuals, and they were justified by racism. Such laws disadvantaged people of color even though they applied equally to whites and non-whites because they enforced the separation of the races and furthered the idea of white supremacy. According to the sex-discrimination argument, sexual-orientation discrimination regulates LGB people, disadvantages women and LGB people, and is justified by sexism. Such laws disadvantage women because, even though they apply equally to men and women, they perpetuate the notion that men and women should play different social roles and thereby reinforce gender stereotypes; for this reason, such laws discriminate on the basis of sex. This stronger form of the sex-discrimination argument sees sexual-orientation discrimination as justified and maintained by sexism. To put the point somewhat differently, this form of the sex-discrimination argument, besides making a formal claim about the connection between sex and sexual orientation, also makes a sociological and a theoretical claim. The sociological claim is that laws which discriminate on the basis of sexual orientation disadvantage women as well as LGB people, because these laws perpetuate a social system in which women play different social roles than men. The theoretical claim is that these laws are justified by sexism.

There is an objection to the stronger version of the sex-discrimination argument: the sociological and the theoretical claims are mistaken because sex and sexual orientation are culturally and conceptually distinct. Various scholars have argued for the need to analyze sexual orientation and sex separately. Cheshire Calhoun, in her article *Separating Lesbian Theory from Feminist Theory*, says that:

> Patriarchy and heterosexual dominance are two, in principle, separable systems. Even when they work together, it is possible conceptually to pull the patriarchal aspect of male–female relationships apart from their heterosexual dimensions.... Even if empirically and historically heterosexual dominance and patriarchy are completely intertwined, it does not follow from this fact that the collapse [or weakening] of patriarchy will bring about the collapse [or weakening] of heterosexual dominance.
>
> *(Calhoun 1994: 562)*

While an advocate of the sex-discrimination argument might admit that sexual-orientation discrimination and homophobia could continue to exist even if there were sex equality and no sexism (Koppelman 1994: 249), following Calhoun, I maintain that there are actual and significant differences between sexism and homophobia in contemporary American and other "Western" societies. Simply put, sexism and homophobia are coming apart. Consider, for example, that it has become unacceptable in most circles to say that women are inferior to men, but it remains acceptable in many contexts to say that someone (or something) is "queer" or "gay" as a way of suggesting weirdness or defectiveness (cf. Chapter 24). This illustrates how homophobia, even as it has gradually become disentangled from sexism, remains entrenched. While many laws that discriminate on the basis of sexual orientation do have origins in sexism, these laws are *maintained* because of homophobia, and despite the repeal of many sexist laws.

That homophobia and sexism have come apart presents a serious problem for the sex-discrimination argument. The existence of these differences calls into question whether sexism—rather than homophobia—is at the core of laws that discriminate on the basis of sexual orientation and whether such laws disadvantage women as much as LGB people. While sexism plays a role in the justification of laws that discriminate against LGB people, homophobia plays a more central role. Sexism and homophobia are mutually supporting but distinct belief systems. It mischaracterizes the nature of laws that discriminate on the basis of sexual orientation to see them as primarily harming women (or even as harming women as much as they harm LGB people) and to see them as primarily justified by sexism rather than (or as much as) homophobia. Rather, even though some women are of course affected by laws that discriminate on the basis of sexual orientation, such laws primarily disadvantage LGB people. Such laws prohibit LGB people from sexually expressing their intimate relationships and from having sex with the people to whom they are sexually attracted. Relatedly, the *theoretical mistake* of the sex-discrimination argument is that homophobia—not sexism—is the primary motivation behind laws that discriminate on the basis of sexual orientation. Despite the fact that sexism played a role in their development, such laws are now maintained primarily by animus towards LGB people and repulsion towards them and the sexual activities in which they engage. Therefore, to deploy the sex-discrimination argument against laws that discriminate on the basis of sexual orientation ignores the central role that conceptions of sexual desire play in such laws.

An advocate of the sex-discrimination argument might respond to the sociological and the theoretical objections raised here by pointing out that just because a law has one problematic feature does not mean that nothing else is wrong with it. Specifically, there might be more than one class disadvantaged by a law and there might be more than one belief system that justifies a law. In particular, in response to the sociological objection, one might say that LGB people *and* women are disadvantaged by sexual-orientation discrimination. Similarly, in response to the theoretical objection, one might say that *both* homophobia and sexism provide the theoretical justification for sexual-orientation discrimination.

Surely some laws that disadvantage one group may also disadvantage another and more than one belief system may undergird some laws. Sometimes, even when this is true, one group may be more disadvantaged than another, and one belief system may play a more central role than another. While women, compared to men, may be more disadvantaged by sexual-orientation discrimination, LGB people are more significantly disadvantaged than women by such laws (of course, these groups—women and LGB people—overlap; my claim here is that sexual-orientation discrimination harms LGB people *qua* LGB people more than it harms women *qua* women). Similarly, while sexism plays a role in maintaining sexual-orientation discrimination, homophobia plays a more central role. Both the sociological and the theoretical objections to the sex-discrimination argument rely on the observation that sexism and homophobia have become disentangled. The sociological objection is that, as a cultural fact, LGB people, not women, suffer the greatest harm from sexual-orientation discrimination. The theoretical objection is that sexual-orientation discrimination is primarily maintained by homophobia, not sexism. Together, the sociological and the theoretical objections create a serious problem for the sex-discrimination argument.

The moral objection to the sex-discrimination argument is that sexual-orientation discrimination should be rejected on the grounds that it invidiously distinguishes between LGB people and heterosexuals, not because it discriminates on the basis of sex. Rejecting sexual-orientation discrimination because it is sex discrimination mischaracterizes the core wrong of sexual-orientation discrimination. Laws restricting the rights of LGB people should be rejected primarily because such laws discriminate on the basis of sexual orientation, *not* because they discriminate on the basis of sex.

In summary, the sex-discrimination argument, even in its strongest form, faces three serious and related objections. By focusing on the harm to women and the sexist assumptions of sexual-orientation discrimination, this argument rests on a cultural mischaracterization and theoretical misalignment. These mistakes lead the sex-discrimination argument to provide the wrong analysis of sexual-orientation discrimination. *LGB people* constitute the class disadvantaged by sexual-orientation discrimination and homophobia is the belief system that justifies it. The sex-discrimination argument focuses on a real connection between sexism and sexual-orientation discrimination, but it does so at the cost of properly emphasizing the deeper connection between homophobia and sexual-orientation discrimination.

An alternative account of why sexual-orientation discrimination is wrong

The problems with the etiological and the sex-discrimination arguments point to a better strategy for critiquing sexual-orientation discrimination, namely to engage in—rather than avoid—the ethical and jurisprudential debate that undergirds the quest for LGB rights (Ball 2002). The etiological argument tries to shift this debate from ethics and public policy to the context of science, while the sex-discrimination argument tries to shift it to the less controversial (at least in most Western democracies) context of sex discrimination. Although it is tempting to try to change the question, especially when discrimination against LGB people seems entrenched and arguments based on the unnatural and non-procreative character of same-sex sexual activities—as well as other equally weak arguments in defense of sexual-orientation discrimination—have continued to hold sway despite their weakness, it is better to talk directly about justice, fairness, and equality for LGB people.

Specifically, the argument needs to be made that same-sex sexual desire is of the same legal and ethical status as different-sex sexual desire, same-sex sexual acts are of the same legal and ethical status as different-sex sexual acts, and relationships between people of the same sex have the same legal and ethical status as relationships between people of different sexes. These ethical claims are at the core of strong arguments against sexual-orientation discrimination; debates about these claims need to be joined rather than ignored in order to obtain and maintain robust LGB rights. In this regard, note that when the U.S. Supreme Court has considered sexual-orientation discrimination in various contexts, it has addressed the issue by talking about fairness, equality, liberty, privacy, and pluralism and not by talking about etiology or sex discrimination (*Romer v. Evans* 1996; *Lawrence v. Texas* 2003; *Obergefell v. Hodges* 2015). For example, Justice Harry Blackmun in his dissent to *Bowers v. Hardwick* (1986) (which upheld Georgia's sodomy law against a constitutional challenge), embraced sexual pluralism as part of his rejection of a law's differential treatment based on sexual orientation and sexual behavior:

> The fact that individuals define themselves in a significant way through their intimate sexual relationships with others suggests that … there may be many "right" ways of conducting those relationships, and that much of the richness of a relationship will come from the freedom an individual has to *choose* the form and nature of these intensely personal bonds.
>
> *(Bowers v. Hardwick 1986: 205)*

Arguments like Blackmun's—and those embraced by many courts in the United States and other jurisdictions in recent years—address differential treatment for LGB people by appeal to moral and legal principles, which is precisely what a discussion of sexual-orientation discrimination warrants.

Notes

1 This chapter draws on some of my previously published works (Stein 1999; Stein 2001; Stein 2009; Stein 2011; Stein 2014).

2 Throughout this chapter, sex and gender are elided in a way that is a non-trivial simplification. Doing so erases transgender people and those who have sexual attraction towards them. This is an unpalatable

result of simplifications necessary given the brevity of this chapter. Dembroff (2016) provides a searching discussion of how transgender people fit into a sophisticated account of sexual orientation.

3 In at least some instances, the non-procreative nature of same-sex sexual activities is offered as a reason for thinking that same-sex sexual activities are unnatural and, thus, since they are unnatural, that discrimination on the basis of sexual orientations is warranted. I do not discuss this possible connection to the unnaturalness argument further, but in some contexts the two arguments in support of discrimination on the basis of sexual orientation are linked.

4 This is a simplification. Virginia law only prohibited whites from marrying "colored" people; "colored" people of different races (for example, a "Negro" woman and an "American Indian" man) were permitted to marry each other.

Bibliography

American Psychological Association. 2009. *Report of the American Psychological Association Task Force on Appropriate Responses to Sexual Orientation*. www.apa.org/pi/lgbc/publications/therapeutic-resp.html.

Bagemihl, B. 1999. *Biological Exuberance: Animal Homosexuality and Natural Diversity*. New York: St. Martin's Press.

Ball, C. 2003. *The Morality of Gay Rights: An Exploration in Political Philosophy*. New York: Routledge.

Bennett, W. 2001. *The Broken Hearth: Reversing the Moral Collapse of the American Family*. New York: Doubleday.

Bowers v. Hardwick. 1986. 478 U.S. 186 (United States Supreme Court).

Burr, C. 1996. *A Separate Creation: The Search for the Biological Origins of Sexual Orientation*. New York: Hyperion.

Calhoun, C. 1994. "Separating Lesbian Theory from Feminist Theory." *Ethics*. 104: 558–581.

Dembroff, R. 2016. "What Is a Sexual Orientation?" *Philosophers' Imprint*. 16(3): 1–27.

Diamond, L. 2008. *Sexual Fluidity: Understanding Women's Love and Desire*. Cambridge: Harvard University Press.

Finnis, J. 1995. "Law, Morality, and 'Sexual Orientation.'" *Notre Dame Journal of Law, Ethics, and Public Policy*. 9: 11–39.

Finnis, J. 1997. "The Good of Marriage and the Morality of Sexual Relations: Some Philosophical and Historical Observations." *American Journal of Jurisprudence*. 42: 97–134.

George, R. 2006. "What's Sex Got to Do with It?: Marriage, Morality, and Rationality." In George, R. and Elshtain, J. (eds) *The Meaning of Marriage: Family, State, Market, and Morals*. Dallas: Spence Publishing.

Goodridge v. Department of Public Health. 2003. 798 N.E.2d 941 (Supreme Judicial Court of Massachusetts).

Grant v. Southwest Trains. 1998. Case C-249/96 (European Court of Justice).

Kelley, K. 1978. "Playboy Interview: Anita Bryant." *Playboy* (May), 73–96 and 232–250.

Koppleman, A. 1994. "Why Sexual Orientation Discrimination is Sex Discrimination." *New York University Law Review*. 69: 197–287.

Koppleman, A. 2002. *The Gay Rights Question in Contemporary American Law*. Chicago: University of Chicago Press.

Lawrence v. Texas. 2003. 539 U.S. 558 (United States Supreme Court).

Levin, M. 1984. "Why Homosexuality Is Immoral." *Monist*. 67: 251–283.

Loving v. Virginia. 1964. 388 U.S. 1 (United States Supreme Court).

Macedo, S. 1995. "Homosexuality and the Conservative Mind." *Georgetown Law Journal*. 84: 261–300.

Marcosson, S. 1992. "Harassment on the Basis of Sexual Orientation: A Claim of Sex Discrimination Under Title VII." *Georgetown Law Journal*. 81: 1–38.

Mohr, R. 1990. *Gays/Justice: A Study in Society, Ethics, and Law*. New York: Columbia University Press.

Moore, G. 1903. *Principia Ethica*. Cambridge, England: Cambridge University Press.

Murphy, T. 1987. "Homosexuality and Nature: Happiness and the Law at Stake." *Journal of Applied Philosophy*. 4: 195–204.

Murphy, T. 1997. *Gay Science: The Ethics of Sexual Orientation Research*. New York: Columbia University Press.

Nussbaum, M. 2002. "Millean Liberty and Sexual Orientation: A Discussion of Edward Stein's *The Mismeasure of Desire*." *Law and Philosophy*. 21: 317–334.

Obergefell v. Hodges. 2015. 135 S. Ct. 2584 (United States Supreme Court).

Perry, M. 1995. "The Morality of Homosexual Conduct: A Reply to John Finnis." *Notre Dame Journal of Law, Ethics, and Public Policy*. 9: 41–73.

Plato. 1934. *The Laws*. Trans. A. Taylor. New York: E.P. Dutton.

Romer v. Evans. 1996. 517 U.S. 620 (United States Supreme Court).

Ruse, M. 1988. *Homosexuality: A Philosophical Inquiry*. New York: Blackwell.

Shidlo, A., Schroeder, M. and Drescher, J. (eds). 2002. *Sexual Conversion Therapy: Ethical, Clinical, and Research Perspectives*. Boca Raton, FL: CRC Press.

Singer v. Hara. 1974. 522 P.2d 1187 (Washington Appellate Court).

Stein, E. 1999. *The Mismeasure of Desire: The Science, Theory and Ethics of Sexual Orientation*. New York: Oxford University Press.

Stein, E. 2001. "Evaluating the Sex Discrimination Argument for Lesbian and Gay Rights." *UCLA Law Review*. 49: 471–518.

Stein, E. 2009. "The 'Accidental Procreation' Argument for Withholding Legal Recognition for Same-Sex Relationships." *Chicago-Kent Law Review*. 84: 403–435.

Stein, E. 2011. "Sexual Orientations, Rights, and the Body: Immutability, Essentialism, and Nativism." *Social Research: An International Quarterly*. 78: 633–658.

Stein, E. 2014. "Immutability and Innateness Arguments about Lesbian and Gay Rights." *Chicago-Kent Law Review*. 89: 597–640.

T. v. M. 1968. 242 A.2d 670 (New Jersey Superior Court Chancery Division).

Further reading

In addition to R. Mohr, *Gays/Justice: A Study in Society, Ethics, and Law* (New York: Columbia University Press, 1990), and C. Ball, *The Morality of Gay Rights: An Exploration in Political Philosophy* (New York: Routledge, 2003), M. Kaplan, *Sexual Justice: Democratic Citizenship and the Political of Desire* (New York: Routledge, 1997) provides an excellent and philosophically sophisticated discussion of LGB rights. W. Eskridge, *Gaylaw: Challenging the Apartheid of the Closet* (Cambridge, MA: Harvard University Press, 2002) provides a rich and thorough discussion of LGB rights in the U.S. legal context.

19
DISCRIMINATION AND DISABILITY

David Wasserman

NATIONAL INSTITUTES OF HEALTH

Sean Aas

GEORGETOWN UNIVERSITY

Introduction

There is little doubt that people with disabilities, even in an affluent country like the United States, are comprehensively disadvantaged. There are however, considerable doubts that wrongful discrimination plays a major role in creating or maintaining that disadvantage. In this chapter, we offer an account of disability discrimination that should help address these doubts.

There is abundant evidence that people with disabilities, as a group, are greatly disadvantaged. The U.S. Bureau of Labor Statistics reports that, despite a significant drop in unemployment in 2015, less than 27% of people with disabilities between 16 and 64 are employed (Bureau of Labor Statistics, 2016). According to a 2014 article on disability and poverty:

> The poverty rate for working-age people with disabilities is nearly two and a half times higher than that for people without disabilities... People with disabilities are also much more likely to experience material hardships—such as food insecurity; inability to pay rent, mortgage, and utilities; or not being able to get needed medical care—than people without disabilities at the same income levels.
>
> *(Vallis and Fremstad, 2014)*

It is unlikely that the material condition of any other salient minority group in the U.S., however despised or feared, approaches this level of destitution.

This depressing state of affairs is hardly limited to the United States. The Organisation for Economic Co-operation and Development (OECD), which includes the world's most developed countries, reported that in the late 2000s, less than half the people with disabilities in the working-age population of its members were employed, while 22% of people with disabilities were living in poverty. In contrast, over 70% of nondisabled working-age people were employed; the poverty rate for nondisabled people was only 14% (OECD, 2010).

Skepticism about the role of discrimination in producing this state of affairs is based on several claims and assumptions, some more plausible than others. The least tenable is the assumption that attitudes towards people with disabilities are less invidious than those toward other disadvantaged minorities (cf. Chapter 22). Even if the condescension, contempt, and discomfort widely displayed toward people with disabilities were somehow more benign when alloyed with pity and excessive solicitude, the latter may be at least as responsible for economic disadvantage. The still-common assumption that most people with disabilities lack the skill and resilience to perform demanding work probably contributes more than aversion to their high unemployment rates – much like Victorian attitudes toward "frail" women.

A second, more plausible claim, is that disability discrimination laws, despite or perhaps because of their redistributive features, have done very little to alleviate the kind of disadvantages described above, and further, that the recalcitrant disadvantage cannot be attributed primarily to lax enforcement or grudging judicial interpretation. Some commentators have argued on these grounds that the focus of disability policy should be on reconstruction and redistribution, rather than on antidiscrimination laws that place the burden of accommodation on individual employers, facilities, and agencies (Russell, 2002; Stein and Stein, 2007; Markel and Barclay, 2009; Maroto and Pettinicchio, 2014).

Far from denying the importance of reconstruction and redistribution, we argue that they are necessary to avoid disability discrimination (by "discrimination" we mean "wrongful discrimination"). The characteristic form of discrimination against people with disabilities, we maintain, involves a failure to recognize their capacities for the various kinds of activity that make life rewarding and meaningful: not only work, but personal decision making, childrearing, friendship and intimate relationships, and wider social and political participation. We do not want to suggest that such "misrecognition" – a term we will discuss later – is the only form of discrimination against people with disabilities, or that it is not also a significant form of discrimination against other social groups. Clearly, people with disabilities also face simple aversion, unmediated by capacity judgments. And just as clearly, other groups, like women and people of color, face the widespread undervaluation of important capacities (cf. Chapters 15 and 16). Nevertheless, we think that the misrecognition of ability is the dominant form, or source, of discrimination against people with disabilities, and that it is more comprehensive toward them than toward other social groups, for whom some capacities, from nurturing to athletic ability, are harmfully over- rather than under-valued.

We could devote a chapter to each of the domains in which people with disabilities face misrecognition. In the limited space we have, we have chosen to focus mainly (though not exclusively) on productive work in the formal economy (cf. Chapter 25). This is so for two reasons. First, as our opening paragraphs suggest, it leads in a direct, quantifiable way to pervasive disadvantage in any society where productive work is closely linked to material welfare.[1] Moreover, the changes required to reduce employment discrimination can be more readily demanded of the relevant decision makers. Employers can be mandated to put in ramps or reconfigure job descriptions, even if such accommodations are costly. Prospective friends and lovers cannot be similarly mandated to recognize people with disabilities as potential partners – which is not to deny that there is a great deal a society can do to facilitate that recognition.

While employment discrimination matters because of its economic impact, it also matters because of the deeper harm it inflicts – the damage to self-respect and the respect of others. Even in a society where income and wealth did not depend on economic productivity, meaningful work would be a central component of well-being. A society that gave to each according to their need and demanded from each according to their abilities would demean people with disabilities if it failed to demand from them the work they were able to do. Indeed, in more familiar societies, where wealth *does* depend on economic productivity, many people find their most meaningful labor in other domains – in volunteer work, unpaid artistic creation, or raising children. The value of work, and its contribution to self-respect, need not depend on remuneration, even if one's remuneration reflects the market value of one's work. So despite our focus on employment, for the reasons given in the last paragraph, it is the capacity for valuable work we regard as central – work that may often be found outside the workplace.

What we hope to do here is explain how the kinds of disadvantage people with disabilities experience are related to disability discrimination. The moral of our chapter is that discrimination, rightly understood, is central to explaining the disadvantages disabled people actually face, and to determining what it would mean for a society like ours to overcome them. The adequate recognition of productive capacities, we will argue, requires *both* 'reasonable accommodation' for specific opportunities, and the creation of a reasonable range of opportunities. Unjust discrimination, we argue, can and does occur at both levels. To avoid it, just societies must establish a comprehensive regime of equality of opportunity, which will not only enable disabled people to compete for specific opportunities, but ensure a wider range of opportunities to compete for in the first place.

Three aspects of disability discrimination

Clearly, it is incumbent on us to provide an account of how disability discrimination should be "rightly understood." The kind of discrimination we are concerned with is, fundamentally, *decisional*: it occurs when individual or collective decision making culpably ignores or underweights reasons to secure valuable opportunities for disabled people to participate in valued aspects of social life. The account we will offer incorporates, and in some ways integrates, features emphasized by competing theories of discrimination: irrationality, distributive injustice, and disrespect (Shin, 2013; Segev, 2014). It treats the denial of reasonable opportunities to people with disabilities as a misweighting of reasons relevant to the exercise of property rights; as a substantive injustice in the allocation of resources; and as a failure to respect or recognize the productive capacities of people with disabilities.

Our account differs from theories that describe discrimination in terms of only one or two of these three aspects. First, we recognize that disability discrimination cannot be regarded as entirely irrational in self-interested terms (cf. Chapter 8). Second, we maintain that a complete theory of distributive justice is neither sufficient nor necessary to determine what counts as disability discrimination. Finally, although disability discrimination involves a failure of respect or recognition, it cannot be assessed without a more extended engagement with distributive issues than other forms of discrimination require. In presenting these differences in more detail, we hope to provide a fuller introduction to our own account. However, we do not claim that all disability discrimination, let alone all discrimination, can be described in these terms; our point is that *disability disadvantage,* often taken to involve substantive injustice more than flawed decision procedures, is more decisional than it might appear.

Disability discrimination as a failure of rationality

Disability discrimination, admittedly, does not seem at first glance to fit the paradigm of irrational prejudice or stereotyping associated with other forms of discrimination, particularly racial and ethnic (Wasserman, 2013). After all, many of the decisions that disadvantage disabled people seem to be at least narrowly rational: an employer decides not to hire someone who cannot lift a small amount of weight, because she does not meet all the requirements of a clerical job; a school decides not to admit a student with a learning disorder, to save the cost of hiring a classroom aide. We argue, though, that closer examination of the structure of the reasons relevant to these sorts of decisions reveals that they are, in an important sense, not appropriately responsive to reasons after all. To appreciate this, it is necessary to understand the character of the reasons relevant to the deployment of socially-protected property rights.

Just societies, we maintain, legitimately constrain the reasons property-holders can take into account as they decide how to deploy their resources. This is part of the discretion societies possess to constitute a just property system. For example, network neutrality rules limit discretion over internet infrastructure; internet service providers are limited in how they can take business relationships or payments into account in deciding how to prioritize internet traffic. Their *reasons* are restricted; they can consider relationships with those who request data in deciding how to prioritize traffic (roughly: you can pay more as a customer for faster access), but not relationships with those who deliver data (roughly: you cannot pay more so that your customers have faster access). Similarly, we argue, societies may restrict the reasons capital owners can take into account in deciding how to deploy their resources with respect to people with disabilities. Decisions that attempt to deploy capital in ways a just society would forbid are defective, in important ways: they misweight relevant reasons.

If, for instance, a just property system requires that capital owners make reasonable accommodations for disabled people, then declining to do so in order to save money involves taking reasons into account which justice precludes. This is a form of decisional discrimination – deciding as justice forbids you to decide – albeit discrimination that has to be defined in an explicitly moralized way. This incorporation of morality into practical rationality will, no doubt, provoke resistance from those who remain committed to a minimalist account of rationality. Their view may appear to be closer to common sense, but in this case common sense is simply wrong, like the common-sense view that we are entitled to our pre-tax income. Liam Murphy and Thomas Nagel (2002) maintain, persuasively, that this view is confused about the relationship between taxes and rights: (just) taxes constrain that to which you can get an entitlement in the first place, and so cannot be construed as taking something to which you are already entitled. We see common sense as similarly confused about reasonable accommodation discrimination mandates: they do not restrict your rights in your capital, but rather, limit the rights you acquire in the first place when you acquire capital.

Disability discrimination as distributive injustice

Resistance to treating disability discrimination as a form of irrationality, even if unwarranted, may suggest that it is better understood simply as a type of distributive injustice. This reductionist or deflationary view gains plausibility when the "currency" of distributive justice is expanded to encompass not only individually held resources, whether tangible or intangible, but also the ways in which society is structured to facilitate or impede individual activities and projects. Such an expansion makes it possible to see a characteristic form of discrimination against people with disabilities as a distributive injustice. We agree with this expansion, but deny that it leads to a view of disability discrimination in which judgments about discrimination are entirely parasitic on judgments about distributive justice.

The notion that discrimination is embedded in ostensibly neutral physical and social structures and practices owes much to feminist critiques of earlier civil rights law, with its narrow focus on the direct and indirect effects of intentional discrimination (see Rebell, 1986; Wegner, 1984). Feminists argued that the design of physical structures and social practices for one group – able-bodied males – constitutes a significant form of discrimination against the rest. The Americans with Disabilities Act can be seen as codifying this notion of structural discrimination. It treats the failure to make reasonable accommodation for people with disabilities in the design of buildings and facilities, and the structuring of jobs, as a form of discrimination. It provides exemptions only for undue burdens, and for changes that would alter the fundamental nature of the activity.

Arguably, the structural discrimination that the ADA attempts to address accounts for most of the disadvantage faced by people with disabilities. One might argue, this is "discrimination" only in a thin sense, parasitic on judgments about justice. An extreme version of this deflationary position would hold that to discriminate against people with disabilities is simply to give them less of the relevant resources than a complete theory of justice would require.[2]

Although, as we argue below, disability discrimination has a closer relationship to distributive injustice than other forms of discrimination, we find the deflationary view untenable in its most extreme forms. A complete theory of justice in holdings is neither sufficient nor necessary for determining what counts as disability discrimination. It is not sufficient, because we cannot ascertain from an individual's share of resources whether he was the victim of discrimination (cf. Chapters 10 and 11). People with disabilities may be comparatively well off despite suffering discrimination, or may be worse off simply because of "brute bad luck." Historical information is needed, and – we will argue – information about the history of material transfers is not enough.

Nor do we need a complete theory of justice to make judgments about discrimination. We have suggested that wrongful discrimination occurs when resource-holders attempt to act on reasons barred from consideration by just property systems. But we need not know everything about justice to know that it must bar certain kinds of reasons. Indeed, if we are to respect reasonable disagreement in the design of public institutions like property systems, we must be able to identify discrimination even without complete agreement. Reasonable people will agree, for example, that any modestly affluent society should require ramps for new buildings, but they will not agree on many closer cases. They might well propose different answers to the rhetorical questions posed by an exasperated judge responding to an early disability discrimination law:

> What must be done to provide handicapped persons with the same right to utilize mass-transportation facilities as other persons? Does each bus have to have special capacity? Must each seat on each bus be removable? Must the bus routes be changed to provide stops at all hospitals, therapy centers, and nursing homes? Is it required that buses be able to accommodate bedridden persons?
>
> *(quoted in Wegner: 1984: 404)*

A complete theory of distributive justice would answer questions like these, and might well require far greater resources for the inclusion of people with disabilities in a variety of contexts. But, we maintain, the failure of individual or collective agents to provide those resources through accommodation does not constitute wrongful discrimination unless that failure is unreasonable. What we need, then, to analyze discrimination as a structurally-inflected individual offense, is not a complete theory of disability justice, but rather an account of when a failure to provide accommodation is unreasonable.

Our view is that, to constitute discrimination, injustices in resources allocation must be informed by objectionable individual attitudes, judgments, or past decisions concerning people with disabilities, or derive from policies and practices which cannot be justified except by reference to objectionable attitudes and judgments. Those include, of course, denying employment to a highly-qualified disabled job applicant requiring no accommodation because of contempt, condescension, or disgust toward people "like" her.[3] More importantly, they encompass decisions made in culpable ignorance of the productive capacities of people with disabilities. Practices and policies informed by false assumptions about those capacities are discriminatory even if established or implemented by individuals who intend no disrespect and think of people with disabilities as their moral and social equals. Finally, they also include those "narrowly rational" decisions, discussed above, that are objectionable not because of the employer's false assumptions but because of the excessive weight she gives her economic interests.

But not all practices and policies that disadvantage people with disabilities, and that would be mistaken under the correct theory of justice, are wrongfully discriminatory. If reasonable individuals, well-informed about the capacities of people with disabilities, can disagree about whether a given accommodation is required by justice, then they can permissibly establish and act within a property system that grants rights-holders latitude to withhold it. The resulting arrangement may be unjust, but not in the particularly serious, disrespectful way that discrimination properly-so-called is unjust.

Disability discrimination as recognitional injustice

In identifying disability discrimination, then, what matters is the extent that the comparative disadvantage of people with disabilities can be attributed to decisional processes that fail to respect their fundamentally equal capacity to take part in social life. A complete theory of justice is not necessary, because a decision or rule that disadvantages people with disabilities can be regarded as discriminatory if it is a recognitional injustice, inconsistent with *any* system of property in capital that recognizes people with disabilities as equal contributors and participants.

Justice as recognition is often discussed in terms of respect for, and appreciation of, the distinctive social identities of individuals (Wasserman et al., 2015). We focus here instead on a different type of recognition – not of their social identity but of their status as equally contributing members of society. Most bodily differences that are classified as "disabilities" do not detract from the ability to contribute to social cooperation, and rules of social cooperation that needlessly prevent people with such disabilities from fully participating display a failure of recognition, a form of injustice that typically has adverse distributive consequences.[4]

This approach to disability discrimination has affinities with more general accounts like those of Richard Wasserstrom (1977), Andrew Koppelman (1998) and Deborah Hellman (2008; Chapter 7), that locate the wrong of discrimination in rules, practices and institutions that deny the moral and political equality of a social group. But we do believe that distributive justice plays a larger role in assessing and rectifying discrimination against people with disabilities than discrimination against other stigmatized social groups. Although various forms of redistribution are necessary to correct practices that discriminate against women and members of minority racial groups, the reconstruction required to avoid disability discrimination is more extensive, and its extent is more debatable. Some, perhaps most, but not all of the distributive injustice faced by people with disabilities is attributable to recognitional injustice – and therefore, to discrimination. Still, as suggested in the last sub-section, people with disabilities, in contrast to most other stigmatized social groups, may also face significant distributive injustice that is not attributable to discrimination.

Two levels of disability discrimination

To flesh out our account of disability discrimination, we will discuss two forms, or levels, of recognitional injustice. First, more narrowly, we argue that a system which does not require employers to make even "reasonable" accommodations grants them excessive latitude to define job descriptions in a way that disrespects the capacities of prospective employees with disabilities. Second, more broadly, we argue that the social system as a whole is disrespectful to disabled people as a class to the extent that it excludes them from productive work without sufficiently good reason.

Discrimination at an individual level: unreasonable failures to accommodate

First, we consider how employment decisions themselves express respect, or disrespect, for people with disabilities. In considering this, it is important to reiterate a point made above, about the conventional understanding of reasonable accommodation mandates as placing burdens on employers. This understanding raises the question of whether those burdens are better assumed by the state and met through taxation or other means. As we argued above, however, this is not the only or best way to understand the distributive import of reasonable accommodation. On the alternative construal we favor, such accommodation is not a cost to private parties at all, because owners of capital are simply not entitled to any proceeds that cannot be realized without unreasonably excluding disabled people from their workforce. Therefore, mandating reasonable accommodations does not force employers to use their resources to help include disabled people; rather, it constrains which rights in resources are "theirs" in the first place.

But why include reasonable accommodation as part of the content of property rights? The reasons are recognitional. The ability to contribute productively to society is central to our social identity; in Rawlsian terms, for the social bases of self-respect. Misrepresentations of capacity, intentional or not, threaten to seriously undermine our self-respect and the respect of others. This kind of recognitional injustice occurs at multiple sites: in the exclusionary decisions of particular decision-makers and in the structural practices – property systems, etc. – that permit and promote these sorts of decisions.

To make this more concrete, consider the case of a paraplegic programmer. Discrimination against him will fall on a spectrum from active animus to a failure of practical imagination. The refusal to hire him could be based on contempt for "cripples," or on the obvious misrecognition in assuming that people who can't walk lack the cognitive skills to program. Harder cases arise where the employer acts, not from animus or uncritical assumptions about capacities, but from concerns regarding the cost or feasibility of accommodation. If these concerns themselves reflect clearly negligent ignorance, there may be insulting disrespect here as well. However, it will often be difficult to assess the cost or feasibility of accommodation. There may still be misrecognition in such cases, but it will be less obvious. Consider a programmer who not only cannot walk, but who experiences fatigue after four or five hours of concentrated work, or who requires medical assistance for which his home but not your office is equipped. You've advertised a "full-time, face-time" job (Travis, 2006), and you quickly conclude that the programmer, however gifted, cannot perform the essential functions of the job, since he cannot work in the office full-time. In a sense, you'd be correct – he can't perform the job as you described it. But taking a step back, the question is whether these requirements are really essential to the tasks you need performed. If you really valued his productive capacities you would ask yourself whether he needed to work a full, uninterrupted day, or could, say, work in four-hour shifts, mostly at home, and still program as effectively and reliably as you required. And although you might reasonably refuse to overhaul your workplace and practices, you should be willing to incur small inconvenience and out-of-pocket costs to accommodate him with a flexible schedule. Your refusal to do so counts as a kind of misrecognition, less culpable than outright animus or gross overgeneralization, but harmful and discriminatory nevertheless (cf. Chapter 23).

The resistance to such accommodations in work schedule and location reflects what Michelle Travis has called "workplace essentialism" – a failure "to distinguish actual job tasks from the default organizational norms regarding when, where, and how the actual tasks get performed" and thereby "to equate the traditional ways of organizing work performance with the underlying work tasks themselves" (2006: 20). Before turning to institutional and other collective misrecognition, we want to consider this local form of misrecognition in situations without animus towards, or culpable underestimation of, disabled applicants.

These situations involve what we could call "job description discrimination": employers, perhaps unknowingly, design roles in ways that unnecessarily exclude disabled people. To take a stylized case: instead of hiring one person to sit at the desk and take orders, and one person to climb the ladders in the warehouse to fulfill them, I hire two people to do each task half the time. I might do this without even realizing that it disadvantages disabled people. Yet, if there is no business rationale for the decision to structure work in this way, then I do seem to be ignorant in a potentially culpable sort of way: proper respect for my fellow citizen requires attention to inclusive ideals as I design work; in the "no-rationale" case, such attention was clearly not paid.

To be sure, in many cases there is a perfectly good rationale for structuring job opportunities in a way that excludes some people from pursuing them. In a variation of our case, the employer can only afford to hire one person to take and fulfill orders. There is a spectrum here, from easy cases of "no-rationale" exclusion, through hard cases where accommodation has substantial but not prohibitive cost, to cases where work needs doing that some people can only do with extremely costly accommodation or simply cannot do, however extensively accommodated. To assess their recognitional import, we need to place individual employment decisions on this spectrum of cost; and (as we argue below), also on a different spectrum, determined by the total social cost of policies permitting decisions like these. We know of no way, a priori, to draw a line on either spectrum between acceptable economy and wrongful discrimination. Indeed, as we have suggested, multiple lines are needed, to indicate different kinds and sources of misrecognition.

It is difficult to say where, exactly, these lines will go. At some point we may need to fall back on judgments about what sorts and degrees of accommodations are "reasonable" or "unreasonable". Still, we can at least hope to describe some of the ideals and values that should influence our judgments of reasonableness. So far, we've suggested that exclusionary decisions – whether at the point of hiring, or at the point of job design – are positively "unreasonable" to the extent that they exclude disabled people for little, or no, good reason. In the next section, we want to suggest much the same for the choice of social structures itself. Structures that exclude people with little, or no good reason, are disrespectful, on that very ground (cf. Chapter 6). This norm, we propose, is more demanding than it might seem.

Discrimination at a collective level: exclusionary rules, practices, and policies

In this section, we argue that what counts as a qualification and an essential function depends to a large extent on the way labor is structured and jobs are configured by broader social institutions and practices. Current divisions and configurations, though not arbitrary, are mutable, and vary greatly across times and places. Those structures and configurations can be made more inclusive by deliberate collective action (Aas and Wasserman, 2016).

It should be easy to see that many rules and practices in the workplace are conventional and mutable. As we have already argued, "workplace essentialism" poses an unnecessary barrier to the employment of disabled people who can perform essential tasks in different ways or places. Moreover, as we observed, many jobs are collections of tasks that vary in their relationship to each other and their importance to the business. The more tasks that are included in a job description, and the more diverse the skills they require, the more likely it is that a disabled individual cannot perform all of them. To be sure, there are certainly jobs for which versatility itself is a legitimate requirement. But the requirement is often unnecessary, and works to the detriment of people with disabilities. U.S. regulations make clear that a task is not an "essential function if it is incidental to the employee's main work and can be easily assumed by other employees" (Kimberlin and Headley, 2000). But as we conceded, it will often be reasonable for individual employers with limited resources to require their employees to perform a variety of unrelated tasks. It is here that we must turn to the role played by social policies, practices, rules in bundling multiple tasks into jobs, and in discouraging flexibility in their performance, so that they cannot be performed by a talented person with an impairment.

For example, well-intentioned but overprotective occupational health and safety regulations may needlessly increase the "essential functions" of a job by preventing people with disabilities from assuming a reasonable level of risk. Various public benefits are tied to either full-time work or full unemployment, making part-time work a losing proposition. Parents with disabilities share with other prospective employees the need for high-quality, flexible, reliable childcare, a need that may be more acute for them because of irregular hours or logistical difficulties in getting to and from their workplaces.

Travis argues that workplace essentialism was entrenched in the eighteenth-to-nineteenth century transition in Western societies from home-based work to a rigid dichotomy between home and workplace: the former the realm of unpaid female domestic labor, the latter the realm of paid male labor (2006: 8–9). She argues that that dichotomy has persisted in the "full-time, face-time" work norm, although the need for it has greatly declined with the advent of telecommuting technology. And, as she points out, that norm imposes unreasonable barriers for people with disabilities who would be fully capable of performing essential tasks if they had flexible hours and work arrangements.

These structural barriers to inclusion are unreasonable, we submit, in the simple sense that there is no good reason for them. As Travis's discussions indicate, the way tasks are bundled into jobs now is often a reflection of arbitrary history, not intelligent design or even adaptive evolution. There is little reason to doubt that more inclusive practices of job organization would have led to a society that is not only more just, but also more efficient and productive. After all, to the extent that thoughtlessly-delineated jobs keep potentially productive people out of the workforce, they reduce the size of the social product. Ongoing structures and practices that perpetuate this sort of exclusion, therefore, have no justification beyond "this is the way we do things around here." And this sort of justification is inadequate to the point of insult when offered to people who lose out on important social goods as a result. Even a justification based on slight gains in overall prosperity trivializes the value to the excluded of the satisfaction and self-respect that come with productive work.

Matters will, of course, be more complicated where there is a true conflict between these values and the values that might be realized by exclusion: where, for instance, excluding some from productive work produces a genuinely large benefit for the society, including those excluded. Thus, the choice of policies that promote the continued automation of work is probably highly beneficial overall. Yet it will predictably make it harder to utilize the productive talents of intellectually disabled people, who may have a less secure place in a service- and information-based economy than a manufacturing-based economy.[5] But it is uncertain how a post-industrial society could change structures so as to alter this trend, let alone whether it should assume the economic, social, and political costs of doing so. More generally, where there is a cost to inclusion, exclusion is less obviously insulting; when the cost is very significant, it need not be insulting at all.

Now to know when exclusion is justified all things considered, we will indeed need a full theory of justice. Where there is a genuinely hard case, it will not be plausible to claim that the less inclusive decision must be insulting to those excluded – even if that decision is, as it turns out, unjust under the best theory of distributive justice. In such cases, societies and individuals "discriminate" against those excluded only in an excessively thin, deflationary, sense of the term. They are not treated as the society or individual has most reason to treat them, but *knowing this* requires insight that none of us possesses. Individual action permitted by not-unreasonably-unjust structures is not discriminatory at all; or at least not in a wrongful sense: it is not wrong to deploy capital in ways that current property norms allow you to, unless those norms are *manifestly* unjust.

Conversely, however, it is wrongfully discriminatory to use capital in ways that just property norms would manifestly require you not to; *especially* to the extent that actual property norms are in this way just, and require you not to. Since actual "reasonable accommodation" mandates are clearly justified, we think that decisions that obviously flout these rules are discriminatory. Thus, the manifest justice of current law on reasonable accommodation makes many actual failures to accommodate discriminatory in a straightforward sense.[6] Many failures, but not all. "Reasonable" is necessarily and intentionally a vague term. This hardly means that there are no clear cases of unreasonable failure to accommodate, but it does mean that many cases will not be clear. In those cases, debating what the law really requires or should require will not, on our account, be well-described as a debate about what constitutes *wrongful* discrimination.

Conclusion

To summarize, many cases in which employers do not provide reasonable accommodation are discrimination *par excellence*: (1) they are in a sense *irrational decisions*; because (2) they take into account putative reasons to exercise property rights which justice *in fact* precludes; and (3) they are, or could be, authorized only by norms that showed disrespect for the productive capacities of people with disabilities. We have no theory to tell us how many decisions will fit this paradigm, though we hope to offer some sense of what one would have to take into account to figure this out. Basically, to the extent that exclusion is the result of *arbitrary history* and lacks *good justifying reasons*, it is disrespectful and therefore wrongly discriminatory. Even if there are coherent reasons for exclusion, discrimination still occurs when those reasons are manifestly inadequate to justify exclusion.

Without an account of which reasons justify exclusion, or when it is obvious that they do, we cannot even estimate how much disability disadvantage comes from paradigm discrimination, rather than from currently-blameless injustices. But it seems clear to us that the proportion will be substantial: after all, many exclusionary policies and practices, including many of those to do with "job description discrimination," are holdovers from a time when disability justice was not on the agenda at all and disabled people were not even thought of as prospective employees. The imposition of these practices was often disrespectful when they were first imposed; it is even more disrespectful now, when we ought to know better.[7,8]

Notes

1 The harm done by failing to recognize other capacities, especially for friendship and intimacy, may result in even greater, albeit less tangible harms, and the assumptions of incapacity that restrict social and political participation surely hinder people with disabilities in achieving recognition. For example, see Kimberley Brownlee's (2016) account of "social contribution injustice" – injustice that "denies us minimally adequate scope and recognition to contribute to social connections according to our abilities" (29). Brownlee illustrates this harmful injustice with the example of a physically impaired

individual denied the opportunity for social contributions by a society that "incorrectly views her as unable to contribute socially" in valuable ways (33–34).

2 Patrick Shin (2013) proposes an equally deflationary (but more consequentialist) account of legal discrimination: "the legal concept *ascribes* the status of discrimination – and with it, a certain measure of opprobrium – to various forms of action that, if unchecked, would undermine the justness of our basic institutional structures."

3 If agents had "brute desires" not to associate with members of a social group that did not reflect an implicit judgment of inferiority, we do not think that discriminating on the basis of those desires would be as wrongful as the discrimination we describe above, contra Lippert-Rasmussen (2012: 72–74).

4 We take no position on the claim that discrimination toward people with disabilities *must* result in injustice or other harm (Lippert-Rasmussen, 2014; Slavny and Parr, 2015).

5 Indeed, automation and artificial intelligence may consign increasingly more people not only to unemployment but to the category of "intellectual disabled." As ever more service and computational tasks can be performed by computers and robots, permanent employment may be limited to the intellectual elite needed to create and oversee them – as well as to govern and teach an increasingly idle human community. It is debatable whether the stigma of unemployment and intellectual deficiency would be mitigated by being so widely shared.

6 This is not to deny that overzealous or unscrupulous lawyers can abuse disability discrimination law to produce unjust results; this is a danger with all law and regulation, however just.

7 Disclaimer: The views expressed are the authors' own. They do not represent the position or policy of the National Institutes of Health, U.S. Public Health Service, or the Department of Health and Human Services.

8 Acknowledgement: Work on the chapter was supported in part by the Intramural Research Program of the NIH, Clinical Center, Department of Bioethics.

Bibliography

Aas, Sean, and David Wasserman. 2016. "Natural and Social Inequality: Disability and Fair Equality of Opportunity." *Journal of Moral Philosophy*. 13: 576–601.

Bureau of Labor Statistics 2016. "Persons with a Disability: Labor Force Characteristics – 2015." *Economic New Release USDL-16-1248*. July 21, 2016. www.bls.gov/news.release/disabl.nr0.htm

Hartley, Christie. 2009. "Justice for the Disabled: A Contractualist Approach." *Journal of Social Philosophy*. 40(1): 17–36.

Hellman, Deborah. 2008. *When Is Discrimination Wrong?* Cambridge, MA: Harvard University Press.

Kimberlin, Diane L., and Linda Ottinger Headley. 2000 "ADA Overview and Update: What Has the Supreme Court Done to Disability Law?" *Review of Litigation*. 19: 579.

Koppelman, Andrew. 1998. *Antidiscrimination Law and Social Equality*. New Haven: Yale University Press.

Lippert-Rasmussen, Kasper. 2012. "Intentions and Discrimination in Hiring." *Journal of Moral Philosophy*. 9(1): 55–74.

Lippert-Rasmussen, Kasper. 2014. *Born Free and equal?: A Philosophical Inquiry into the Nature of Discrimination*. Oxford: Oxford University Press.

Markel, Karen S., and Lizabeth A. Barclay. 2009. "Addressing the Underemployment of Persons with Disabilities: Recommendations for Expanding Organizational Social Responsibility." *Employee Responsibilities and Rights Journal*. 21(4): 305–318.

Maroto, Michelle, and David Pettinicchio. 2014. "The Limitations of Disability Antidiscrimination Legislation: Policymaking and the Economic Well-being of People with Disabilities." *Law & Policy*. 36(4): 370–407.

Murphy, Liam, and Thomas Nagel. 2002. *The Myth of Ownership: Taxes and Justice*. Oxford: Oxford University Press.

Rebell, Michael A. 1985. "Structural Discrimination and the Rights of the Disabled." *Geo. LJ*.74: 1435.

Russell, Marta. 2002. "What Disability Civil Rights Cannot Do: Employment and Political Economy." *Disability & Society*. 17(2): 117–135.
Segev, Re'em. 2014. "Making Sense of Discrimination." *Ratio Juris*. 27(1): 47–78.
Shin, Patrick S. 2013. "Is There a Unitary Concept of Discrimination?" In Hellman, Deborah, and Moreau, Sophia, (eds.) *Philosophical Foundations of Discrimination Law*. Oxford: Oxford University Press: Chapter 8.
Slavny, Adam, and Tom Parr. 2015. "Harmless Discrimination." *Legal Theory*. 21: 100–114.
Stein, Michael Ashley, and Penelope J. S. Stein. 2007. "Beyond Disability Civil Rights." *Hastings Law Journal*. 58: 1203.
Strudler, Alan. 1994. "The Social Construction of Genetic Abnormality: Ethical Implications for Managerial Decisions in the Workplace." *Journal of Business Ethics*. 13(11): 839–848.
Travis, Michelle A. 2005. "Recapturing the Transformative Potential of Employment Discrimination Law." *Washington and Lee Law Review*. 62(3).
Vallas, Rebecca, and Shawn Fremstad. 2014. "Disability is a Cause and Consequence of Poverty." *Talk Poverty*. September 19, 2014, https://talkpoverty.org/2014/09/19/disability-cause-consequence-poverty/
Wasserman, David. 2013. "Is Disability Discrimination Different?" In Hellman, Deborah, and Moreau, Sophia (eds) *Philosophical Foundations of Discrimination Law*. Oxford: Oxford University Press: Chapter 13.
Wasserman, David, Adrienne Asch, Jeffrey Blustein and Daniel Putnam. 2015. "Disability and Justice." *The Stanford Encyclopedia of Philosophy* (Summer 2015 Edition), Edward N. Zalta (ed.) http://plato.stanford.edu/archives/sum2015/entries/disability-justice/
Wasserstrom, Richard A. 1977. "Racism, Sexism, and Preferential Treatment: An Approach to the Topics." *UCLA Law Review*. 24: 603–615.
Wegner, Judith. 1984. "The Antidiscrimination Model Reconsidered: Ensuring Equal Opportunity Without Respect to Handicap Under Section 504 of the Rehabilitation Act of 1973." *Cornell Law Review*. 69: 401.

20
DISCRIMINATION AND AGE

Juliana Bidadanure

STANFORD UNIVERSITY

Introductory remarks

Consider the following series of hypothetical examples.

> Vote 1: individuals racialized as Black are denied the right to vote.
> Vote 2: individuals below the age of 18 years old are denied the right to vote.
>
> Jobs 1: in a context of job scarcity, a government urges employers to give priority to male workers in the labor market, making gender discrimination legal.
> Jobs 2: in a context of job scarcity, a government urges employers to give priority to young workers in the labor market, making age-based discrimination legal.
>
> Airline 1: an airline refuses to employ a qualified Black candidate unless he shaves his hair while not requiring the same of White candidates.
> Airline 2: an airline refuses to employ a qualified 60-year-old candidate, because they consider 60 years old to be too old an age to pilot a plane.
>
> Premium 1: an insurance company charges men a higher premium than women, because men statistically cause more accidents than women.
> Premium 2: an insurance company charges drivers below the age of 25 years old a higher premium than older drivers, because younger drivers statistically cause more accidents than older drivers.

Differential treatments based on race and gender often strike us as more clearly wrong than age-based differential treatments. This is so even when exactly the same important rights or opportunities are being denied – such as the right to vote or to a job opportunity. In all the examples above, for instance, where cases numbered 1 are instances of gender or race-based discrimination while cases numbered 2 are instances of age-based discrimination, most of us are likely to consider the first versions of each case as far more serious than the second versions. At the very least, we will think that *Vote 1*, *Jobs 1* and *Airline 1* are more concerning than their counterparts. In fact, *Vote 2*, *Jobs 2* and *Airline 2* are fairly realistic scenarios: most countries do deny the right to vote to children and teenagers; we often seem to deem some unfit for a job because of their age; and we sometimes force people to retire after a certain age. *Premium 1* is perhaps less straightforwardly worse than *Premium 2*. Indeed, some readers may not find *Premium 1* very serious in the first place and will thus be equally unbothered by *Premium 2*. The European Court of Justice certainly thinks differently. Gender has recently been ruled out as an acceptable basis for differential treatment in fixing insurance premiums. Appealing to age to fix such premiums remains lawful.[1]

Our social fabric, our relationships, obligations and entitlements are structured around age membership without it being widely recognized as a cause of concern. In fact, as John Macnicol points out: "Age distinctions, age stratifications, age judgments and 'age-appropriate behaviors' are subtly woven into our patterns of thinking, as a way of making sense of the world" (Macnicol 2006: 4). We are all well aware of this, and yet we do not consider most of those cases to be wrongful. This is made clear by the comparatively low state of advancement of anti-age-discrimination law. In the UK, for instance, legislation to prevent race, gender and disability discrimination is well established, but age discrimination has only recently been legally recognized and legislation is still comparatively underdeveloped (Macnicol 2006). As Gosseries (2014) claims, it seems that anti-discrimination law is treated with *more leniency* than race and gender in the US as well: there, "age is not covered by *title VII of the 1964 Civil Rights Act* and *the 1967 Age Discrimination in Employment Act* deals with differential treatment above the age of 40 only". The EU Court also seems to treat age more leniently as a ground for discrimination: "Directive 2000/78/EC includes specific provisions for age – notably Article 6 – that leave more room to Member States than it does for other suspect grounds" (Gosseries 2014).

Whereas considerable attention has been given to the 'Equality of What?' debate in political philosophy, the question of how the value of equality applies through time has not been a central focus of attention. As a result, issues of age-based inequalities in general and age discrimination in particular remain under-theorized.[2] In fact, it is interesting to note that, when philosophers wrestle with what Hellman has called 'the puzzle of discrimination', they often appeal to cases of age-based discrimination to illustrate the fact that some forms of discrimination are not wrongful. Hellman starts her book on discrimination by giving the example of a parent who treats children differently based on their age – putting the two-year-old to bed earlier and letting the four-year-old play. Later on, she mentions an airline that refuses to employ pilots older than 62 (Hellman 2008: 2) and a State that refuses to license drivers under the age of 16 years old (Hellman 2008: 2). These examples, for Hellman, are taken to be exemplar of the fact that distinction drawing is not always wrong. In other words, age-based differential treatment often serves to illustrate discrimination that is *not* wrongful.

The question that I want to ask in this chapter is thus the following: Are we mistaken to often tolerate differential treatment by age? After all, age, not unlike gender and race, is a feature of our identity we do not choose. We do not have control over it and yet others may fail to treat us as equals on the basis of it (cf. Chapter 18). The most common and emblematic image of wrongful age-based discrimination is that of a 50+ worker being laid off because of her age. In such case, unless the government steps in to prevent employers from systematically discriminating against older workers, she will be condemned to join the ranks of the long-term unemployed. Perhaps we should simply treat age discrimination no more leniently than race and gender discrimination as a matter of general rule. If age is not relevantly different, let us get over our bigoted intuitions that the age-based differential treatment of the kind involved in the *Voting*, *Jobs*, *Airlines* and *Premium* examples should be tolerated more than their counterparts. Or perhaps that would be a mistaken move. If some cases of age-based discrimination will be found to be almost un-controversially problematic, some others will persistently strike us as acceptable, even in cases where important rights are denied. But then what – if anything – is the morally relevant difference between age discrimination and other forms of discrimination? For shorter, is age relevantly 'special', as Gosseries (2014) puts it? If so, the singularity of our attitudes towards age would be explained and, more importantly, justified.

Accepting the basic view that drawing distinctions between people is not always wrong, this chapter asks when drawing distinctions based on age is normatively dubious. I first explain why we seem to feel differently about age discrimination than we do about race or gender discrimination. I argue, like Axel Gosseries and Norman Daniels have before, that age is indeed special in one relevant way – we pass through the different age categories over time, whereas we do not change gender or race in the same predictable way. As a result, treating people unequally based on their age can be compatible with equal treatment of persons over time (cf. Chapters 10 and 11). More than that, in some cases, treating people unequally based on their age may be our best chance to treat people fairly over time (Section 2 of this chapter). Drawing on Deborah Hellman's account of wrongful discrimination and on my previous work on age-group justice, I then argue that we should still be concerned about instances of age-based discrimination that are demeaning – such as the exclusion of elderly people premised on ageism (Section 3). I then express concerns about drawing connections too tightly between what counts as demeaning and the history of domination suffered by a given group. I argue that it may blind us to the wrongness of discrimination experienced by the young (Section 4).

The puzzle of age discrimination

The *puzzle of age discrimination* can be phrased in the following manner: we seem to feel more strongly about race and gender discrimination than about age discrimination – are we right to treat age as a special category, or should we treat it more like gender and race? To answer this question, we do not need quite yet to commit to a fully-fledged theory of what makes discrimination wrongful. We may just focus on whether we have reasons to believe that there is something about age that sets it apart from race and gender as grounds for discrimination. If we start from the broad idea that discrimination is wrongful when it fails to treat persons as equals, we may ask whether there is something about age discrimination that makes it less likely to offend this general norm. Whether we answer this first question by the affirmative or not, we will then have to explain why some cases of age discrimination may be problematic and others not – why 'ageist' discrimination against the elderly may offend the norm of equal treatment, but not excluding children from voting in elections, for instance. This second question can hardly be answered without committing to a theory of discrimination. In this section, I will focus on answering the first question. I will then move on to the second question in the next section, this time appealing to Hellman's theory of discrimination.

So, is age special – and if so, what makes it special? Let me consider two answers: (1) relevance: age may be a better proxy for morally relevant traits than gender and race; (2) purpose: age-based differential treatment may serve more acceptable purposes than gender or race discrimination. Directly or indirectly, most theories of discrimination will find relevance and purpose to play some role (even if only instrumental) in explaining the wrongness of discrimination. So let's see if age-based discrimination can be distinguished from other forms of discrimination by appealing to purpose or relevance.

First, one could make the argument that at least some age ranges – like very young or very old age – are better proxies for morally relevant properties like ability, competence, or experience than gender and race (cf. Chapter 3). This is a hypothesis that Gosseries (2014) puts forward in his paper on age discrimination. This could help explain our peculiar reaction to age. In the *Voting* example above, we can explain our intuitions by appealing to the differences in competence, and capacity for autonomy, of children compared to adults. The process of ageing, from birth to adulthood, is correlated with various developmental and cognitive processes that make it *relevant* to ascribe differential responsibility, ability to consent and autonomy to children than to adults (cf. Chapter 8). Age is also often a fairly accurate proxy for predicting behaviors. British men over 30 are four times less likely to commit crime than younger British men, for instance, and this basic fact underpins justifications for youth profiling by the police (Macnicol 2006: 4). The effect of age on attitudes and behavior, at least in some cases, is quite important, which reinforces the view that age is different – it is simply a more reliable proxy for relevant traits like competence, experience and attitude.

The basic observation that age is often an accurate proxy is not sufficient on its own to set age discrimination apart from race and gender discrimination, however. Discrimination scholars are often reluctant to tolerate race or gender discrimination in cases where gender and race are accurate proxies for risky behavior or likeliness to commit crime, for instance. As Hellman forcefully argues, discrimination is often wrongful *and* an accurate proxy at the same time. A firm may refuse to hire women between 20 and 40 because pregnancies imposes a cost on the firm and women outside that age bracket are much less likely to become pregnant. And yet, we do feel that these forms of exclusion are precisely the ones we should oppose when we regulate (cf. Chapter 15). So, when addressing the issue of discrimination, the discussion of whether or not a category is a relevant proxy may be part of the equation, but it hardly suffices to establish the moral status of an instance of discrimination. In sum, the reliable proxy argument fails to help us isolate age discrimination because whether or not something is a reliable proxy is often an unnecessary condition for a discrimination to be found wrongful. It may help us understand why we often *feel* differently about age, but it does not provide a sufficient reason to isolate age.

A second (compatible) justification for our special treatment of age could be that race and gender inequalities generally serve a worse purpose. The idea here is that depending on what one is trying to achieve when discriminating, we will be able to determine whether it is wrong or not. We may exclude a group we deem inferior; or we may be trying to achieve a respectable goal: efficiency, security, stability, etc. Consider *Airline 2*. The airline may simply be trying to ensure that its pilots are in perfect physical condition (including good eyesight, good hearing, and good endurance). They know that it will cost them a lot to screen their pilots too often, so they prefer to avoid the age bracket that will require more regular check-ups. The purposes of age discrimination here are security and efficiency. In *Airline 1*, the overt purpose of the discrimination is more trivial than security – it has to do with the professional presentation of the staff. The company accommodates biases to maximize profit, thus serving to reproduce an idea of beauty that is grounded on racial prejudice and white privilege.

The second explanation that age discrimination differs in terms of its purpose does not work as an explanation for what makes age special, though. Age discrimination can be grounded on ageism, just like gender discrimination may serve the sexist purpose of keeping women out. Consider *Airline 2*, for instance. Safety is a serious concern, but the alternative of testing individual workers' ability is available to the company. More importantly, it is just by chance that here age discrimination is justified by efficiency or safety, whereas the race case is not. Gender and race discrimination is in fact also often justified in this manner. Think of the previous example of discrimination in hiring of women aged 20–40, or think of racial profiling – those who argue in favor of these practices defend them on the basis of efficiency or security: in the first case for the companies to avoid costs and in the second case to save on 'un-necessary' stopping of white people, also saving costs. So the basic idea that age may typically serve more justifiable purposes is likely not factually true. In any case, in general, if purpose may matter in deciding whether an instance of age discrimination is tolerable, like relevance, it is not a sufficient condition. The purpose explanation does not set age apart because similar purpose justifications apply to age, gender or race; and because purpose does not seem sufficient, at least on most accounts, to justify discrimination anyway.

Insofar as we are willing to accept some instances of age discrimination, in cases where age is an adequate proxy or in cases where the purpose is noble and important, we are *still* in search of a reason why putting in jeopardy the principle of equal treatment would be acceptable in age cases where it is not for the race and gender equivalent. So what else (if anything) makes age special?

Here is what is truly different about age. Contrary to gender and race, age is not a discrete and immutable feature. As Macnicol (2006) puts it, age is not a club you are born in. We expect to pass through the various stages of a life and old age is a club we know we will most probably join one day. As a result, differential treatment by age does not necessarily generate inequalities between persons over time, whereas treating people differently based on their ethnicity and sex does: "a society that relentlessly discriminates between people on grounds of age can still treat them equally over their complete lives (…). Everyone's turn [at being discriminated against] comes" (Gosseries 2007). At first sight, it might seem like a wrongful discrimination between persons that some rights, such as voting rights, are only granted after a certain age (cf. Chapter 29). However, this is fundamentally different from a case in which women cannot vote, for instance, since age restrictions on voting rights do not treat individuals unequally over time, while sex discrimination does. Over time there is no differential treatment: young and old will have been treated equally with respect to their rights to vote. If we understand persons diachronically (and we do, since we tend to believe in a continuous identity of persons between childhood and old age), then age discrimination is compatible with equal treatment of persons. If there is no differential treatment between persons, then it makes sense to think that there is no wrongful discrimination either.

The fact that age-based differential treatment may not create unequal treatment of diachronic persons still does not give us *reasons* to treat persons differently based on their age. This is where purpose and relevance can be linked back in. Youth profiling by the police, the denial of the right to vote to children, and age rationing for some jobs or healthcare opportunities, can all be justified by appeal to purposes like efficiency or safety. But it is only the fact that those treatments may be compatible with equal treatments of diachronic persons that sets it apart in a morally relevant way from similar cases of discrimination based on gender or race.

There is a particular kind of efficiency that often gives us reasons to treat different age groups differently. I call it lifespan efficiency (Bidadanure 2016). As Norman Daniels (1988) has suggested, we may convert our interpersonal problem of justice between age groups into an intrapersonal procedure where we ask how one would distribute resources to maximize utility over a life course. Some scarce resources may be better distributed early in life (in childhood or young adulthood) even if this means denying your older self some of those resources. Lifespan efficiency may give us good reasons to justify unequal but adapted treatment by age that benefit us all in the long run. Some resources may be better distributed without attention to age membership – either because they are not scarce (voting rights) or because we want to ensure that people have enough of them at any point in their lives. Appealing to this procedure, we may in fact not simply accept synchronic inequalities as long as they do not generate diachronic inequalities; we may in fact have reasons to do so: maximizing well-being over a life course.

Most importantly, we also often have reasons to distribute scarce resources unequally between age groups in order to *ensure* equality between persons over time. Take the example of the youth job guarantee,[3] which aims to protect young people from unemployment in contexts where they risk becoming a comparatively disadvantaged birth cohort in the labor market. Or think of expensive healthcare resources such as organ transplants, which we allocate as a matter of priority to younger patients (all other things being equal) to ensure the general principle that every person gets a chance to live a life of normal length. Here, equal treatment of diachronic persons not only *permits* but may *require* an unequal treatment of synchronic persons (cf. Chapters 10 and 11). These cases are not uncontroversial or unproblematic. But they help us see what makes age special in at least one morally relevant manner. If discrimination is wrongful when it fails to treat people as equals, and if age discrimination is such that it often is compatible with, or required for, an equal treatment of diachronic persons, then it seems like we have a valid reason to think of age discrimination as special.

When age discrimination is demeaning: the case of ageism

Now, we need a theory of discrimination to answer a further question. Age discrimination is special and we have good reason to treat it somewhat more leniently than race and gender discrimination. But which cases of age discrimination are nonetheless wrongful? None? Some? Which ones?

For Hellman (2008), what matters primarily to decide whether a case of discrimination is wrongful is whether a given discrimination is *demeaning* (cf. Chapter 7). The bedrock principle is that discrimination is wrong when it treats some individuals as if they were not equally morally worthy as persons. Humans have an inherent dignity that requires that they be treated with respect. Traits like race, sex, merit, talent or age do not affect this inherent dignity. So the question then becomes, when does differential treatment based on some traits undermine our commitment to this basic principle? Another way to pose this question, Hellman argues, is to ask when discrimination demeans: "To demean is to treat another as not fully human or not of equal moral worth" (Hellman 2008: 35). To demean means to put down and diminish; to degrade or debase another. It is to denigrate with the power (hierarchical or institutional) to do so, even if it fails to achieve that goal.

When do we know whether an instance of discrimination is demeaning and offends the norm of equality? Hellman gives the example of a woman being denied a job by virtue of being a woman, for instance, compared to a case where people are being denied a job because their first name starts with an A. While the latter case may be silly and arbitrary, she argues, the first case is an instance of wrongful discrimination because it denies women the status of equal beings. We know that the two cases are different because there is no history of wrongful treatment of people whose names start with the letter A, whereas there is such history of mistreatment in the case of women. Moreover, women are still members of a disadvantaged group – they are more likely to be victims of violence, whether domestic, in the workplace or in public spaces; they often enjoy inferior socio-economic status and are still not equally politically represented, for instance. This is not the case for people whose names start with an A, so we can see that the exclusion of women is demeaning when the other case is not.

Where does this leave us in terms of our initial project to decide which instances of age discrimination are wrongful? The relevant question here becomes 'can age discrimination be demeaning and if so in what way?' Does our unequal treatment of people by age run afoul of the commitment to honor their equal moral worth? We have already seen that age inequality can be compatible with an equal treatment of persons over time. So perhaps sometimes we can treat people differently at a time without denying their moral worth as diachronic persons. In a paper on age-group justice,[4] I argued that we have egalitarian reasons to be concerned with inequalities between age groups, even if they do not generate diachronic inequalities, insofar as they generate synchronic relational inequalities between people. If elderly people are vulnerable to domination, exclusion, marginalization or demonization, I argued, then the requirements of relational equality are not met. In the context of discrimination, I think that my principle of synchronic relational equality nicely translates into the following principle about age discrimination: even if age discrimination is compatible with diachronic equality in treatment (and does not offend the equal moral worth of diachronic persons), we should refrain from treating people in a way that is demeaning to their synchronic persons too. Just like the fact that women live longer than men on average does not alter the basic fact that unequal pay is demeaning, the fact that unequal treatment by age may even out over time does not amend the fact that a particular age group is systematically treated in a demeaning way.

In practice, identifying which instances of age discrimination actually demean is difficult. Perhaps forbidding children to vote is not demeaning while disenfranchising elderly people is demeaning, for instance; but why? A possible answer can be offered by introducing one particular instance of demeaning age discrimination – age discrimination that is grounded on ageism.

Ageism, Confort argues, "is the notion that people cease to be people, cease to be the same people or become people of a distinct and inferior kind, by virtue of having lived a specified number of years" (Confort in Macnicol 2006: 10). The term 'ageism' was first coined by Robert Butler in the 1960s to describe "a process of systematic stereotyping and discrimination against people because they are old, just as racism and sexism accomplish this for skin color or gender. Older people are characterized as senile, rigid in thought and manner, and old-fashioned in morality and skills" (Butler in Macnicol 2006: 7). Ageism is often implicit and commonly expressed through patronizing and infantilizing treatment of elderly people, who are shown pity but not respect. The aged are lumped together and stereotyped as lacking the qualities that younger people have. They are tarred with the same brush instead of being treated according to their own merits, talents and competences. Ageism exists both at the interpersonal and institutional levels (legal, medical, welfare, political, educational, media etc.).

Age discrimination is often underpinned by crude and negative stereotypes about the aged, which then guide decisions relating to hiring, firing and promotion. As a result, on the labor market, for instance, the 60+ remain overrepresented among the long-term unemployed. If we follow Hellman, whether age is an adequate or a crude proxy for competence is only indirectly relevant if it contributes to a demeaning process. Hellman argues that discrimination is more likely to demean when it targets a member of a group that has a history of mistreatment: "differentiating on the basis of features that define a historically mistreated group or a group that currently occupies a low social position is more likely to demean than doing so on the basis of other features. This is because the history and current status of the group concerned affects the meaning of the distinction drawing" (Hellman 2008: 57). There is no history of lynching and enslavement of elderly people as there is for women and black people, but one only needs to think about the poor law infirmary in Victorian England, where elderly people were segregated in prison-like houses, and the general fact of total destitution that accompanies old age in most of history, for instance, to know that the treatment of elderly people has been abusive too. Currently, old age is also often associated with poverty, loneliness, depression and loss of purpose. On that basis, it is easy to understand how ageist discrimination can demean. If we think that age is partly socially constructed, then elderly people can be more than what we allow them to be. We can avoid the self-fulfilling prophecy that unfolds when older people are segregated and put in a situation where they are under-stimulated or feel like a burden.

Technologies, health, transportation and community life all play important parts in what elderly people are able to be and do.

Moreover, it is important to point out that various forms of exclusion often work together. Sociologists tell us that people may be oppressed or discriminated against because they find themselves at the intersection of various categories. Ageism often works in combination with sexism, for instance. As Macnicol argues, societies often see ageing in women as a process of gradual sexual disqualification, so older women are more likely to experience ageism. Similarly, when Butler coined the concept of ageism, it was in relation to elderly black people being subjected to the hatred of affluent middle aged whites around a housing project. So even though ageism is defined as a distinct kind of prejudiced approach, it often comes with other forms of discriminations (cf. Chapter 5). This is particularly important if we subscribe to Hellman's account of wrongful discrimination as demeaning: if one is excluded as an elderly person and as a woman, for instance, the discrimination is even more likely to be demeaning than if it was only based on ageism.

Because age is special, it may be that using it as a proxy for experience, competence and ability may be less problematic than using gender as a proxy. The fact that discriminatory treatments fall disproportionally on the same groups over time increases the demeaning potential of any given discrimination aimed at members of this group. To understand this, think of cases where black people have to endure a racist joke, or think of women being catcalled. Because the individuals subjected to those treatments have to go through them over and over again, each instance of mistreatment has more power to demean than if it was not persistent over time. Insofar as this is the right way to think about the demeaning potential of discrimination, and because age discrimination does not fall on the same people over time, it is plausible to think that it has less demeaning potential than gender and race discrimination. However, because it does affect people for an important portion of their life, because it tends to happen to groups that are otherwise disadvantaged disproportionally, and because it normalizes widespread negative stereotypes about old age, ageist discrimination should be taken to be a demeaning form of discrimination.

Just like other forms of discrimination, therefore, age discrimination can be wrong when it is demeaning. Whether a particular instance is demeaning or not may depend on many factors. When crude generalizations or stereotypes are used, when the vulnerabilities of an elderly person are ridiculed or taken to be the most important thing about them, the discrimination will be more likely to demean. When age discrimination simply amounts to a differential treatment of different age groups in ways that do not treat an age group in such a stereotypical manner (in a non-ageist manner), it may not be demeaning. For instance, think of the example of *Jobs 1* and *2*, where under conditions of job scarcity, we make age discrimination legal. In *Jobs 1*, we give priority to men on the labor market and in *Jobs 2*, we give priority to young people. We can see that *Jobs 2* is fundamentally different from *Jobs 1* in that (1) it is compatible with equal treatment of persons over time; and (2) may actually promote diachronic fairness by ensuring that new entrants get access to jobs too. What's more, it does not rely on the view that the aged are incompetent or of lower worth. It attempts to distribute a scarce resource between diachronic persons in an equal manner, and so it may not be demeaning.

The wrongness of youth discrimination

Macnicol and Butler mainly describe cases of discrimination that are related to the process of 'ageing'. As a result, they focus primarily on anti-elderly discrimination and they conflate this with age discrimination. Similarly, as we have seen before, Hellman associates quite strongly the question of knowing whether a particular instance of discrimination is demeaning with the question of whether the group that is discriminated against has been dominated and oppressed historically. As a result, she also focuses mainly on ageism and anti-elderly discrimination, and does not discuss the possibility of wrongful youth discrimination. If, as Butler and Macnicol postulate, we live (and have always lived, perhaps) in a youth-centered society – a society that despises ageing and valorizes youth – then we should indeed not worry much about cases where young adults are discriminated against since it is unlikely to be demeaning. Take the example of a white applicant being denied entry at a school and filing a discrimination complaint. Hellman responds: "There is no history of whites qua whites being excluded that gives this interpretation traction. More plausible is the claim that the school's decision demeans blacks because the lowering of standards seems to track the stereotype of blacks as intellectually inferior" (Hellman 2008: 80; cf. Chapter 7). If a form of discrimination does not track a historical exclusion, then it is less likely to demean, and so it may not be a wrongful instance of discrimination.

I worry that this reveals a risk of circularity in Hellman's account – if we have failed to see an inequality as wrongful in the past, and we still fail to recognize some groups as disadvantaged, will we tend to underestimate the extent to which discrimination against them can be demeaning? Young people may not have been historically oppressed and excluded as a group, but they are victims of negative stereotypes and are often set aside in morally dubious manners. They are more likely to be infantilized, patronized and demonized as lazy and violent, and marginalized from the labor market and from political institutions (Devlin 2006; Interparliamentary Union 2014; Chauvel 2010). This should I think urge us to be concerned with discrimination against the young, even if there is no history (or at least no recognized history) of mistreatment of young people.

Hellman uses a telling example involving young people: a case where a one-time landlord refuses to rent a flat to young men. She concludes: "Though the implication of my refusal to rent can surely be read as insulting ("they are going to trash the place") and would-be tenants surely are denied the possibility of renting a house they may like, my action does not demean them" (Hellman 2008: 37). Among the reasons that she gives is the following: "the implication that young men just out of college like to party and do not take good care of possessions does not implicate their equal moral worth – in part because they do not form a group that has been subordinated in our culture" (Hellman 2008: 37). In this example, we are considering a discrimination against young, educated men. But let us now imagine that the landlord refused to rent the place to young people in general, based on the crude generalization that young people will trash the place. I am not sure that we should think of this as acceptable so quickly, drawing on the fact that there is no history of youth oppression. This is especially true when we see that those seemingly unproblematic stereotypes are found in various institutions and have an impact on the opportunities and benefits young people have access to. Indeed, in addition to voting at disproportionately lower rates than other age groups, young people below the age of 30 years old are almost absent from parliaments. This is an objection of limited impact to Hellman since she does not believe that a history of domination is *necessary* for demeaning treatment.

Let me thus take what I take to be a serious example of anti-youth discrimination: the denial of a guaranteed minimum income in France to young adults below the age of 25 years old.[5] This was considered a wrongful discrimination by the French highest discrimination authority (HALDE) in 2009. Hellman interestingly appeals to a very similar case in Québec – *Gosselin v. Québec*. Citizens below the age of 30 years old were denied full social security and the Supreme Court then declared the age-based differential treatment unlawful. One way to respond to those two cases would be to recognize that young people also form a stereotyped group and are denied important social and political rights as a result. The differential treatments in question signify to the young that they are second-class citizens who can't behave, are not sufficiently virtuous and can't be trusted to make good decisions. One natural conclusion here would be to conclude, therefore, that such anti-youth discrimination is demeaning and therefore wrongful. Interestingly, Hellman offers another response. She suggests that in the *Gosselin v. Québec* case, the discrimination may be unjustified for justice-based reasons. On this view, the discrimination may not be demeaning, or therefore wrongful; it may be unjust in that young people were not getting the minimum they deserved. I think this is an awkward move that is made without sufficient justification. When young people are denied an important social right without adequate justification and against a background of marginalization from political and labor institutions, it is natural to worry that discrimination against them can be demeaning.

Conclusion

To recap, age inequalities are in principle compatible with equal treatment of persons over time, and this makes age somewhat special. We often have good reasons to treat age groups differently: to maximize lifespan utility (granting more of some resources to elderly people to bring them to a sufficient level of functioning, or reserving some expensive educational resources for childhood), or to ensure diachronic fairness. But such calculus is only acceptable because it is compatible with equal treatment of diachronic persons. As we saw in Section 2, reasons of efficiency would be far from sufficient to justify differential treatment in other cases. The intuitive sense that age discrimination is special and should be treated as such is thus explained and, at least to some extent, justified. If we follow Hellman's insightful theory of when discriminations are wrong, one may nonetheless object to a range of cases of age-based differential treatment – those that demean. Ageist discrimination, I have argued, is a clear example of age discrimination that has the potential to demean. Youth discrimination, when it is grounded on negative stereotypes of young adults as inadequate citizens who cannot be trusted, I have argued, can also be demeaning and should therefore concern us too. This is especially true in contexts of youth socio-political marginalization.

Notes

1 For a very interesting and detailed discussion of how the European Court of Justice treats age, see Gosseries (2014) and Gosseries and Colla (2013).
2 For more on age group justice see, for instance, Daniels (1988), McKerlie (2013) and Bidadanure (2016).
3 The proposal consists in guaranteeing a job to all young adults under the age of 25 years if they have been unemployed for more than four months.
4 Bidadanure (2016).
5 Bidadanure (2012).

Bibliography

Bidadanure, Juliana. 2012. "Short-sightedness in Youth Welfare Provision: The Case of RSA in France." *Intergenerational Justice Review*. 1(12): 22–28.

Bidadanure, Juliana. 2016. "Making Sense of Age-Group Justice: A Time for Relational Equality?" *Philosophy, Politics & Economics*. 15(3): 234–260.

Chauvel, Louis. 2010. "The Long-Term Destabilization of Youth, Scarring Effects, and the Future of the Welfare Regime in Post-Trente Glorieuses France." *French Politics, Culture & Society* 28(3): 74–96.

Daniels, Norman. 1988. *Am I My Parents' Keeper?* New York: Oxford University Press.

Devlin, Maurice. 2006. *Inequality and the Stereotyping of Young People*. Dublin: The Equality Authority/National Youth Council of Ireland.
Gosseries, Axel. 2014. "What Makes Age Discrimination Special? A Philosophical Look at the ECJ Case Law." *Netherlands Journal of Legal Philosophy* 43(1): 59–80.
Gosseries, Axel, and Colla, Anne-France. 2013. "Discrimination par l'âge et droit transitoire. Réflexions à partir de Commission/Hongrie (C-286/12)." *Journal des tribunaux du travail*. 43: 69–81.
Hellman, Deborah. 2008. *When is Discrimination Wrong?* Cambridge, MA: Harvard University Press.
Interparliamentary Union. 2014. Youth Participation in Parliaments.
Macnicol, John. 2006. *Age Discrimination: An Historical and Contemporary Analysis*. Cambridge: Cambridge University Press.
McKerlie, Dennis. 2013. Justice between the young and the old. Oxford: Oxford University Press.
Sargeant, Malcolm (ed.) 2011. *Age Discrimination and Diversity*. Cambridge: Cambridge University Press.
Sargeant, Malcolm. 2011. "Ageism and Age Discrimination" in *Discrimination and Diversity*. Cambridge: Cambridge University Press.

21

DISCRIMINATION AND IMMIGRATION

José Jorge Mendoza

UNIVERSITY OF MASSACHUSETTS LOWELL

Introduction

For some time now, moral and political philosophers have debated the ethics of immigration. These debates have focused on a wide array of issues that come up when discussing the topic of immigration. Central to this debate has been the question of whether a political community has the presumptive right to exclude non-members who wish to join the community or if commitments to liberal principles—such as universal equality or individual freedom—give immigrants a presumptive right to enter any and all political communities they choose. Keeping in mind that the rights under consideration are mainly thought to be presumptive (meaning that under certain circumstances they can be defeated), a corollary question that has naturally followed from these discussions has been when, or should, these rights be superseded? In response to this question, it has been suggested, both in defense and opposition to immigration, that such overriding situations may include the cases of refugees, natural calamities (e.g., natural disasters or threats of overpopulation), threats of chaos (e.g., terrorism, drug cartels, or social mistrust), and even economic interests (both at the national and international level).

Along these lines, another potentially overriding situation that philosophers have discussed is the concern over discrimination: does the potential for invidious discrimination provide a sufficiently strong reason for suspending a political community's right to control immigration, or even for an individual to lose their right to emigrate? This concern will be the focus of this chapter. In what follows, I will outline what philosophers working on the issue of immigration have had to say about the potential for invidious discrimination, both at the level of official immigration policy and at the level of implementation and enforcement.

The first section of this chapter will look at what philosophers have had to say about direct discrimination, by which I mean discrimination that is explicitly stated in official immigration policy. This section will primarily focus on philosophers who defend a political community's right to control immigration because they have had the harder time dealing with issues of discrimination. The second section will then look at the issue of indirect discrimination, by which I mean cases where the implementation or enforcement of facially "neutral" policies nonetheless targets or favors members of a particular class or has a disparate impact on members of a particular class. This section will focus on the work of philosophers who primarily work on the issue of race, because they are the ones who have taken the issue of indirect discrimination in the immigration context more seriously (cf. Chapter 16). The end goal of this chapter is therefore not necessarily to take sides on any of these debates, but to outline the terrain and provide the reader with an adequate entryway into these philosophical discussions over discrimination and immigration.

Direct discrimination in immigration policy

For the purposes of this chapter, I will refer to direct discrimination as any explicit (i.e., in the letter of the law) favoring or excluding of potential immigrants based on their membership in a particular group or class. Now depending on how groups or classes get defined, it is true that one could easily make the case that any sort of immigration control is by definition discriminatory. After all, any kind of immigration policy (with the possible exception of an open-border policy) seems to give preference to members of certain groups while excluding others. For example, even a completely closed-border policy would appear to give preference to fellow citizens over non-citizen foreigners.

If we are of the opinion that all forms of direct discrimination are inherently unjust, then it would stand to reason that the only appropriate solution to the immigration question would be open borders. This does not necessarily need to follow, however, if we make the assumption—as I will in this chapter—that there are in fact forms of direct discrimination that are not necessarily unjust in themselves (cf. Introduction and Chapter 1). Given this assumption, the primary focus of this section will therefore be on locating and identifying unjustifiable or invidious forms of direct discrimination. In this respect, I believe that there are two ways in which direct discrimination in immigration policy is almost always considered invidious.

The first is when policies explicitly use membership in what today are called protected classes (e.g., race, religion, national origin, sex, sexual orientation, and disability) as a criterion for exclusion. As an example of such a policy we have the now infamous 1882 Chinese Exclusion Act. That act was in effect in the United States up until 1943, and it directly discriminated against Chinese nationals by explicitly denying them entry into the United States. This policy is now roundly condemned as racist for targeting a particular class of persons (i.e., Chinese nationals) who are now considered members of a protected class (either in terms of race or national origin). So even if not all forms of direct discrimination are necessarily unjust, an immigration policy can be considered invidiously discriminatory, and therefore unjust, if it explicitly targets members of a protected class because they are members of that class.

A second way in which an immigration policy can be invidiously discriminatory is when it favors or rewards members of historically advantaged groups, while at the same time not extending those same rewards or opportunities to members of historically disadvantaged groups. For example, Argentina currently places restrictions on immigrants from all over the world with one glaring exception: Europe. The reason for this exception is Article 25 of its constitution, which states explicitly that the government of Argentina may not restrict or burden the migration of Europeans into Argentina. In this case, Argentina's immigration policy is not necessarily excluding members of a protected class, but it is explicitly favoring a group that historically has already enjoyed many advantages in Argentine society, while not extending those same benefits to members of historically disadvantaged groups. Again, even if some forms of direct discrimination can be justified, an immigration policy that explicitly favors historically advantaged groups over historically disadvantaged groups is now widely considered invidiously discriminatory.

I leave it to others in this volume to further explain (or dispute) why the two forms of direct discrimination I have picked out above should (or should not) be considered unjust. For my purposes, it seems sufficient that most philosophers working on the ethics of immigration are in agreement that these two forms of direct discrimination are unjust, and that no account of immigration justice can be satisfactory if it does not avoid or reject them outright or in principle. While philosophers who endorse a more open-borders position have had an easier time dealing with these two forms of invidious direct discrimination—after all, they exclude almost no one and make the benefit of immigration available to everyone—philosophers who endorse a political community's right to control immigration have had a much more difficult time. In the rest of this section, I will outline the source of this difficulty and how some defenders of immigration restrictions have tried to respond. Ultimately, I want to suggest that they do not go far enough because even if their accounts can address invidious forms of direct discrimination, they fail to do so for invidious forms of indirect discrimination, which will be the subject of the second section of this chapter.

Many credit Michael Walzer's *Spheres of Justice* as the starting point for current philosophical debate over immigration. In that book, Walzer put forth a communitarian case for immigration restrictions by arguing that political communities have a vital interest in shaping their collective character and that in order to shape their character they must have control over membership. According to Walzer, the issue of immigration is therefore "a matter of political choice and moral constraint [for political communities]" (Walzer 1983, 62). By that, Walzer meant that the interest a political community has in shaping its character is so important that, with only a few exceptions, it should be free to choose which foreigners it will admit and which it will exclude. Political communities are morally constrained, however, in that once they do admit foreigners they must then extend to them access to full membership. As Walzer notes: "Naturalization ... is entirely constrained: every new immigrant, every refugee taken in, every resident and worker must be offered the opportunities of citizenship" (Walzer 1983, 62). On his account, this is necessary because even the slightest tint of second-class status, which could easily result if some residents were permanently barred from membership, could undermine a political community's claim to legitimacy (i.e., its claim to be democratically self-determined).

Walzer is clear that a political community's right to exclude is only presumptive, meaning that it could possibly be defeated under certain circumstances. The prime example he gives is that of refugees, whom he defines as "needy outsiders whose claims [in justice] cannot be met by yielding territory or exporting wealth [and] can be met only by taking [them] in" (Walzer 1983, 48). He also suggests that there might be cases where a political community must be forced to give up some of its land, such as when they have a surplus but refuse to take in needy outsiders (Walzer 1983, 47). A political community, however, can never be forced to take in non-refugee foreigners as members of their community.

An unfortunate entailment of Walzer's view is that it seems to justify (albeit in a modified version) policies like the infamous "White Australia" policy. For those unfamiliar with this policy, it was a policy in effect in Australia from about 1901–1973. This policy explicitly favored white northern European immigrants and at the same time explicitly discouraged or prevented non-white immigration. To be fair, Walzer does not himself support this policy, but he is forced to recognize that some version of it would be allowable under his account. This is because Walzer bases a political community's right to control immigration on its strong interest in shaping its own character and if a community desires to have a racially or ethnically homogenous character, then it seems that the kind of immigration policy necessary to promote such a character (i.e., an invidiously discriminatory policy) would be permissible on Walzer's account.

For most of us such a policy is simply wrong and we would reject it out of hand, but coming up with a consistent and principled way of rejecting that sort of policy, while still defending a political community's right to control immigration, has proven difficult. David Miller, for example, has tried to temper his own nationalist defense of immigration controls by supplementing his view with the following caveat. Miller believes that characteristics such as race, ethnicity, sex, and gender—traits of what we now consider protected classes—should not be used as criteria for exclusion because "[for immigrants to] be told that they belong to the wrong race, or sex … is insulting, given that these features do not connect to anything of real significance to the society they want to join" (Miller 2005, 204).

While this is a laudable attempt at reconciling anti-discriminatory commitments with a principled support for immigration restrictions, not everyone has found Miller's account very convincing. For example, Christopher Heath Wellman has on this point used Miller's own marriage analogy against him. In defending a political community's right to exclude from the potential charge that it would also deny people the right to exit, Miller had stated that the right to exit is a lot like the right to marry: "where by no means everyone is able to wed the partner they would ideally like to have, but most have the opportunity to marry someone" (Miller 2005, 197). Sticking closely to this analogy, Wellman notes that if it would also be wrong to force racist individuals to marry someone outside of their race, then why is it okay to force a racist political community to admit foreigners belonging to a race they would rather not associate with (Wellman 2008, 138; cf. Chapters 22–23, 30–31)? In other words, if something is a right—like the right to rebuff a marriage proposal or to exclude non-citizen foreigners—why does it matter that those who get rebuffed or excluded (or possibly even a third party) find the reasons for this rejection insulting? Sure, getting rebuffed for reasons that are beyond one's control is always hurtful, but if we stick to the analogy, no one has any more of a presumptive right to be admitted into a political community than they do of forcing someone into marriage.

In this regard, Michael Blake has presented a very interesting and original alternative to Miller's caveat. Blake has argued that: "In all cases in which there are national or ethnic minorities … to restrict [or show preference in] immigration for national or ethnic reasons is to make some citizens politically inferior to others" (Blake 2003, 232–233). In other words, immigration policies that directly discriminate against members of a protected class or favor historically advantaged groups over historically disadvantaged groups should be rejected, not because they are insulting or hurtful to foreigners, but because they undermine the social and civic standing of citizens who also happen to share the race, ethnicity, religion, sex, or gender that is being excluded or being shown disfavor in immigration policy. According to Blake, this is the principled reason why a presumptive right to control immigration does not necessarily entail a right to invidiously discriminate in immigration policy. If the right to control immigration is derived from a political community's democratic self-determination, and if democratic self-determination is threatened when some segments of the citizenry come to occupy a kind of second-class status, then an immigration policy that invidiously discriminates should be rejected as self-defeating.

Up to now, Blake's argument has been the best response defenders of a political community's right to control immigration have been able to produce in an effort to address the problem of invidious discrimination. This argument, however, is not without some drawbacks. First, it seems to come undone in cases where a political community is already homogenous or where certain groups are not represented. As Wellman has stated in response to Blake: "If [hypothetically] all Australians were of European descent … then no existing Australians would [on Blake's account] be treated as second class citizens by an immigration policy that excluded all non-Europeans" (Wellman 2011, 149). One possible counter-response might be to say that in the real world no political communities are literally homogenous. This, however, would seem to be dependent at best on current realities, but would not be an unconditional response to Wellman's objection.

A second objection is that direct discrimination against a protected class or historically disadvantaged group might actually be necessary in order to obtain other more important forms of justice. For example, in the case of global "brain drain," where the best and brightest of a depressed region of the world (e.g., the Global South) immigrate in large numbers to more affluent regions of the world (e.g., the Global North). This usually occurs because countries in the affluent region give preferences in their immigration policies to "skilled" immigrants, but this is not the only reason skilled professionals decide to move from depressed regions of the world—where their skills are desperately needed—to regions where their skills are less urgently needed, but still in demand. Nonetheless, the loss of skilled professionals, such as doctors, has led to abysmal conditions in many poor countries and this has disproportionally harmed those who, globally speaking, are already the least well off. For these reasons, Peter Higgins and Gillian Brock have argued that restrictions (both in the sense of entering and exiting) should be placed on professionals attempting to migrate from regions like the Global South—which historically have been the most disadvantaged regions and whose members primarily belong to what we would consider protected classes—to historically more advantaged regions like the Global North (Brock and Blake 2015, 11–107; Higgins 2015). In other words, there might be good reasons for justifying exclusions in immigration policy (and also denying some people the right to exit) that, at least on the surface, seem like invidious forms of discrimination.

Various philosophers have challenged the veracity and legitimacy of responding to brain drain through the use of discriminatory restrictions, but most of these responses either begin from an open-borders position or seek to dispute the claim that political communities have a presumptive right to control immigration (Oberman 2013; Sager 2014; Mendoza 2015a). This means that they tell us very little about whether, in theory, a political community's right to control immigration could be made compatible with the kinds of anti-discriminatory commitments that are now commonly accepted.

Indirect discrimination in immigration policy

Given that most countries today try to avoid explicitly invidious forms of discrimination in their immigration policy, the use of indirect methods of discrimination has now become a much more important topic of discussion within the immigration debate. By indirect methods I have in mind two sorts of cases. The first involves an intention to discriminate, but where the desired outcome must be masked because it can no longer be obtained through direct means. The second does not require any sort of intention, but can be driven solely by the implicit or unconscious biases of individuals or the inertia of institutions that continue to produce systematic forms of invidious discrimination.

For the purposes of this chapter, we will therefore say that immigration policy indirectly discriminates when the policy is facially neutral, meaning it does not explicitly discriminate according to the letter of the law, but where either (a) this facially neutral criterion is covertly used to target members of a protected class or unfairly benefit members of historically advantaged groups or (b) this facially neutral criterion has a disparate impact that leads to a similar discriminatory outcome—even when that outcome was not the intention of the policymakers or enforcers (cf. Chapter 2). Most philosophers working on the ethics of immigration have not given indirect discrimination serious consideration in their work. This is a blind spot in the literature that only recently has been pointed out (Mendoza 2014; Fine 2016). Fortunately, philosophers who work on the issue of race have paid attention to indirect discrimination in the context of immigration, so we turn primarily to their work in this section.

Indirect discrimination in the immigration context can occur in two distinct places: in how a policy gets implemented, and how it gets enforced. By implementation, I have in mind the way official policy gets actualized in the real world. In other words, who or which groups ultimately are granted official permission to enter the country and which are denied entry. Enforcement, on the other hand, has to do with the entire coercive apparatus that a state has at its disposal to prevent or remove foreigners who have not been granted official permission to enter or remain in the country. Unlike with the implementation of a policy—which is where the pools of potential and precluded immigrants officially get determined—enforcement has to do instead with determining where and on whom a state's coercive apparatus will be focused. In both cases, indirect discrimination can be intentional, meaning it is motivated by something like ill will or favoritism, or it can be unintentional, meaning it is propelled largely by the implicit biases of individuals or the inherent structures underlining institutions. In neither case, however, is the discrimination explicit.

In *The Huddled Masses Myth*, Kevin Johnson provides an excellent summary of how, throughout much of the twentieth century, the United States excluded immigrants not just on the basis of race, class, sex, or sexual orientation—grounds that are now considered classic examples of invidious direct discrimination—but also on the basis of being either "criminals" (e.g., gangsters or prostitutes), "political subversives" (e.g., communists or anarchists), or people with "infectious diseases" (e.g., people with HIV or AIDS). Exclusions based on membership in groups like the former are now loathed by most liberal democracies, but exclusions based on membership in categories like the latter often are not. For most people, there appears to be nothing inherently wrong with an immigration policy that discriminates against non-protected classes of people, especially when it's done for the sake of protecting the health and well-being of its citizens or maintaining social and political stability. These sorts of exceptions become problematic, however, when they are used merely as proxies for the more invidious forms of discrimination. In other words, when the real motivation behind supposedly "neutral" exclusions is to keep out people of certain races, ethnicities, or of a certain sex or sexual orientation.

In *The Biopolitics of Race*, Sokthan Yeng suggests that something like this is at work in liberal democracies today. She suggests that because maintaining national health and social welfare are considered laudable goals for states to pursue, discriminatory criteria in immigration policy that appears to meet these goals is not immediately recognized as being problematic. Yeng believes that these sorts of exclusions in immigration policy are really only proxies through which bigots covertly smuggle in their racist, sexist, or homophobic agendas. For example, immigration policies can be drafted to exclude people who are "likely to be a burden on the economy" or that are "likely to pose a terrorist threat." These exclusions do not on the surface seem unreasonable to most people, especially since they make no explicit reference to race, ethnicity, sex, sexual orientation, or even national origin, but those who craft this policy are fully cognizant that the way these exclusions will be implemented is such that they will virtually have the same effect as a policy that explicitly discriminates against members of protected classes. In other words, it is understood that in practice these sorts of "neutral" exclusions will have the effect of disproportionately denying official entry to women, members of the LGBTQ community and people from certain parts of the world (e.g., Latin America or the Middle East).

Indirect discrimination can also occur unintentionally. For example, when the US implemented its 1965 Immigration and Nationality Act it did so as part of a larger effort to end centuries of invidious discrimination in the US. In other words, this immigration reform was motivated by anti-discriminatory sentiments that at the time were sweeping the nation (e.g., the Civil Rights Movement). The implementation of this policy, however, had different effects than the policymakers had foreseen. The designers of this policy were guided, maybe naïvely, by the belief that the last vestiges of invidious discrimination in US immigration policy could be removed if the national origin quotas were repealed and replaced with yearly numerical caps that gave every country the same number of visas (1965 Immigration and Nationality Act). In theory, this policy would treat every country the same and in doing so would no longer advantage or disadvantage potential immigrants based on their national origin.

The implementation of this policy, however, had different and unintended consequences. First, in treating all countries the same, despite their obvious differences in size, immigrants from much smaller countries (e.g., Finland and Denmark) gained a competitive advantage in admissions over immigrants from much larger countries (e.g., China and India). As it just so happens to be, most smaller countries were also countries that historically had been favored in previous US immigration policies, while the larger countries tended to be those that historically had been disadvantaged in US immigration policies. Second, this policy ignored important social–historical differences that led to or were the cause of why some countries (e.g., Norway) had less demand for US visas while other countries (e.g., Mexico) had acquired more of a demand. Given the social–historical situation in 1965, the policy of evenly distributed numerical caps did not have much of an effect on potential immigrants from what turned out to be largely "white" countries, but it did have an adverse effect on the prospects of potential immigrants from what turned out to be largely "non-white" countries (Mendoza 2015b).

These examples represent the ways in which facially neutral immigration policies can, when *implemented*, indirectly discriminate in an invidious manner. They are not, however, the only ways in which immigration policies can indirectly discriminate. Immigration policies can also indirectly discriminate in how they get *enforced*. The enforcement of immigration policies can intentionally, although covertly, be used as a pretext for harassing minority groups without the obvious tinge of bigotry. In these sorts of cases, facially neutral categories like "legal status" can be used as a kind of stand-in or proxy for something more nefarious like race or ethnicity. The enforcement of immigration policies can also unintentionally discriminate when it, either because of the unconscious biases of officers or institutionalized prejudices of the agencies, has a disparate impact on minority or already disadvantaged groups.

Grant J. Silva and Carlos Alberto Sánchez have made arguments along the lines of the former, suggesting that for the sake of enforcement, terms like "illegal alien" function not so much as terms of art, but as proxies that hide the true discriminatory intentions of immigration enforcers (Silva 2015). As Sánchez points out, even when the official guidelines for enforcement make no mention of race or ethnicity (and even when discrimination was not the intention of policymakers), in reality the biases or ill will of enforcement agents can often lead to discriminatory results.

> Who is to be harassed, abused, and attacked by [immigration enforcement]? [Answer:] Anyone who might be an illegal alien, that is, "where reasonable suspicion exists that the person is an alien who is unlawfully present in the United States." The question, of course, is: what constitutes "reasonable suspicion"? The reasonable thing to say to this question is that reasonable suspicion is grounded on any sort of suspicious behavior. But if the person is not acting "suspiciously" given the context in which she finds herself, then how is this law to be enforced? The person enforcing such laws must appeal to their own better judgment and rely on established beliefs about how "illegal aliens" act and who they are—this, as a matter of official duty. The enforcer must appeal to criteria which necessarily include racial, cultural, linguistic, and ethnic filters. As such, everyone captured by such filters is under suspicion.
>
> *(Sánchez 2011)*

In the sorts of cases highlighted in the work of Silva and Sánchez, the connection between biased enforcers and invidious discrimination is clear and easy to identify. In these cases, discrimination might not be part of the official policy (i.e., there is no direct discrimination in the letter of the law), but the enforcers of this policy, who are motivated by racial or ethnic prejudice, use facially neutral terms like "illegal alien" as a kind of stand-in or "dog whistle" for race and ethnicity that can be picked up by other fellow racists or xenophobes even when largely inaudible to the rest of the population (Silva 2015, 73–74).

Indirect discrimination in enforcement also does not need to be intentional. Given that the resources devoted to enforcing laws are always finite, it is understandable that agencies look for ways to make their use of resources as efficient as possible. In the case of immigration enforcement, this has meant focusing on areas that are more likely to yield higher capture rates. It is also a fact about the world that communities in which members of minority groups predominantly live and workplaces where members of minority groups are predominantly employed are also areas where there is a higher percentage of undocumented immigrants. It is therefore easy to see why, even when immigration agents are not motivated by ill will or prejudice, minority groups can still be disproportionately subjected to more intense scrutiny by immigration enforcement. For this reason some have argued that this kind of intense scrutiny can lead to a violation of basic liberties and can socially stigmatize citizens and permanent residents that live and work in those areas. The end result is that certain segments of the citizenry, by being treated or branded as perpetual foreigners, are wrongfully discriminated against (Mendoza 2014; Mendoza 2016; Reed-Sandoval 2016).

Given the different possible ways in which an immigration policy can indirectly discriminate, it is not surprising that there are also various (and at times competing) proposals for how to diagnose and respond to this kind of invidious discrimination. One approach, which I see as championed by Yeng, Silva, and Sánchez, is to see indirect discrimination as merely a covert extension of direct discrimination. On this view, discrimination based on race, ethnicity, national origin, sex, gender, or disability might no longer be socially acceptable, but the discriminatory attitudes and beliefs of individuals and of the state in general remain deeply engrained and get cashed out in non-explicit ways, either in the implementation or enforcement of so-called "neutral" immigration policies. On this view, indirect discrimination is the result of a racist, xenophobic, sexist, ableist, or heteronormative society. This implies that the best way to combat invidious indirect discrimination is not through a more "neutral" policy, but by combating the racism, xenophobia, sexism, ableism, and heteronormativity in society head-on.

One difficulty with this sort of view is that it seems hard pressed to account for indirect discrimination that is not consciously or intentionally motivated. Earlier I brought up the example of the 1965 US immigration reform act. That act was intended to end discrimination in US immigration policy and for a lot of ethnic groups (e.g., Irish, Italian, Polish, and Jewish Americans) it did just that. Ironically, one group that historically benefited from prior US immigration policies, Mexican nationals, were disadvantaged by the 1965 reform. Before 1965 the US had terribly racist immigration policies with respect to most of the world, but at the same time it had an open-border policy with countries in the western hemisphere (which included Mexico). After 1965, the US started to cap immigration from every country at 20,000 immigrants per year. As mentioned already, this cap appeared neutral, but as the historian Mai Ngai explains, it had some unintended and unfortunate consequences for Mexican nationals when it was implemented:

> The imposition of a 20,000 annual quota on Mexico recast Mexican migration as "illegal." When one considers that in the early 1960s annual "legal" Mexican migration comprised some 200,000 braceros and 35,000 regular admissions for permanent residency, the transfer of migration to "illegal" form should have surprised no one. The number of deportations of undocumented Mexicans increased by 40 percent in 1968 to 151,000 … [by 1976] the

> INS expelled 781,000 Mexicans from the United States. Meanwhile, the total number of apprehensions for all others in the world, *combined*, remained below 100,000 a year.
> (*Ngai 2004, 261*)

In short, because of the immigration reform of 1965, Mexican nationals went from comprising one of the largest groups of newly arriving "legal" immigrants to the US, to becoming the largest segment of the undocumented immigrant population.

The implementation of this policy had indirect discriminatory affects on people of Mexican origin, even if that was not the intention of policymakers. It also had a further indirect discriminatory affect when the policy was enforced. After 1965 the Mexican-American community (and the Latin American community in general) began to experience a process similar to racial profiling (cf. Chapter 27). Since most undocumented immigrants were now coming from Mexico, people with even the slightest hint of Mexican nationality came to be regarded as somehow more likely to be unlawfully present. This profiling practice was upheld in two Supreme Court cases. In the 1975 case of *United States v. Brignoni-Ponce* the court ruled that roving border patrol agents could not stop people solely for "appearing Mexican," but that because of the recent spike in undocumented immigration from Mexico, "Mexican appearance" could be used as one of the relevant factors for such stops (*United States v. Brignoni-Ponce* 1975; Johnson 2004, 30–31). A year later the Supreme Court ruled that referring a car to secondary inspection based solely on a "Mexican appearance" of the driver was warranted and not in violation of the constitution. Again, this was because of the recent increase in undocumented immigration from Mexico (*United States v. Martinez-Fuerte* 1976).

What the case of Mexican-Americans in the US shows is that it is not just bigoted attitudes that motivate invidious indirect discrimination, but the implementation and enforcement of immigration policy, when it does not pay sufficient enough attention to socio-historical realities, can also produce invidiously discriminatory results that then engender bigoted views about certain groups, which might not have necessarily existed before. In other words, discriminatory immigration policy is not just the result of bigotry, but can also cause bigotry. Falguni Sheth has argued for something along these lines in suggesting that categories like "race" need to be thought of less as biological or social constructions and more as products of legal and political structures that seek to divide and pit groups against one another (Sheth 2009). In these sorts of cases, it is therefore not enough to combat what might merely turn out to be symptoms (e.g., racism, xenophobia, sexism, ableism, or heteronormativity), but instead we must get at the larger causes (e.g., capitalism, liberalism, or nativism) that give rise to these forms of invidious discrimination.

Conclusion

Given all the terrain that has been covered, it might be good to conclude by summarizing some of the key takeaways of this chapter. First, it should be made clear that virtually no philosopher endorses any form of invidious discrimination, which I have generally defined as discrimination against members of protected classes (e.g., race, religion, national origin, sex, sexual orientation, or disability) or that favors members of historically advantaged groups, while not extending those same benefits to members of historically disadvantaged groups. Second, it remains unclear whether proponents of a political community's right to exclude can consistently reject every immigration policy that contains some form of invidious direct discrimination. Third, even if that were possible, most of these philosophers have not given the potential for invidious indirect discrimination serious consideration. However, the bulk of philosophers who work on the issue of immigration from a philosophy of race perspective have, by focusing on how so-called "neutral" immigration polices get implemented and enforced. Lastly, within this literature there is a split between those who place more of an emphasis on indirect discrimination that intentionally uses facially "neutral" criteria as a veiled or roundabout way of targeting or favoring members of a particular group and those that worry that facially "neutral" criteria will, regardless of the intentions of policymakers and enforcers, have a disparate impact on certain groups because of such unconscious things as implicit biases or institutionalized prejudices. With that said, there is no reason to believe that these two approaches are mutually exclusive. They could in theory be used in tandem, although typically one or the other is given priority.

Bibliography

1965 Immigration and Nationality Act, H.R. 2580; Pub.L. 89-236; 79 Stat. 911. 89th Cong., 2nd sess., (October 3, 1965).

Blake, M. 2003. "Immigration." In Frey, R. G. and Wellman, C. H. (eds), *A Companion to Applied Ethics*. Oxford: Blackwell Publishing: 224–237.

Brock, G. and Blake, M. 2015. *Debating Brain Drain: May Governments Restrict Emigration?* New York: Oxford University Press.

Fine, S. 2016. "Immigration and Discrimination." In Fine, S. and Ypi, L. (eds), *Migration in Political Theory: The Ethics of Movement and Membership*. New York: Oxford University Press.

Higgins, P. 2013. *Immigration Justice*. Edinburgh: Edinburgh University Press.

Johnson, K. 2004. *The Huddled Masses Myth: Immigration and Civil Rights*. Philadelphia: Temple University Press.

Mendoza, J. 2014. "Discrimination and the Presumptive Rights of Immigrants." *Critical Philosophy of Race*. 2(1): 68–83.

Mendoza, J. 2015a. "Does Cosmopolitan Justice Ever Require Restrictions on Migration?" *Public Affairs Quarterly*. 29(2): 175–186.

Mendoza, J. 2015b. "Latino/a Immigration: A Refutation of the Social Trust Argument." In Bauder, H. and Matheis, C. (eds), *Migration Policy and Practice: Interventions and Solutions*. New York: Palgrave Macmillan: 37–57.

Mendoza, J. 2016. *The Moral and Political Philosophy of Immigration: Liberty, Security, and Equality*. Blue Ridge Summit, PA: Lexington Books.

Miller, D. 2005. "Immigration: The Case for Limits." In Cohen, A. I. and Wellman, C. H. (eds), *Contemporary Debates in Applied Ethics*. Malden, MA: Blackwell Publishing: 193–206.

Ngai, M. 2004. *Impossible Subjects: Illegal Aliens and the Making of Modern America*. Princeton, NJ: Princeton University Press.

Oberman, K. 2013. "Can Brain Drain Justify Immigration Restrictions?" *Ethics*. 123(3): 427–455.

Reed-Sandoval, A. 2016. "Locating the Injustice of Undocumented Migrant Oppression." *Journal of Social Philosophy*. 47(4): 374–398.

Sager, A. 2014. "Reframing the Brain Drain." *Critical Review of International Social and Political Philosophy*. 17(5): 560–579.

Sánchez, C. 2011. "On Documents and Subjectivity: The Formation and De-Formation of the Immigrant Identity." *Radical Philosophy Review*. 14(2): 197–205.

Sheth, F. 2009. *Toward a Political Philosophy of Race*. Albany: SUNY Press.

Silva, G. 2015. "Embodying a 'New' Color Line: Racism, Anti-Immigrant Sentiment and Racial Identities in the 'Postracial' Era." *Knowledge Cultures*. 3(1): 65–90.

United States v. Brignoni-Ponce, 422 U.S. 873 (1975).

United States v. Martinez-Fuerte, 428 U.S. 543 (1976).

Walzer, M. 1983. *Spheres of Justice: A Defense of Pluralism and Equality*. New York: Basic Books.

Wellman, C. 2008. "Immigration and Freedom of Association." *Ethics*. 119: 109–141.

Wellman, C. and Cole, P. 2011. *Debating the Ethics of Immigration: Is There a Right to Exclude*? New York: Oxford University Press.

Yeng, S. 2013. *Biopolitics of Race: State Racism and U.S. Immigration*. Blue Ridge Summit, PA: Lexington Books.

22
DISCRIMINATION AND OBESITY

Garrath Williams

UNIVERSITY OF LANCASTER

Introduction

The fat activist Marilyn Wann has said, 'The only thing that anyone can diagnose, with any certainty, by looking at a fat person, is their own level of stereotype and prejudice toward fat people' (in Rothblum and Solovay 2009: xiv). In this chapter I argue that even if – as popular prejudice suggests – it were possible to draw other inferences from the amount of body fat a person carries, this would do nothing to justify discrimination.

In the first section, I briefly indicate the evidence for widespread discrimination against obese people in modern developed societies, and note some debates about appropriate language. In the second section, I highlight some distinctive features of obesity as a ground of discrimination. Most importantly, weight bias is still widely acceptable, and its justifications find institutional support insofar as medicine stresses that obesity is bad and, perhaps, remediable. This brings us to some facts about health and obesity, which are too often simplified in public discussions. I then turn to the wrong of obesity-based discrimination. I argue that the standard rationalisations are untenable, and not only because their factual premises are so dubious. Philosophically, they rest on illiberal confusions about the appropriate place for personal judgments. In our private lives, we may well respond to others on the basis of their body shape or our personal estimates of their virtues or abilities. (Just as they may respond to us in their turn!) When we engage in different forms of civil association, however, anti-discrimination provisions remind us what is, and what is not, 'our business.' They thereby help to uphold norms of equality, freedom and respect.

Background and terminology

Discrimination on the grounds of a person's body weight – or more specifically, the amount of body fat he or she is perceived to carry – is ubiquitous in modern Western societies (Crandall *et al.* 2009; Puhl *et al.* 2015). It belongs to the social attitudes and relations of almost every group, from very young children to adults who pride themselves on their freedom from prejudice. Bullying, exclusion and discrimination are found throughout school systems (Puhl 2011). Discrimination affects job prospects and earnings; it occurs in workplaces of every sort (Rudolph *et al.* 2009). It affects health care: many studies testify to the prejudicial attitudes and inferior care that obese people experience (Phelan *et al.* 2015). Many public and commercial facilities do not serve obese people well – seating or aisles or other facilities may be ill-suited, attractive clothing is hard to find, some forms of insurance may be more expensive or denied. In social interactions, fatter people are often excluded and marginalised, and may face greater difficulties in finding a partner. Some evidence suggests that prejudice and discrimination have worsened in the past few decades (Andreyeva *et al.* 2008). Moreover, the distribution of obesity intersects with other forms of disadvantage, including race and class (McLaren 2007; Chapter 5). Discrimination against fatter women tends to be more severe (Fikkan and Rothblum 2011).

This discrimination occurs against the background of a steady increase in rates of obesity. This has happened most markedly in the US since about 1975; it also affects most other developed countries, and increasingly developing countries too. (See NCD Risk Factor Collaboration 2016 and the graphic representation by Galka 2016.) The causes are still not wholly clear, but all authors agree on one central factor. Our food systems have shifted toward commodity crops (wheat, corn, soy, sugar, oils) and factory-farmed animal products. Commerce drives relentless promotion of calorie-dense processed foods based on these ingredients (Bleich *et al.* 2008).

As with other prejudicial ways of categorising people, the appropriate language is contested. 'Obesity' is a medical term, standardly defined either as body mass index over $30kg/m^2$, or as 'abnormal or excessive fat accumulation that may impair health' (WHO 2016). There are well-known problems in using BMI as an index of fatness (Okorodudu 2010). Definitions of 'normality' are never neutral, while 'excess' is a relative term and the health consequences of extra body fat are less clear than we are often told. Moreover, the medical profession has a sad record of discriminating on the grounds of weight and body shape. For these reasons, some authors reject the word. There are attempts to reclaim the word 'fat' (as in 'fat activism' and 'fat studies' [Rothblum and Solovay 2009; Cooper 2010]) or to find less loaded terms (perhaps 'heavy' or 'plus size'), as well as to separate the condition from the person (so: 'person with obesity' rather than 'obese person'). These efforts and debates are bound to continue. In the absence of agreement on acceptable alternatives, I will speak of both 'obesity' and 'fatness.' I will also use the now-standard (if euphemistic) term 'weight bias' to describe attitudes and actions that are prejudicial to fatter people.

Some distinctive aspects of obesity

Obesity provides one of the clearest examples of discrimination on the grounds of individual bodily features. 'Race' is generally caught up with family and cultural identities; religion is usually visible by conventional signs or observances; sexual identities must be signalled. Even sex is apparent largely to the extent that people adopt gendered cultural markers or emphasise sexed aspects of the body. Obesity belongs to the body and it cannot be hidden.

At the same time, obesity provides none of the consolations of shared fate. Attempts to foster solidarity among obese persons, as in fat activism, have so far reached only a small number of people. Many fatter people have struggled, and may struggle throughout their lives, with shame and body dissatisfaction (Schwartz *et al.* 2006).

Moreover, obesity is rendered painfully visible by our image-conscious societies. Whole industries promote ideals of the slim or muscular human body. Except in protest against these unrealistic norms, no one represents the fatter body as desirable or normal. In the mainstream media, we mostly see pictures of 'headless fatties' (Charlotte Cooper's [2007] phrase nicely captures the pejorative force of such images) or, worse still, slim actors in 'fat suits' who portray obesity as ridiculous.

As this suggests, the continued social acceptability of obesity discrimination is striking. One index of its acceptability is how few jurisdictions have prohibited discrimination on the grounds of body weight (Michigan is the only state to do so in the US: Puhl and Heuer 2010: 1025). Obesity is not a disability, except at its extremes; most obese people cannot, therefore, claim the protection of disability discrimination law (e.g. Court of Justice of the European Union 2014; cf. Chapter 19).

The acceptability of weight bias is also shown by widespread stereotypes of fatter people as lazy, lower in intelligence, slovenly, greedy and lacking in self-control. Of course, every form of unjust prejudice is accompanied by *rationalisations* – that is, putative justifications that do not withstand scrutiny. Racism involves the attribution of innate deficiencies and character flaws, for example, while sexism is inseparable from stereotypes that denigrate women. Such ideas are no longer acceptable in most spheres of Western societies, but rationalisations for weight bias remain current.

They are supported by two widely-held beliefs: first, that obesity is unhealthy; and second, that it is subject to individual control. Combining these two claims, it follows (more or less) that fatter people are choosing to damage their health and impose costs on others, for example in terms of sick leave and health care costs. Such ideas gain credibility by their association with some of the most prestigious institutions of our societies: medicine and science. Daily news headlines relate obesity to ill-health, often prompted by the 'latest research.' Many magazines feature regular advice on how to lose fat or 'get in shape.' An immense diet industry also contributes, since its profitability depends on beliefs that fatness is bad and can be reduced.

Unlike other chapters in this collection, then, one regrettable task of this chapter is to tackle the rationalisations for stigma and discrimination. I will first say a word about obesity, health and weight loss, since this factual background is often misrepresented. I then turn to some normative problems with these rationalisations.

Health, harm and control of body weight

Obesity might be considered naturally discriminatory, so to speak. Human physiology means that body fat has adverse implications for health. Thus the WHO definition quoted above: 'excessive fat accumulation that may impair health.' These assumptions are less well-grounded than we usually assume.

There is clear evidence that obesity is *correlated* with a range of health problems, such as type II diabetes and cardiovascular disease. At severe levels, where mobility and physical fitness are impaired, the health risks are incontrovertible. Before this point, however, the correlations are not stark. With 'overweight,' people's longevity is not markedly less than for 'normal weight.' With obesity, rates of premature death start to increase, but it is a matter of judgment how severely one evaluates the risks. A recent study synthesised data on 900,000 adults aged 35–89. It found that the risk of death doubles at BMI in the range 37.5–40kg/m^2 (considerably higher than the 30kg/m^2 threshold for obesity), as against the range with the lowest risk of death, BMI 22.5–25kg/m^2.[1]

Correlations do not tell us about causality, however. To what extent is 'excess' fat actually the cause of ill-health and early death, and how far is deliberate weight loss possible or healthy? It is well-established that quite obese people can be physically fit and healthy in terms of various metabolic markers, such as blood pressure or insulin resistance (Phillips 2013). Conversely, quite thin people can eat badly, take too little exercise, and suffer various metabolic problems associated with obesity. Hence the position of 'Health At Every Size' advocates (Bacon 2010): we all have reasons to keep physically active and eat a healthy diet, but doing these things may or may not lead to weight loss. In any case, we should not value weight loss as such – partly because we should repudiate our culture's thin ideal and the body dissatisfaction and discrimination that come with it, and partly because many methods of weight loss, or repeated weight loss and regain, may damage health (not to mention enjoyment!).

This line of thinking is compatible with another argument, one too rarely made. Adverse discrimination, prejudice and shame not only spoil people's lives; they are themselves detrimental to health. Some research points to their role in causing increases in body weight (Vartanian and Porter 2016). (Compare one rationalisation for stigma, that it encourages fat people to lose weight: Callahan 2013.) There has been much less research as to how far weight bias causes ill-health. But we know that stigma and discrimination are major stressors and cause profound misery; more generally, we know that lower social status is damaging to health. To an extent not yet known, the health risks are caused not by obesity but by weight bias (Muennig 2008).

It is easy to find superficial support for the idea that individuals can control their body weight. The historical emergence of obesity shows that fewer people would be obese if social and economic conditions were different. Every person will lose weight (fat *and* muscle) if starved. Many of us have gained or lost some body fat by changing our diets, or perhaps by exercising more or less.

Nonetheless, one individual cannot alter our social and economic systems, and human physiology is remarkably variable. Energy intake and expenditure, appetite regulation, the metabolism of fat deposit and use – all are extremely complex. Variations in these mechanisms mean that different people have different weight 'set-points,' a relatively small range beyond which it is extremely hard to lose (or gain) weight. Obesogenic chemicals and some pharmaceutical drugs (such as the Pill or some anti-depressants) seem to increase this set-point; age and hormonal changes (such as menopause) can do the same (McAllister *et al.* 2009). Prolonged dieting may also damage the mechanisms involved, as the body responds by eking out fat deposits as long as possible.

Bearing out these claims, the track record of interventions to guide or assist people in losing body fat is poor. In general, it seems that only modest reductions are possible without surgery (Dombrowski *et al.* 2014). Most obese people have repeatedly attempted to lose weight, and found that initial success is followed by weight regain. The prevalence of this pattern and the physiological factors that cause it (Greenway 2015) suggest that, for many people, it is not possible to achieve sizeable reductions in body weight by changes in behaviour (Ochner *et al.* 2015). At the individual level, however, initial success may reinforce the sense that control is possible, while later 'relapse' may support the sense that lack of self-control is to blame.

Overall, it is clear that maintaining leanness or losing body fat are much more difficult and painful for some people than others. I have stressed variations in individual physiology. Bearing in mind how obesity tends to intersect with other forms of disadvantage, we might also recall the varying conditions that people face in their everyday lives. Obviously, wealth and status tend to give people more control over these conditions. Disadvantage does the opposite.

Approaching the wrong of obesity discrimination

Our assessment of the wrongness of obesity discrimination will depend, in large part, on how seriously we take the rationalisations for these practices. Perhaps the most trenchant way to understand the wrong is as simply one more form of appearance-based discrimination. No surprise that, like other forms of prejudice, it has rationalisations and defenders. But we should take these no more seriously than claims that some races are more or less intelligent than others. Treating people differently on the basis of body fat is a basic failure of equality; not to make suitable accommodations for different body sizes is a basic failure of respect. Failing to acknowledge bodily diversity and bodily vulnerability fosters an unjust status hierarchy based on disgust. Any supporting reasoning is corrupt and does not dignify a reply. The important question is what sorts of legal measures and social activism can overcome the discrimination and underlying attitudes.

I have much sympathy for this view. As mentioned, however, the currency and credibility of the rationalisations is remarkable. They have weighty institutional anchors, in the form of the medical profession, scientific research, and the media that convey (no doubt simplified versions of) their claims to an audience that already idealises leanness and youth. Anyone convinced that our societies seriously wrong fatter people must also be curious how popular framings ignore the burden of stigma and discrimination facing obese people, and instead figure obesity as a burden on the body politic. And curious too, that the association between obesity and ill-health generates so little empathy for fatter people, and instead rationalises attitudes and practices that make their situation much worse.

This moral perversity is interesting in itself. Understanding it is surely important to effective challenge, even if one would prefer not to fight a purely rearguard battle. But I also think that the normative structure of the rationalisations can teach us an important lesson about the meaning of equality and mutual respect. Setting aside their empirical problems, the rationalisations cannot justify discrimination: they fail to respect the separation of spheres that is central to liberal societies. The purported concern for others is free-floating and irresponsible; the assumed moral authority proves intrusive and malign.

Obesity as a matter of personal responsibility

Let me state frankly the central rationalisations for obesity discrimination: *Obese people show a lack of self-control and individual responsibility; they are blameworthy and bring adverse consequences upon themselves; their needs do not call for accommodations in public and civic life; they do not merit anti-discrimination safeguards; to the extent that collective arrangements support their health needs, they impose a burden on society.*

There are many lines of argument one might offer against this mindset. One strategy is to point out the complexity of the facts. As noted above, individual physiology varies; control over body weight is very limited; body fat does not necessarily cause ill-health. Relatedly, one might argue that the causal processes are economic and systemic. Widespread obesity emerges alongside commercial food systems involving commodity agriculture and factory farming; hence obesity is not an individual failing but a social product. Another route would be to examine the psychology of weight bias. Over and over again, psychologists find that its core motivation lies in feelings of disgust (e.g. Vartanian *et al.* 2016). Even if the above rationalisations had some validity, we ought to repudiate the underlying animus.

These arguments are important, although each has its limits. In the remainder of this chapter, however, I want to pursue a more philosophical argument: that judgments of personal responsibility play no defensible role in justifying discrimination or the collective failure to prohibit discrimination (cf. Chapter 18). More colloquially: even if one holds that many obese people could lose some body fat and give more priority to their long-term health – well, *so what?* How could this warrant negative responses to those persons?

One initial point is sociological. Alongside the aesthetic value attached to thinness and (for men) muscularity, and the disvalue attached to fat, note that ideas of individual responsibility enjoy an unprecedented prominence in modern Western societies. Poor people are blamed for their fecklessness, the unemployed for their laziness – although a shortage of reasonably paid jobs already explains both poverty and unemployment. Many illnesses, especially those not well-understood, are still attributed to psychological failings (Sontag 1978). Conversely, the wealthy and the healthy may be congratulated on their hard work and responsibility, not merely their good fortune. Even if we do not moralise inequalities quite so freely, they may be understood as the result of the 'free market,' ameliorable only by *il*liberal state intervention.

Social psychology (Chapter 32) has highlighted several factors behind Western societies' fondness for individualising explanations. Perhaps most important is our tendency to 'just world' thinking (Ebneter *et al.* 2011). Assuming that the world is basically just, this mindset rationalises suffering and disadvantage as deserved, at least where we cannot easily remedy them. This insulates us from the harsh truth that bad things happen to good people – not to mention the even harsher truth that we ourselves might suffer undeservedly. Obese persons are responsible for their condition, or at least guilty until proven innocent; their suffering reflects their moral failings.

These observations should put us on our guard, but they do not disprove the standard rationalisations. To do so, we need to adapt an argument already familiar in the context of discrimination on grounds of sexuality (LeBesco 2004: Chapter 9). Many manifestos for equal rights emphasise that sexuality is not a choice, making discrimination *unfair*. Bigots can respond that while sexuality may be unchosen, sexual conduct certainly is. A more radical argument is that choice is irrelevant. Even if someone chooses a sexual or romantic relationship with someone of the same sex, and even if she is fully aware that disapproval and discrimination will follow – this can hardly *justify* those responses (cf. Chapter 18). A parallel argument applies to obesity.

Separate spheres as the basis for anti-discrimination provisions

For the sake of argument, let us grant some factual ground to social prejudice. Suppose that fatness is *prima facie* evidence that a person has struck a faulty balance between her health and some aspect of her personal conduct, such as her eating habits. What follows from this?

Note first that the alleged failings are unlikely to generalise as broader character traits. To recur to the familiar stereotypes: wanting to eat generously does not imply greed with regard to anything else; a compulsive 'relation to food' does not imply compulsiveness in other domains; dislike of physical activity is not laziness *per se*; a lack of self-understanding of one's 'eating behaviour' or a faulty estimation of various health risks do not imply general stupidity. It is not only that such failings are attributed on inadequate evidence (after all, we generally know very little about the pressures and conditions that another person faces in her life). As everyone should know from his or her own peccadillos, at issue are quite specific tendencies of feeling and behaviour, that bear no particular implications for other activities or spheres of life. Even conceding simplistic claims about control, it would be foolish to treat obesity as 'a window into men's souls,' and cruel 'to pinch them' because of it.

I quote Elizabeth I's famous words against religious persecution because they bring out a more fundamental point. A liberal society grants each person a special responsibility for his or her own life. To make a person accountable to others for how he or she leads her life would be to subject that person to other people's standards of conduct or, indeed, appearance. It would give others demeaning authority over a person, licensing intrusive scrutiny and reproaches (Schoeman 1992; Anderson 1999). So it would undermine liberty and equality alike. To bear personal responsibility means that others may not impose their own standards on you. With the important exception of personal relationships, this means that they may *not* hold you responsible on their terms (Williams 2013).

This concern with freedom has another implication that is less often appreciated. Liberalism not only limits state authority and prohibits individuals from imposing their values on one another; it must also foster different forms of civil association. To stay with the example of religious belief: alongside prohibitions on persecution, freedom of religion also depends on believers' rights to associate in churches of their choice. That is, the liberal state must also uphold a framework for separate spheres of association, each populated by many different groups and organisations (Walzer 1984). To give another illustration: economic freedom depends not just on individual rights to property and contract, which limit state action and prohibit theft and other infringements. Economic freedom also depends on the ability to form, enter and leave business associations such as partnerships, cooperatives and corporations.

Each of these spheres has its own proper criteria for judging persons. Some criteria are essential if groups or organisations within that sphere are to uphold the purposes defining that form of association. A church, for instance, may exclude those who reject its central practices or doctrines – just as those excluded must be free to form their own church and make similar exclusions. In other words, different grounds of discrimination are warranted in different spheres. Depending on the context, we may take account of a person's ability to pay, or her ability to do a given job, or need for health care, not to mention her willingness to participate. Likewise, different norms and forms of accountability apply in different spheres.

At the same time, in order to uphold equality and liberty, safeguards are needed. Certain forms of discrimination, legitimate in one sphere, become arbitrary, intrusive or demeaning when carried over into other forms of association. People may not, for example, be excluded or held accountable by employers because of their political affiliation or sexual behaviour or religious practices. This is not because those things are necessarily private, nor because they are always outside of a person's control, nor because the relevant choices are good or valid. It is not even because such characteristics are irrelevant to that sphere of association. (An employer might benefit from a socially homogenous workforce, for example.) Instead, it owes to a moral and political decision to separate spheres, so that the authority that is necessary to each does not tip over into domination. Each form of authority is defined by its proper modes of assessing and governing persons. This implies that there can be improper exercises of authority, such as inadmissible forms of accountability or unjust grounds for discrimination. In sum, each of us is prohibited from imposing our own standards on others *except* when we act within forms of civic association that depend on such standards and *so long as* others are free to associate in terms of *their* standards.

Obesity discrimination as a failure to separate spheres

This broader political perspective enables us to appreciate the wrong of obesity discrimination. It is an important fact about a prejudiced society that fatness will often be or seem relevant. Employers will perceive good reasons to discriminate if they are swayed by rationalisations for weight bias, and may have good reasons to prefer slimmer employees if their customers are prejudiced (cf. Chapter 8). Likewise, it is a basic fact about human diversity that accommodating different people can be more or less convenient or costly. To permit discrimination in terms of the immediate goals of organisations would leave considerable scope for weight bias and other invidious forms of discrimination (Kirkland 2008: 32–36).

I have suggested that liberal societies create separate spheres in order to ensure that people are not broadly accountable for their decisions and characteristics, so that they can conduct their lives on their own terms while still associating with others. Each of us may refuse to spend our lives counting calories, for example, just as we may refuse to be friends with particular people (cf. Chapters 30 and 31). To uphold these freedoms, however, places requirements on different civic associations and organisations, as well as on the state. In all these spheres, a certain degree of impersonality becomes requisite. That is to say, as role-holders (employees or service providers, for example), we are obliged to judge others on their merits. But these 'merits' are not whatever criteria seem relevant, let alone the criteria that we may each adopt in our private lives. They are, rather, the criteria that define and constitute that sphere of association.

Two implications of this point bring out the wrongs of obesity discrimination. First, consider stereotyping, in the form of quasi-statistical generalisations by which bodily appearance is taken as a sign of abilities or character traits that are relevant to a given form of association. After all, however we separate personal and public spheres, or different spheres of civil association, it is one and the same person who moves between them. Suppose it were true that body fat is an avoidable evil for many people. And though liberals should hesitate to presume such moral consensus, let us also grant that failure to redress this evil is a sign of wider moral failings. Even conceding this serpent's nest of factual and moral claims, by what title might groups and organisations take account of an indicator that would, of course, remain highly fallible?

On the liberal understanding sketched above, there is no need to demonstrate that stereotypes are false in order to show their illegitimacy as bases of discrimination. (We can set aside, then, the epistemic problems involved in refuting *or* vindicating such generalisations.[2]) The overarching principle is that people should be able to participate in civic life on equal terms. If an ability or character trait *is* relevant to a specific form of association, then it must be judged as such, even if an appearance-based generalisation might provide a cheap or easy rule of thumb. To judge someone by the average merits of others with a similar appearance is to create a status hierarchy (cf. Chapter 3). Fatter people face the special burden of demonstrating that they do not conform to one or other stereotype, and all the double binds that come with this. (Thus the reproach of 'having a chip on one's shoulder,' for example.) Discriminators shrug off their responsibility to consider people's actual merits in favour of a crude proxy. No general truth in the stereotype can overcome this basic unfairness.

Second, consider questions of cost. These need not invoke dubious stereotypes or claims of culpability. Larger people cannot fit in such confined spaces as smaller people; health insurers must pay more to cover the needs of less healthy people. We cannot dismiss these financial concerns as mere greed: no business can run if unprofitable, and non-profit organisations must care about their finances too. Are service providers entitled to charge some customers more, then? I am not sure that this question can be answered *a priori*. What does bear emphasising, however, is how profoundly important a decision it is to *ignore* the greater costs of serving some people. To do so is to endorse the principles of equal respect and inclusiveness – 'to put your money where your mouth is,' in the old phrase. It recognises that service providers belong to civil society, and that a strong presumption of equal treatment applies there. Consider how outrageous it would be for a transport company to charge for carrying wheelchairs, for example: to make an issue of the relatively small cost involved would be disrespectful and exclusionary. As regards obesity, it is quite rare for costs per person to be much higher. The obvious cases are providing two airline seats for one person (assuming those seats could have been sold to two people), and health insurance for those at elevated risk of illness. However one finally judges the first case, I suggest the overarching imperative is to institute clear rules that are implemented in a way that respects all passengers (Poria and Beal 2016). If an organization imposes additional fees in a way that exacerbates stigma and humiliation, or causes painful uncertainty for a particular group, it cannot claim to be merely respecting financial realities.[3] The second case points to an important argument for socializing health care costs. It shows that the logic of private health insurance is inherently perverse: insurers have strong motivations not to serve those who need their services (cf. Chapter 28). It also returns us to the previous point that grounds of discrimination should be properly judged. As noted, body mass index is easy to measure and socially salient, but also a very crude measure of risk.

Finally, let me mention another cost-based argument encouraged by the medicalisation of obesity. (By which I mean: the way that medical institutions and public discourse link obesity to adverse health outcomes.) This is the charge that, by indulging in an 'unhealthy lifestyle,' fatter people impose costs upon the rest of us, especially under any system that pools health care costs. The central injustice of this assertion is to ignore the costs that attach to obesity – as if there were not already, beyond whatever health risks attach to obesity, plentiful social disincentives to avoid this fate. Never mind all scientific evidence about appetite, metabolism, weight set-points and the rest: the stigma and discrimination facing obese people should already discredit the idea that fatness is largely voluntary. In other words, the argument is so inattentive to social reality and so psychologically implausible that it betrays its own discreditable motivations. It is as if, granted this extra dose of blame and opprobrium, fatter people might finally wake up and realise that they are not only widely disliked and harming themselves, but also taking more than their fair share of health care resources. Only by ignoring the immense social burden that fatter people already face could someone frame those persons as 'a burden on society.'

Conclusion

As many authors remark, obesity is one of the last publicly acceptable grounds for discrimination. However unwittingly, medical authority feeds into social prejudice; so too do wider norms of attractiveness and our societies' fondness for individualising explanations. Assumptions about harm and avoidability channel prejudice and disgust into allegations of personal culpability.

Apart from the dubious factual premises invoked, I have argued that these rationalisations provide no support for obesity discrimination. Claims about personal responsibility cannot warrant the careless application of institutional penalties and exclusions. Basic norms of equality, respect and freedom mean that, when we fulfil responsibilities as members of civil society, we should understand such judgments as demeaning, intrusive and out of order. They take standards that may or may not be relevant to personal decisions (about what to eat or how to care for one's appearance, and so on) and casually use them as justifications for making someone else's life harder. Even if it is meaningful, the 'self-control' needed to 'stay in shape' has no public relevance. The self-control needed to mind one's own business certainly does.[4]

I have only hinted at the practical measures required to tackle obesity discrimination. My own view is that obesity should join other grounds mentioned in anti-discrimination legislation. Nonetheless, legislation can only go so far (cf. Chapter 35). Organisations may be able to do more – for instance, if they adopt policies and procedures to uphold respectful treatment of all employees or customers. Still, legislative and organisational measures are bound – especially when they respect the liberal principles stressed here – to leave untouched many daily manifestations of weight bias, not to mention the shame and self-hatred by which we internalise these norms. Here we enter the sphere of social activism – not just to encourage legislative change and improve organisational policies, but also to promote acceptance of bodily diversity.[5]

Notes

1 In absolute terms, this BMI increase (from 22.5–25 to 37.5–40kg/m^2) correlates with an increase from 14.5 to 28.2 deaths per annum per 1,000 persons. To translate the midpoints of these BMI ranges into more familiar terms: for someone who is 172cm tall (= 5'8", roughly between the averages for British men and woman), this corresponds to body weights of roughly 70kg and 115kg,

or 11st v. 18st, or a difference of nearly 100lbs. Note too, that BMI of 22.5–25kg/m^2 represents the *upper* part of the so-called normal weight category (18.5–25kg/m^2). In other words, by the same logic that many people are told to lose weight for the sake of their health (anyone with a BMI over 25kg/m^2 being classified as 'overweight' or obese), a lot of people should be told to *gain* weight. Mortality figures are from Prospective Studies Collaboration 2009. A more recent and even larger synthesis reports similar findings: Global BMI Mortality Collaboration 2016.

2 But see Roehling *et al.* 2008 for discussion and empirical studies that disprove them.

3 Advocates of differential pricing often contend that it is fair(er). But to charge someone double while offering facilities that remain inadequate (the discomfort of a double seat with an armrest jammed against your back, unusable toilets, and so on) can hardly be described as fair, either.

4 My thanks to Myfanwy Williams for this reversal of the self-control trope.

5 For advice, discussion and feedback, I am very grateful to Reuven Brandt, Rachel Cooper, Morris Kaplan, Kasper Lippert-Rasmussen, Elena Loizidou, Neil Manson, Mari Mikkola, Kristin Voigt, Steve Wilkinson and Myfanwy Williams.

Bibliography

Anderson, E. S. 1999. "What Is the Point of Equality?" *Ethics*. 109(2): 287–337.

Andreyeva, T., Puhl, R. M., and Brownell, K. D. 2008. "Changes in Perceived Weight Discrimination Among Americans, 1995–1996 Through 2004–2006." *Obesity*. 16(5): 1129–1134.

Bacon, L. 2010. *Health at Every Size: The Surprising Truth about Your Weight*. 2nd edition. Dallas: BenBella Books.

Bleich, S. N., Cutler, D., Murray, C., and Adams, A. 2008. "Why Is the Developed World Obese?" *Annual Review of Public Health*. 29: 273–295.

Callahan, D. 2013. "Obesity: Chasing an Elusive Epidemic." *Hastings Center Report*. 43(1): 34–40.

Cooper, C. 2007. 'Headless Fatties.' Online at: http://charlottecooper.net/publishing/digital/headless-fatties-01-07

Cooper, C. 2010. "Fat Studies: Mapping the Field." *Sociology Compass*. 4(12): 1020–1034.

Court of Justice of the European Union. 2014. "Advocate General Jääskinen Considers That Morbid Obesity May Amount to a 'Disability' for the Purposes of the Equal Treatment in Employment Directive," 17 July, http://curia.europa.eu/jcms/upload/docs/application/pdf/2014-07/cp140112en.pdf

Crandall, C. S., Nierman, A., and Hebl, M. 2009. "Anti-Fat Prejudice." In Nelson, T. D. (ed). *Handbook of Prejudice, Stereotyping, and Discrimination*. New York: Psychology Press, 469–487.

Dombrowski, S. U., Knittle, K., Avenell, A., Araujo-Soares, V., and Sniehotta, F. 2014. "Long Term Maintenance of Weight Loss with Non-Surgical Interventions in Obese Adults: Systematic Review and Meta-Analyses of Randomised Controlled Trials." *BMJ*. 348: g2646.

Ebneter, D. S., Latner, J. D., and O'Brien, K. S. 2011. "Just World Beliefs, Causal Beliefs, and Acquaintance: Associations with Stigma Toward Eating Disorders and Obesity." *Personality and Individual Differences*. 51(5): 618–622.

Fikkan, J. L. and Rothblum, E. D. 2011. "Is Fat a Feminist Issue? Exploring the Gendered Nature of Weight Bias." *Sex Roles*. 66(9–10): 575–592.

Galka, M. 2016. "Watch How Fast the World Became Obese." *Metrocosm*. July 18. http://metrocosm.com/map-world-obesity/

Global BMI Mortality Collaboration. 2016. "Body-Mass Index and All-Cause Mortality: Individual-Participant-Data Meta-Analysis of 239 Prospective Studies in Four Continents." *The Lancet*. 388: 10046.

Greenway, F. L. 2015. "Physiological Adaptations to Weight Loss and Factors Favouring Weight Regain." *International Journal of Obesity*. 39(8): 1188–1196.

Kirkland, A. 2008. *Fat Rights: Dilemmas of Difference and Personhood*. New York: New York University Press.

LeBesco, K. 2004. *Revolting Bodies? The Struggle to Redefine Fat Identity*. Amherst, MA: University Massachusetts Press.

McAllister, E. J., Dhurandhar, N. V., Keith, S. W., Aronne, L. J., Barger, J., Baskin, M., Benca, R. M., *et al.* 2009. "Ten Putative Contributors to the Obesity Epidemic." *Critical Reviews in Food Science and Nutrition*. 49(10): 868–913.

McLaren, L. 2007. "Socioeconomic Status and Obesity." *Epidemiologic Reviews*. 29(1): 29–48.

Muennig, P. 2008. "The Body Politic: The Relationship Between Stigma and Obesity-Associated Disease." *BMC Public Health*. 8: 128.

NCD Risk Factor Collaboration. 2016. "Trends in Adult Body-Mass Index in 200 Countries From 1975 to 2014: a Pooled Analysis of 1698 Population-Based Measurement Studies with 19.2 Million Participants." *The Lancet*. 387: 1377–1396.

Ochner, C. N., Tsai, A. G., Kushner, R. F., and Wadden, T. A. 2015. "Treating Obesity Seriously: When Recommendations for Lifestyle Change Confront Biological Adaptations." *The Lancet Diabetes & Endocrinology*. 3(4): 232–234.

Okorodudu, D. O., Jumean, M. F., Montori, V. M., Romero-Corral, A., Somers, V. K., Erwin, P. J., and Lopez-Jimenez, F. 2010. "Diagnostic Performance of Body Mass Index to Identify Obesity as Defined by Body Adiposity: a Systematic Review and Meta-Analysis." *International Journal of Obesity*. 34(5): 791–799.

Phelan, S. M., Burgess, D. J., Yeazel, M. W., Hellerstedt, W. L., Griffin, J. M. and van Ryn, M. 2015. "Impact of Weight Bias and Stigma on Quality of Care and Outcomes for Patients with Obesity." *Obesity Reviews*. 16(4): 319–326.

Phillips, C. M. 2013. "Metabolically Healthy Obesity: Definitions, Determinants and Clinical Implications." *Reviews in Endocrine and Metabolic Disorders*. 14(3): 219–227.

Poria, Y. and Beal, J. 2017. "An Exploratory Study About Obese People's Flight Experience." *Journal of Travel Research*. 56(3): 370–380.

Prospective Studies Collaboration. 2009. "Body-Mass Index and Cause-Specific Mortality in 900,000 Adults: Collaborative Analyses of 57 Prospective Studies." *The Lancet*. 373 (9669): 1083–1096.

Puhl, R. M. 2011. "Weight Stigmatization Toward Youth: a Significant Problem in Need of Societal Solutions." *Childhood Obesity*. 7: 359–363.

Puhl, R. M. and Heuer, C. A. 2010. "Obesity Stigma: Important Considerations for Public Health." *American Journal of Public Health*. 100(6): 1019–1028.

Puhl, R. M., Latner, J. D., O'Brien, K. S., Luedicke, J., Daníelsdóttir, S., and Ramos Salas, X. 2015. "Potential Policies and Laws to Prohibit Weight Discrimination: Public Views From 4 Countries." *The Milbank Quarterly*. 93(4): 691–731.

Roehling, M. V., Roehling, P. V., and Odland, L. M. 2008. "Investigating the Validity of Stereotypes About Overweight Employees: the Relationship Between Body Weight and Normal Personality Traits." *Group & Organization Management*. 33(4): 392–424.

Rothblum, E. and Solovay, S. (eds). 2009. *The Fat Studies Reader*. New York: NYU Press.

Rudolph, C. W., Wells, C. L., Weller, M. D., and Baltes, B. B. 2009. "A Meta-Analysis of Empirical Studies of Weight-Based Bias in the Workplace." *Journal of Vocational Behavior*. 74(1): 1–10.

Schoeman, F. D. 1992. *Privacy and Social Freedom*. New York: Cambridge University Press.

Schwartz, M. B., Vartanian, L. R., Nosek, B. A., and Brownell, K. D. 2006. "The Influence of One's Own Body Weight on Implicit and Explicit Anti-Fat Bias." *Obesity*. 14(3): 440–447.

Sontag, S. 1978. *Illness as Metaphor*. New York: Farrar, Straus and Giroux.

Vartanian, L. R. and Porter, A. M. 2016. "Weight Stigma and Eating Behavior: a Review of the Literature." *Appetite*. 102: 3–14.

Vartanian, L. R., Trewartha, T., and Vanman, E. J. 2016. "Disgust Predicts Prejudice and Discrimination Toward Individuals with Obesity." *Journal of Applied Social Psychology*. 46(6): 369–375.

Walzer, M. 1984. "Liberalism and the Art of Separation." *Political Theory*. 12(3): 315–330.

Williams, G. 2013. "Sharing Responsibility and Holding Responsible." *Journal of Applied Philosophy*. 30(4): 351–364.

World Health Organization (WHO). 2016. "Obesity and Overweight: Fact Sheet." Online at: http://www.who.int/mediacentre/factsheets/fs311/en/

Web resources

www.lindabacon.org: website of Linda Bacon, advocate of Health At Every Size.

www.naafaonline.com: National Association to Advance Fat Acceptance (US).

http://biastoolkit.uconnruddcenter.org: Rudd Center For Food Policy And Obesity, *Preventing Weight Bias: Helping Without Harming in Clinical Practice.*

https://medium.com/@thefatshadow: series of thoughtful essays by an anonymous writer ('Your Fat Friend').

23
DISCRIMINATION AND LOOKISM

Xiaofei Liu

XIAMEN UNIVERSITY

Introduction

A recent post on the Chinese *Microblog* by a computer engineer provoked heated discussion on looks-based discrimination. This computer engineer received a reduced annual employee bonus because he was considered "too ugly" by his new supervisor.[1] While many readers of this post were outraged by this incident of looks-based discrimination, economic "penalties" for being "ugly" are actually not rare at all. According to a 1994 study in the United States, working men considered the least attractive "are penalized about 9 percent in hourly earnings" (Hamermesh and Biddle 1994). Other studies show that less attractive individuals are less likely to be hired or promoted (Hosoda *et al.* 2003; Mobius and Rosenblat 2006). Moreover, plainness in looks may disadvantage a person not just economically, but also relationally. Studies showed that plain-looking people have fewer opportunities for social interaction than the better looking (Juhnke 1987; Mulford *et al.* 1998; Chapter 31). An article recently published on an LGBT community website, *Advocate*, serves as an illustration. Citing a frequent caveat in online dating profiles – "No Fats, Femmes, or Asians", the author criticized the looks-based biases in the North American gay community (Nguyen 2011). Unlike the Chinese *Microblog* post, the response this article received was less than sympathetic.

Lookism, differential attitude or treatment based solely on a person's physical appearance, has been receiving increasing attention, especially in socioeconomic and legal circles. Many point to its harm to the disadvantaged, the costs it brings upon society through pressure to look more beautiful, and its apparent violation of equality, and ask for legal actions to redress it (Solovay 1999; Kirkland 2008; Rhode 2010). Some compare it to racial discrimination, and call it "the new racism" (Salkeld 2011). Yet others believe there are important differences between lookism and more notorious forms of discrimination, such as racism (Alexander 1992; Ford 2008; cf. Chapter 16). And when it comes to personal relationships, people's attitudes toward lookism are even more permissive, as the reaction to that *Advocate* article testifies.

Is lookism the same as racism? Is it morally objectionable? And, if so, in what ways? In order to answer these questions, we need first to understand the complexity behind the phenomena that we call "lookism". I start by examining lookist practice at three levels, and the potentially morally relevant issues related to each. I then consider the moral problems bound up with various kinds of lookist practice because of these issues.

Understanding lookism

Lookism stands for a complex set of phenomena. Part of its complexity comes from the many facets of appearance – height, weight, symmetry, skin tone, body shape, etc. One could discriminate or be discriminated against on the basis of any of these facets. Adding to this complexity, judgments based on appearance can be purely aesthetic, or involving moral and other considerations. We can divide these judgments into roughly three levels. On one level, appearance is used as the basis for judging how attractive one finds a person; on another level, it is used as the basis for judging a person's moral character or personality; on a third level, appearance is used as the basis for judging how well a person is going to perform a certain function. In reality, judgments at one level often influence those at another; but each of these three levels forms a more or less distinct space of assessment. Thus, the rest of this section will discuss each of these levels in turn.

Lookism and attractiveness

The most basic form of lookism concerns physical attractiveness. Some physical features, such as a symmetrical face, blonde hair, and a V-shaped torso, are generally considered attractive; other features, such as rough-looking skin, jagged teeth, or a chubby belly, are often considered unattractive. How attractive we find another person can then affect whom we date, befriend, or even share an office with. This subsection focuses on the aesthetic judgment itself, and its impact on our interpersonal relationships is left for later sections.

It is usually believed that aesthetic judgment is beyond the scope of moral evaluation. As a common saying goes: "Beauty is in the eye of the beholder". This is often taken to mean two things: first, that there is no objective standard for beauty; second, that we need no reason for finding someone attractive – it is simply a personal taste. Researchers have actually found a high degree of consensus regarding the attractiveness of a face among individuals of different sex, race, age, socioeconomic status, and cultural backgrounds (Ritts *et al.* 1992). But this discovery does not necessarily mean that these shared standards of beauty are objective, nor does it mean that individual aesthetic opinions should conform to these shared standards. Nevertheless, there are reasons to believe that aesthetic preference is not always "simply a personal taste"; it might have some moral implications.[2]

We can distinguish between three kinds of lookism. First, there is *simple lookism* – judging someone's attractiveness based solely on appearance. Let's use the caveat mentioned at the beginning, "No Fats, Femmes, or Asians", as an illustration. Regarding fat people as unattractive because of their body size, for example, can be viewed as a case of simple lookism. Appearance is also related to many salient social identities, such as race, sex, and age. Our assessment of attractiveness is often intricately intertwined with our opinions of these social identities. We may judge a certain appearance as unattractive because we disvalue a certain social group characterized by that appearance. We may call this kind of lookism *loaded lookism* – judging someone's attractiveness based on a certain appearance as a result of the group identity implied by that appearance. For example, regarding feminine men as unattractive because one considers this group as inferior in character can be viewed as a case of loaded lookism. Lastly, because some social groups are commonly associated with a certain appearance (e.g. old people with gray hair, and Chinese people with epicanthic fold), appearance could become a proxy for group identity and be used as the basis for aesthetic judgment of the whole group, which we may call *group lookism* – judging someone's attractiveness based on a group identity as a result of one's aesthetic opinion of the appearance said to be characteristic of that group. Regarding all Asians as unattractive because one finds characteristic traits of Asians (e.g. epicanthic fold) unattractive can be viewed as a case of group lookism.[3]

We should distinguish these three forms of discrimination, because they have different moral implications. For example, loaded lookism seems to involve presuming an inferior value for a certain social group, and thus seems more analogous to typical racism and sexism. Group lookism judges an entire social group on the basis of some alleged common trait, which may not be true for every individual of that group. For example, even though most people from East Asia have epicanthic fold, some nevertheless do not. Thus, group lookism seems to involve some kind of overgeneralization.

Lookism and character

Let's now turn to the second level – using looks as the ground for judging a person's moral character or personality. At first, it may appear odd to associate appearance with moral character, as appearance is often taken to be beyond control. But actually many aspects of physical appearance change at some point in life as a result of choice – from hairstyle, tattoo, and tooth form, to skin tone, body size, and even facial configuration (e.g. by means of makeup or plastic surgery).

Consider the following case. Ms. Nedder, who taught at a small Catholic college in New Hampshire, had demonstrated her ability to teach. However, the college decided not to renew her contract, because she, then weighing 375 pounds and standing five feet six inches tall, was considered not a good role model for the students. In the college's opinion, her contract would not sit well with the college's mission that urges its members "to take responsibilities for [oneself] and for others" (Kirkland 2008: 38).

Many ordinary people associate obesity with gluttony, laziness, and lack of self-control (Oliver and Lee 2005: 933; cf. Chapter 22). Since "taking responsibility for oneself" is among the core values of this religious institution, a demonstrated moral weakness such as lack of self-control would indeed be unfitting. But let's leave aside judgments about capability, and focus on the judgment about moral character for the moment.

Appearance, such as body size, seems related to dietary habits and other lifestyle factors. It is common to attribute obesity to blameworthy choices. This belief that fatness is a result of some moral flaw is under fire. For example, Deborah L. Rhode forcefully argues that, contrary to what most people believe, obesity is not something that can easily be modified by choices of dieting and exercising. Citing numerous recent studies on weight loss, she writes: "Weight reflects a complex interaction of physiological, psychological, socioeconomic, and cultural factors. Genetically determined set-points work to keep bodies within a predetermined range; furthermore, when dieters reduce their caloric intake and increase their exercise, their metabolism slows down to compensate and makes any weight loss difficult to sustain" (2009: 1050). She also mentions that "only about five percent of dieters manage to achieve long-term weight loss, and those who do frequently require surgical and lifestyle interventions that are anything but moderate" (2009: 1062–3). What Rhode points out is that weight is not as controllable through voluntary choices as people often believe (cf. Chapter 22). Some obese people may not have much choice about their obesity, as a genetically determined "set-point" often keeps their body fat within a certain range. Of course, this is not to deny that weight can be causally related to choice. Studies show that worldwide obesity "has nearly doubled since 1980"; and that while obesity rates are high in countries like the USA (33.9%) and the UK (22.7%), it is relatively low in countries like Austria (11.0%), the Netherlands (10.0%), and Italy (9.8%).[4] Unless we are ready to say that the span of three decades or the division by the Atlantic could cause such divergence in people's genetic makeup, these data provide good evidence for believing that diet and lifestyle are partially responsible for the current state of obesity. However, even if diet and lifestyle are partly to blame, it does not mean such factors necessarily make the relevant agents blameworthy. People may be forced to take sedentary jobs with long working hours, or acquire bad dietary habits in early childhood which are very difficult to alter later on. In such cases, diets and lifestyles that cause obesity do not necessarily manifest a moral flaw such as greed or lack of self-control.

Thus, before we associate appearance with moral character, we need to be aware that, for some people, the appearance may not be a result of their choices, and that, even if it is, they may not be fully blameworthy for those choices, as their choices may be severely limited so as to reflect little or no moral fault on their part.

In addition to controllability, another issue that has moral implications is whether a certain sort of appearance should be regarded as undesirable. Some people choose to pierce a bodily part, as a mode of self-expression; some choose to gain excessive weight, because they actually prefer their body that way. Although excessive weight and extreme forms of body piercing are usually looked upon unfavorably by the general society, there is the question – should they be? Voluntarily acquiring such appearance does not always manifest a moral flaw; it may simply be a matter of difference in aesthetic opinion, or even represent a moral protest against conformism and in favor of diversity.

There is yet a third issue. People may associate looks with moral character or personality not because they believe a sort of appearance is the result of any choice, but because they believe that appearance is a reliable indicator of a certain moral character or personality. There is a long history of physiognomy both in the East and the West: for example, bigger cheekbones are taken to mean aggressiveness, small slant eyes untrustworthiness, and so on. Though regarded by most scientists as a pseudoscience, some recent studies show that there is some truth to this ancient art: some sorts of appearance are related to personality through factors such as "testosterone levels" (Highfield *et al.* 2009). Bigger cheekbones, for example, are likely associated with higher testosterone levels and thus with aggression. This suggests that certain sorts of appearance can indeed be physiologically connected to some character traits. However, these studies also quickly point out that personality judgments based on appearance are usually "overgeneralizations". In other words, appearance is often an unreliable indicator of personality in an individual case.

Therefore, to evaluate lookism at this level we should take into consideration three issues. First, there is the issue of whether an appearance is a result of choices for which the agent is fully responsible. Second, even if a person's appearance is a result of such choices, there is the issue of whether it should be regarded as undesirable. And last, for appearances not causally related to any choice, there is the issue of whether they can be a reliable indicator of any character trait, physiologically or otherwise.

Lookism and capability

Let's turn to the third level – using looks as the ground for judging a person's capability to perform a certain function. It is sometimes believed that discrimination based on appearance is justified because appearance is relevant to one's capability to function in a certain way. Consider the following two cases:

> *Cheerleader*: Lian dreams of being a member of her university cheerleading squad. But she is barely five feet tall, with visible facial deformity. She went to the tryout, and the judges thought that her height was unfitting for the current team and that her facial deformity would prevent her from making a good, sweet smile. She was thus denied a position in the squad.

> *Policeman*: Jian dreams of being a police officer. He passed all the physical tests except for one: he is one inch shorter than the minimum height required. The local government introduced this requirement because they feel that taller police officers provide better protection for the public.

When we evaluate judgments about functional capability relating to appearance, one critical issue is whether that appearance is actually directly connected to having or lacking that functional capability. Lian's height and facial deformity indeed make her incapable of performing the expected tasks, whereas Jian's height does not in fact hamper his capability to function as a police officer. This difference in the actual connection between the appearance and the relevant capability explains why the treatment in *cheerleader* is acceptable, but that in *policeman* is not.

Sometimes, even though a certain sort of appearance is connected to a functional capability in general, this connection is nevertheless false in particular cases. For example, it might be true that muscular police officers usually do a better job at physically overpowering dangerous suspects; but it does not mean a non-muscular police officer will necessarily be inferior in this regard. We need to conduct an individualized inquiry to determine whether a person's bodily appearance indeed shows or undermines a functional capability in her particular case (cf. Chapter 3). Merely relying on some crude statistics about a group overgeneralizes, and does not represent a proper assessment based on individual qualities.

Moreover, appearance may be connected to a functional capability only indirectly – through some third-person opinion.[5] A plain-looking applicant may be denied a job as a marketing agent at a cosmetic clinic not because she lacks marketing skills, but because her looks will negatively affect potential customers' opinion of the clinic's service. Her appearance negatively affects her ability to attract more customers via third-person opinions that connect the appearance of a sales agent with the quality of a cosmetic clinic's service. When such opinions are widespread in society, they have real potential to damage the success of businesses that do not heed them. If there exists no external measure to counter such opinions, employers have a *prima facie* reason to act in accord with these opinions.[6]

Lastly, looks may be connected to a functional capability through judgments about the person's moral character, personality, or physical attraction. For example, an employer may like to work with cooperative people, and thus prefers applicants whose appearance supposedly signifies such traits. Evaluation of such lookist practice will require evaluation of lookist judgments at the level of aesthetics and character.

To sum up, this section has examined three levels of lookism, and the various potentially morally relevant issues that each raises. In particular, three kinds of lookism potentially raise moral concern.[7]

A) *Ungrounded lookism*, which involves taking a certain sort of appearance as embodying some aesthetic, character, or functional inferiority based on no ground or an unreasonable ground. For example, taking small hands as indicating mental weakness, or taking an appearance unrelated to choice as indicating a moral flaw, are instances of this kind. Loaded lookism, when there is no good reason to ground one's negative attitude towards the relevant group, also belongs to this category.

B) *Statistical lookism*, which involves taking a certain sort of appearance as embodying some aesthetic, character, or functional inferiority based on a crude group-based statistical association. Group lookism is one such example. Using cheekbones to judge someone's moral character or functional capability is another example.

C) *Individualized and norm-conforming lookism*, which involves taking a certain sort of appearance as embodying some aesthetic, character, or functional inferiority based on an individualized assessment that appeals to some commonly accepted, yet questionable, standard. Disliking a fat person because the social standard of beauty favors thinness, or refusing to hire a person with a pierced nose because the social standard morally condemns body piercing, are cases of this kind.

By highlighting these three kinds of lookism, I don't mean that they must be mutually exclusive. The point is rather that each kind raises a unique type of moral concern, and thus is subject to a specific type of moral criticism. Let's now proceed to consider the moral questions.

Evaluating lookism

Lookism is a complex set of phenomena, as is discrimination in general. People find different forms of discrimination objectionable for different reasons (cf. Chapters 6–14). Theorists of discrimination have proposed various accounts of why discrimination is wrong. These accounts can be divided into two major approaches: one approach finds the wrongness mainly in the discriminator's act or mental state; the other approach finds it mainly in the deprivation suffered by the discriminatee.

Within the first approach, some propose that discrimination such as racism or sexism is wrong because it involves disrespect for people's equal moral worth (e.g. Alexander 1992; cf. Chapter 6). Others propose that it is wrong because it fails to properly value people's merits: decisions on hiring and admission should be based on who has the best relevant qualification (e.g. Hook 1995; cf. Chapter 8). Still others propose that it is wrong because such acts carry the message that the discriminatees are fundamentally inferior, and thereby objectively demeans them (e.g. Hellman 2008; Chapter 7).

Within the second approach, discrimination is thought to be wrong because, for example, it undermines the discriminatees' equal opportunity to access various social resources (e.g. Segall 2012; Chapters 10 and 11); or it injures the discriminatees' deliberative freedoms, "freedoms to have our decisions about how to live insulated from the effects of normatively extraneous features of us, such as our skin color or gender" (Moreau 2010; Chapter 13); or it makes the discriminatees worse off than they ought to be (Lippert-Rasmussen 2014: 154–5; Chapter 12).

We do not need to decide which of these accounts has the greatest theoretical merit here. They offer us various perspectives from which we can understand why discrimination is morally objectionable. In light of these perspectives, let's proceed to examine the three kinds of lookism, and in the process of this examination we will also see two other approaches to understanding the wrongfulness of discrimination.

Ungrounded lookism

Ungrounded lookism takes the discriminatee as having a certain sort of inferiority, when there is no ground or no reasonable ground for doing so. The computer engineer mentioned at the beginning received a reduced bonus simply because his supervisor found him unattractive; Jian was denied a police officer's job simply because some people feel that they are safer with taller police officers. Such treatment denies the discriminatee benefits or respect that he or she actually merits, and thus harms the discriminatee. Ungrounded lookism in hiring and admission also undermines people's equal opportunity to work or receive education, and it places burdens on them because of "normatively extraneous" features, and thereby limits their deliberative freedoms.

Furthermore, discriminating against people who have a certain sort of appearance, while there is no reasonable ground for doing so, is often motivated by a disrespectful attitude on the part of the discriminator – "I just do not like them." Even when such an attitude is absent, treatment like this often objectively conveys a demeaning message that these people's worth is devalued by their appearance so much that their other qualities do not matter. In such treatment, not only is the discriminatee regarded as inferior, but also his or her value as a person is reduced to the superficial level of mere appearance.

This is so even in cases where appearance is indeed connected to a certain function. For instance, being good-looking can be relevant for being an effective service person or a pleasant friend, but other factors such as personality and integrity are equally, if not more, important. Denying people employment or friendship merely by virtue of their appearance would fail to respect a person's value in its full sense, and convey the demeaning message that their appearance makes them so undesirable that their other relevant qualities do not matter.

Statistical lookism

Unlike ungrounded lookism, statistical lookism has a factual ground: there is a statistical connection between the sort of appearance and some defect. People with bigger cheekbones have a higher chance of being aggressive, fat people tend to be less agile, and people with an East Asian origin usually have single-fold eyelids. If one does not want an aggressive or clumsy employee, or aesthetically disfavors single-fold eyelids, then there appears to be good reason to discriminate against people with such traits.

However, such judgments involve overgeneralization – not every individual with such a physical trait has the "defect", and thus treating a person based on some group statistic will deny that person individualized assessment. I have argued elsewhere (Liu 2015) that the wrongfulness of discrimination, no matter which approach one takes, is grounded on an implicit premise that people's pursuit of basic well-being – basic material, educational, and relational needs – ought to be properly honored. And part of the duty to honor that pursuit is to give everybody a fair consideration based on his or her relevant individual qualities when it comes to work, education, and relationship opportunities that are important for satisfying basic needs. "Everybody deserves to be treated based on what kind of person he or she is, not based on what kind of person other people are" (Liu 2015: 260). Treating a person with an East Asian origin as unattractive because one aesthetically disfavors single-fold eyelids, an alleged Asian characteristic, would risk denial of a fair consideration based on individual qualities. Likewise, treating a fat person as being clumsy because many fat people are like this would also deny that person a fair consideration.

Compared to ungrounded lookism, which is offensive mainly because it disrespects equality or demeans human value, statistical lookism is offensive mainly because it denies people's individuality and treats them as exchangeable tokens of a type of human being.

Individualized and norm-conforming lookism

Some lookist practice, however, involves an individualized assessment based on a seemingly reasonable standard. For example, Lian was denied a cheerleader role because her height and facial deformity in fact prevented her from performing the expected tasks; people with jagged teeth are found unattractive, because tooth form is a standard aspect of physical attractiveness. I think none of the aforementioned approaches enables us to say that this type of lookist practice is definitely wrong.

First of all, it is much harder to claim that a differential treatment implicates a disrespectful attitude or a demeaning message that the discriminatee is fundamentally inferior, or that the treatment denies individuality, when such treatment is based on an individualized assessment with a seemingly reasonable standard. Second, it is also hard to prove that such lookism causes unjust harm. Lookism of this kind indeed deprives the discriminatee of some benefits; but whether that deprivation constitutes a harm depends on where the discriminatee would otherwise be – i.e. her baseline. Baseline is often determined by a set of commonsensical social norms, such as which physical trait is reasonably connected to which functional capability and what kind of basic well-being a person ought to have. Since the standards on which the aforementioned lookism operates are often part of this set of social norms, it is hard to see how the resulting deprivation makes the discriminatee worse off than he or she would otherwise be.[8]

It is thus unclear that such lookism is wrong, considered from either of the above three perspectives – disrespect, denial of individuality, and harm. There is, however, a different ground for resisting this type of lookism. Some anti-lookism theorists try to draw an analogy between ugliness and disability, and to apply to lookism the logic behind the Americans with Disabilities Act of 1990. This logic acknowledges that "persons function in different ways, some of which will appear as dysfunctional in certain environments or according to certain norms", but such difference is something that society should try to accommodate, rather than a ground for discrimination (Kirkland 2008: 22). A wheelchair user, for example, will be able to move around like a normal person, with the assistance of an elevator (cf. Chapter 19). It is thus argued that the problem lies not in the discriminatee, but in the standards which are tacitly incorporated into the structure of physical and social environments – they often favor the dominant group.

This accommodation approach has its support from the Rawlsian theory of justice. Rawls argued that natural talents such as beauty and intelligence are contingent and undeserved. Although eliminating their influence on how we distribute social resources is unfeasible, our social structure can and should be arranged "so that these contingencies work for the good of the least fortunate" (Rawls 1971: 102; cf. Chapter 11). Suppose that the aesthetically least gifted are indeed the worst off in terms of basic well-being,[9] and that accommodating them would not drastically decrease the overall well-being of the whole society. There would be a duty to assist them. Thus, even individualized and norm-conforming lookism should be subject to closer scrutiny. When widespread social opinions disfavor a certain group of people such that they lack adequate opportunities to access the goods essential to their basic well-being, we may still have a moral obligation not to discriminate against them.

That said, the positive duty to assist needs to be balanced against the negative duty to respect self-ownership (see, for example, Nozick 1974). Natural gifts such as appearance, no matter how arbitrary and undeserved, are what their bearer is entitled to have, and the relevant ownership should be respected. Even if we have a duty to accommodate the aesthetically least gifted, this duty still needs to be balanced against the duty to respect others' self-ownership. And thus there should be limits on how far this duty to accommodate can go. Moreover, because of the need to balance between the interests of different groups (e.g. the employee, the employer, and often the customers), the costs of accommodation should not disproportionately fall on one party, but be shared by all – a point that I will return to later.

The accommodation approach raises greater suspicion when it comes to lookist practice in personal relationships. Consider simple lookism: an obvious worry is that we cannot help how attractive we find another person. Unlike the wheelchair case, in which we can adjust the physical environment to accommodate the disability, it might be argued that we cannot "adjust" our taste in order to find someone attractive. But this "control-centered" worry is problematic, for we do seem to have some long-range control over our preferences, including aesthetic preferences. For example, studies have found that people can come to like a group whom they previously disliked by lengthy exposure to their positive traits (Dasgupta and Greenwald 2001). The real issue is that a moral view that requires people to change even their most personal preferences seems too demanding – at too great a cost of personal freedom.[10] For example, we all agree that no employer should require employees to change their religious beliefs or undergo cosmetic surgery.

But accommodation need not require us to find a way to like people we find unattractive. A more reasonable requirement would ask us to help, in the first place, (re)build social standards of beauty that are more diverse and inclusive. Every person deserves a fair opportunity to pursue a life of basic well-being, which includes not just basic material and educational needs, but also basic relational needs. Opportunities to be appreciated are a prerequisite for such important relationships as friendships and loving relationships. If a society's social standards are set up in such a way that makes appreciation for some people more difficult from the beginning, these people would be deprived of a fair opportunity to have flourishing relationships.[11]

A reasonable duty to accommodate would require us, especially those with great social influence (e.g. multinational corporations and social media), to advocate for more inclusive concepts of beauty. It would require us to fight against lookist practices that reinforce or introduce an exclusionary and overly narrow standard of beauty, such as advertisements portraying blonde hair or a slender body as the only or highest form of beauty. Such practices, especially by influential organizations and social media, make appreciation of a diverse range of appearance less possible, and thereby diminish some people's chances of satisfying their basic relational needs.

Conclusion

In many ways lookism is similar to racism: it can be caused by a demeaning attitude that disrespects equality, or an overgeneralization that disregards individuality, or a popular social opinion or standard that commands one's heeding; and it often deprives people of important social goods (cf. Chapter 16). There are also notable differences. First, race is hereditarily stable, and thus the victims of racism often suffer from generationally accumulated deprivation; while this is usually not the case with appearance. Second, racism has been discussed mostly in relation to the distribution of public goods, while lookism also draws increasing attention to biases in the private realm. Third, unlike race, most aspects of appearance are alterable (though sometimes at great cost), which is a reason why many victims of lookist practice choose to modify their appearance instead of standing up firmly against such discrimination. The most important difference, perhaps, is that lookism often operates on a set of norms that are *still* unreflectively accepted or, at least, regarded as benign by most people. The battle against lookism has yet to win the fight over the norms.

Historically, many racist prejudices (e.g. beliefs that certain races are intellectually, morally, and aesthetically inferior) were widely accepted in some societies. Overcoming such prejudices involved what Elizabeth Anderson calls "contentious politics": active mass resistance to the normative claims "embodied in social institutions enforced by and catering to the powerful" (Anderson 2015: 39; cf. Chapter 35). Such resistance ranges from moral arguments, petitioning, and theatrical performances, to street demonstrations, litigation, and political campaigns, with the goal of eliciting public recognition of the illegitimacy of the old norms. Its success requires coordinated efforts from all levels of society, especially the victims of discrimination – they need to actively "demand respect" and, through their action, "demonstrate worthiness of respect" (Anderson 2015: 37).

"Contentious politics" against lookism thus would involve, first, active mass resistance to exclusionary and overly narrow standards of beauty – for example, demonstrations against such standards or boycotting the products of companies that introduce or reinforce them. Second, it would involve active efforts to advocate for inclusive and diverse concepts of beauty and value

– for example, supporting or participating in such events as the fat-acceptance movement so as to create more opportunities for appreciation of those underappreciated.[12]

Notes

1 "Man Received Reduced Annual Bonus for Being 'Ugly'," *Sina News*, http://news.sina.com.cn/s/2015-02-13/115931517781.shtml.

2 I argued for this point in Liu (2015: 266).

3 For a real-life example of group lookism, see Liu (2015: 255–256).

4 From the website of European Association for the Study of Obesity (EASO), http://easo.org/education-portal/obesity-facts-figures/.

5 This type of discrimination is often called "reaction qualifications". For in-depth discussion, see Lippert-Rasmussen (2014), Chapter 9, and Mason (2016).

6 When a society establishes laws to prohibit employers from discriminating against people whom some widespread social opinions disfavor, this practice is better interpreted as an effort to establish some external measure to counteract these social opinions, than as a declaration that employers' compliance with these opinions is totally unjustified.

7 These three kinds of lookism echo K. Anthony Appiah's division of stereotype. Appiah distinguishes between three kinds of stereotype: false stereotype, statistical stereotype, and normative stereotype. Ungrounded lookism and statistical lookism correspond roughly to Appiah's first two types of stereotype. While Appiah's normative stereotype concerns how the discriminatee ought to behave to conform to norms concerning her group identity, individualized and norm-conforming lookism is more inclusive, concerning all those seemingly reasonable social standards of what is beautiful, what is good, and so on. See Appiah (2001).

8 Of course, the norms within that set can be questioned, through which the baseline can then be revised. But we need first to provide justification for changing a certain social norm before we can revise the baseline, on the basis of which a claim of harm may be grounded.

9 The basic well-being – satisfaction of basic material, educational, and relational needs – are included in the "primary goods", which Rawls takes to include liberties, income and wealth, the social bases of self-respect, etc.

10 Mason (2016) argues that the degree of control that the discriminator has over his response to the discriminatee's appearance is relevant in accessing the morality of lookist practice. I think that control matters only in relation to the costs of the corresponding accommodation – the harder the control, the higher the costs.

11 For a detailed argument, see Liu (2015: 262–267).

12 I want to thank Kasper Lippert-Rasmussen, Peter Vallentyne, Crystal Allen Gunasekera, Wilfried Hinsch, Sheng Zhang, and an anonymous reviewer for this chapter for very helpful comments and criticisms on earlier drafts.

Bibliography

Alexander, L. 1992. "What Makes Wrongful Discrimination Wrong: Biases, Preferences, Stereotypes, and Proxies." *University of Pennsylvania Law Review*. 141: 149–219.

Anderson, E. 2015. "Moral Bias and Corrective Practices." *Proceedings and Addresses of the APA*. 89: 21–47.

Appiah, K. A. 2001. "Stereotypes and the Shaping of Identity," in Post, R. *et al.* (eds), *Prejudicial Appearances: The Logic of American Antidiscrimination Law*. Durham: Duke University Press.

Cotter, A. 2006. *Race Matters: An International Legal Analysis of Race Discrimination*. Burlington: Ashgate.

Dasgupta, N. and Greenwald, A. G. 2001. "On the Malleability of Automatic Attitudes: Combating Automatic Prejudice with Images of Admired and Disliked Individuals."*Journal of Personality and Social Psychology*. 81: 800–814.

Fara, P. 2003. "Marginalized Practices," in R. Porter (ed.), *The Cambridge History of Science Volume 4: Eighteenth-century Science*. Cambridge: Cambridge University Press, 485–508.

Ford, R. T. 2008. *The Race Card: How Bluffing about Bias Makes Race Relations Worse*. New York: Farrar, Straus and Giroux.

Hamermesh, D. S. and Biddle, J. E. 1994. "Beauty and the Labor Market." *American Economic Review*. 84: 1174–1194.

Hellman, D. 2008. *Why is Discrimination Wrong?* Cambridge: Harvard University Press.

Highfield, R. *et al.* 2009. "How Your Looks Betray Your Personality," *New Scientist*. www.newscientist.com/article/mg20126957-300-how-your-looks-betray-your-personality/.

Hook, S. 1995. "Reverse Discrimination," in S. Cahn (ed.), *The Affirmative Action Debate*. New York: Routledge, 145–152.

Hosoda, M. *et al.* 2003. "The Effects of Physical Attractiveness on Job-Related Outcomes: A Meta-Analysis of Experimental Studies." *Personnel Psychology*. 56: 431–462.

Juhnke, R. *et al.* 1987. "Effects of Attractiveness and Nature of Request on Helping Behavior." *Journal of Social Psychology*. 127: 317–322.

Kirkland, A. 2008. *Fat Rights: Dilemmas of Difference and Personhood*. New York: New York University Press.

Lippert-Rasmussen, K. 2014. *Born Free and Equal? A Philosophical Inquiry into the Nature of Discrimination*. New York: Oxford University Press.

Liu, X. F. 2015. "No Fats, Femmes, or Asians." *Moral Philosophy and Politics*. 2: 255–276.

Mason, A. 2016. "Appearance, Discrimination, and Reaction Qualifications." *The Journal of Political Philosophy*. 25(1): 48–71.

Mobius, M. and Rosenblat, T. S. 2006. "Why Beauty Matters," *American Economic Review*. 96: 222–235.

Moreau, S. 2010. "What is Discrimination?" *Philosophy and Public Affairs*. 38: 143–179.

Mulford, M. and Orbell, J. 1998. "Physical Attractiveness, Opportunity, and Success in Everyday Exchange," *American Journal of Sociology*. 103: 1565–1592.

Nguyen, J. 2011. "Gaysians Are Beautiful," *The Advocate*. www.advocate.com/politics/commentary/2011/03/03/gaysians-are-beautiful-jimmy-nguyen.

Nozick, R. 1974. *Anarchy, State, and Utopia*. New York: Basic Books.

Oliver, E., and Lee, T. 2005. "Public Opinion and the Politics of Obesity in America." *Journal of Health Politics, Policy and Law*. 30: 923–954.

Post, R. *et al.* 2001. *Prejudicial Appearances: The Logic of American Antidiscrimination Law*. Durham: Duke University Press.

Rawls, J. 1971. *A Theory of Justice*. Cambridge: Harvard University Press.

Rhode, D. L. 2009. "The Injustice of Appearance." *Stanford Law Review*. 61: 1033–1101.

Rhode, D. L. 2010. *The Beauty Bias: The Injustice of Appearance in Life and Law*. New York: Oxford University Press.

Ritts, V. *et al.* 1992. "Expectations, Impressions, and Judgments of Physically Attractive Students: A Review." *Review of Educational Research*. 62: 413–426.

Salkeld, L. 2011. "Didn't Get the Job? Blame 'Lookism', as Discrimination against the Ugly 'Is the New Racism'," *DailyMail*. www.dailymail.co.uk/news/article-2033782/Didnt-job-Blame-lookism-discrimination-ugly-new-racism.html.

Segall, S. 2012. "What's so Bad about Discrimination." *Utilitas*. 24: 82–100.

Solovay, S. 1999. *Tipping the Scales of Justice: Fighting Weight-based Discrimination*. Amherst: Prometheus.

Further reading

D. S. Hamermesh, *Beauty Pays: Why Attractive People Are More Successful* (Princeton, NJ: Princeton University Press, 2011); and D. L. Rhode, *The Beauty Bias: The Injustice of Appearance in Life and Law* (New York: Oxford University Press, 2010) provide a fine overview of various forms of looks-based discrimination. X. F. Liu, "No Fats, Femmes, or Asians," *Moral Philosophy and Politics* (2015); and A. Mason, "Appearance, Discrimination, and Reaction Qualifications," *The Journal of Political Philosophy* (2016) discuss the moral issues related to some cases of looks-based discrimination.

24

DISCRIMINATION AND TRANS IDENTITIES

Mari Mikkola

UNIVERSITY OF OXFORD

Introduction

A recent study portrays a devastating picture of material disadvantages trans people in the USA face. Many live in extreme poverty; they face unemployment at twice the rate of the general population; 90% of those surveyed reported having experienced workplace harassment, mistreatment or discrimination (or tried to non-disclose their trans status to avoid this); 47% reported having had experienced adverse job outcomes (like being denied promotion); one-fifth had experienced homelessness at some point due to their trans status; 53% reported having been verbally harassed or disrespected in public places, such as hotels, restaurants, buses, airports and government agencies; and 41% of the respondents reported having attempted suicide compared to 1.6% of the general population. Although respondents from all backgrounds were found to have suffered discrimination, trans people of color were particularly adversely affected due to the interaction of anti-trans bias and structural racism (Grant *et al.* 2011, 2–5).

In the light of such statistics, the former US Vice-President Joe Biden's recent declaration that "transgender rights" are the "civil rights issue of our time"[1] looks welcome and timely. Civil rights struggles are commonly linked to those that took place in the USA during the 1950s and 1960s in order for African-Americans to gain equal citizenship rights with white Americans. Being the legal basis and constitutive of free and equal citizenship, civil rights typically include personal, political, and economic rights that are crucially connected to autonomy in some sense. First, free and equal citizens have legal guarantees to partake in public discussion and decision-making. All citizens ought to have a voice and a vote in democratic deliberation. Second, citizens' "moral independence" (Dworkin 1995) is guaranteed by legal protections. This means that they have the ability to decide for themselves what to value and to live in conformity with those values. Equal citizenship has to do with 'public autonomy', which is about an individual's freedom to partake in democratic deliberation and decision-making, as well as with 'private autonomy', that is to do with individual freedom to choose a worthwhile way of life (for more, see Altman 2013).

Although civil rights violations conceivably involve material deprivation and disadvantage, the connection looks to be contingent rather than necessary. After all, one might say that those who (for instance) come from socio-economically disadvantaged backgrounds still have civil rights: their socio-economic status does not prevent them from partaking in democratic deliberation, deny them a vote or a voice, or necessarily hamper their (public or private) autonomy (cf. Chapters 20 and 35). One might point out that economic disadvantages experienced by some groups, like the Amish, are precisely the result of exercising moral independence and pursuing a way of life that group members find valuable (cf. Cudd 2006). Material inequalities can and do co-exist with civil rights' protections. With this in mind, how does Biden's claim square with the material disadvantages that trans persons face? What forms of discrimination stand in the way of trans people's civil rights and material well-being? This chapter examines these questions. The point is not to question whether trans people face discrimination; rather, the point is to clarify different ways in which this happens. Furthermore, I am not questioning the truth of Biden's claim; rather, another aim of this chapter is to elucidate in what sense trans discrimination involves civil rights violations and how these are connected to discrimination that results in material deprivation.[2] I will outline how trans discrimination involves a complex intermingling of (what I call) material and symbolic discriminatory forces. This not only tells us something important about political strategies of resistance, but it also tells us something interesting about the notion of sex discrimination, particularly as it has been understood in feminist discussions and anti-discrimination legislation. I will start by clarifying some terminology. I will then consider what sex discrimination amounts to, and how to understand trans discrimination.

Terminology

Above I talked about 'trans people'. This is somewhat fast and loose, and demands a modification. First, the term 'transsexual' is typically used to refer to individuals who use medical means and technologies to alter their bodies, so that their bodily presentation conforms to their gendered sense of self (Bettcher 2009a). Understanding this requires that we distinguish sex and gender. Speakers ordinarily seem to think that 'gender' and 'sex' are coextensive: women and men are human females and males, respectively, and the former is just the politically correct way to talk about the latter. Feminists typically disagree and many have historically endorsed a sex/gender distinction. Its standard formulation holds that 'sex' denotes human females and males, and depends on *biological* features (chromosomes, sex organs, hormones, other physical features). Then again, 'gender' denotes women and men, and depends on *social* factors (social roles, positions, behavior, self-ascription). The main feminist motivation for making this distinction was to counter biological determinism: the view that one's sex determines one's social and cultural traits and roles. Instead, feminists have argued that the latter are culturally learned or acquired, not caused by anatomy. In order to distinguish biological differences from social/psychological ones, and to talk about the latter, feminists appropriated the term 'gender'. Psychological writings on transsexuality were the first to employ gender terminology in this sense. Until the 1950s and 1960s, the term 'gender' was used to refer to masculine and feminine words, like *le* and *la* in French (Nicholson 1994, 80). But, in order to explain why some people felt that they were "trapped in wrong bodies", some psychologists (famously, John Money and Robert Stoller) began using 'sex' to pick out biological traits and 'gender identity' to pick out the amount of femininity and masculinity a person exhibited. Although (by and large) a person's sex and gender complement one another, separating them made theoretical sense and seemingly explained transsexuality: transsexuals' sex and gender do not match.

Contra this earlier usage, it is more common nowadays to employ 'transgender' to refer to:

> people who 'do not conform to prevailing expectations about gender' by presenting and living genders that were not assigned to them at birth or by presenting and living genders

> in ways that may not be readily intelligible in terms of more traditional conceptions of gender. Used as an umbrella term, it generally aims to group several different kinds of people such as transsexuals, drag queens and kings, some butch lesbians, and (heterosexual) male cross dressers.
>
> *(Bettcher 2009a)*

In many activist circles, the denotation 'trans*' has recently been used to refer to: "Transgender, transsexual, genderqueer, non-binary, genderfluid, genderfuck, intersex, third gender, transvestite, cross-dresser, bi-gender, trans man, trans women, agender."[3] Trans* is contrasted with 'cis' that denotes (roughly) women-born-female and men-born-male, who have gender identities and presentations that conform to the sex assigned at birth. 'Trans*' is also considered to be more inclusive than 'trans' in encompassing gender non-conforming individuals too, who may or may not consider themselves to be transgendered. For the remainder of this chapter, then, I will use 'trans*' as an inclusive umbrella term.

Discrimination

Philosophical literature on discrimination is extensive, and surveying it in full here is not possible. At its most basic, discrimination amounts to group-based differential treatment. It can be understood in a moralized or a neutral sense. For instance, adults and children are treated differentially along many social axes (e.g. one group is allowed to drive, the other is not). We do not usually find such differential treatment problematic though. In its moralized sense, discrimination consists in differential treatment of one group relative to another insofar as some acts, practices, or policies impose a *wrongful* disadvantage on that group. Furthermore, discrimination as a form of social injustice is due to some salient facet of our social identities and it is systematic, structural, and sometimes also organizational. The relevant groups facing discrimination must be somehow socially salient and public: they are groups "important to the structures of social interactions across a wide range of social contexts" (Lippert-Rasmussen 2006, 169; cf. Introduction). Being structural means that such discrimination has its causes in norms, habits, symbolic meanings, and assumptions unquestionably embedded in and underlying our institutional and social arrangements (cf. Young 1990). Such structural or institutional discrimination may also be organizational, where certain public bodies (corporations, universities, government agencies, other collective agents) act in discriminatory ways. (It need not be, though; more on this shortly.) In being systematic, discriminatory practices typically exist "throughout a society, usually over a substantial period of time", where "the institutions of society interlock and reinforce each other in ways that create and maintain" such practices (Clatterbaugh 1996, 290). Additionally, discrimination may be *direct* (some people are explicitly and intentionally singled out for disadvantaging treatment due to socially salient features), or it may be *indirect* (cf. Chapters 1 and 2). In the latter case, some rule disproportionately affects a group of people due to a socially salient feature they possess, although the rule is at face value neutral. With this in mind, we can see that structural discrimination need not be organizational: some corporations may have entirely gender-neutral rules about promotions and no overt discriminatory behavior takes place. But if only or mostly male employees are able to fulfill promotion requirements given background work and family-life arrangements, the rule indirectly disadvantages female employees.[4]

Well-known feminist writings on discrimination have focused on employment sex discrimination (cf. Chapter 15). The idea that sex discrimination in workplaces is the obstacle to women's liberation was prominent in the 'second wave' of feminist theory (late 1960s to early 1990s). Many US feminists saw equal access to employment outside the home, which was hampered by employment sex discrimination, as bringing an end to women's oppression (cf. Friedan 1963). On these feminist views, sex discrimination is a form of arbitrary differential treatment of individuals on the grounds of sex. People are treated differently because of their sex when sex is not a legitimate factor to take into account – it does not justify differential treatment (cf. Goldman 1979; Hook 1995). If one has a *legitimate* reason to take a person's sex into account, then the decision to hire (say) only females for a particular job is not discriminatory in the moralized sense (cf. Chapter 8). And if (for some reason) males simply were more able to do some job and more males than females were employed to do this job, this would also be morally (and legally) permissible. Anti-sex discrimination laws, then, are typically designed to stop employers treating people differently on sexed grounds, where sex is irrelevant for the particular job.

The feminist legal theorist and philosopher, Catharine MacKinnon, has famously argued that this understanding of sex discrimination misunderstands the source of such discrimination (MacKinnon 1987). She calls the above the 'difference approach' to discrimination. On this approach, women and men are fundamentally alike but their sex differences muddle this. Employers come falsely to think that sex differences result in women and men also differing in their abilities; as a result, they illegitimately treat women less favorably. Sex discrimination legislation is meant to correct this: the key idea is that once sex differences are not allowed to justify differential treatment, women and men will have the same employment opportunities. MacKinnon argues that the difference approach and sex and/or gender neutrality do not preclude women from being unjustly disadvantaged. Many well-paid jobs with good career prospects require that those hired for them can work long hours, do overtime, perhaps regularly travel abroad, or relocate easily. Those who are primary caretakers of small children – statistically women – are often unable to meet these requirements. On the difference approach this is not, however, discriminatory. If a job requires that the employee works 60 hours a week, the employer is perfectly entitled to hire only those who can work these hours. If only male applicants are able to fulfill this requirement, it is perfectly legitimate for the employer to hire only men. Even though this is formally not discriminatory, nonetheless, it seriously disadvantages women by making it difficult for those with caretaking responsibilities to gain well-paid jobs with good career prospects (cf. Chapter 15). That is, sex- and/or gender-neutral workplace arrangements can still indirectly discriminate against women. Instead, MacKinnon's alternative dominance approach acknowledges that sex differences exist, but it denies that these differences are responsible for discrimination. Rather, unequal distribution of power is: men as a group simply are more powerful socially, politically, and economically than women, and so the standards of work (and many other areas of life) are defined from a male perspective. The problem is not sex difference, but sexism and androcentricism in how we organize work and family lives (along with many other social institutions).

The discussion so far has looked at what discrimination amounts to. But given that we are dealing with wrongful discrimination, what grounds the wrongfulness? Answers to this question diverge considerably; I will note merely a few that are relevant for the discussion at hand.[5] If sex discrimination is arbitrary, so that the trait on the basis of which one is discriminated against is irrelevant for some job, the discriminator's judgments are irrational (Chapter 8). The irrationality might be explicated in a number of ways. For instance, one might say that if an employer fails to treat its employees on the basis of merit, this would be irrational and unfair. Alternatively, the irrationality might be grounded in the employer being influenced by false or misleading stereotypes about someone's social kind membership, such as thinking that since women are 'naturally' more emotional, they are unsuited for leadership roles (cf. Altman 2015; cf. Chapter

32). Being treated on the basis of misleading stereotypes may not suffice, though. Rather, some hold that such treatment must involve an instance of motivated irrationality, where the motivating force derives from *prejudice* (Dworkin 1985; Ely 1980) understood as a negatively-valenced attitude. To clarify: being influenced by false or misleading stereotypes may not be prejudicial. After all, I may be influenced by a positively-valenced mistaken stereotype that (say) women are particularly good at some specific job. In basing my hiring decisions on such a stereotype, my decision is not prejudicial because it is not based on any negative attitudes towards *men* – I simply hold (falsely) that women are particularly suited for the jobs that I am hiring for. On some views, this would still be an instance of sex discrimination. But it would be an instance that is based on stereotyping rather than prejudice.

That said, this explication of why sex discrimination is wrongful ill fits the idea of discrimination as civil rights violation. Rather, in such cases of differential discriminatory treatment the discriminator fails to respect something about the discriminatee, like their dignity or personal autonomy. Deborah Hellman (2011; Chapter 7) holds that wrongful discrimination involves drawing distinctions between people that count as demeaning. 'Demeaning' for Hellman means: "to treat someone in a way that denies her equal moral worth…To demean is not merely to insult but also to put down, to diminish or denigrate" (2011, 29). It is to treat another as morally inferior. Alternatively, one might hold that civil rights violations are wrongful in hampering some crucial human interests (cf. Mikkola 2016). For instance, Sophia Moreau holds that unjust discrimination injures our crucial interest in *deliberative freedoms*: "freedoms to deliberate about and decide how to live in a way that is insulated from pressures stemming from [normatively] extraneous traits of ours", such as our skin color or reproductive organs (2010, 147; cf. Chapter 13). Deliberative freedoms are those that we think members of liberal societies have a right to, namely freedom of thought and action (Moreau 2010, 148). Decision-making and deliberation are about making commitments, and taking steps to bring about what we are committed to. A necessary condition for me having a particular deliberative freedom is that "I really have the opportunity to do the thing I may decide to do" (Moreau 2010, 170). Normatively extraneous traits, then again, are those that "people should not have to factor into their deliberations…*as costs*" when thinking about where to live or what job to pursue (Moreau 2010, 149). Discrimination is wrongful in that our right to deliberative freedoms is not insulated from pressures based on extraneous traits: due to some trait, I do not have the opportunity to do something I may decide to undertake. And this undermines citizens' moral independence.

Trans* discrimination

With the above theoretical tools at hand, how can we understand trans* discrimination? In exploring this question, it is useful to distinguish material and symbolic discrimination (although I take the two to be intertwined). What follows is not an exhaustive list of ways in which trans* people face discrimination, but it is nevertheless still illuminating.

Material discrimination

One of the most disturbing forms of trans* material discrimination is transphobic violence and harassment. According to Talia Mae Bettcher, transphobia is not necessarily the fear of trans* people, but "any negative attitudes (hatred, loathing, rage, or moral indignation) harbored towards transpeople on the basis of our enactments of gender" (2007, 46). Transphobic violence and homicide are considered to be urgent and serious problems, and in the USA trans* women of color are especially at increased risk for violence, according to the Human Rights Campaign's

2015 study.[6] Instances of transphobic violence and harassment are directly discriminatory: the perpetrators explicitly intend to discriminate and their motivation to do so hinges on trans* persons' gender presentation – trans* persons face violence and harassment because of their gender presentation, although this is often also intertwined with their race and class markers.

There are of course many other types of material discrimination, and many of the material deprivations trans* people face are also faced by females and people of color (employment discrimination, poverty, rates of homelessness, adverse job outcomes). Clearly this does not make these discriminatory forces identical, but it does raise an issue: can we analyze trans* discrimination using the same theoretical frameworks feminists have used to theorize discrimination against women? Consider employment discrimination. According to the U.S. Equal Employment Opportunity Commission, sex discrimination "involves treating someone (an applicant or employee) unfavorably because of that person's sex. Discrimination against an individual because of gender identity, including transgender status, or because of sexual orientation is discrimination because of sex in violation of Title VII."[7] This way of putting employment sex discrimination of trans* people is, however, tricky for a number of reasons. Given that trans* identities are about not conforming to prevailing gender expectations by presenting and living genders that come apart from those gender presentations assigned at birth, how fitting is the idea that trans* discrimination involves *sex* discrimination? And does sex discrimination of trans* people involve discrimination on the basis of traits that are arbitrary or irrelevant for a job?

Consider the latter question first. In an obvious sense, the answer is yes. For most jobs (if not almost all), I contend, a person's sex is irrelevant. However, reflecting on why this is morally problematic in the case of trans* people is instructive. In many instances of employment discrimination that females face, employers seemingly fail to treat their employees on the basis of merit, and instead do so on the basis of false or misleading stereotypes about women. But in the case of trans* employees, stereotyping *per se* does not quite home in on the relevant wrong. Rather, what seems to be doing the work is prejudice (negatively-valenced stereotyping).[8] For one thing, trans* identities are still highly pathologized: trans* people allegedly suffer from 'gender dysphoria' or 'gender identity disorder' in gender identifying contrary to their birth-assigned sex. The latest 2013 *Diagnostic and Statistical Manual of Mental Disorders* still classifies trans* identity as a disorder. This sort of pathologization is connected to transphobia.[9] So employment discrimination of trans* people seems to involve negative – often visceral and non-cognitive – attitudes (hatred, loathing, rage, moral indignation), rather than 'merely' mistaken beliefs about a trans* person's employment performance. Trans* employment discrimination, then, is seemingly wrongful in a specific sense: it is not about arbitrarily taking sex into account when making hiring and firing decisions; it is about such decisions involving prejudicial, negatively-valenced attitudes. To put the point differently: while employment discrimination of women involves structural discrimination (as MacKinnon argues), trans* employment discrimination involves more organizational discrimination that is made wrongful by employers' prejudicial attitudes (rather than misleading stereotypical beliefs about sex differences).

Now, what about the idea that trans* discrimination involves *sex* discrimination? This is not so straightforward, if by 'sex' we mean anatomical features (chromosomes, sex organs, genitalia, hormones, other physical features). Bettcher considers two common ways to understand trans* identities. First, the 'wrong body' model whereby "transsexuality is construed as a misalignment between gender identity and sexed body where identity is innate and determines one's *real* sex" (Bettcher 2013, 53). One's identity shows that one inhabits a 'wrong' body in need of medical alteration. Second, the transgender model: trans* people challenge the existence of two "nontransversible mutually exclusive categories in which all individuals belong" (Bettcher

2013, 53). On this view, they go 'beyond the binary'. However, Bettcher holds, both models fail to do justice to some trans★ persons' self-identifications (see also Bettcher 2014 for a detailed discussion of these models). Instead, she proposes that trans★ discrimination and oppression is about trans★ people opposing "the *meanings* of mainstream gender terms and practices", so that there is a conflict between dominant culture and "subcultural formations" (Bettcher 2013, 53; my italics). Again, the upshot of this is that sex discrimination in the sense of being about anatomy illegitimately affecting job opportunities does *not*, on Bettcher's account, accurately capture the situation of trans★ people facing employment discrimination. This is because the dominant understanding of sex is simply rejected, opposed, or revised in trans-friendly settings, and so the dominant conception of 'sex discrimination' is meaningless and unacceptable to many coming from trans-subcultures. Bluntly put, sex discrimination that trans★ people face derives from their *opposing* mainstream understandings of sex. But this phenomenon looks very different to the one more commonly understood under the rubric of sex discrimination by feminist philosophers and policy makers.

With this in mind, MacKinnon's critique of the difference approach might actually reveal something about trans★ employment discrimination that helps us understand such discrimination better (although MacKinnon herself does not realize or acknowledge this). In discussing employment discrimination against women, MacKinnon argues that sexism, androcentricism, and male dominance are responsible for the discrimination, not sex difference. That is, although females historically have faced overt and direct sex discrimination, they nowadays more frequently encounter more covert structural discrimination due to workplace arrangements that take being a heterosexual, cis-male (who is typically white, able-bodied and middle-class) as the standard against which everyone is measured. Now, analyzing workplace arrangements with an expanded version of her dominance approach will probably reveal that in addition to male dominance, our workplace arrangements are heteronormative and trans-unfriendly. And so, there is an added layer of trans★ discrimination: employment arrangements not only tend to display overt direct discrimination owing to transphobic prejudice, but dominant heteronormative workplace practices can also fail to promote trans★ people's well-being at work (such as failures to provide adequate toilet facilities). Employment discrimination resulting from heteronormative workplace arrangements might involve less overt prejudicial discrimination, but it may well involve what Moreau took unjust discrimination to involve: failures to ensure that our deliberative freedoms are insulated from pressures based on normatively extraneous traits. Due to one's trans★ identity, one may not have the opportunity to do something one may decide to undertake (like apply for a particular job or pursue a particular career). But being trans★ should not figure as a cost in one's freedom to deliberate and decide about how to live one's life, or which employment goals to pursue. Assuming that citizens in liberal societies have a *prima facie* right to deliberative freedoms, such costs incurred by trans★ people seemingly hamper free and equal citizenship – which is in line with Biden's characterization of trans rights being the civil rights issue of our time.

Symbolic discrimination

The above demonstrates a way to connect material discrimination and civil rights struggles. We can explicate the connection further by thinking about (what I am calling) symbolic discrimination that to a significant extent undergirds material deprivation. By 'symbolic', I do not mean that discrimination is somehow 'in the head'. I take symbolic discriminatory forces to be very real indeed. However, the point is that rather than being about material forces, symbolic discrimination is about prevalent social and cultural meanings attached to being trans★

(intertwined with meanings pertaining to other social identity facets), which play a significant role in the forms of discrimination trans* people face.

I noted above that Bettcher (2013) understands trans* discrimination and oppression to be about trans* people opposing mainstream meanings of gender and gendered practices, which results in a conflict between dominant cultural meanings and subcultural trans-meanings. This conflict hinges on what Bettcher takes gender presentation to communicate. In short, "public gender presentation can be seen to euphemistically communicate or symbolically represent genital status" (Bettcher 2013, 58). In her view, we all regularly communicate something about our private genital status in public, which makes asking near-strangers intimate questions about their genitalia a boundary violation, a form of abuse and harassment. (Just think of one's co-worker making such inquiries out of the blue.) Trans* people, however, on Bettcher's view opt out of this system: they do not take gender presentation to communicate intimate information about genital status. That is, they reject such dominant cultural practices and ways of generating meanings. As a result, she holds, trans* people are subject to 'reality enforcement': "a mechanism by which acquiescence to the mandate to communicate genital status is enforced" (Bettcher 2013, 58). This sort of enforcement involves invalidation of self-identity claims made by trans* people (like, "you are *really* just a man" uttered to trans women by cis-people). Reality enforcement further involves thinking about trans* identities as mere appearances (such as trans* people being told that they are engaging in some form of 'gender-deception') (Bettcher 2013, 59). Finally, reality enforcement involves a kind of sexual abuse via attempts to verify trans* people's genital status (such as being asked "Have you had *the* surgery?"). This sort of questioning "involves the effort to reinforce the cultural mandate to symbolically declare genital status that trans people have effectively opted out of" (Bettcher 2013, 59), which is abusive in being a privacy and intimacy violation. Some cis-individuals feel entitled to inquire about trans* people's genital presentation even when they are near (or full) strangers. By contrast, inquiring about cis-people's genital presentation is typically not considered to be appropriate (such as asking a near-stranger "so, what is the size of your penis then?"). These sorts of inquiries about trans* people's genital presentation, then, are violations of bodily privacy and intimacy.

Reality enforcement is a type of symbolic discrimination against trans* people. It is symbolic (in my terminology) because it involves a conflict between different *meanings* over gender and gendered practices. It is a form of differential treatment in that cis-people generally do not face reality enforcement of this kind. And it is wrongful in that reality enforcement involves denial of identity claims, being seen as a 'deceiver', and privacy violations. This relates to Hellman's view above on what is wrongful about discrimination: it involves demeaning differential treatment that aims not only to insult, but also "to put down, to diminish or denigrate" (Hellman 2011, 29; Chapter 7). We can see that this sort of symbolic discrimination is closely connected to the idea of civil rights struggles, and it goes against trans* citizens' moral independence in being a kind of autonomy violation. Unfortunately, reality enforcement and genital verification do not always involve just asking, but also physical violence and homicide when trans* people are attacked and forcibly made to 'reveal' their genital presentation. This connects to the very real material discrimination discussed above. In this sense, material discrimination of trans* people involves an attack on public and private autonomy that equal citizens are entitled to, which hinges on transphobic practices of reality enforcement – or, what I have here called 'symbolic discrimination'.

In order to combat reality enforcement, Bettcher argues that, rather than thinking of trans* identities as being aberrant or somehow in need of explanation, we ought to "accept the self-identity claims of all trans people as presumptively valid and true without requesting justification as a condition of acceptance" (Bettcher 2013, 52). She holds that trans* politics should proceed with "the principle that transpeople have *first-person authority* (FPA) over their own gender" (2009b, 98). FPA is a kind of ethical authority (Bettcher 2009b, 100), which fits the idea that dominant practices violate trans* people's civil rights in being both public- and private-autonomy hindering. What Bettcher means by this is the following: FPA involves a kind of first person avowal that is connected to privacy and the ownership of one's own mental attitudes. Avowal generally is about an acknowledgement that one takes responsibility for one's mental states (like feelings). It is further a sort of confession of mental attitudes that are otherwise private (Bettcher 2009b, 101). And so, in a "publicly avowing attitude, the first person has in some sense staked a social claim and certified a view about their mental life on which we can 'bank'" (Bettcher 2009b, 102). In this sense, then, FPA is not merely epistemic but ethical: something has gone not only epistemically but also ethically seriously wrong when another person tells me with alleged authority what my 'real' attitudes about my own identity are or should be. This involves a kind of autonomy violation in that the other is inappropriately treating their interpretation and assessment of my attitudes as authoritative (Bettcher 2009b, 103). Following Bettcher, we see here again how the idea of civil rights struggles fits trans* politics: trans* people are fighting for authority over their own identities and self-definition, and against pathologization of trans* identities and reality enforcement. Again, this echoes Hellman's view that discrimination is wrongful when it involves demeaning another: when someone is treated as morally inferior. One clear way in which this takes place is when others take their assessments of our attitudes to be authoritative over our own assessments. And trans* struggles for authority also echo Moreau's view that discrimination involves normatively extraneous traits hampering our deliberative freedoms: fearing denials of FPA, trans* people may and do avoid certain situations and actions that they would otherwise decide to engage in and undertake. Being trans* is a cost that hinders moral independence when it should not.

Conclusion

What do the preceding sections tell us about sex discrimination? For one thing, they shows that although both trans* politics and feminism fight against employment discrimination, the problems faced are of a subtly different kind. The manner in which women have (and do) face employment discrimination is not the same as the manner in which trans* people do. The above also suggests that the wrongfulness of employment discrimination comes apart, depending on who faces such discrimination. Although I am sure that many Western cis-women still face misogyny, this does not suffice to explain their diminished employment prospects. And appealing to stereotyping does not sufficiently explain trans* employment discrimination. Anti-discrimination laws may then not be able to mitigate both, and these subtle differences make a real difference to the efficacy of such legislation.

Furthermore, thinking about different discriminatory forces (for instance, material and symbolic discrimination) demonstrates that there is no such thing as trans* discrimination *simpliciter*. This tells us something about the wrongfulness of discrimination, which makes a difference to strategies of resistance. While trans* employment and housing discrimination may (principally) involve disadvantaged treatment that is wrongful due to hostile and prejudicial attitudes, other forms of trans* discrimination involve autonomy and privacy violations. Such violations do not just involve prejudicial attitudes but (as demonstrated by reality enforcement) violations that are more grounded in disrespect against trans* people and in their democratic interests not being protected (as discussed by Hellman and Moreau). With this in mind, there is a sense in which Biden is right: symbolic discriminatory forces, most notably reality enforcement, do hinder trans* people's public and private autonomy. And this demonstrates that different interventions are needed to fight against different discriminatory forces. Employment and housing discrimination are unlikely to end simply by enacting anti-sex discrimination legislation, like that cited above. Rather, justice demands urgent interventions on the symbolic level too. Importantly, this demands the depathologization of trans* identities. It also involves acceptance of subcultural meanings of gender and gendered practices. Anti-sex discrimination laws do not alter people's affective reactions and the social meanings that they accept. And so, in order for those laws to be effective, being trans* has to have the kind of legitimacy that bearers of civil rights are afforded.

Notes

1 www.huffingtonpost.com/entry/joe-biden-transgender- military_us_56113679e4b0af3706e11c97.

2 I make this point in response to a furore in the USA about toilet use, which took place at the time of writing this piece. Many US conservatives, including some prominent African-Americans, are fiercely opposing the idea that struggles to secure trans rights are akin to African-American civil rights struggles.

3 *You Know When You're Trans* When…Blog*, http://youknowyouretrans.tumblr.com/.

4 The above still neglects some further important distinctions; for more, see Altman 2015; Mikkola 2016; Moreau 2010; Chapter 2.

5 For more on the wrongfulness of discrimination, see Chapters 6–14.

6 http://hrc-assets.s3-website-us-east-1.amazonaws.com//files/assets/resources/HRC-Anti TransgenderViolence-0519.pdf

7 https://www.eeoc.gov//laws/types/sex.cfm

8 Much of the same is true of how trans* people are treated on the housing market. Family rejection, inability to find accommodation due to renters' prejudiced attitudes and homeless shelters' inability to create safe spaces for trans* people result in serious material obstacles for trans* people on the housing market. (For more, see www.transequality.org/issues/housing-homelessness.)

9 Pathologization is particularly worrying when we bear in mind that in some countries medical access to transitioning comes with a particularly insidious cost: trans* people are forcibly sterilized in the process of transitioning. Until a few years ago, this was standard practice for instance in Sweden, Germany, and Italy.

Bibliography

Altman, Andrew. 2013. "Civil Rights." *The Stanford Encyclopedia of Philosophy* (Summer 2013 Edition), edited by Edward N. Zalta. Online at http://plato.stanford.edu/archives/sum2013/entries/civil-rights/

Altman, Andrew. 2015. "Discrimination." *The Stanford Encyclopedia of Philosophy* (Fall 2015 Edition), edited by Edward N. Zalta. Online at http://plato.stanford.edu/archives/fall2015/entries/discrimination/

Bettcher, Talia Mae. 2007. "Evil Deceivers and Make-Believers: On Transphobic Violence and the Politics of Illusion." *Hypatia*. 22(3): 43–65.

Bettcher, Talia Mae. 2009a. "Feminist Perspectives on Trans Issues." *The Stanford Encyclopedia of Philosophy* (Winter 2009 Edition), edited by Edward N. Zalta. Online at http://plato.stanford.edu/archives/win2009/entries/feminism-trans/

Bettcher, Talia Mae. 2009b. "Trans Identities and First-Person Authority." In *You've Changed: Sex Reassignment and Personal Identity*, edited by Laurie Shrage, 98–120. Oxford: Oxford University Press.

Bettcher, Talia Mae. 2013. "Trans Women and 'Interpretive Intimacy': Some Initial Reflections." In *The Essential Handbook of Women's Sexuality* (volume two), edited by Donna Marie Castañeda, 51–68. Santa Barbara: Praeger.

Bettcher, Talia Mae. 2014. "Trapped in the Wrong Theory: Re-Thinking Trans Oppression and Resistance." *Signs: Journal of Women in Culture and Society*. 39(2): 383–406.

Clatterbaugh, Kenneth. 1996. "Are Men Oppressed?" In *Rethinking Masculinity: Philosophical Explorations in Light of Feminism*, edited by Larry May, Robert Strikwerda and Patrick Hopkins, 298–306. Lanham, ML: Rowman & Littlefield.

Cudd, Ann. 2006. *Analyzing Oppression*. NY: Oxford University Press.

Dworkin, Ronald. 1985. *A Matter of Principle*. Cambridge, MA: Harvard University Press.

Dworkin, Ronald. 1995. *Freedom's Law*. Cambridge, MA: Harvard University Press.

Ely, John Hart. 1980. *Democracy and Distrust*. Cambridge, MA: Harvard University Press.

Friedan, Betty. 1963. *The Feminine Mystique*. Harmondsworth: Penguin Books Ltd.

Goldman, Alan. 1979. *Justice and Reverse Discrimination*. Princeton: Princeton University Press.

Grant, Jaime M., Lisa A. Mottet, Justin Tanis, Jack Harrison, Jody L. Herman, and Mara Keisling. 2011. *Injustice at Every Turn: A Report of the National Transgender Discrimination Survey*. Washington: National Center for Transgender Equality and National Gay and Lesbian Task Force. Online at www.thetaskforce.org/static_html/downloads/reports/reports/ntds_full.pdf

Hellman, Deborah. 2011. *When is Discrimination Wrong?* Cambridge, MA: Harvard University Press.

Hook, Sidney. 1995. "Reverse Discrimination." In *The Affirmative Action Debate*, edited by Steven Cahn, 145–152. New York: Routledge.

Lippert-Rasmussen, Kasper. 2006. "The Badness of Discrimination." *Ethical Theory and Moral Practice* 9(2): 167–185.

MacKinnon, Catharine. 1987. *Feminism Unmodified*. Cambridge, MA: Harvard University Press.

Mikkola, Mari. 2016. *The Wrong of Injustice: Dehumanization and its Role in Feminist Philosophy*. New York: Oxford University Press.

Moreau, Sophia. 2010. "What is Discrimination?" *Philosophy & Public Affairs*. 38: 143–179.

Nicholson, Linda. 1994. "Interpreting Gender." *Signs*. 20: 79–105.

Young, I. M. 1990. *Justice and the Politics of Difference*. Princeton: Princeton University Press.

PART IV
Sites of discrimination

25
DISCRIMINATION AND THE JOB MARKET

Sarah Goff

UNIVERSITY OF HONG KONG

Introduction

Comparisons between men and women, blacks and whites, and other groups show different patterns of employment and different average levels of compensation for work. These differences persist, to a lesser degree, in comparisons of individuals with similar levels of educational attainment and job experience. When individuals of different genders and racial groups are matched on these characteristics and other observable traits, white males enjoy higher wages, higher non-wage compensation, a lower probability of experiencing unemployment, and other advantages. Economists and sociologists cannot fully explain these patterns on the basis of observable differences between members of these groups, other than group membership itself. Empirical research in this field seeks to identify the impact of discriminatory decision-making in the job market, and distinguish it from the knock-on effects of personal choices and differential treatment in society's other institutions.

In this chapter, I will describe common points of reference and topics of interest for both the empirical literature and the philosophical literature on discrimination in the job market. A first point of reference is the pattern of job allocation that would result from non-discriminatory hiring practices. A second is the mental states of employers and other economic decision-makers, particularly how their tastes and factual beliefs influence their assessments of job seekers and employees. A third is the nature of the relationship between discrimination in the job market and differential treatment in the broader society.

Estimations and explanations of discrimination in the job market

This section describes empirical social scientists' efforts to explain race- and sex-based patterns of labor market outcomes. In what follows, I provide a brief overview of three leading theoretical explanations for the observed patterns, namely: human capital theory, taste discrimination, and statistical discrimination.

Wage differences by race and gender are the most visible, and most widely recognized, pattern of labor market outcomes. Altonji and Blank (1999) note that the wage gaps among racial and ethnic groups have been stable in the U.S. since the mid-1970s. Another notable pattern is racial and ethnic segregation within the labor market, with black and Hispanic men concentrated in low-skilled jobs (ibid: 3153). Blau and Kahn (2007) observe that the pay gap between American men and women has narrowed since the late 1970s, but that the convergence in wages has slowed in recent years. Significant sex segregation by occupation also remains. Even when both men and women have substantial representation in an occupational category, there is often significant segregation of the sexes between organizations and within organizations according to job title. Empirical researchers generally seek to understand the causes of the gender wage gap and wage differentials between blacks and whites, although there is extensive documentation of wage differentials among other groups as well.

Human capital theory assumes that employers allocate jobs according to job seekers' capacities to make productive contributions, also known as their "human capital." Human capital theorists argue that labor market patterns track broader social inequalities, because employers allocate jobs on the basis of job seekers' actual levels of accumulated human capital (Polachek 1987). Women have a greater tendency to take interruptions from formal employment due to the division of labor in the family, and thus on average women have less work experience (cf. Chapter 15). Members of racial minority groups are more likely to have restricted access to quality public educational institutions, and geographical racial segregation may reduce their access to jobs that provide training and experience. Women's and racial minorities' lower average wage levels are not attributable to discrimination, if the observed patterns can be explained by the lower levels of human capital held by these groups. However, the theory's capacity to explain sex segregation in the labor market has been disputed (England 1982).

The theory of taste discrimination, which was first described in Gary Becker's influential book *The Economics of Discrimination* (Becker 1971 [1957]), provides an explanation for the residual patterns of unequal wages and segregation within the labor market that persist after accounting for differences in human capital. Taste discrimination occurs whenever a person pays or forgoes income for the privilege of associating with some people over others, either as a result of prejudicial preferences or ignorance about others' capacities to make economically productive contributions (ibid: 14). One implication of Becker's analysis is that employers can discriminate more within monopolistic industries, because they have greater capacity to bear the costs of their preferences for job seekers. Another implication is that heterogeneity in employers' tastes for discrimination will result in segregation in the labor market, with non-discriminatory employers hiring more members of the disadvantaged group. While taste discrimination has been a highly influential theory, economists generally favor models of discrimination that depend on imperfect information, which are discussed below. Taste discrimination's lack of popularity among economists may be due to the fact that the theory can explain lower average wages for women and racial minority groups only if prejudice is widespread or markets are not competitive.

Theories of "statistical discrimination" seek to explain employers' differential treatment of women and racial minority groups on the basis of imperfect information (cf. Chapter 3). Employers aim to hire workers whose productive contributions will exceed the cost of paying them, but they also aim to limit the costs of searching for qualified workers and training them (Arrow 1973). When two job seekers provide evidence of having similar qualifications, an employer may maximize profit by taking account of information about the job seekers' respective groups, particularly the average levels of human capital in the group and the credibility of signals about their members' levels of human capital (Phelps 1972). Differential treatment on this basis has the effect of advantaging a less qualified job seeker from a group whose median member is highly qualified, and disadvantaging a highly-qualified job seeker from a group whose median member has low qualifications. However, Aigner and Cain (1977) note that this differential treatment does not lead to a difference in the average wage levels of groups that have the same average productivity, and therefore, they argue, it does not constitute discrimination. Lundberg and Startz (1983) argue that differential treatment on the basis of credible signaling could lead to a difference in average wage levels if individuals' anticipation of this treatment disincentivizes their investments in human capital, and thus it reduces a group's average level of productivity. Some groups may be disadvantaged by use of statistical discrimination because credible signals about their productivity are relatively scarce, such as young workers at the beginning of their working lives (Altonji and Pierret 2001), and not because they are otherwise disadvantaged.

The inability to directly observe employers' tastes and beliefs, and the lack of a precise measure for human capital, pose significant obstacles to researchers' efforts to measure the impact of employers' discrimination on labor market outcomes. The best available evidence may come from experiments, such as correspondence and audit studies, which manipulate signals about the race and sex of job seekers to measure the extent to which this information affects employers' decision-making. One prominent correspondence study provided employers with identical résumés from fictitious job seekers whose names strongly signaled their race. The résumés with names that strongly signaled white applicants received significantly more callbacks for interviews, particularly for résumés from highly qualified applicants (Bertrand and Mullainathan 2004). Other evidence comes from quasi-experiments, such as Goldin and Rouse's influential study of orchestras' use of screens to conceal the identities of musicians, which accounted for up to 25% of the increase in women hired between 1970 and 1996 (2000). It is believed that most discrimination in the job market takes the form of indirect discrimination, since it is illegal for employers to directly discriminate against women and racial minorities, but these studies indicate there may be a significant contribution from employers' implicit biases against these groups (cf. Chapters 2 and 32). While there are many studies following these approaches, experiments can provide only suggestive evidence of the extent of discrimination and the forms it takes within the broader labor market. This is also a limitation of laboratory research, showing that women and men differ on average in psychological attributes, such as risk aversion and attitudes to competition, which are theoretically relevant but have not been demonstrated to influence labor market outcomes (Bertrand 2010: 1583).

I note three points of particular interest for philosophical accounts of discrimination in the job market. First, economists generally assume that the job seekers' human capital is the primary basis for the allocation of jobs. Employers deviate from this standard if they hire in accordance with their own preferences over the identities of job seekers. Second, employers' preferences and factual beliefs are fundamental to the leading explanations for how discrimination occurs in the job market. Third, discrimination in the job market may have complex linkages with differential treatment in society's other fundamental institutions. The household division of labor and inequalities in the public educational system, for instance, may be highly significant for explaining the lower levels of human capital held by women and racial minorities, on average (cf. Chapter 15). However, anticipated experiences of discrimination in the job market also may be important, if they disincentivize labor force participation and educational attainment.

The philosophical literature on discrimination in the job market

This section provides an overview of three philosophical debates about how to define discrimination in the job market and explain when it is wrong. First, there is debate over normative standards for the allocation of jobs, particularly over whether a wrong is done to the most qualified applicant when she is passed over for a job. A second debate concerns the significance of decision-makers' mental states for identifying whether discrimination has occurred and whether it is wrongful. A final debate concerns the relationship between discrimination in the job market and broader differences in society's treatment of its members: if an employer hires on the basis of idiosyncratic prejudices, for instance, this may not be wrongful discrimination because it does not correspond to broader social divisions.

Discrimination as the misallocation of jobs

It is a commonly held belief that the most qualified applicant for a job should receive it, either because she deserves the job or due to her superior merit. A person is judged as deserving of a job on the basis of past actions and achievements; a person's merits are judged on the basis of the qualities she currently possesses. It has been argued there is a close link between a person's deservingness and her meriting of a particular position (Miller 1996; Sher 1988; cf. Chapter 9). A job seeker is deserving on the basis of her past acquisition of skills and qualifications, and she is meritorious for possessing these acquired qualities. An important point is that the job seeker need not be morally responsible for her possession of the relevant qualities (Miller 1992). Since job seekers necessarily make use of their own natural talents and fortunate circumstances, for which they are not responsible, such a requirement would be problematic. However, a central question is why a person's superior desert or merit supports her moral claim to a job. For George Sher, hiring by merit "is a way of taking seriously the potential agency of both the successful and the unsuccessful applicants" (Sher 1988: 120). David Miller argues that the most qualified job seeker deserves the job, so that she also may deserve the remuneration to be received for the contributions she will make in the job (1992).

Some critics of meritocratic hiring argue that it is merely derivative of employers' rational self-interest or the requirements of an efficient job market, which are commonly viewed as inadequate grounds for the most qualified job seeker to have a claim to a position (Daniels 1978; Cavanagh 2002: 43–48, 63–69; Hellman 2008: 105–108). Thus, a central question concerns the extent of difference between, on the one hand, meritocracy and desert as normative standards for how employers *should* allocate jobs and, on the other, economic models describing how employers *do* in fact allocate them. According to Miller's argument for meritocracy, jobs should be allocated on the basis of job seekers' prior acquisition of talents and skills, because these are predictive of their future contributions in work. If an employer allocates a job on the basis of a job seeker's superior education and work experience, he may simultaneously satisfy the predictions of human capital theory and this interpretation of the meritocratic standard. However, if meritocratic hiring requires the employer to forgo the use of statistical discrimination or to overlook his customers' prejudices when specifying the requirements of a job (these "reaction qualifications" will be discussed later in this chapter), adopting the meritocratic standard may be very costly for him, and for the efficiency of the job market also.

Another debate about meritocratic hiring concerns its relationship with equality of opportunity (Chapters 10 and 11). Matt Cavanagh sketches and criticizes a set of views in which equality of opportunity plays a supporting role for meritocratic hiring. On his sketch, equality of opportunity is merely derivative: it creates favorable conditions of competition in which job seekers' natural potential for desert can be identified, job seekers can demonstrate their deservingness, and individuals can be rewarded in accordance with their responsibility for their own deservingness (2002: 88–90). Andrew Mason, by contrast, argues for embedding meritocratic hiring within a theory of equality of opportunity (2006). Taking inspiration from George Sher's argument for allocating jobs to the best qualified as a way to respect job seekers' agency (1988), Mason argues that meritocratic hiring is a requirement of justice for respecting persons. According to Mason's theory of equality of opportunity, hiring by merit is one of several requirements of justice relating to the allocation of jobs, which also include open competition for positions and access to qualifications. This set of institutional requirements creates conditions in which individuals arc allocated jobs in accordance with their responsible choices.

There are two important objections to meritocratic hiring's justification as a requirement of equality of opportunity. First, when equality of opportunity is not realized in society's other fundamental institutions, such as the family and the public educational system, meritocratic hiring may fail to provide equal opportunities for job seekers. Instead, equalizing opportunities may require employers to engage in "affirmative action" through quotas or other special considerations for socially disadvantaged job seekers (cf. Chapter 33). Affirmative action may be understood as a requirement for achieving meritocratic hiring under non-ideal conditions, or viewed as a justified deviation from meritocratic hiring in order to achieve equality of opportunity (Mason 2001: 780–781). Therefore, under non-ideal conditions, meritocratic hiring is either significantly revised in the content of its standards for employers or it is secondary to other requirements of justice. The second set of objections to meritocratic hiring, when justified as a required component of equality of opportunity, is against equality of opportunity as a theory of justice. These objections to equality of opportunity in the job market are also targeted against Rawls' argument for the lexical priority of fair equality of opportunity over the difference principle (1971).

In his rejection of Rawls' theory of equality of opportunity, Richard Arneson argues for an organization of society, including an arrangement of the job market, that maximally fulfills a prioritarian theory of justice (1999: 109; cf. Chapter 12). Arneson indicates that certain practices conventionally regarded as discriminatory can be judged morally wrong on the grounds that they detract from the achievement of justice: "Discrimination on the basis of race, sex, sexual orientation, and so on, is wrongful because (to the extent that) discrimination on these bases is not a good means to achieve fulfillment of fundamental justice values" (1999: 95). Kasper Lippert-Rasmussen also endorses a prioritarian theory of justice, but one that has sensitivity to individuals' moral deservingness. A wrongful act of discriminatory hiring is additionally wrong, according to a theory that is sensitive to desert, when the successful applicant is less deserving than the passed-over job seeker (2013: 165–170). By contrast, Shlomi Segall proposes a luck egalitarian account of justice in hiring with an "add on" proviso of non-discrimination, following from his view that non-meritocratic theories of justice cannot account for why discriminatory hiring is morally wrong (2012a: 44).

This concludes the chapter's brief overview of the first approach to discriminatory hiring, which understands discriminatory hiring to be wrong when it results in the misallocation of jobs. One issue of interest for this approach is how it specifies the employer's role in bringing about the correct allocation of jobs. Meritocratic hiring is generally taken to imply the employer has a duty to the most qualified applicant to allocate him a job. On prioritarian, desert prioritarian, or luck egalitarian theories, employers might be required to allocate jobs to candidates with the highest levels of human capital in order to improve economic efficiency, and thereby promote the achievement of justice. Another possibility is that justice requires employers to allocate jobs with concern for the welfare, and also the deservingness, of individual job seekers; this may require large deviations from hiring on the basis of human capital.

Discrimination as a feature of the discriminator's preferences and beliefs

In subsequent paragraphs, I describe an approach to defining wrongful discrimination on the basis of the discriminator's mental state and the costs imposed on others. Larry Alexander's influential article (1992) remains the most fully described theory of wrongful discrimination that follows this approach, and several other theorists take a similar line of argument in their analysis of the significance of the discriminator's unwarranted contempt (Cavanagh 2002) or unwarranted animus (Arneson 2006). On Alexander's view, discriminatory treatment is intrinsically wrong only when it occurs because of the discriminator's "biases," defined as incorrect judgments that other people have inferior moral worth. "When a person is judged incorrectly to be of lesser moral worth and is treated accordingly, that treatment is morally wrong regardless of the gravity of its effects. It represents a failure to show the moral respect due the recipient, a failure which is by itself sufficient to be judged immoral" (1992: 159). When an employer passes over the most qualified applicant for a position, Alexander's view implies that this treatment is intrinsically wrongful when it reflects an erroneous judgment of the applicant's moral worth. Intrinsically wrongful discrimination can also be wrong extrinsically, due to the effects it has on others, and an act of intrinsically wrongful discrimination may be much more wrong because it imposes social costs.

This approach to defining wrongful discrimination requires a distinction between morally problematic preferences and factual beliefs, and those that are morally benign. Alexander distinguishes between preferences and factual beliefs that reflect incorrect moral judgments of persons, and those that do not reflect these judgments. An employer's decision-making may be biased because it reflects certain kinds of problematic preferences, such as "shallow aversions" to association with groups of people, or problematic factual beliefs, such as inaccurate negative stereotypes. Alexander argues that these preferences and factual beliefs originate in society's historical legacy of bias against certain groups, and reflect erroneous judgments of others' moral worth (1992: 218). It is relevant whether bias has a causal influence on the formation of a preference or factual belief, but a causal influence does not entail that there is bias in the discriminator's treatment of others. For instance, a preference may be "tainted" by its origins in a society's history of widespread bias against members of a group. Alexander argues that it is not biased to have "tainted" preferences for a trait frequently held by members of certain groups, while it is biased to have a preference for non-association with persons as members of a group (1992: 178–179). A more difficult item to categorize is "implicit bias," defined as an unconscious aversion to people as members of groups. Alexander argues that implicit biases are benign because the unconscious nature of an implicit bias implies that it does not constitute a judgment that other persons are morally inferior (1992: 179–183).

One question for this approach is how it evaluates the effects of wrongful discrimination. On Cavanagh's definition of discrimination as the expression of unwarranted contempt for others, this treatment is wrong regardless of its effects on the distribution of jobs (2002: 197–207). Cavanagh argues that his account identifies what is distinctive about discrimination, since there are other causes for a problematic distribution of jobs (ibid: 155–157). However, a job seeker may be successful on account of an employer's prejudice against other applicants, and Segall finds it unpersuasive that this success would be discriminatory, as Cavanagh's account implies (2012b: 88). Arneson proposes an account of discrimination in which it is wrong to act on the basis of unwarranted animus or prejudice against persons of a certain type, but he argues that this non-consequentialist theory of discrimination "does not help in formulating policies" for complex issues, such as concerning suspect classifications (2006: 796). Alexander does not view his account of intrinsically wrongful discrimination as a comprehensive definition of wrongful discrimination, and he argues that taste discrimination and statistical discrimination also may be wrong extrinsically (1992: 191).

Reaction qualifications

This second approach to defining wrongful discrimination also informs the debate over how employers should take account of customer preferences, and the preferences of existing employees, in the specification of a job and in the evaluation of job seekers' qualifications. Alan Wertheimer has defined "reaction qualifications" as "the abilities and characteristics that contribute to job effectiveness by serving as the basis for appropriate reactions in the recipients" (1983: 100). To predict a job seeker's ability to make productive contributions in a given position, an employer must identify preferences among his customers, and his existing employees, that may be relevant to the job seeker's reaction qualifications. Wertheimer proposes that several kinds of preferences are illegitimate by nature, although to variable degrees: preferences corresponding to others' innate characteristics, those based on hierarchical judgments about social groups, preferences among a historically dominant group for their own members, and reactions that can be controlled (1983: 107–108). If some relevant preferences and reactions are intrinsically immoral, this ought to be taken into consideration when deciding whether to discount them, Wertheimer suggests. Mason endorses a narrower, "moralized" account of qualifications that excludes prejudice, on the grounds that it is unjust for a person to be deemed deficient in qualifications due to prejudice against his group (2006: 34–35).

Wertheimer and others (Alexander 1992: 173–176) argue for consideration of the likely social consequences of counting and discounting reaction qualifications. An important consideration against discounting reactions is the potential cost to the person having the reaction. Nursing home residents who have aversions to male nursing aides but are accepting of male doctors, for instance, might have a moral right to their preferences even if these are prejudicial. Kimberly Yuracko argues that U.S. courts are rightly lenient on this form of sex-discrimination, due to patients' interests in privacy and its limited effects on equality of opportunity, while they are rightly less accepting of claims for sex-titillation as a job requirement (2004).

There is general agreement on the difficulty of assessing when reaction qualifications ought to be counted or discounted (Miller 1992), and several of the leading views are self-acknowledged to be "messy" (Alexander 1992: 218), "complex," and "pluralistic" (Wertheimer 1983). Typically it is the employer who is thought to be in a position to disregard or appropriately weigh the reactions of his customers and existing employees, when specifying the requirements of a job or evaluating a job seeker's suitability. One question is how to justify the costs the employer may incur in making decisions to discount other people's morally problematic preferences. Some have argued that customers should bear some of the burdens, through the non-satisfaction of their problematic preferences (Kelman 2001: 847–849). Lippert-Rasmussen proposes a "symmetric view" of meritocratic norms, so that if employers may not satisfy their tastes for discrimination when selecting amongst job seekers, customers may not do so in their reactions to job-holders (2009).

Statistical discrimination

Another debate concerns when employers may make use of particular kinds of factual information that is predictive of a job seeker's performance. The use of statistical inferences to predict a job seeker's likely levels of productivity, on the basis of the performance of other members of her group, has been described as "statistical discrimination" (cf. Chapter 3). Lippert-Rasmussen argues that a hiring strategy disadvantaging certain groups on the basis of statistical information may be wrong when it is a "self-fulfilling" expectation that creates disincentives for members of low performing groups to acquire additional qualifications (2007: 400–401). A different line of criticism against employers' use of statistical information is that this fails to respect the job seeker, because she is treated as a member of her group and not as an individual (cf. Chapter 6). When an employer predicts that a female job seeker will take parental leave, for instance, it is argued that the employer fails to respect her as an individual (Miller 1999: 168–169). Benjamin Eidelson argues that selectors are not required to ignore statistical evidence in order to respect people as individuals; however, selectors should take into account other relevant evidence that reflects the choices individuals have made in acquiring their traits (2013). Requiring individualized attention to job seekers' choices, however, seems to recommend restricted use of statistical discrimination and other strategies for reducing employers' search costs.

Discrimination and broader social divisions

Thus far, this chapter has described two approaches to wrongful discrimination in the job market, defined as: first, the misallocation of jobs and, second, treatment of job seekers following from problematic features of decision-makers' mental states. On a third approach, wrongful discrimination in any social context tracks broader social divisions. In order to identify wrongful discrimination in the job market, arguments following this approach make reference to broader patterns of social differentiation. Two leading examples come from Hellman (2008) and Lippert-Rasmussen (2013), whose respective theories of wrongful discrimination are each accompanied by an account of social divisions.

Hellman's definition of wrongful discrimination is the drawing of distinctions between people in a way that demeans them, and this is wrong because it treats people as morally inferior. In the employment context, Hellman argues that the employer has the capacity to demean others, due to his status and power over employees (2008: 42–43). When the employer makes distinctions amongst employees, his differentiations are demeaning if they have conventional meanings of disrespect in the broader culture. A casino's policy requiring different standards of dress and personal care for its male and female employees is judged to be demeaning, on the grounds that "it conveys the idea that a woman's body is for adorning and the enjoyment by others" (ibid: 42). By contrast, a nursing home's refusal to hire male aides to attend to elderly female patients does not express that men are of unequal moral worth, because "the practice of preferring that only people of the same sex see one's body and help with private functions does not demean either men or women" (ibid: 45; Chapter 7). Hellman identifies wrongful discrimination in the former case and not the latter, by referencing an account of social differentiation in which employers have power and some forms of gender differentiation have disrespectful cultural meanings.

One question is whether Hellman's argument would identify many, or relatively few cases of wrongful discrimination in the job market. The casino case involves differential treatment of male and female employees occupying the same role within an organization, while the nursing case contributes to the segregation of the workforce by gender. As mentioned previously in this chapter, empirical social scientists disagree about the primary causes of gender segregation in the labor market. Some argue that employers restrict women's access to positions generally held by men. However, as argued by human capital theorists and recently by Claudia Goldin in her comparison of the "family friendly" pharmacy industry with other professions (2014), women may tend to train for occupations that are compatible with care for dependents. It is unclear whether Hellman's argument requires a correct account of the underlying causes of sex segregation in the labor market, in order to accurately interpret the cultural meaning of an employer's decision to hire a woman in a "family friendly" occupational role.

While Hellman's argument relies on an account of society's power relations and cultural meanings, Lippert-Rasmussen understands society to be differentiated into "socially salient groups." "A group is socially salient if perceived membership of it is important to the structure of social interactions across a wide range of social contexts" (2013: 30). A job seeker can experience disadvantageous treatment due to his membership in a socially salient group, and this would be discrimination, but he cannot experience discrimination due to his membership in the group of "untalented workers." Lippert-Rasmussen argues that discrimination is only wrongful when it produces harms, which are assessed by comparison to a desert-prioritarian baseline. Not all discriminatory treatment produces harms in comparison to this baseline, and it is possible that employers' discrimination against women can make them worse off than men without it being the case that this discrimination is morally wrong (ibid: 167). While discrimination does not necessarily cause wrongful harms, features of socially salient groups make it more likely. Discrimination against a job seeker may contribute to stigmatic harms for other members of the socially salient group, and it may be cumulative with other harms suffered by that individual in other social contexts (ibid: 168–170). When a job seeker is disadvantaged by an employer's idiosyncratic prejudices, this is less likely to be morally wrong than a disadvantage that is due to discrimination, all else being equal.

Conclusion

This chapter's overview of discrimination in the job market has focused on several connections between empirical social science and the leading philosophical approaches. First, I have described economists' efforts to estimate discrimination in the labor market, measured as the deviation from an allocation of jobs on the basis of human capital. As discussed above, there is philosophical debate over the normative standard for how jobs ought to be allocated. Meritocratic hiring may be the standard that adheres most closely to the predictions of human capital theory. In this case, its specification of non-discriminatory hiring would make relatively modest demands on employers. However, its demands may be substantial if there are large cost savings from statistical discrimination and from taking account of "reaction qualifications," which may be prohibited on some interpretations of the meritocratic standard.

Second, economists define taste discrimination and statistical discrimination on the basis of decision-makers' preferences and factual beliefs. This corresponds to an approach to defining wrongful discrimination on the basis of discriminators' moral judgments of others, as reflected in their preferences and factual beliefs. Intrinsically wrongful discrimination may not have problematic consequences, even for those who are discriminated against. Thus, the approach is sometimes complemented by an account of discrimination that is wrong because of its costs. However, economic actors sometimes may have moral rights to act on preferences and factual beliefs that impose costs to others and to the achievement of justice.

Finally, empirical social scientists are interested in the causal linkages between discrimination in the job market and broader sociological divisions. I have described theories in which differential treatment in one social context, such as the job market, can be wrongful discrimination only when it corresponds to broader patterns of social differentiation. Discrimination in the job market may take on a certain meaning due to power hierarchies and social conventions, or it may tend to cause wrongful harms, due to the nature of groups and their treatment in society.

Bibliography

Aigner, D. J. and Cain, G. G. 1977. "Statistical Theories of Discrimination in Labor Markets." *Industrial and Labor Relations Review*. 30: 175–187.

Alexander, L. 1992. "What Makes Wrongful Discrimination Wrong?" *University of Pennsylvania Law Review*. 141: 149–219.

Altonji, J. G. and Blank, R. M. 1999. "Race and Gender in the Labor Market." In O. Ashenfelter and D. Card (eds) *Handbook of Labor Economics: Volume 3C*. Amsterdam: North-Holland. 3143–3259.

Altonji, J. G. and Pierret, C. R. 2001. "Employer Learning and Statistical Discrimination." *The Quarterly Journal of Economics*. 116: 313–350.

Arneson, R. 1999. "Against Rawlsian Equality of Opportunity." *Philosophical Studies*. 93: 77–112.

Arneson, R. 2006. "What is Wrongful Discrimination?" *San Diego Law Review*. 43: 775–808.

Arrow, K. J. 1973. "The Theory of Discrimination." In O. Ashenfelter and A. Rees (eds) *Discrimination in Labor Markets*. Princeton: Princeton University Press. 3–33.

Becker, G. S. (1971 [1957]). *The Economics of Discrimination*, 2nd edition. Chicago: University of Chicago Press.

Bertrand, M. 2010. "New Perspectives on Gender." In O. Ashenfelter and D. Card (eds) *Handbook of Labor Economics: Volume 4B*. Amsterdam: North-Holland. 1545–1592.

Bertrand, M. and Mullainathan, S. 2004. "Are Emily and Greg More Employable than Lakisha and Jamal? A Field Experiment on Labor Market Discrimination." *American Economic Review*. 94: 991–1013.

Blau, F. and Kahn, L. 2007. "The Gender Pay Gap: Have Women Gone as Far as they Can?" *Academy of Management Perspectives*. 21: 7–23.

Cavanagh, M. 2002. *Against Equality of Opportunity*. Oxford: Oxford University Press.

Daniels, N. 1978. "Merit and Meritocracy." *Philosophy and Public Affairs*. 7: 206–223.

Eidelson, B. 2013. "Treating People as Individuals." In D. Hellman and S. Moreau (eds) *Philosophical Foundations of Discrimination Law*. Oxford: Oxford University Press. 203–227.

England, P. 1982. "The Failure of Human Capital Theory to Explain Occupational Sex Segregation." *The Journal of Human Resources*. 17: 358–370.

Goldin, C. 2014. "A Grand Gender Convergence: Its Last Chapter." *American Economic Review*. 104: 1091–1119.

Goldin, C. and Rouse, C. 2000. "Orchestrating Impartiality: The Impact of 'Blind' Auditions on Female Musicians." *The American Economic Review*. 90: 715–741.

Hellman, D. 2008. *When is Discrimination Wrong?* Cambridge, MA: Harvard University Press.

Kelman, M. 2001. "Market Discrimination and Groups." *Stanford Law Review*. 53: 833–896.

Lippert-Rasmussen, K. 2006. "Private Discrimination: A Prioritarian, Desert-Accommodating Account," *San Diego Law Review*. 43: 817–856.

Lippert-Rasmussen, K. 2007. "Nothing Personal: On Statistical Discrimination." *Journal of Political Philosophy*. 15: 385–403.

Lippert-Rasmussen, K. 2009. "Reaction Qualifications Revisited." *Social Theory and Practice*. 35: 413–439.

Lippert-Rasmussen, K. 2013. *Born Free and Equal? A Philosophical Inquiry into the Nature of Discrimination*. Oxford University Press.

Lundberg, S. and Startz, R. 1983. "Private Discrimination and Social Intervention in Competitive Labor Markets." *American Economic Review*. 73: 340–347.

Mason, A. 2001. "Equality of Opportunity: Old and New." *Ethics*. 111: 760–781.

Mason, A. 2006. *Levelling the Playing Field: The Idea of Equal Opportunity and its Place in Egalitarian Thought*. Oxford: Oxford University Press.

Miller, D. 1992. "Deserving Jobs." *Philosophical Quarterly*. 42: 161–181.

Miller, D. 1996. "Two Cheers for Meritocracy." *The Journal of Political Philosophy*. 4: 277–301.

Miller, D. 1999. *Principles of Social Justice*. Cambridge, MA: Harvard University Press.

Phelps, E. S. 1972. "The Statistical Theory of Racism and Sexism." *The American Economic Review*. 62: 659–661.

Polachek, S. W. 1987. "Occupational Segregation and the Gender Wage Gap." *Population Research and Policy Review*. 6: 47–67.

Rawls, J. 1971. *A Theory of Justice*. Cambridge, MA: Harvard University Press.

Segall, S. 2012a. "Should the Best Qualified Be Appointed?" *Journal of Moral Philosophy*. 9: 31–54.

Segall, S. 2012b. "What's so Bad about Discrimination?" *Utilitas*. 24: 82–100.

Sher, G. 1988. "Qualifications, Fairness, Desert." In N. E. Bowie (ed.) *Equal Opportunity*. Boulder: Westview Press. 113–127.

Wertheimer, A. 1983. "Jobs, Qualifications, and Preferences." *Ethics*. 94: 99–112.

Yuracko, K. A. 2004. "Private Nurses and Playboy Bunnies: Explaining Permissible Sex Discrimination." *California Law Review*. 92: 147–213.

Further reading

Ayres, I. and Siegelman, P. (1995) "Race and Gender Discrimination in Bargaining for a New Car," *American Economic Association* 85, pp. 304–321 is an important experimental study of employees' discrimination against customers. Goff, S. (2016) "How to Trade Fairly in an Unjust Society: The Problem of Gender Discrimination in the Labor Market," *Social Theory and Practice* 42, pp. 555–580 describes a relationship between women's loss of job opportunities from discrimination and unfairly exploitative wages. Zwolinski, M. (2006) "Why Not Regulate Private Discrimination?" *San Diego Law Review* 43, pp. 1043–1061 criticizes the differential legal treatment of commercial and private practices of discrimination.

26

DISCRIMINATION AND EDUCATION

Gideon Elford

UNIVERSITY OF OXFORD

Introduction

Like many other areas of social life, education is an area replete with issues pertinent to discrimination. Here I am interested in dimensions of education which give rise to questions of discrimination in ways that are of particular import in that domain. Those questions include whether and what kind of discrimination is implicated in the different ways students are assessed in education; in respect of the academic standards according to which students are admitted to educational institutions; and in the grouping of students on the basis of non-academic criteria.[1] With that in mind the focus in the following is on two different ways in which students are differentiated in the context of education. First, through the use of academic tests and qualifications that are both administered by educational institutions, say by having students sit exams and grading them accordingly, and also used by educational institutions to inform decisions as to how opportunities for education are distributed, for instance in the context of competitive admissions processes for positions in higher education. Second, differentiation on explicitly non-academic grounds, including on the basis of fees, gender,[2] and faith. Given that the moralized character of 'discrimination' as a term is contested, I will endeavor to avoid conceptual confusion and controversy by often using the language of 'differentiating', 'selecting' or 'grouping' when referring to the descriptive, non-moralized sense of discrimination and often using the language of 'wrongful discrimination' when referring to the sense of discrimination with that thick moral import (cf. Introduction).

Academic tests and qualifications

Academic tests and qualifications standardly play a dual role in systems of education. Qualifications and the like are among the goods that are provided through a system of education (some examples being a high school diploma in the US, or GCSEs and A-Levels in the UK). Schools and universities award qualifications that are both markers of achievement with a value in their own right and also a part of what I will term 'portfolios of accomplishment' for students to use in competitive applications to further roles and positions. Educational institutions also stand on the other side of such application processes and themselves make use of test results, qualifications and assessments when making decisions about how to distribute opportunities for education. When an educational institution is selective, as, for instance, most universities are, the process of admitting students into the institution involves differentiating between applicants partly on the basis of the aforementioned portfolios of accomplishment which include the qualifications they have already obtained through the education system. Here academic tests and qualifications are used as a basis for differentiating between students in order to decide which students should be offered educational opportunities. So educational institutions differentiate between students by handing out qualifications of different kinds, and also use the qualifications students have obtained as a way of differentiating between students with regard to what opportunities they will be offered. Call the former educational 'assessment' and the latter educational 'admission'.

I am going to explore the possible issues of discrimination connected with academic tests and qualifications first and foremost through the lens of their role in those admissions processes. As will become clear, many of the questions of wrongful discrimination that arise in this context mirror and encompass possible discrimination relating to the earlier stage of educational assessment.[3] Indeed, whilst it is in principle possible to distinguish between these dual roles, in practice they are sometimes more difficult to disentangle. For instance, where some universities conduct interviews as part of their admissions process, the university is simultaneously running an 'admissions' process at the same time as conducting an 'assessment' test, on the basis of which they might give each candidate an 'interview score' that functions much like a qualification or grade would.

There are, of course, many familiar requirements of non-discrimination often recognized to be important constraints on admissions procedures. Excepting the more controversial issue of positive discrimination, to which I will later return, the norm condemning bias, explicit or implicit, against race, gender (apart from cases of single-sex schooling) or class, in an education selection process is widely affirmed. Perhaps less obviously, elements of educational institutions' admissions processes are also potentially implicated in forms of so-called indirect discrimination (cf. Chapter 2). Whilst the precise contours of the category of 'indirect discrimination' are contested, the broad idea is that such discrimination involves an act or process imposing, or failing to take due account of, disadvantages pertaining to a certain group, even though the act or process does not itself reflect any kind of objectionable bias or intention. A paradigm case in a non-specifically educational context would be favoring applications for employment from men over women on the grounds that men are less likely to require time away from work for the purposes of child-bearing, meaning they will be more productive employees. Whilst it might not be objectionable in its own right to differentiate between applicants on the grounds of expected productivity, doing so in this case systematically disadvantages women in a way that is thought to indirectly discriminate against them as a group. It is in respect of this notion of indirect discrimination that several of the interesting issues in the context of admissions arise.

Whilst I focus here on admissions to higher education institutions, many of the relevant issues translate to admissions in earlier stages of education, including selective schools and so-called 'streaming' within schools. Consider, then, admissions processes to higher education institutions. Typically the educational institution runs a selection procedure which differentiates between students on the basis of the applications those students submit which might include, among other things, their academic grades, predicted grades, a statement of purpose, extra-curricular activities and achievements, references, further specific application tests and interviews. Such are all possible constitutive elements in what I'll continue to refer to as students' 'portfolios of accomplishment'.[4] So on what basis might this kind of selection procedure be thought to wrongfully indirectly discriminate against some of those applicants? To address this, it's worth first considering what rationale can be given for differentiating between students on the basis of their respective portfolios. An oft-cited thought is that, for competitive applications generally, the right selection procedure to use is one which seeks to select the best qualified candidates. For this reason educational institutions should assess which of the portfolios reflect the best qualified and fill their places accordingly.

Amongst the range of reasons offered in support of following a 'best qualified' criterion for selecting between candidates we find appeal to considerations of desert, legitimate expectations, productivity, merit and respect. In order, it is sometimes suggested that obtaining good grades and putting together a high caliber portfolio of accomplishment reflects the past performance of the candidate which is *deserving* of reward through the award of a place over less qualified candidates (Miller 1999: Ch. 8; Sher 1988). Alternatively, but relatedly, where students have *legitimate expectations* that better qualifications will enhance their prospects for university acceptance, it is claimed that we have a reason to satisfy such expectations by distributing university places accordingly. A further proffered reason is that of *productivity*, where on the one hand it is suggested that university selection in line with that criterion best improves human capital, which in turn enhances social productivity, and on the other that universities have a role, through their admissions processes, in signaling to future employers who thereby gain valuable information with regard to who they should employ (cf. Chapter 9). On a popular further understanding of how educational opportunities should be distributed, selection should be governed by a *meritocratic principle* under which opportunities ought to be distributed on the basis of talent and effort but not social class (Brighouse and Swift 2008).[5] It is also sometimes argued that failing to distribute opportunities like university places according to a best qualified criterion (perhaps one based upon meritocratic considerations) represents a failure to *respect* those candidates passed over in favor of less qualified candidates, who can legitimately feel like their agency has been disrespected (Sher 1988; Mason 2006: Ch. 2).

I cannot hope to offer an exhaustive assessment of each of these bases for supporting a 'best qualified' criterion for university admissions. Instead I will concentrate on one of these – the meritocratic view – largely because of the popularity of that view in the context of admissions in education, and because it offers a fruitful entry-point to uncover potential ways in which university admissions guided by a 'best qualified' criterion might nevertheless be thought to indirectly wrongfully discriminate against unsuccessful student applicants.

Under this meritocratic view, educational opportunities should be distributed in accordance with merit, understood in terms of the talent and effort of students.[6] Now, it's seldom thought that qualifications and the like are important in their own right as opposed to what they represent, either in terms of the value of the achievement they reflect, or in terms of the ability or future potential they indicate. To think otherwise would seem to fetishize qualifications over whatever it is they are designed to capture. So although qualifications are thought to be of use in differentiating between students on grounds of merit, this is not necessarily because the better qualifications are *constitutive* of greater merit but because qualifications are thought appropriate proxies or indicators for merit. For instance, if a lazy and intellectually limited student somehow flukes a higher set of grades than a diligent and intellectually able one, we need not hold that the former is actually more meritorious than the latter even if we think it best to use such grades as commonly the most reliable indicators of students' respective merit in general.

The potential gap between portfolios of accomplishment and merit is significant. A meritocratic university admissions procedure, in the above sense, uses qualifications and other elements of those portfolios to differentiate between students by taking those qualifications and grades as indicators of merit. It is clear, however, that those qualifications might be *imperfect* as indicators for merit and, as such, have the potential to conceal background inequalities. In this way, for instance, social class, gender and race might in different ways underpin differential opportunities to attain the qualifications used as evidence for merit. As such, disadvantages some students face in opportunities to obtain the qualifications translate into disadvantages to obtain opportunities in further education offered by universities. Consider the well-recognized differences in the level of education many students receive from state schools in deprived areas compared with what is offered by expensive private schools. One of the advantages of a private school education is precisely that those schools are better able to ensure that their students receive higher grades. It is arguable, then, that for any given student level of merit, private schooling gives students advantages in the form of enhanced opportunities to acquire evidence of merit that might place them at a competitive advantage when it comes to applying for university places.

Now, even if it proves to be the case that state school students are disadvantaged when it comes to opportunities to obtain qualifications, this might not be sufficient to establish indirect wrongful discrimination. After all, not all inequalities manifest wrongful discrimination and it's manifestly not the case that where individuals are at a competitive disadvantage in a selection procedure they are necessarily discriminated against. One further dimension often thought to be relevant to classifying some procedure as involving *discrimination* is whether the disadvantages in question are disproportionately visited upon a socially salient group (Lippert-Rasmussen, 2013: Ch. 2; Introduction). On this view, it can't just be a random assortment of students who are disadvantaged through a university admissions process; rather, in order to count as wrongful indirect discrimination it is necessary for the process to impose systematic disadvantages on a socially salient group in a way that is suitably explained by their membership of the group. In the case under consideration here, one might contest whether 'state school students' are a socially salient group in the relevant sense. However, even if 'state school students' are not considered a socially salient group, it could be that state schooling is a constitutive or correlate of a grouping that is socially salient, such as membership of a stratum of social class. Indeed, if a stratum of social class is the relevant socially salient group which underpins the inequalities between students when it comes to university admission, then the ways in which these are produced go beyond formal schooling. They might be thought to include family life more generally, including the education provided in the home and the ambitions and aspirations instilled in students by parents, siblings and friends. All of these factors might plausibly be thought to have an influence on a child's potential to achieve good grades, and evidence an attractive profile of life experiences and achievements. In short, there might be a cluster of dimensions of social class that affect the caliber of the portfolio of accomplishment a student is able to present to support their application. Differentiating between students on the basis of those portfolios has the potential, at least in principle, to indirectly wrongfully discriminate.

The focus in the foregoing is primarily on indirect discrimination related to social class, rather than either of the other aforementioned bases for discrimination, gender and race. I will return to gender in the following but, before continuing, note that even though the above discussion emphasizes the *social class* basis for discrimination at the level of university admissions, it is similarly possible to connect that line of argument with race. If the suggested disadvantages underpinned by social class map onto, and are explained in the right ways by, the disadvantages faced by a given racial group, this might be thought to represent a case of indirect discrimination against that racial group.

Thus far I have considered the potential for indirect wrongful discrimination in the context of university admissions against members of more deprived social classes when a 'best qualified' criterion is used for selection. One might ask whether, pushed to its logical conclusion, this has the implication that adopting a 'best qualified' criterion potentially involves 'discriminating' against those with lower merit, understood as those students who are less talented or less disposed to exert effort. One straightforward response to this thought would be to emphasize that the 'less meritorious' are not necessarily a socially salient group. Thus understood, even if those lacking in merit face disadvantages that are regrettable for egalitarian reasons, they are not subject to 'discrimination', properly understood. An objection of this sort does, however, draw into focus a further wrinkle, particularly in view of the context being education. To this point I have explored the issue of indirect wrongful discrimination in terms of the influence of social background, including schooling and upbringing, on students' opportunities to *evidence merit* through qualifications in their applications for university places. In fact, whether one thinks of these disadvantages in terms of 'discrimination' or not, it is often thought to be a desideratum of university admissions processes to discount for over- or under-inflated qualifications that fail to suitably track the underlying merit of some students compared with others. Policies of this kind make absolute sense if universities seek to select the best qualified only insofar as this is thought to reflect underlying merit. If social disadvantages lead to imperfections in the extent to which qualifications tally with merit then there is an inbuilt rationale for universities to take account of this. For this reason it is a mistake to identify any such discounting as positive discrimination proper.

But, of course, social background, including schooling, doesn't just frustrate some students' ability to manifest merit in grades but influences the very development of talent and cultivation of effort. With that in mind, one can ask the further question, as to whether adopting 'merit' as the underlying standard has the potential to involve indirect wrongful discrimination against those students from less advantaged social classes, whose opportunity to develop the skills, aptitudes and diligence that would place them among the more meritorious is systemically limited by the way advantage is socially stratified.

On many accounts, whether some act or procedure qualifies as indirectly wrongfully discriminating depends in part on whether the justification for the act or procedure is sufficient to justify the disadvantages suffered by the would-be discriminatees. If this is accepted, the discriminatory character of university admissions governed according to merit will depend on the broader justification for that criterion. Rather than explore the positive reasons that are offered in favor of the merit or 'best qualified' criterion for university admissions I want to simply sketch a claim that there might be something particular about educational institutions which counsels against taking merit as the guiding criterion for differentiating between students.

Education is widely accepted to be an important determinant of talent and effort at various stages of a child's development. If part of the purpose of an education system is to *develop* merit, and if there are egalitarian reasons against allowing a child's social class to influence inequalities in that regard, then one might suppose that there are reasons that apply to an education system in particular to offset inequalities in merit, rather than take them as given (cf. Chapter 11). In this way the merit-developing purpose of education distinguishes it from other domains like employment, where it's not clear that any given employer has, *qua* employer, a particular role responsibility to discount for background inequalities between candidates' ability to fulfill the selection criteria. In contrast, one might think of admissions processes in education as part of a wider education system which has a role responsibility for the allocation of educational resources, a part of which involves taking into consideration the desirability of ensuring that social class inequalities do not translate into differential opportunities provided by education. All of this falls far short of a case in favor of taking less meritorious students whose comparative lack of merit is partly a result of their social class. Whether this kind of so-called positive discrimination is permissible (or required) depends on considering the range of reasons *in favor* of using merit as the criterion for admissions. If accepted it would merely count in support of that positive discrimination case.

One 'admissions' process at earlier stages of education which involves selecting between students on the basis of testing and distributing educational resources accordingly is the so called 'streaming' of students, by teaching them in groups separated by ability. In university admissions, the differentiation the educational institution engages in is tied to the distribution of opportunities of explicitly different value – acceptance: good; rejection: bad. In contrast, streaming does not necessarily recognize the differential value of the educational opportunities differently grouped students receive. Although students have their learning environments segregated, the higher or lower ability groups are not necessarily supposed to receive education of greater or lesser value than one another. Instead, it is simply that they are given different education tailored to their particular educational needs. If that claim bears out, it would appear that, on many accounts of what discrimination consists of, differentiating between students through educational streaming *isn't* discriminatory, given that (the argument goes) no students are disadvantaged. In that case, even if the aforementioned influence of social class on merit obtains in these earlier stages of education, there is no indirect discrimination against less able students, as the groups into which they are sorted offer them no less valuable an education than the other more able students from whom they are separated. Whether streaming does involve unequal education for the different ability groups is, as one might expect, contested. Even where the quality of the teaching and resources devoted to the different groups and tailored to their needs is in relevant respects equal in value, the mere fact of being grouped together in a particular 'ability' group, particularly in the lower ability group, could have a tendency to dampen ambitions, lessen self-esteem and corrode motivation among students so grouped. This might be said to exact a negative influence on such students' future opportunities to achieve through education. Further, it is often claimed that grouping according to ability has the propensity to invite social stigma from the student community within the institution against the members of the lower ability groups. So even if the 'untalented' are not a socially salient group in society more broadly, streaming becomes the architect of a new set of socially salient groups internal to educational institutions, where differences in talent are made more visible and, moreover, publicly recognized by the institution itself. The worry here, then, is that the very process of streaming creates certain disadvantages which are unequally distributed. In principle, this can be conceptualized in terms of discrimination, particularly where there are social class, gender or race-based explanations of the stratification of students across those ability groups.

In the above I have chiefly concentrated on social class as a basis for potential indirect discrimination when it comes to the differentiating role that qualifications play in admissions processes, also noting how this might be connected with race. Gender also gives rise to related issues of potential discrimination, particularly in respect of the role that tests and qualifications have in the context of educational *assessment*. Indeed, indirect gender discrimination is often flagged where educational assessment processes tend to systematically favor students of one gender over another. For instance, where there are statistically significant differences in math test scores between male and female students it may be that the design of the math test rewards one gender compared with another when it comes to evidencing ability at math. This has the straightforward consequence that insofar as such test scores are taken by higher educational institutions as markers of merit for the purpose of admissions, those gender inequalities at the level of assessment may translate into inequalities in the distribution of subsequent educational opportunities.[7] Indeed, the same concerns arise when it comes to some of the components specific to university admissions, such as the use of statements of purpose and interviews as a basis for differentiating between students. If, say, the tendency of male applicants to be more confident and intellectually combative in interviews, or to be comfortable at accentuating their achievements in cover letters, results in their gaining more favorable assessments, this might be thought of in terms of indirect wrongful discrimination of a certain kind.

Beyond such forms of discrimination there are further forms of discrimination relating to implicit bias pertaining to the admissions process. For instance, a hazard of such admissions interviews in respect of discrimination might be a tendency of interviewers to implicitly favor candidates who are 'like them' according to dimensions of class, sex or race. In a similar vein, indirect discrimination worries might arise where assessors favor statements of purpose which embody a certain writing style, or reflect a set of experiences and activities, if writing style or common experiences correlate with class, gender or race. Differentiation on such grounds, whether through implicit bias or as a part of the explicit criteria for admission, might also be thought to involve wrongful discrimination.

The kind of would-be gender indirect discrimination discussed in the above concerning gender in educational assessment processes relates to the improper influence of gender-correlated ability to obtain more highly-rated portfolios of accomplishment. However, as noted in the context of indirect discrimination and social class, the same issues are relevant to the question of whether merit itself ought to be taken as the relevant differentiating selection criterion at all. In other words, if the issue isn't gender inequalities in the *ability to evidence* math ability with high math test scores but gender inequalities *in genuine math ability*, then rewarding differential math ability with different grades or by distributing subsequent educational opportunities in accordance with math ability might similarly be considered, at least in principle, indirect gender discrimination.

Fees, gender and faith

Much of the above reflects on some of the ways in which the use of tests and qualifications informing merit-based differentiation might involve indirect wrongful discrimination on the basis of social class. A further way that social class might be connected with indirect discrimination is by way of the use of fees as a basis for selecting in education. There are two main ways in which fees are used in the context of education that tend to be the subject of debate. The first is the availability of fee-paying private education, and the tendency such private schooling has to exacerbate social inequalities. The second is that charging of fees for higher education, such as for university places, in a way that either makes it more difficult for some to attend university, or has the propensity to diminish the perceived attractiveness of the option of a university education, given its price.

So, it might be argued that expensive private schools that admit students on the basis of their parents' ability and willingness to pay, indirectly discriminate against students from poorer social classes. Moreover, when this is not simply any individual school but a whole tier of the education sector, the system of fee-paying private education might be thought to systematically exclude them from accessing a valuable social good. Of course, it might be objected that if free, state education is available then students from poorer backgrounds aren't deprived of the opportunity for education, only restricted in the range of education choices they can access. There may be something to this when it comes to assessing the discriminatory pedigree of fees for education. After all, I suspect many would feel the charge of wrongful discrimination to be a stronger one were education *only* available at significant private cost. Still, it's worth bearing in mind the positional dimension of education; namely that its value depends in part on how much of it others have (Swift 2003: Ch. 2; Brighouse and Swift 2006). For instance, in a competitive application process having B grades is worth more when most other applicants have only C grades, compared with a situation in which most other applicants have As. In this case, then, the worry is not simply that students from poorer backgrounds are effectively excluded from some educational goods that other, more privileged students get to enjoy, rendering the former *comparatively* worse off; it's that the students from poorer backgrounds are in a real sense made worse off in an *absolute* sense by being placed at a competitive disadvantage in applications for further education and employment. Further, in the case of fees for higher education, even though students at the application stage have, in the usual case, already enjoyed significant education, concerns about the discriminatory potential of university fees are thought to militate in favor of some systems of higher education funding, and against others. For instance, it is sometimes argued that means-tested student loan terms or a graduate tax are each preferable to a funding system with upfront fees and market rate loans, on the basis that the latter presents a considerable barrier to students from poorer backgrounds, not to mention a system that strongly dissuades the uptake of university places among such parts of society (Brighouse 2004).

I have concentrated here on the ways fees might be thought to discriminate on the basis of social class. However, there are further ways in which fees are claimed to manifest discrimination. One such basis is nationality, where universities often charge different fees to foreign students than they do for domestic students, for study of the same courses. Indeed, in the UK claims of discrimination were voiced against Scottish universities offering free education to Scottish students but charging tuition fees to students from other parts of the UK (Hubble 2012). In an interesting further case, it has also been argued that charging fees has the potential to discriminate on religious lines, where certain loan-based university fee systems are claimed to wrongfully discriminate against Muslim students, some of whom interpret Islamic law to forbid certain interest-accruing loans (McPherson 2011; cf. Chapter 17).

Whilst I have noted ways in which assessment and admissions might be thought to involve indirect gender discrimination, those cases don't involve explicit differentiation on grounds of gender, but differentiation which is claimed to have a disproportionately disadvantageous impact on a gender group, typically women. It is also worth mentioning differentiation between genders of a more direct kind, in the form of single-sex schooling. One way of looking at single-sex schooling is as a kind of streaming writ large, with students grouped between schools, rather than classes, and selected according to sex and not merit or test results. Again, as with streaming, there is no explicit suggestion that this will involve inequalities in educational quality. And, again as with streaming, one can see the discriminatory potential of differentiation of this sex-based kind if one considers what it would look like if there *were* manifest and publicly recognized differences in the quality of education given to different groups. If it could be shown that all-female schools had systematically higher funding, and uniformly offered education of a vastly superior caliber to the male-only or mixed counterparts, many would find it very intuitive to think of this in terms of direct wrongful discrimination. However, partly because the range of single-sex schools and the mixed-sex alternatives are of varying quality, the claim that one sex is advantaged by such forms of selection is more difficult to sustain.[8]

In any case, there is a supposition amongst defenders of single-sex schooling that there are good reasons in favor of separating sexes during various stages of education which include a range of benefits from doing so. Such benefits are said to include, for instance, that single-sex education tends to involve fewer of the kind of distractions which exist on account of the mixing of sexes; and that boys and girls develop at different rates and in different ways, meaning single-sex education offers a kind of flexibility to tailor education provision to students' specific educational needs. In contrast, though, if it could be shown that there were genuine disadvantages for some pertaining to single-sex schooling, such separation might have more in common with racially segregated schooling which has long been considered a paradigm reference point regarding past wrongfully discriminatory practices.[9] Of course the picture here is an undoubtedly complicated one, and there are several dimensions on which racial segregation might be thought to differ from single-sex schooling, including, and especially, the point and purpose, historically, of that racial segregation and the public designation of inferiority for African-Americans it unquestionably involved (Sumner, 1870).

In many contexts differentiation on grounds of faith is seen as wrongful discrimination. Yet there are also a variety of contexts in which it's considered eminently acceptable. Consider religious institutions like churches or mosques. Few would consider it wrongful discrimination on grounds of faith to exclude non-Christians or non-Muslims respectively from certain leadership positions within those institutions (cf. Chapter 17). After all, it is a part of the mission of such associations to foster, sustain and cultivate a range of shared values which members must genuinely affirm in order to take up many of the roles and fulfill the purposes of such bodies. One way of approaching the issue of faith discrimination in education, then, is to consider whether any similar such supporting considerations can be used to justify differentiation between students on grounds of faith when it comes to education, such as in faith schools. Of course, the wider debate over the value and permissibility of faith schools is deep and complex, traversing a range of further issues, including the very point and purpose of education and the rights of both parents and children. Indeed, the justifiability of state funding for faith schools – itself a matter of considerable controversy – raises its own discrimination issues (Callan 2000). I offer here only a limited sketch of some of those issues pertinent to the possibly discriminatory character of selecting students on faith-based grounds.

At least in the United Kingdom, the selection of students on faith grounds is only permitted under limited conditions, including that the school is oversubscribed; that the selection must be on the basis of faith and not ethnicity; and that differentiation on faith grounds must be restricted to admissions (Department for Education 2014). With the comparison between religious institutions and faith schools in mind, it might be claimed that whilst religious institutions have as a central part of their point and purpose to foster and sustain faith and worship according to the tenets of the particular religion, educational institutions, including faith schools, have a point and purpose that goes beyond specifically religious faith and involves the training of children in various ways to be able to function in society in later life. In response, and in defense of selection on religious grounds, it might be said that the cultivation of certain religious values is, in fact, inseparable from a program of early education where the aim ought to be not only to equip with skills for later life but also to shape the values and outlook of students.

Even so, it's worth asking how far the selection of *students* on faith grounds is necessary in order to sustain institutions which offer the kind of faith-inspired education that faith schools provide. One might think, for instance, that insofar as students are *recipients* rather than *providers* of the education, there is stronger reason to select *teachers* partly on faith grounds than there is to select *students*, if the guiding thought is that common motivations and values of the right sort are important in order to offer a faith-inspired education. Indeed, to echo some of the earlier observations about the role of the education system concerning cultivation of merit, part of the mission of faith schools is precisely to cultivate and inspire the values and outlook counseled by that faith. If so, it's unclear how far this would favor selecting on the basis of the pre-existing affirmation of such values on the part of the students being admitted.[10] In fact, where faith schools select between students on grounds of faith this is typically on the basis of the faith of the students' parents, rather than the students' own. In which case it's harder to see the faith of the students themselves as a relevant reason supporting that faith-based differentiation. Indeed, this suggests that it is at least partly the interests of the parents that are served by selecting on the basis of faith; namely that parents have an interest in their children being educated in an environment and in a way that accords and promotes the values and worldview which those parents consider it important for their children to share.

A further contrast between schools and other religious institutions concerns the potential rights at stake. Whilst rights to education and rights to freedom of religion and association arc all widely affirmed in some form, the case for a *positive* right to education (under which there would be a duty to provide education) is often thought to be stronger and less contestable than any *positive* right to religious associations of particular kinds (as opposed to the negative right to be unobstructed in forming religious associations and institutions with similarly-minded others). Again, these are deep and difficult philosophical waters but the idea, crudely put, is that children might have a positive right to the provision of education, whereas persons generally do not have a positive right to the provision of membership of a religious community. In other words, if such communities did not exist we would not in general have a positive right to their invention. It would not follow, of course, that any child would have a right to the provision of education by any particular educational institution, so this does not support the thought that by not being selected by a given school on faith grounds, the child is necessarily having their rights transgressed. But it may reflect a further relevant difference between other religious institutions and associations, as opposed to faith schools in particular, that only in the case of the latter is it true that the goods they provide are ones that the would-be recipients have a positive right to in some form. This suggests that, as with gender, it is possible that the availability of similarly good educational alternatives bears on whether selection on faith grounds qualifies as wrongful discrimination.

Conclusion

The foregoing brief survey of some of the issues of discrimination in education illustrates that the academic standards educational institutions use both to assess and to admit students have the potential to involve indirect discrimination across a range of dimensions, including social class, race and gender. It also illustrated that the use of non-academic criteria for selection by educational institutions can give rise to similar issues of discrimination. The fact that education is a context in which issues of discrimination arise should not be surprising. After all, it involves the distribution of a scarce good which has considerable importance, both in its own right and as a means to further goods and opportunities. The questions of who gets education, how much of it and of what kind are therefore significant ones, and the answers will naturally involve forms of differentiation that have discrimination potential. What's more, the provision of education has itself characteristically involved internal tests and standards of achievement, which themselves seem to imply differentiation with scope for discrimination, at least of an indirect form.

Notes

1 One further issue that is commonly associated with education is so-called positive discrimination, an example of which in the educational context might involve admitting students from underrepresented groups, despite their satisfying to a lesser degree whatever are otherwise judged to be the appropriate criteria for admission. As the permissibility of this form of discrimination is a contested issue across contexts beyond the specifically educational, I do not offer an in-depth analysis of the issue beyond noting its intersection with the issues in education that I do discuss. For more on positive discrimination in admissions to education see Clayton 2012.

2 For the sake of simplicity and consistency with the language in which many of the issues are discussed, I treat 'gender' and 'sex' coterminously, whilst recognizing that they might be distinguished.

3 As a result, discrimination at earlier stages can have further consequences for students' success in later competitive education admissions processes.

4 It's worth noting that the extent to which each of the constitutive elements of such portfolios of accomplishment are accorded significance may depend on the perceived point and purpose of the institution to which candidates are applying. To wit, a music college will no doubt accord greater significance to grades in various instruments, and a sports academy more significance to experience in competitive sport. The broader question of whether any given admissions process involves wrongful discrimination or not will, then, often be thought to depend, at least in part, on whether that process is congruent with the point and purpose that an institution has (see the discussion of faith schools below).

5 The meritocratic view is endorsed here in a limited but not an unqualified sense by Brighouse and Swift.

6 There is a further question of how talent and effort are themselves to be understood; whether, for instance, talent is to be understood in terms of current ability or future potential, and effort understood to relate to past or future efforts. The plausibility of a given meritocratic conception will no doubt depend on the answers to these questions.

7 Of course, gender inequalities with respect to any given subject may not necessarily result in inequalities at a later stage of education, if and when any such subject-related inequalities balance out across subjects, say if female students score comparatively poorly in math tests but male students score comparatively poorly in English tests. However, when there are particular subjects, such as Math for instance, for which test scores more strongly influence the future opportunities students enjoy (educational or otherwise), it may be more likely that systematic gender inequalities in the attainment of good scores in those subjects will reflect wrongful indirect discrimination.

8 What's more, if there are groups who are advantaged and disadvantaged by single-sex schooling, it's not always clear which group is the relevant one with respect to specifying the putative discrimination (Lippert-Rasmussen 2013: Ch. 2).

9 Witness the US Supreme Court case *Brown v. Board of Education of Topeka* 347 U.S. 483 (1954).

10 Though it's worth recognizing that the mission is to *sustain* as well as to cultivate.

Bibliography

Brighouse, H. 2004. "Paying for Higher Education: Are Top-Up Fees Fair?" Éthique et économique/ Ethics and Economics. 2(1).

Brighouse, H. and Swift, A. 2006. "Equality, Priority and Positional Goods." *Ethics*. 116: 471–497.

Brighouse, H. and Swift, A. 2008. "Putting Educational Equality in its Place." *Educational Policy and Finance*. 3(4): 444–466.

Callan, E. 2000. "Discrimination and Religious Schooling." In W. Kymlicka and W. Norman (eds) *Citizenship in Diverse Societies*. Oxford: Oxford University Press. 45–67.

Clayton, M. 2012. "On Widening Participation in Higher Education Through Positive Discrimination." *Journal of Philosophy in Education*. 46: 414–431.

Department for Education. 2014. *Schools Admission Code*, www.gov.uk/government/uploads/system/uploads/attachment_data/file/389388/School_Admissions_Code_2014_-_19_Dec.pdf

Gilby, N. 2011. "Amplifying the Voice of Muslim Students: Findings from Literature Review." *BIS Research Paper*. 55.

Hubble, S. 2012. "Higher Education Student Support Across the UK Regions from September 2012." *Commons Briefing Paper* SN06217. http://researchbriefings.parliament.uk/ResearchBriefing/Summary/SN06217#fullreport

Lippert-Rasmussen, K. 2013. *Born Free and Equal*. Oxford: Oxford University Press.

Mason, A. 2006. *Levelling the Playing Field: The Idea of Equal Opportunity and its Place in Egalitarian Thought*. Oxford: Oxford University Press.

McPherson, P. 2011. "Tuition Fee System is Discriminatory, say Muslims." *The Independent*. 21st August 2011.

Miller, D. 1999. *Principles of Social Justice*, Cambridge, MA: Harvard University Press.

Sher, G. 1988. "Qualifications, Fairness, and Desert." In N. E. Bowie (ed.) *Equal Opportunity*. Boulder, CO: Westview Press. 113–127.

Sumner, C. 1870. *Equality Before the Law: Unconstitutionality of Separate Colored Schools in Massachusetts*. Washington: F. & J. Rives & Geo. A. Bailey.

Swift, A. 2003. *How Not to be a Hypocrite: School Choice for the Morally Perplexed Parent*. London: Routledge.

27

DISCRIMINATION AND LAW ENFORCEMENT

Re'em Segev

THE HEBREW UNIVERSITY OF JERUSALEM

Introduction

Law enforcement – namely actions performed by police officers, prosecutors and judges in executing the criminal law, such as questioning, searching, arresting, prosecuting, convicting and sentencing people – is one context in which the question of the moral status of discrimination is salient. The answer to the question of what amounts to wrongful discrimination in this context depends on the answer to the controversial question of what amounts to wrongful discrimination in general. Yet my focus in this chapter is on aspects that are especially salient in the context of law enforcement.[1]

Law enforcement and discrimination

Several related features are especially noteworthy in the context of law enforcement. First, in the most common contexts in which discrimination is discussed – employment and education – the prevailing assumption is that the proper action is giving the benefit to the most qualified candidate. In contrast, the common assumption in the context of law enforcement appears to be that the proper action is enforcing the law when the relevant person is guilty of violating the law (assuming that the law is justified). This difference might reflect a deeper difference in terms of the underlying considerations, although this is more controversial: the more significant consideration for the criterion of qualifications seems to be maximizing utility, while the more prominent basis for the criterion of guilt appears to be moral desert (although both considerations might support both criteria to some degree).

A second feature is that the relevant agents in the context of law enforcement are public officials. This is significant because public officials do not have the moral permission that, according to a common view, other individuals have to perform actions that are not morally recommended in some cases, and since discrimination by public officials is often especially objectionable (since it often involves worse consequences and, according to one view, because it violates a special requirement of "equality before the law").[2]

Finally, discrimination in the context of law enforcement might take many forms, such as, for example, in terms of the common legal doctrines, both "direct discrimination" and "indirect discrimination" (cf. Chapters 1 and 2). In this chapter, I focus on rational discrimination – namely discrimination that is supported by a good *pro tanto* consideration, or, in other words, based on a morally significant fact (as opposed to an unfounded prejudice) – and particularly of statistical discrimination that is rational – namely discrimination that is based on sound statistical evidence (cf. Chapter 3). The context of law enforcement highlights the question of whether rational and statistical discrimination are morally justified, since, on the one hand, it is often claimed that certain forms of law enforcement policies, such as racial profiling, might be justified when they are rational and specifically statistically sound, but, on the other hand, many object to these forms of discrimination, especially in this context.

The moral status of rational and statistical discrimination is important in general. On the one hand, such forms of discrimination are often considered morally dubious (and are sometimes legally prohibited). The law, for example, often prohibits some forms of "indirect discrimination" and requires some forms of "accommodation" also when the relevant actions are rational in the stipulated sense. On the other hand, other forms of rational discrimination are typically not considered as wrong. This too is reflected in the law, which typically includes defenses that exempt from the prohibition on discrimination actions that are supported by a (good) reason, especially relating to the relevant qualifications of the candidates (cf. Chapters 9 and 25).[3]

Moreover, it is at least doubtful whether common theoretical accounts of discrimination entail conclusions that align with the common view (and the law) regarding rational discrimination. For example, accounts that focus on the mental state of the agent do not seem to apply when the relevant action is based on a good reason. And accounts that associate discrimination and distributive injustice might condemn some cases of rational discrimination but in a way that diverges from the common view. For example, they seem to condemn cases in which the most qualified candidate is preferred if the less qualified candidate is not responsible for her lesser qualifications, even if this preference is not related to a classical ground of discrimination. While such a preference in itself is not a case of discrimination, according to the conventional understanding of discrimination (even if it is wrongful), the moral fault in this case and in cases of discrimination is the same according to distributive theories. Such theories diverge from the common view, that seems to draw a sharper distinction in this regard. Moreover, even at a less fundamental level, the common suggestion regarding the common denominator of the grounds of discrimination – their significant effects on the lives of people in many contexts ("social salience") – seems to apply to qualifications that are relatively general. For example, general intelligence, as measured by common psychometric tests, affects the nature of the education one receives and, independently or as a result, the nature of employment one gets, and, again independently or as a result, one's social status.

The question as to which forms of rational and particularly statistical discrimination are wrong, and which are not, is especially salient in the context of law enforcement, also due to the fact that law enforcement is typically very selective in general.[4] This is typically considered to be justified given the cost of enforcement. As a result, the main concern in this context is whether specific forms of selective enforcement are (particularly) objectionable, specifically as wrongful discrimination.[5] This is especially the case given that law enforcement is particularly very selective with regard to the classical grounds of discrimination, such as race and sex, at least in terms of its consequences. However, there is a difference between different grounds of discrimination in this context: while statistical discrimination in the context of law enforcement is often considered troubling regarding race, this is not the case regarding sex – presumably since it is assumed that the (statistical) discrimination in this context is rational.

The doubt regarding the moral status of statistical discrimination that is rational is especially salient in the context of law enforcement. This is evident, *inter alia*, in the empirical research in this field. Sometimes, there is evidence that the number of people questioned, searched or convicted, or the severity of sentences, for example, do not represent the ratio of the relevant racial groups in the relevant community.[6] Some assume that this disparity itself constitutes wrongful discrimination, or at least is necessarily due to wrongful discrimination. Others argue that this is not necessarily the case, mainly since it is possible that the relative number of persons that violate the law is not identical in every racial group. Therefore, research in this context often considers also whether such differences persist even after controlling for various factors, especially ones that are (or might be considered as) good reasons to distinguish persons in the context of law enforcement, for example prior convictions with regard to the severity of punishment (it is obviously very difficult to control for every such factor). This reflects the assumption that a mere difference between racial groups does not constitute or conclusively demonstrate wrongful discrimination.[7] One explanation for this assumption is the view that rational discrimination does not (necessarily or ever) constitute wrongful discrimination. This difference in the nature of the inquiry might have a significant effect on the conclusion, since while there is often evidence for substantial disparities between racial groups without controlling for other factors, the existence and especially the extent of such disparities are unclear or controversial when controlling for such factors.[8]

The doubt concerning the question as to whether or when rational discrimination and especially statistical discrimination (that is rational) is wrong, in the context of law enforcement, is demonstrated also in the ambivalent legal position regarding, for example, racial profiling: while racial profiling is sometimes considered to be illegal, this is not so in every case and it is difficult to identify a coherent legal principle in this regard.[9]

Statistical discrimination

A preliminary difficulty in considering the moral status of discrimination in general and statistical discrimination in particular is conceptual: it is unclear and controversial what exactly amounts to discrimination and specifically to statistical discrimination. The standard definition of discrimination is roughly the allocation of a benefit (including avoiding a burden) in a way that is sensitive to traits such as race, religion or gender. However, this leaves many questions unanswered. One example that is conspicuous (*inter alia*) in the context of law enforcement is whether what matters for discrimination in general is the mental state of the agent (her motivating reason) or the outcome of the action (or both).

Regarding statistical discrimination, the puzzle is even more significant, as it is unclear what distinguishes statistical evidence – and thus statistical discrimination (that is based on statistical evidence) – from non-statistical evidence (and non-statistical discrimination). There are specific examples that are commonly classified as statistical evidence (and statistical discrimination) – such as racial profiling – as well as cases that are commonly classified as non-statistical evidence – such as the report of an eyewitness (who saw, for instance, a person running away from a crime scene). However, it is unclear what makes the former a case of statistical evidence and the latter a case of non-statistical evidence, and accordingly it is unclear how to generalize these examples. Since what matters ultimately is not whether there is some difference between statistical and non-statistical evidence and discrimination but whether there is a *morally significant* difference between them, I discuss the nature of statistical discrimination when evaluating the arguments for and against it.

Two points are, however, worth noting at the outset. First, statistical evidence should presumably not be defined in a way that entails that it is necessarily based on *false* evidence, as paradigmatic cases of statistical evidence are based on sound data. This is compatible of course with the possibility that many actual generalizations on the basis of the paradigm grounds of discrimination, such as race and gender, are statistically unsound.[10] Second, statistical discrimination should not be defined in a way that includes a normative component according to which it is necessarily morally wrong overall (despite the fact that the discrimination is rational in the sense that there is a good reason for it). For this would cover only some of the paradigm cases of statistical discrimination (and it would be less misleading to refer instead to "wrongful statistical discrimination").

Considerations in favor of statistical discrimination

In order to determine whether statistical discrimination in law enforcement, such as racial profiling, is justified, it might be useful to consider first the considerations in its favor (that make it rational in the stipulated sense), before considering whether there are considerations against it.

There is a wide agreement regarding the normative premise that there is a *pro tanto* consideration in favor of statistical discrimination (in the context of law enforcement) *if or to the extent that*, it is the most efficient way of promoting the standard goals of the (criminal) law, such as preventing wrongful actions[11] or promoting retributive justice by punishing blameworthy wrongdoers in proportion to their blame.[12] Indeed, these considerations in favor of law enforcement are not unique to the context of statistical discrimination.

The main doubt in this context is thus empirical rather than normative: whether, or when, is statistical discrimination an efficient means of promoting these goals. This question is especially salient in the context of law enforcement, given the background assumption that full enforcement is impossible or too costly.

More specifically, the main doubt with respect to this empirical question is whether there is a statistical correlation between the probability of committing actions that are wrongful and illegal and the grounds of discrimination (in themselves or combined with other factors). The main controversy in this regard concerns race (as opposed to gender, for example, regarding which there do not seem to be significant doubts). One doubt is that evidence that suggests that such a correlation exists is typically based on the previous actions of officials – for example, as reflected in police records – that might themselves be due to misguided assumptions concerning such a correlation.[13] Another doubt is that even when there is such a correlation, race might receive weight beyond what is warranted by the evidence.[14] Therefore, it is controversial, specifically, whether racial profiling is indeed efficient in achieving proper moral goals overall.[15] However, it is clearly possible that statistical discrimination would be efficient in this sense and it seems likely that it is in fact efficient in some actual cases.

The fact that there is often a consideration in favor of relying on statistical evidence does not entail of course that additional (non-statistical) evidence should be ignored or that further inquiry regarding additional evidence is redundant. Indeed, there is a consideration in favor of considering additional relevant evidence that is available, and therefore there is a consideration in favor of conducting further inquiry if there is a chance that it would produce additional evidence. But when this involves a cost (that is morally significant), as is often the case, there is also a consideration against further inquiry.[16] Thus, the optimal course of action is not necessarily to conduct every possible inquiry.

Considerations against statistical discrimination

The next question – which is practically important mainly when statistical discrimination is efficient in promoting proper moral goals – is whether there are considerations against statistical discrimination. There seem to be two considerations of this type that are clear and compelling in terms of their normative premises. The first is that statistical discrimination based on the paradigm grounds of discrimination, especially race, might trigger negative reactions (particularly given the history of wrongful discrimination based on race). These include, first, the reactions of those who are targeted by racial profiling. These reactions might be due to the fact that these people often believe that the relevant form of racial profiling is irrational or at least wrong overall (whether this belief is correct is immaterial in this regard). These reactions might have negative effects, for example, in terms of well-being, both directly and indirectly, for example to the extent that they have a negative effect on the willingness of the relevant persons to trust, and therefore to cooperate with, law enforcement officials, and thus on the efficiency of law enforcement in general.[17] Racial profiling might also lead to unwelcome reactions by other people, beyond those who are targeted by it, for example by exacerbating the phenomenon of wrongful discrimination (again, this might be the case even due to an action that is not wrong in itself, that is, apart from this consequence).[18] Here again the main question is empirical – the extent to which such negative outcomes would be the result of statistical discrimination and specifically racial profiling.

Another consideration against statistical discrimination (and discrimination in general)[19] reflects a concern for justice – particularly distributive and retributive justice (a concern that is not merely instrumental and therefore exists even if it is not accompanied by an additional bad result).[20] The general concern is that one outcome of statistical discrimination would be that the burdens of law enforcement are not allocated justly and, moreover, fall on those who already have less than their just share.

The content of distributive and retributive justice is of course controversial, as well as their interaction. One complication, which is especially important in the context of law enforcement, and concerns the relation between distributive and retributive justice, is that many distributive accounts hold that distributive justice is sensitive to responsibility – including responsibility for wrongdoing. This is especially noteworthy in the context of law enforcement, given the common assumption that the appropriate allocative pattern in this context requires distinguishing those who are responsible for wrongdoing (that is also illegal). The view that distributive justice includes an element of responsibility take various forms, along several dimensions. For example, one version considers responsibility as morally significant *in addition* to another distributive concern, such as equality or priority for the worse-off (so that these distinct considerations might clash), while another version holds that responsibility is the *only* (non-instrumental) distributive factor.[21] According to this view, we should not be concerned with inequality between those who are blameworthy for wrongdoing and those who are not (at least if the positions of the relevant persons, or the inequality, are proportional to the degree of the relevant wrongdoing).[22] In other words, this view entails that the relevant burdens of law enforcement do not include legal punishment, to the extent to which it is imposed on those who are blameworthy for wrongdoing in a proportional manner.

However, all of these views converge in terms of their implications in some cases. For example, all hold that an unequal allocation of the burdens of law enforcement is (*pro tanto*) unjust when the relevant persons do not deserve these burdens, given their situation or behavior. This might be the case, *inter alia*, because the relevant person did not commit the action of which he is suspected or for which he is charged – as might often be the case with respect to the victims of statistical discrimination in law enforcement.[23] This is especially unjust if these burdens are borne by people who have less than what they deserve, in terms of distributive or retributive justice, regardless of these burdens. And this might be often the case with respect to statistical discrimination in the context of law enforcement, such as racial profiling against members of minority groups who are generally unjustifiably worse-off. Indeed, this might be the case not only when race is part of the relevant profile, but also, for example, when law enforcement relies on strategies such as the "broken windows" model (prioritizing preventing offenses relating to urban disorder in light of the assumption that this would also be effective in preventing more serious offenses), or the "hot spots" model (focusing on locations in which the crime rate is relatively high).[24]

It is sometimes noted in this regard that minorities are often not only those who bear the costs of statistical discrimination, such as racial profiling, but also those who benefit from it – since many victims of crimes committed by members of minority groups are also members of minority groups, indeed often the same group.[25] To the extent that this is the case, there might be a justice-based consideration both for and against statistical discrimination. The overall balance in terms of justice is likely to be different in different cases and regarding different individuals (assuming, as seems plausible, that the ultimate concern of justice is individuals rather than groups). For although a significant part of the benefits and burdens of statistical discrimination is borne by many members of such minority groups (for instance, on the one hand, a sense of security and, on the other hand, fear of being targeted by law enforcers), there are likely to be differences between individual members in this regard. Specifically, statistical discrimination might mitigate injustice with regard to those who would otherwise be the victims of crimes (sometimes even if they also bear the burdens of statistical discrimination, assuming that it is less significant than the burden of the relevant crime), but exacerbate it regarding others.

Other objections to statistical discrimination

It is sometimes claimed that relying on statistical evidence, specifically in the form of statistical discrimination, is objectionable in a way that does not apply to reliance on non-statistical evidence and goes beyond the considerations discussed so far. Exploring every argument in this regard is beyond the scope of this chapter,[26] but a few points are worth noting in this context.[27]

One of the most common claims against the reliance on statistical evidence, including as a basis for statistical discrimination, is that it violates the requirement to treat each person as an individual, rather than as a member of a certain group (for instance, a racial group), or to respect the autonomy of each person. This idea is often associated with the idea that discrimination in general involves disrespect for individuals[28] and undermines the autonomy of individuals (cf. Chapter 6). It was claimed, for example, that relying on statistical evidence regarding the question of whether an individual had engaged in wrongful conduct "shows a lack of respect for the autonomy of an individual to infer his morally significant behavior from the average behavior of a reference group to which he belongs".[29] This objection seems to be sometimes reflected in the law as well, including in the context of law enforcement. An example is the legal rule in the United States according to which an "individual" suspicion is required in order to stop a person.[30]

However, it is difficult to identify an objectionable sense in which statistical discrimination is not personal, and in this sense disrespects individuals. Statistical evidence is, after all, evidence that relies on a property of the relevant person, for example her race. And while statistical evidence does not include *every* "personal" property of the relevant person, this is not necessarily objectionable if, as is typically the case, further inquiry involves a morally significant cost and therefore should not be conducted in every case. Indeed, paradigm cases of *non*-statistical evidence also do not take account of every (pertinent) fact about the relevant person (consider the eyewitness case, for instance). The fact that statistical evidence is probabilistic rather than certain is also not objectionable in itself, given the fact that we often face uncertainty that could not be completely resolved or that its resolution involves a prohibitive cost. Again, common examples of non-statistical evidence are also of this type (for example that it is more likely that a person who runs away from a crime scene is guilty, compared to a person who does not). This leaves us with the fact that the probabilistic nature of statistical evidence is based on a generalization that also reflects facts about others, and in this sense does not depend *merely* on facts about the relevant person and specifically on the actions of the relevant person. However, this does not entail in itself that this evidence is irrelevant or objectionable. Indeed, common examples of non-statistical evidence are also not completely within the control of the relevant person. A person does not control, for example, what an eyewitness thinks she sees.

According to a different claim, statistical discrimination is objectionable since the consideration in favor of it – the fact that it is efficient in promoting various goals – is due to injustice, specifically in the form of wrongful discrimination, for example since higher crime rates among minorities are the result of wrongful discrimination in the past.[31] This objection is based *inter alia* on an analogy to Jerry Cohen's criticism of John Rawls' incentive argument for the Difference Principle:[32] the consideration in favor of inequality that is (also) for the benefit of the worse-off, is that the people who are more talented in terms of producing resources are willing to utilize their talents only if they are compensated more than others.[33] In both cases, a certain consideration exists only due to wrongful actions, and specifically wrongful actions of agents who contemplate acting in light of this consideration, rather than the people who would bear the cost of these actions.

What is the implication of the observation that a certain consideration exists due to injustice? Clearly, there is a reason in favor of discontinuing injustice[34] and rectifying its results.[35] And to the extent that these are impossible or too costly – at all or, more commonly, for a certain agent or during a certain period of time – this observation highlights the fact that the consideration of efficiency in favor of statistical discrimination might clash with a consideration of (distributive or retributive) justice against it. However, the fact that injustice is the cause of a certain state of affairs does not provide in itself a reason to ignore this state of affairs – and therefore does not undermine the consideration in favor of statistical discrimination, if there is no better alternative that is available for the relevant agent. Indeed, this seems to be the case even if it is impossible or too costly (for the relevant agent) to discontinue or remedy the injustice. Thus, it does not seem that the existence of injustice provides a reason that is independent of the distributive (or retributive) reason against statistical discrimination.[36]

Conclusion

Thus, there might be clashing considerations with respect to statistical discrimination: in favor of it there might be a consideration of efficiency in promoting moral goals such as preventing wrongdoing or exacting retributive justice, and, for example, a consideration of distributive justice against it. When this is the case, the relative importance of the clashing considerations should be evaluated. The importance of the relevant considerations depends on normative questions and on the relevant facts. Therefore, it seems that all we can say in general is that the force of all the relevant considerations appears to be a matter of degree and to be different in different types of cases. For example, the importance of preventing a wrongful action, through statistical discrimination, depends, *inter alia*, on the degree to which the relevant action is wrongful and the degree to which statistical discrimination is more efficient – involves lesser moral costs – compared to other means of preventing such actions. Similarly, while it is difficult to determine the importance of the retributive consideration in favor of punishing blameworthy wrongdoers, it seems plausible to assume that this depends, *inter alia*, on the degree to which the relevant person is blameworthy. The same appears to be true with regard to the considerations against statistical discrimination. Clearly, the considerations relating to the negative reactions to statistical discrimination vary in the degree to which these reactions have a negative effect in terms of well-being, for example, directly or indirectly – for instance, through their effect on the extent of cooperation with the police. And the importance of the distributive (or retributive) consideration against statistical discrimination depends on the degree to which the persons who are negatively affected by it are worse-off or the degree to which this effect does not properly reflect what they deserve in light of their actions (or both) (cf. Chapter 28). Since the importance of all the relevant considerations is a matter of degree, and varies in different factual settings, the overall conclusion is presumably that law enforcement by way of statistical discrimination is sometimes justified and sometimes not.

The proper resolution of the clash between the consideration for and against statistical discrimination might involve an element of compensation, namely enforcing the law by way of statistical discrimination while compensating the persons who are targeted by it if they bear its costs unjustifiably. This might be appropriate given the considerations against statistical discrimination. For compensation might, first, at least mitigate some of the negative reactions to statistical discrimination as well as the distributive or retributive injustice that is due to the fact that those who bear the cost of statistical discrimination often do not deserve it. Sometimes, statistical discrimination might be justified *only* if it is accompanied by such compensation. At other times, it might be justified without compensation (especially when compensation is impossible or very costly for some reason).[37] It seems reasonable to assume that compensation would be typically effective overall only if it is not trivial and provided in a way that conveys the message that the intentions of the relevant agents are not objectionable. Otherwise, it might be seen as disrespectful.

According to one suggestion, compensation is in order when the law enforcement action, the stop-and-search for example, was unjustified, given the level of the risk.[38] However, while the moral status of the action, specifically under uncertainty, is relevant to some of the applicable considerations, it is irrelevant to others and it seems mostly irrelevant particularly to the considerations in favor of compensation. The moral status of the action is relevant, for instance, to the extent to which the concern is deterring police officers from performing unjustified stops and searches. In contrast, in terms of the considerations against statistical discrimination, that often support compensation, the moral status of the relevant action is beside the point. In these respects, what matters is not whether the action was justified given the limited information, but rather the result – the degree to which the person who was (negatively) affected by the action is harmed or is worse-off or deserves this result (cf. Chapter 12).

According to a different claim, racial profiling is "reasonable" even if it involves "differential burdens", namely even if it involves distributive injustice, provided that certain conditions are met, including that the goal is important, an equal allocation of the burden involved in producing the good is impossible, and it is widely acknowledged that similar "differential burdens are imposed on others" with respect to other goods.[39] This claim is unclear in several respects, for example whether the claim is that, when the relevant conditions are met, racial profiling is justified *despite* the cost in terms of distributive justice or rather that *there is no* cost in this respect. If distributive justice should be evaluated in a way that takes account of (and aggregates) all benefits and burdens for each person, in every aspect of her life, then *if* the overall allocation of benefits and burdens is just, there is indeed no cost in terms of distributive injustice, even if some people carry a specific burden that others do not (in terms of law enforcement). However, it seems unlikely that this condition is often met in the context of statistical discrimination in general and in the context of law enforcement in particular. For example, those who bear most of the burden of racial profiling are often members of minorities that are worse-off in other respects as well (cf. Chapter 28). In addition, what *ultimately* matters regarding distributive and retributive justice is not what people think, and specifically what it is "widely acknowledged", but rather the actual facts regarding the allocation of benefits and burdens (although what people think might be of instrumental significance in this respect).

Law enforcement in just one context in which we should consider the moral status of discrimination, and the considerations that are relevant in this context are, it is reasonable to assume, pertinent in other contexts as well. Yet the context of law enforcement highlights, and provides an important test case for, questions of general importance, such as the moral status of rational discrimination, and specifically statistical discrimination that is rational. The answers to these questions are not simple, I suggest, since there are considerations both for and against such discrimination, and the conclusion depends on their relative importance, which vary in different types of cases. This suggests that it might be necessary to explore these questions in an even more specific way that distinguishes different types of cases within the law enforcement category.

Notes

1 I do not discuss discrimination in the *content* of the law (for example of offenses, defenses and sentences) to the extent that it is distinct from its enforcement, although this distinction is to a significant degree arbitrary, and many issues are relevant in both contexts. I also do not discuss the *legal* status of the law enforcement actions. Yet the moral status of these actions is pertinent both to the question of what the law should be and to the question of how positive law should be interpreted, especially since the legal status of the relevant actions is often unclear.

2 It was claimed that discrimination in law enforcement is special since security is a public good that requires quick variables (Risse and Zeckhauser 2004: 135). The question is whether these variables are morally significant in themselves.

3 See Segev 2014: 50–51.

4 Namely, the law is not enforced equally in response to every (type of) violation.

5 See, for example, Chiao 2012; Friedman and Ponomarenko 2015: 1869, 1896; Kennedy 1994: 1257–1259.

6 See recently, Fryer 2016.

7 A similar phenomenon exists, for example, regarding the disparity between the numbers of men and women in certain occupations or the gap between the salaries of men and women.

8 See Harcourt and Meares 2011: 854–856; Spohn 2000.

9 See, for example, *Floyd v. City of New York*, 959 F. Supp. 2d 540 (S.D.N.Y. 2013); Chiao 2012: 309.

10 Schauer 2006: 22.

11 This might not apply to every wrongful action. For example, one view limits the criminal law to "harmful" actions (Mill 1859) and another to "public" actions (Duff 2007). And perhaps there is a reason only in favor of preventing wrongdoing that consists in the violation of a decisive consequential, as opposed to a deontological, reason (Segev 2016).

12 Risse and Zeckhauser 2004 note that there is a "utilitarian" consideration in favor of racial profiling. This is misleading since the utility consideration in favor of racial profiling is compatible not only with a utilitarian view.

13 See Engel, Calnton and Bernard 2002: 252.

14 See Schauer 2006: 196; Risse and Zeckhauser 2004: 138–141; Lippert-Rasmussen 2014.

15 For general doubts as to the efficiency of racial profiling, see, for example, Bjerk 2007: 522, 536–538; Harcourt 2007: 215; Thomsen 2011; Wasserman 2011: 124; Durlauf 2006: 413.

16 See Lippert-Rasmussen 2011; Lippert-Rasmussen 2014: 276.

17 See Schauer 2006.

18 For negative effects of racial profiling, see, for example, Lever 2004; Lever 2007: 9; Durlauf 2006: 409; Manning 2010: 251-252.

19 See Lippert-Rasmussen 2014; Segev 2014.

20 Compare Schauer 2006: 190. Distributive justice might be relevant in the context of discrimination and law enforcement in other ways too. For example, if the currency of justice is *overall* well-being, it implies a reason against punishing a person who is already worse-off to the degree required in light of her overall moral status, even if she has performed a wrongful action. In contrast, if the relevant currency is the impact of punishment on well-being, it implies a reason against punishing the sensitive (which might often correlate with the rich). For relevant discussions, see Kolber 2009a: 230–235; Kolber 2009b; Husak 2010: 444–445.

21 Kagan 1998.

22 Compare Temkin 2003: 767.

23 This might also be the case since the offense applies to a morally permissible action.

24 See, for example, Manning 2010: 137, 153, 168; Ong Hing 2016.

25 See, for example, Kennedy 1994: 1259–1260, 1266–1267.

26 For recent discussions, see Enoch, Spectre and Fisher 2012; Lippert-Rasmussen 2014: 82–83.

27 Evaluating arguments regarding statistical discrimination is often difficult given the difficulty in explaining the distinction between statistical and non-statistical evidence (in general terms), due to which it is also difficult to explore the question of whether there is a morally significant difference between statistical and non-statistical discrimination.

28 For this general idea, see, for example, Alexander 1992.

29 Wasserman 2011: 126. See also Eidelson 2015.

30 See Harcourt and Meares 2011.

31 This objection, and the analogy to Cohen's argument, are discussed by Lippert-Rasmussen 2014: 283–299.

32 Rawls 1999.

33 Cohen 2008.

34 A situation might be unjust even if no unjust actions are being performed anymore if some people were unjustifiably worse-off in the past, and justice is evaluated in light of life as a whole.

35 The enduring results of past discrimination are noted, for example, by Thomson 1973: 381–384; Roithmayr 2014: 4–10.

36 Thus, Cohen might be right that the incentive consideration is not a consideration of *justice*, but this does not imply that it should be ignored if it is impossible or too costly to prevent the injustice.

37 Risse and Zeckhauser 2004: 157, 160 claim that there are usually various considerations against compensation. However, these considerations are not necessarily decisive, especially since compensation can take various forms.

38 Harcourt and Meares 2011: 868.

39 Risse and Zeckhauser 2004: 157.

Bibliography

Alexander, L. 1992. "What Makes Wrongful Discrimination Wrong? Biases, Preferences, Stereotypes, and Proxies." *University of Pennsylvania Law Review*. 141: 149–219.

Bjerk, D. 2007. "Racial Profiling, Statistical Discrimination, and the effect of a Colorblind Policy on the Crime Rate." *Journal of Public Economic Theory*. 9: 521–545.

Chiao, V. 2012. "Ex Ante Fairness in Criminal Law and Procedure." *New Criminal Law Review*. 15: 277–332.

Cohen, G. A. 2008. *Rescuing Justice and Equality*. Cambridge: Harvard University Press.

Duff, R. A. 2007. *Answering for Crime: Responsibility and Liability in the Criminal Law*. Oxford: Hart.

Durlauf, S. N. 2006. "Assessing Racial Profiling." *The Economic Journal*. 116: F402-F426.

Eidelson, B. 2015. *Discrimination and Disrespect*. Oxford: Oxford University Press.

Engel, R. S., Calnton, J. M., and Bernard, T. J. 2002. "Theory and Racial Profiling: Shortcomings and Future Directions in Research." *Justice Quarterly*. 19: 249–273.

Enoch, D., Spectre, L., and Fisher, T. 2012. "Statistical Evidence, Sensitivity, and the Legal Value of Knowledge." *Philosophy & Public Affairs*. 40: 197–224.

Friedman, B. and Ponomarenko, M. 2015. "Democratic Policing." *New York University Law Review*. 90: 1827–1907.

Fryer, R. G. 2016. "An Empirical Analysis of Racial Differences in Police Use of Force" (working paper).

Harcourt, Bernard E. 2007. *Against Prediction: Profiling, Policing, and Punishing in an Actuarial Age*. Chicago: University of Chicago Press.

Harcourt, B. E. and Meares, T. 2011. "Randomization and the Fourth Amendment." *University of Chicago Law Review*. 78: 809–877.

Husak, D. 2010. "Already Punished Enough." In *The Philosophy of Criminal Law: Selected Essays*. Oxford: Oxford University Press.

Kagan, S. 1998. "Equality and Desert." In McLeod, O. and Pojman, L. (eds), *What Do We Deserve?* Oxford: Oxford University Press. 298–314.

Kennedy, R. 1994. "The State, Criminal Law, and Racial Discrimination: A Comment." *Harvard Law Review*. 107: 1255–1278.

Kolber, A. J. 2009a. "The Subjective Experience of Punishment." *Columbia Law Review*. 109: 182–236.

Kolber, Adam J. 2009b. "The Comparative Nature of Punishment." *Boston University Law Review*. 89: 1565–1608.

Lever, A. 2004. "Why Racial Profiling Is Hard to Justify: A Response to Risse and Zeckhauser." *Philosophy and Public Affairs*. 33: 94–110.

Lever, A. 2007. "What's Wrong with Racial Profiling? Another Look at the Problem." *Criminal Justice Ethics*. 26: 20–28.

Lippert-Rasmussen, K. 2011. "We are all Different: Statistical Discrimination and the Right to be Treated as an Individual." *Journal of Ethics*. 15: 47–59.

Lippert-Rasmussen, K. 2014. *Born Free and Equal? A Philosophical Inquiry into the Nature of Discrimination*. Oxford: Oxford University Press.

Manning, P. K. 2010. *Democratic Policing in a Changing World*. Boulder: Paradigm.

Mill, J. S. 1859. *On Liberty*. London: Parker & Son.

Ong Hing, B. 2016. "From Ferguson to Palestine: Disrupting Race-Based Policing." *Howard Law Journal* 59.

Rawls, J. 1999. *A Theory of Justice*. Cambridge, MA: Harvard University Press. (First edition 1971).

Risse, M. and Zeckhauser, R. 2004. "Racial Profiling." *Philosophy and Public Affairs*. 32: 131–170.

Roithmayr, D. 2014. *Reproducing Racism: How Everyday Choices Lock in White Advantage*. New York: New York University Press.

Schauer, F. 2006. Profiles, Probabilities, and Stereotypes. Cambridge, MA: Harvard University Press.

Segev, Re'em. 2014. "Making Sense of Discrimination." *Ratio Juris*. 27: 47–78.

Segev, Re'em. 2016. "Should We Prevent Deontological Wrongdoing?" *Philosophical Studies*. 173: 2049–2068.

Spohn, C. 2000. "Thirty Years of Sentencing Reform: The Quest for a Racially Neutral Sentencing Policy." *Criminal Justice*. 3: 427–501.

Temkin, L. S. 2003. "Egalitarianism Defended." *Ethics*. 113: 764–782.

Thomsen, F. K. 2011. "The Art of the Unseen: Three Challenges for Racial Profiling." *The Journal of Ethics*. 15: 89–117.

Thomson, J. J. 1973. "Preferential Hiring." *Philosophy & Public Affairs*. 2: 364–384.

Wasserman, D. 2011. "Is Racial Profiling More Benign in Medicine Than Law Enforcement?" *Journal of Ethics*. 15: 119–129.

28
DISCRIMINATION AND INSURANCE

Ronen Avraham

UNIVERSITY OF TEXAS

Introduction

Private insurance is everywhere. As the primary device to reduce risk of loss and uncertainty, insurance is one of the most important institutions around us. It provides financial support in business and human life, it encourages safety and saving behaviors, and it provides security from catastrophic losses as well as peace of mind when aging. Insurance even promotes economic growth and international trade. And yet, very little is known about the requirements of justice and specifically of equal and fair non-discrimination norms from private insurance providers. As entities that offer services to the public, are they subject to the same norms as public entities? As entities whose core business is to classify people based on their actuarial risk, are they not allowed to discriminate between various groups?

Indeed, what is unique about insurance is that even statistical discrimination (the act by which an insurer uses a characteristic of an insured or potential insured as a statistic for the risk it poses to an insurer), which by definition is absent of any malicious intentions, poses significant moral and legal challenges. Why? Because on the one hand, policy makers would like insurers to treat their insureds equally, without discriminating based on race, gender, age, or other characteristics, even if it makes statistical sense to discriminate. Indeed, the US Supreme Court has expressed this aim of policy makers regarding insurance: "[e]ven a true generalization about [a] class cannot justify class-based treatment" (*Norris 1983*). On the other hand, at the *core* of insurance business lies discrimination between risky and non-risky insureds. But riskiness often statistically correlates with the same characteristics policy makers would like to prohibit insurers from taking into account. In fact, historically, courts in the EU and the US have permitted insurers to account for these characteristics; some because such a practice is required to maintain healthy insurance markets, and others because in their view the practice (in the absence of malicious intentions) is a *manifestation* of the equality principle. As one American court wrote: "[r]isk discrimination is not race discrimination" *(Nat'l Assoc. For The Advancement Of Colored People, 1992)*.

The picture is further complicated by the fact that insurance is both a social and a private enterprise. While social, government-provided insurance reflects ideals of solidarity and cross-subsidization of risk among the citizens, private insurance is profit-driven, thus requiring different risk pricing. But even private insurance requires a license from the state and states often require their citizens to purchase various types of insurance. The protection from competition and the guaranteed demand for their products can justify imposing anti-discrimination norms on private actors. Indeed, states have struggled to find a middle ground between complete prohibition and complete permission, by prohibiting risk differentiation if it amounts to "unfair discrimination." The problem, however, remained because "unfair discrimination" remained undefined. Indeed, states' constitutions and the main human rights documents only provide a list of prohibited grounds for discrimination, without ever defining discrimination.

The goal of this chapter is to try to reimagine private insurance as an institution complying with the fundamental requirements of justice, and specifically with fairness and non-discrimination norms. My first goal is to highlight the unique features required for the understanding of the seeming oxymoron *fair* discrimination in insurance. My second goal is to introduce a nuanced way to understand how costs matter in the determination of whether insurance discrimination is overall *just*. (I use the word "fair" for the deontological, cost-blind requirement to not discriminate, as discrimination is *prima facie* wrong, and the word "just" for the consequentialist, costs-conscious requirement to not wrongfully discriminate, all things—including costs—considered.)

Given the scope here, I do not attempt to develop an original and robust account of the wrongfulness of discrimination, which would capture all our intuitions and be resistant to all philosophical objections. Others have already brilliantly failed at this undertaking before. Instead, I draw on other philosophers' work on discrimination, most of which is not directly on insurance, in order to extract insights relevant to fair insurance practice. Then, because I believe that justice cannot be blind to costs, I also build on the literature on the social costs of prohibition on discrimination in insurance markets in my attempt to draw a skeleton for a theoretical framework for a just discrimination in insurance. Ultimately, I argue that there is no one-size-fits-all answer to the questions of what a fair and just insurance policy is. Rather, the answer varies from one line of insurance to another and from one characteristic to another, as well as from one type of discriminatory treatment to another. To illustrate this point, consider the following two examples:

> *Example 1:* In a landmark case in 2011, the European Court of Justice entirely forbade charging women *less* than men for their life insurance, even though on average, women live longer than men and therefore are less likely to die in any given year (*Test-Achats 2011*). By contrast, this practice is not entirely forbidden in many US states.
>
> *Example 2:* In a couple of landmark cases in the late 1970s and early 1980s, the US Supreme Court entirely forbade charging women *more* than men for their employer-provided pension insurance funds, or providing them with smaller monthly benefits, even though on average, women live longer than men and therefore require pension benefits for a longer period of time (*Manhart 1978, Norris 1983*). By contrast, this practice is not entirely forbidden in the EU.

Which approach does equality support? What can and should explain the differences between the EU and the US? Besides the cross-continental difference, an internal inconsistency exists as well. Life insurance provides coverage for dying too early, whereas pension insurance provides coverage for dying too late, so to speak. It seems that norms of anti-discrimination should have the same impact in both types of insurance; yet each legal system reverses its own treatment of gender discrimination between pension insurance and life insurance.

The puzzle is not limited to any one line of insurance or insurer characteristic; rather, it pervades the entire institution. It might be obvious that people should not be denied insurance or charged a higher premium because of their race, but what about people who are overweight (cf. Chapters 16 and 22)? Is this class protected? And even if it is protected, is it protected no matter what the costs to the rest of the pool or society are?

The existing approach for statistical discrimination by insurers

With some notable exceptions, in most of the cases both the EU and the US require insurers to balance equality and efficient business practices by refraining from "unfair discrimination." However, how they should strike that balance remains a normative mystery. In the following sections, I scan the legal landscape in both the EU and the US. My goal is to expose in more detail the inconsistency already revealed in the examples above. It remains an open question whether this inconsistency reflects substantive disagreements about moral first principles, about the proper implementation of (otherwise consensual) first principles, or about second-order considerations such as market conditions or path dependency. This question can only be answered once philosophers provide a robust theoretical framework for unfair discrimination in insurance and economists provide evidence about the social cost of the prohibition on unfair discrimination.

The EU legal landscape

Article 5(1) of Council Directive 2004/113/EC of 13 December 2004 implemented the principle of equal treatment between men and women in the access to and supply of goods and services.[1] It provides that "the use of sex as an actuarial factor in the calculation of premiums and benefits must not result in differences in individuals' premiums and benefits." Article 5(2), however, allowed deviation from the prohibition if the use of sex is "based on relevant and accurate actuarial and statistical data." In the above-mentioned landmark case (the 2011 *Test-Achats* ruling), the Court of Justice of the European Union declared Article 5(2) invalid, meaning that gender can no longer be taken into account, even if it makes actuarial sense.

Despite its seeming applicability to all lines of insurance, the *Test-Achats* ruling did not create a reliable bright line. As the European Commission has subsequently clarified, it remains possible for insurers to offer gender-specific insurance products to cover gender-specific conditions such as prostate cancer or breast cancer.[2] On the other hand, and to further complicate matters, this option is prohibited when it comes to pregnancy and maternity, in light of the specific solidarity mechanism created by Article 5(3). But that is not all. The line continues to blur because the use of risk factors that might be correlated with gender remains permissible as long as they comprise real risk factors in their own right. For example, in the field of auto insurance, price differentiation based on the size of a car engine is acceptable, even if statistically, men drive cars with engines that are more powerful. In other words, while direct statistical discrimination was prohibited, indirect statistical discrimination was not (cf. Chapters 1 and 2).

Certain other inconsistencies remain in the wake of the *Test-Achats* ruling. For example, Article 9[1][h] of Directive 2006/54/EC, which applies to pension plans, allows for the setting of different levels of benefits between males and females when justified by actuarial factors. One would expect that because pension and life insurance cover similar risk (the risk of not knowing when one would die) the *Test-Achats* ruling will apply to pension plans as well. And yet, according to the European Commission, *Test-Achats* has no impact on this provision. Lastly, the European Commission also explained that the *Test-Achats* ruling does not affect the use of other, in many ways similar, risk-rating factors such as age or disability.

The US legal landscape

In the US, the situation is somewhat different, though equally inconsistent. To date, most states in the US have adopted some form of a baseline prohibition against "unfair discrimination between individuals of the same class and essentially the same hazard." Typically, this prohibition does not apply: "where the refusal, limitation, or rate differential is based on sound actuarial principles or is related to actual or reasonably anticipated experience." (See, e.g., NY Code—Section 4224.) What are those "sound actuarial principles" or "reasonably anticipated experience[s]" that justify discrimination? No one really knows. Indeed, a great deal of inconsistency exists in the treatment of anti-discrimination norms in the US. This inconsistency exists in federal laws and state laws, across coverage lines and policyholder characteristics, and in both the substance and the intensity of regulation.

Inconsistent treatment of discrimination across states' statutes. In the US, insurance law is primarily governed by the states, not the federal government. The variation of the specific laws governing discrimination practices exists not only across states, but also internally, across lines of insurance and policyholder characteristics. Whereas Montana flatly forbids gender discrimination, California requires it—comprising an example of *cross-state variation* (Avraham *et al.* 2014). State regulation of discrimination in the automobile and property lines of insurance is more robust than in the cases of health, life, or disability insurance—comprising *cross-line variations.* One particular example of cross-line variation is that many states prohibited insurers' use of genetic information in health insurance. However, states hardly regulate the use of such information for other lines of insurance, including life or disability insurance, where genetic information matters. An example of a *cross-characteristics variation* is that before Obamacare, insurers were allowed to use gender in health insurance underwriting decisions, but were not allowed to use race for the same purpose. The *cross-state*, *cross-line*, and *cross-characteristics* variations of states' specific laws remain normatively unexplained (but see Avraham *et al.* 2015).

Inconsistent treatment of discrimination by courts. The inconsistent treatment of discrimination by states' legislatures is further reflected in courts' interpretation of the statutory term, "unfair discrimination." In the context of auto insurance, for example, courts found that automobile insurance rates based upon sex and age are fair unless those sex- and age-based rating factors are found to be actuarially unsound.[3] Yet, other courts have forbidden auto insurers from discriminating based on age, sex, or zip code.[4] A similar dynamic exists with respect to race. Some courts permitted life insurers[5] or homeowner insurers[6] to charge African-Americans higher premiums than Caucasians, since the difference was based on statistical risk, while other courts prohibited such practices.

Inconsistent treatment of discrimination by legal commentators. The vast majority of legal and philosophy scholars writing on discrimination did not write about it in the context of insurance; the vast majority of scholars writing on insurance have not considered questions of discrimination. An important exception happened in the US around the years when the Supreme Court delivered the aforementioned cases of *Norris* and *Manhart* decisions, when a lively debate on the permissibility of gender discrimination in pension insurance emerged between lawyers and economists. Some scholars argue that actuarial fairness *is* fair (Gerber 1975; Kimball 1979; Benston 1982; Bailey *et al.* 1976) or can be *made* fair (Gaulding 1995; Wortham 1985). Other scholars consider "rational" discrimination to be repugnant (Sydlaske 1975; Laycock and Sullivan 1981; Brilmayer *et al.* 1984).

Interestingly, neither camp can justify the tremendous variation that exists in the law. For example, neither camp can explain why race discrimination is considered repugnant, while gender discrimination is so often deemed acceptable in the insurance context. Commentators on both sides of the debate have noted this inconsistency and have argued that the laws should be changed to eliminate it. One camp argues that both race and sex discrimination should be allowed because both race and sex are statistically correlated with risk, whereas the other camp, by contrast, argues that neither form of discrimination should be allowed because both race and sex are categories over which individuals have no control or are historically invidious classifiers, or because using such classifications perpetuates undesirable stereotypes about race and gender—or some combination of these arguments.

With a few important exceptions (Wortham 1986; Gaulding 1985), commentary has focused on whether *particular* classifications should be forbidden from an anti-discrimination perspective. The commentary usually focuses on one or two insurance lines, such as life insurance and pensions (Brilmayer *et al.* 1984; Hoffman 2003). Developing a general normative framework, however, comprises a different challenge, requiring legal, economic, and philosophical foundations in order to determine the appropriate contours of discrimination in the entire universe of insurance. Such an undertaking also requires empirical investigation to account for the costs of implementing those norms in light of the market conditions. I now turn to highlighting the unique features of insurance that require philosophers to think more deeply about what unfair discrimination is in the insurance context.

Unique features of a theoretical framework

For egalitarians, "fair" practices mean "just" or "equal" practices, meaning that insurers should drop from their analysis and calculations any characteristics whose use is normatively repugnant, such as race or gender. For actuaries and economists, "fair" practices means "actuarially fair," which also means "efficient." Accordingly, each insured pays a premium that reflects his or her risk. Risk is proxied by any classifier that substantially correlates with risk, including race and gender, even when the particular classification characterizes socially salient groups that might deserve constitutional protection. Proponents of this approach thus believe that the use of such proxies amounts to rational actuarial discrimination; namely, permissible discrimination founded in business necessity (cf. Chapter 3). So how should we reconcile the competing anti-discrimination norms and fundamental insurance practices?

Philosophers seem to agree that any conception of unfair discrimination must include some disadvantageous (and not merely differential) treatment of people based on their perceived membership of a socially salient group. However, philosophers disagree on what such discrimination exactly means and what makes it unfair. In recent insurance practices the issue is complicated further as insurers usually no longer intentionally attempt to disadvantage insureds for belonging to a certain group (the so-called disparate *treatment*), but rather evaluate in good faith insureds' individual risk based on the readily available statistical data for that group (for the so-called disparate *impact*). In short, discrimination in insurance no longer deals with the problem of intentional discrimination, but rather with the problem of *statistical* discrimination. Moreover, even the limited discussion of statistical discrimination that exists deals with direct statistical discrimination and almost completely ignores the hard problem of indirect statistical discrimination, such as when insurers discriminate based on a characteristic (such as the size of a car engine) that correlates with a protected class (such as gender).

Moreau's view is that discrimination is wrong because it violates our deliberative freedoms, which are our "freedoms to have our decisions about how to live insulated from the effects of normatively extraneous features of us, such as our skin color or gender" (Moreau 2010, 147; Chapter 13). It is unclear, however, whether Moreau would consider actuary risks, such as the different mortality risks men and women face, as normatively extraneous features. Another view is that discrimination is wrong when it treats people disadvantageously based on immutable traits (Kahlenberg 1996; cf. Chapter 18). Sometimes, however, protection from discrimination is given even to mutable traits such as religion, while in other instances protection from discrimination is not given to immutable traits, such as denying blind people car insurance (Boxill 1992). Dworkin has argued that discriminatory acts are those that could be justified only if a certain prejudiced belief were correct. The absence of a "prejudice-free justification" thus makes a law or policy discriminatory (Dworkin 1985). Suppose, however, that there are bad ways of treating women that are unjustifiable no matter which prejudiced beliefs may be true, such as preventing women from undertaking physical jobs because on average they are shorter than men. Surely, treating women in that way while treating men much better could be discriminatory, even though the stereotype might be correct. Indeed, Fred Schauer has argued that discrimination is wrong even when it relies on somewhat accurate stereotypes, which may apply to many but not all members of the group (Schauer 2003). A related view is that discrimination is wrong because it fails to treat people based on their individual merit (Hook 1995). The problem with this approach, however, is that it cannot explain what is distinctively wrong about failing to treat people based on merit (Cavanagh 2002). Does any disrespectful treatment of members of disadvantaged groups constitute discrimination?

Hellman holds that direct discrimination is wrong because it demeans those against whom it is directed, treating them as morally inferior rather than morally equal (Hellman 2008; Chapter 7). A related view argues that people are entitled to as much respect or concern as the dominant group not merely from the state but also in their daily relationships with other individuals or corporations (cf. Chapters 6 and 35). To be in a "just relationship" with others, participants must interact with each other in a way that respects the individuality of each (Dagan and Dorfman 2015). Of course, what counts as *demeaning* and what the idea of "just relationship" requires in the context of insurance remains to be worked out. Is charging women a lower life insurance premium demeaning? What about charging a higher pension contribution? Lippert-Rasmussen disagrees with the broad school of thought under which Hellman's approach falls, which he calls "[t]he disrespect-based account of the badness of discrimination" (Lippert-Rasmussen 2013). Lippert-Rasmussen argues that discrimination is wrong primarily because of its *harmful effects* (cf. Chapter 12). But harmful compared to what? His view is that it should be harmful compared to the counterfactual situation whereby such discrimination does not exist. But what if prohibition on discrimination harms the disadvantaged group in the short run, yet advantages it in the long run? Scholars have argued that the EU's recent prohibition on gender discrimination in insurance raised premiums for both genders, allegedly making them both worse off. But what if such a prohibition would benefit women in the long run? Lippert-Rasmussen's approach seems to enable such a forward-looking costs and benefits analysis.

Obviously, in this chapter I cannot fully discuss all or even the few previously noted conceptions of discrimination. Still, my reading of the philosophical literature leaves me with the impression that very rarely does it apply neatly to insurance, where factors such as the relevant line of insurance, the characteristic, as well as the type of discrimination, are extremely important for the determination of what fair discrimination really is. For example, charging the elderly a higher premium for life insurance based on their higher actuarial risk is probably not as bad, if it is bad at all, as completely refusing to sell life insurance to old people, which in turn is probably also not as bad, if it is bad at all, as refusing to sell life insurance to black people even if their actuarial risk is as high as that of the elderly. Nor is refusing to sell the elderly life insurance as bad as refusing to sell the elderly health insurance. But most of the approaches noted above do not seem to advance the conceptualization much in these nuanced contexts.

Moreover, most of the previous conceptions do not place adequate emphasis on costs. But costs also matter. If forbidding discrimination will unravel an entire insurance market or kill hundreds of people a year because bad drivers no longer take caution on the roads because they are insured, policy makers need to pause before they require such insurance practices.

The moral requirements from a theoretical framework

To start filling in the gaps in the existing literature, in what follows I offer a two-stage process policy makers must undertake in order to determine what a *fair* and *just* insurance regime is. I provide a pragmatic sketch of how a more nuanced analysis can help determine whether a specific regime is *fair*. I then show how costs need to be integrated in order to determine whether a specific regime is also *just*.

At the first stage, policy makers must determine whether specific discrimination is *fair*; namely, that it is not *prima facie* wrong. The answer to this deontological question depends on at least three factors: the characteristic in question, the line of insurance, and the nature of the discriminatory treatment. Once one concludes that some specific insurance practice is *fair* (or unfair), the second stage becomes relevant. In the second stage, one examines whether a specific discrimination (whether fair or unfair) is also *just*, as the social costs of allowing or prohibiting discrimination are taken into account. Such costs might come in three forms: first, a higher premium to the same group the prohibition on discrimination purported to protect; second, potentially in the form of what economists call adverse selection; or third, even worse, in the form of adverse primary behavior. In other words, whereas the first stage examines the deontological fairness-related commitments private insurers have to their customers, the second stage engages in the tradeoff between equality and its consequences. I now describe these two stages in more detail.

Stage one: the relevant factors for fair discrimination

A. The first factor: the characteristics

Not all characteristics are the same. Both race and age are immutable, and yet in life insurance we accept age discrimination but usually do not accept discrimination for race (cf. Chapters 16 and 20). Indeed, the literature highlights several features that are relevant for the analysis, which is why the analysis is so complicated. First, we must determine whether a characteristic is controllable or immutable. There is some intuitive appeal to prohibiting discrimination that is based on immutable traits, as one should not be disadvantaged for things one has no control over. Indeed, people tend to tolerate discrimination more when choice is perceived to be involved, such as in the contexts of sexual orientation, obesity, and parenthood (Kricheli-Katz 2014). Of course, that does not mean that choice must be a factor, from a normative perspective. Indeed, as the previous example shows, not all immutable characteristics are treated the same. In fact, for discrimination to be wrong, mutability is probably neither a necessary condition (i.e., religion is mutable yet a protected trait) nor a sufficient condition (i.e., blind people are prevented from driving).

The second relevant feature for the analysis is whether the characteristic changes over one's lifetime (such as age) or stays fixed (Lippert-Rasmussen 2013). It is possible that age discrimination is more tolerable because we all get the same chance to be on the winning side and the losing side of it over the course of our lifetime. Third, we must determine whether a characteristic constitutes a *cause* of the risk, rather than merely *correlating* with it. Legal commentators usually demand a causal relationship between the classifier and the risk for the classifier to be taken into account, whereas actuaries often believe that correlation is sufficient. Fourth, the characteristics' predictive value (of the underlying risk) must be considered; that is, to what extent is the characteristic a good predictor for the risk? The better predictor of risk the characteristic is, the more tolerable such discrimination becomes (cf. Chapter 3). Fifth, we should determine whether discrimination on the basis of the characteristic perpetuates negative stereotypes, or otherwise subordinates disadvantaged groups (Hasnas 2002). Sixth, the historical use of the characteristic as a method of discrimination is relevant; that is, whether the characteristic defines a socially salient group that has been disadvantaged in the past. In that sense, discrimination based on skin color is more problematic than discrimination based on eye color. Whether a characteristic is socially suspect, of course, is context-dependent. For example, religion might be a more sensitive category in Catholic countries such as Italy, whereas race might be more sensitive in the US. In this context, it is interesting to reflect on the normative classification of "new" socially-suspect classes such as the obese, HIV-positive individuals, or parents.

B. The second factor: the line of insurance

The importance of each insurance line varies. By importance, I refer to the importance of the insurance to the insured's autonomy and participation in the polity. For example, health insurance is more determinative of citizens' ability to participate in the polity than are some other forms of insurance, such as traveler's insurance. When considering the disparate importance of these two lines of insurance to society at large, arguments for or against discrimination in the healthcare context have greater moral, economic, (and constitutional) implications than those in the context of traveler's insurance. While health insurance is more like a social good, or what Rawls called a "primary good," and many others will consider a basic human right, traveler's insurance is more like an economic commodity. If a good is an economic commodity, no moral duty necessarily exists to ensure equitable access. But where do life insurance or disability insurance, for example, fall on this spectrum? And what about homeowner's insurance, car insurance, or mortgage insurance?

C. The third factor: the nature of the discriminatory treatment

Insurance companies might discriminate against insureds or potential insureds in various ways. I focus here on discrimination in the underwriting process, and not in the coverage decisions they make after an occurrence. The harshest type of discrimination is to never issue a policy because of some characteristic, such as a blanket refusal to insure blacks. A somewhat similar type of discrimination happens when insurers refuse to renew or when they cancel policies based on some characteristic. Indeed, many states have statutes that limit and others have statutes that prohibit the use of a particular characteristic in issuance, renewal, or cancellation. Another form of discrimination involves restricting coverage in ways that might harm disadvantaged groups. For example, insurance companies might limit disability coverage to disabilities that do not stem from having HIV. But even with statutes limiting such discrimination, insurance companies can still discriminate against their insureds by simply charging a higher premium. Indeed, some states have statutes that limit but do not completely prohibit the use of a particular characteristic in rate-setting. Other states have statutes that expressly prohibit insurers from taking into account a specific characteristic, even in setting rates. These discrepancies call for a more nuanced fairness-based analysis of discrimination in insurance. For example, it is possible that fairness requires insurance companies to admit people with various diseases and disabilities to their pool, and yet fairness might still allow insurers to charge these people a higher premium.

The philosophical literature does not provide a nuanced analysis of the three factors described above as applied to insurance. Indeed, this literature rarely expressly relates to insurance at all, as rarely can its general insights be applied directly to insurance. As a result, and as we just saw, crucial legal nuances such as the nature of the insured's characteristics, the specific line of insurance, and the exact nature of discrimination remain unanalyzed. In what follows, I focus on another issue that the literature on discrimination overlooks: the role of costs in the analysis.

Stage two: the tradeoff between equality and its consequences

Whether discrimination is just overall, even when it is not fair, depends on the social costs involved. Therefore, policy makers should attempt to account for the actual cost related to discrimination. In this context, three types of costs must be considered. The first is the impact of the prohibition on discrimination on the disadvantaged group it purports to help, in terms of refusal to insure, refusal to renew or higher premium. For example, imagine a prohibition on a comprehensive auto insurance policy providing *free* roadside assistance to women (but not to men). Such a prohibition can be justified in Stage One as fair on the ground that the policy demeans women (Hellman 2008; Chapter 7) because it assumes they cannot or do not want to change a flat tire themselves, thus perpetuating a stereotype that women are physically weaker, are deterred from physical tasks, or cannot handle a car—stereotypes that might hurt them in other markets such as the employment one. (Of course, a policy of free roadside assistance to women might be deemed fair in Stage One on the ground that society should be able to entertain the thought that women on average are less good than men at car maintenance, and at the same time that women are morally equal to men. But let us assume for now that a Stage One analysis determined the policy to be unfair and therefore upheld the prohibition.)

Such a prohibition, however, might increase the premium to women, potentially causing some of them—the poorer ones—not to buy comprehensive coverage, thus making them worse off. Oxera (2011) found that after the *Test-Achats* case, which required insurance companies in the EU to have unisex premiums, life insurance premiums increased for women. Similarly, Aseervatham *et al.* (2014) found that following the *Test-Achats* case auto insurance premiums increased for young females. Is it self-evident that a policy that boosts fairness (Stage One) but harms the very same group it purported to help is just? Does the magnitude of the harm to that group not matter?

Policy makers should also consider a second type of losses—efficiency losses in the insurance markets stemming from the fact that due to prohibition on discrimination, one group cross-subsidizes another, which might lead to a problem known to economists as *adverse selection*. If the insurer prices both races equally, all else being the same, blacks, for example, might pay less than the risk they pose. Insurers fear that certain whites cross-subsidizing blacks will drop out of the insurance pool. The absence of those less risky people will then raise the average riskiness of the pool, raising the cost of premiums for the entire pool and reducing the net benefit that participating in the insurance pool provides to the remaining members of both races. This situation in and of itself is an efficiency loss. But that might not be all. The reduction in the net benefit might further lead to whites that were previously on the cusp of dropping their participation in the pool to reconsider, causing them to leave the pool as well. Insurers argue that these events happening repeatedly comprise a chain reaction they call a *death spiral*, which might not end until the entire insurance pool unravels. A similar phenomenon can occur if insurers are banned from using genetic information. People who know they have defective genes will opt into the pool, driving out people without such genes. The end result might be that in the name of equality for everyone, we provide insurance to no one.

Another possibility is that a prohibition on discrimination might lead insurers to conduct a more detailed investigation of each applicant, and that in turn will raise premiums for everyone, dropping the poorer would-be insureds outside of the pool. The outcome would be that equality between the races comes at the expense of the poor of both races. The bottom line is this: can one seriously argue that costs associated with adverse selection never matter for the normative analysis?

Notably, while higher adverse selection costs and costs associated with death spirals are theories well accepted by economists, the empirical evidence of the extent to which they accurately describe the real world is mixed. Cutler and Reber (1998) conducted a detailed analysis of health insurance plans. They show that when Harvard University increased the premium of the most generous health plans for its policyholders regardless of the risk they imposed, the best risks in the pool (the ones with lower medical expenses) left this plan for a less generous one with a lower premium. Other evidence for adverse selection in health insurance markets exists (Cutler and Zeckhauser [2000]). However, in line with my claim in this chapter, in surveying the literature Cohen and Siegleman (2010) found that the significance of the adverse selection effect may vary by line of insurance, the characteristic discriminated against, and the nature of the discrimination. The upshot from all this is that in this regard as well, the analysis must be specific and cannot remain at the general level at which the literature in philosophy comfortably remains.

The third type of costs policy makers need to incorporate is the impact of allowing and prohibiting discrimination on insureds' *primary behavior*. Let us start with the impact of *allowing* discrimination. Suppose we conclude in Stage One that discriminating on the basis of genetics is fair, for example because it is not conceptually different from discrimination based on health conditions, which was allowed in the US until Obamacare. Our support of such discrimination may increase once we do our Stage Two analysis and consider the risk of adverse selection discussed above. And yet, we must also consider the impact of such policy on insureds' primary behavior. In our case, if insurers were allowed to discriminate based on clients' genetics, people might be deterred from having genetic tests. This, in turn, might prevent them from getting preemptive help, as well as prevent society from improving the science of genetic diseases (Hellman 2003). These costs might justify prohibiting genetic discrimination, at least in lines of insurance where people might be deterred from taking the tests, despite such discrimination being fair and despite the costs associated with the risk of adverse selection.

A similar analysis can be conducted for the case when discrimination is *prohibited*. Let us assume that in the first stage, one concludes that credit score discrimination (which scholars believe to be an alternative insurance companies found to race discrimination, once the latter was prohibited) should be prohibited in auto insurance. Still, policy makers should be hesitant to forbid credit score discrimination before they understand the empirical picture. In states that to prohibit such discrimination in auto insurance, premiums may be lower for drivers with a low credit score. But if low credit score is correlated with substance abuse, such a policy might cause more risky drivers to drive, potentially decreasing overall safety. Is it not crucial to know whether car accident rates rise? What about the number of fatalities and severe injuries? Avraham, Cohen and Shurtz (2016) found that states that prohibited discrimination based on credit score faced an increase of about 3% in fatalities. This extrapolates to about one thousand fatalities a year nationwide. One must pause here and reflect on whether the prohibition on credit discrimination is at all just.

To be sure, it might still be the case that a prohibition on credit score discrimination is not only *fair* (Stage One) but also *just*, even once the costs in terms of lost human lives are taken into account (Stage Two). My point, however, is that the impact on primary behavior involves important empirical questions that policy makers should not ignore.

More generally, I argued in this section that for pragmatic reasons a two-stage analysis is desirable. In the first stage, policy makers should focus on the deontological requirements a fair insurance regime necessitates. My main point there was that a more nuanced analysis, one that takes into account the specific characteristic, the specific line of insurance, and the specific nature of discrimination, is required. In the second stage, policy makers should focus on the costs associated with a fair anti-discrimination regime in order to determine whether it is also just. My main point there was again that a nuanced analysis is extremely important: one that takes into account the impact on the protected groups' welfare, the impact on insurance markets, and the impact on the primary behavior.

Conclusion

In this chapter, I sketched a contemporary mapping of anti-discrimination insurance laws (statutes, courts decisions, and directives) in both the EU and the US. Of course, inconsistency in legal treatment across and within jurisdictions is rampant in countless areas. Here, I conjectured that the complete legal mess might imply that policy makers still lack the necessary nuanced normative framework regarding optimal insurance anti-discrimination policy. I attempted to start filling in this gap with my two-stage analysis hereby offered.

One question left unanswered is why private insurance companies need to be subject to norms, such as anti-discrimination norm, usually applicable to the government. We never think about asking a grocery store to sell milk or bread to minorities below its costs, and yet we do ask insurance companies to do so when pricing policies. The answer might be that modern life makes insurance companies so large, in terms of their political, economic, and legal influence, that the same rationales originally applied to the relationship between citizens and governments are also relevant to citizens and insurance companies. Insurance companies sell services and spread risks across millions of people, thus serving a large chunk of the polity. Insurance companies are often protected from competition, especially from abroad, thanks to government regulation. Governments routinely mandate and encourage their citizens to buy coverage—a benefit no other private industry enjoys. Insurance companies manage trillions of our dollars, for example our pension funds, which comprise a large proportion of the public's wealth. Insurance companies are often too big to fail, which grants them important influence with governments. And yet, it is not entirely clear that costs of equality should not be spread across all citizens rather than just the insurance company's customers. For example, if a minority neighborhood suffers from a high crime rate due to the government's neglect, which would naturally result in higher property insurance premiums in that neighborhood, it is not clear that insurance companies (and their customers) should bear the costs for such neglect by being prohibited from charging higher premiums in that neighborhood. Rather, perhaps a sounder regime will be one where the government reimburses insurers for the various costs associated with requiring them to charge an equal premium. This example highlights possible interesting intersections between markets, anti-discrimination norms, and mechanisms of distributive justice. However, adequately addressing these issues lies well beyond the scope of this chapter.

Notes

1 Official Journal of the European Union L 373, 21.12.2004, p. 37.

2 Guidelines on the application of Council Directive 2004/113/EC to insurance, in the light of the judgment of the Court of Justice of the European Union in Case C-236/09 (*Test-Achats*).

3 *Insurance Services Office v. Commissioner of Ins.* (1979, La App) 381 So 2d 515, cert den (La) 382 So 2d 1391.
4 *Government Employees Ins. Co. v. Insurance Comm'r* (1993) 332 Md 124, 630 A2d 713.
5 *Guidry v. Pellerin Life Ins. Co.* 364 F.Supp.2d 592 W.D.La., 2005. And see also *Young v. Farmers' Mut. Life Ins. Co.*, 1 S.W.2d 74 Ark., 1928.
6 *Toledo Fair Hous. Ctr. v. Nationwide Mut. Ins. Co.*, 704 N.E.2d 667 Ohio.Com.Pl., 1997.

Bibliography

Aseervatham, V., Lex, C., and Spindler, M. "How do Unisex Rating Regulations Affect Gender Differences in Insurance Premiums?" *The Geneva Papers on Risk and Insurance – Issues and Practice.* 41(1): 128–160.

Avraham, R., Logue, K. D., and Schwarcz, D. 2014. "The Anatomy of Insurance Anti-Discrimination Laws." *University of Southern California Law Review.* 87(2): 195–274.

Avraham, R., Logue, K. D., and Schwarcz, D. 2015. "Towards a Universal Framework for Insurance Anti-Discrimination Laws." *Connecticut Insurance Law Journal* 21(1).

Bailey, H. T. *et al.* 1976. "The Regulatory Challenge to Life Insurance Classification." *Drake Law Review.* 25: 779–827.

Benston, G. J. 1982. "The Economics of Gender Discrimination in Employee Fringe Benefits: Manhart Revisited." *The University of Chicago Law Review.* 49(2): 489.

B. Boxill. 1992. *Blacks and Social Justice*, revised ed. Lanham, MD: Rowman and Littlefield.

Brilmayer, L., Laycock, D., and Sullivan, T. A. 1983. "The Efficient Use of Group Averages as Nondiscrimination: A Rejoinder to Professor Benston." *University of Chicago Law Review.* 50: 222–249.

Cavanagh, M. 2002. *Against Equality of Opportunity*, Oxford: Oxford University Press.

Cohen, A. and Siegelman, P. 2010. "Testing for Adverse Selection in Insurance Markets." *Journal of Risk and Insurance.* 77(1): 39–84.

Cotter, A. 2006. *Race Matters: An International Legal Analysis of Race Discrimination.* Burlington, VT: Ashgate.

Cutler, D. M. and Reber, S. J. 1998. "Paying for Health Insurance: The Trade-off Between Competition and Adverse Selection." *The Quarterly Journal of Economics.* 113: 433–466.

Cutler, D. M. and Zeckhauser, R. J. 2000. "The Anatomy of Health Insurance." In: A. J. Culyer and J. P. Newhouse (eds), *Handbook of Health Economics.* New York: Elsevier.

Dagan, H. and Dorfman, A. 2015. "Just Relationships." *Columbia Law Review.* 116 (6).

Dworkin, R. 1985. *A Matter of Principle.* Cambridge, MA: Harvard University Press.

Gardner, J. 1998. "On the Ground of Her Sex(uality)." *Oxford Journal of Legal Studies.* 18: 167–187.

Gaulding, J. 1995. *Race, Sex and Genetic Discrimination in Insurance: What's Fair? Cornell Law Review.* 80: 1646.

Gerber, J. "The Economic and Actuarial Aspects of Selection and Classification." *The Forum.* 10(4): 1205–1230.

Hasnas, J. 2002. "Equal Opportunity, Affirmative Action, and the Anti Discrimination Principle: The Philosophical Basis for The Legal Prohibition of Discrimination." *Fordham Law Review.* 71: 424–542.

Hellman, D. 2003. "What Makes Genetic Discrimination Exceptional?" *American Journal of Law and Medicine.* 29: 77–116.

Hellman, D. 2008. *When is Discrimination Wrong?* Cambridge, MA: Harvard University Press.

Hoffman, S. 2003. "Unmanaged Care: Toward Moral Fairness in Health Care Coverage." *Indiana Law Journal.* 78(2): 659–721.

Kimball, S. L. 1979. "Reverse Sex Discrimination: Manhart." *American Bar Foundation Research Journal.* 83: 85–139.

Laycock, D. and Sullivan, T. A. 1981. "Sex Discrimination's 'Actuarial Equality': A Rejoinder to Kimball." *American Bar Foundation Research Journal.* 6(1): 221–228.

Lippert-Rasmussen, K. 2013. *Born Free and Equal?* Oxford: Oxford University Press.

Moreau, S. 2010. "What is Discrimination?" *Philosophy and Public Affairs.* 38(2): 143–179.

Oxera. 2011. *The Impact of a Ban on the Use of Gender in Insurance*. Oxford: Oxera.

Perkins, J. D. 2002. "Life Insurance Risk Classification: Finding the Boundary between Antitrust and Unfair Discrimination." *Connecticutt Insurance Law Journal*. 9: 527.

Schauer, F. 2003. *Profiles, Probabilities, and Stereotypes*. Cambridge, MA: Harvard University Press.

Segal, S. 2012. "What's So bad About Discrimination?" *Utilitas*. 241: 82–100.

Sydlaske, J. 1975. "Gender Classifications in the Insurance Industry." *Columbia Law Review*. 75(7): 1381–1403.

Wortham, L. 1985. "Insurance Classification: Too Important to Be Left to the Actuaries." *University of Michigan Journal of Law Reform*. 19: 349.

Wortham, L. 1986. "The Economics of Insurance Classification: the Sound of One Invisible Hand Clapping." *Ohio State Law Journal*. 47: 863.

Case law

Norris, 463 U.S. 1073. (1983).

Los Angeles Dept. of Water and Power v. Manhart. 435 U.S. 702. (1978).

The National Association for The Advancement Of Colored People, et al., v. American Family Mutual Insurance Company, 978 F.2d 287 (7th Circ, 1992).

29

DISCRIMINATION AND POLITICS

Nenad Stojanović

UNIVERSITÄT LUZERN

Introduction

Political philosophers and legal theorists working on the concept of discrimination hardly ever mention the sphere of electoral politics (see, e.g., the various essays in Hellman and Moreau 2013; Altman 2015). They mostly refer to discrimination arising in areas such as employment, education and housing (cf. Chapters 25 and 26). And yet, as numerous empirical studies show (see, e.g., Fisher et al. 2015; Street 2014), discrimination is present in politics too. Hence, the aim of this chapter is to elaborate a conceptual roadmap – supported by selected empirical examples – that shall help to address the concept of discrimination in the political–electoral sphere of liberal democracies.

To accomplish this I distinguish between three key political actors in representative democracies: voters, political parties and candidates. While they often overlap – in any given election a citizen can be both a voter and a candidate running on a party ballot – it is useful to keep them separated for analytical purposes. Also, I will address discriminations against these three political actors on grounds of morally objectionable and (supposedly) politically irrelevant identity characteristics such as race, ethnicity and gender (cf. Chapters 15 and 16).

A couple of additional remarks are in order. First, my account of discrimination in politics draws upon a *moralized* concept of discrimination, as defined by Altman (2015: §1.2; cf. Introduction), that is applied to

> …acts, practices or policies that meet two conditions: (a) they wrongfully impose a relative disadvantage or deprivation on persons based on their membership in some salient social group, and (b) the wrongfulness rests (in part) on the fact that the imposition of the disadvantage is on account of the group membership of the victims.
>
> *(Altman 2015)*

Second, as in most accounts of discrimination, it will be useful to distinguish between direct and indirect, as well as between explicit and implicit forms of discrimination in politics (cf. Chapters 1 and 2). Third, for reasons of space I will focus mainly on cases of morally wrongful discrimination (discrimination *against*) and will not address instances of morally justified "positive" discrimination (discrimination *in favor*) and discrimination *between* (see Lippert-Rasmussen 2014: 14). Finally, at the end of each section I will mention a number of difficult, borderline cases.

Discrimination of citizens *qua* voters

The right to vote – also called suffrage or the franchise – is a political right and a central element of democratic political systems (Beckman 2009). The main idea is that in a democracy *every* citizen, in principle, should have the right to participate in the body politic. In the wording of the *Universal Declaration of Human Rights* of 1948 (article 21.1), "everyone has the right to take part in the government of his country, directly or through freely chosen representative."

The most frequent exceptions to this principle – considered as not unreasonable and, thus, legitimate in contemporary democracies – are grounded on *age* (no country allows children to vote), on basic *mental capacity* (in nine out of ten democracies the mentally impaired cannot vote) and on *citizenship* (resident non-citizens are almost never enfranchised in national elections) (López-Guerra 2014; cf. Chapter 20).

Nowadays there is a general consensus that the distribution of the right to vote "should not discriminate unfairly between individuals on the basis of *irrelevant* distinctions" (Beckman 2009: 1; emphasis added). In this regard, the most commonly cited politically irrelevant traits are "race, color, sex, language and religion".[1] These traits are typically considered as next to immutable ("ascriptive") and the groups based on them are in most contexts *socially salient*. This remark is important, because, arguably, in any viable account of discrimination only the socially salient groups can qualify as potential grounds of discrimination (Altman 2015: §1.2; Lippert-Rasmussen 2014: 30–36).

In the remaining part of this section I will map the possible discriminations, drawn from real-world examples, indicating discriminatory laws and practices grounded on such ascriptive and socially salient traits of citizens *qua* voters.

Direct and explicit discrimination against citizens qua *voters*

The most clear-cut case of legal, direct and explicit discrimination against citizens *qua* (potential) voters is the history of women's suffrage. Before the late nineteenth century, certain states or sub-state entities had granted the right to vote to women. But it was a history of partial enfranchisement *and* disenfranchisement. For example, women could vote in Sweden between 1718 and 1771 and in the state of New Jersey from 1776 to 1806. The first country to grant the right to vote to women (without restrictions), and not to revoke it, was New Zealand in 1893, followed by Finland in 1906 and Norway in 1913. The major waves of women's enfranchisement came after the First World War and then again after the Second World War. Today, women's suffrage exists in almost all countries that use elections.[2]

In some cases, the enfranchisement of women was accompanied by a restatement of discriminatory practice on the basis of illegitimate criteria *other* than sex. In 1902 New Zealand, for example, explicitly excluded aboriginal men and women from the franchise.[3]

Direct and implicit discrimination against citizens qua *voters*

Legal provisions can also implicitly deny the franchise to certain groups of citizens. Consider a law stipulating that only people with a basic level of literacy can vote. Depending on the context, this might amount to a form of discrimination against individuals who belong to socially salient, minority groups. That kind of discrimination can be seen as "structural", because it "concerns the rules that constitute and regulate the major sectors of life such as [...] political powers and responsibilities (Altman 2015: §2.3; see Lippert-Rasmussen 2014: 77–78). For example, the literacy tests that Southern states in the US began to adopt in 1890 had a large differential racial *impact*, since 40–60 percent of blacks were illiterate, compared to 8–18 percent of whites (Kousser 1974). So, until the 1965 Voting Rights Act, literacy tests as well as poll taxes and various other bureaucratic restrictions *de facto* disenfranchised large numbers of African-Americans. The Voting Rights Act, however, did not completely eradicate this form of discrimination. An amendment to the Act was introduced in 1975, and again in 1982 and 2007, to address the discrimination against language minorities (Sher 2011: 65–69). In recent years, other and more subtle devices – such as voter ID laws, requiring citizens to provide an official identity card before they are permitted to vote – have been devised in some US states to make it harder for citizens belonging to minority groups to participate, *qua* voters, in elections.[4]

Notice that structural discrimination cuts across the distinction between direct and indirect discrimination. As a *conceptual* matter, it is necessarily indirect "by its very nature" (Lippert-Rasmussen 2014: 78). Nevertheless, as an *empirical* matter, "direct discrimination is (almost) always part of the story of how structural discrimination came to be and continues to exist" (Altman 2015: §2.3). The aim of the agents who had designed the literacy tests in the US was to keep off the polls as many African-Americans as possible. Indeed, Altman (2015: §2.1) cites precisely this example as a case of *direct* discrimination even though such a policy, "on its face, makes no explicit reference to the group that [its agent] aims to disadvantage."

Discrimination against citizens qua *voters by parties*

A peculiar, but rare, form of discrimination against citizens *qua* voters does not concern their right to vote in elections but rather the way in which parties excluded them from the democratic process. The "White Primaries", practiced by the Democratic party in southern US states up to the 1940s, are an example in point. This practice excluded African-Americans until the Supreme Court declared it unconstitutional (*Smith v. Allwright*, 1944).

Difficult cases

Plural voting

Provided that there is universal suffrage and that, in principle, everyone has the right to vote, can we say that the problem of discrimination against citizens *qua* voters has been solved? Not necessarily. Indeed, (a) equal rights of participation (that include also the rights of association and political expression, as well as the right to run for office) constitute only one of three components of political equality. The other two components are (b) the idea that every vote should have an equal weight and (c) that there should be "equal opportunities for effective political influence" (Cohen 2009: 271).

As for the second of these components, John Stuart Mill famously argued in favor of "plural voting": everyone should have the right to vote but the votes of more educated citizens should have more weight. Many thinkers have rejected this proposition, claiming that it would undermine the principle of political equality (e.g., Beitz 1989). In the past, some democracies did allow certain categories of citizens to cast more votes, on the basis of their level of education or wealth. For example, Belgium practiced plural voting between 1894 and 1919. Citizens with higher education and certain abilities received two extra votes, while householders and other wealthy citizens had one additional vote. So it was possible to accumulate up to three extra votes (Bartolini 2007: 352).

Nevertheless, I reckon that *prima facie* this kind of treatment appears less wrongful than, say, the (imaginary) proposition to grant white citizens two votes each and one vote each to black citizens. Again, the reason is that, in principle, given proper background conditions (in particular, equal chances and equal access to education), being less educated or poor is not a permanent human condition, nor a socially salient group identity.

A form of legal "plural voting" exists, however, in many contemporary democracies, especially in federal systems. It does not concern the question of how many votes citizens can cast, but how their votes are counted. In the second chambers of the US and Swiss parliaments every federal entity (each of the states and cantons) has the same number of representatives (two), irrespective of its population. This means that in the second chamber the votes of citizens of Wyoming (564,000 in 2010) have the same weight as the votes of citizens of California (37.2 million), or that a vote from the canton of Uri (36,000 in 2015) counts the same as a vote from the canton of Zurich (1.47 million).

The rules governing citizens' representation in the second chambers of federal countries might be considered blatant examples of democratic *injustice* but not, by themselves, instances of *discrimination*. While some people may feel a certain pride in being, say, citizens of Zurich and not of Uri, their cantonal identity is not (if at all) as salient socially as being black or Muslim. (Also, notice that a citizen of Zurich is legally entitled to move his official residence to Uri anytime.) So, in the US context, Beitz (1989: 94) argues that white primaries or the exclusion of women from the franchise were "clearly objectionable" as they were experienced as "demeaning" by the victims of such exclusion, whereas "few [...] feel insulted or degraded by the patent inequality of representation in the U.S. Senate". Possibly, citizens tend to see such arrangements as an acceptable price of federalism.

Racial vote dilution

If anyone has the right to vote, and if all votes have equal weight, is there still room for discrimination against citizens *qua* voters? Possibly, if we turn our attention to the third component of the principle of political equality, that is, the idea that my vote should have an equal opportunity of effective *influence* as your vote. To see this, consider elections in single-member districts held under the first-past-the-post system (e.g., as used in Canada, the UK, the US). In such contexts, citizens have the right to vote and every vote has the same weight. And yet voters who support a political party or candidates who can obtain only a minority of ballots will lack parliamentary representation and, thus, their vote will hardly have any influence in the parliamentary decision-making process. This is not a problem *per se* but may become one – it has been known as the "problem of permanent minorities" in democratic theory (Williams 1998: 77) – if citizens' voting patterns are more or less stable and systematic over time.

It is easy to imagine cases where the permanent electoral minority is a racial, ethnic or religious group. While it is difficult to see this fact, by itself, as an instance of discrimination, the charge of discrimination could be raised if, say, the borders of electoral districts were deliberately drawn in such a way as to permanently harm the effective influence of the minority vote.

Imagine a minority group A that is concentrated within the core area (e.g., the downtown of a large city) of a given territory where it constitutes 45 percent of the population of the whole territory. The majority group B occupies the surrounding areas (e.g., the suburban parts of that city) and has a population share of 55 percent. The electoral system obliges the authorities to divide the territory into two electoral districts, each electing one representative to Parliament. How should the district lines be drawn? There is presumptive discrimination if authorities use morally objectionable criteria – such as race – for districting purposes. The term "racial vote dilution", coined in the US, describes precisely districting schemes through which authorities intentionally drew the district lines to make sure that African-Americans and Latinos become a minority in each district. In a series of decisions the Supreme Court struck such districting schemes as discriminatory and obliged the authorities to concentrate minorities in a way to allow them to form (permanent) demographic *majorities* (Altman 1998). In other words, discriminatory gerrymandering was replaced by a form of affirmative-action re-districting producing the so-called "minority-majority districts" (cf. Chapter 33).

Political parties

Legal bans of ethnic parties

In some countries minorities tend to form their own parties. We can speak of direct discrimination if the constitution or electoral laws explicitly ban the formation of such parties (see Rosenblum 2007). The Venice Commission of the Council of Europe, for example, stresses that electoral law "must guarantee equality for persons belonging to national minorities, which includes prohibiting any discrimination against them" (Venice Commission 2003: 19; see also Lécuyer 2014). In particular, this implies that "the national minorities must be allowed to set up their parties".

However, there are not so many examples of countries that have legally banned ethnic minority parties. The Venice Commission lists Albania, Bulgaria, Georgia and Turkey as countries that have "prohibit[ed] parties representing minorities" (Venice Commission 2000: 7). But this assertion is misleading. In reality, in these countries the electoral law does not target the parties of *specific* minorities. The Bulgarian constitution, for example, defines the ban as follows: "There shall be no political parties on ethnic, racial or religious lines, nor parties which seek the violent seizure of state power" (Lublin 2014: 205).

Yet if a country is dominated by an ethnic majority, a ban on ethnic parties amounts *de facto* to the ban of ethnic *minority* parties and can be considered a case of legal and direct, albeit implicit, discrimination. In Albania, for example, the Albanians make up 98 percent of the population and do not have problems in forming parties that bear "Albanian" in their name. So the ban on ethnic parties *de facto* prohibits the Greek minority (0.9 percent) from forming their own ethnic party. Generally speaking, legal bans on ethnic and regional parties are found in Africa (Benin, Cape Verde, Ghana, Lesotho, Mali, Namibia, and Sao Tomé and Principe) and less so on other continents (Lublin 2014: 203).

Some party bans have been successfully challenged in courts. In 2001 the European Court of Human Rights declared in a 6-1 ruling (*Stankov and the United Macedonian Organisation Ilinden v. Bulgaria*) that the Bulgarian government had violated Article 11 of the European Convention on Human Rights – "Everyone has the right to freedom of peaceful assembly and to freedom of association with others" – when it refused to register an ethnic Macedonian organization in 1991. Nonetheless, the Turkish minority in Bulgaria was able to circumvent the ban by forming the Movement for Rights and Freedoms, which has won seats in every election (9 percent on average) since 1991 (Lublin 2014: 205).

Other cases of discrimination against ethnic minority parties

There are a number of other ways by which countries can legally but implicitly discriminate against ethnic minorities by preventing them from setting up their own parties. The measures include registration and ballot-access requirements, as well as electoral thresholds. Such rules are typically applied to all parties but "can have a disproportionate [negative] impact on ethnoregional parties" (Lublin 2014: 209). Territorially dispersed (even if relatively large), as well as smaller (even if territorially concentrated) minorities are vulnerable to such rules.

Take Slovakia as an example (Lublin 2014: 214–215). Its Hungarian minority has a population share of 10 percent and is concentrated along the Slovak–Hungarian border. The initial electoral threshold of 3 percent, in 1990, was not an obstacle to the two Hungarian parties, which gained 9 percent of the seats. In 1998, the government of Vladimír Mečiar, a Slovak nationalist, required coalitions of two or more parties to gain at least 5 percent of the vote for *each* party in the alliance and to have at least 10,000 members. The Hungarian parties avoided the obstacle by merging into a single party that won 9 percent of the vote and 10 percent of seats in 1998. Nonetheless, as Lublin (2014: 218) remarks, "Slovakia demonstrated how governments can cloak attacks on minority parties in seemingly neutral electoral rules".

That being said, it is not easy to establish whether a given legal provision hides an *intentional* attempt to discriminate against ethnic minorities (cf. Chapter 1). Electoral thresholds, in particular, are typically established with purposes that are not intentionally discriminating (such as avoiding excessive partisan fragmentation), even though they could still have discriminatory effects. So the final answer will necessarily be context-dependent and a matter of empirical inquiry. The electoral law in Turkey sets up an electoral threshold of 10 percent that makes it difficult for Kurdish parties to gain seats. But consider the Turkish citizens (including the Kurds from Turkey) in the canton of Geneva, Switzerland, who make up about 1 percent of the population (Stojanović 2013: 104). Does the electoral law, establishing a threshold of 7.5 percent for parties to enter the cantonal parliament, discriminate against the Turkish (or Kurdish) minority in Geneva? It is clearly difficult to sustain such a claim. There is no evidence that the authorities of Geneva had any intention of harming ethnic minorities, nor that the Turkish (or Kurdish) citizens have ever intended to form their own party. Hence, the analysis of the specific contexts of Turkey and Geneva allows us to claim that only the electoral law in Turkey is discriminatory.[5]

As a matter of fact, democracies can intervene if they realize that a given electoral threshold, deemed necessary to avoid excessive partisan fragmentation, has negative consequences upon minorities. For example, Germany has a general threshold of 5 percent, but it made an exception for the parties of the Danish minority in the region of Schleswig-Holstein, by lowering the threshold to 3 percent. In Italy, too, lower thresholds have been applied in the province of Alto Adige/South Tyrol, where two-thirds of the population speak German (Stojanović 2013: 273).

Difficult cases

A difficult case concerns ethnic party bans in countries where there is no clear ethnic majority. In such places, a general ethnic party ban could be justified for reasons of peace and stability, or indeed to preserve the democracy itself according to the precepts of "militant democracy" (see, e.g., Kirshner 2014). It does not necessarily conceal a preference for the dominant ethnic group because, by definition, no ethnicity is dominant. For example, a general ethnic party ban was declared in Bosnia and Herzegovina in early 1990, two years before the war. It was later declared unconstitutional by the Constitutional court, so the ethnic parties representing the three main ethnic groups, none of which had a demographic majority, could be formed. They eventually won 75 percent of the vote in the November 1990 elections (Stojanović 2014).

Candidates

The third kind of political actors who are potential victims of discrimination in politics are citizens *qua* candidates. Notice that by "candidates" I refer not only to citizens who actually run for office but also to *potential* candidates, or aspirants, who are *prevented* from standing for office. So in this section I will (a) examine the cases of direct discrimination in which the constitution or law prevents certain groups of citizens from running for office on grounds of their membership of socially salient groups. I will then (b) address the cases of legal but indirect discrimination. If neither problem subsists, however, we still face two discriminatory practices performed by (c) party selectors and (d) by citizens *qua* electors.

Direct discrimination against candidates

The cases of legal and direct discrimination concern countries where certain categories of citizens are not allowed to run for office because of their ascriptive group identities. The examples in point are Bosnia and Herzegovina, and South Tyrol. In Bosnia, candidates who do not belong to any of the three "constitutive peoples" (Bosniaks, Croats, and Serbs) cannot run for the three-member Presidency and cannot be appointed to the second chamber of Parliament (the House of Peoples). The European Court of Human Rights – in *Sejdić and Finci v. Bosnia and Herzegovina* (2009) and *Zornić v. Bosnia and Herzegovina* (2014) – declared such practices as "discriminatory" and defended the right of Bosnian citizens belonging to the group of "Others" – such as Roma (Mr. Sejdić), Jews (Mr. Finci), or Bosnians (*sic*; Ms. Zornić) – to run for any political office of the country (Lécuyer 2014). A similar case in point is South Tyrol, where since 1980 the ethnic census data have been used to check whether candidates belong to one of the three recognized groups (German, Italian, or Ladino). A group of citizens – called "ethnic objectors" – refused any affiliation. As a consequence, the provincial authorities prevented the ethnic objectors from running for office (Stojanović 2013: 200–206).[6]

Notice, however, that in many countries not all enfranchised citizens have a right to run for specific political offices, although it appears *prima facie* inappropriate to consider such practices as cases of discrimination. Nobody would argue, I assume, that Barack Obama is discriminated against because after his two terms in office he is not allowed to run for a third time. Other countries restrict access to office by age (cf. Chapter 20). In France, only citizens who are over 24 years of age are eligible for the Senate. We do not consider this a form of discrimination as most citizens are expected to reach the age of 24 in their lives. In Rehfeld's (2010: 249) words, "[reaching a certain age] is an acquirable trait that is purportedly necessary for the job". There are borderline cases, however. For example, the age limit of 40, required to become a senator in Italy, appears far too excessive. Also, according to the US Constitution (Article 2.1), only "a natural born citizen" can hold the office of President or Vice-President. This provision discriminates against citizens who are not Americans at birth, but it appears less problematic than the political discrimination against ethnic minorities and of citizens without an ethnic affiliation in the consociational regimes of Bosnia or South Tyrol.

Indirect discrimination against candidates

The Constitution or laws can contain provisions that do not directly aim at preventing citizens belonging to minority groups from running for office, but that still produce similar effects. As an example, take the financial provisions in electoral laws.

If candidates are legally required to pay large sums of money – either to the state or to their parties – in order to participate in elections, this might hinder potential candidates from economically disadvantaged groups. Whether or not it amounts to an instance of indirect discrimination against socially salient groups is context-specific. This might be the case in places where there is a sufficiently strong correlation between socio-economic status and ethnicity, for example in the US, where African-Americans and Hispanics are generally less well-off than whites. But generally speaking, better educated and better-off people are over-represented in politics everywhere, as the systematic political under-representation of workers demonstrates (Mansbridge 2015). And even within economically disadvantaged ethnic minorities we will always find better-off individuals who can afford to run for office. Therefore, I do not think that, in most developed democracies, this kind of discrimination is problematic *per se*.

Of course, winning an election – especially at the national level – can be very costly even if there are no laws requiring candidates to pay large sums of money in advance (Cohen 2009). This might put more pressure upon economically disadvantaged ethnic minorities but does not amount to a form of indirect discrimination. Rehfeld (2010: 262), therefore, argues that an *equal* right to run for office entails not only that citizens must be allowed to run for office but also that "the citizen's voter-exogenous probability of success in her run for office must be equal to any other citizen's". Among voter-exogenous factors we can mention financial resources, but also redistricting schemes and other special provisions, such as quotas, that favor some groups over others. Rehfeld excludes, thus, the idea that an equal chance to run for office entails any intervention within the realm of voter-*endogenous* factors: "When a voter is a racist, or sexist, or merely votes with an eye to his own good despite the harm it will cause the whole, it expresses the venality, ignorance, or simply unjustness of voters, but it is not an obvious violation of anyone's right to run" (Rehfeld 2010: 263). He never uses the notion of discrimination to describe such patterns of voters' behavior. And yet, I think, we ought to try to make sense of the idea that voters can discriminate against candidates. But before addressing that problem (§4.4), we shall discuss the discrimination happening at an earlier stage, when party members or party leaders are called upon to select aspirant candidates and allow them to run for office in the first place (§4.3).

Discrimination against candidates by party selectors

In most democracies all enfranchised citizens are allowed not only to vote but also to stand for any political office. Generally speaking, while citizens can certainly participate in elections as independent candidates, in most cases they can be elected only if they run on a party ballot. Hence, the role of individuals who select candidates within the parties becomes decisive. Empirical research in the UK and France has found out that selectors may perform three forms of discrimination against aspirants: direct, indirect and imputed discrimination (Norris and Lovenduski 1993; Childs 2008: 61; Murray 2010).[7]

- Direct discrimination reflects the racial, sexist and other forms of selectors' prejudice, and takes place when selectors judge aspirants not as individuals but on the basis of characteristics seen as common to their group.

- Indirect discrimination refers to cases where the idea of what constitutes a "good politician" counts against aspirants coming from minority groups.
- Another form of indirect discrimination, also called "imputed discrimination", is when selectors are not necessarily racists or sexists but exclude potential candidates from minority groups because they think that most voters will not support them. In other words, party selectors act on the basis of the perceived lack of electability of minority candidates and try to avoid losing votes. As one selector from the Labour Party in the UK told an Asian Labour candidate who had failed to receive support in the selection process: "Well, the reason I didn't vote for you was because we [the Labour Party selectors] were worried that we might lose the vote" (Norris and Lovenduski 1993: 393).

It should be noted that imputed discrimination is probably more pronounced in majoritarian single-member district electoral systems than in multi-member districts and/or PR systems. A Venice Commission (2009) study thus affirms that "[b]oth the First-Past-the-Post system and the French Two-Round system tend to work against women". Most European countries, apart from the UK and France, use PR or mixed electoral systems in national parliamentary elections. With regard to ethnic minorities, however, the empirical evidence is much more complex and there is not general scholarly consensus on the merits of PR over majoritarian systems (see, e.g., Moser 2008; Lublin 2014).

Discrimination of minority candidates by electors

Once a minority aspirant has passed the party gates and become a candidate, he or she might still face discrimination by citizens *qua* electors. Consider, for example, the Gallup surveys in the US revealing that a considerable number of respondents would not vote for a *generally competent* candidate from their *own* party if this candidate was a woman, a black or a Muslim. Consequently, many empirical studies have tried to measure this kind of voting behavior, by referring explicitly to the notion of discrimination (see, e.g., Highton 2004; Fisher *et al.* 2015; Street 2014).

At the theoretical level, however, it is far from evident that we can use the concept of discrimination to make sense of such voting patterns. Indeed, no recent work on discrimination in political philosophy or legal theory ever mentions electoral discrimination (e.g., Hellman and Moreau 2013; Lippert-Rasmussen 2014; Altman 2015). Here is a (non-exhaustive) list of reasons that might explain this reticence:

- The freedom of choice is an important principle in the theory and the practice of democracy. If political equality entails that citizens "have the right to be ruled by anyone they choose" (Rehfeld 2010: 256), then the very notion of discrimination does not fit well into this picture.
- It is very difficult to assess the kind of competence that candidates need to possess in order to access political office. It is actually controversial whether there should be *any* test of competence at all (should we be ruled only by people with college degrees?). In the job market the competence is typically seen as a morally permissible motive for employing Applicant A (more competent) instead of Applicant B (less competent) and, generally speaking, there is agreement on the kind of skills that applicants need to have in order to perform a specific job (cf. Chapter 25). So an employer acts in a discriminatory way if she systematically refuses to employ people belonging to minority groups even though they are objectively as competent as the successful applicants (or even more competent). So, if there

is no agreement on what constitutes competence in politics, it is much more difficult to raise the charge of discrimination – an "inherently comparative" concept (Altman 2015; see Lippert-Rasmussen 2014: 16)[8] – if a voter prefers Candidate A (belonging to the majority group) over Candidate B (belonging to a minority group).

- Even if we suppose, for the sake of argument, that all candidates can be ranked according to their political skills and competences, we still face at least two difficulties. The first difficulty is of an empirical nature: voters simply lack time, resources or interest to collect information on the skills and competences of individual candidates. This happens in contexts with few candidates competing for one seat – in single-member district systems – but becomes dramatic in open-list PR systems where voters can allocate preference votes to a limited number of candidates out of a slot comprising *hundreds* of candidates. The second difficulty is conceptual: even if there were an agreement on the competence-driven candidate ranking, and even if voters had all necessary information for assessing such competence, it is a core principle of democracy to allow voters to support candidates on the basis of their purely political and ideological preferences: I can openly opt for a less competent candidate and democratically justify that choice by the candidate's proximity to my political views. In other words, I discriminate *between* but not *against* candidates.
- The secret ballot, while less clearly a requisite of democracy, is a widely accepted practice that is supported both by theoretical and practical considerations (to fight against corruption, in particular). Further, voting is an individual act and in a typical election no single vote will decide the outcome of the election. Therefore, while on a moral level one might argue that certain voters have a discriminatory voting behavior, no single voter can be accused of preventing anyone from being elected.

Difficult cases

Our debate over discrimination by citizens *qua* (potential or real) candidates in elections is not exhaustive. There are many difficult cases. Sometimes candidates can be prevented from running for office if they engage in hate speech or if they incite violence. This looks *prima facie* a legitimate restriction. But what if, in reality, it conceals attempts to block candidates from minority groups? In a 2003 ruling, for example, a divided Israeli Supreme Court voted 7–4 against the disqualification of a prominent Israeli–Arab politician, Ahmad Tibi, accused by the majority of the Knesset of supporting the second Intifada (Rosenblum 2007: 47–48).

Another difficult case is the electoral penalty suffered by less attractive politicians (see, e.g., Rosar *et al.* 2012). Less attractive people do not form a socially salient group. Hence, this kind of electoral penalty should be excluded from our account of discrimination. We do perceive such practices as unjust, however, and perhaps discriminatory in a more generic sense of the term (see Lippert-Rasmussen 2014: 34).

Finally, in many ethnically divided places people tend to vote only for candidates belonging to their own group. Is ethnic voting a form of discrimination? Is it discriminatory if people vote for candidates who resemble them? According to Rosenblum (2007) there is nothing wrong when people form ethnic parties and when they perform bloc (i.e. ethnic) voting. She considers them "key instruments" of political conflict and of political integration.

Conclusion

In this chapter we have explored instances of political discrimination against voters, parties and candidates belonging to socially salient groups. We have seen that in many democracies each of these core political actors have been subjected to direct or indirect, explicit or implicit forms of discrimination.

Conceptually, the most puzzling part concerns the cases in which the purported discriminators are citizens *qua* electors whereas the discriminatees are citizens *qua* candidates. In such cases, one could argue, there ought to be a legal right *not* to be prevented – for example, by means of fines or prison – from engaging in morally objectionable forms of discrimination. The reason is that the right of citizens to run for offices clashes with the right of citizens *qua* electors to vote for any party or candidate they wish.

Notes

1 See the *International Covenant on Civil and Political Rights*, Article 2.1.

2 The Vatican is an exception. In Saudi Arabia women were allowed to vote for the first time in the municipal elections held in December 2015.

3 See the *Commonwealth Franchise Act* (Article 4, sub-section "Disqualification of coloured races"): "No aboriginal native of Australia Asia Africa or the Islands of the Pacific except New Zealand shall be entitled to have his [sic] name placed on the Electoral Roll [...]." Source: Museum of Australian Democracy (http://www.foundingdocs.gov.au/scan-sid-164.html; accessed 27 June 2016).

4 This amounts to indirect discrimination as the possession of ID is disproportionately lower among minorities and the poor. See "How voter ID laws are being used to disenfranchise minorities and the poor", *The Atlantic*, 16 March 2012.

5 Recall that, being a form of structural discrimination, the Turkish electoral law is conceptually an instance of indirect discrimination but, as an empirical matter, it amounts to direct discrimination against Kurdish parties.

6 See the case of Alexander Langer – a member of the European Parliament from 1989 to 1995, where he chaired the Green Group – who in 1995 was denied the right to run for the office of mayor of the provincial capital Bolzano/Bozen.

7 To be sure, Norris and Lovenduski (1993) referred to direct versus indirect *prejudice* and not *discrimination* (albeit in their conclusion they state that women candidates "seem to experience some discrimination against them by Labour, but not Conservative, party members", p. 406). Interestingly, however, subsequent studies on the same topic (e.g., Childs 2008) transformed the notion of prejudice into discrimination.

8 Not all theorists of discrimination agree with this approach. For a critique, see Réaume (2013).

Bibliography

Altman, A. 1998. "Race and Democracy: The Controversy over the Racial Vote Dilution." *Philosophy & Public Affairs*. 27(3): 175–201.

Altman, A. 2015. "Discrimination." In E.N. Zalta (ed.) *The Stanford Encyclopedia of Philosophy,* Fall 2015 edition. Available online: http://plato.stanford.edu/archives/fall2015/entries/discrimination/

Bartolini, S. 2007. *The Political Mobilization of the European Left, 1860–1980. The Class Cleavage.* Cambridge: Cambridge University Press.

Beckman, L. 2009. *The Frontiers of Democracy. The Right to Vote and Its Limits.* London: Palgrave Macmillan.

Beitz, C. 1989. *Political Equality. An Essay in Democratic Theory.* Princeton: Princeton University Press.

Childs, S. 2008. *Women and British Party Politics. Descriptive, Substantive and Symbolic Representation.* London: Routledge.

Cohen, J. 2009. "Money, Politics, Political Equality." In *Philosophy, Politics, Democracy. Selected Essays.* Cambridge, MA.: Harvard University Press. 268–303.

Fisher, S.D., Heath, A.F., Sanders, D., and Sobolewska, M. 2015. "Candidate Ethnicity and Vote Choice in Britain." *British Journal of Political Science.* 45(4): 883–905.

Hellman, D. and Moreau, S. (eds). 2013. *Philosophical Foundations of Discrimination Law.* Oxford: Oxford University Press.

Highton, B. 2004. "White Voters and African American Candidates for Congress." *Political Behavior.* 26(1): 1–25.

Kirshner, A. 2014. *A Theory of Militant Democracy. The Ethics of Combatting Political Extremism.* New Haven: Yale University Press.

Kousser, J.M. 1974. *The Shaping of Southern Politics: Suffrage Restriction and the Establishment of the One-Party South, 1880–1910.* New Haven: Yale University Press.

Lécuyer, Y. 2014. *Le droit à des élections libres.* Strasbourg: Editions du Conseil de l'Europe.

Lippert-Rasmussen, K. 2014. *Born Free and Equal? A Philosophical Inquiry into the Nature of Discrimination.* Oxford: Oxford University Press.

López-Guerra, C. 2014. *Democracy and Disenfranchisment. The Morality of Electoral Exclusions.* Oxford: Oxford University Press.

Lublin, D. 2014. *Minority Rules. Electoral Systems, Decentralization, and Ethnoregional Party Success.* New York: Oxford University Press.

Mansbridge, J. 2015. "Should Workers Represent Workers?" *Swiss Political Science Review.* 21(2): 261–270.

Moser, R.G. 2008. "Electoral Systems and the Representation of Ethnic Minorities: Evidence from Russia." *Comparative Politics.* 40(3): 273–292.

Murray, R. 2010. *Parties, Gender Quotas and Candidate Selection in France.* London: Palgrave Macmillan.

Norris, P. and Lovenduski, J. 1993. "'If Only More Candidates Came Forward': Supply-Side Explanations of Candidate Selection in Britain." *British Journal of Political Science.* 23(3): 373–408.

Réaume, D. 2013. "Dignity, Equality, and Comparison." In D. Hellman and S. Moreau (eds) *Philosophical Foundations of Discrimination Law.* Oxford: Oxford University Press. 7–27.

Rehfeld, A. 2010. "On Quotas and Qualifications for Office." In I. Shapiro, S.C. Strokes, E. J.Wood and A.S. Kirshner (eds). *Political Representation.* Cambridge: Cambridge University Press. 236–268.

Rosar, U., Klein, M. and Beckers, T. 2012. "Magic Mayors: Predicting Electoral Success from Candidates' Physical Attractiveness under the Conditions of a Presidential Electoral System." *German Politics.* 21(4): 372–391.

Rosenblum, N.L. 2007. "Banning Parties: Religious and Ethnic Partisanship in Multicultural Democracies." *Law & Ethics of Human Rights.* 1(1): 17–75.

Sher, R.K. 2011. *The Politics of Disenfranchisement. Why Is It So Hard to Vote in America?* Armonk and London: M. E. Sharpe.

Stojanović, N. 2013. *Dialogue sur les quotas. Penser la représentation dans une démocratie multiculturelle.* Paris: Presses de Sciences Po. Italian ed. (2014) *Dialogo sulle quote.* Bologna: Il Mulino.

Stojanović, N. 2014. "When Non-nationalist Voters Support Ethno-nationalist Parties: The 1990 Elections in Bosnia and Herzegovina as a Prisoner's Dilemma Game." *Southeast European and Black Sea Studies.* 14(4): 607–625.

Street, A. 2014. "Representation Despite Discrimination: Minority Candidates in Germany." *Political Research Quarterly.* 67(2): 374–385.

Venice Commission. 2000. *Electoral Law and National Minorities.* Strasbourg: Council of Europe.

Venice Commission. 2003. *Code of Good Practice in Electoral Matters.* Opinion no. 190/2002, Strasbourg: Council of Europe.

Venice Commission. 2009. *Report on the Impact of Electoral Systems on Women's Representation in Politics.* Study nr. 482/2008. Strasbourg: Council of Europe.

Williams, M.S. 1998. *Voice, Trust, and Memory. Marginalized Groups and the Failings of Liberal Representation.* Princeton: Princeton University Press.

30

DISCRIMINATION AND THE PRIVATE SPHERE

Hugh Collins

UNIVERSITY OF OXFORD

The need for a private sphere

Should laws against discrimination apply to all economic and social relations? Or should there be limits on the application of those laws in respect of private, personal or intimate relations? It is generally accepted today, for instance, that discrimination laws should apply to actions and decisions of the government and of private sector employers, but should discrimination law apply to the decisions of consumers with regard to the shops where they buy their goods, to workers in their choice of employer, or to individuals in the choice of their guests, friends and lovers? If limits are placed on the scope of application of discrimination laws with respect to such examples, what moral or ethical principles should determine the boundary of a private sphere within which actionable claims against discrimination are unavailable?

This is not the same question as asking why and when discrimination is wrong. It assumes the moral wrongfulness of many instances of discrimination on grounds of race, sex, and other protected characteristics in private and personal relationships. The question is rather what instances of morally wrong discrimination should be prohibited and sanctioned by the law. For instance, it seems objectionable for parents to refuse to permit their daughter to bring her boyfriend to dinner on the ground of his skin color, but should the law interfere with this exercise of freedom and privacy? Similarly, it may be unfair for parents to discriminate between their children by sending their sons to expensive schools whilst sending their daughters to be educated at cheaper, inferior schools, but the issue here is whether the law should forbid this practice or tolerate it as a necessary feature of respect for the freedom of individuals, and perhaps parental rights. In a further example suggested by the facts in *Pla and Puncernau v. Andorra* (2006) 42 EHRR 25, it may be unfair and morally wrong for a wealthy lady to exclude an illegitimate or adopted grandson from her will, but should the law invalidate that choice on the ground that it is an act of discrimination against a protected class of children? Unless legal prohibitions track exactly the scope of the moral wrong of discrimination, there must be a private sphere in which law permits or at least tolerates discrimination against individuals on prohibited grounds such as sex, race, and religion. Within this private sphere, parents would be permitted to discriminate against their daughters with regard to their education, and a grandmother could leave an illegitimate or adopted grandson out of her will.

Historically, with respect to this determination of the scope of the private sphere, the law drew a sharp distinction between actions of the state and actions of everyone else. It was said that only the state should be placed under a legal duty never to discriminate, whereas private actors and non-state institutions should enjoy unfettered liberty with respect to their personal preferences (subject to the ordinary laws of civil and criminal wrongs). That duty placed on states is confirmed by Article 2(1) of the United Nations Covenant on Civil and Political Rights:

> Each State Party to the present Covenant undertakes to respect and to ensure to all individuals within its territory and subject to its jurisdiction the rights recognized in the present Covenant, without distinction of any kind, such as race, color, sex, language, religion, political or other opinion, national or social origin, property, birth or other status.

This stance is supported by liberal political theorists such as Dworkin who insist that the state should be placed under a duty to treat citizens with equal concern and respect (Dworkin 1985). Many constitutions such as that in the United States apply the principle of equality solely to actions of the state, with the consequence that constitutional equality duties do not normally apply to non-state actors such as private employers, retailers, and landlords. That demarcation between the public and the private sphere could be justified by saying that whilst all state action must conform to the law and the principles of the constitution, such as equal protection of the laws, in contrast, in order to respect individual liberty and the freedom to pursue personal preferences and individual goals, actions by private individuals should in general be unfettered by constitutional principles, except for those legal prohibitions that are designed to protect the freedoms of others (Gardner 1989; cf. Chapter 13).

The advent of anti-discrimination laws from the 1960s onwards marked a shift in that boundary between state action and private conduct. The Civil Rights Act of 1964 in the USA rejected that boundary because it needed to address broader structures of segregation practiced against African Americans, that were causing severe economic disadvantage and social exclusion. These structures were not confined to state action with regard to voting rights and education, but harmful racist practices and institutional segregation were discoverable in the restrictions on access to transport, restaurants, clubs, and to private sector employment. Subsequent legislation in the UK and the EU followed the pattern set by the USA for sex and race discrimination and included within its scope private employers, landlords, shopkeepers, and restaurants. Thus, the limitation of the scope of anti-discrimination laws to the public sector or state action was decisively rejected on the ground that otherwise discrimination law would be ineffective in the pursuit of its goals.

The abandonment of the boundary between public and private spheres based upon the criterion of state action poses the problem of devising a new delimitation of the scope of the private sphere that should be kept outside the scope of anti-discrimination laws that is based on moral and political principles. The terminology of the contrast between public and private spheres seems unlikely to be very helpful in this context, however. This is because we are now searching for a dividing line within the sphere that was once regarded as private, such as private sector employment, but which now must be labeled as public in order to explain the application of discrimination laws to this sphere, whilst at the same time inventing a new narrower private sphere to which anti-discrimination laws do not apply. Moreover, the terms public and private often serve as verbal contrasts, with the terms merely signifying what has been excluded from the other, rather than demarcating a particular sphere of conduct (Collins 1987), and to call something private is often no more than an assertion that it should be unregulated.

An alternative strategy for defining the proper sphere of application of discrimination laws is to seek guidance from the liberal principle that individual liberty should be respected except where harm is caused to others. This 'harm principle' would permit the application of discrimination laws whenever the action of one person causes harm, or at least non-trivial harm, to another. Discrimination may cause various kinds of harms such as the denial of a job opportunity, a block to promotion, or the distress and offense caused by demeaning someone. The problem with this application of the harm principle is that if 'offense' or 'demeaning treatment' are treated as significant harms, that would almost certainly eliminate an unregulated private sphere altogether, for there is likely to be offense whenever discrimination occurs even between family and friends. Indeed, it seems likely that any consequentialist approach that uses law to combat harm or moral wrong will have difficulty in separating out an unregulated private sphere (Lippert-Rasmussen 2013: 264).

An alternative approach is to identify a realm of intimate and affective relationships where the meaning and success of those relationships depends on sentiment, and on the affective quality of the relationships. In such relationships, it seems likely that paternalistic supervision by the state of choices and preferences would undermine the meaning and success of such relationships, in which spontaneous feelings rather than rational calculation often make for the best experiences (Gardner 1992). With respect to such intimate relationships, the state should try to secure equal legal treatment for a wide variety of sexual and personal relationships, but out of respect for individual liberty and personal autonomy, individual choices within that framework should not be legally controlled (Emmens 2009). In choosing a marriage partner, a friend with whom to go on holiday, or networks on social media, this respect for the realm of intimate and affective relationships should permit discriminatory preferences (cf. Chapters 31 and 35).

Whilst helpful in establishing the need for at least a small unregulated private sphere in order to preserve the character of spontaneous and affective relationships, the previous argument seems insufficiently broad as a delimitation of a private sphere that is immune from the application of anti-discrimination laws. For instance, if I plan to rent out a room in my home to a lodger, my preferences with respect to the age and gender of the lodger are not clearly appropriate to being subject to legal control, not because it will be an intimate relationship, but because I will need to feel comfortable about the identity of someone living in my home. Similarly, if I receive two job offers, one from a male employer and the other from a woman, my preference to work for a woman may be based on discriminatory stereotypes about male and female bosses, but it is questionable whether it is any of the law's business to control my choice of employer. In both these cases, my personal preferences, even though tainted by discriminatory stereotypes, may have to be respected in order to avoid excessive intrusion into my personal choices. Furthermore, to apply discrimination laws to such choices may raise concerns about the disproportionate costs of compliance with the law, the possible interference with some fundamental rights of the alleged discriminator, and more generally about the need to respect the freedom of individuals to choose their own way of life without intrusive surveillance by government.

Although these concerns about respect for spontaneous and affective relationships, and respect for the freedom of individuals to make personal choices without excessive intrusion by the state explain the existence of an unregulated private sphere, they do not provide much guidance as to where the boundary should be drawn. We turn next to examine how the law has in practice drawn that boundary.

The scope of the unregulated sphere of conduct

In general, the law defines the scope of the public or regulated sphere by reference to the nature of the activity and the nature of the proposed duty-bearer. The private sphere becomes the remaining field of activity that is constituted either by not being one of the specified activities, or not being an action of one of the specified duty-bearers. In this brief description of the contemporary legal framework of discrimination laws, I will omit particular exclusions that may apply to particular instances of discrimination, such as the exemption from sex discrimination where sex is a genuine occupational qualification, as in the example of the choice of an actor for reasons of authenticity. The task at this point is to discover the broad picture of the scope of anti-discrimination laws and, by implication, the scope of the private sphere.

Discrimination laws generally apply to employment and employment-like relationships, to landlord and tenant relationships, to associations including trade unions and political parties, to educational institutions, and to commerce where goods and services are being offered to the public. These prohibitions on discrimination are only addressed to one party to the relationship: the employer, the landlord, the governing or managing committee of the association or the educational institution, and the retailer of goods and services to the public. The duty does not apply to the worker, to the tenant, to the individual member of an association, to the student, or to the consumer. An employer is normally understood as someone who exercises the power of direction over someone providing services, so that where there is no relation of subordination between the employing entity and the person providing services, as in the case illustrated by *Jivraj v. Hashwani* [2011] UKSC 40, of an arbitrator for contractual disputes, the relationship or choice of arbitrator is excluded from the scope of anti-discrimination laws. There are some further typical limitations worth noting. Small clubs or associations may be excluded, perhaps because they rely on friendship as the principal bond of membership, as for example in the UK with associations which have fewer than 25 members (Equality Act 2010, s.107). Associations may be gender-specific (but not race-specific) in their membership, as in the case of all-female sports clubs or 'Gentlemen's Clubs' (Equality Act 2010, Sched 16). Some landlords may be excluded from all but laws against race discrimination if either the rental property is in effect part of the landlord's home, or if the residential accommodation is communal, such as a dormitory (Equality Act 2010 Sched 24). In various contexts, such as schools and religious organizations, special exclusions from discrimination law apply.

That list of exclusions from the regulated sphere seems to indicate that there are two overlapping boundaries that define the scope of anti-discrimination laws in the private sphere. First, normally, the relationship has to be a contractual one, or must be expected to be a contractual one if it comes to fruition, as in the case of applicants for jobs and membership of associations. Anti-discrimination laws do not generally apply to social relationships where there is no contractual relation, as in the case of invitations to dinner or dispositions in a will. The law of contract excludes such agreements from the scope of contract law on the ground that either there is no material exchange taking place (in the common law this is called the absence of consideration), or there is no intention to enter into legal relations. However, it has to be acknowledged that not every instance of prohibited discrimination neatly fits this line fixed by the limits of the law of contract. In some cases there may be a contract, but discrimination law is excluded, as in the case of the choice of a marriage partner (assuming that marriage is a kind of contract). In other cases, there may not be a contract for reasons such as the absence of consideration, but discrimination law may apply. Section 29 of the Equality Act 2010 describes its scope as 'the provision of a service to the public or a section of the public (for payment or not)'. By the inclusion of services offered to the public without payment, the section seems to include the work of voluntary bodies, such as the provision of first aid services at sports events by the St John Ambulance, or assistance by The Red Cross in the event of an emergency. It is unlikely that this first aid is provided under a contract with the patient, but clearly the service of offering first aid to the public would be governed by discrimination laws. The boundary provided by the law of contract is therefore not completely reliable as a guide to the scope of discrimination laws. It is not surprising, however, that the guidance provided by the law of contract normally serves this purpose of indicating the scope of discrimination law, for the rules on determining the scope of legally enforceable contracts tackle a similar problem to that posed by the private sphere, that excludes the law of discrimination. In both instances, the law is protecting a private sphere where moral standards, but not state enforced legal standards, should operate to guide people in their social and economic interactions. In general, therefore, this absence of an actual or expected contractual relationship places the first limit on the scope of anti-discrimination laws and provides an initial guide to the scope of the private sphere in discrimination law.

The second dimension of the boundary of the private sphere in discrimination law seems to be determined by the character of the person subject to the duty. It is invariably only one party to the contractual relationship who is designated as the duty-bearer: an employer, a landlord, or an institutional managing committee. Consumers, employees, tenants, and members of trades unions or golf clubs are not subject to the duties of anti-discrimination law. The regulations do not apply to an ordinary consumer out shopping, or hiring a self-employed craftsman such as a plumber, a painter, or a portrait artist. Similarly, employees are not duty-bearers, unless they are exercising the power of the employer, as in the case of a manager hiring a recruit, though the employer may be vicariously liable for actions of employees against other employees, as in the case of harassment. We will need to explore further the reasons for this restriction on the category of duty-bearers, but at first glance it is evident that it is the more powerful actor, in the sense of the person who controls access to the benefit envisaged by the contract, such as a job or membership of a club, who is the duty-bearer.

Although the two broad criteria that define the scope of the private sphere in the law of discrimination – actions referable to contracts, and duties connected to the person or institution that controls access to the contracts – may not capture every nuance of the regulatory boundaries, they appear to supply the main themes governing the scope of the law. The question now becomes as to what moral and political principles might justify these criteria for the determination of a private sphere in which the law of discrimination does not apply.

Justifications for the scope of the private sphere

Three kinds of argument might be used to justify these limits on the application of anti-discrimination laws.

1 *Scope defined by purpose.* It could be the case that the purpose or goal of anti-discrimination laws does not apply to these excluded relationships or persons, because they fall outside the aims of the law and therefore need not be regulated.
2 *Purpose limited by a proportionality test.* Alternatively, some or all of these excluded relationships might fall within the purpose or goal of the anti-discrimination laws, but the scope of the laws might also be required to satisfy a proportionality test in order to prevent excessive interference with the liberty of individual duty-bearers.
3 *Balancing competing rights.* Alternatively, limits on the scope of the anti-discrimination laws might be set by balancing the right of the victim or protected group member not

to suffer discriminatory adverse treatment against the rights of the alleged perpetrator to make its own choices and express its own values.

These three kinds of argument could be used separately and cumulatively to explain and justify the limits on the scope of the anti-discrimination laws with respect to a private sphere. All three may be needed to account for the current law, though often points can be quickly reformulated within each framework to achieve the same outcome.

Limited scope defined by purpose

The general structure of this kind of justification for the scope of the private sphere stresses the point that the aim of discrimination law must guide the shape of the unregulated private sphere. Just as the aim of the law does not include (at present) the elimination of discrimination against obese people, so too the aim of the law may not encompass the regulation of discriminatory preferences within certain kinds of activities and relationships (cf. Chapter 22).

Many theories of discrimination law suggest, however, that it is founded on broad principles that render the existence of any unregulated sphere puzzling and problematic. For instance, if we say that the aim of the law is to require everyone to treat others with equal respect (at least to the extent that they should not treat a person differently simply on the ground of a protected characteristic), it would be hard to identify any scope for a private sphere, for we can show disrespect or unequal treatment in any kind of social or economic relationship.

Nevertheless, there are some theories of discrimination law that would explain more directly the scope of the unregulated private sphere by reference to a narrower aim attributed to the law. For instance, if the goal of discrimination law is regarded as the reduction of social exclusion, this relatively precise goal might point towards a more determinate guide to the proper scope of an unregulated private sphere. Social exclusion might be associated with certain kinds of contracts and institutions, in particular those to do with employment and a permanent home. If so, the law might focus on the decisions of employers and landlords, who tend to control access to employment and housing. Other social and economic relations might be regarded as less significant fields for the law to address, and beyond the aim of the law. These fields would then comprise the unregulated sphere.

It is not always easy to tease out the extent to which a theory of the aim of discrimination law would provide some space for an unregulated sphere. For instance, following Gardner and Khaitan (Gardner 1989: 17–21; Khaitan 2015: 148; cf. Chapter 13) in the direction of Raz's perfectionist account of autonomy (Raz 1986: 416), if the aim of anti-discrimination laws is to protect individual autonomy in the broad sense of positive freedom or access to valuable life opportunities for an individual or the protected group against irrelevant or unnecessary discriminatory rules, that kind of aim would appear to justify the application of the law to all the key ingredients in a worthwhile life, such as education, housing, travel, the purchase of goods and services, and employment. With this aim in mind, the scope of anti-discrimination law might be narrower than envisaged by a simple principle of formal equality or equal respect, but the exclusions would be mainly oriented towards activities and actions that were not thought to contribute much, if at all, to a worthwhile or meaningful life. Assuming that the formation of close personal relationships and friendships would be regarded as a key part of a worthwhile or meaningful life, the putative general aim of the law would not apparently account for the exclusion of intimate relationships from the law. It would have to be argued, as described above, that legal regulation of this kind would in practice hinder all spontaneous and intimate relations, so that despite the risk of permitting such relations to be suffused with unwelcome discriminatory practices, the law should not intervene for fear of more widely damaging social relationships.

Goal limited by a proportionality test

A second kind of theory of the scope of the unregulated private sphere does not rely on the general aim of the law, about which it can be pluralistic, accepting that the law embraces many different aims. Instead, this approach holds that since anti-discrimination laws necessarily interfere with the liberty of individuals who are subject to the duties imposed by them, their scope should be subject to a proportionality test. In other words, it must be shown that in the pursuit of its goal the law does not disproportionately interfere with the liberty or privacy of the discriminator. Under the test of proportionality, we need to consider whether the interference is necessary and appropriate in the pursuit of a legitimate aim. Assuming that the aim of eradicating discrimination on protected grounds is legitimate in general, the first question is whether the precise law in question serves that legitimate aim. The answer to that question lies at the core of the analysis of the previous approach to fixing the scope of the private sphere, by reference to the general justifying aim of the law. The remaining questions are whether the regulation is necessary, in the sense that no other measure that is less invasive of liberty and privacy would suffice to achieve the aim effectively, and whether the regulation is appropriate, bearing in mind the costs imposed and the degree of interference with liberty and privacy.

Using this proportionality approach, Khaitan produces an insightful account of the scope of the unregulated private sphere which focuses on the issue of who should be duty-bearers (as opposed to the kinds of social and economic relationships to which the law should apply). He argues that proportionality depends, first, on the severity of the impact that the duty has on the bearer's negative freedom (*i.e.* interference with liberty) (Khaitan 2015: 200). He suggests that if a person has a more 'public' character, that person's interest in negative freedom will be less than a person acting privately. He argues that employers have a public character because of their power to determine access to and success in employment (Khaitan 2015). In contrast, Khaitan suggests that, like those professing a common calling such as an innkeeper (for whom, as illustrated by *Constantine v. Imperial Hotels Ltd* [1944] KB 693, unreasonable discrimination was always prohibited), other duty-bearers such as landlords, retailers, and some associations have 'assumed a degree of public-ness by offering to serve the public generally' (Khaitan 2015: 204). The second determinant of the application of the proportionality test, according to Khaitan, is the optimality or effectiveness of a proposed duty-bearer in furthering the goal or goals of anti-discrimination law such as the reduction of the disadvantage of particular groups in accessing valuable opportunities. If the goal of the law will not be supported or furthered to any significant extent by imposing the duty on this particular individual or institution, in the absence of some kind of symbolic importance connected to the imposition of the duty, it does not seem to be an appropriate measure and its costs will probably exceed its potential benefits.

Balancing competing rights

A third approach to the determination of the unregulated private sphere analyses the issue in terms of a balance between the competing rights of the parties (Collins 2013). On the one side, the victim of discrimination can claim an interference with social and economic rights such as the right to work on an unjustifiable, discriminatory basis. It is also possible to argue that individuals have a self-standing fundamental right not to be discriminated against on the ground of one of their protected characteristics, as is perhaps indicated in Article 21(1) of the Charter of the Fundamental Rights of the European Union, which states:

> Any discrimination based on any ground such as sex, race, colour, ethnic or social origin, genetic features, language, religion or belief, political or any other opinion, membership of a national minority, property, birth, disability, age or sexual orientation shall be prohibited.

On the other side of the dispute, the discriminator can claim a right to negative liberty or freedom to exercise personal preferences, combined with possibly other social and economic rights such as the freedom to conduct a business and freedom of contract.

A number of ways might be developed for balancing these competing rights against each other. One requirement when balancing competing rights is usually to ensure that neither party is deprived of the essence of their right. Consider, for instance, the case where a testator wants to discriminate in a will between different classes of beneficiaries on grounds of sex, religion, legitimacy, or sexual orientation. On the one hand the testator enjoys a right to the peaceful enjoyment of property, including its voluntary alienation by contract or a will, and also a general liberal right to express his or her preferences. On the other hand, the potential beneficiaries can claim a right to equal protection of the laws, and the protection of their dignity and privacy from infringements based on discriminatory prejudices against protected characteristics. If a will discriminates between potential heirs on prohibited grounds, we might ask whether invalidating the will would deprive the testator of the essence of his or her right, as argued by dissenting Judge Garlicki in *Pla and Puncernau v. Andorra* (2006) 42 EHRR 25: 'The whole idea of a will is to depart from the general system of inheritance, that is, to discriminate between potential heirs.' If, however, the testator still enjoys much of his or her freedom of testamentary disposition despite the invalidity of the discriminatory provision, we need to ask whether a failure to invalidate this discriminatory provision would deprive the excluded beneficiaries of the essence of their right to be treated as an equal.

Another possible approach to the balancing of the rights of the parties is to apply a double proportionality test, so that the interference with the rights of both parties is assessed to determine whether it is necessary and appropriate (Collins 2014: 49). For instance, in Case 236/09 *Test-Achats ASBL*, [2011] ECR I-773, the general question posed to the Court of Justice of the EU was whether insurance policies that discriminated in their terms between men and women according to actuarial factors were prohibited on the ground of sex discrimination. In declaring such policies invalid, even if they benefitted women with cheaper prices, the Court was clearly not persuaded that the rejection of such policies would interfere disproportionately with the right of insurance companies to conduct their business freely. On the other hand it seems to have regarded any action involving sex discrimination as substantial interference with the rights of individuals and the principles on which the EU is based.

Other rights may become involved in this balancing exercise in particular cases, such as a right to manifest a religion. For example, in *Bull and Bull v. Hall and Preddy* (2013) UKSC 73, the issue was whether the religiously committed proprietors of a small hotel could refuse double-bedded accommodation to a gay couple on the ground that their religion regarded sexual relations between men as immoral. The UK Supreme Court determined that this refusal of a double bed amounted to discrimination on the ground of sexual orientation. But there remained a further question whether this protection of the rights of the gay couple by anti-discrimination laws amounted itself to a disproportionate interference with the right of the proprietors to manifest their religion, to which the court answered in the negative, having performed a balancing test with respect to the significance of, and the degree of, interference with the rights concerned.

Conclusion

The moral justification for the legal model that permits an unregulated private sphere remains contested and indeterminate. The precise boundary of the unregulated private sphere seems likely to be set by a combination of views about the legitimate aim of the law, the proportionality of interference with the choices of individuals, and the need to balance the rights of all the parties concerned.

Bibliography

Collins, H. 1987. "The Decline of Privacy in Private Law." *Journal of Law and Society*. 14: 91.
Collins, H. 2013. "The Vanishing Freedom to Choose a Contractual Partner." *Law and Contemporary Problems*. 76: 71.
Collins, H. 2014. "On the (In)compatibility of Human Rights Discourse and Private Law." In H.-W. Micklitz (ed.) *Constitutionalization of European Private Law*. Oxford: Oxford University Press.
Dworkin, R. 1985. "Liberalism." In R. Dworkin, *A Matter of Principle*. Oxford: Clarendon Press. 181.
Emmens, E. 2009. "Intimate Discrimination." *Harvard Law Review*. 122: 1307.
Gardner, J. 1989. "Liberals and Unlawful Discrimination." *Oxford Journal of Legal Studies*. 9: 1.
Gardner, J. 1992. "Private Activities and Personal Autonomy: At the Margin of Anti-discrimination Law." In Bob Hepple and Erika Szyszczak (eds), *Discrimination: The Limits of the Law*. London: Mansell.
Khaitan, T. 2015. *A Theory of Discrimination Law*. Oxford: Oxford University Press.
Lippert-Rasmussen, K. 2013. *Born Free and Equal?* Oxford: Oxford University Press.
Raz, J. 1986. *The Morality of Freedom*. Oxford: Oxford University Press.

31

DISCRIMINATION AND THE PERSONAL SPHERE

Hugh Lazenby

UNIVERSITY OF GLASGOW

Paul Butterfield

CITY UNIVERSITY OF NEW YORK

Introduction

Data from the Quickmatch function of OKCupid, a large dating website, shows that on average people who identify as part of a particular racial group will rate other members who share that identity as more attractive than the mean.[1] This is true for all groups listed on the website: Asian, Black, Latino and White.[2] The data also shows that particular groups face distinct ratings 'penalties'. Here the outcome of the data is more gender-specific. Black and Asian men are rated as less attractive than the mean by members of all groups other than their own, while Black (but not Asian) women are rated as less attractive than the mean by members of all groups other than their own. These preferences are reflected in the number of messages and responses individuals receive. For example, compared to women of other races, Black women receive roughly 75% as many first messages from other users on the site and roughly 75% as many responses to their own first messages.[3]

How should we view the fact that people select their romantic partners in this way (cf. Chapter 23)? Is it different from choosing to date people who are tall or who have clear skin? Perhaps most interestingly, does it count as discriminatory and, if it does, is it morally objectionable? The practical import of these questions is clear. We want to know whether we are wronging others when we select our romantic partners. However, these questions also bear on more theoretical questions about the moral limits of discrimination. Our romantic choices are some of the most personal we have. If they can count as morally objectionable discrimination, we may have reason to believe that all of our choices can.

In this chapter, we investigate these questions through the lens of a particular theory of discrimination – Kasper Lippert-Rasmussen's (KLR) *desert-prioritarian* account.[4] The chapter has two sections. Section one presents KLR's account of the wrongfulness of discrimination and introduces four possible causal explanations of the online dating referenced above. We argue that on all of the possible explanations, KLR's account will consider the case to involve discrimination that is at least *pro tanto* wrongful. Section two seeks to analyze this result and so, in turn, the plausibility of KLR's account. We suggest that the ascriptions of the desert-prioritarian account conflict with ordinary intuition, which we speculate to be that discrimination in romance, if it is wrong at all, will only be wrongful under certain explanations. We go on to consider how KLR might respond to this objection before finally considering whether an alternative rights-based account of the wrongfulness of discrimination, such as the one provided by Sophia Moreau, can better capture ordinary intuition.

Is it wrongful discrimination?

A preliminary question is whether the choice of one's romantic partner is the kind of choice that could count as discriminatory. Should we not limit discrimination to choices that are undertaken by the state, or at least only include individual choices when they are in some sense public? For our purposes, it is sufficient to note that many personal choices, including selecting partners according to their race, count as discriminatory not only on broader definitions of discrimination, which include all differential treatment on the basis of an individual's group membership, but also on KLR's own more narrow definition of discrimination, which limits discrimination to the negative treatment of individuals on the basis of their membership in *socially salient* groups; racial identity is socially salient, if anything is.[5,6]

The important question, then, is not whether the choices in question count as discrimination, but whether they are wrongful and, in particular, whether they are wrongful on KLR's desert-prioritarian account. That account is harm-based: it considers discrimination wrong when, and because, it is harmful. The prioritarian component of the view holds that the harm of discrimination is worse the lower the absolute level of well-being of the person it falls upon. The desert component holds that the harm of discrimination is worse if it is undeserved. This second component allows KLR to capture the idea that those who perpetrate discrimination are fairer targets for the harm of that discrimination than their victims.[7] In addition, KLR views the wrong of discrimination as a *pro tanto* wrong as opposed to an all-things-considered wrong. On this pluralist account of morality there are many competing moral considerations, of which the demand to avoid discrimination is only one. This means that discrimination can be justified if there are sufficiently strong countervailing moral reasons to discriminate.

Putting these points together, we can say that *in principle* selecting by race in romantic partnerships will count as wrongful if it is harmful, and how wrongful it is will vary in proportion to three factors: (1) the level of harm it causes; (2) the absolute level of well-being of the victim(s); and (3) whether the harm is deserved. To determine whether the case actually involves wrong-doing, then, we need to know how far the factors are instantiated. Here an interesting question arises as to whether different possible explanations of the data might lead to different factors being instantiated to different degrees. Consider below some candidate explanations (we will take Black women as the subject of the discrimination since they suffer the worst discrimination):

> *Explicit Racism*: Black women are selected against because members of other races, in particular those selected, consciously hold racist views. For example, they believe that Black women are inferior to women of other races, and/or endorse racist stereotypes that cause them to consider Black women to be sexually and romantically unattractive.

> *Implicit Bias*: Black women are selected against as a result of implicit bias, arising from pervasive negative stereotypes against Black women in society. These include the ideas that Black women are more sexually promiscuous, less intelligent, and so forth. Although members of other races do not consciously accept these stereotypes – and, indeed, if asked would sincerely deny that they believed them – they still act unconsciously to shape people's views of Black women. When selecting sexual and romantic partners, these stereotypes act to prejudice members of other races against Black women, albeit unconsciously.

Income Preference: Black women are selected against because they are poor, relative to women of other races. Here race plays no direct role in the decision of members of other races to select against Black women. Rather, individuals selecting partners filter by income, and Black women are on average in a lower income class, which causes members of other races to select against them. Importantly, members of other races are not using Black women's racial identity as a means of predicting income: they are simply observing facts about income (which are disclosed explicitly on the website) without making any conscious judgment about how this factor varies with race.

Innate Preference: Black women are selected against because members of other races find them unattractive. On this view there is no explanation of this preference beyond human biology. Some people simply have innate, pre-social preferences for certain physical features that are constitutive of racial identity, such as skin color, and these preferences cause them to select against Black women.

We do not mean to suggest that all of these explanations are equally plausible. In fact, we doubt that the last explanation has any plausibility (although we suspect it is also widely accepted outside of academic circles). Further, we do not mean to suggest that the data is to be explained by any one factor. It is likely to be a mixture of more than one. The question we want to address is simply whether, if one or other was (more or less) causally responsible for the discrimination, would this affect the instantiation of the different factors?

There are at least two different kinds of harm that we might expect to result from the discrimination. First, it might impact the opportunities for romantic partnership that Black women have. As we mentioned earlier, Black women receive roughly 75% of the messages women in other groups do.[8] Insofar as the opportunity for romantic partnership is an important good that they are being denied, this may count as a harm in itself (cf. Chapter 12). Second, the fact that people discriminate in this way may send a message of inferiority, demeaning Black women and harming their self-respect (cf. Chapter 7). The key thought here is that being told that a large section of others in your community find people of your race unattractive is something that can be psychologically damaging, akin to being told that you are actually worth less than others.

There is good reason to believe that all of the above explanations, were they true, would involve harm of the two kinds described in the last paragraph, and so will appear similar from the perspective of KLR's account. To support this point, consider first that whatever the reason for the discrimination, the effect in terms of the availability of partners seems the same. That is, whether a person is being selected against as a result of explicit bias, innate preference, or for some other reason, the effect is always that that person has fewer opportunities for romantic partnership. Now consider, second, that whatever the reason for the discrimination, having fewer partners available on account of one's race is likely to be experienced as a message of inferiority. This becomes clear when we remember that the person who is discriminated against will typically not be aware of the precise reason the discrimination is taking place. From the discriminatee's perspective, what is immediately clear is only that people of their race are being selected against.

Can we distinguish between the cases on the basis of priority, or desert? Again, this seems unlikely. In each case we have exactly the same set of victims of discrimination: Black women in the romantic marketplace. It does not make sense, then, to talk of any targeted agents having a greater or lesser level of well-being prior to discrimination taking place in any of these cases. And, of course, since the parties are the same, they are also no more or less deserving in one case or another.

This leads us to our first conclusion: desert-prioritarianism will treat all of the four scenarios we have sketched in this section similarly, since the level of harm is at least similar between the different explanations and there are no other relevant differences.[9] We do not mean to defend the strong conclusion that the harm will be exactly the same, although for the reasons we have given one might think that is true. Again, our conclusion is only that insofar as each explanation will involve harm of the two sorts identified earlier, each will be considered *pro tanto* wrongful and, further, that there is good reason to believe that the level of harm is similar, making each explanation similarly wrongful.

Analysis

We have argued that for each of the explanations of the data, the act of selecting partners according to race will constitute wrongful discrimination on the desert-prioritarian account. In this section we want to ask whether this conclusion is plausible. That is, we want to ask whether we should think that all of the explanations we have considered are cases of wrongful discrimination.

We will start with a speculative claim: many people do not believe that all cases of discrimination involving harm are cases of wrongful discrimination. More precisely, many people think either that the label of wrongful discrimination is not something that can apply to the choice of a romantic partner at all or, perhaps more commonly, that if it does apply to some cases, such as the case of explicit racism, it should not apply to all cases, such as the case of innate preference.[10] We can only appeal to anecdotal evidence to support this claim. One such piece of evidence is that in our experience people are typically willing and unashamed to admit a preference for a certain race if they believe their preference is innate, but the same is not true if they believe their preference is explicitly racist. For example, it is not uncommon for someone to say 'I just have a thing for Asians' or 'I've always had a type: Black men', but it is much harder to imagine someone saying in polite company that their preference was explained by their belief in that group's racial superiority.

Let us accept for sake of argument that most people actually do believe that at least not all of the above explanations of the data involve wrongful discrimination. How should we respond to this fact? One response would be to reject the intuition. If there are sufficient other reasons in favor of believing KLR's view, we could simply think that the problematic intuition is an outlier that should be discounted. However, if we want to hold on to the intuition, two other strategies suggest themselves. First, we could attempt to accommodate the intuition, explaining how it tracks some other feature of the cases rather than their wrongfulness. Second, we might reject KLR's view and search for a different account of discrimination that can provide justification for the distinction the intuition aims at. We will consider these possibilities in turn.

Accommodating the intuition

We are looking to show that the intuition is tracking some feature of the cases other than moral wrongdoing. In other words, the intuition is tracking something morally significant, but not the fact that only some (or none) of the cases involve wrongdoing.

A first possibility is that the intuition is tracking blameworthiness. Blameworthiness and wrongdoing may come apart. In Parfit's famous example, an individual, Clare, has a choice between benefiting her child, whom she loves, and some strangers.[11] The strangers will benefit more from her benevolence, but Clare chooses to benefit her child. This, Parfit claims, looks like an instance of blameless wrongdoing. If blameworthiness and wrongdoing can come apart here, maybe the same is true in the case of discrimination. Perhaps both *Explicit Racism* and *Innate Preference* involve wrongdoing, but only *Explicit Racism* involves blameworthy action.

Parfit initially defends Clare in terms of the fact that her love for her child is part of a set of motivations which, taken as a whole, would do the most good. That is, loving one's child is a motivation which, taken in conjunction with her other motivations, tends to the good even if it does not achieve the most good in this particular case. However, this defense does not seem available in *Innate Preference*. It is not at all clear that the preferences in this case do tend to the good. Quite the opposite. Still, we might try to defend the distinction in a different way. For example, we might claim that blameworthiness requires some element of control. If we cannot change our innate preferences, then we cannot be blamed for them. Our innate preferences, including (we are assuming) who we are attracted to, are simply pieces of good or bad brute luck – and attaching blame to pieces of good or bad brute luck is inappropriate.

Here it is worth noting that the issue is not whether people's innate preferences are *actually* of this sort, or even whether people have innate preferences, but whether people *believe* they have innate preferences that are beyond their control. If that is true, and people also believe that explicit racist preferences have a different, controllable, and so blameworthy character, then that is enough to explain the difference in intuition about the cases. We can discount people's intuition that the *Innate Preference* case is not wrong, because their intuition is merely reflecting their (possibly false) beliefs about the structure of their own preferences, and how blameworthy they are in light of that structure.

This line of argument also suggests another that is not to do with blame. Perhaps the judgment is not tracking *pro tanto* wronging but all-things-considered wronging. Imagine that innate preferences exist, and that they are immutable or, at least, very costly to change. Imagine also that the same is not true of preferences that reflect explicit racist attitudes: those can be changed comparatively easily. Now suppose further that when you are considering what you should do, and in particular whether you should discriminate in the context of your relationships, the right thing to do may depend in part on how good any potential relationship will be, both for your partner *and* for you. If you know in advance that your preferences are innate and so are fixed, you may reason that any potential relationship with someone that you are not innately attracted to will ultimately be miserable for you. As such, not discriminating may ultimately be the wrong thing to do because, even if discriminating harms the prospective partners that you discriminate against, the harm to you of not discriminating outweighs this harm.[12] By contrast, if your preferences are not innate, and so can be changed comparatively easily, then this will not be true. It would be better if you were not to discriminate and simply adjust your preferences. Thus, what the intuition in question is tracking might *not* be a difference in the *pro tanto* wrongdoing that KLR is interested in, but a difference in all-things-considered wrongdoing between the two cases. In the innate preference case, the discrimination is all-things-considered justified and merely *pro tanto* wrongful. In the explicit racism case the discrimination is both *pro tanto* wrongful and all-things-considered wrongful.

An alternative account of discrimination

We have offered two possible avenues that KLR might use to defend his position against our intuition. No doubt there may be others too. But suppose now that the intuition is correct. It tracks the fact that not all, and perhaps none, of the explanations we considered in Section one are *pro tanto* wrongful. In that case, we need a theory to explain why this is so. In this section, we want to consider an alternative account of discrimination that can do this. The account we have in mind locates the wrong of discrimination in the violation of a person's rights. We will call this type of account a 'rights-based account' (cf. Chapter 10).

A rights-based account of discrimination must have a foundation. That is, it must include a description of what function rights serve. The idea that rights serve to protect either an individual's 'interests' or their 'autonomous will' is traditionally popular. As well as determining the function of rights, a rights-based account must also include a description of how, given that function, rights are to be assigned. For example, if we assume that the function of rights is the protection of interests, one might think that rights should be assigned so as to maximize the overall satisfaction of interests. Alternatively, one might think that rights should be assigned according to some hypothetical decision procedure where individuals, idealized in accordance with a given account of interests, choose how to assign rights under certain informational constraints.

Sophia Moreau defends a rights-based view that grounds our rights against discrimination in the protection of our *deliberative freedoms* (cf. Chapter 13). For Moreau, these are freedoms 'to deliberate about and decide how to live in a way that is insulated from pressures stemming from extraneous traits of ours', such as our skin color and gender.[13] On her account, our rights against discrimination exist because it is important that we can navigate our lives without having to worry that we will be obstructed by these traits. However, Moreau is also conscious of the fact there are other values – indeed other freedoms – that will compete with our deliberative freedoms for the purpose of determining how rights should be assigned. Considering why anti-discrimination law does not extend to our private lives, she writes:

> One of these may be the value of deep personal relationships. One plausible reason why anti-discrimination law does not regulate personal dealings between family members and friends is that, for caring relationships to flourish, people need to be able to choose whom they wish to be close to and how they are going to treat each other and they need to be able to treat their loved ones in special ways, ways in which they would not treat every other person … Another value that seems to be fostered by limiting anti-discrimination law to these public transactions is the value of autonomy. We need to have some spheres of activity in which we can associate with whomever we wish if we are truly to be able to develop and live out our own life plans.[14]

Moreau is concerned with legal rather than moral rights, but there is no reason to think that the same thoughts cannot be extended to apply to morality. Further, her arguments about the limits of our rights against discrimination, and in particular her argument concerning autonomy, seem to have direct import for our question. They suggest that when seeking to determine how rights against discrimination operate in our romantic lives, we must consider both the freedoms of the parties that are being selected against and also the freedom of the choosing party to develop and live out their own life plans. The challenge, then, is to determine what someone adopting this kind of rights-based view will say about the different explanations. We cannot offer a definitive answer to this, partly because as we have mentioned there are a number of ways we might weigh freedoms to assign rights, but we can note that in principle it offers two ways in which one could reject KLR's conclusion that all of the explanations involve *pro tanto* wrongfulness.

First, one might think that the value of our freedom to choose our romantic partners for our own reasons always outweighs the freedom of our prospective partners not to be chosen against. On this interpretation, whom we date or have sex with is entirely up to us, and we should be free to choose on whatever reasons we think fit in order that we can live out our lives autonomously. This allows that our reasons may be bad reasons and that the life we choose may in fact be bad for us. It also allows that our choices may be harmful to others. But it stipulates that even when we act on bad reasons, and harm others through these choices, we do so permissibly, since no other party has a right that we have contravened.

This interpretation is compatible with holding that there is discrimination at other levels that is wrongful, and even that that discrimination is wrongful in part because of the fact that it leads to discrimination at this level. In the case of income discrimination, for example, the fact that certain groups face discrimination over pay is wrongful (cf. Chapter 25). And the right against that discrimination may be supported in part by the fact that discrimination in pay will spill over into discrimination and reduced freedom in other domains. However, the interpretation asserts that even if discrimination at the level of pay is wrongful because it contravenes a right, and that right is supported partly because the discrimination leads to reduced freedom in romantic partnership, there is no distinct right against discrimination in romantic partnership.

Second, one might think that the value of our freedom to choose our romantic partners for our own reasons outweighs the freedom of our prospective partners not to be chosen against for some reasons but not others. For example, you might think that people have a right not to be chosen against for explicitly racist reasons but not for reasons of innate preference. Supporting this requires showing that somehow the weight of the grounds of the right differs between the explanations.

Moreau discusses how discrimination may be permissible for some reasons and not others in the context of hiring:

> Consider, for instance, a basic case of indirect discrimination, such as the adoption by an English tearoom of a policy that waiters must speak only English at all times while on the job, even when on their breaks. This policy would likely disproportionately burden people from certain ethnic groups. Now consider three different scenarios. Suppose, firstly, that eliminating the English-only rule would cause the tearoom to lose some profits, because it would thereby seem less of an authentically English tearoom to its clients. Suppose, secondly, that the tearoom would lose so many clients for this reason that it would have to close. And suppose, finally, that the clients would go elsewhere because they were prejudiced and did not wish to be served by non-English staff.[15]

In the first case, she argues that the prospective employees' deliberative freedom is the only significant freedom at issue, as the employer's freedom to do whatever he thinks will increase his income should not be considered weighty. Therefore, the employees have a right against discrimination *for that reason*, and the employer acts wrongfully. In the second case, Moreau argues that the freedom to be able to run a viable business should be considered weighty, and, indeed, should be considered of greater weight than the freedom of the employees to speak their native language. Therefore, the employees do not have a right against discrimination *for that reason*, and the employer's actions are permissible. In the final case, Moreau argues that while the shop will still have to close, permitting discrimination in this context would encourage the persistence of the prejudicial attitudes that cause this loss. And these are the kinds of attitudes that result in limitations on the freedom of claimants from victimized groups. So the law cannot recognize business losses that stem from client prejudice without undermining its goal of promoting and protecting each individual's right to these deliberative freedoms.[16] In essence, the permission in the law would be bad for the promotion of deliberative freedom in the long term. This means that deliberative freedoms are best protected by assigning a right against discrimination *for that reason* and the employer acts wrongfully.

Can we similarly differentiate between the explanations of the romantic selection? There is at least one reason to think that we might. Imagine, as evidence might be thought to suggest, that racist attitudes can be changed by exposure to people who are the object of that attitude.[17] Deeming it permissible for people to discriminate on the basis of their racist preferences would then result in these attitudes and their harmful effects being perpetuated longer than they needed to be. Instead, accepting a right against discrimination on racist grounds could serve to create greater exposure to those of other races and so ameliorate the prevalence of racist attitudes. This might allow us to distinguish between discrimination in the case of explicit racism and the other cases.

Conclusion

We have examined whether discrimination in the selection of romantic partners is wrongful on two prominent accounts. Further, we have raised concerns about the fact that one of those accounts, desert-prioritarianism, seems to consider the discrimination wrongful whatever its explanation. This, we have suggested, conflicts with ordinary intuition. We have left open how exactly the alternative rights-based account will view the different explanations, but we think it is promising in that it offers some way to reject the claim that discrimination in our romantic choices is likely to be *pro tanto* wrongful because of its harmful effects, whatever its explanation. In closing, let us reiterate that we do not consider all of the explanations of the data we have considered to be equally plausible. On the contrary, we believe that the data is likely to be explained entirely by some combination of the first three explanations. We have included the possibility of *innate preference* because if it were true, there is reason to believe it would make a difference to our moral assessment of the case, and a good theory should be able to capture that difference. In the real world, it is unfortunate, and probably self-serving, that many people accept that explanation.[18]

Notes

1 Rudder 2014: 110.

2 In this chapter we will talk about racial groups. It is important to be clear that we do not mean by this that racial identity is a biological category.

3 Rudder 2014: 111.

4 Lippert-Rasmussen 2014.

5 KLR's full definition of discrimination is as follows: "X discriminates against Y in relation to Z by Φ-ing if, and only if, (i) there is a property, P, such that (X believes that) Y has P and (X believes that) Z does not have P, (ii) X treats Y worse than Z by Φ-ing, (iii) it is because (X believes that) Y has P and (X believes that) Z does not have P that X treats Y worse than Z by Φ-ing, (iv) P is the property of being a member of a certain socially salient group (to which Z does not belong), and (v) Φ-ing is a relevant type of act etc., and there are many acts etc. of this type, and this fact makes people with P (or some subgroup of these people) worse off relative to others, or Φ-ing is a relevant type of act etc., and many acts etc. of this type would make people with P worse off relative to others, or X's Φ-ing is motivated by animosity towards individuals with P or by the belief that individuals who have P are inferior or ought not to intermingle with others." An earlier version of this chapter showed how each of these conditions was met in the case under discussion. However, in the end we judged that this was a distraction from the main point of the chapter. The additional justification is available upon request.

6 Adopting KLR's definition (which counts a group as salient 'if perceived membership of it is important to the structure of social interactions across a wide range of social contexts') does have one further interesting implication. While racial identity clearly has social salience, other features such as clear skin and height do not. We can say, then, that selecting a partner on *those* bases will not count as

discriminatory. This raises the possibility that the data, which appears to show discrimination on the basis of race, might actually reflect selection on the basis of some other feature, which is not itself constitutive of membership in a socially salient group but which is correlated with race. In that case, what appears as discrimination will in fact not be discrimination. We accept that this is a live possibility, but as will be clear, it has no importance for argument. This is because our argument in no way depends on the actual empirical explanation of the data. It concerns the ability of KLR's view to properly account for our (different) attitudes towards different explanations of the data.

7 More fully, KLR says the following, "Suppose that someone engages in an act of blatant, racial discrimination against another. As a result someone is harmed or made worse off than the other. In one variant of the case it is the discriminator himself who suffers the harm. In the other variant it is the discriminatee who suffers an equally great harm. According to [standard] prioritarianism these outcomes contain equal amounts of moral value. Hence, if a third agent can make the harm fall either on the discriminator or on the discriminatee, she has no reason to do one rather than the other as far as [standard] prioritarianism goes" (Lippert-Rasmussen 2014: 166).

8 Rudder 2014: 111.

9 We do not mean to say that someone who endorses KLR's account cannot, for independent reasons, think that those things are morally significant. The point is that if they were to think that, it would have to be explained by appeal to some additional moral theory.

10 The existing academic work on this topic argues against this intuition. In his article 'Sexual racism: intimacy as a matter of justice', Sonu Bedi identifies reciprocal intimacy as a primary social good, which makes its distribution across racial lines a distinct matter of justice from a Rawlsian or Nussbaumian liberal perspective (Bedi 2015). Bedi proposes that discriminatory sexual preferences reinforce hierarchical stereotypes about racial groups (Bedi 2015: 1001), and, in so doing, violate the demands of justice.

11 Parfit 1984: 33–35.

12 One might think that discriminating against potential partners based on their race will, in fact, *not* be harmful to those potential partners if you hold racist beliefs. This is because potential partners who belong to social groups you do not respect will not be made worse off through being unable to date you, or enter into a relationship with you. It is not valuable, after all, to be in a relationship with someone who holds racist views against oneself. But there is reason to think that actually, if someone who held racist views against a certain group genuinely did not discriminate against that group in her sexual or romantic life, she would be likely to ultimately disavow her prior racism. In their article 'Seeing is believing: Exposure to counterstereotypic women leaders and its effect on the malleability of automatic gender stereotyping' (Dasgupta and Asgari 2004: 642–658), Nilanjana Dasgupta and Shaki Asgari observe that exposure to counterexamples of stereotypes about a social group undermined subjects' belief in the stereotypes in question. In an experiment detailed in the article, subjects were exposed to examples of women who hold leadership roles, and it was found that their stereotypical attitudes towards women were diminished in the process. We speculate that the process of dating would have a comparable effect. The racist who does not discriminate in the dating world would, in the course of dating those who she holds racist views against, be likely to reduce or remove the aspect about her personality (her racism) that would make her a poor fit for those she holds the view against in the first place.

13 Moreau 2010: 147.

14 Moreau 2010: 161.

15 Moreau 2010: 166.

16 Moreau 2010: 167.

17 See footnote 12.

18 For comments on earlier versions of this chapter we would like to thank Iason Gabriel, Kasper Lippert-Rasmussen, Tom Parr and an anonymous referee.

Bibliography

Bedi, Sonu. 2015. 'Sexual Racism: Intimacy as a Matter of Justice.' *Journal of Politics*. 77: 998–1011.

Dasgupta, Nilanjana and Asgari, Shaki. 2004. 'Seeing is believing: Exposure to counterstereotypic women leaders and its effect on the malleability of automatic gender stereotyping.' *Journal of Experimental Social Psychology*. 40: 642–658.

Lippert-Rasmussen, Kasper. 2014. *Born Free and Equal?* Oxford: Oxford University Press.

Moreau, Sophia. 2010. 'What is Discrimination?' *Philosophy & Public Affairs*. 38: 143–179.

Parfit, Derek. 1984. *Reasons and Persons*. Oxford: Oxford University Press.

Rudder, Christian. 2014. *Dataclysm*. London: 4th Estate.

PART V

Causes and means

32

THE SOCIAL PSYCHOLOGY OF DISCRIMINATION

Jules Holroyd

UNIVERSITY OF SHEFFIELD

Introduction

Research in social psychology focuses on the psychological mechanisms involved in and underpinning discrimination. The research program is vast (for accessible overviews, see Ramiah *et al.* 2010; for research on gender discrimination in particular see Valian 1999; on racial discrimination see Blank *et al.* 2004). In this chapter I focus on three areas of research from social psychology that have been taken up by philosophers: in-group/out-group favoritism, implicit bias, and stereotype threat. Whilst each has garnered some philosophical attention, little attempt has been made to tease out the implications of this research for philosophical analyses of discrimination. In this chapter I explore some of the ways in which insights from research in social psychology may require revision or fine-tuning to philosophical analyses of discrimination. Philosophers have good reason to attend to the findings of social psychology: not only to gain an understanding of the mechanisms that may underpin discrimination, but also to inform philosophical analyses of discrimination and ensure that they are suitably formulated to capture the full range of the phenomenon.

Discrimination

In order to evaluate the implications of this research for analyses of discrimination, it will help to have an understanding of discrimination in view. For present purposes, we will focus on the analysis offered by Lippert-Rasmussen (2013), which has been recently elaborated and defended. The conditions are intended to capture the notion of group discrimination, which is arguably at issue in common usage of the notion of discrimination. Lippert-Rasmussen proposes the following set of conditions for group (direct) discrimination:

> An agent, X, discriminates against someone, Y, in relation to another, Z, by Φ-ing (e.g. hiring Z rather than Y) if and only if:
>
> (i) There is a property, P, such that Y has P or X believes that Y has P, and Z does not have P or X believes that Z does not have P,

(ii) X treats Y worse than he treats or would treat Z by Φ-ing, and
(iii) It is because (X believes that) Y has P and (X believes that) Z does not have P that X treats Y worse than Z by Φ-ing (Lippert-Rasmussen 2013: 15).
(iv) P is the property of being a member of a certain socially salient group (to which Z does not belong) (Lippert-Rasmussen 2013: 26).
(v) Φ is a relevant type of act, policy or practice, and there are many acts etc. of this type, and this fact makes people with P (or some subgroup of these people) worse off relative to others, or Φ is a relevant type of act etc., and many acts etc. of this type would make people with P worse off relative to others, or X's Φ-ing is motivated by animosity towards or dislike of individuals with P or by the belief that individuals who have P are inferior or ought not to intermingle with others (Lippert-Rasmussen 2013: 28).

Lippert-Rasmussen clarifies that conditions i–iii are part of an analysis of generic discrimination (Lippert-Rasmussen 2013: 15-22) – a broad notion of discrimination that captures differential treatment of persons such as exclusion of unqualified candidates from consideration for a job, or judicial conviction of individuals found to be guilty (Lippert-Rasmussen 2013: 15). The addition of conditions (iv) and (v) narrows down the analysis to one that captures those cases in which individuals are differentially treated on the basis of membership of a socially salient group, where social salience is a matter of perceived membership being important to the structure of social interactions in a range of social contexts (e.g. race, gender, age) (Lippert-Rasmussen 2013: 30). This idea is accommodated by condition (iv). Finally, condition (v) of Lippert-Rasmussen's analysis is needed in order to give an analysis that excludes one-shot, unproblematically motivated differential treatment that does not, or would not, constitute a pattern of disadvantaging treatment (Lippert-Rasmussen 2013: 28–30). Accordingly, condition (v) captures the idea that it is differential treatment which involves actions, or patterns of action, that do or would disadvantage, or which express hostility or judgments of inferiority, with which we are concerned.[1]

We should note that it is this idea of *group* discrimination with which much research in social psychology has been concerned: the driving motivation behind much of the social psychological research is to understand discrimination and the mechanisms underpinning it as it tracks and structures our social identities. Ramiah *et al.* (2010) motivate their field of research by observing that 'the pervasiveness of discrimination and its systematic, and often subtle, expression shapes society in ways that perpetuate inequities' (Ramiah *et al.* 2010: 90). This much indicates that at stake for these authors is discrimination that tracks social identities taken to be important and with significance for the ways in which society is structured.

Note, moreover, that our focus for the most part in this chapter is on *direct discrimination*: cases in which an individual (or organization) treats another person or group disadvantageously, because of their social group membership (race, age, gender and so on). This is because much of the psychological research is relevant to direct discrimination, since it speaks to the cognitive mechanisms underpinning differential treatment in this sense. I set aside, for the most part, the important related phenomenon of *indirect discrimination*, which concerns cases where a policy or procedure is on the face of it neutral, but in fact disproportionately disadvantages members of a particular social group.

With this analysis on the table, and a sense of its relationship to the concerns of social psychological research, we can examine some of the research programs which focus on the cognitive mechanisms that underpin discriminatory judgments and behavior. We will then be in a position to consider what revisions or refinements, if any, this understanding of group discrimination may benefit from.

Discrimination involving in-group favoritism

Social psychologists have identified in-group favoritism as one of the mechanisms by which differential treatment is perpetrated. So called 'categorization effects' – whether individuals are categorized as 'in-group' or 'out-group' members – have been shown to impact on a wide array of behaviors, from what is credited to the agent, to the sorts of benefits allocated to her.

For example, various studies have prompted individuals to consider whether behaviors or outcomes, which may have been positive or negative, were the result of an agent's traits (e.g. her hard work or talents), or due to factors external to the agent (such as luck or other people's actions). These studies have focused on different in-group/out-group identities, with Hindu participants being asked to evaluate the described behaviors of Hindu (in-group) or Muslim (out-group) individuals (Taylor and Jaggi 1974), Israeli and Arab American students being asked to evaluate actions from other Israeli and Arab agents (Rosenberg and Wolfsfeld 1977), and even individuals with preferences for Super Bowl teams (Dallas Cowboys vs Pittsburgh Steelers) being asked to evaluate the causes of events involving their respective teams in a game (Winkler and Taylor 1979).

In these studies, the findings indicated that when individuals evaluated out-group members, negative behaviors or outcomes were more frequently attributed to failings on the part of the out-group agent (bad character, lack of effort, and so on). Meanwhile, positive outcomes were explained by situational factors, thereby removing credit from the out-group individual. The converse pattern was found when participants made evaluations of in-group members: positive outcomes were more frequently attributed to traits of the agent, whilst negative actions or outcomes were attributed to situational factors out of the agent's control.[2]

In another study, participants viewed video recordings of behaviors (a 'shove') that could be interpreted in different ways. The responses analyzed showed that white participants attributed the behavior as due to personal factors, such as violent dispositions, when the perpetrator was racialized black; and more frequently interpreted the same behavior as due to situational factors when the perpetrator was racialized white (Duncan 1976). In these studies, then, in-group favoritism manifests itself in the disposition to reach for explanatory resources that are favorable to members of our in-group.

A notable feature of this research paradigm, however, is that whilst in some of the studies above the in-group identities tracked social identities that are consequential in structuring social arrangements, and indeed are sometimes identities with which group members positively identify, the in-group bias need not depend on such social identities. In studies that asked participants to allocate rewards to in-group and out-group members, the group identities activated were entirely arbitrary, and artificially constructed by the experimental context: e.g., the tendency to over-estimate or under-estimate the number of dots presented in a prior task (Taifel and Turner 1986). Yet, even so, being a member of one or other of these groups sufficed to activate in-group bias: members of each group typically favored the allocation of resources to in-group members, and sought to maximize the difference in resources allocated to in-group and out-group members.[3] Other studies focused on arbitrarily constructed group statuses that tracked the team color to which participants belonged (being assigned to the 'green' group, or the 'red' group, say) (Dawes *et al.* 1990). The key point to note, then, is that whilst the tendency to form such in-group preferences seems a pervasive feature of our psychology, the in-group/out-group statuses that this form of favoritism may track seem to be highly malleable. That is to say: who counts as in one's in-group may be variable, with new (sometimes arbitrary) group statuses being formed depending on social contextual features or prompts.

Note that analyses of discrimination have characterized group discrimination such that these sorts of arbitrary, in-group preferences would not meet the criteria for social salience. For example, the notion of social salience incorporated by Lippert-Rasmussen has it that 'A group is socially salient if perceived membership of it is important to the structure of social interactions across a wide range of social contexts' (Lippert-Rasmussen 2013: 30).[4]

This analysis of social salience permits us to capture the notion of discrimination as it is used to explain what is wrong with certain kinds of treatment that disadvantage women, racial minorities, certain religious identities, or the elderly, for example. These kinds of social identities clearly structure social interactions and social hierarchies in a broad range of contexts. Note, though, that this analysis will not allow the sort of differential treatment manifested in some of the studies on in-group favoritism to be diagnosed as discrimination. Certainly the disposition to over- or under-estimate dots is not socially salient in this sense: it does not structure interactions across a wide range of social contexts. Yet it is precisely because the experimenters brought this status to salience – as structuring *that* social context - that we saw patterns of differential treatment emerge within the laboratory studies.

Moreover, the experimentally-found tendency for in-group bias has been identified by philosophers as one of the mechanisms by which structures of hierarchy and inequality might be perpetuated. Consider Elizabeth Anderson's remarks, in the context of epistemic discrimination, whereby some agents are judged to be less credible than others. She observes that if in-group biases in this context line up with social identities that are already the basis of systematic disadvantages, then we should see this sort of epistemic discrimination as structural (Anderson 2012: 170). For example, if in-group bias about credibility judgments tracks race, then this will reinforce epistemic and other dimensions of disadvantage that black and minority ethnicity individuals may already face. Compare this with a context in which in-group bias about credibility judgments track whether one is an over- or under-estimator of dots. This will not track any pre-existing systemic disadvantage. Anderson's remarks alert us to the distinction between the identities that populate an in-group/out-group bias, and the social salience of those identities in structuring or perpetuating wider patterns of social disadvantage.

The point of this observation is to show that analyses of group discrimination that aim to focus on the socially salient identity have a choice to make about the scope of the phenomena to be captured. The choice made will have implications for how social salience is characterized. For example, on the one hand, we may seek to restrict discrimination to those cases that meet the social salience criteria as characterized above. One motivation for doing so is to capture ordinary usage of the notion of discrimination. This would be to maintain that differential treatment on the basis of these arbitrarily drawn and artificially constructed in-group identities is not discrimination. On this construal, dispositions to favor in-group members may be present across a range of differential treatments, but only some of those instances constitute group discrimination proper.

On the other hand, we might seek to treat the in-group biases revealed in various experimental contexts as continuous with the notion of discrimination as captured by the analysis offered at the beginning of the chapter. In that case, we could refine our analysis of social salience, indexing it to a context, such that:

> A group is socially salient, in context C, if perceived membership of it is important to the structure of social interactions in that context, C.

On this construction, in-lab differential treatment such as that described above will count as discrimination, though this manifestly will not transmit to other contexts, in which other identities are salient. What may be socially salient for the purposes of an individual's differential treatment may not coincide with what is socially salient in structuring broader patterns of social disadvantage.

What attention to the social psychological research helps us to see, then, is that the original analysis of group discrimination builds in certain strong conditions for social salience, present only in some of the cases of differential treatment, albeit those which garner great concern and feature in ordinary usage of the notion of discrimination. But this is just one option: a context sensitive account of salience may be preferred, if one seeks to capture all cases of differential treatment based on in-group bias, and identify the continuity, in terms of operative cognitive mechanism, between the 'in-lab' and 'real-world' phenomena.

Discrimination involving implicit bias

In the past couple of decades, social psychologists have focused on the measurement of 'implicit bias', or what is sometimes called 'aversive racism', or unconscious or automatic discrimination. In this section I set out some of the research on implicit bias, and show how our understanding of discrimination – in particular, condition (iii) of the analysis from earlier – requires revision.

Implicit biases are automatic patterns of thought or feeling.[5] Notably, these patterns may not be transparent to us, and it may be difficult for us to detect and control when they are operating in our minds or influencing our judgments and behaviors. Those which have occupied the attention of philosophers typically involve attaching some negative property or stereotypic trait to membership of a social group. For example, indirect measures have indicated that men are more strongly associated with leadership and women more strongly associated with nurturing and supporting roles (AAUW report 2016).[6] Other studies have found that white people are more strongly associated with intellectual features and black people more strongly associated with physical traits (Amodio and Devine 2006). Other measures have focused on the problematic biases we might have towards people on the basis of religion, age, disability or sexuality (see Jost *et al.* 2009 for an overview of research on implicit biases). Crucially, individuals who sincerely profess egalitarian values and beliefs may display negative associations on these indirect measures. Whilst the mere presence of such biases is troubling, their potential to influence action is particularly relevant to concerns about discrimination. Various studies indicate that behavior may be influenced by implicit bias.[7] Consider first a study on hiring selections by Dovidio and Gaertner (2000). These studies indicated that individuals were more likely to make hiring recommendations in the case of moderately good white candidates than moderately good black candidates. (In cases where the candidates were obviously stellar or unqualified, the decisions tracked quality of application rather than race.) The moderately good candidates had exactly the same credentials, but differed only with respect to the race indicated on their application materials (cued with racially stereotyped names). Accordingly, the differential recommendations appear to be race-based discrimination, and involve a pattern of treatment that would – does – significantly disadvantage black individuals. Yet individuals who made such discriminatory recommendations may not have been aware that they were discriminating, and indeed may avow anti-racist norms of fair treatment when asked to report on their explicit or endorsed beliefs and values.

Second, consider the now well known 'shooter bias' tests (Glaser *et al.* 2006; Correll *et al.* 2007). In these studies, individuals participate in a simulation task whereby they are shown images of males in different postures holding a range of objects. In some cases the object is a weapon (gun); in other cases, it is not (mobile phone). Some of the images are of black males, others of white males. Participants in the simulation are instructed to 'shoot' at only those individuals who are armed. Results indicate that the participants are more likely (and faster) to shoot black males with weapons than white males with weapons, and more likely to make the error of shooting an unarmed black male. It is clear how such biases and discriminatory behavior could have gravely disadvantaging effects for black individuals.

Cases such as these – where individuals are discriminating based on race – may not fit our usual understanding of discrimination: the discriminatory treatment may be unintentional. Indeed, that she is engaging in unequal treatment may be something of which the discriminator is unaware, and, were she cognizant of it, would disavow. Nonetheless, I take it as uncontroversial that such patterns of race-based differential treatment, that are obviously disadvantageous, do count as discrimination, and should be captured by an analysis of the notion.[8] However, the conditions we set out above need refinement if they are to be able to do so. Let us consider the first three conditions for group discrimination set out on pp. 381–382:

> An agent, X, discriminates against someone, Y, in relation to another, Z, by Φ-ing (e.g. hiring Z rather than Y) if and only if:
>
> (i) There is a property, P, such that Y has P or X believes that Y has P, and Z does not have P or X believes that Z does not have P,
> (ii) X treats Y worse than he treats or would treat Z by Φ-ing, and
> (iii) It is because (X believes that) Y has P and (X believes that) Z does not have P that X treats Y worse than Z by Φ-ing.

Take the shooter bias studies. The discriminator (X) is in this case one of the participants in the study. The property in question, P, is the race of the individual in the scenario – P denotes the fact that an individual (Y) is racialized black (or believed to be black). In shooting an unarmed black male in the study images, X treats that individual worse than he treats other individuals in the study images who are not black, with potentially fatal consequences.[9] Insofar as the race of the individuals in the images appears to be the only factor that could explain the differential responses, it appears that it is this perceived property (P) (possessed by Y but not by Z) which explains why X treats Y in that way. In our current context, race is a socially salient group, clearly, and the kind of action at issue – shooting – is such that it is of a relevant type of act of which there are many which make black individuals worse off (facing increased risk of violence in their daily lives).[10] The point I want to press is that some refinement is needed to the analysis of direct discrimination if it is to be able to adequately capture this sort of discriminatory behavior. The adequacy of the analysis turns on the way in which the third condition is understood. Recall this condition requires that:

> (iii) It is because (X believes that) Y has P and (X believes that) Z does not have P that X treats Y worse than Z by Φ-ing.

We should want to say that it is because (the discriminator – the participant in the test – believes that) the individual is black – and (the discriminator believes that) other individuals in the simulation images are white – that the discriminator treats the black individuals worse (shooting more readily, including at unarmed individuals) than the white individuals.

However, we need to see further what it means to say that someone acted *because* the individual has (or is believed to have) the relevant property (in this case, being black). Lippert-Rasmussen suggests that, in the case of direct discrimination:

> X treats Y worse than Z by Φ-ing because (X believes that) Y has P and (X believes that) Z does not have P if, and only if, the thought that Y, and not Z, has P is part of X's direct, motivating reason for Φ-ing.[11]

This is intended to capture the relation that holds between (perceived or imagined) membership of a socially salient group and disadvantageous treatment as we find it in cases of direct discrimination.

This characterization seems to serve well in cases of discrimination in which explicit bias has a role; that is, in which someone's perceived group membership is considered by the agent to be a reason for treating them disadvantageously. Such cases of explicit bias include, for example, if an individual is believed to be less suitable for a job – represented as incompetent – *because* of beliefs about race and competence, or judged less likely to be an effective leader – represented as indecisive – *because* of beliefs about gender and leadership.

Cases of implicit bias discrimination seem not to involve such clear beliefs or judgments that are taken to justify differential treatment. Yet we should expect discrimination due to implicit bias to be captured by an analysis of direct discrimination:[12] it is a matter of an individual treating another individual disadvantageously on account of her race (or gender, or age etc.). But in fact, whether the analysis offered can capture these cases of discrimination will depend on exactly how condition (iii) is glossed, and in particular on how we understand the notion of a 'motivating reason' for action. On one broad rendering of this notion, we might follow a Williams-inspired understanding of motivating reason, which is to say that an agent has a motivating reason for some action (φ-ing) when she 'has some motive which will be served or furthered by [her] φ-ing' (1981: 101). On this reading of what it is to have a motivating reason, we commit only to the idea that the agent has some motive that causes her to act. She need not be aware of this motive, or the role it plays in her action; indeed, she may disavow it. Thus construed, the shooter bias case could be understood such that the fact that the individual is racialized black *does* serve as a motivating reason for the participant's differential (worse) treatment – even though the participant is unaware of this motive and its role in her action. Note that we must also suppose, on this reading, that 'the thought that' the individual is racialized black must also be construed permissively: as including unconscious thoughts, as well as explicitly entertained reflections.

Whilst this interpretation of Lippert-Rasmussen's understanding – of what it is to treat someone differently 'because' of her perceived group membership – can accommodate cases of discrimination due to implicit bias, there is perhaps something inelegant or unsatisfying about it. In particular, it seems to require some specification of the motive that is furthered by the agent's discriminatory action. There may be answers to be given here – vested and unarticulated or disavowed interests in preserving racial hierarchy (for racialized white participants, at least); or perhaps more simply an interest in efficient cognizing, which promulgates dependency on such fast associative thought. But we will need an answer (or answers) that cover all of the cases in which discrimination due to implicit bias is found, and that is not an *ad hoc* postulate to ensure the agent comes out as having the requisite motivating reason(s). Perhaps there is work to do in pinning this part of the analysis down so that apprehension of the individual's group membership is the cause – the motivating reason – for the differential treatment.

Note that there are some interpretations of 'motivating reasons' that will not be compatible with Lippert-Rasmussen's analysis. For example, on another rendering of the notion, a motivating reason is 'a reason for which someone does something, a reason that, in the agent's eyes, counts in favor of her acting in a certain way' (Alvarez 2016).[13] But note that on this latter reading, in many cases of discrimination due to implicit bias, 'the thought that Y has P' (e.g. the individual is black) cannot properly be construed as the agent's 'motivating reason' for action. This is because in many cases, the agent who is influenced by implicit bias disavows the associations (or associated propositions) that are implicated in the discriminatory actions. For example, in the shooter bias case, individuals who display this discriminatory pattern of shooting may nonetheless deny that 'the thought that the individual is black' counts in favor of her acting a certain way. On explicit self-reports, the agent may strongly resist subscribing to propositions such as 'black people are more likely to carry weapons', and repudiate any such racist stereotypes. That the individual is black does not provide the agent with a motivating reason for differential treatment, then. Of course, we might uncharitably take such self-reports as disingenuous and insincere. But a further reason for maintaining that this cannot be posited as the agent's motivating reason is that, in the case of implicit bias, individuals may not intend to discriminate, and indeed may not be aware that they have been implicated in differential treatment.

The upshot of this is that the gloss on motivating reasons needs to be spelled out in more detail. If one spells it out in terms of the broader reading – the motive for or cause of the agent's action – then implicit bias discrimination may be captured by condition (iii). However, if for independent reasons one endorses the narrower construal of motivating reasons, a different articulation of condition (iii) will be needed in order to capture the phenomenon of discrimination that results from implicit bias. In these cases, what is needed is a more direct connection between the socially salient group membership and the differential treatment; one that is not mediated by the agent's thoughts about her reasons for action. Various options are available. For example, we might say that:

> X treats Y worse than Z by Φ-ing because (X believes that) Y has P and (X believes that) Z does not have P if, and only if, (1) the thought that Y, and not Z, has P is part of X's direct, motivating reason for Φ-ing, or **(2) X's categorization of Y, and not Z, as P influences her Φ-ing**.

Whilst (1) continues to deal with the cases where discrimination is intentional and based on explicit prejudice, this additional clause, (2), should capture cases where the agent's automatic processing of social identity, and automatically activated stereotypes or affective states, influence the agent's behavior without her awareness, and without her intention. The mere (and perhaps non-conscious or sub-personal) categorization of the individual as belonging to a socially salient group may suffice to activate the automatic processes that influence the agent's behavior.

This might seem excessively complicated. An alternative fix would be to appeal to a contrast class that is on the table with talk of motivating reasons: namely, explanatory reasons. An explanatory reason is one that *explains* an agent's action, and it certainly seems clear that we should want to appeal to social category information (that the individual was racialized black) to explain the agent's differential treatment. This would lead us to the following specification of condition (iii):

> X treats Y worse than Z by Φ-ing because (X believes that) Y has P and (X believes that) Z does not have P if, and only if, Y having (or being believed to have) P, and not Z, **is the explanatory reason for X's Φ-ing**.

This is certainly a more elegant fix. However, one reason to worry about this way of capturing implicit bias discrimination is that we may then lose the distinction between direct and indirect discrimination. This is because in cases of indirect discrimination, the fact (for example) that the agent is racialized black will also *explain* the differential treatment, but indirectly, via the proxy consideration that ends up yielding racial discrimination. To accommodate this, one could restrict explanatory reasons to those which are psychological: namely, those which feature in the agent's psychology, rather than those which have *any* explanatory role. Since (I assume) we should want to maintain the distinction between direct and indirect discrimination, and see discrimination due to implicit bias falling on the direct discrimination side of the distinction, this fix will have to be understood in this way to do the work required.

There may be further reasons to object to these modified conditions, or to favor one over the other. The main concern here, though, is to demonstrate that attention to the research in social psychology has import for analyses of discrimination. If these analyses seek to capture such phenomena as discrimination due to implicit bias, then some revisions – of the sort proposed above – may be in order.

Stereotype threat

A third domain of research in social psychology that is worth turning our attention to concerns the phenomenon known as 'stereotype threat'. As detailed by Steele (1997, 2010), 'stereotype threat' refers to the cases in which the perceived threat of confirming a stereotype has a deleterious effect on an individual's performance on a task.

For example, Steele and Aronson (1995) asked black and white college students to take a study comprised of questions from the GRE (Graduate Record Examination). Some of the participants were told the test was diagnostic of intellectual ability, whilst others were explicitly told it was not diagnostic of abilities. The diagnostic condition activated stereotypes about the lower intellectual abilities of black people. In this condition, black students underperformed compared to the white students; no such effect was found in the non-diagnostic condition. Shih *et al.* (1999) found that stereotypes about gender had a similar effect: when gender – and the perceived threat of the stereotype that women are poor at math – was made salient, women students' performances suffered. Interestingly, this effect disappeared when another aspect of the women's identities was made salient, namely their Asian-American identity, which is stereotyped as skilled at quantitative reasoning.

These studies, and others, are taken to support a variety of hypotheses about the mechanism by which perceived stereotype hinders performance. Candidate explanations contend that the activation of a stereotype, and an individual's awareness of this stereotype – even if they do not endorse it – may provoke anxiety. Alternatively, such awareness may decrease motivation on the task; or cause subjects to unintentionally imitate and express the stereotype in their engagement with the task; or simply create self-doubt which distracts from the task in hand.[14]

The phenomenon of stereotype threat raises some interesting questions for proposed analyses of discrimination. In particular, we may press for greater precision with respect to our understanding of what it is to 'treat' individual X worse than Y – the framing that appears in condition (ii) of the analysis above. Does the sort of behavior that is described as 'activating a stereotype', in the context of these studies, constitute a form of differential (worse) treatment? In some cases this 'activation' amounted to no more than merely mentioning gender, or the mere mention of some feature of the task associated with a stereotype – for example, whether a test is diagnostic of intellectual abilities. Steele and Aronson (1995) simply told their participants (black and white) in the diagnostic condition that:

> ...because we want an accurate measure of your ability in these domains, we want to ask you to try as hard as you can to perform well on these tasks. At the end of this study, we can give you feedback which may be helpful by pointing out your strengths and weaknesses.
> *(Steele and Aronson 1995: 803)*

It is rather surprising to consider this prompt as a form of differential and disadvantageous treatment that partially constitutes discrimination. This will be especially so in cases in which the individual is not at all aware that such words activate stereotypes that can have a deleterious effect on performance. Nonetheless, it is true that this mere mention did, under some description, involve treating individuals involved in the study differently and disadvantageously. For black students, this constituted *activating a negative stereotype* – since this prompt sufficed to activate negative stereotypes concerning black people and intellectual abilities, and thereby caused (via one or other of the candidate mechanisms mentioned above) lower levels of performance. For the white students who were given this very same prompt, no negative stereotype was activated.

Should we capture such behaviors, which (perhaps unknowingly) activate stereotypes, as directly discriminatory *treatment*? How one might unpack the notion of 'treatment' will depend on whether one is inclined to subsume the phenomenon of stereotype threat under the rubric of direct – rather than indirect – discrimination. It seems unclear to me what intuition or ordinary usage supports, and broader theoretical concerns might guide one's choice here. However one chooses, there is some work to do. If one is so inclined to see stereotype threat as a form of direct discrimination, then a notion of 'treatment' that can handle the various and subtle ways of *activating stereotypes* will be needed. On the other hand, one may not want to extend the analysis of direct discrimination to include stereotype threat. On this line of thought, we could leave such cases to be captured by the analysis of indirect discrimination.[15] Then an understanding of 'treatment' should be developed, as part of the analysis of direct discrimination that excludes such activation. This might be a delicate matter, however, since manifestly, we have reason to maintain that treating (in the standard common-sense way) according to stereotypes is a form of discrimination (cf. Lippert-Rasmussen 2013: 21). Yet, we have seen that direct discrimination need not be intentional (above; see also Lippert-Rasmussen fn 70). So, circumscribing the notion of 'treating' in a way that maps these complex contours, and allowing us to allocate stereotype threat to the desired side of the direct/indirect distinction, may be a demanding task.

Conclusion

We have seen three domains of research from social psychology, concerning in-group favoritism, implicit bias, and stereotype threat. Each poses distinctive challenges to philosophical analyses of discrimination: the first concerns how we might characterize the 'social salience' of group membership on the basis of which one is disadvantageously treated, and whether this should include all cases of in-group favoritism, or only those that track groups that have widespread social salience. The second concerns how the basis for a discriminator's differential treatment is understood, and whether it need make reference to the explicit beliefs of the discriminator, or include mere automatic categorizations that instigate implicit biases. Finally, we saw that some refinements may be needed to what is included within the scope of differential *treatment*, and whether it includes seemingly innocuous behavior that nonetheless activates stereotypes, and thereby stereotype threat. Whilst these matters are philosophical, and cannot be settled simply by appeal to empirical research, my hope is that these observations provide further motivation for philosophers interested in discrimination to mine the rich seams of research on the social psychology of discrimination.[16]

Notes

1 Note that whilst these conditions capture the sorts of treatment that we find morally objectionable, no moral evaluation is built into the conditions themselves: it is thus a contingent empirical fact that these conditions pick out treatment that is often morally objectionable – often in a way that makes it wrong – when they do. (Lippert-Rasmussen's later analysis of the wrong as to do with the harm that discrimination imposes fills out that part of the account – see Chapter 6 of Lippert-Rasmussen 2013.)

2 However, for a more complex pattern of results, see Hewstone and Ward (1985), which focused on Malay/Chinese identities; and Stephan (1977) which examined attributions of Anglo-Chicano and black American high school students. All these studies are discussed in the overview by Hewstone (1990).

3 Also worth noting is that in-group favoritism need not coincide with antipathy towards an out-group (Brewer 1999; see also Ramiah *et al.* 2010: 88).

4 Compare also Baber's notion of *social salience*, which focuses on the extent to which a property is taken to 'predict and explain beliefs, character traits, tastes or other socially significant psychological characteristics' (2001: 53). This characterization will also exclude from salience those arbitrary and artificial in-group statuses, insofar as whether one is (e.g.) an under- or over-estimator is clearly not taken to predict or explain much at all.

5 Contention abounds as to how to characterize these automatic thought processes – whether they involve associative mental states, states with propositional content, affective or representational content, and whether they are mental states at all. For discussion see Mandelbaum (2015), Levy (2015), Machery (2016) and Holroyd (2016).

6 Downloadable here: www.aauw.org/resource/barriers-and-bias/

7 There is contention over the predictive validity of implicit biases: see discussion in Machery (2016), and Oswald *et al.* (2013). The important point to take away from the research, it seems, is that biases may lead to discriminatory behavior, though it is difficult to determine when this is so. Given this, we cannot be confident that our behavior is not influenced in these discriminatory ways. For debate about these concerns regarding predictive validity, see the roundtable discussion at The Brains Blog: http://philosophyofbrains.com/2017/01/17/how-can-we-measure-implicit-bias-a-brains-blog-roundtable.aspx

8 See discussion from Christopher Lebron (2016) of the wide reaching impact of shootings of black males, by police, on the lives of all racialized as black. Of course, we need not believe all such cases are due to implicit bias.

9 This is slightly complicated by the fact that we are talking about a fictional individual, portrayed in the study images. However, I do not take this complication to affect the substantive point at issue here: that such discriminatory behavior cannot be captured by the conditions as stated.

10 Of course, the study is alarming insofar as it indicates that such behavioral propensities might be found outside of laboratory simulations. As such, we might cautiously say that such studies are evidence of discrimination outside the lab, rather than acts of discrimination themselves. But my point is not that the laboratory setting cannot be accommodated by this set of conditions. The point is that the analysis cannot as it stands capture differential treatment that results from such biases.

11 Note that Lippert-Rasmussen appears to endorse this condition as an analysis of direct discrimination (37), but rejects it as an analysis of discrimination *tout court*, since indirect discrimination cannot be accommodated by this analysis. The final and full articulation of this condition for group discrimination is disjunctive, whereby: 'X treats Y worse than Z by Φ-ing because (X believes that) Y has P and (X believes that) Z does not have P if, and only if, (i) the thought that Y, and not Z, has P is part of X's direct, motivating reason for Φ-ing, or (ii) the fact that Y, and not Z, has P causally explains X's Φ-ing and this in turn is causally explained by the fact that people with P are often treated worse than those without P in the sense given by (i)' (38). The second disjunct here is supposed to capture the

phenomena of indirect discrimination. However, I take it for our purposes, our attention should be on the first disjunct (i) since discrimination due to implicit bias should be captured by an analysis of direct, rather than indirect, discrimination.

12 Note that in some cases, implicit bias is revealed across groups of individuals. For example, consider studies, such as the CV studies mentioned above, where the structure is a 'between participants' study, such that no participant makes judgements about or interacts with both black and white individuals, and differential treatment emerges in patterns of behavior across participants – some of whom interact with or make evaluations about black individuals, others of whom interact with or make evaluations about white individuals. In such cases, our understanding of discrimination due to implicit bias may pose additional difficulties for this model of direct discrimination. The analysis will perhaps only hold on the assumption that, in these 'between participants' studies, each individual *would have judged differently* were the race of the applicant different. My remarks in the text above apply to cases where implicit bias is revealed by differential treatment, by one person, of individuals differentially racialized.

13 See also Dancy's view of motivating reasons, whereby for something to be a motivating reason for the agent, she has to take that consideration to be a normative reason for acting (Dancy 2000). This construal of motivating reasons similarly seems to require that the consideration 'in the agent's eyes' is a reason for – a consideration in favor of – action.

14 For an overview of a range of studies on stereotype threat, and an evaluation of the competing hypotheses, see Mallon (2016).

15 For the statement of the analysis of indirect discrimination, see footnote 11. The key difference is the focus on the causal role of social category information, rather than the role it plays in the psychological dispositions of the individual who disadvantageously treats another.

16 This research was completed with the support of the Leverhulme Trust project grant on Bias and Blame (RPG-2013-326).

Bibliography

AAUW report 2016. www.aauw.org/resource/barriers-and-bias/

Al Ramiah, A., Hewstone, M., Dovidio, J. F. and Penner, L. A. 2010. "The Social Psychology of Discrimination: Theory, Measurement and Consequences." In L. Bond, F. McGinnity and H. Russell (eds) *Irish and International Approaches to Measuring Discrimination*. Dublin: Liffey Press. 84–112.

Alvarez, M. 2016. "Reasons for Action: Justification, Motivation, Explanation." *The Stanford Encyclopedia of Philosophy* (Winter 2016 Edition). Edward N. Zalta (ed.), https://plato.stanford.edu/archives/win2016/entries/reasons-just-vs-expl/

Amodio, D. M., and Devine, P. G. 2006. "Stereotyping and Evaluation in Implicit Race Bias: Evidence for Independent Constructs and Unique Effects on Behavior." *Journal of Personality and Social Psychology*. 91(4): 652–661.

Anderson, E. 2012 "Epistemic Justice as a Virtue of Social Institutions." *Social Epistemology*. 26(2): 163–173.

Baber, H. E. 2001. "Gender Conscious." *Journal of Applied Philosophy*. 18(1): 53–63.

Blank, R. M., Dabady, M. and Citro, C. F. (eds) 2004. *Measuring Racial Discrimination*. Washington, DC: The National Academies Press.

Brewer, M. 1999. "The Psychology of Prejudice. Ingroup Love or Outgroup Hate?" *Journal of Social Issues*. 55(3): 429–444.

Correll, J., Park, B., Judd, C. M., Wittenbrink, B., Sadler, M. S. and Keesee, T. 2007. "Across the Thin Blue Line: Police Officers and Racial Bias in the Decision to Shoot." *Journal of Personality and Social Psychology*. 92: 1006–1023.

Dancy, J. 2000. *Practical Reality*. New York: Oxford University Press.

Dawes, R., van de Kragt, A. and Orbell, J. 1990. "Cooperation for the Benefit of Us—Not Me, or My Conscience." In J. Mansbridge (ed.) *Beyond Self-interest*. Chicago: University of Chicago Press. 97–110.

Dovidio, J. F. and Gaertner, S. L. 2004. "Aversive Racism." In M. Zanna (ed.), *Advances in Experimental Social Psychology*. San Diego, CA: Academic Press. 1–52.

Duncan, B. L. 1976. "Differential Social Perception and Attribution of Intergroup Violence: Testing the Lower Limits of Stereotyping of Blacks." *Journal of Personality and Social Psychology*. 34: 590–598.

Glaser, J. and Knowles, E. 2008. "Implicit Motivation to Control Prejudice." *Journal of Experimental Social Psychology*. 44: 164–172.

Hewstone, M. 1990. "The 'Ultimate Attribution Error'? A Review of the Literature on Intergroup Causal Attribution." *European Journal of Social Psychology*. 20: 311–335.

Hewstone, M. and Ward, C. 1985. "Ethnocentrism and Causal Attribution in Southeast Asia." *Journal of Personality and Social Psychology*. 48: 614–623.

Holroyd, J. 2016. "What do we Want from a Model of Implicit Cognition?" *Proceedings of the Aristotelian Society*. 116(2): 153–179.

Lebron, C. 2016. "I'm Black. Does America Have a Plan for My Life?" *The Stone*. Sept 26, www.nytimes.com/2016/09/26/opinion/im-black-does-america-have-a-plan-for-my-life.html

Levy, N. 2014. "Neither Fish nor Fowl: Implicit Attitudes as Patchy Endorsements." *Noûs*. 49(4): 800–823.

Lippert-Rasmussen, K. 2013 *Born Free and Equal: A Philosophical Analysis of Discrimination*. Oxford: Oxford University Press.

Machery, E. 2016. "De-Freuding Implicit Attitudes." In Brownstein, M. and Saul, J. (eds) *Implicit Bias and Philosophy, Volume 1: Metaphysics and Epistemology*. Oxford: Oxford University Press.

Mallon, R. 2016. "Stereotype Threat and Persons." In Brownstein, M. and Saul, J. (eds) *Implicit Bias and Philosophy, Volume 1: Metaphysics and Epistemology*. Oxford: Oxford University Press. 131–154.

Mandelbaum, E. 2015. "Attitude Inference and Association: On the Propositional Structure of Implicit Bias." *Noûs*. 50(3): 629–658.

Oswald, F. L., Mitchel, G., Blanton, H., Jaccard, J. and Tetlock, P. E. 2013. "Predicting Ethnic and Racial Discrimination: A Meta-analysis of IAT Criterion Studies." *Journal of Personality and Social Psychology*. 105(2): 171–192.

Rosenberg, S. W. and Wolfsfeld, G. 1977. "International Conflict and the Problem of Attribution." *Journal of Conflict Resolution*. 21: 75–103.

Shih, M., Pittinsky, T. L., *et al.* 1999. "Stereotype Susceptibility: Identity Salience and Shifts in Quantitative Performance." *Psychological Science*. 10: 80–83.

Steele, C. 2010. *Whistling Vivaldi: And Other Clues to how Stereotypes Affect Us*. New York, NY: W. W. Norton and Company.

Steele, C. M. 1997. "A Threat in the Air: How Stereotypes Shape Intellectual Identity and Performance. "*American Psychologist*. 52: 613–629.

Steele, C. M., and Aronson, J. 1995. "Stereotype Threat and the Intellectual Test Performance of African Americans." *Journal of Personality and Social Psychology*. 69: 797–811.

Stephan, W. G. 1977. "Stereotyping: The Role of Ingroup-Outgroup Differences in Causal Attribution of Behavior." *Journal of Social Psychology*. 101: 255–266.

Tajfel, H. and Turner, J. C. 1979. "An Integrative Theory of Intergroup Conflict." In Austin, W. G. and Worchel, S. (eds). *The Social Psychology of Intergroup Relations*. Monterey, CA: Brooks/Cole.

Taylor, D. M. and Jaggi, V. 1974. "Ethnocentrism and Causal Attribution in a South Indian Context." *Journal of Cross-Cultural Psychology*. 5: 162–171.

Valian, V. 1999. *Why So Slow? The Advancement of Women*. Cambridge, MA: MIT Press.

Williams, B. 1981. *Moral Luck*. Cambridge: Cambridge University Press.

Winkler, J. D. and Taylor, S. E. 1979. "Preference, Expectations, and Attributional Bias: Two Field Studies." *Journal of Applied Social Psychology*. 9: 183–197.

33
DISCRIMINATION AND AFFIRMATIVE ACTION

Julie Suk

YESHIVA UNIVERSITY

Introduction

It may seem obvious that a discussion of affirmative action belongs in a book about the ethics of discrimination. But there are at least two quite different understandings of the relationship of affirmative action to the idea of discrimination. On one view, affirmative action has been called "positive discrimination," "affirmative discrimination," and "reverse discrimination," revealing the baseline understanding that affirmative action is a form of discrimination, and shares with discrimination some significant feature that has moral salience. On another view, affirmative action is in the DNA of the norm *against* discrimination. On the latter conception, affirmative action shares with the concept of *non*-discrimination a significant feature that has moral salience. This chapter lays out these two conceptions and explores how the law of many legal orders treats affirmative action as discrimination, which may or may not be justified. This chapter challenges this conceptual framework, and argues that it fundamentally misapprehends the essential features of discrimination.

Affirmative action has been attacked on the grounds that it violates meritocratic norms, that it stigmatizes its beneficiaries, and that it causes social division. In legal conflicts about the validity of specific affirmative action policies, these arguments tend to gain moral ground through the rhetorical framing of affirmative action as a form of discrimination. Today, many legal orders around the world begin with the premise that affirmative action is a form of discrimination. Some proceed to conclude that affirmative action is *wrongful* discrimination, and therefore impermissible, but others permit some forms of affirmative action as *justified* discrimination. Neither conclusion challenges the notion that affirmative action is *discrimination*, that it shares some morally significant features in common with the paradigmatic forms of discrimination that are more obviously morally wrongful, and which antidiscrimination law was adopted to condemn. For instance, a policy of excluding blacks because they are black from admission to law school at a public university[1] is easily understood as morally wrongful discrimination. Indeed, the prevalence of similar policies of racial exclusion and segregation across the United States led to the adoption of legislation and judicial decisions prohibiting discrimination.

Categorizing an act or policy as discrimination does not necessarily make it legally or morally invalid (cf. Introduction). But it does cast a cloud of illegitimacy over that act or policy, and in the absence of a countervailing justification, anything that can be described as "discrimination" is invalid. Judges then determine whether the justifications for these policies are sufficiently compelling to outweigh the presumption of wrongfulness in any act or policy initially described as race discrimination. This legal approach to affirmative action is thus structurally similar to the way we might conceptualize the relationship between killing in self-defense and murder. Both acts end the life of a human being, and the former may be justified while the latter is clearly not justified. When we say that affirmative action is justified discrimination, we assume that affirmative action does something similar to the paradigmatic act of racial discrimination, that it creates a similar moral problem or harm which has to be justified, and in the absence of justification, affirmative action is the moral equivalent of racial exclusion. On this view, the difference between affirmative action and racial exclusion is that affirmative action might have morally compelling justifications, whereas racial exclusion simply does not. This chapter unpacks and ultimately rejects the description of affirmative action as discrimination, because it misleadingly borrows normative weight from a cosmetic similarity. The taking of a human life is a necessary common feature of killing in self-defense and murder, and whether justified or not, the human life that has been taken carries some moral weight in the equation. But I shall argue that affirmative action and paradigmatic discrimination do not share an analogous common moral feature; they do not both involve the diminishment of something of moral value. In many judicial opinions and some philosophical accounts, discrimination is defined as unequal treatment that fails to treat individuals as individuals capable of exercising freedom. This chapter shall argue that the imperative to treat individuals as individuals is inadequate to explain what's morally wrong with the paradigmatic form of discrimination, i.e., the exclusion of African Americans through segregated public institutions. Dissecting the paradigmatic form of discrimination helps isolate discrimination's essential features, which are missing from affirmative action.

The dominant legal approach: affirmative action as discrimination

The U.S. Supreme Court struck down a race-based affirmative action program for the first time in the 1978 Bakke case,[2] with Justice Powell's concurring opinion articulating the moral reasoning that shaped the twenty-first century law of affirmative action in the United States[3] and influenced other legal orders.[4] The Bakke decision treated a racial quota in a public university as discrimination against a white applicant, which was presumed to be morally wrong unless it could be justified by a compelling state interest. The racial quota was struck down, but the court left open the possibility of justifying racial preferences properly designed to achieve the compelling state interest in diversity in the competitive selection of university students. The Supreme Court reaffirmed this approach to strictly scrutinize affirmative action as discrimination, even while upholding racial preferences, most recently in *Fisher v. Texas*.[5]

In *Fisher v. Texas*, a white applicant who was not admitted to the university argued that a policy of treating membership in a disadvantaged race as a plus factor in admissions constitutes racial discrimination and thus violates the U.S. Constitution's guarantee of equal protection. The affirmative action policy was deemed constitutionally valid, *even though it discriminated* against white applicants, because the university had a compelling interest in admitting a student body that was diverse, and the university did so without imposing racial quotas or making race the determinative factor (cf. Chapter 34). The Court noted that "racial characteristics so seldom provide a relevant basis for disparate treatment," and that "any official action that treats a person differently on account of his race or ethnic origin is inherently suspect" (Fisher 2016, at 2208, citing Fisher 2013, at 2418). Discrimination is implicitly defined as different treatment of different races, which carries a presumption of moral wrong. That presumption can be overcome, but not easily. The justification must be "compelling," and diversity of the student body has been recognized as a compelling interest, whereas remedying past societal discrimination has not. Furthermore, even when the policymaker's interest in diversity is compelling, there are some means that can never be employed. For instance, the Court has rejected quotas; diversity cannot be defined as a specified percentage of a racial group. Nonetheless, the U.S. Supreme Court ultimately validated a policy in which a racial preference was used in the context of a highly individualized assessment of each applicant, in which race was one of many factors considered to determine what the individual would contribute to diversity at an elite public university.

This legal approach, developed by the U.S. Supreme Court over the last forty years, subjects affirmative action to the same moral scrutiny to which one would subject a policy of excluding African Americans from university.[6] According to this conceptual framework, both policies classify and treat people differently on the basis of race, and should thus be presumed to be morally wrong unless a countervailing justification can be given. A well-designed pursuit of diversity can overcome the morally wrongful discrimination in the case of affirmative action, whereas no moral value can justify the morally wrongful discrimination in the case of black exclusion.

The general approach of treating affirmative action as discrimination subject to a high standard of justification is not exceptional to the United States. Consider, for example, the legal struggle over legislative efforts to advance women in politics, civil service employment, and corporate boards in Europe. The Court of Justice of the European Union (CJEU) has interpreted the Equal Treatment Directive to prohibit gender quotas[7] but to permit some flexible preferences for women in employment.[8] Article 2(1) of the directive prohibits discrimination: "For the purposes of the following provisions, the principle of equal treatment shall mean that there shall be no discrimination whatsoever on grounds of sex …"[9] The Court of Justice held in 1995 that giving a preference to female candidates for civil service jobs in which women were under-represented "involves discrimination" (Kalanke para. 16). Once discrimination is "involved," the next question is whether the policy, "although discriminatory in appearance," comes within the legal exception written into the text of the directive at Article 2(4): "This Directive shall be without prejudice to measures to promote equal opportunity for men and women, in particular by removing existing inequalities which affect women's opportunities." One way of reading the language of Article 2(4) would be to conclude that affirmative action policies to remove women's inequalities can never constitute sex discrimination prohibited by Article 2(1). One might say that affirmative action is good policy or bad policy, but not discrimination and therefore not a problem under Article 2(1). But the Court of Justice has invalidated some affirmative action policies that were intended to remove existing women's inequalities, by applying a proportionality analysis that bears some resemblance to heightened scrutiny in the United States. Because sex classifications "involve discrimination," the Court has required affirmative action for women to be not only intended to remove women's inequalities, as stated in Article 2(4), but also proportionately designed to mitigate the impact on the man who is not selected. This impact is presumed to be a form of discrimination that bears a moral resemblance to the more obviously wrong forms of sex discrimination, such as the historic exclusion of women from the civil service.

Without changing this framework, the European Court upheld sex-based affirmative action programs in two subsequent decisions. In those decisions, men who had been denied promotions attempted to invalidate German civil service promotion schemes that gave preferences to female candidates because women were the underrepresented sex in that job category. In both of those cases, the court acknowledged that the women's advancement plans were "discriminatory in appearance" against men (Badeck 2000: para. 19), but could be justified because they were proportionate and narrowly designed. Specifically, the affirmative action programs that were upheld by the European Court were not rigid quotas giving automatic preferences to equally qualified women, but preferences that left room for the male candidate to show that his special individual circumstances "tilted the balance" in his favor. This analysis is consistent with the following set of moral assumptions. When a race- or sex-based preference is utilized, every individual subject to it is discriminated against, and this raises a moral problem that must be overcome by a morally compelling justification. Note that, even under European law, which textually authorizes affirmative action, many affirmative action programs have been invalidated on the grounds that they were designed in a manner that was insufficiently respectful of the individual right to non-discrimination.

Treating people as individuals

In the prevailing affirmative action jurisprudence across many legal orders, it is assumed that both affirmative action and the paradigm case of discrimination entail the denial of a freedom-enhancing opportunity to the individual who is not admitted because of the policy. Classifying a person by race is presumptively contrary to understanding a person as autonomous and free. This rhetoric dominates the cases that have invalidated quotas and affirmative action programs, and it is frequently deployed to explain why the state must carry the heavy burden of justification for any race-conscious affirmative action policy. The idea is that "[d]istinctions between citizens solely because of their ancestry are by their very nature odious to a free people whose institutions are founded upon the doctrine of equality." These words appear in numerous U.S. Supreme Court opinions on affirmative action.

What makes racial distinctions "by their very nature odious to a free people"? Recent commentators in the philosophical literature about discrimination have defended the view that discrimination is wrong because it violates the individual's entitlement to freedom. Sophia Moreau, for instance, takes the view that an individual is entitled to make decisions about how to live, and when that "deliberative freedom" is impeded by the operation of normatively extraneous traits, that individual has been morally wronged (Moreau 2010; Chapter 13). Benjamin Eidelson argues that discrimination law protects an individual's moral entitlement to be treated as an individual. On Eidelson's account, being treated as an individual does not only mean being subjected to a decision making process that is procedurally fair and sufficiently sensitive to qualities that are relevant to the judgment being made. When a person is subject to morally wrongful discrimination,

> in focusing on particular socially salient traits to the exclusion of others, the decision-maker has failed to take appropriate account of the life a person has chosen for herself; maligned her capacity to continue to make such choices through an exercise of reflective choice, and thereby demeaned her standing as an autonomous individual.
>
> *(Eidelson 2014: 205)*

Tarunabh Khaitan argues that the point of discrimination law is to protect individuals' secured access to negative liberty, an adequate range of valuable opportunities, and self-respect (Khaitan 2015: 126; cf. Chapter 2). While troubled by U.S. courts' implied moral equivalence between affirmative action and malicious or intentional direct discrimination, Khaitan characterizes affirmative action as "technically" "collateral discrimination," which could be wrong if it lacks adequate justification (Khaitan 2015: 221).

And, while these individual freedom-based philosophical accounts of what makes discrimination wrong are not directly addressing affirmative action, courts have embraced the idea of treating individuals as individuals to justify the rejection of affirmative action programs in strong moral terms. In Bakke, for instance, the U.S. Supreme Court objected to setting aside 16 out of 100 spots for admission to a prestigious medical school for racial minorities, because it tells "other individuals" that they are "totally foreclosed from competition for the 16 admissions seats."[10] In J.A. *Croson v. Richmond*, the Court described a set-aside of 30 percent of public subcontracts to minority business owners as a violation of white business owners' "'personal rights' to be treated with equal dignity and respect."[11] (Croson 1989: 319). In *Gratz v. Bollinger*, the Supreme Court invalidated the University of Michigan's undergraduate admissions policy of awarding extra points in a competitive admission process to candidates belonging to underrepresented minorities on the grounds that university admissions should consider "each particular applicant as an individual, assessing all of the qualities that the individual possesses."[12]

Affirmative action as non-discrimination

Although many legal orders treat affirmative action as discrimination that must be justified if it is to survive, this approach departs from an older account of affirmative action's relationship to discrimination. Arguably, Article 2(4) of the EU Equal Treatment Directive authorizes affirmative action, not as an *exception* to the norm of non-discrimination as the CJEU suggests in passing, but as a *necessary feature* of the non-discrimination norm. On this view, the moral duty not to discriminate on grounds of sex is simply one subsidiary duty stemming from a broader moral imperative to eradicate inegalitarian social relations between men and women. These inegalitaran social relations, derived from women's historic exclusion from political and economic power, undermine the legitimacy of public institutions of governance and economic life. The duty to maintain legitimate public institutions might at times require increasing the proportion of the underrepresented sex in major political, economic, and social institutions. In this vein, Kasper Lippert-Rasmussen focuses on "the motivational idea that proportional representation is a way of nullifying the repressive effects of discrimination on underrepresented groups" (Lippert-Rasmussen 2013: 194). Tarunabh Khaitan includes affirmative action in enumerating the "complex list of tools" of antidiscrimination law, along with direct and indirect discrimination, harassment, reasonable adjustments, and positive duties (Khaitan 2015: 23). Although neither Lippert-Rasmussen nor Khaitan defend the idea that affirmative action is an essential feature of non-discrimination, they both assume that this view has a significant following. Khaitan observes that "the practitioners – lawyers, judges, litigants, legislators – all assume that there is an essential connection between affirmative action and discrimination … Insofar as the practice is concerned, discrimination and affirmative action seem to be inseparable" (Khaitan 2015: 81).

As an historical matter, the policy of giving preferences to African Americans for jobs originated as an extension of antidiscrimination law. President Kennedy issued Executive Order 10925 in 1961 to prohibit race discrimination in employment by companies contracting with the federal government. The executive order commanded, "The contractor will not discriminate against any employee or applicant for employment because of race, creed, color, or national origin. The contractor will take affirmative action to ensure that applicants are employed, and that employees are treated during employment without regard to their race, creed, color or national origin." The term "affirmative action" did not necessarily refer to racial preferences in this context; the order was using the term to refer to aggressive efforts to avoid excluding qualified black employees or applicants for employment because of their race.

By 1965, a year following the passage of the Civil Rights Act, President Johnson issued another executive order (No. 11246) calling for "affirmative action" by federal contractors, authorizing the Secretary of Labor to investigate the employment practices of government contractors and subcontractors for discrimination. In a commencement address shortly before the issuance of the executive order, President Johnson famously declared the "revolution of the American Negro" as involving "not just legal equity but human ability, not just equality as a right and a theory but equality as a fact and equality as a result." In that speech, he used the word "discrimination" twice; once to refer to the racial segregation in education struck down by the *Supreme Court in Brown v. Board of Education*, and then to explain why the African American family was so weak – due to "centuries of oppression and persecution of the Negro man;" "the long years of degradation and discrimination, which have attacked his dignity and assaulted his ability to produce for his family." Thus, when affirmative action was first conceptualized, the concept of "discrimination" was conceptually adjacent to oppression, persecution, attacks on dignity and economic agency. Affirmative action was thus introduced as a logical extension of antidiscrimination policy. If there is a duty, not only to refrain from morally wrongful discrimination, but also to take steps to prevent, eliminate, or nullify the effects of morally wrongful discrimination, affirmative action simply refers to the steps necessary to fulfill that duty. "Affirmative action" thus referred initially to aggressive efforts to prevent the oppression of blacks. In 1967, these aggressive efforts included quotas and goals imposed on federal contractors for the hiring of African Americans in the Philadelphia Plan. The Philadelphia Plan set concrete goals for the hiring of minorities in an effort to integrate building and construction trades unions in the industrial North and West. These trades unions controlled large-scale projects contracted by the federal government, and membership in these unions was largely passed down through generations of white fathers, sons, uncles, and nephews (Golland 2011).

What makes discrimination discriminatory?

The imperative to treat people as individuals can explain what's wrong with discrimination in the paradigmatic case, but it does not adequately capture the full moral magnitude of the historic wrong of excluding African Americans from good schools, universities, good jobs, and the suffrage. It is plain that such policies focused on a socially salient trait – dark skin – to the exclusion of other more relevant traits – academic potential, talent, wisdom – such that the individual's capacity for making decisions about how to live was insufficiently recognized. Furthermore, it is also apparent that these policies deprived African Americans of meaningful opportunities, based on the socially salient characteristic, and failed to appreciate their capacities as individual human beings to choose how to live. Under this account of what makes discrimination wrong, a white candidate whose individual efforts and traits are disregarded when he is rejected under an affirmative action program sustains the same moral wrong as the black candidate who is excluded on the basis of race. The failure to recognize individuals as individuals is the problem one would come up with if one were required to identify a common thread between affirmative action and paradigmatic discrimination. But that's all it is – an insignificant thread – in a thick fabric of a deeply problematic moral practice.

Discrimination fails to respect each individual's capacity for freedom, but as an historic matter, the actual forms of race and sex discrimination enacted other, more serious moral wrongs. A policy of excluding African Americans from good schools, including elite public universities, concentrated privilege and the public power that emanates from higher education in the hands of a few. This created and sustained political and economic institutions that did not serve the public interest. Joseph Fishkin has characterized entrenched power as a "bottleneck" that is problematic because it diminishes individuals' opportunities to flourish (Fishkin 2014). In addition to inhibiting individual opportunities, a political system in which only a fraction of the population has access to the education that would enable it to exercise governing power is undemocratic. An economic system in which wealth is concentrated in the hands of a few, and sustained through inherited wealth, is oligarchic. Discrimination is a twentieth-century concept that describes a set of social practices, namely distinguishing between people along racial lines, by which it was determined who would be excluded from public power. These practices were morally wrong because they sustained a corrupt political and economic system based on undeserved, entrenched privilege. What made discrimination wrong was not merely its failure to treat individuals as individuals, but its creation of oligarchic political, economic, and social institutions.

In *Democracy and Distrust*, John Hart Ely observed that the unequal treatment of individuals by the state, in itself, could not be wrong, because all legislation necessarily classifies, generalizes, and treats various circumstances differently. At the same time, some of these classifications – including, in many instances, race – are morally repugnant. For Ely, a policy of excluding African Americans from higher education would be contrary to Equal Protection not merely because there was race-based unequal treatment, but because this race-based unequal treatment was part of a larger political malfunction blocking the possibility of a legitimate representative democracy:

> When the (1) ins are choking off the channels of political change to ensure that they will stay in and the outs will stay out, or (2) though no one is actually denied a voice or a vote, representatives beholden to an effective majority are systematically disadvantaging some minority out of simple hostility or a prejudiced refusal to recognize commonalities of interest, and thereby denying that minority of the protection afforded other groups by a representative system.
>
> *(Ely 1980: 103)*

The U.S. Supreme Court has, on occasion, embraced this political process theory of constitutional antidiscrimination norms. In *Hunter v. Erickson*, it found that a city had discriminated by enacting a charter provision that prohibited the city council from adopting any ordinances dealing with racial, religious, or ancestral discrimination, unless a majority of the voters of the city approved by referendum. The city argued that this new city charter amendment was not discrimination in violation of Equal Protection because the law did not distinguish between persons on the basis of race, but rather, removed a certain subject (housing discrimination) from the city council's legislative domain and placed that subject under the majoritarian democratic control of the voters.[13] In the absence of unequal treatment of persons as individuals on grounds of race, how could this law register as wrongful discrimination?

The answer was that the city charter amendment significantly burdened racial minorities' ability to participate in democratic self-government. "The majority needs no protection against discrimination and if it did, a referendum might be bothersome but no more than that," the Court noted. Even though "the law on its face treats Negro and white, Jew and gentile in an identical manner," the Court nonetheless applied strict scrutiny "[b]ecause the core of the Fourteenth Amendment is the *prevention* of *meaningful and unjustified* official distinctions based on race" (emphasis added) (*Hunter v. Erickson: 391*). Even when there was no racial distinction in the statute, and no formal unequal treatment, the Court referred to the city charter amendment as a "discrimination" requiring justification under strict scrutiny. Thus, the "discrimination" that carries with it a presumption of wrongfulness that must be justified is not defined as unequal treatment of individuals based on race. Rather, discrimination is defined as an act that distorts the political process to effectively diminish the minority's voice. The distortion goes beyond the ordinary imbalance of political power that comes from being a minority. The city's act imposed additional burdens on the minority by requiring a referendum to adopt policies likely to be in the minority's interest. These additional burdens created an illegitimate blockage in the political process, an institutional mechanism by which the incumbent majority could shield its power and privilege from challenge.

Similarly, over a decade later, the U.S. Supreme Court understood the judicially enforced antidiscrimination norm in constitutional Equal Protection as "safeguarding the interests of those groups that are 'relegated to such a position of political powerlessness as to command extraordinary protection from the majoritarian political process.'"[14] A presumption of morally wrongful discrimination could then be made even without formally unequal treatment of members of different races, and without evidence of hostility towards any racial group. The presumption of morally wrongful discrimination arises when governmental power is assigned in such a way as to exclude particular racial groups from effective participation in the political process. In that case, the Court invalidated a legislative enactment that terminated a Seattle school board's policy of mandatory busing to desegregate its schools. The Court understood the desegregation program as a policy that "at bottom inures primarily to the benefit of the minority" (*Washington v. Seattle*: 472). When a legislative referendum repealed the school board's integration policy, it discriminated in violation of Equal Protection in two ways. First, it singled out a racial issue for special treatment; it allowed the school board to use mandatory busing for reasons other than racial integration (such as special education). But second, and more importantly, the legislative attack restructured the political process in a way that made it impossible for minorities to participate in self-government. Racial minorities, even if they convinced their local school boards to integrate by busing, were legislatively overridden. Again, this enabled the majority to shield its power and privilege by requiring monumental political efforts to integrate schools.

In these cases, the U.S. Supreme Court established that restructuring the political process to the disadvantage of a racial minority could be a sufficient condition to trigger a presumption of wrongful discrimination subject to heightened scrutiny and thorough justification. A background assumption against which the Court was reasoning was that the race-based different treatment of an individual was a necessary condition for heightened scrutiny. The Court suggested in these cases that heightened Equal Protection scrutiny could be applied even if there was no race-based unequal treatment of an individual. This move did not directly attack the assumption that race-based unequal treatment of an individual would be sufficient, even if not necessary, to trigger heightened scrutiny. And indeed, in recent years, the U.S. Supreme Court has declined to strike down a state constitutional ban of affirmative action based on the reasoning of these earlier political process cases.[15]

At the same time, other countries have demonstrated more openness to the political process approach, at least when it comes to sex discrimination. In France, for instance, Article 1 of the Constitution pronounces that the law shall promote equal access by women and men to the electoral mandate and positions of social and professional responsibility.[16] This amendment makes it impossible to regard gender quotas as wrongful discrimination violative of the equality guaranteed in Article 6 of the Declaration of the Rights of Man.[17] Under a political process approach to wrongful discrimination, distinguishing by sex or race is not wrong when or because it fails to treat individuals as individuals. The institutional use of these classifications is wrong only when it distorts the political process. The distortion entrenches the power of the incumbent group and compounds the difficulty encountered by a disempowered group in governing to protect its interests, or those of the public. This distortion of the institutions necessary to sustain a legitimate, well-functioning democracy is the core moral wrong of discrimination (cf. Chapter 29). These institutions include the governance organs of the state, but also include schools, universities, and the economic institutions that exert enough power to govern, in effect, social life and human civilization.

What happens when we regard the distortion of important public institutions as an essential feature of discrimination? The relationship of affirmative action to discrimination looks very different from the way courts have construed it over the past generation. Giving a preference, or even reserving positions for blacks in university admissions would not register as discrimination at all. These racial quotas would be regarded as different in kind from the covert racial quotas and other strategies utilized by elite American universities in the early and mid-twentieth century to limit the enrollment numbers of Jews.

A distinctive feature of university admissions in the United States, by contrast with the systems in place in many other advanced democracies, is that American universities use highly individualized processes to select their students. They do not base admissions on academic qualifications alone. They have complex admissions regimes that evaluate students' personal and moral characteristics, as demonstrated by extracurricular activities, personal essays, and face-to-face interviews. There is no admissions system in the world that is as deeply concerned with treating each individual as an individual and with fully recognizing each person's choices in authoring one's life. If we regard the wrong of discrimination as the failure to treat individuals as individuals, it would make sense to say that an admissions regime is less discriminatory if it is more individualized. Based on this understanding of what discrimination is, this individualized admissions regime is less discriminatory than a system that selects students based on a lottery that was completely indifferent to individual characteristics (including race) among students who met the minimum academic qualifications as determined by high school grades or an entrance exam.

As an historical matter, elite American universities' highly individualized admissions systems were created as a deliberate mechanism to limit the number of Jewish students and to preserve the white, Protestant majority in these institutions and in the institutions' pipeline to the political and economic leadership of the nation (Karabel 2005). At the beginning of the twentieth century, Harvard and other similar universities in the United States based admission on academic criteria, requiring applicants to pass exams in several academic subjects. Under this system, the proportion of Jewish students grew over time. Although a formal quota officially limiting the number of Jews was rejected, Harvard University adopted a new admissions regime in 1926 that would require interviews, photos, and an assessment of character and fitness. Similarly, Columbia University was the first university in the United States (and perhaps in the world) to create an Office of Admissions in 1910 in direct response to the "Jewish Problem" of the high number of Jews admitted through competitive academic exams. The Office of Admissions rejected scholastically brilliant boys if they did not sufficiently display the qualities of character and leadership, and it permitted the admission of academically weak candidates of good background and character (Karabel 2005: 131). This highly individualized – and highly subjective – admissions system had the purpose and effect of entrenching Protestants' access to education and positions of wealth, leadership, and power in American life. One might view this regime as "affirmative action for white Protestants." Whatever we call it, it is obviously discrimination that is morally wrong.

Today, a university admissions regime that treats individuals as individuals risks entrenching the power and privilege of the wealthy. There is an ever-widening gap between poor and affluent children's extracurricular activities and enriching life experiences.[18] By contrast, imagine an admissions process that refuses to take into account the applicants' individual characteristics and self-authorship choices, but rather, relies on a random lottery among all minimally qualified students. This regime refuses to recognize each person's individualized efforts at excellence and self-definition; yet it seems more likely to distribute higher education opportunities to those who lack wealth, privilege, and family connections.

Which system of opportunity distribution is closer to the ideal of non-discrimination? If our intuitions gravitate towards the random lottery, the concept of discrimination cannot primarily be about the norm of treating individuals as individuals. On the contrary, the highly-individualized admissions regime is what can coherently be described as *discriminatory* if it prevents a disfavored group from entering into the pipeline to political and economic power. That tells us something about the core of the discrimination concept. What makes discrimination discriminatory is the entrenchment of incumbent power by a privileged group.

When the moral wrong of discrimination is understood in this way, there is no morally significant conceptual similarity between the early twentieth-century anti-Semitic quotas (formal or informal) that intended to limit the proportion of Jews at elite American universities to preserve white Anglo-Saxon privilege, and the late-twentieth-century quotas that had the effect of limiting the proportion of whites in order to make seats available to disadvantaged minorities. The similarity between anti-Semitic quotas of the early twentieth century and racial quotas for disadvantaged groups of the late twentieth century is cosmetic, not moral. There is a morally significant difference, however: the beneficiaries of the Jewish quotas were the incumbently privileged Protestants, who had the power to enact the quotas for their own benefit. By contrast, the very purpose of twentieth-century racial quotas and affirmative action programs is to bring underrepresented groups into a powerful institution. Twenty-first century gender and race quotas have the intention and effect of opening up rather than blocking the pathways to the exercise of economic and political power.

At the same time, not all affirmative action policies and quotas intending to democratize power are fair. Fairness may require that the costs of nullifying the wrongs of racial discrimination should be spread broadly across the economy or political community, rather than being imposed on a few individuals (Fallon and Weiler 1984). The unfairness of affirmative action, however, is morally and conceptually distinct from the wrong of discrimination. Unfortunately, legal actors challenging affirmative action policies have squeezed into the concept of discrimination all the problems of unfairness of varying degrees, and even the problems of poor policy design and inefficiency, associated with affirmative action. This creates the mistaken and morally dangerous impression that the reasons for rejecting an affirmative action policy carry the same moral force as the struggle against racial exclusion.

Consider, for example, the situation at issue in two cases that invalidated affirmative action programs in the United States. In *Firefighters v. Stotts*[19] and *Wygant v. Jackson Board of Education*,[20] the government sought to maintain the proportion of racial minorities in public jobs – firefighting and teaching – to nullify the consequences of excluding African Americans in the past. To maintain a diverse workforce, they adopted a policy of laying off white employees who had more seniority than some of the minority employees who were retained. The white employees who were laid off claimed that they were subject to morally wrongful discrimination. In these cases, it is easy to understand why these employees experienced the layoff as unfair. They had relied on an expectation that seniority would give them priority in the event of layoffs. That expectation had a long tradition. But nullifying the effects of past societal discrimination required the unsettling of these expectations. This meant that a few individuals would bear a disproportionate burden in the society's efforts to make public employment legitimate and just. Arguably, the burdens should be absorbed by the state or distributed evenly, which could have been done if the seniority of all workers had been eradicated, even that of the most senior white workers who had been retained. If a random lottery had been used, for instance, the racial proportions would likely have been retained without causing this sense of unfairness. Nonetheless, when the state imposes a disproportionate and undeserved burden on an individual to carry out a legitimate public purpose, the unfair treatment of the individual presents a moral problem. But that problem is not properly understood as discrimination. The unfairness of affirmative action in the layoff scenario is more similar to that occasioned by takings. The U.S. Constitution, and public law in many other countries, authorizes the compensation of individuals subject to the taking of their property for public use in certain circumstances. The unfairness of affirmative action should be understood as morally analogous to takings, not to discrimination.

Conclusion

One may be left wondering why it matters whether we begin with the premise that affirmative action is discrimination, when courts around the world have recognized the possibility of justifying affirmative action nonetheless. I shall conclude by highlighting a line from the sitting Chief Justice of the U.S. Supreme Court. In explaining his view that the constitution required the rejection of a public school integration plan that took students' race into account, he wrote, "The way to stop discrimination on the basis of race is to stop discriminating on the basis of race."[21] He deploys the moral outrage against racial segregation to stop the very policies that could mitigate this moral wrong. This rhetorical move is made possible by taking the cosmetic similarity between a race-conscious integration and a race-conscious segregation and turning it into a moral similarity. But a better way to stop discrimination on the basis of race is to attempt to achieve genuine clarity about the core features of discrimination and what makes discrimination wrong.

Notes

1 See, e.g., *Sweatt v. Painter*, 339 U.S. 629 (1950), in which the U.S. Supreme Court invalidated the University of Texas's policy of excluding African Americans from its law school.

2 See *Regents of the Univ. of California v. Bakke*, 438 U.S. 265 (1978).

3 Justice Powell's concurring opinion was embraced by a majority of the U.S. Supreme Court a quarter of a century later, in *Grutter v. Bollinger*, 539 U.S. 306 (2003).

4 Brazil's highest court, the Supremo Tribunal Federal, discussed Bakke and Grutter at length in its landmark 2012 decision upholding race-based affirmative action. See S.T.F., A.D.P.F. No. 186, Orgão Julgador: Tribunal Pleno, Relator: Ricardo Lewandowski, 26.04.2012, 205, D.J.e., 17.10.2014, 1, http://www.stf.jus.br.

5 *Fisher v. University of Texas at Austin*, Slip Op., June 23, 2016; see also *Fisher v. University of Texas at Austin*, 570 U.S. __ (2013) ("Fisher I").

6 The rule of applying the same strict scrutiny was explicitly embraced by a majority of the *Court in Adarand Constructors v. Peña*, 515 U.S. 200 (1995) and reaffirmed in the context of analyzing affirmative action in university admissions in Fisher I, *ibid*.

7 See Case C-450/93, *Kalanke v. Freie Hansestadt Bremen*, E.C.R. I-03051 (1995).

8 See Case C-409/95, *Marschall v. Land Nordrhein-Westfalen*, E.C.R. I-06363 (1997); Case C-158-97, *Badeck v. Hessicher Ministerpräsident*, E.C.R. I-1902 (2000).

9 Council Directive 76/207/EEC of 9 February 1976 on the implementation of the principle of equal treatment for men and women as regards access to employment, vocational training and promotion, and working conditions.

10 Bakke, n. 2, p. 319.

11 *J.A. Croson v. Richmond*, 488 U.S. 469, 493 (1989).

12 *Gratz v. Bollinger*, 539 U.S. 244, 271 (2003).

13 See *Hunter v. Erickson*, 393 U.S. 385 (1969)

14 *Washington v. Seattle School District No. 1*, 458 U.S. 457, 486 (1982) (quoting *San Antonio v. Rodriguez*).

15 *Schuette v. BAMN*, 134 U.S. 1623 (2014).

16 French Constitution, art. 1.
17 See, e.g., Conseil Constitutionnel, Décision no. 2015-465 QPC du 24 avril 2015.
18 See Kaisa Snellman, Jennifer M. Silva, Carl B. Frederick, and Robert D. Putnam, The Engagement Gap: Social Mobility and Extracurricular Participation Among American Youth, 657 Annals of the American Academy of Political and Social Science 197 (2015).
19 *Firefighters v. Stotts*, 467 U.S. 559 (1984).
20 *Wygant v. Jackson Board of Education*, 476 U.S. 267 (1986).
21 *Parents Involved in Community Schools v. Seattle School District No. 1*, 551 U.S. 701, 748.

Bibliography

Legal Materials

Sweatt v. Painter, 339 U.S. 629 (1950).
Regents of the Univ. of California v. Bakke, 438 U.S. 265 (1978).
Grutter v. Bollinger, 539 U.S. 306 (2003).
S.T.F., A.D.P.F. No. 186, Orgão Julgador: Tribunal Pleno, Relator: Ricardo Lewandowski, 26.04.2012, 205, D.J.e., 17.10.2014, 1, http://www.stf.jus.br.
Fisher v. University of Texas at Austin, 136 S.Ct. 2198 (2016) ("Fisher 2016").
Fisher v. University of Texas at Austin, 133 S.Ct. 2411 (2013) ("Fisher 2013").
Adarand Constructors v. Peña, 515 U.S. 200 (1995).
Case C-450/93, *Kalanke v. Freie Hansestadt Bremen*, E.C.R. I-03051 (1995).
Case C-409/95, *Marschall v. Land Nordrhein-Westfalen*, E.C.R. I-06363 (1997).
Case C-158-97, *Badeck v. Hessicher Ministerpräsident*, E.C.R. I-1902 (2000).
Council Directive 76/207/EEC of 9 February 1976 on the implementation of the principle of equal treatment for men and women as regards access to employment, vocational training and promotion, and working conditions.
J.A. Croson v. Richmond, 488 U.S. 469, 493 (1989).
Gratz v. Bollinger, 539 U.S. 244, 271 (2003).
Hunter v. Erickson, 393 U.S. 385 (1969).
Washington v. Seattle School District No. 1, 458 U.S. 457, 486 (1982).
French Constitution.
U.S. Constitution.
Conseil Constitutionnel, Décision no. 2015-465 QPC du 24 avril 2015.
Firefighters v. Stotts, 467 U.S. 559 (1984).
Wygant v. Jackson Board of Education, 476 U.S. 267 (1986).

Other

Eidelson, B. 2014. "Treating People as Individuals." In D. Hellman and S. Moreau (eds) *Philosophical Foundations of Discrimination Law*. Oxford: Oxford University Press. 203–227.
Ely, J. H. 1980. *Democracy and Distrust*. Cambridge MA: Harvard University Press.
Fallon, R. H., Jr. and Weiler, P. C. 1984. "Firefighters v. Stotts: *Conflicting Models of Racial Justice*." *The Supreme Court Review* 1984: 1–68.
Fishkin, J. 2014. *Bottlenecks: A New Theory of Equal Opportunity*. Oxford: Oxford University Press.
Golland, D. H. 2011. *Constructing Affirmative Action: The Struggle for Equal Employment Opportunity*. Lexington: The University Press of Kentucky.
Hellman, D. 2008. *When is Discrimination Wrong?* Cambridge MA: Harvard University Press.
Hellman, D. and Moreau, S. 2014. *Philosophical Foundations of Discrimination Law*. Oxford: Oxford University Press.
Karabel, J. 2005. *The Chosen: The Hidden History of Admission and Exclusion at Harvard, Yale, and Princeton*. Boston: Houghton Mifflin.

Kennedy, R. 2013. *For Discrimination: Race, Affirmative Action, and the Law*. New York: Pantheon Books.
Khaitan, T. 2014. *A Theory of Discrimination Law*. Oxford: Oxford University Press.
Lippert-Rasmussen, K. 2014. *Born Free and Equal? A Philosophical Inquiry into the Nature of Discrimination*. Oxford: Oxford University Press.
Moreau, S. 2010. *What Is Discrimination?* 38 Philosophy & Public Affairs 143.
Snellman, K., Silva, J. M., Frederick, C. B. and Putnam, R. D. 2015. "The Engagement Gap: Social Mobility and Extracurricular Participation Among American Youth." *Annals of the American Academy of Political and Social Science*. 657: 194–207.
Suk, Julie C. 2014. "Quotas and Consequences: A Transnational Re-evaluation." In D. Hellman and S. Moreau (eds). *Philosophical Foundations of Discrimination Law*. Oxford: Oxford University Press. 228–249.

34
DISCRIMINATION AND DIVERSITY

George Hull

UNIVERSITY OF CAPE TOWN

Introduction

When an institution (*e.g.*, a business or a university) has exhibited a pattern of unjust discrimination against certain societal groups over a period of time, it often lacks *diversity* as a consequence. Homogeneity—all white Christian male managers, say, or all heterosexual able-bodied students—is in such cases an artefact of the pattern of unjust discrimination. When steps are taken to end unjust discrimination, one should expect such an institution to become more diverse. If, beyond ending discrimination, a policy of preference is implemented to make redress to those people unjustly discriminated against, one should expect it to become more diverse more quickly.

But increasing diversity is not always merely a side-effect of anti-discrimination and redress policies. Sometimes diversity itself is a goal of policy. Educational institutions, for example, strive for diversity in their student body, in what is taught, and in who teaches. Businesses pay attention to the degree of diversity of their workforce and in their boardroom. Government—local, regional and national—encourages, or insists on, diverse residential neighborhoods, diverse sports teams, diverse government contractors, a diverse civil service.

When diversity is itself a policy goal, a different set of relations between diversity and discrimination becomes salient. First, advocates of diversity argue that diversity not only is caused by, but also causes, a reduction in unjust discrimination, since it tends to destroy negative prejudices. So policies aiming to increase diversity often have as their ultimate goal a reduction in unjust discrimination. Second, some of the further positive effects attributed to diversity (including more efficient deliberative processes and distributive justice gains across society) are expected not to ensue unless a sufficient number of members of groups which have been unjustly discriminated against are present in a workplace, classroom, neighborhood, or other context. Third, policies of preference with diversification as their goal have themselves been accused of being forms of unjust discrimination (cf. Chapters 33 and 36). Defenders of such policies have to supply a rebuttal of this charge.

Much philosophical discussion of diversity has occurred in the context of the debate about *affirmative action*—policies of preference ("positive discrimination") in favor of applicants from certain societal groups, on the basis of more than just their qualifications for the educational place, employment position or supply contract they are applying for. The expected benefits of diversity are frequently invoked as constituting a "forward-looking" justification of affirmative action. This is contrasted with a "backward-looking" justification which presents affirmative action as a way of making amends to applicants, or providing applicants with compensation, for unjust discrimination and resultant wrongful harm they have suffered (*e.g.*, Cohen 2003: 23–45; Sterba 2009: 31–35). However, as will become clear below, not all policies of preference implemented for the sake of the expected benefits of diversity can be counted as affirmative action (cf. Chapter 33).

This chapter first considers the question of what diversity is. After that, it outlines the social gains to which increased diversity is supposed to give rise: on the one hand efficiency gains, on the other hand justice gains (including a reduction in unjust discrimination). It discusses what recent research tells us about how likely these gains are to ensue, and assesses the charge that policies of preference aimed at diversity are themselves forms of unjust discrimination. Finally, it turns to the issue of whether policies aimed at diversity are too socially divisive, or—as some theorists have provocatively argued—not divisive enough.

What is diversity?

If it is said that an institution should diversify, we can ask, first, which types of social group it should aim to include members of; second, what kinds of inclusion it should aim for; third, roughly what proportions of each social group it should aim to include.

Which social groups?

When theorists advocate diversity, they are not arguing for diversity along just any lines (*e.g.*, height, hair color, which soccer team one supports). Rather, it is the importance of diversity of *socially relevant groups* in a professional, educational, residential, or other context which these theorists stress (*e.g.*, Anderson 2010: 113). In the writings of diversity advocates, socially relevant groups are typically differentiated along two main axes of comparison: on the one hand, the doctrinal and ethno-cultural differences to which theories of pluralism and multiculturalism draw our attention; on the other hand, the degree to which (and manners in which) groups of people have been stigmatized, unjustly discriminated against, or otherwise unfairly disadvantaged.[1]

Comprehensive doctrines

Most modern societies are made up of individuals with widely differing conceptions of the human good. These conceptions are often embedded within what John Rawls calls a "comprehensive doctrine," a relatively systematic framework of theoretical and normative beliefs, which may be backed up by a tradition of textual exegesis (Rawls 1996: xviii–xx, 12–15). Such comprehensive doctrines may be religious (*e.g.*, Islam) or secular (*e.g.*, utilitarianism). If diversity is expected to generate benefits via the confrontation, or mutual illumination, of diverse opinions and worldviews, it will make sense for comprehensive-doctrine diversity to be the focus of policy. This could be achieved through ensuring that proponents of diverse comprehensive doctrines are present in the same institutional setting, but also through other measures, such as ensuring that diverse comprehensive doctrines feature in school textbooks.

Ethno-cultural groups

Besides being plural in the sense that they contain proponents of different comprehensive doctrines, modern societies are also usually plural in the sense that they contain adherents of different ethno-cultures.[2] Adherents of different ethno-cultures tend to differ along any or all of the following dimensions:

- language or dialect
- habits of greeting and hospitality
- family structure and conventions of affiliation
- religious practices and observances
- artistic products.

For example, South African society contains adherents of Pedi, Tswana, Chinese, Zulu, Indian and Afrikaner ethno-cultures, among others.

Ethno-cultural differences and differences of comprehensive doctrine often coincide—for example, when the religious practices of a group are accompanied by a shared comprehensive doctrine founded on a tradition of textual exegesis. But they do not always coincide. Philosophers such as Charles Taylor have argued that ethno-cultural adherence requires societal recognition in its own right (Taylor 1994: 64), and philosophers such as Will Kymlicka have argued that it can ground "group-differentiated rights" for "ethnic and national minorities" (Kymlicka 1995: 34). Whether such recognition has been afforded, and whether such rights claims have been met, are different questions from the Rawlsian question of whether the principles governing the basic structure of a society are justifiable by the lights of the different reasonable comprehensive doctrines propounded by members of that society (Rawls 1996: 12).

Disadvantaged groups

Socially relevant groups can also be constituted via processes of stigmatization, unjust discrimination, and other unfair disadvantaging. Disadvantaged groups sometimes coincide with ethno-cultural groups. This can happen when adherents of a given ethno-culture are excluded from job referral networks and access to critical resources controlled by a dominant group—*e.g.*, when they are vulnerable newly arrived immigrants. To rationalize its continued in-group favoritism, the dominant group might develop stigmatizing representations of adherents of the ethno-culture in question: they are lazy, dirty, sly, untrustworthy. These stigmatizing representations could then motivate violent attacks on members of the stigmatized group, or legislation excluding them from high-status jobs or public amenities. Even in the absence of open hostility or formal unjust discrimination, stigmatizing narratives about the ethno-culture in question might (consciously and subconsciously) shape dominant group members' treatment of members of the stigmatized group, to marginalizing and disadvantaging effect.[3]

Such a process of stigmatization and discrimination can also center on a non-ethno-cultural social identity. It can, for example, center on the identity of propounding a particular comprehensive doctrine (*e.g.*, communism). But it often centers on social identities whose boundaries cross-cut those both of comprehensive doctrine and of ethno-culture, such as sex, disability status, and sexual orientation.

It is possible for the group identity of an unfairly disadvantaged group to be entirely constituted by the manner in which it is disadvantaged. Economic classes into which society members are born should arguably be understood in this way: there would be no social identity left to distinguish a lower economic class were its members' economic position to become equivalent to that of all other society members (Blum 2008: 195). In contrast, comprehensive-doctrine groups, ethno-cultural groups, sexual-orientation groups, women and disabled people would retain their social identities as groups even if they were no longer stigmatized or discriminated against. In these cases, justice demands not that the social identities in question be done away with, but that they no longer "be taken as a badge of inferiority" (Blum 1998: 61).

Racial identity is an interesting problem case. There is disagreement about whether racial identities are entirely constituted by peculiar social processes of stigmatizing, discrimination and privileging, or are at least partly constituted by quasi-ethno-cultural differences, which could, and should, survive the end of racial stigma and discrimination (Jeffers 2013).

As will be discussed below, many of the benefits of diversifying an institution are expected not to ensue unless members of groups which have been unjustly discriminated against are represented in that institution in sufficient numbers.

What kind of inclusion?

Not all ways in which members of an as yet unrepresented group can be included in a context are expected to yield diversity gains. Some are even thought to have significant negative consequences.

Bare presence

The *bare presence* of diverse socially relevant groups in an institution, neighborhood, or other context, is usually held to be insufficient to trigger the benefits of diversity. Diversity gains are thought to be particularly unlikely to arise when:

- members of diverse groups, though present in the same context, remain spatially apart from each other (*e.g.*, eating meals with in-group members at different tables)
- members of diverse groups, though they come into contact with one another, do so only fleetingly or intermittently (*e.g.*, just to greet one another in the corridors)
- members of diverse groups, though interacting extensively for protracted periods of time, do so in a hierarchically ordered fashion (*e.g.*, all managers in a workplace are members of group G_1, and all subordinates members of group G_2).

Integration

Integration is a form of inclusion of diverse socially relevant groups which goes beyond their bare compresence in the same context. Diverse groups are *integrated* in a context when their members regularly interact co-operatively in that context for protracted periods of time on terms of equality. This can be achieved in a hierarchical context, such as a business firm or a navy, so long as members of all the groups in question occupy all levels of the hierarchy.

One theorist who has argued powerfully for the goal of integration across societal contexts is Elizabeth Anderson. The ideal of integration which Anderson advocates is "the full participation on terms of equality of socially significant groups in all domains of society" (2010: 113).[4]

Assimilation

A form of inclusion of diverse groups in a context counts as *assimilation* when it occurs on condition that, or otherwise has the result that, at least one of the groups adapts its behavior, beliefs or practices (*e.g.*, dress, social activities, political views, language, manner of speech) so that they conform to those of another of the groups. The bare presence of a group in a context is unlikely to give rise to assimilation. But many forms of integration count as, or are conditional on, assimilation.

Whether a given instance of assimilation is good, bad, or indifferent, will depend on which types of socially relevant group are involved. If integration of a lower economic class across societal contexts were to result in their conforming to middle-class practices such as more hygienic food preparation and overseas holidaymaking, this would surely be, if anything, a positive form of assimilation. However, when a group's social identity is not exhausted by the manner in which it is disadvantaged, assimilation will often be a negative phenomenon. For example, gay people might be integrated into a profession on condition that they conceal their sexual orientation; or members of an ethno-cultural group might find that they cannot participate at school on terms of equality unless they conform to most of the ethno-cultural practices of the majority group in that context. These two cases of assimilation do seem objectionable. In the former case, the manner in which the group in question is integrated contributes to stigmatizing a sexual-orientation identity; in the latter case, the manner of inclusion of members of the group in question is arguably incompatible with proper recognition of their ethno-cultural identity, and might even threaten the survival of their ethno-culture.

In the long run, assimilation poses a threat to diversity—and thus to any expected benefits of diversity. Some degree of ethno-cultural homogeneity in certain domains (*e.g.*, family, church, even school) is plausibly a condition on the possibility of ongoing ethno-cultural diversity in other domains (*e.g.*, workplace, parliament).

What proportions?

If a corporation, government, or other organization is to introduce policies aimed at diversity, with concrete goals and a timeline, it will need to know not just which groups it should include, but also roughly what proportions of those groups it should aim to include.

Demographic proportionality

Government policies aimed at diversity often use national or regional demographics as a benchmark for the proportions of socially relevant groups institutions should include.[5] However, though departures from demographic proportionality are sometimes symptomatic of unjust discrimination, in many cases there are innocent explanations for them—*e.g.*, occupational traditions within ethno-cultural groups (Sowell 2004: 184–190; Benatar 2008: 298–299). Philosophers who advocate diversity tend not to argue for demographic proportionality. Often they explicitly disavow it (*e.g.*, Sterba 2009: 28; Anderson 2010: 109).

Equal proportions

A flag made up of three equally large sections of blue, white and red is likely to strike us as "more multi-colored" than a flag on which two tiny spots—one blue, one white—appear against a red background. A related intuitive notion can influence our thinking about social contexts, with the result that an institution in which three social groups are represented strikes us intuitively as most diverse when those three groups are represented in equal proportions. However, in the absence of further justification, we ought not to permit this geometrical intuition associated with "diversity" to guide policy-making on social inclusion.

Critical mass

Much theoretical work on diversity employs the notion of a *critical mass*. This is the minimum proportion of a social group that needs to be included in a context if the diversity gains its inclusion can generate are to be triggered.

It is useful to expand the notion of a critical mass into that of a *critical range*, bounded by a *lower critical threshold* (*e.g.*, 5 per cent), below which no diversity gains can be expected from the inclusion of a given group, and an *upper critical threshold* (*e.g.*, 20 per cent), above which no more diversity gains can be expected from the inclusion of more members of the group in question. For example, James Sterba puts the critical range of "under-represented minority students" needed in a college class to trigger "the educational benefits of diversity" at "three to five for a class of thirty" (2009: 71).

In a society with a majority group and a small minority group, demographic proportionality could often translate into minority representation below the upper critical threshold—or even below the lower critical threshold. Thus the notion of a critical range helps us articulate a potential problem with diversification policies which aim at demographic proportionality.

Efficiency gains from diversity

Policies fostering diversity are often adopted partly on the basis that they will improve *efficiency*. Diversity advocates particularly emphasize diversity's potential to improve the quality of group deliberative processes with a problem-solving or truth-seeking purpose. For this reason, many theorists expect that, other things being equal, bodies such as juries, parliaments, student laboratory teams, product development teams and research clusters will perform to a higher standard when they are made up of members of diverse socially relevant groups.

We can distinguish at least four different—though not mutually exclusive—models of how diversity might improve the quality of group deliberation. First, it can create an environment in which there is *confrontation of opinions*. Liberals such as John Stuart Mill have argued that there are epistemic benefits to be expected from an environment in which people espousing different beliefs, values and conceptions of the human good mix together and can freely state and debate their disagreements. In such an environment, people are both more likely to advance toward true beliefs and correct values through debate, and likely to understand those true beliefs and correct values better through having critiqued or defended them (Mill [1859] 1974: 75–118). As noted in the previous section, the confrontation-of-opinions model will particularly speak in favor of comprehensive-doctrine diversity.

Diversity can, second, improve group deliberation through the inclusion of *expert witnesses*. For example, a public relations firm based in Dublin, tasked by a corporate client with developing a strategy for marketing cigarettes to women in Latvia, would be well advised to include at least one Latvian woman in its team. In this case, as in many others, insider knowledge—whether of an ethno-culture or of another type of socially relevant group identity—constitutes a form of expertise. The type of diversity the expert-witnesses model speaks in favor of will normally be quite narrowly tailored to the task at hand.

Third, though, diversity could improve deliberation by enabling it to draw upon many and various *springs of creativity*. The sources of innovative ideas are unpredictable; even with the benefit of hindsight they can be obscure. Focusing on scientific research, Joseph LeFevre notes that "there is no 'mechanical' method for devising hypotheses." Rather, "the creation of a hypothesis is affected by everything that is involved in forming a person," including "education, culture, ethnicity, sexuality, racial identity" (2003: 129), and more. The decisive brainwave—

whether in science or in other problem-solving and truth-seeking endeavors—will not always originate in the content of a person's education and training. It could also stem from a (consciously or subconsciously) perceived analogy with an ethno-cultural practice, an element of a comprehensive doctrine, or even a characteristic experience of a disadvantaged group. The springs-of-creativity model speaks in favor of diversity along as many dimensions as possible, to maximize the variety of experiential, cultural and doctrinal material from which a deliberating group can draw its inspiration. Focusing on science, LeFevre concludes: "The more diverse the community of scientists in all ways other than their common scientific education, ... the more diverse will be the relevant and responsible hypotheses which will be tested in the search for truth, and the more truth will be discovered" (*ibid.*).

Fourth, diversity might improve the quality of group deliberation by inducing participants to deliberate with greater *responsibility*. If members of a dominant social group are the only participants in a deliberative forum such as a parliament, a boardroom or a jury, there can be a risk that problem-solving and truth-seeking will be subverted by in-group-favoring rationalizations (and, indeed, out-group-stigmatizing narratives and stereotypes), which are mutually reinforced and go unchecked. It has been proposed that the inclusion of members of subordinate or disadvantaged groups in such settings will make dominant group members more hesitant to put forward in-group-favoring rationalizations, and in general more critically reflective on their contributions to discussion, thus making the deliberation better able to serve its truth-seeking or problem-solving purpose (Anderson 2010: 130–132). The responsibility model will tend to speak in favor of diversity along the dimensions of disadvantage, stigmatization and discrimination.

The practice of awarding educational places, employment positions or supply contracts to people on the basis that doing so will improve efficiency in the educational, professional, or other context in question by increasing diversity is often counted as a form of affirmative action (*e.g.*, LeFevre 2003; Sterba 2009). However, this is misleading. Employing somebody on the basis that their inclusion in a team will increase its overall efficiency is the single most normal and, *pro tanto*, justifiable rationale for an employment decision; calling it "affirmative action" suggests there is something special or exceptional about this rationale. Many opponents of affirmative action recognize this, and consequently oppose hiring and employment on the basis of the expected efficiency gains from diversity chiefly because they believe that the alleged efficiency gains will not actually ensue (*e.g.*, Cohen 2003).

Social and organizational psychologists have dedicated a great deal of empirical research to the effects of diversity, and in particular to testing the springs-of-creativity hypothesis. Researchers occupying what Daan van Knippenberg calls the "social categorization perspective" (2007: 12) have also contributed a counter-hypothesis: what we can call the *inter-group friction* hypothesis. This says that in diverse workplaces, members of different groups will tend to like, trust and understand those they categorize as out-group members less than those they categorize as in-group members. According to the inter-group-friction hypothesis, misunderstandings, uncooperativeness and other tensions will tend to reduce the problem-solving or truth-seeking effectiveness of diverse work groups.

Meta-analyses of research on multicultural and mixed-gender teams tend to conclude that there is no overall correlation between team diversity and either improved or decreased task efficiency across the board. Both springs-of-creativity efficiency gains and inter-group-friction efficiency losses are frequently observed, often in one and the same team (*e.g.*, Stahl *et al.* 2010). Empirical research has begun to focus on isolating the factors which determine whether springs-of-creativity effects or inter-group-friction effects prevail in a given context. Some findings suggest that inter-group-friction effects are prone to be more pronounced when team members are from groups which differ from one another in more than one socially relevant respect, creating a "faultline" (Homan *et al.* 2007a). This could mean that, for example, if a disadvantaged black group in a society is also ethno-culturally distinct from the rest of society, then integrating members of that group into a mainly white work team could not be expected to yield net efficiency gains unless it was preceded, or accompanied, by some degree of ethno-cultural assimilation. Disconcertingly, one factor which may contribute significantly to determining whether diversity increases work-group efficiency is whether or not the team members expect it to (Homan *et al.* 2007b)!

There is some empirical support for the responsibility hypothesis. For example, a study conducted by Samuel Sommers in the United States found that deliberation by mixed black-and-white juries in a simulated trial tended to be superior to deliberation by all-white juries. This was not simply because of the "broader informational exchange" on the former—*i.e.*, not just due to confrontation-of-opinions and expert-witness effects. Rather, on mixed black-and-white juries "White participants were largely responsible for the influence of racial composition, as they raised more case facts, made fewer factual errors, and were more amenable to discussion of race-related issues" (Sommers 2006: 606). A plausible explanation for this finding is that the presence of members of a disadvantaged group made the white jurors more aware of the risk of putting forward in-group-favoring rationalizations and thus more critically reflective about what they said (Sommers 2006: 607).

Justice gains from diversity

Policies fostering diversity are often adopted not just because they are expected to improve efficiency, but also on the basis that they will help make society more *just*. At the same time, policies of preference aimed at reaping justice gains from diversity have themselves been branded as unjust discrimination which fails to treat people equally.

Diversity advocates claim diversification in business firms, educational institutions, the civil service, and other contexts can contribute to social justice because:

(a) it tends to *equalize opportunities* across societal groups
(b) it tends to *make the provision of important services more equitable* across societal groups
(c) it tends to *destroy negative stereotypes or antipathetic attitudes* which lead to unjust discrimination against some societal groups, and to a limiting sense of inferiority on the part of some members of those groups.

The practice of awarding educational places, employment positions or supply contracts to members of particular societal groups on the basis that doing so will help make society more just is a form of affirmative action. The forward-looking rationale for affirmative action under discussion here, which invokes the goal of achieving distributive justice in the future, is to be distinguished from the backward-looking rationale for affirmative action, which invokes the necessity of rectificatory or compensatory justice for those who have been wronged or wrongfully harmed by unjust discrimination in the past (Sterba 2009: 34–35).[6]

Whether the forward-looking or the backward-looking rationale is invoked, the policy recommended is one of preference ("positive discrimination") in favor of applicants from certain societal groups, on the basis of something other than their qualification—*i.e.*, how efficiently they can be expected to do the job, carry out the service contracted, or make use of the educational place. Many opponents of affirmative action hold this to be a violation of the *equal treatment* due to all (*e.g.*, Cohen 2003: 23-45).

However, defenders of affirmative action have pointed out that, even in the absence of "positive discrimination" for the sake of increased justice, applicants for places, positions or contracts are not "treated equally," if this means each having an equal chance of being successful in their application (as they would if there was a lottery, say). They are not even "treated equally" in the sense that each has an equal chance of being successful in their application if they put in equal effort (and thus, arguably, are equally deserving).[7] Rather than an abstract ideal of equal treatment, it is society's interest in being served by skilled and effective professionals in all domains (law, medicine, municipal administration, teaching, accounting, and so on) which justifies permitting—even compelling—organizations to allocate places, positions and contracts to the most qualified applicants.

But if increasing overall welfare is an important societal goal, achieving justice is surely at least as important a goal. So if the former goal can justify policies of preference in favor of the best trained, most skilled and most diligent applicants, it is reasonable to infer that the latter goal could justify policies of preference along different lines when they could be expected to make society more just (Dworkin 1977: 228). Clearly, the two goals can come into conflict. Policies aimed at achieving justice gains from diversity can be objectionable if, by inducing employers and educational institutions to take on very poorly qualified applicants, they reduce overall social welfare excessively (Cohen 2003: 143–145; Sowell 2004: 187; Benatar 2008: 303–304).

What this response helpfully emphasizes, though, is that the question of whether meritocratic hiring should be supplemented with some degree of preferential hiring for the sake of justice gains from diversity should not be understood as the question of whether equal treatment of applicants may be violated. It is more properly understood as asking what balance the institutional framework within which applicants compete for places, positions and contracts should strike between the aims of *overall social welfare*, on the one hand, and, on the other, *social justice* (while also properly respecting *individual freedom*). Applicants should of course be treated equally within whichever institutional framework it is determined strikes the right balance between these goals.

One way in which diversity advocates claim diversity can increase justice is by (a) equalizing opportunities. Diversity can contribute to equality of opportunity by increasing the social and cultural capital which members of disadvantaged groups possess. If policies of preference lead to increased inclusion of members of disadvantaged groups in neighborhoods, schools and workplaces dominated by members of advantaged groups, this can give them access to information networks, job-referral networks and other support networks (social capital) they were previously excluded from, thus increasing their ability to become apprised of and take advantage of opportunities for advancement. It can also enable them to pick up habits, social norms and points of reference (cultural capital) which make them more attractive prospects to employers or higher-education institutions.

Studies of neighborhood desegregation projects such as the Gautreaux Project in Chicago suggest that diversity can indeed contribute to equality of opportunity via the mechanisms just mentioned (Anderson 2010: 118–119). For diversity to equalize opportunities by widening the distribution of social and cultural capital it must be along the dimension of advantage and disadvantage. It should also take the form of integration, since members of advantaged groups are unlikely to include others in their networks unless they are well acquainted with them and interact with them as equals. Gains in equality of opportunity through integration leading to the acquisition of cultural capital are likely to come at the price of problematic forms of assimilation—which may also be a tacit condition on the acquisition of social capital.

When disadvantaged societal groups live in communities which are very separate from the rest of society, another way in which policies of preference can contribute to distributive justice is by (b) making the provision of important services more equitable across society. Diversity advocates have proposed that qualified doctors, lawyers, accountants, managers, administrators, and other professionals, who come from disadvantaged communities themselves are more likely to practice in those communities than those who come from advantaged backgrounds. To the extent that this is so, increasing the representation of disadvantaged groups in degree and training programs can be expected to increase the extent and quality of service provision in disadvantaged communities (Nagel 1973: 361; Dworkin 1977: 228).[8]

Diversity is also championed on the basis that it can (c) destroy negative stereotypes and break down antipathetic attitudes towards stigmatized and disadvantaged groups (cf. Chapter 32). It thereby helps create a more just society, firstly, because it reduces the extent to which certain social identities—*e.g.*, lesbian, transgender, black, female—are stigmatized and counted as a badge of inferiority. Secondly, a reduction in prejudice is thought to lead to a reduction in unjust discrimination, so the destruction of negative stereotypes and antipathy should also make a contribution to (a) equalizing opportunities, and ending unfair disadvantaging.

The hypothesis that contact between members of different societal groups in contexts of diversity leads to a reduction in prejudice is called the "contact hypothesis." American social psychologist Gordon Allport's canonical statement of the contact hypothesis dates from 1954. It predicts that prejudice—defined as "an antipathy based upon a faulty and inflexible generalization" (Allport 1954: 9)—against disadvantaged minority groups will be reduced by contact between members of advantaged majority groups and members of disadvantaged minority groups which:

- is frequent enough to lead to personal acquaintance (*e.g.*, daily encounters in the workplace)
- involves encountering each other as equals (*e.g.*, as fellow students or as employees at the same rank)
- involves the co-operative pursuit of common goals (*e.g.*, work tasks)
- is supported by institutional structures (*e.g.*, a teacher instructing individuals to work together on a project) (Allport 1954: 281).

In response to the contact hypothesis, critics of affirmative action have objected that, when employers and educational institutions give preference to much less qualified members of disadvantaged groups to achieve diversity, their underperformance may in fact reinforce existing stereotypes and prejudices against them (Cohen 2003: 110; Benatar 2008: 292–293). However, one would think this effect could be obviated by a policy of moderate preference supplemented by some degree of on-the-job training (Sterba 2009: 85).

In any case, empirical studies overwhelmingly confirm Allport's contact hypothesis. A comprehensive meta-analysis (Pettigrew *et al.* 2006) found "an inverse relationship between intergroup contact and prejudice" in 94 per cent of the 515 studies it reviewed (766). Moreover, not only direct contact but also indirect contact—*e.g.*, "knowing that a member of the ingroup has a close relationship with a member of an outgroup" (Lemmer *et al.* 2015: 153)—has been shown to reduce negative stereotypes and antipathetic attitudes toward disadvantaged groups. This is not to say that the inter-group contact promoted by diversity always reduces prejudice. But when it does not, it can usually be established that one of Allport's four conditions does not hold (*e.g.*, Vincent 2008).

Today, theoretical controversy attaches less to the idea that inter-group contact reduces prejudice than to the distinct idea that reduction in prejudice must lead to a reduction in unjust discrimination. In the last few years a new current in social psychology has emerged which challenges "the paradigm of prejudice." Theorists associated with this current have, firstly, pointed to evidence that practices of in-group favoritism which harm disadvantaged groups often co-exist with positive stereotypes about, and sympathetic attitudes toward, the disadvantaged groups which are harmed (Glick *et al.* 2012; Dixon *et al.* 2012: 413–417). Secondly, they have argued that, though inter-group contact impacts positively upon the attitudes of dominant group members, by making them less prejudiced, there is reason to believe it impacts negatively upon the attitudes of subordinate and disadvantaged group members, by making them more doubtful and hesitant about joining together in collective action when this is needed to overcome injustices of which they are victims (Dixon *et al.* 2012: 417–421). Inter-group contact inhibits *mobilization* (Reicher 2012).

Diversity and divisiveness

Critics of policies of preference aimed at diversity have for a long time highlighted the potential of such policies to *polarize* a society.[9] By making individuals' group membership a condition on their ability to access important goods and opportunities, they can make it rational for people to club together with other members of their societal group to maximize the share of resources their group attains and minimize that attained by other groups. Thomas Sowell has argued that this dynamic, exacerbated by demagogic politicians, contributed to the ethnic polarization in countries such as Sri Lanka and Nigeria, resulting in civil war (Sowell 2004). In South Africa, the scholar, anti-*Apartheid* activist and former Robben Island detainee Neville Alexander lamented the African National Congress-led government's introduction of policies of preference making use of *Apartheid*-era population categories. In Alexander's eyes, the ensuing formation of organizations such as the "*Bruin Belange Inisiatief*"—set up to further the interests of South Africans classified as "Coloured"—was "the thin end of the genocidal wedge" (2013: 166).

In response to these criticisms one can point out, in the first place, that some evidence suggests diversification policies can induce members of different societal groups to regard each other as members of a common in-group (*e.g.*, South African, Malaysian, American), thus potentially reducing polarization (*e.g.*, Gaertner *et al.* 2009). But, in the second place, though extreme, violent scenarios such as genocide and civil war must undoubtedly be avoided, it is far from clear that social cohesion should always trump social justice as an aim of public policy. Some degree of polarization within society could be an acceptable price to pay for the justice gains to be expected from diversity.

The new current in social psychology which challenges the "paradigm of prejudice" adds an interesting new twist to the academic debate on divisiveness. Theorists such as Steve Reicher, Kevin Durrheim and John Dixon claim that "prejudice reduction" is not a reliable way of making extremely unequal societies more just, and may actually put a brake on this process. Even when dominant group members generally have positive beliefs about, and positive attitudes toward, subordinate group members, they "rarely (if ever) give away their power and privileges. Rather, these must be wrested from them by members of subordinate groups" (Dixon *et al.* 2012: 418). To the extent that diversity gives rise to positive attitudes among members of subordinate groups toward dominant group members, or causes them to regard dominant group members as members of a common in-group, it can make them "more likely to abandon the project of collective action to change inequitable societies"[10] (Dixon *et al.* 2012: 421). In a nutshell, *diversity is not divisive enough.*

While certainly not uncontested,[11] the ideas of this new current in social psychology resonate with some of the separatist thinking of twentieth-century liberation movements—particularly black liberation movements in the United States and in South Africa.[12] At the least these theorists remind us that diversity's benefits need to be weighed against important benefits which can arise, in certain social contexts, from homogeneity.

Notes

1 Lawrence Blum (2008) stresses the "distinction between cultures-of-ethnocultural-groups and persons-in-devalued-groups" (204), as well as other important distinctions, in a critical survey of recent literature to which the discussion in this subsection of the text is indebted.
2 Blum (1998: 53) helpfully distinguishes between "*ethno*-culture" and other types of culture, such as "professional cultures, … institutional cultures, neighbourhood cultures, family cultures."
3 Elizabeth Anderson (2010: 7–16) provides a perspicuous account of how such mechanisms of stigmatization, discrimination and disadvantaging can combine and reinforce one another, which draws on the work of the sociologist Charles Tilly (Tilly 1998).
4 Anderson's position is by no means uncontested. For example, see the critical responses of political theorists to Anderson (2010) at 345–375 of *Political Studies Review* (12[3]).
5 This is true of recent South African government policies (Maré 2014: 67, 76–89), for instance, and Nigerian government policies stretching further back (Sowell 2004: 106–107).
6 The forward-looking rationale and the backward-looking rationale are not mutually exclusive. For example, a government might choose to make amends to a group it has wrongfully discriminated against in the past via an affirmative action program, rather than by some other means, due to the fact that affirmative action has the additional virtue of tending to equalize opportunities in the future (Hull 2015: 132).
7 Thus Thomas Nagel (1973: 362) remarks, "When racial and sexual injustice have been reduced, we shall still be left with the great injustice of the smart and the dumb, who are so differently rewarded for comparable effort."
8 However, this positive outcome could potentially be achieved without increasing the diversity of individual educational institutions: all-black or all-Hispanic universities, for example, might have the same effect. (I owe this point to Kasper Lippert-Rasmussen.)
9 See Blum's (2008) helpful discussion of the "divisiveness paradigm" in recent literature on diversity.
10 This chimes with a concern Lawrie Balfour (2014: 350) has raised about Anderson's advocacy of racial integration under the banner of a shared national identity: "[P]rioritizing a national identity effaces the historical importance of race as a *political* concept—both as an instrument of oppressive power and as a source for liberationist thinking and action."
11 For example, see the critical commentaries on Dixon *et al.* (2012) by other social psychologists at 425–451 of the issue of *Behavioral and Brain Sciences* (35[6]) in which their article appeared.
12 For discussion of separatist currents in U.S. black nationalism, see Shelby (2005); on the South African Black Consciousness Movement's qualified separatism, see Hull (forthcoming).

Bibliography

Alexander, N. 2013. *Thoughts on the New South Africa.* Auckland Park: Jacana Media.

Allport, G. 1954. *The Nature of Prejudice.* Reading, Palo Alto, London and Don Mills: Addison-Wesley Publishing.

Anderson, E. 2010. *The Imperative of Integration.* Princeton and Oxford: Princeton University Press.

Balfour, L. 2014. "Integration, Desegregation and the Work of the Past." *Political Studies Review.* 12(3): 347–352.

Benatar, D. 2008. "Justice, Diversity and Racial Preference: A Critique of Affirmative Action." *South African Law Journal.* 125(2): 274–306.

Blum, L. 1998. "Recognition, Value, and Equality: A Critique of Charles Taylor's and Nancy Fraser's Accounts of Multiculturalism." *Constellations.* 5(1): 51–68.

Blum, L. 2008. "Ethnicity, Disunity, and Equality." In L. Thomas (ed.), *Contemporary Debates in Social Philosophy.* Malden, Oxford and Carlton: Blackwell Publishing. 193–211.

Cohen, C. 2003. "Why Race Preference is Wrong and Bad." In C. Cohen and J. Sterba, *Affirmative Action and Racial Preference: A Debate*. New York: Oxford University Press. 1–188.

Dixon, J., Levine, M., Reicher, S. and Durrheim, K. 2012. "Beyond Prejudice: Are Negative Evaluations the Problem and Is Getting Us to Like One Another More the Solution?" *Behavioral and Brain Sciences*. 35(6): 411–425.

Dworkin, R. 1977. *Taking Rights Seriously*. London: Duckworth.

Gaertner, S. and Dovidio, J. 2009. "Common Ingroup Identity: A Categorization-based Approach for Reducing Intergroup Bias." In T. Nelson (ed.), *Handbook of Prejudice, Stereotyping, and Discrimination*. New York and London: Psychology Press. 489–506.

Glick, P. and Fiske, S. 2012. "An Ambivalent Alliance: Hostile and Benevolent Sexism as Complementary Justifications for Gender Inequality." In J. Dixon and M. Levine (eds), *Beyond Prejudice: Extending the Social Psychology of Conflict, Inequality and Social Change*. Cambridge and London: Cambridge University Press. 70–88.

Homan, A., Van Knippenberg, D., Van Kleef, G. and De Dreu, C. 2007a. "Interacting Dimensions of Diversity: Cross-categorization and the Functioning of Diverse Work Groups." *Group Dynamics: Theory, Research, and Practice*. 11(2): 79–94.

Homan, A., Van Knippenberg, D., Van Kleef, G. and De Dreu, C. 2007b. "Bridging Faultlines by Valuing Diversity: Diversity Beliefs, Information Elaboration, and Performance in Diverse Work Groups." *Journal of Applied Psychology*. 92(5): 1189–1199.

Hull, G. 2015. "Affirmative Action and the Choice of Amends." *Philosophia*. 43(1): 113–134.

Hull, G. (forthcoming). "Black Consciousness as Overcoming Hermeneutical Injustice." *Journal of Applied Philosophy*. DOI: 10.1111/japp.12201.

Jeffers, C. 2013. "The Cultural Theory of Race: Yet Another Look at Du Bois's 'The Conservation of Races.'" *Ethics*. 123(3): 403–426.

Kymlicka, W. 1995. *Multicultural Citizenship: A Liberal Theory of Minority Rights*. Oxford: Clarendon Press.

LeFevre, J. 2003. "The Value of Diversity: A Justification of Affirmative Action." *Journal of Social Philosophy*. 34(1): 125–133.

Lemmer, G. and Wagner, U. 2015. "Can We Really Reduce Ethnic Prejudice Outside the Lab? A Meta-analysis of Direct and Indirect Contact Interventions." *European Journal of Social Psychology*. 45(2): 152–168.

Maré, G. 2014. *Declassified: Moving Beyond the Dead End of Race in South Africa*. Auckland Park: Jacana Media.

Mill, J. S. [1859] 1974. *On Liberty*. London: Penguin Books.

Nagel, T. 1973. "Equal Treatment and Compensatory Discrimination." *Philosophy and Public Affairs*. 2(4): 348–363.

Pettigrew, T. and Tropp, L. 2006. "A Meta-analytic Test of Intergroup Contact Theory." *Journal of Personality and Social Psychology*. 90(5): 751–783.

Rawls, J. 1996. *Political Liberalism* (expanded edition). New York: Columbia University Press.

Reicher, S. 2012. "From Perception to Mobilization: The Shifting Paradigm of Prejudice." In J. Dixon and M. Levine (eds), *Beyond Prejudice: Extending the Social Psychology of Conflict, Inequality and Social Change*. Cambridge and London: Cambridge University Press. 27–47.

Shelby, T. 2005. *We Who Are Dark: The Philosophical Foundations of Black Solidarity*. Cambridge and London: Belknap Press.

Sommers, S. 2006. "On Racial Diversity and Group Decision Making: Identifying Multiple Effects of Racial Composition on Jury Deliberations." *Journal of Personality and Social Psychology*. 90(4): 597–612.

Sowell, T. 2004. *Affirmative Action Around the World: An Empirical Study*. New Haven and London: Yale University Press.

Stahl, G., Maznevski, M., Voigt, A. and Johnson, K. 2010. "Unraveling the Effects of Cultural Diversity in Teams: A Meta-analysis of Research on Multicultural Work Groups." *Journal of International Business Studies*. 41(4): 690–709.

Sterba, J. 2009. *Affirmative Action for the Future*. Ithaca and London: Cornell University Press.

Taylor, C. 1994. "The Politics of Recognition." In C. Taylor, K. Appiah, J. Habermas, S. Rockefeller, M. Walzer, S. Wolf and A. Gutmann, *Multiculturalism: Examining the Politics of Recognition*. Princeton: Princeton University Press.

Tilly, C. 1998. *Durable Inequality*. Berkeley, Los Angeles and London: University of California Press.

Van Knippenberg, D. 2007. *Understanding Diversity*. Rotterdam: Erasmus Research Institute of Management.

Vincent, L. 2008. "The Limitations of 'Inter-racial Contact': Stories from Young South Africa." *Ethnic and Racial Studies*. 31(8): 1426–1451.

Further reading

L. Blum, "Ethnicity, Disunity, and Equality," in L. Thomas (ed.), *Contemporary Debates in Social Philosophy* (Malden, Oxford and Carlton: Blackwell Publishing, 193–211) constructively discusses different types of societal group relevant to diversification policies. Some classic philosophical essays on policies of preference are collected in M. Cohen, T. Nagel and T. Scanlon (eds), *Equality and Preferential Treatment: A* Philosophy and Public Affairs *Reader* (Princeton: Princeton University Press, 1977). C. Cohen and J. Sterba, *Affirmative Action and Racial Preference: A Debate* (New York: Oxford University Press, 2003) debates the pros and cons of affirmative action in the U.S. context. An accessible overview of empirical research into the effect of diversity on team performance is D. van Knippenberg, *Understanding Diversity* (Rotterdam: Erasmus Research Institute of Management, 2007). J. Dixon and M. Levine (eds), *Beyond Prejudice: Extending the Social Psychology of Conflict, Inequality and Social Change* (Cambridge and London: Cambridge University Press, 2012) collects essays exemplifying the new current in social psychology which challenges the "paradigm of prejudice." For a powerful defense of integration across social contexts, turn to E. Anderson, *The Imperative of Integration* (Princeton and Oxford: Princeton University Press, 2010).

35
WRONGFUL PRIVATE DISCRIMINATION AND THE EGALITARIAN ETHOS

Carina Fourie

UNIVERSITY OF WASHINGTON

Introduction

A gay white man does not date black men because they are black (cf. Chapters 23, 30 and 31). Is this wrongful discrimination? What would a common-sense answer to this question be? One might be tempted to say 'yes' – this seems so much like typical cases of wrongful racial discrimination, such as a refusal to hire black people for employment, that it is difficult to see why it should not also be wrongful discrimination. One might also be tempted to say 'no' – wrongful discrimination does not apply to individuals acting in their private capacities. At face value, each of these conflicting answers has some ring of truth. What does the philosophical literature tell us in this case? These kinds of questions, what we can call questions about private discrimination, are seldom explicitly addressed in detail.[1]

It may be difficult to see what is at stake here. Is this merely a terminological concern of interest only to theorists of discrimination? One reason why it could be of further significance is that equality has been said to require an egalitarian ethos (Wolff, 1998). Imagine that we take as a starting point the following: we want to live in a society of equals, that is, a society where people foremost *are* equals; they have relationships of equality. The commitment to living in a society of equals can be described as a commitment to social–relational egalitarianism (e.g. see Anderson 1999, Fourie *et al.* 2015). According to such an ideal, relationships of equality could include those relationships between individuals acting in private capacities, as friends or neighbors, and thus beyond their roles in the economy or political life, e.g. as workers and employers, or as citizens and their political representatives. An egalitarian ethos is a means of describing which norms should guide individuals' interactions, including their private interactions, in a community or society of equals.[2] A *prima facie* candidate norm for an egalitarian ethos would be a principle of non-discrimination. The intuitive understanding of non-discrimination – that we should not discriminate against people on the basis of race, gender, sexuality, etc. – fits well with the commitment to equal relationships. Investigating how discrimination might be said to apply in the private could thus be a fruitful line of enquiry for determining the content of an egalitarian ethos. It can contribute, thus, not only to filling out the literature on discrimination, which does not often deal with private discrimination in detail, but by contributing to a better understanding of what a genuinely equal society would look like.

In this chapter I will examine how a particular theory of discrimination – the objective-egalitarian account developed by Deborah Hellman – can be applied to cases of private differential treatment, such as dating preferences, in order to help stipulate a norm of non-discrimination for an egalitarian ethos. During the course of my analysis I will also indicate how aspects of the theory need to be revised to provide a compelling framework for understanding the ethical status of private discrimination.

In the first section, I indicate on what basis the objective-egalitarian account would distinguish wrongful differential treatment (i.e. wrongful discrimination) from acceptable differential treatment. I will apply this to dating preferences as an example of private discrimination, and I will then defend the application of the objective-egalitarian account to the private. In the process I will revise the notion of 'efficacy' (the power to demean) so that it is an adaptation of Hellman's original notion. In the last section I will gesture towards what else may be required of an egalitarian ethos besides the requirement of non-discrimination.

To qualify before I move on to the next section – I do not examine further implications of private wrongful discrimination, e.g. in terms of how much, if at all, a community or society can attempt to influence this form of discrimination. This may seem unsatisfactory – some of the more controversial questions are going to concern what, if anything, we can do about this kind of behavior, rather than whether or not the behavior is wrongful. However, it would be premature to take up these further complications here. The initial steps – how to identify wrongful private discrimination – are thus the subject of this chapter, and necessarily so.

What is wrongful discrimination?

There is a variety of theories as to what makes discrimination wrongful.[3] The discussion in this chapter is being set up as a potential contribution to social–relational egalitarianism (from now on, and for short I will refer to 'social egalitarianism' and 'social equality'), and more specifically to exploring, non-systematically, what might be the content on an egalitarian ethos. If we wanted to determine how a principle of non-discrimination could be used to stipulate the norms of an egalitarian ethos in a society of equals, we would need to rely on a notion of discrimination that is a good fit with a social egalitarian framework. Social egalitarians, to clarify, do not claim that all inequalities, such as those of power and social status, are necessarily morally problematic. Rather, they are particularly interested in identifying when and why these kinds of inequalities can be said to be problematic. At a minimum, problematic inequalities are those that result from or lead to people being treated as inferior (see Anderson, 1999; Scheffler, 2003; Anderson, 2008; Fourie *et al.*, 2015). As I will explain below, Deborah Hellman's theory of what makes discrimination wrongful (Hellman, 2011; see Chapter 7) is a *prima facie* good fit with social egalitarianism.

Hellman claims "that it is morally wrong to distinguish among people on the basis of a given attribute when doing so demeans any of the people affected" (Hellman 2011: 7; Chapter 7). This is what Hellman refers to as 'wrongful discrimination'. It has two significant aspects. The first is a certain kind of *treatment*: to demean, according to Hellman, is to debase, to treat another as lesser. The second is the *efficacy* of that treatment: you can only demean someone if you are in a dominant position in terms of status or power (Hellman 2011: 35). I will use an intuitive notion of which kinds of hierarchies should be used to determine efficacy; I will include the positions in race and gender hierarchies as examples of 'dominance' and 'subordination' relevant to determining efficacy.[4] As I will discuss in the following sections, however, this requires further analysis and I will be specifying and adapting the notion of 'efficacy'.

Demeaning is wrongful, Hellman claims, because it violates the respect each person deserves on the basis of having equal moral worth (Hellman 2011: 14–21). *Differential* treatment merely treats people differently; wrongful discrimination treats them differently in a way that violates a morally fundamental form of equality. Two aspects of this theory are especially important to emphasize here: its objectivity and its egalitarianism. I refer to Hellman's account as the objective-egalitarian account of discrimination (for short, the objective-egalitarian account) because of these two factors.

First, the theory rests on an objective notion of what it is to demean. To demean means to treat someone as a lesser objectively. Behavior can be judged to be demeaning according to what is considered demeaning in the particular society in which it occurs. That it is objective means that treatment can still demean even if the person demeaned does not *feel* demeaned; the prejudice or intention of the discriminator also does not necessarily determine whether or not someone has been demeaned (Hellman 2011: 24–27; 138–168). Additionally, whether or not behavior is demeaning is not related to its effects – thus even if no harm follows from the treatment, it remains demeaning.

Second, this notion of discrimination has egalitarian elements which make it particularly suitable to social egalitarianism. All theories of discrimination seem somehow related to theories of equality because they aim to explain why certain forms of differential behavior (unequal treatment) are impermissible while others are not. However, there are two (further) explicitly egalitarian aspects to Hellman's theory, which you will not necessarily find in other theories of discrimination. First, the wrongness of discrimination has to do with a violation of equality *per se*, that is, the violation of equal moral worth. Second, discrimination is only wrongful if it is efficacious and efficacy is related to inequality – to the relative positions of the agents in a power or status hierarchy. For these reasons, a principle of non-discrimination based on Hellman's theory seems particularly apt as a candidate principle for an egalitarian ethos. That is not to say, however, that it is the only theory of discrimination that may be useful for developing the egalitarian ethos of social equality further.

A society of equals would be one in which we would apply a principle of non-discrimination understood according to the objective-egalitarian account. How would this account apply to private discrimination (cf. Chapters 30 and 31)?

Wrongful private discrimination and racial preferences in dating

The concept 'private discrimination', when it is mentioned at all, is used variously in the literature. For example, it can be understood broadly to include "discrimination by individuals as citizens, as opposed to *state* discrimination", (Vallentyne 2006: 982; Chapter 10) or, and as I will understand it here, more narrowly applying to "discrimination by private individuals, acting in roles generally understood to be outside the realms of the marketplace and political life" (Blake 2006: 1018). For example, it relates to whom one dates or marries, or with whom one socializes or lives. Note, however, it is definitely not part of the definition that I am using that these kinds of decisions cannot be judged to be morally problematic, even abhorrent; nor does it imply that society might not have an interest in influencing these decisions, or even be justified in trying to encourage certain kinds of choices rather than others.

Now let us consider applying the objective-egalitarian account to two examples of private discrimination, both of which are examples of racial preferences in dating. These are particularly suitable cases to use for elaborating what may be required of an egalitarian ethos in terms of the norms it sets for private relationships. First, topics like these – dating preferences – are often considered to be paradigmatic cases of the private. Second, the general category of inequality involved, differential treatment on the basis of race, is considered particularly morally questionable in a society of equals, at least outside of the private.

As context is important for determining whether behavior is demeaning according to the objective-egalitarian account, let us say that all of these cases occur currently in the USA:

1 *Not dating black men*: A gay white man does not date black men because they are black.[5] This is even in cases where, were the men white but the same in all other respects (e.g. in terms of socioeconomic status, body size, intelligence, attractiveness, etc.), he would indeed ask them out on dates or accept their offers for dates.[6] He will admit to friends that he does not want to date black men, and insinuates such to acquaintances and colleagues.
2 *Not dating white men*: A straight black woman does not date white men because they are white. This is even in cases where, were the men black but the same in all other respects, she would indeed ask them out on dates or accept their offers for dates. She will admit to friends that she does not want to date white men, and insinuates such to acquaintances and colleagues.

Considering the objective-egalitarian account, case 1 is wrongful discrimination. It seems plausible to claim that the specific treatment in 'not dating black men' is objectively demeaning in the current USA as black men are being treated as inferior to white men, following current and historical social and political patterns. Additionally, the treatment appears to be efficacious in its ability to demean as it is a *white* man who refuses to date *black men* – his position in the relevant (racial) power hierarchy is one of dominance. According to the objective-egalitarian account, in contrast to the first case and even though the behavior itself is the same, case 2, '*not dating white men*', is not wrongful discrimination, because the positions of subordination are reversed – it is the black woman who is doing the differentiating and she has the lower status in the current context of the US because of her race. Thus, although the treatment seems as if it could demean white men, it is not efficacious.[7]

Foremost in applying a principle of non-discrimination, we are using the objective-egalitarian account to analyze these cases ethically and make a *pro tanto* moral claim about them. We are claiming that there is something morally wrong with what is happening in case 1, '*not dating black men*', and that something is wrongful discrimination. In terms of an egalitarian ethos then, the claim is that case 1 is incompatible with such an ethos, but case 2, '*not dating white men*', is not, at least not according to a standard of discrimination. In other words, an egalitarian ethos would morally condemn the behavior in case 1 but not in case 2.

There are strong commonsense reasons to support using the objective-egalitarian account's judgments in these cases. First, case 1 seems so similar to quite uncontroversial cases of wrongful racial discrimination outside of the private, e.g. not hiring or promoting someone because they are black, that it seems we need good reason *not* to see this as wrongful discrimination. Second, I think it would be strange if our theory of discrimination were unable to make a moral distinction between cases 1 and 2 – there seems to be something normatively important about the context of current racial inequality that would make us want to distinguish between a black person treating whites differentially and a white person treating blacks in such a way. The objective-egalitarian account provides us with a plausible, principled way of explaining the difference between them.[8]

I would suggest, however, that we modify the definition of efficacy slightly, to move it away from claiming that you necessarily need to be in a *dominant* position in order to have the power to demean. Rather, we should use *subordination* rather than dominance to define efficacy. In other words, if the person you are discriminating against is subordinate in the status hierarchy and your behavior appears to treat her as inferior (for example, by tapping into and reinforcing a pervasive social hierarchy that treats people of her race as inferior) then you are discriminating wrongfully, even if you do not belong to the dominant group.

Consider this example:

3 *Not dating black women*: A straight black man does not date black women because they are black. This is even in cases where, were the women white but the same in all other respects, he would indeed ask them out on dates or accept their offers for dates.

If we stick to the idea that you need to be in a dominant position in order to wrongfully discriminate, we would have to say that case 3 is not wrongful discrimination as it is a *black man* treating white and black women differentially. In this way, cases 2 and 3 are not wrongful discrimination for the same reason. According to our original definition of efficacy which specifies that the discriminators must be dominant, we would have to say that the discriminator in each of these cases is not dominant and thus neither has the power to demean. I am not sure that this conclusion is convincing, however. There is an important moral difference between cases 1 and 3 on the one hand, and case 2 on the other, that is not being picked up by our analysis. In case 2, not only is the discriminator (a black woman) not dominant, she is discriminating against those who are not subordinate (white men). However, in case 3, those discriminated against are subordinate. The discriminator in this case is helping to maintain the narrative of black women's inferiority. If we claim that neither case 2 nor 3 are wrongful discrimination, and that they are not so for the same reason, we seem to be neglecting a factor of primary moral significance that distinguishes the cases.

On reflection, I think we should be able to claim that the treatment in case 3 is efficacious. Case 3 fits the overall understanding of wrongful discrimination – people are being treated differentially in a way that implies that they are inferior. The only thing stopping us from calling this wrongful discrimination is the definition of efficacy. It makes sense, however, to center the wrongness of discrimination around those who are discriminated against and their implied inferiority, rather than centering its wrongness on the discriminators and their dominance. To reflect this, I recommend we adapt our understanding of efficacy so that even those who are themselves subordinated by power hierarchies can be efficacious; they can be understood to have the power to demean because they are reinforcing the supposed inferiority of the subordinated given by pervasive hierarchies of moral worth. The defining characteristic of efficacy should thus be based on whether the person or people discriminated against are subordinate in the relevant social hierarchy; if they are, then the discriminator has the power to demean.

Now that we have a preliminary understanding of the objective-egalitarian account and how it could be plausibly applied to the private, with, thus far, a slight amendment to the notion of efficacy, I would like to address two objections. Working through the first of these objections will help us to specify and modify efficacy even further.

Objections: the problems of efficacy and gender preferences

The first objection has to do with claiming that private discrimination generally could be wrongful; the second with claiming that racial preferences in dating specifically could be wrongful. Examining the first objection – the problem of efficacy – will help us to develop further, and modify the notion of efficacy in the objective-egalitarian account in a way that will make its application even more intuitively plausible.

The problem of efficacy

The first objection claims that private discrimination, such as racial preferences in dating, is not efficacious, or it is unlikely to be. This objection seems essential to address at this stage because it is an internal objection – it comes from Hellman herself. Hellman claims that private individuals do not, or often do not, have the power to demean each other through differential treatment (e.g. Hellman 2011: 36–37, 44; Chapter 7). This implies that private discrimination cannot be wrongful or is usually not wrongful. In this handbook, for example, Hellman claims that "Wrongfully discriminatory actions, on the account presented here, are denials of equal status by individuals and institutions with actual power" and that this means "the individual who chooses his friends on the basis of race may not, on this account, wrongfully discriminate" seemingly because these kinds of choices are usually not efficacious (Chapter 7).

In the first section I mentioned that the power to demean comes from the discriminator being in a dominant position. In the previous section I modified this to claim that a discriminator has the power to demean, even if she herself is in a subordinate position, as long as she discriminates against others who, like her, are subordinate. My interpretation has been that the status or power hierarchies that should be used to determine efficacy include the social hierarchies that designate dominance and subordination merely by virtue of group membership. In other words, whites could be considered to have power over blacks, men have power over women, the rich over the poor, and so on. It seems, however, that my interpretation of efficacy and Hellman's have come apart in this sense – she does not seem to include racial or gender hierarchies as determinants of dominance and subordination for establishing efficacy. If she did include these kinds of hierarchies, then it seems that she would have to recognize that a white person who refuses to be friends with black people is likely to be discriminating wrongfully.

How should we understand efficacy then, according to Hellman, in order to explain why private discrimination is unlikely to be wrongful? If we unpack her analysis further, there appear to be at least two factors that affect the efficacy of private discrimination. The first has to do with the extent of the power to demean; the second has to do with the power to lower someone's status. I do not have the scope to provide a detailed defense of my interpretation of the power to demean in contrast to Hellman's, but I will raise what I consider to be problems with these two aspects of Hellman's notions of efficacy, which would make me hesitant to endorse it.

First, at times, Hellman implies that once-off or infrequent cases of discrimination do not have the power to demean. For example, she compares a person in their private capacity renting out their house once-off to a professional landlord, and claims that while the former does not have the power to demean, the latter does (Hellman, 2011: 36–37). Is it the frequency with which the dominant person can affect others or the number of people that they are able to affect that determines efficacy, then? Let's call the frequency of discrimination or the number of people affected, or a measure of both of these, the 'extent' of efficacy. This, however, would not explain why private discrimination cannot be efficacious. If a white man refuses to date black women, refuses to live in a black neighborhood, refuses to shop at stores owned by black people, and so on, this is private discrimination but he does not act 'once-off'. Isolation could be a characteristic of both private and non-private discrimination, and should not then be used to claim that private discrimination cannot be wrongful because it is not efficacious.

Furthermore, if an employer promotes a white employee at the expense of a black employee once-off (thus, seemingly constituting an isolated case of non-private discrimination) it seems strange not to call this wrongful discrimination, even if the extent of power in this case appears to be minimal. Besides the fact, then, that once-off or infrequent differential treatment cannot be used to distinguish private from non-private discrimination, I cannot see that the extent of power should make a difference to whether demeaning treatment is efficacious or not. It might be an indication of how *harmful* discrimination is likely to be, but it seems to be an odd defining feature of efficacy, especially for a theory, as discussed in the first section, that refuses to define demeaning treatment according to its harmful effects.

Additionally, so-called isolated cases are probably rarely isolated. A seemingly isolated act of racial discrimination, whether private or not, can help to maintain and reinforce the social norms which make hierarchies of moral worth acceptable, and which probably help to maintain institutional and structural discrimination (see Haslanger 2012: e.g. 11, on the complex interplay between individuals and structures).

Let's turn to the second possibility for helping us to distinguish between private and non-private discrimination which might explain why the former is unlikely to be efficacious. Hellman has also claimed that a discriminator is efficacious only when she could actually lower the status of the person being discriminated against (Chapter 7). When someone in a dominant position treats someone who is subordinate differentially, and they actually lower the subordinate's status, then discrimination is wrongful. The implication of this for our present purposes is that when it comes to private discrimination, the discriminator is unlikely to be in a position where they could lower another's status, and thus the discrimination cannot be wrongful. I find the idea that the power to demean has to do with the power to actually lower someone's status puzzling. Let me illustrate using one of Hellman's examples:

> I spit on a homeless man lying on the street... This act of spitting constitutes demeaning [treatment] because (a) spitting is a conventional way of showing disrespect and (b) the relative disparity in status between a homeless person and myself allows my expression of disrespect to put him down.
>
> *(Hellman 2011: 35)*

According to both Hellman's account and mine, this is an example of demeaning treatment that is efficacious (although it is not discrimination because it is not differential treatment). It is interesting to note that this is actually an example of individuals acting in their private capacity. If Hellman recognizes that in this case of the private, an individual does have the power to demean, it seems that private discrimination would also have the potential to be wrongful. This is not the main point I want to make here, however.

According to my account of efficacy, the subordinate position of the homeless person explains the power I have to demean him in this example. For Hellman, there appears to be an additional factor at play – that by spitting at him, I actually lower his status. What does it mean that the homeless person's status is lowered? There appear to be two primary ways of understanding status in this context. However, neither of these provides us with the basis for a compelling additional factor for determining efficacy.

First, there is what could be called fundamental status – each person has equal moral worth. Second, there is someone's social status, e.g. where they stand in a socially determined hierarchy of resources, esteem, or power. I cannot see that spitting at a homeless person actually does or can lower his status according to either of these understandings. First, the treatment, i.e. the spitting, indicates that I am treating him *as if he were inferior* but I cannot actually lower someone's fundamental status. The homeless person is not my inferior and does not have lower equal moral worth than I do – nothing I do can change that. I am acting wrongly in this situation precisely because I am acting as if he were inferior to me when he is not. Second, I cannot see that I have lowered his *social* status any further – he is no more genuinely powerless, homeless, or lacking in resources than he was before I spat at him. Rather, I am treating him as if I accept, and am reinforcing, his position in the social hierarchy and his supposed inferiority; this is all that seems to be true of this situation, and this seems to be all that need be true of demeaning treatment to be efficacious. 'Lowering someone's status' does not appear to be adding a factor of moral importance to this example.

In conclusion to this section, I would not recommend using these additional factors – the extent of the power to demean or the lowering of someone's status – for determining efficacy and thus for specifying wrongful discrimination. It is for these reasons that I do not find convincing the objection that private discrimination does not have the power to demean.

The problem of gender preferences

By insisting, however, that individuals in their private capacities and in terms of their dating preferences could have the power to demean each other, my account opens itself up to an objection that would not be applied to the original objective-egalitarian account. This objection claims that once one opens the door to the possibility of dating preferences being classified as wrongful discrimination, many kinds of intuitively acceptable preferences become morally suspect, and this undermines the idea that they could be wrongful discrimination. Consider this objection based on the problem of gender preferences: if we are going to say that case 1, '*not dating black men*', is wrongful discrimination in terms of race, would this not imply that the case of straight men refusing to date other men, for example, is also wrongful discrimination? If the (modified) objective-egalitarian account cannot explain a difference between cases of racial preferences and cases of gender preferences, then that implies both are wrongful discrimination. Yet, the idea that straight men are doing something wrongful by not wanting to date other men does not seem to match many people's intuitions. If we cannot claim that both kinds of dating preferences are wrongful, according to this objection, we should then abandon referring to any private dating preferences, including racial preferences, as wrongful discrimination.

The objective-egalitarian account is able to respond convincingly to this objection, providing us with a principled distinction between the cases of wrongful discrimination in racial preferences, on the one hand, and acceptable discrimination in terms of gender, on the other hand. At face value the objection may seem to have something to it in terms of my understanding of efficacy: straight men, it could be claimed, have the power to demean gay men by tapping into the social hierarchy which has favored straight people over members of the LGBTQ community, and treated the latter as inferior. The problem with this objection, however, is that in the case of dating preferences and in the current context in which we are examining these cases, it does not seem to apply. While it is true that LGBTQ-identified individuals have been treated as inferior, this particular case – men choosing not to date other men – is not related to a hierarchy of moral worth associated with sexuality or gender. Note, these straight men are refusing to date other men; they are not refusing to date gay men specifically. For this differential treatment to be demeaning, it needs to be demeaning to those being treated differentially, and it needs to indicate that they are inferior. However, it seems odd to claim that straight men's preference for women is related to norms that indicate men's inferiority and women's superiority. Currently in the US, no pattern of discourse or treatment exists that could support the idea that men refusing to date other men *is demeaning to men*. In contrast, think back to our racial preferences – we can match the pattern of whites refusing to date blacks to a systematic social pattern that treats black people as inferior to whites. Once we examine the preferences based on gender in more detail we realize that they do not follow the required pattern to be wrongful discrimination. I agree that there are many ways in which differential treatment on the basis of gender or sexuality is demeaning and does indicate inferiority. However, as an analogy to racial preferences in dating, and thus as an objection to my claim that case 1 is wrongful discrimination, this claim fails.

I find that the objections from efficacy and gender preferences do not convince that private discrimination cannot be, or is unlikely to be, wrongful, nor that racial preferences in dating cannot be wrongful discrimination. It is possible that a number of other objections could be formulated that challenge the notion that wrongful differential treatment occurs in the private. Defending the application of the objective-egalitarian account to the private from additional objections would be a further step in this line of argument for which we do not have the scope here. I will say, though, that many of the objections that are likely to be raised are not about the claim that these forms of treatment are morally wrong but rather about *what may follow* from the claim that they are morally wrong. For example, what kind of social pressure, if any, is justified in trying to get people to conform to a principle of non-discrimination in the private? Is the state allowed to do anything to encourage people to make egalitarian choices in their relationships? These are significant questions but beyond the scope of the argument I am presenting here.

The insufficiency of a principle of non-discrimination for an egalitarian ethos

The objective-egalitarian account, with modifications to its notion of efficacy, can be used to provide a principled distinction between wrongful private discrimination and acceptable private discrimination. If we want to describe a society of equals, we might claim that even private decisions in such a society would be guided by an egalitarian ethos. Among the norms that this ethos reflects could be a principle of non-discrimination that would morally condemn wrongful private discrimination. I have not argued here for an egalitarian ethos. Rather, I have shown how we could use and modify a particularly compelling theory of discrimination to identify wrongful private discrimination with a view to spelling out an egalitarian ethos.

It seems unlikely, however, that if we had to describe which principles of equality might guide interactions between people acting as private individuals, that we would stop at a principle of non-discrimination. Setting aside the private and speaking of society generally, discrimination is far from the only threat to equality; indeed, many theorists worry that an ongoing focus on discrimination distracts from (other dimensions of) oppression (e.g. Loury 2003; see also Young 1990 for an influential account of the dimensions of oppression). Additionally, proponents of an egalitarian ethos have identified a number of norms that threaten equality but are not related to discrimination – e.g. the selfish attitudes of the advantaged (Cohen 2001: 117–133).

If we accept that a principle of non-discrimination derived from the objective-egalitarian account is necessary, but probably not sufficient for an egalitarian ethos, what else might be necessary for such an ethos? I cannot make detailed claims or provide a comprehensive list here. I gesture, however, to a problem which would likely undermine an egalitarian ethos, which is implicit in my analysis thus far.

As we have seen, the objective-egalitarian account of wrongful discrimination has two elements to it: the actual differential treatment, which debases, and the efficacy of the treatment. It is possible for treatment to attempt to demean but it will not be efficacious because it is not directed at subordinates (using our modified definition of efficacy). I think we can accept that this kind of treatment is in itself insufficient to be discrimination; however, I would find it doubtful to claim that this kind of treatment is compatible with an ideal of social equality. It appears to violate equality even if it is expressed by someone who is subordinate towards someone who is dominant, or if it occurs between equals.

Take the example of spitting that Hellman uses: she claims that spitting at a colleague or boss is disrespectful but not (efficaciously) demeaning because it has no power to demean, considering the relevant power hierarchy (Hellman 2011: 35). In a society of equals it seems to be a moral problem, however, for people to treat each other in ways that indicate inferiority – e.g. spitting at them, expecting them to bow in our presence – no matter how efficacious it is in terms of the power hierarchy of the agents involved. This behavior still attempts to demean, and this in itself seems out of place for *egalitarian* reasons. Besides its condemnation of wrongful discrimination, an egalitarian ethos is thus also likely to condemn attempts to demean that are not efficacious. This claim is perfectly compatible with the objective-egalitarian account of discrimination: Hellman emphasizes that her concern is only to determine wrongful discrimination; she is not arguing that wrongful discrimination constitutes all instances of demeaning treatment or violations of equal moral worth (Hellman 2011: 29–32, 34–37).

This problem of attempting to demean – as well as other threats to equality – needs fleshing out and will require much further investigation;[9] however, it is useful to point in the direction of the other norms of an egalitarian ethos, albeit briefly, to indicate what equality between private individuals would look like, besides being compliant with a principle of non-discrimination.

Conclusion

The objective-egalitarian account can distinguish wrongful private discrimination from acceptable private discrimination in a way that fits considered judgments of cases of racial preferences in dating. As I have argued, however, the definition of efficacy needs to be modified and to be adapted from the original in order to be most suitable as a framework for private discrimination. Besides contributing to the literature on discrimination, analysis of private discrimination can help to contribute to the burgeoning contemporary literature aimed at describing an egalitarian ethos. While a principle of non-discrimination might be a compelling requirement of an egalitarian ethos, it is clearly not sufficient for such an ethos; it would be useful to explore further which norms of equality would be upheld by individuals in their private capacities in a society of equals.[10]

Notes

1 For one of the rare extended debates on private discrimination, see the special edition of the *San Diego Law Review* 2016, 43(4), especially Blake, 2006; Dripps, 2006; Lippert-Rasmussen, 2006; Nelkin, 2006; Zwolinski, 2006. See also Lippert-Rasmussen (2013: 261–271) on this gap in the literature.

2 I do not defend the need for an egalitarian ethos but assume it can be defended. For arguments that show why we might need an egalitarian ethos, see e.g. Wolff, 1998; Cohen, 2001: 117–147. Describing an egalitarian ethos can also be understood as continuous with numerous projects pursued in critical race theories, feminist theories, and broader theories of justice and equality. See the following, for example: Lebron (2015) on the virtues required for a racially equal society, Hampton (2006) on feminist social contract theory, and Scheffler (2015) on the egalitarian norms of private relationships.

3 See, e.g., Richards and Lucas, 1985; Alexander, 1992; Lippert-Rasmussen, 2013.

4 For want of a clearer way to put this, I am going to use the terms 'dominant' and 'subordinate' as short-hand to refer to those who have greater power or status (within society as a whole or within a particular domain), and those who have lesser power or status, respectively. I definitely do not endorse

the hierarchies behind these terms, nor do I imply that those who are subordinate are lacking in agency or are simply victims of those who are dominant. Examples of those who are dominant, depending on context, are the rich, white people, employers, teachers and social systems, such as the policing system, whereas the subordinate would be, respectively, the poor, people of color, employees, students, and citizens. My discussion in this chapter is predominantly about discrimination between individuals rather than organizational and structural discrimination (Pincus 1996); however, in recognition of the importance of both organizational and structural discrimination, I mention institutions here, such as the policing system, to indicate how they can be understood according to dominance and subordination.

5 I take race to be a social construct with no genuine biological basis; however, while "racial characteristics ... distinguishable by observable bodily marks... may be of no intrinsic significance, they nevertheless can serve as useful indices around which human agents organize their expectations" (Loury 2003: 27), and around which discrimination, exploitation and oppression have been built.

6 For ease of discussion I will refer to these dating preferences as if there are only two (socially constructed) races – black and white. I recognize that this is not a reflection of reality and also that there are problems with considering racial inequalities in the US to be dominated by white–black relations. I think this problematic simplification is (arguably) justified, however, for the sake of brevity.

7 For the purposes of this chapter, I use hierarchies where, in social context, the positions of dominance and subordination are uncontroversial. An interesting complication would be where numerous social hierarchies – e.g. gender, race, sexuality, ability – confuse dominance and subordination in a particular case.

8 Note, this assessment relies on the idea that someone can feel that they have no choice when it comes to whom they are attracted and yet we can still say that when a person acts on that kind of attraction, it is morally wrong. I can imagine the following response to my claims: 'I can't help to whom I am attracted. I simply am attracted to white men and I am not attracted to black men.' I am claiming that even if we can accept this response at face value, discriminating on this basis can still be (*pro tanto*) wrongful. This seems like a reasonable assumption: we still tend to judge actions as wrongful even if the actors involved feel compelled to act in that way; pedophilia would be an extreme example here.

9 See, for example, Anderson, 2008 on inequalities of standing, esteem and power. Also, see Coleman, 2013 on duties of miscegenation. For the problem of treating people as superior, see Fourie 2012, and for problems of inequalities of esteem, see Neuhouser on Rousseau, 2014; Fourie 2015: 87–106.

10 I have received exceptionally useful comments which have helped me substantially revise initial drafts of this chapter – many thanks to Kasper Lippert-Rasmussen, an anonymous reviewer, Agomoni Ganguli Mitra, Jan-Christoph Heilinger, Sabine Hohl and Colin Marshall. I am also grateful to Michael Blake and Julio Covarrubias Cabeza for sharing their work on this topic with me.

Bibliography

Alexander, L. 1992. "What Makes Wrongful Discrimination Wrong? Biases, Preferences, Stereotypes, and Proxies." *University of Pennsylvania Law Review*. 141(1): 149–219.

Anderson, E. 1999. "What Is the Point of Equality?" *Ethics*. 109: 287–337.

Anderson, E. 2008. "Expanding the Egalitarian Toolbox: Equality and Bureaucracy." *Aristotelian Society Supplementary Volume*. 82: 139–160.

Blake, M. 2006. "The Discriminating Shopper: The Rights and Wrongs of Discrimination." *San Diego Law Review*. 43: 1017–1034.

Cohen, G.A. 2001. *If You're an Egalitarian, How Come You're So Rich?* Cambridge, MA: Harvard University Press.

Coleman, N.A.T. 2013. *The Duty to Miscegenate*. Ph.D. Dissertation. University of Michigan.

Dripps, D.A. 2006. "Is the Privilege of Private Discrimination an Artifact of an Icon?" *San Diego Law Review*. 43: 1063–1070.

Fourie, C. 2012. "What is Social Equality? An Analysis of Status Equality as a Strongly Egalitarian Ideal." *Res Publica*. 18: 107–126.

Fourie, C. 2015. "To Praise and to Scorn: the Problem of Inequalities of Esteem for Social Egalitarians." In: Fourie, C., Schuppert, F., Wallimann-Helmer, I. (eds), *Social Equality: On What It Means to Be Equals*. New York: Oxford University Press. 87–106.

Fourie, C., Schuppert, F., Wallimann-Helmer, I. (eds). 2015. *Social Equality: On What It Means to Be Equals*. New York: Oxford University Press.

Hampton, J. 2006. *The Intrinsic Worth of Persons: Contractarianism in Moral and Political Philosophy*. New York: Cambridge University Press.

Haslanger, S. 2012. *Resisting Reality: Social Construction and Social Critique*. New York: Oxford University Press.

Hellman, D. 2011. *When Is Discrimination Wrong?* Cambridge, MA: Harvard University Press.

Lebron, C. J. 2015. *The Color of Our Shame: Race and Justice in Our Time*. Oxford: Oxford University Press.

Lippert-Rasmussen, K. 2006. "Private Discrimination: A Prioritarian, Desert-Accommodating Account." *San Diego Law Review*. 43: 817–856.

Lippert-Rasmussen, K. 2013. *Born Free and Equal?: A Philosophical Inquiry into the Nature of Discrimination*. Oxford: Oxford University Press.

Loury, G.C. 2003. *The Anatomy of Racial Inequality*. Cambridge, MA: Harvard University Press.

Nelkin, D.K. 2006. "Discriminating Shoppers Beware." *San Diego Law Review*. 43: 1035–1042.

Neuhouser, F. 2014. *Rousseau's Critique of Inequality: Reconstructing the Second Discourse*. Cambridge: Cambridge University Press.

Pincus, F.L. 1996. "Discrimination Comes in Many Forms: Individual, Institutional, and Structural." *American Behavioral Scientist*. 40: 186–194.

Richards, J.R., Lucas, J.R. 1985. "Discrimination." *Proceedings of the Aristotelian Society. Supplementary Volumes*. 59: 53–83.

Vallentyne, P. 2006. "Left Libertarianism and Private Discrimination." *San Diego Law Review*. 43: 981–994.

Wolff, J. 1998. "Fairness, Respect, and the Egalitarian Ethos." *Philosophy and Public Affairs*. 27: 97–122.

Zwolinski, M. 2006. "Why Not Regulate Private Discrimination?" *San Diego Law Review*. 43: 1043–1062.

PART VI

History

36

DISCRIMINATION

Word, concept, anti-norm – some historical sketches

Robert K. Fullinwider

Introduction

In the sections that follow I offer glimpses of the concept of discrimination at work and trace its eventual transformation into a dominant political and legal idea. These glimpses include Charles Dickens' reactions to slavery in America, the Congressional debate after the American Civil War over amending the Constitution, the fate of minority protection-clauses in peace treaties after World War I and World War II, and recent developments in American civil rights law and affirmative action policy. My recountings are opportunistic rather than comprehensive.

Once upon a time

Although heavy reliance on the word "discrimination" in law, policy, and social critique is a relatively recent phenomenon, the rudimentary *concept* behind the word has been available to humans from the time they were able to oppress one another. The root idea refers to differential treatment. The idea of its converse likewise was available: uniform treatment. To illustrate: Sometime after the escape of the Jews from Egypt, God instructed Moses on the proper modes of offerings and sacrifices, adding, "All who are native-born shall do these things in this manner … [a]nd if a stranger dwells with you … just as you do, so shall he do. One ordinance shall be for you … and for the stranger" (Bible: Numbers 15:13–15).

Discrimination would involve treating the native-born and the stranger differently; the "one ordinance" prescribed nondiscrimination. However, a similar "one ordinance" provision assumed a less embracing form when, earlier, God, having just gotten the Jews out of Egypt, taught them how to celebrate.

> And the Lord said unto Moses and Aaron, this is the ordinance of the passover: There shall no stranger eat thereof … And when a stranger shall sojourn with thee, and will keep the passover to the Lord, let all his males be circumcised, and then let him come near and keep it; and he shall be as one that is born in the land: for no uncircumcised person shall eat thereof. One law shall be to him that is homeborn, and unto the stranger that sojourneth among you.
>
> *(Bible: Exodus 12:43–49)*

The one law here does not distinguish between homeborn and stranger but it does distinguish between circumcised and uncircumcised; and the latter are excluded from eating the Passover meal. Nondiscrimination has its limits.

The apostle Paul urged on the early Christian community the *annihilation* of all such distinctions. The Christian must become a *new* person in Christ, in whose image "there is neither Greek nor Jew, circumcised nor uncircumcised, barbarian, Scythian, slave nor free" (Bible: Romans 10:12, Colossians 3:10–11). The annihilation recommended by Paul has not been the norm, before or after. Humans from all times have busily divided themselves into families, tribes, clans, religions, nations, and peoples; into different castes, classes, stations, orders, and offices acquired by birth and blood, all of these marked by distinction piled upon distinction.

In the Middle Ages, sumptuary laws defined appropriate dress and equipage so that each person could recognize his superior or inferior in any encounter and accord the appropriate deference or condescension. Distinction and discrimination were the warp and woof of life. Uniformity as equality, as the putting aside of difference, was not a real concern – according to my potted tale – until the American and French revolutions ushered in a new mentality about citizenship and political equality.

The American Revolution, of course, began with the Declaration of Independence: "We hold these truths to be self-evident, that all men are created equal." Eleven years after the Declaration, in trying to put together a workable government out of the disparate political entities emerging from the successful revolution against England, the members of the Constitutional Convention in Philadelphia compromised on the embarrassment of slavery, which existed from North to South but was particularly embedded in the South. The Constitution that resulted contained this provision among others:

> Representatives and direct Taxes shall be apportioned among the several States which may be included within this Union, according to their respective Numbers, *which shall be determined by adding to the whole Number of free Persons … three fifths of all other Persons.*

The Constitution acknowledged among the American population a distinct degraded class of "all other Persons," not free.

An observer

In 1842, Charles Dickens toured the United States and wrote a book about his travels, *American Notes for General Circulation.* He was particularly appalled by slavery and his eye was alert to the awful inequalities and hypocrisies this institution bred. He depicted other social "distinctions" as well, some he may not have thought so outlandish. Here is Dickens on railroads:

> There are no first and second class carriages [on American railroads] as with us; but there is a gentleman's car and a ladies' car: the main distinction between which is that in the first, everybody smokes; and in the second, nobody does. As a black man never travels with a white one, there is also a negro car; which is a great, blundering, clumsy chest, such as Gulliver put to sea in, from the kingdom of Brobdingnag.
>
> *(Dickens 1842/1985: 111)*

Different social classes, different genders, different races – all distinguished and put in their proper places, here and there.

In Philadelphia, visiting a wretched prison, Dickens noticed

> [s]itting upon the stairs, engaged in some slight work … a pretty coloured boy. 'Is there no refuge for young criminals in Philadelphia, then?' said I. 'Yes, but only for white children.' Noble aristocracy in crime!
>
> *(Dickens 1842/1985: 151)*

Travelling into Virginia, Dickens offered this description:

> In the negro car belonging to the train in which we made this journey, were a mother and her children who had just been purchased; the husband and father being left behind with their old owner. The children cried the whole way, and the mother was misery's picture. The champion of Life, Liberty, and the Pursuit of Happiness, who had bought them, rode in the same train; and, every time we stopped, got down to see that they were safe. The black in Sinbad's Travels with one eye in the middle of his forehead which shone like a burning coal, was nature's aristocrat compared with this white gentleman.
>
> *(Dickens 1842/1985: 180–1)*

While in Richmond, he had occasion to cross the James River.

> Crossing this bridge, on my way back, I saw a notice painted on the gate, cautioning all persons to drive slowly: under a penalty, if the offender were a white man, of five dollars; if a negro, fifteen stripes.
>
> *(Dickens1842/1985: 183)*

Nowhere in *American Notes for General Circulation* did Dickens use the word "discrimination." He had many other words at his disposal to describe the exclusions, distinctions, and differentiations he saw in slavery and in the treatment of blacks generally: "abuse of power," "cruelty," "horrors," "corruption," "atrocities," "torture," "injustice," "outrages," "brutality," "savagery," "ugliness," to list a few.

Post bellum

The American Constitution in its compromise on slavery opened a boil that eventually had to be lanced by a terrible civil war. In the aftermath of that war, the United States Congress proposed and secured the ratification of three amendments to the Constitution: the Thirteenth, abolishing slavery; the Fourteenth, making the freed slaves citizens of the United States and extending to everyone the "equal protection of the laws;" and the Fifteenth, securing the electoral franchise to citizens regardless of race.

The Congressional debate on the Fourteenth Amendment was especially intense and in it we find the word "discrimination" deployed in ways quite recognizable to our contemporary ears.

The first two sections of the Fourteenth Amendment read:

> Section 1: All persons born or naturalized in the United States, and subject to the jurisdiction thereof, are citizens of the United States and of the state wherein they reside. No state shall make or enforce any law which shall abridge the privileges or immunities of citizens of the United States; nor shall any state deprive any person of life, liberty, or property, without

> due process of law; nor deny to any person within its jurisdiction the equal protection of the laws.
>
> Section 2: Representatives shall be apportioned among the several states according to their respective numbers, counting the whole number of persons in each state … . *But when the right to vote … is denied to any of the male inhabitants of such state, being twenty-one years of age, and citizens of the United States … the basis of representation therein shall be reduced in the proportion which the number of such male citizens shall bear to the whole number of male citizens twenty-one years of age in such state.*

It's obvious that Section 2 related to the article in the Constitution counting each slave as three-fifths of a person for purposes of representation. This original article had given the antebellum Southern states extra representation in Congress, which they had used to their advantage. Now the ex-slaves would count fully for purposes of representation, even though the former slave states would prevent the freedmen from having the franchise. These states would be able to come back into Congress with an even greater number of representatives and, allied with Northern Democrats, basically achieve by legislation what they had failed to gain on the battlefield. The Republicans in Congress were determined to avert this outcome.

Debate over this section of the Fourteenth Amendment was especially prolonged. Some opponents objected that the language of Section 2 was obscure, so at one point Senator Benjamin Wade of Ohio offered to amend it:

> Section 2. No class of persons … [against which] suffrage *discrimination* shall be made, by any State, shall be included in the basis of representation, unless such *discrimination* be in virtue of impartial qualifications founded on intelligence or property, or because of alienage, or for participation in rebellion or other crime.

Senator Wade explained:

> I think my amendment in this respect is plainer and more practicable than the [original] proposition … The entire population [of a state] is taken in the first instance, as a basis. The [Federal] census always *discriminates* between the black and the white population, and it makes several other *discriminations*; and therefore it is, and will be at all times, perfectly easy and practicable to ascertain exactly how much of the population of a State shall be counted in the basis of representation under my amendment … Under this amendment you ascertain the classes of the population, and when any *discrimination* shall be made upon any of these subjects the whole of that particular class will be excluded.
>
> (Congressional Globe *1866: 2769)*

Senator Wade's substitute was hardly a model of clarification but, had it gained adoption, the word "discrimination" would have been written into the Constitution. As Senator Wade's text and comments illustrate, the word "discrimination" took on morally neutral and non-neutral roles promiscuously (cf. Introduction). The census discriminates between blacks and whites, Senator Wade tells us. That is to say, it categorized each individual surveyed as either black or white. This was a good thing, for Stevens' purposes, since it facilitated identifying classes that might be denied the vote because of color. If a state then proceeded to discriminate – i.e., *wrongfully* exclude – on account of race, it would suffer: that was the thrust of Section 2. Throughout the debates, opponents and proponents of the Fourteenth Amendment shifted back and forth between these different usages – discrimination plain (making some sort of distinction or other) and discrimination plus (making some sort of wrongful distinction or other).

In defending Section 1, the Fourteenth Amendment's proponents expressed the need to protect the freedmen by putting a check on the power of states. The equality proposed in that section was explicitly comparative. Like God instructing Moses on sacrifices, the Fourteenth Amendment (according to its proponents) instructed the states:

> Whatever law punishes a white man for a crime shall punish the black man precisely in the same way and to the same degree. Whatever law protects the white man shall afford "equal" protection to the black man. Whatever means of redress is afforded to one shall be afforded to all. Whatever law allows the white man to testify in court shall allow the man of color to do the same.
>
> (Congressional Globe *1866: 2459)*

This instruction was necessitated by the immediate post-war condition in the South, where, asserted one defender of the Amendment,

> color disqualifies a man from testifying in courts, or being tried in the same way as white men. I need not enumerate these partial and oppressive laws. Unless the Constitution should restrain them, those States will all, I fear, keep up this *discrimination*, and crush to death the hated freedmen.
>
> (Congressional Globe *1866: 2459)*

President Andrew Johnson, who succeeded to the office after Lincoln's assassination, assumed a substantial place in the Congressional debates, excoriated by Republicans and defended by Democrats. The sources of Republican ire? Johnson had given a blanket pardon to former Confederates, allowed the rebel states to reconstitute themselves, vetoed the Second Freedmen's Bureau Act in early 1866, and vetoed the Civil Rights Act of 1866. The latter veto was overridden immediately by Congress and the Civil Rights Act became law. Indeed, it was because the Republicans so strongly valued the rights this law extended to the former slaves that they acted by means of the Fourteenth Amendment to entrench them, in a general way, in the Constitution, where they could not be swept away in the future by a simple majority vote in Congress.

As soon as Congress completed work on the Fourteenth Amendment, it repassed the Second Freedmen's Bureau Act. Johnson again vetoed it and this time Congress overrode the President's veto. The Freedmen's Bureau, created in the War Department in 1865 to bring relief to the newly freed slaves while war was still raging, was authorized among other things to distribute abandoned or expropriated lands to the freedmen and assist them in becoming self-sufficient. The Second Freedman's Bureau Act extended this authorization and, in addition, gave the Bureau Commissioners power to protect a panoply of civil rights belonging to the freedmen. President Johnson had many objections to the new bill but one feature prompted him to complain of what we would now call "reverse discrimination" and "affirmative action." He wrote:

> [T]he *discrimination* [in the disposing of land] made in the bill seems objectionable … . It may deprive persons of their property who are equally deserving objects of the nation's bounty as those [i.e., the freedmen] whom by this legislation Congress seeks to benefit.

Johnson went on to characterize the legislation as advantaging "a favored class of citizens" and warned Congress against the "danger of class legislation" (*Congressional Globe* 1866: 3850).

Soon legal cases under the Fourteenth Amendment found their way to the Supreme Court. In the first case in which the Court used the Fourteenth Amendment to invalidate a state law, *Stauder v. West Virginia* (1880), the word "discrimination" is used a dozen and a half times in a relatively brief opinion. In Justice Harlan's long dissent in a later decision, the *Civil Rights Cases of 1883*, the word "discrimination" recurs repeatedly. We see, in other words, "discrimination" emerging as *a term of art*, foreshadowing its ubiquitous place in law and policy a century later.

In 1910, Gilbert Thomas Stephenson, a lawyer in North Carolina, published a survey of all race-based legislation in the United States since the Civil War, *Race Distinctions in American Law*. Stephenson thought it useful to mark out the difference between racial "distinctions" and "discriminations" because they were often confused. "A race distinction in the law," he wrote,

> is a requirement imposed by statute, constitutional enactment, or judicial decision, prescribing for a person of one race a rule of conduct different from that prescribed for a person of another race.
>
> *(Stephenson 1910: 1)*

Many people, said Stephenson, especially blacks, take distinction to be discrimination, but

> there is an essential difference … North Carolina, for example, has a law that white and Negro children shall not attend the same schools, but that separate schools shall be maintained. If the terms for all the public schools in the State are equal in length, if the teaching force is equal in numbers and ability, if the school buildings are equal in convenience, accommodations, and appointments; a race distinction exists but not a discrimination … There is no discrimination so long as there is equality of opportunity, and this equality may often be attained only by a difference in methods.
>
> *(Stephenson 1910: 2–3)*

But if the schools attended by black students are shabby, the teachers fewer and undertrained, the school year only half as long:

> if such conditions exist under the law, race distinctions exist which are at the same time discriminations against Negroes.
>
> *(Stephenson 1910: 3)*

Thus, "[a] race distinction connotes a difference and nothing more." By contrast, "[a] discrimination necessarily implies partiality and favoritism;" discriminations, but not distinctions, should be "obliterated" from society (Stephenson 1910: 4, 361).

Stephenson offered readers a *moralized* definition of discrimination. That he took the time to distinguish "distinction" from "discrimination" in order to forestall confusion indicates that a moralized notion had already gained currency in both legal and public commentary at the end of the nineteenth century. The foundation was already there for the role "discrimination" came to play in the second half of the twentieth century.

The minorities treaties

We could hardly discuss discrimination and the origins of a nondiscrimination principle without taking up religion. Although the inhabitants of various empires, kingdoms, and principalities have been fighting, conquering, and oppressing one another from earliest times, the Protestant

Reformation in the sixteenth century ushered in an especially terrible time of war and persecution that engulfed all of Europe. Religious strife spiraled out of control in the seventeenth century with the onset in 1618 of the Thirty Years War. Originally a conflict within minor German principalities, eventually the violent struggle involved the monarchies of the Holy Roman Empire, Sweden, France, and Spain. Their involvement turned the initial religion-based contest into a major geopolitical struggle. Millions died. The Treaty of Westphalia that ended the war resulted in the recognition of a balance of power in Europe based on state sovereignty and non-interference, and on a modest establishment of religious toleration.

The next two centuries in Europe were not free of war and conquest, but these were largely dynastic quarrels, imperial adventures, or ripples from the French Revolution and Napoleonic conquests. The Congress of Vienna in 1814 aimed for stability, but its extensive redrawing of political boundaries meant that various ethno-religious groups lived as not-always-welcomed minorities in their countries, separated from their kinsmen in other states. More importantly, the dissolution in the latter part of the nineteenth century of the Ottoman Empire saw the emergence in Eastern Europe of new states containing turbulent populations of Muslim and Christian, Orthodox and Roman Catholic, Slav and non-Slav, all intermixed. In this cauldron the spark was struck that precipitated World War I.

At the end of that war, the victorious powers created new states out of the collapsed Austro-Hungarian Empire, established an independent Poland, and readjusted the borders of other Eastern European states. Already, mass expulsions of ethnic and religious minorities had occurred in the unruly decades before. The Allied Powers wanted to forestall such ethnic cleansing and achieve stability in the states as configured in 1919. The mechanism they chose was a series of "minorities treaties" protecting the rights of religious, ethnic, and linguistic minorities.

The first country affected was Poland. As hostilities ceased in 1918, many Eastern European countries were creating "facts on the ground," enlarging themselves, seizing territory, and the like. Polish troops marched into Lwow in western Ukraine and staged a three-day massacre of Jews. Alarmed at this and other events in Poland, the Allied Powers at Versailles demanded that, in return for a guarantee of its borders, Poland submit to the following articles:

> Article 2. Poland undertakes to assure full and complete protection of life and liberty to all inhabitants of Poland without distinction of birth, nationality, language, race or religion.
>
> Article 7. All Polish nationals shall be equal before the law and shall enjoy the same civil and political rights without distinction as to race, language or religion.
>
> Article 8. Polish nationals who belong to racial, religious or linguistic minorities shall enjoy the same treatment and security in law and in fact as the other Polish nationals.
>
> Article 10. Educational Committees appointed locally by the Jewish communities of Poland … will provide for the distribution of the proportional share of public funds allocated to Jewish schools … .
>
> Article 11. Jews shall not be compelled to perform any act which constitutes a violation of their Sabbath …
>
> *(Temperley 1924: 439–42)*

Poland resented this demand but signed the treaty in June 1919. Similar articles went into the treaty signed by the newly created Serb–Croat–Slovene State, though in place of articles especially protecting Jews was an article specifically protecting the "Musulman." Apart from these special safeguards, the treaties with Czechoslovakia, Austria, and Hungary mirrored the terms of the Polish treaty by acknowledging minority rights.

These provisions were not novel. Earlier, as Greece and other states gained independence from the Ottoman Empire, the guarantees of their sovereignty by the European powers contained expectations of equality and nondiscrimination. The "minorities treaties" after World War I extended these expectations. They had slight effect, however. The League of Nations could entertain "petitions" from aggrieved minorities but possessed little power to do anything about their grievances. In 1934 Poland tore up its treaty and the others remained mostly dead letters.

World War II brought with it further changes in borders, mass expulsions, and the large-scale slaughter of Jews and other "inferior" people. At the end of the war the victors once again tried to put Europe back together through a series of peace treaties. As at the end of the earlier war, the Allied Powers attempted to secure rights – this time "human rights" rather than "minority rights" – in the peace accords.

In each treaty, the submitting nations agreed to secure basic "human rights" and "fundamental freedoms" to all "*without distinction* as to race, sex, language or religion." Bulgaria, Hungary, and Finland undertook, as well, to repeal any discriminatory legislation imposed because of racial origin. These articles were there to protect Jews. The same is true of the special articles that applied to Hungary and Romania: the laws "in force" in these countries "shall not … discriminate" among persons because of "their race, sex, language or religion." The *concept* of discrimination was at work in the treaties imposed after both World Wars (governments "shall make no distinctions") but it appeared in its own name (though fleetingly) only in the World War II treaties (Leiss 1954: 252, 275, 299, 324).

The United Nations initially was not much better than the League of Nations at enforcing these treaty provisions, but after World War II a "human rights"/"nondiscrimination" regime slowly came to acquire a much greater purchase in world opinion and international institutions.

The new American revolution

Gilbert Stephenson, in his 1910 book, could illustrate the difference between racial *distinctions* and *discriminations* by using the example of North Carolina's racially separate schools because a decade and a half earlier in *Plessy v. Ferguson* the Supreme Court had established "separate but equal" as a proper interpretation of the Fourteenth Amendment when states legislated on social affairs. Upholding a Louisiana statute requiring blacks and whites to travel in different railroad cars, Justice Brown wrote for the Court:

> A statute which implies merely a legal distinction between the white and colored races … has no tendency to destroy the legal equality of the two races, or reestablish a state of involuntary servitude … Laws permitting, and even requiring, their separation … do not necessarily imply the inferiority of either race to the other … We consider the underlying fallacy of the plaintiff's argument to consist in the assumption that the enforced separation of the two races stamps the colored race with a badge of inferiority. If this be so, it is not by reason of anything found in the act, but solely because the colored race chooses to put that construction upon it.
>
> *(Plessy 1896: 543, 544, 551)*

This last remark was amazingly obtuse even for its time. Justice Harlan, in his famous dissent, more accurately pegged the issue as about

> state enactments which, in fact, proceed on the ground that colored citizens are so inferior and degraded that they cannot be allowed to sit in public coaches occupied by white citizens. That, as all will admit, is the real meaning of such legislation as was enacted in Louisiana.
>
> *(Plessy 1896: 560)*

Nevertheless, "separate but equal" remained the law for another half century. The Court, over the ensuing decades, chipped away here and there at racial segregation but finally gathered its forces in its historic 1954 decision, *Brown v. Board of Education*, to sweep *Plessy* away entirely (cf. Chapter 33). The several cases that were consolidated under *Brown* were actually argued before the Court in 1952. The Court then deferred its decision and requested further argument in 1953. Its finding, announced in 1954, was unanimous: school segregation was *inherently* unequal (Brown 1954: 495). Chief Justice Earl Warren, a former governor of California, had used the two years since initial argument to win over any wavering Justices. He wanted a united front as the Court legally undercut deeply-rooted institutional patterns in the South and elsewhere. This may account for one of *Brown*'s singular features: it is a momentous decision with almost no argumentation. Once readers set aside the opinion's description of the case history and other legal preliminaries, they find five short paragraphs in support of the Court's conclusion that racial segregation in schools is fundamentally unequal and cannot be made equal by parity in facilities, funding, teachers, and the like (Brown 1954: 493–495).

Even in the 1954 decision, however, the Court temporized. Though the plaintiffs' rights were vindicated, the Court offered no remedy. Instead it set further argument by the parties and only in 1955 ordered that schools be integrated "with all deliberate speed" (Brown 1955: 301), a process that began in 1956. The Court knew its decision marked a dramatic turning point, but its unanimity did not prevent decades of discord and strife. The resistance of the Southern states, the unpopularity of forced busing, and the subsequent white flight from public schools both North and South yielded a depressing present-day fact: a remaining high level of racial segregation in schools.

While *Brown* had enormous symbolic impact and considerable practical force (among other things it was the springboard for several subsequent Supreme Court decisions that swept away the remaining legal vestiges of American apartheid), the real revolution in American race relations came with the Civil Rights Act of 1964 (as amended in 1972), and President Lyndon Johnson's Executive Order 11246 the following year. The Civil Rights Act forbade discrimination on the basis of race, color, religion, or national origin in elections, education, federally supported programs, and public accommodations. Most importantly, in Title VII of the Act, Congress forbade discrimination in employment and added gender to the list of proscribed bases.

Under Title VII, federal courts who found companies guilty of discriminating were empowered, among other things, "to order such affirmative action as may be appropriate" (Civil Rights Act of 1964: Sec. 706g). Those fateful words, "affirmative action," were to appear again in Lyndon Johnson's 1965 Executive Order, requiring all federal contractors to take affirmative action to comply with the Order's nondiscrimination mandate (Executive Order 1965: Sec. 202.1). Under Title VII, affirmative action was something a company did to *make up for* its discrimination. Under the Executive Order, affirmative action was something companies did to *avoid* discrimination. This ambiguity portended trouble and it soon came. In 1972, when the Labor Department issued a slew of implementing regulations requiring employers to formulate numerical goals and timetables for hiring and promoting minorities and women, a great national tumult erupted about "preferential hiring," "quotas," and "reverse discrimination" that, though now playing out on different terrain, remains unfinished.

A double bind

According to the Labor Department's rules, those goals and timetables required an employer's good faith efforts to "achieve prompt and full utilization of minorities and women, at all levels and in all segments of his work force where deficiencies exist" (Fullinwider 1980: 163, quoting 41 Code of Federal Regulations 60–2.10; this section of the Code reads much differently today.) At jeopardy if an employer failed: eligibility for federal contracts.

Related to the pressure employers felt to remedy their workforce "deficiencies," the very definition of discrimination underwent a dramatic change. In a landmark ruling in 1971, the Supreme Court, in *Griggs v. Duke Power Company*, held that under Title VII *any* employment practice adversely affecting minorities amounted to discrimination – unless the employer could show the practice to be justified by "business necessity" (Griggs 1971: 431). Thus, employers were doubly motivated to revise their modes of operation; yet almost any selection process was likely to yield disparate impact, while "prompt" correction of deficiencies seemed unattainable. What to do? One obvious solution presented its own difficulties. The solution: employers could put their fingers on the racial scales – recruit and employ racial minorities at a faster clip than their (revised) procedures would allow. The problem: if such fingers on the scales were obvious, employers could be sued by disgruntled whites for "reverse discrimination."

Under the *Griggs* interpretation, discrimination meant two things: disparate treatment and disparate impact. How could employers be faithful to one of the Title's mandates without transgressing the other?

In her dissenting opinion in a 2009 Supreme Court case, *Ricci v. DeStefano*, Justice Ginsburg pooh-poohed the idea that the two strands of Title VII generated any kind of tension.

> Neither Congress' enactments nor this Court's Title VII precedents … offer even a hint of "conflict" between an employer's obligations under the statute's disparate-treatment and disparate-impact provisions … Standing on an equal footing, these twin pillars of Title VII advance the same objectives: ending workplace discrimination and promoting genuinely equal opportunity.
>
> *(Ricci 2009: 624)*

The *Ricci* case involved the city of New Haven, Connecticut, which threw out a fire department promotion exam when it became apparent the exam would qualify hardly any blacks. When the city tossed the tests, white firefighters sued. Justice Kennedy, who wrote the lead opinion for the Court, framed the problem before him as a dilemma.

> [The complaining firefighters] would have us hold that, under Title VII, avoiding unintentional discrimination cannot justify intentional discrimination. That assertion, however, ignores the fact that, by codifying the disparate-impact provision in 1991, Congress has expressly prohibited both types of discrimination. We must interpret the statute to give effect to both provisions where possible … At the opposite end of the spectrum, [the city asserts] that an employer's good-faith belief that its actions are necessary to comply with Title VII's disparate-impact provision should be enough to justify race-conscious conduct.
>
> *(Ricci 2009: 580, 581)*

Nor was Justice Kennedy alone in seeing a tension at work in Title VII. "Hints" abounded throughout the 1970s, 1980s, and 1990s. In one early litigation, Judge John Minor Wisdom of the Court of Appeals in the Fifth Circuit, writing in dissent, characterized the defendants in the case (a company and its union) as required

> to walk a high tightrope without a net beneath them. On one side [lay] the possibility of liability to minorities in private actions, federal pattern and practice suits, and sanctions under Executive Order 11246. On the other side [lay] the threat of private suits by white employees and, potentially, federal action.
>
> (*Weber v. Kaiser Aluminum 1977: 230*)

To "promptly" correct deficiencies in its workforce and to avoid causing disparate impact, the company and its union had entered into an agreement in which black and white employees on a one-for-one basis would be promoted into a new in-house job-training program for skilled craft jobs. Inevitably, the agreement sparked a lawsuit.

The "tightrope-without-a-net" problem was apparent not only to employers but to the federal government as well, which hastened to issue a new set of regulations in 1978, "Affirmative Action Appropriate Under Title VII of the Civil Rights Act of 1964," telling companies and unions that if they took "actions appropriate to *overcome the effects of past or present practices, policies, or other barriers to equal employment opportunity*," they would be "allowed *flexibility* in modifying employment systems and practices to comport with the purposes of Title VII" (Affirmative Action 1978: Subsection c). In other words, companies and unions would be shielded from government pressure and defended against lawsuits if their "modifications" arose from affirmative action plans, even though the modifications might involve a finger on the racial scales.

A history of the future

Today, anti-discrimination is a giant industry. Layers of federal, state, and municipal laws and court rulings protect individuals in a variety of transactions and settings from discrimination on account of *race, color, national origin, religion or creed, gender, age, disability, sexual orientation, gender-identification, genetic make-up, reproductive health, and marital status* (cf. Chapters 15–24). The state of Connecticut, for example, lists 3 provisions in its constitution, 80 general statutes, 11 public acts, 7 sets of regulations, and 5 executive orders all directed to preventing discrimination – this in addition to the 11 federal laws, 12 sets of federal regulations, 6 federal guidelines, and 14 federal executive orders directed to the same effect.

European countries possess similar bundles of regulation. For example, anti-discrimination law in the United Kingdom includes the familiar range of protected personal characteristics and also carves out buffer zones for "positive" choices based on socio-economic disadvantage, the need to enhance equality of opportunity for some groups, and the desire to increase the number of women in political office (Equality Act 2010).

Surely, readers might think, we've now reached a limit and identified all the oppressed groups among us that need legal protection from discrimination. I demur. Many groups are yet likely to claim candidacy. Prostitutes, for example, remain a degraded and stigmatized class, victimized by discriminatory statutes and selective law enforcement (Johnson 2014). Perhaps they, too, can find policy and litigation champions to promote their cause, though I doubt it. "Lookism," the practice of favoring people based on their physical appearance, already possesses a name and animates a coterie of "anti-lookist" acolytes, though it has yet to acquire legal status as a wrong. Of course, the largest class of oppressed people among us is made up of children. Why should 12-year-olds be subject to the tyranny of their parents, confounded by law from making their own way in the world, subjected to a daily stream of microaggressions, treated by all of our institutions and practices as if they were – children? Their day will come.

Bibliography

Affirmative Action Appropriate Under Title VII of the Civil Rights Act of 1964, 29 CFR Ch. 14, Part 1608 (1978).

Bible (King James Version).

Brown v. Board of Education, 347 U.S. 483 (1954).

Brown v. Board of Education, 349 U.S. 294 (1955).

Civil Rights Act of 1964, Public Law 88–352 (1964).

Civil Rights Cases of 1883, 109 U.S. 3 (1883).

Congressional Globe, 1866.

Dickens, Charles. 1842/1985. *American Notes for General Circulation*. New York: Penguin Books.

Equality Act 2010, Chapter 15.

Executive Order 11246, 30 F.R. 12319 (1965).

Fullinwider, Robert K. 1980. *The Reverse Discrimination Controversy: A Moral and Legal Analysis*. Totowa, New Jersey: Rowman and Littlefield.

Johnson, Elizabeth M. 2014. "Buyers Without Remorse: Ending the Discriminatory Enforcement of Prostitution Laws." *Texas Law Review*. 92: 717–748.

Leiss, Amelia C. (ed.). 1954. *European Peace Treaties after World War II: Negotiations and Texts of Treaties with Italy, Bulgaria, Hungary, Rumania, and Finland*. Boston: World Peace Foundation.

Plessy v. Ferguson, 163 U.S. 537 (1896).

Ricci v. DeStefano, 557 U.S. 557 (2009).

Stauder v. West Virginia, 100 U.S. 303 (1880).

Stephenson, Gilbert Thomas. 1910. *Race Distinctions in American Law*. New York: D. Appleton and Company.

Temperley, H.W.V. (ed.) 1924. *The History of the Peace Conference of Paris*, Volume 5: *Economic Reconstruction and Protection of Minorities*. Oxford: Oxford University Press.

Weber v. Kaiser Aluminum & Chemical Corporation, 563 F.2d 216 (1977).

INDEX

Page numbers in *italic* refer to tables.